Lecture Notes in Computer Science   13967

Advanced Research in Computing and Software Science
Subline of Lecture Notes in Computer Science

More information about this series at https://link.springer.com/bookseries/558

Gianluca Della Vedova · Besik Dundua ·
Steffen Lempp · Florin Manea
Editors

Unity of Logic and Computation

19th Conference on Computability in Europe, CiE 2023
Batumi, Georgia, July 24–28, 2023
Proceedings

 Springer

Editors
Gianluca Della Vedova 🔟
University of Milano-Bicocca
Milan, Italy

Besik Dundua 🔟
Kutaisi International University
Kutaisi, Georgia

Steffen Lempp 🔟
University of Wisconsin
Madison, WI, USA

Florin Manea 🔟
University of Göttingen
Göttingen, Germany

ISSN 0302-9743   ISSN 1611-3349   (electronic)
Lecture Notes in Computer Science
ISBN 978-3-031-36977-3   ISBN 978-3-031-36978-0   (eBook)
https://doi.org/10.1007/978-3-031-36978-0

This Springer imprint is published by the registered company Springer Nature Switzerland AG
The registered company address is: Gewerbestrasse 11, 6330 Cham, Switzerland

Preface

The conference *Computability in Europe* (CiE) is organized yearly under the auspices of the Association CiE, a European association of mathematicians, logicians, computer scientists, philosophers, physicists, biologists, historians, and others interested in new developments in computability and their underlying significance for the real world. CiE promotes the development of computability-related science, ranging over mathematics, computer science and applications in various natural and engineering sciences, such as physics and biology, as well as related fields, such as philosophy and history of computing. CiE 2023 had as its motto *Unity of Logic and Computation*, reflecting the interest of CiE in research that is able unify research fields that are traditionally considered disjoint.

CiE 2023 was the 19th conference in the series, and took place in Batumi, Georgia. We are grateful to the Batumi Shota Rustaveli State University and Institute of Applied Mathematics, Tbilisi State University for hosting and supporting our conference. The Russian invasion of Ukraine forced us to organize CiE 2023 as a hybrid event.

The previous CiE conferences have been held in Amsterdam (The Netherlands) in 2005, Swansea (UK) in 2006, Siena (Italy) in 2007, Athens (Greece) in 2008, Heidelberg (Germany) in 2009, Ponta Delgada (Portugal) in 2010, Sofia (Bulgaria) in 2011, Cambridge (UK) in 2012, Milan (Italy) in 2013, Budapest (Hungary) in 2014, Bucharest (Romania) in 2015, Paris (France) in 2016, Turku (Finland) in 2017, Kiel (Germany) in 2018, Durham (UK) in 2019, virtually in Salerno (Italy) in 2020, virtually in Ghent (Belgium) in 2021, and in Swansea (UK) in 2022.

Structure and Program of the Conference

The conference program was centered around two tutorials, six invited lectures, five special sessions as well as contributed papers and informal presentations.

The Program Committee of CiE 2023 was co-chaired by Gianluca Della Vedova (University of Milano–Bicocca, Italy) and Steffen Lempp (University of Wisconsin–Madison, USA). The Program Committee had 21 additional members, selected the invited and tutorial speakers and the special session organizers, and coordinated the reviewing process of all submitted contributions.

The members of the Program Committee of CiE 2023 selected for publication in this volume and for presentation at the conference 21 of the 36 non-invited submitted papers. All non-invited submissions received at least three single-blind reviews. In addition to the contributed papers, the volume contains two invited papers and 13 abstracts. The production of the volume would have been impossible without the diligent work of our expert referees, consisting of both Program Committee members and subreviewers. We would like to thank all of them for their excellent work.

Tutorials

- *Impact of Quantum Computing to Cryptography.* Ludovic Perret (Sorbonne University, France)
- *Ramsey's theory computes through sparsity.* Ludovic Levy Patey (CNRS, France)

Invited Speakers

- Andrei Bulatov (Simon Fraser University, Canada)
- Anne Condon (University of British Columbia, Canada)
- Stephanie Dick (University of Pennsylvania, USA)
- Kirsten Eisenträger (Pennsylvania State University, USA)
- Neil Lutz (Swarthmore College and Iowa State University, USA)
- Mark Steedman (University of Edinburgh, UK)

Special Sessions

Computational Sciences. Organizers: Jonathan Gryak (City University of New York, USA) and V. Anne Smith (University of St. Andrews, UK)

- Franziska Matthäus
- Jon Paul Janet
- Karianne Bergen
- Arjen Hommersom

Classical Theories of Degrees. Organizers: Keng Meng Ng (Nanyang Technological University, Singapore) and Andrea Sorbi (University of Siena, Italy)

- Klaus Ambos-Spies
- Iskander Kalimullin
- Mariya Soskova
- Guohua Wu

Proof Theory. Organizers: Anupam Das (University of Birmingham, UK) and Gilda Ferreira (University of Lisbon, Portugal)

- Willem Heijltjes
- Emil Jeřábek
- Marie Kerjean
- Sam Sanders

Weihrauch complexity. Organizers: Damir Dzhafarov (University of Connecticut, USA) and Arno Pauly (Swansea University, UK)

- Andrej Bauer
- Vasco Brattka

- Tonicha Crook
- Manlio Valenti

Scalable computational genomics. Organizers: Giovanna Rosone (University of Pisa, Italy) and Alexandru Tomescu (University of Helsinki, Finland)

- Jasmijn Baaijens
- Erik Garrison
- Chirag Jain
- Camille Marchet

Final Considerations

All authors who have contributed to this conference are encouraged to submit significantly extended versions of their papers, with additional unpublished research content, to *Computability. The Journal of the Association CiE*.

The Steering Committee of the conference series CiE is concerned about the representation of female researchers in the field of computability. In order to increase female participation, the series started the Women in Computability (WiC) program in 2007. In 2016, after the new constitution of the Association CiE allowed for the possibility of creating special interest groups, a Special Interest Group named Women in Computability was established. Also since 2016, the WiC program is sponsored by ACM's Women in Computing. This program includes a workshop, the annual WiC dinner, the mentorship program and a grant program for young female researchers. The Women in Computability workshop continued in 2023, coordinated by Liesbeth de Mol.

The organizers of CiE 2023 would like to acknowledge and thank the following entities for their financial support: the *Association for Symbolic Logic* (ASL) and *Springer-Verlag*.

We gratefully thank all the members of the entire Organizing Committee of CiE 2023 for their work towards making the conference a successful event.

May 2023

Gianluca Della Vedova
Besik Dundua
Steffen Lempp
Florin Manea

Organization

Program Committee Chairs

Gianluca Della Vedova (Co-chair)	University of Milano–Bicocca, Italy
Steffen Lempp (Co-chair)	University of Wisconsin–Madison, USA

Steering Committee

Marcella Anselmo	University of Salerno, Italy
Verónica Becher	University of Buenos Aires, Argentina
Liesbeth De Mol	University of Lille, France
Gianluca Della Vedova	University of Milano–Bicocca, Italy
Nataša Jonoska	University of South Florida, USA
Benedikt Löwe	University of Amsterdam, The Netherlands
Florin Manea (Chair)	Göttingen University, Germany
Elvira Mayordomo	University of Zaragoza, Spain
Klaus Meer	Cottbus University, Germany
Russell Miller	City University of New York, USA
Mariya Soskova	University of Wisconsin–Madison, USA

Program Committee

Nikolay Bazhenov	Novosibirsk State University, Russia
Manuel Bodirsky	TU Dresden, Germany
Vasco Brattka	University of the Bundeswehr Munich, Germany
Liesbeth De Mol	University of Lille, France
Besik Dundua	Kutaisi International University, Georgia
Juan Luis Gastaldi	ETH Zurich, Switzerland
Thomas Graf	Stony Brook University, USA
Delaram Kahrobaei	City University of New York, USA
Ekaterina Komendantskaya	Heriot-Watt University, UK
Angeliki Koutsoukou-Argyraki	Cambridge University, UK
Florin Manea	Göttingen University, Germany
Klaus Meer	Cottbus University, Germany
Isabel Oitavem	Nova University Lisbon, Portugal
Roland Omanadze	Ivane Javakhishvili Tbilisi State University, Georgia
Daniel Paulusma	Durham University, UK
Elaine Pimentel	University College London, UK
Markus Schmid	Humboldt University Berlin, Germany
Shinnosuke Seki	University of Electro-Communications, Tokyo, Japan

Sebastiaan Terwijn	Radboud University Nijmegen, The Netherlands
Dan Turetsky	Victoria University of Wellington, New Zealand
Linda Westrick	Pennsylvania State University, USA

Organizing Committee

Anzor Beridze	Batumi Shota Rustaveli State University, Georgia
Mikheil Donadze	Batumi Shota Rustaveli State University, Georgia
Besik Dundua (Chair)	Kutaisi International University and Institute of Applied Mathematics, Tbilisi State University, Georgia
Mikheil Rukhaia (Co-chair)	Institute of Applied Mathematics, Tbilisi State University, Georgia
Lela Turmanidze	Batumi Shota Rustaveli State University, Georgia

Additional Reviewers

Arrighi, Emmanuel
Batyrshin, Ilnur
Berndt, Sebastian
Bienvenu, Laurent
Blanc, Manon
Bollig, Benedikt
Brice, Léonard
Brown, Joseph Alexander
Cai, Jin-Yi
Carl, Merlin
Carvalho, Margarida
Casel, Katrin
Chen, Lijie
Chitaia, Irakli
Curticapean, Radu
de Brecht, Matthew
Duncan, Adamson
Eastaugh, Benedict
Erlebach, Thomas
Fernau, Henning
Fiori Carones, Marta
Fiorino, Guido
Freund, Anton
Gabelaia, David
Graça, Daniel
Grigoriev, Dima
Hausmann, Daniel

Heller, Jonah
Hirahara, Shuichi
Hirst, Jeff
Kari, Jarkko
Kihara, Takayuki
Kirst, Dominik
Knäuer, Simon
Krebbers, Robbert
Kristiansen, Lars
Köhler, Ekkehard
Le Coz, Corentin
Lisitsa, Alexei
Lutfalla, Victor
Löding, Christof
Mariot, Luca
McCauley, Samuel
Melnikov, Alexander
Miller, Russell
Mottet, Antoine
Nikolaev, Andrey
Noce, Marialaura
Ospichev, Sergei
Pauly, Arno
Rauzy, Emmanuel
Ribeiro, João
Richerby, David
Richter, Linus

Roman'kov, Vitaly
Rukhaia, Mikheil
Salo, Ville
San Mauro, Luca
Santos, Paulo Guilherme
Schlicht, Philipp
Schmidt, Christiane
Schroeder, Matthias
Seisenberger, Monika
Selivanov, Victor
Sergei, Artemov
Sorbi, Andrea

Spicher, Antoine
Stephan, Frank
Ushakov, Alexander
Valenti, Manlio
von Oertzen, Timo
Welch, Philip
Wicke, Kristina
Wilson, James
Wrona, Michał
Yamaleev, Mars
Zimand, Marius

Invited Tutorial

Ramsey's Theory Computes Through Sparsity

Ludovic Patey[1,2,3]

[1] Équipe de Logique Mathématique
[2] IMJ-PRG - Université Paris Cité
[3] Bâtiment Sophie Germain

Abstract. Ramsey's theory is a branch of combinatorics which studies the conditions under which structural phenomena appear within sufficiently large amount of data.

The most famous such example is probably Ramsey's theorem for graphs, asserting for every infinite graph, the existence of an infinite subset of vertices whose induced graph is either a clique, or an anticlique.

Many of such statements can be seen as mathematical problems, formulated in terms of instances and solutions. For example, an instance of Ramsey's theorem for graphs is an infinite graph, and a solution is any infinite subset of vertices whose induced subgraph satisfies the desired properties.

One can measure the computational power of these statements in terms of the Turing degrees of their solutions.

In this tutorial, we will learn how the combinatorial nature of these statements affect their computational power through various examples, and will see a recurring theme emerge: the computational power of theorems coming from Ramsey's theory comes from the sparsity of their solutions.

Invited Speakers

The Complexity of CSP-Based Ideal Membership Problems

Andrei Bulatov

School of Computing Science, Simon Fraser University, Burnaby BC, Canada

Abstract. In this talk we consider the Ideal Membership Problem (IMP for short), in which we are given polynomials $f_0, f_1, \ldots, f_k$ and the question is to decide whether f_0 belongs to the ideal generated by $f_1, \ldots, f_k$. In the more stringent version the task is also to find a proof of this fact. The IMP underlies many proof systems based on polynomials such as Nullstellensatz, Polynomial Calculus, and Sum-of-Squares (SOS). In such applications the IMP usually involves so-called combinatorial ideals that arise from a variety of discrete combinatorial problems. This restriction makes the IMP significantly easier and in some cases allows for an efficient solution algorithm.

The first part of this talk follows the work of Mastrolilli [SODA 2019] who initiated a systematic study of IMPs arising from Constraint Satisfaction Problems (CSP) of the form CSP(G), that is, CSPs in which the type of constraints is limited to relations from a set G.

We show that many CSP techniques can be translated to IMPs thus allowing us to significantly improve the methods of studying the complexity of the IMP. In particular, we use them to prove a general necessary condition for the tractability of the IMP, and three sufficient ones. The sufficient conditions include IMPs arising from systems of linear equations over $GF(p)$, p prime, and also some conditions defined through similar conditions.

Our work has several consequences and applications. We mention one of them - a variation of the IMP and based on this propose a unified framework, different from the celebrated Buchberger's algorithm, to construct a bounded degree Groebner Basis. Our algorithm, combined with CSP techniques, leads to polynomial-time construction of Groebner Basis for many combinatorial problems.

Towards More Robust Schemes
for Programming Molecules

Anne Condon

Department of Computer Science, University of British Columbia,
Vancouver, Canada

Abstract. In this talk I'll provide an introduction to two widely-studied molecular programming models, and describe recent work on two questions:

- Chemical reaction networks (CRNs) are an elegant molecular programming language, capable of simulating logic circuits, neural networks, and more. Runtime analysis of CRNs usually relies on a "well mixed" assumption. How might we relax that assumption to obtain more insight on the robustness of CRN programs under more realistic, or even adversarial, conditions?
- DNA strand displacement systems (DSDs) are a lower-level programming language, and a very useful intermediate description of molecular computations, between CRNs and a real DNA implementation. However, current schemes for translating abstract CRNs down to DSDs haven't scaled well. How might we do better?

Invited Abstracts

Primitive Recursive Degree Spectra
of Structures

Iskander Kalimullin 🆔

Kazan Federal University, Kremlevskaya st. 18, 420008, Kazan, Russia
ikalimul@gmail.com

Abstract. We present some new results on the degrees of presentations of algebraic structures under primitive recursive reducibility.

Keywords: Algebraic structure · Primitive recursive function · Primitive recursive reducibility

We say that a function g is *primitive recursively reducible* to a function f ($g \leq_{PR} f$) if g can be obtained from f and the basic (sometimes called initial) primitve recursive functions $o(x), s(x), I_m^n$ by the composition and primitive recursion operators. It is easy to check that this relation satisfies all necessary properties of reducibility (reflexivity, transitivity, etc.), so that we can introduce the *PR*-equivalence $\equiv_{PR}$ and the *PR*-degrees. As usual, identifying the sets and predicates with their characteristic functions allows us to consider primitive recursive reducibility on sets. Note that the graph of a function is primitive recursively reducible to the function itself but the reverse reducibility can fail. In general, only functions dominated by primitive recursive functions are *PR*-reducible to sets.

Extending the definition of fully primitive recursive (punctual) structures from [1] we now say that an algebraic structure $\mathcal{A}$ in a finite signature with domain ω is *primitive recursively reducible* to a function f ($\mathcal{A} \leq_{PR} f$) if each operation and predicate from $\mathcal{A}$ is primitive recursively reducible to f. Then similarly to the Turing reducibility case the *PR-degree spectrum* of an infinite structure $\mathcal{A}$ can be defined as the collection of all functions f to which some isomorphic copy is primitive recursive:
$$DS_{PR}(\mathcal{A}) = \{f : (\exists \mathcal{B} \cong \mathcal{A})[\mathcal{B} \leq_{PR} f]\}.$$

For example, we can easily present the upper *PR*-cone of a set $A \subseteq \omega$ as a *PR*-degree spectra of a structure:
$$DS_{PR}(\omega; 0, 1, +, A) = \{f : A \leq_{PR} f\}.$$

A simple forcing argument shows that a non-trivial union of two or more upper *PR*-cones can not form a *PR*-degree spectra of a structure.

By Theorem 3.2 from [2] the *PR*-degree spectra of a structure $\mathcal{A}$ forms a cone $\{f : A \leq_{PR} f\}$ only if the set A is primitive recursively coded into the quantifier-free theory of the structure $\mathcal{A}$. Note that an arbitrary functional cone $\{f : g \leq_{PR} f\}$ may be not possible. Moreover, the following proposition holds:

Proposition 1. *(See the proof of Theorem 3.2 from [2]). Let* $\mathcal{A} \leq_{PR} f$ *be a structure in a finite signature. Then there is a structure* $\mathcal{B} \cong \mathcal{A}$ *such that* $\mathcal{B} \leq_{PR} f$ *and all*

operations in $\mathcal{B}$ are domintated by primitive recursive functions, and so, they are PR-equivalent to some sets. Therefore, if $f \in DS_{PR}(\mathcal{A})$ then for some set $X \in DS_{PR}(\mathcal{A})$ we have $X \leq_{PR} f$.

The property of PR-degree spectra described in the conclusion of the previous proposition will be called below the *set-basis property*.

Other examples of PR-degree spectra can be found among the complements of lower PR-cones, i.e., the collections $\{f : f \not\leq_{PR} g\}$. The easiest case $g = \emptyset$ is covered by the following result:

Theorem 1. *[3] There is an algebraic structure $\mathcal{A}$ with two unary operations and one unary predicate such that*

1. there is no primitive recursive structure $\mathcal{B} \cong \mathcal{A}$;

2. if a functuion f is not primitive recursive then there is a structure $\mathcal{B} \leq_{PR} f$ such that $\mathcal{B} \cong \mathcal{A}$.

In other words, $DS_{PR}(\mathcal{A}) = \{f : f \not\leq_{PR} \emptyset\}$.

The essential part of the proof is the examination of the set-basis property for the collection $\{f : f \not\leq_{PR} \emptyset\}$:

Proposition 2. *([3]). If a function f is not primitive recursive then there is a set $X \leq_{PR} f$ such that X is not primitive recursive.*

Extending this proposition we can see that some other complements of lower PR-cones also satisfy the set-basis property.

Proposition 3. *If $f \not\leq_{PR} g$ and the graph of g is primitive recursive then there is a set $X \leq_{PR} f$ such that $X \not\leq_{PR} g$.*

As a corollary, we can then extend Theorem 1 as follows:

Theorem 2. *If the graph of a computable function g is primitive recursive then there is an algebraic structure $\mathcal{A}$ with two unary operations and one unary predicate such that $DS_{PR}(\mathcal{A}) = \{f : f \not\leq_{PR} g\}$.*

If a function g is computable then the set-basis property is the main difficulty towards building a structure with PR-spectrum $\{f : f \not\leq_{PR} g\}$. And this property can fail for some specific g. Indeed, let h be any computable function not dominated by primitive recursive functions (e.g., let h be the Ackerman function). Let $P_0, P_1, P_2, \ldots$ be all sets primitive recursively reducible to h, and let P be a set such that $P_i \leq_{PR} P$ for each $i \in \omega$ (e.g., let P be the uniform join of all P_i's). Then $h \not\leq_{PR} P$ due the non-domination property of h, but

$$X \leq_{PR} h \Rightarrow (\exists i)[X = P_i] \Rightarrow X \leq_{PR} P$$

for every set X, so that the set-basis property for the collection $\{f : f \not\leq_{PR} P\}$ fails.

Proposition 4. *There is a computable set P such that the collection $\{f : f \not\leq_{PR} P\}$ does not equal the PR-degree spectrum of any structure.*

Note that the study of the PR-degree spectra of the form $\{f : f \not\leq_{PR} g\}$, where g is a non-computable function, can cause more problems similar to the situation with Turing degree spectra [4–6].

Acknowledgements. The work is supported by the Russian Science Foundation (grant no. 23-21-00181) and performed under the development program of Volga Region Mathematical Center (agreement no. 075-02-2023-944).

References

1. Kalimullin, I., Melnikov, A., Ng, K.M.: Algebraic structures computable without delay. Theor. Comput. Sci. **674**, 73–98 (2017)
2. Kalimullin, I., Melnikov, A., Montalban, A.: Punctual definability on structures. Ann. Pure Appl. Logic **172**, 102987 (2021)
3. Kalimullin, I.S.: Punctual structures and primitive recursive reducibility. Lobachevskii J. Math. **43**, 582–586 (2022)
4. Kalimullin, I.S.: Spectra of degrees of some structures. Algebra Logic. **46**, 399–408 (2007)
5. Kalimullin, I.S.: Almost computably enumerable families of sets. Sb. Math. **199**, 1451–1458 (2008)
6. Andrews, U., Cai, M., Kalimullin, I.S., Lempp, S., Miller, J.S., Montalban A.: The complements of lower cones of degrees and the degree spectra of structures. J. Symbol. Logic **81**, 997–1006 (2016)

Simultaneous Cupping and Continuity in Bounded Turing Degrees

Guohua Wu

Division of Mathematical Sciences, School of Physical and Mathematical
Sciences, Nanyang Technological University, 21 Nanyang Link,
Singapore 637371
guohua@ntu.edu.sg

A computably enumerable (c.e. for short) degree $\mathbf{a}$ is cuppable if there is an incomplete c.e. degree $\mathbf{c}$ such that $\mathbf{a} \cup \mathbf{c} = \mathbf{0}'$. Correspondingly, $\mathbf{a}$ is low_n-cuppable with $n \geq 1$ if $\mathbf{c}$ above can be chosen as a low_n c.e. degree. As usual, low_1 is simply denoted by low.

In 1984, Ambos-Spies, Jockusch, Shore and Soare proved in [2] that $\mathbf{a}$ is low cuppable if and only if $\mathbf{a}$ is noncappable if and only if $\mathbf{a}$ is promtly simple. In [6], Li, Wu and Zhang proved the existence of a c.e. degree $\mathbf{a}$ which is cappable (hence not low cuppable) and low_2 cuppable, and raised a hierarchy of cuppable c.e. degrees as $\mathbf{LC}_1 \subseteq \mathbf{LC}_2 \subseteq \mathbf{LC}_3 \subseteq \cdots$, where $\mathbf{LC}_n$ denotes the class of low_n-cuppable degrees. Recently, Greenberg, Ng and Wu proved in [4] that there exist incomplete cuppable degrees which can only be cupped to $\mathbf{0}'$ by high degrees (in fact, superhigh).

Fix $n \geq 1$. Say that a collection $\mathcal{A}$ of n many c.e. degrees is simultaneously cuppable is simultaneously cuppable, if there exists an incomplete computably enumerable degree cupping all degrees in $\mathcal{A}$ to $\mathbf{0}'$. We thus have the notion of cuppable degrees, when $n = 1$. A recent result of Tran and Wu [7] says that for each $n \geq 1$, there exists a collection of n many c.e. degrees, such that any $n - 1$ of $\mathcal{A}$ is simultaneously cuppable, but $\mathcal{A}$ itself is not simultaneously cuppable. For $n = 2$ this was originally proved by Li, Wu and Yang in [5].

In this talk, I will present the idea of constructing simultaneously cuppable degrees in c.e. bounded Turing degrees, also known as weak-truth-table degrees. Constructions in bounded Turing degrees are usually mild and simpler than those for Turing degrees due to the change of convergence modes of computations. Unlike Lachlan's non-splitting for c.e. Turing degrees, in this structure, splitting and density can be combined. Cupping properties in bounded Turing degrees have been extensively studied by Ambos-Spies in [1].

We will also present some results on the continuity property of simultaneous cupping in bounded Turing degrees. That is, in bounded Turing degrees, if $\mathbf{c}$ cups all degrees in a finite collection $\mathcal{A}$ to $\mathbf{0}'_{bT}$, then there exists $\mathbf{a} < \mathbf{c}$ cupping all degrees in $\mathcal{A}$ to $\mathbf{0}'_{bT}$.

The author is partially supported by MOE Tier 1 grant RG111/19, Singapore.

References

1. Ambos-Spies, K.: Cupping and noncapping in the r.e. weak truth table and Turing degrees. Arch. für Math. Logik und Grund. **25**, 109–126 (1985)
2. Ambos-Spies, K., Jockusch, C.G., Shore, R.A., Soare, R.I.: An algebraic decomposition of the recursively enumerable degrees and the coincidence of several degree classes with the promptly simple degrees. Tran. Amer. Math. Soc. **281**, 109–128 (1984)
3. Cooper, S.B.: On a theorem of C. E. M. Yates. Handwritten Notes (1974)
4. Greenberg, N., Ng, K.M., Wu, G.: Cupping and jump classes in the computably enumerable degrees. J. Symbolic Logic **85**(4), 1499–1545 (2020)
5. Li, A., Wu, G., Yang, Y.: On the quotient structure of computably enumerable degrees modulo the noncuppable ideal. In: Cai, JY., Cooper, S.B., Li, A. (eds.) Theory and Applications of Models of Computation. TAMC 2006. LNCS, vol. 3959, pp. 731–736. Springer, Berlin (2006). https://doi.org/10.1007/11750321_69
6. Li, A., Wu, G., Zhang, Z.: A hierarchy for cuppable degrees. Illinois J. Math. **44**(3), 619–632 (2000)
7. Tran, H.H., Wu, G.: A hierarchy for cuppable degrees. This volume
8. Soare, R.I.: Recursively Enumerable Sets and Degrees. Perspectives in Mathematical Logic. Springer-Verlag, Berlin (1987)

Multiple Permitting Notions for the Not Totally ω-C.A. Computably Enumerable Degrees

Klaus Ambos-Spies

Department of Mathematics and Computer Science, Universität Heidelberg,
Im Neuenheimer Feld 205 D-69120, Heidelberg, Germany
ambos@math.uni-heidelberg.de

Abstract. Downey and Greenberg [5] introduced an infinite hierarchy of the computably enumerable sets and degrees by classifying the computational power of such sets and degrees according to the mind-change complexity of the functions computable from them. A degree is computationally weak in this sense if it can only compute functions which possess computable approximations which have few mind changes. The two lowest levels of this hierarchy are the classes of the array computable degrees and the totally ω-c.a. degrees. Here a c.e. degree **a** is array computable if there is a computable function h such that any function f computed by **a** is h-computably approximable (h-c.a.), i.e., possesses a computable approximation where the mind-change function is bounded by h. The latter property is a nonuniform version of the former, i.e., **a** is totally ω-c.a. if, for any function $f \leq_T \mathbf{a}$, there is a computable function h such that f is h-c.a. Both degree classes and their complements, the array noncomputable c.e. degrees and the not totally ω-c.a. c.e. degrees, turned out to be quite important and allowed the classification of quite a few properties of the c.e. sets and degrees (see [5]).

Originally, the array computable degrees have been introduced by Downey, Jockusch and Stob [6] in a different way. In [6] array noncomputable (a.n.c.) sets are introduced which are tailored for capturing certain multiple permitting arguments, and a c.e. degree is called array computable if it does not contain any a.n.c. set. Since the permitting technique yields wtt-reductions, the definition of the a.n.c. sets is based on the complexity of the functions wtt-computable from the sets (while the previously stated definition is concerned with the functions which are Turing-computable from the sets).

In our talk we introduce analogs of the array noncomputable sets, defined in terms of multiple permittings, which capture the permitting strength of the not totally ω-c.a. Turing degrees. In particular, we introduce the universally array noncomputable (u.a.n.c.) sets and the uniformly multiply permitting (u.m.p.) sets. The former notion is derived from the a.n.c. sets of Downey, Jockusch and Stob [6] while the latter notion is based on a closely related but somewhat more explicit multiple permitting notion for the a.n.c. degrees which we introduced in [1]. Both notions coincide up to wtt-equivalence, the latter – but not the former – being wtt-invariant. As we show, the (Turing) degrees of the uniformly permitting sets are just the c.e. degrees which are not totally ω-c.a., and any such degree contains a c.e. wtt-degree of u.m.p. sets and a c.e. wtt-degree which does not contain any u.m.p. set. The latter shows that not all c.e. sets in a not totally ω-c.a. degree have the same permitting power (with respect to wtt-reducibility).

We discuss the advantages provided by our alternative characterizations of the not totally ω-c.a. degrees. In particular we show how, by working with the newly introduced 'generic' sets for the considered degree class, we may strengthen some results and at the same time obtain some simplified, modular proofs which eliminate redundancies in the arguments based on the original mind-change characterization of the not totally ω-c.a. degrees.

Finally, we introduce and discuss some variations of the a.n.c. sets and our new multiply permitting notions for the almost-c.e. sets (i.e., left-c.e. reals) in place of the c.e. sets.

Most of the results presented in our talk are taken from some joint works with Nan Fang, Nadine Losert, Martin Monath and Wolfgang Merkle (see [2–4]).

Keywords: Computably enumerable sets and degrees · Array noncomputable sets and degrees · Totally ω-c.a. sets and degrees · Weak truth table reducibility · Permitting.

References

1. Ambos-Spies, K.: Multiple permitting and array noncomputability. In: Manea, F., Miller, R., Nowotka, D. (eds.) Sailing Routes in the World of Computation. CiE 2018. LNCS, vol. 10936, pp. 30–39. Springer, Cham (2018). https://doi.org/10.1007/978-3-319-94418-0_3
2. Ambos-Spies, K., Fang, N., Losert, N., Merkle, W., Monath, M.: Array noncomputability: a modular approach. Unpublished Notes
3. Ambos-Spies, K., Losert, N.: Universally array noncomputable sets. To appear
4. Ambos-Spies, K., Losert, N., Monath, M.: Array noncomputable left-c.e. reals. To appear
5. Downey, R., Greenberg, N.: A hierarchy of Turing degrees. A transfinite hierarchy of lowness notions in the computably enumerable degrees, unifying classes, and natural definability. Annals of Mathematics Studies, 206, pp. xii+222. Princeton University Press, Princeton (2020)
6. Downey, R., Jockusch, C., Stob, M.: Array nonrecursive sets and multiple permitting arguments. In: Ambos-Spies, K., Müller, G.H., Sacks, G.E. (eds.) Recursion Theory Week. LNM, vol. 1432, pp. 141–173. Springer, Berlin (1990). https://doi.org/10.1007/BFb0086116

Is there a Jump in the Weihrauch Lattice?

Manlio Valenti (iD)

Department of Mathematics, University of Wisconsin - Madison, Madison, USA
manlio.valenti@wisc.edu

A very important notion in the study of Weihrauch reducibility is the jump operator. The jump of the multi-valued function $f : \subseteq X \rightrightarrows Y$ is the problem $f' : \subseteq X' \rightrightarrows Y$ defined as $f'(x) := f(x)$, where X' is the represented space $(X, \delta_{X'})$ *and* $\delta_{X'}$ maps a convergent sequence $(p_n)_{n \in \mathbb{N}}$ in $\mathbb{N}^{\mathbb{N}}$ to $\delta_X(\lim_{n \to \infty} p_n)$. In other words, f' takes in input a sequence that converges to a name of an f-instance and produces an f-solution to that instance.

In a more general context, we say that a partial order $(P, \leq)$ admits a jump if there is a map $J : P \to P$ s.t. for every $p, q \in P, p < J(p)$ and $p \leq q \Rightarrow J(p) \leq J(q)$. We show that the existence of a jump on countable partial orders is a Σ_1^1-complete property, and hence no easier characterization is possible.

Despite its name, the jump in the Weihrauch lattice fails to satisfy both these properties: it is not degree-theoretic and there are functions f s.t. $f \equiv_W f'$. This raises the natural question: is there a (better) jump in the Weihrauch lattice?

We answer this question positively and provide an explicit definition for an operator on multi-valued functions that, when lifted to the Weihrauch degrees, induces a jump operator. We explore its algebraic properties and provide explicit characterizations for the jump of some milestone problems in the Weihrauch lattice.

This is joint work with Uri Andrews, Steffen Lempp, Alberto Marcone, and Joe Miller.

Exploring the Non-Computability of Machine Learning Classifiers

Tonicha Crook[1] , Jay Paul Morgan[2] , Arno Pauly[1] ,
and Markus Roggenbach[1]

[1]Department of Computer Science, Swansea University, Swansea, Wales, UK
t.m.crook15@outlook.com, arno.m.pauly@gmail.com,
m.roggenbach@swansea.ac.uk
[2]Université de Toulon, Aix Marseille Univ, CNRS, LIS, Marseille, France
jay.morgan@univ-tln.fr

This paper is a follow-on from our previous paper [3] where we presented methods using Computable Analysis to verify Machine Learning (ML) techniques. Algorithmic issues of ML can be studied in the abstract setting of Computable Analysis as most ML notions are based on real numbers. Classifiers are a basic concept of ML, we define these classifiers using represented spaces; a classifier is a continuous function that takes some $x \in \mathbf{X}$ as input, and either outputs a colour $j \in \mathbf{k}$, or diverges ($\perp$). Therefore, an implementable classifier has to be a computable function and therefore has to be continuous.

We successfully answered verification questions given different classifiers. For example, we can verify whether a DDOS-attack returns false negatives, or whether all points in the attack are classified as expected. Finding and preventing adversarial examples is of high interest in the ML community. Adversarial examples occur when a small change to the input results in a miss-classified output. We defined a notion of an instance using computable metric spaces. This allows us to perform the principle method of robustness and verification – checking if a classifier is susceptible to adversarial examples by checking each of the adherent points for catastrophic changes in output classification [2].

An important aspect of ML procedures is the learning process. Continuing the idea that learning is a computable process, the learners themselves can be assumed to be continuous [4]. From this, we can ask how robust the classifier that we are learning with the training data is. Using computable compactness and computable overtness we can show that telling whether a point or region is robust (i.e. does not change class) are computable operations. Another notion we introduce is sparse or dense training data, where data is dense at a point x if adding an additional data point far from x does not change its classification, but sparse does [5]. The operation defining if a point is sparse or dense is also computable using computably compact, computable metric space.

These results are generally optimal, meaning that providing less information on the input, demanding more information about the output, or relaxing the restrictions on the

This work is supported by the UKRI AIMLAC CDT, cdt-aimlac.org, grant no. EP/S023992/1.

ambient space will in general render the maps non-computable. A feature of all our "decision" procedures is that we allow for a case of *no information given*, i.e. that we include $\perp$ in the range of potential answers.

Here, we use Weihrauch degrees to examine *how* non-computable certain problems become [1]. Such an approach reveals whether relaxing our demands for the nature of computation permits us to answer more questions. A typical example could be, to be satisfied with any algorithm that is going to converge to a correct answer, even if nothing is known about the convergence speed.

We also compare the following kind: Consider an ML-inspired problem that is computable for compact sets, but not for closed sets. How does its Weihrauch degree for closed sets compare to the Weihrauch degree for translating a closed set into a compact set? To enable this, we provide some new results concerning the translations between different spaces of subsets.

A verification question is computable given a specific type of set, according to our findings in [3]. What transpires, though, if the set that we are provided is of a different type? Usually, compact or overt information is required. We study what happens when we have closed information instead. If a given closed set is bounded, there is a name as a compact set for it. The same holds for overt. In general, these translations fail to be computable. What is the Weihrauch degree of such a translation? How do we compare the complexity of the solution on closed sets with the complexity of a solution obtained through translation?

It turns out that the Weihrauch degree of translating from closed to compact is Π^0_1Bound. Translating from closed to overt is already known to be lim [6]. Concerning the second question, for instance, the complexity is isInfinite$_\mathsf{S}$ for the question if a classifier outputs one specific colour for all inputs for a given closed set in $\mathbb{R}^n$. We prove that isInfinite$_\mathsf{S}$ is strictly weaker than Π^0_1Bound but they coincide up to unbounded finite parallelisation [7]. That means for this verification task that the complexity of direct verification on closed sets is as close to the complexity of the translation task as could be expected.

References

1. Brattka, V., Gherardi, G., Pauly, A.: Weihrauch complexity in computable analysis. In: Brattka, V., Hertling, P. (eds.) Handbook of Computability and Complexity in Analysis. Theory and Applications of Computability, pp. 367–417. Springer, Cham (2021). https://doi.org/10.1007/978-3-030-59234-911
2. Casadio, M., et al.: Neural network robustness as a verification property: a principled case study. In: Shoham, S., Vizel, Y. (eds.) Computer Aided Verification. CAV 2022. LNCS, vol. 13371, pp. 219–231. Springer, Cham (2022). https://doi.org/10.1007/978-3-031-13185-1_11
3. Crook, T., Morgan, J., Pauly, A., Roggenbach, M.: A computability perspective on (verified) machine learning (2021). https://arxiv.org/abs/2102.06585
4. Kwiatkowska, M.: Safety and robustness for deep learning with provable guarantees. In: Proceedings of the 35th IEEE/ACM International Conference on Automated Software Engineering, pp. 1–3 (2020)

5. Morgan, J., Paiement, A., Pauly, A., Seisenberger, M.: Adaptive neighbourhoods for the discovery of adversarial examples (2021). https://arxiv.org/abs/2101.09108
6. Pauly, A., Fouché, W.L.: How constructive is constructing measures? J. Log. Anal. **9** (2017). http://logicandanalysis.org/index.php/jla/article/view/241/121
7. Solda, G., Valenti, M.: Algebraic properties of the first-order part of a problem (2022). https://doi.org/10.48550/ARXIV.2203.16298

Gödel's Dialectica Transformation is Reverse Differentiation

Marie Kerjean[1] and Pierre-Marie Pédrot[2]

[1] Speaker, CNRS, LIPN, Université Sorbonne Nord, Paris, France
kerjean@lipn.fr
[2] Inria, France
pedrot@inria.fr

Dialectica was originally introduced by Gödel in a famous paper [7] as a way to constructively interpret an extension of HA [1], and turned out to be a very fertile object of its own. Judged too complex, it was quickly simplified by Kreisel into the well-known realizability interpretation that now bears his name. Soon after the inception of Linear Logic (LL), Dialectica was shown to factorize through Girard's embedding of LJ into LL, purveying an expressive technique to build categorical models of LL [13]. In its logical outfit, Dialectica led to numerous applications and was tweaked into an unending array of variations in the proof mining community [10].

The modern way to look at Dialectica is however to consider it as a program translation, or more precisely *two* mutually defined translations of the λ-calculus exposing intensional information [14].

In a different scientific universe, Automatic Differentiation [8] (AD) is the field that studies the design and implementation of *efficient* algorithms computing the differentiation of mathematical expression and numerical programs. Indeed, due to the chain rule, computing the differential of a sequence of expressions involves a choice, namely when to compute the value of a given expression and when to compute the value of its derivative. Two extremal algorithms coexist. On the one hand, forward differentiation [16] computes functions and their derivatives pairwise in the order they are provided, while on the other hand reverse differentiation [12] computes all functions first and then their derivative in reverse order. Depending on the setting, one can behave more efficiently than the other. Notably, reverse differentiation has been critically used in the fashionable context of deep learning.

Differentiable programming is a rather new and lively research domain aiming at expressing automatic differentiation techniques through the prism of the traditional tools of the programming language theory community. As such, it has been studied through continuations [15], functoriality [6], and linear types [4]. It led to a myriad of implementation over rich programming languages, proven correct through semantics of higher-order differentiable functions [11]. Surprisingly, these various principled explorations of automatic differentiation are what allows us to draw a link between Dialectica and differentiation in logic.

The simple, albeit fundamental claim of this talk is that, behind its different logical avatars, the Dialectica translation is in fact a reverse differentiation algorithm, where the linearity and involutivity of differentiation have been forgotten. In the domain of proof theory, differentiation has been very much studied from the point of view of *linear logic*. This led to Differential Linear Logic [5] (DiLL), differential categories [3], or the differential λ-calculus. To support our thesis with evidence, I will formally state a correspondence between each of these objects and the corresponding Dialectica interpretation.

More generally, Dialectica is known for extracting *quantitative* information from proofs [10], and this relates very much with the quantitative point of view that differentiation has brought to λ-calculus [2]. Herbelin also notices at the end of its paper realizing Markov's rule through delimited continuations that this axiom has the type of a differentiation operator [9]. If time permits, I will explore the possible consequences of formally relating reverse differentiation and Dialectica to proof mining and Herbelin's work in the conclusion.

References

1. Avigad, J., Feferman, S.: Gödel's functional ('dialectica') interpretation. In: Buss, S.R. (ed.) Handbook of Proof Theory. Elsevier Science Publishers (1998)
2. Barbarossa, D., Manzonetto, G.: Taylor subsumes scott, berry, kahn and plotkin. Proc. ACM Program. Lang. **4**(POPL), **1**(1–1), 23 (2020)
3. Blute, R.F., Cockett, J.R.B., Seely, R.A.G.: Differential categories. Math. Structures Comput. Sci. **16**(6), 1049–1083 (2006)
4. Brunel, A., Mazza, D., Pagani, M.: Backpropagation in the simply typed lambda-calculus with linear negation. POPL (2020)
5. Ehrhard, T., Regnier, L.: Differential interaction nets. Theoretical Computer Science **364**(2) (2006)
6. Elliott, C.: The simple essence of automatic differentiation. In: Proceedings of the ACM on Programming Languages (ICFP) (2018)
7. Gödel, K.: Über eine bisher noch nicht benützte Erweiterung des finiten Standpunktes. Dialectica **12**, 280–287 (1958)
8. Griewank, A., Walther, A.: Evaluating Derivatives: Principles and Techniques of Algorithmic Differentiation. Society for Industrial and Applied Mathematics, USA, 2nd edn. (2008)
9. Herbelin, H.: An intuitionistic logic that proves markov's principle. LICS 2010
10. Kohlenbach, U.: Applied Proof Theory - Proof Interpretations and their Use in Mathematics. Springer Monographs in Mathematics, Springer, Cham (2008). https://doi.org/10.1007/978-3-540-77533-1
11. Krawiec, F., Peyton Jones, S., Krishnaswami, N., Ellis, T., Eisenberg, R.A., Fitzgibbon, A.: Provably correct, asymptotically efficient, higher-order reverse-mode automatic differentiation. Proc. ACM Program. Lang. **6**(POPL), 1–30 (2022)
12. Linnainmaa, S.: Taylor expansion of the accumulated rounding error. BIT Numerical Mathematics **16**, 146–160 (1976)
13. de Paiva, V.: A dialectica-like model of linear logic. In: Category Theory and Computer Science (1989)
14. Pédrot, P.: A functional functional interpretation. CSL-LICS '14, Vienna, Austria, pp. 14–18 (2014)
15. Wang, F., Zheng, D., Decker, J., Wu, X., Essertel, G.M., Rompf, T.: Demystifying differentiable programming: Shift/reset the penultimate backpropagator **3**(ICFP), 1–31 (2019)
16. Wengert, R.E.: A simple automatic derivative evaluation program. Commun. ACM **7**(8), 463–464 (1964)

Disjunction-Free Disjunction Property

Emil Jeřábek

Institute of Mathematics, Czech Academy of Sciences, Czechia
jerabek@math.cas.cz
https://math.cas.cz/~jerabek

Frege proof systems (often called Hilbert-style systems outside proof complexity) are among the simplest and most natural proof systems for classical and nonclassical propositional logics; they are polynomially equivalent to sequent calculi and natural deduction systems, which further testifies to their robustness and fundamental status. Although it is commonly assumed for all classical propositional proof systems that some tautologies require exponentially large proofs, this has been proven so far only for relatively weak proof systems; unrestricted Frege systems are far beyond the reach of current lower bound techniques.

Curiously, the state of affairs is much better in nonclassical logics: Hrubeš [3–5] proved exponential lower bounds on the number of lines in Frege proofs for some modal logics and intuitionistic logic, which was generalized by Jeřábek [7] to all transitive modal and superintuitionistic logics with unbounded branching, and by Jalali [6] to substructural logics.

Under the hood, all these lower bounds are based on variants of the *feasible disjunction property*: given a proof of $\varphi_0 \vee \varphi_1$ (or $\Box\varphi_0 \vee \Box\varphi_1$ in the modal case), we can efficiently pinpoint $i \in \{0, 1\}$ such that $\vdash \varphi_i$. (This plays the role of *feasible interpolation* as used in classical proof complexity.) This might suggest that in the intuitionistic case, the lower bounds essentially rely on presence of $\vee$ in the language. Despite that, Jeřábek [8] showed that the intuitionistic lower bounds hold for a sequence of purely implicational tautologies, but he used an indirect argument exploiting implicational translations of intuitionistic tautologies and proofs.

In this talk, we will present a simple direct proof of a disjunction-free formulation of the feasible disjunction property for implicational intuitionistic logic, based on an efficient version of Kleene's slash. More generally, we show an implicational formulation of Hrubeš-style feasible monotone interpolation, which yields a direct proof of an exponential lower bound on explicit intuitionistic implicational tautologies expressing the Clique–Colouring disjoint NP pair. This argument avoids the implicational translation of intuitionistic proofs, and it applies with minimal adaptations to Frege (and Extended Frege) systems, sequent calculi, and natural deduction (even dag-like), obviating the need for polynomial simulation of these proof systems by Frege.

One motivation for this talk comes from recent claims by Gordeev and Haeusler [2], who purport to show that all intuitionistic implicational tautologies have

Supported by the Czech Academy of Sciences (RVO 67985840) and GA CR project 23-04825S.

polynomial-size dag-like natural deduction proofs, implying NP = PSPACE. These claims are wrong as they contradict the above-mentioned exponential lower bounds on intuitionistic implicational proofs, but for a non-specialist, understanding this may require some chasing down the literature and reading between the lines. Using the approach shown in this talk, the proof of the lower bound becomes much simpler, it explicitly covers the Gordeev and Haeusler proof system, and it is self-contained except for monotone circuit lower bounds (Alon and Boppana [1], improving Razborov [10]).

The talk is based on [9].

Keywords: Proof complexity · Intuitionistic implicational logic · Feasible disjunction property · Exponential lower bound.

References

1. Alon, N., Boppana, R.B.: The monotone circuit complexity of Boolean functions. Combinatorica **7**(1), 1–22 (1987)
2. Gordeev, L., Haeusler, E.H.: Proof compression and NP versus PSPACE II. Bulletin of the Section of Logic **49**(3), 213–230 (2020)
3. Hrubeš, P.: Lower bounds for modal logics. J. Symbolic Logic **72**(3), 941–958 (2007)
4. Hrubeš, P.: A lower bound for intuitionistic logic. Annals Pure Appl. Logic **146**(1), 72–90 (2007)
5. Hrubeš, P.: On lengths of proofs in non-classical logics. Annals Pure Appl. Logic **157**(2–3), 194–205 (2009)
6. Jalali, R.: Proof complexity of substructural logics. Annals Pure Appl. Logic **172**(7), 102972, 31 (2021)
7. Jerábek, E.: Substitution Frege and extended Frege proof systems in non-classical logics. Annals Pure Appl. Logic **159**(1–2), 1–48 (2009)
8. Jerábek, E.: Proof complexity of intuitionistic implicational formulas. Annals Pure Appl. Logic **168**(1), 150–190 (2017)
9. Jerábek, E.: A simplified lower bound for implicational logic. arXiv:2303.15090 [cs.LO] (2023). https://arxiv.org/abs/2303.15090
10. Razborov, A.A.: Lower bounds on the monotone complexity of some Boolean functions. Mathematics of the USSR, Doklady **31**, 354–357 (1985)

Exploring the Abyss in Reverse Mathematics and Computability Theory

Sam Sanders

Department of Philosophy II, RUB Bochum, Germany
sasander@me.com
https://sasander.wixsite.com/academic

Abstract. I will present some results from my ongoing project with Dag Normann on the logical and computational properties of the uncountable. In particular, I will discuss recent results (and their connections) in Kohlenbach's *higher-order* Reverse Mathematics (RM for short; see [2]) and Kleene's computability theory based on S1-S9 [1, 3] and our recent lambda calculus formulation [6]. The aforementioned fields constitute generalisations to more abstract objects of Friedman-Simpson's RM [11] and Turing computability [12], which are essentially limited to real numbers and similar second-order constructs.

First of all, we discuss numerous basic third-order theorems from analysis that exhibit 'vanilla' behaviour, both in RM and computability theory. These theorems pertain to well-known function classes (Baire 1, regulated, bounded variation, semi-continuous, cadlag, quasi-continuous...) and are even *equivalent* to the Big Five in RM, with similar results in computability theory ([7], §2.1-7).

Secondly, we also show that *slight* variations or generalisations of these theorems fall far outside of the Big Five, and *much* stronger systems, as full second-order arithmetic comes to the fore ([7], §2.8). Similar (less prissy) results exist in computability theory [8, 9]. The function classes at hand are also well-known: Baire 2, cliquish, semi-continuous, Baire one star.

We have no explanation of the observed 'abyss' between e.g. Baire 1 and Baire 2 or between quasi-continuous and cliquish, especially as these are closely related classes. There also does not seem to be any known philosophy of mathematics that identifies this abyss.

Finally, we explain how the logical and computational properties of the uncountability of the reals as follows:

there is no injection from $\mathbb{R}$ to $\mathbb{N}$.   (NIN)

plays a central role in our project [4, 5, 10].

References

1. Kleene, S.C.: Recursive functionals and quantifiers of finite types. I, Trans. Amer. Math. Soc. **91**, 1–52 (1959)

This research was supported by the *Deutsche Forschungsgemeinschaft* (DFG) (grant nr. SA3418/1-1) and the *Klaus Tschira Boost Fund* (grant nr. GSO/KT 43).

2. Kohlenbach, U.: Higher order reverse mathematics, Reverse mathematics 2001. LNL, vol. 21, ASL, pp. 281–295 (2005)
3. Longley, J., Normann, D.: Higher-order Computability, Theory and Applications of Computability. Springer, Berlin (2015). https://doi.org/10.1007/978-3-662-47992-6
4. Normann, D., Sanders, S.: On robust theorems due to bolzano, weierstrass, and cantor in reverse mathematics. J. Symbolic Logic 1–51 (2022). https://doi.org/10.1017/jsl.2022.71
5. Normann, D., Sanders, S.: On the uncountability of R. J. Symbolic Logic **87**(4),1474–1521 (2022)
6. Normann, D., Sanders, S.: On the computational properties of basic mathematical notions. J. Logic Comput. **32**(8), 1747–1795 (2022)
7. Normann, D., Sanders, S.: The Biggest Five of Reverse Mathematics, Submitted, p. 39 (2023). https://arxiv.org/abs/2212.00489
8. Sanders, S.: On the computational properties of the uncountability of the real numbers. In: Ciabattoni, A., Pimentel, E., de Queiroz, R.J.G.B. (eds.) Logic, Language, Information, and Computation. WoLLIC 2022. LNCS, vol. 13468, pp. 362–377. Springer, Cham (2022). https://doi.org/10.1007/978-3-031-15298-6_23
9. Sanders, S.: On the computational properties of the Baire category theorem, Submitted (2022). https://arxiv.org/abs/2210.05251
10. Sanders, S.: Big in Reverse Mathematics: the uncountability of the real numbers, Submitted, p. 21 (2022). https://arxiv.org/abs/2208.03027
11. Simpson, S.G.: Subsystems of second order arithmetic, 2nd ed. Perspectives in Logic, CUP (2009)
12. Turing, A.: On computable numbers, with an application to the Entscheidungsproblem. Proc. London Math. Soc. **42**, 230–265 (1936)

Willem's Adventures in Curry–Howard Land

Willem Heijltjes

Department of Computer Science, University of Bath, UK
w.b.heijltjes@bath.ac.uk
http://willem.heijltj.es

Abstract. From the start, the Curry–Howard–De Bruijn correspondence linking proof theory to computation was more than an isolated case: it covered not only the isomorphism between simply-typed lambda-calculus and intuitionistic natural deduction, but also that between combinatory logic and Frege–Hilbert systems. Since then, it has grown into a rich landscape of connections between proof systems and typed calculi, to the point that the immediate question for any proof system is, what is its computational meaning?

In this talk I will share my experience over the past decade in exploring new parts of this landscape. Firstly we will look at the question, what is the computational content of deep-inference proof systems? As it shares the basic syntax of category theory, it is no surprise that past work (by Brünnler and McKinley) has linked deep inference to categorical combinators. Here, we go further, and consider how the characteristic "medial" and "switch" rules relate to fine-grained notions of computation in the lambda-calculus: full laziness, end-of-scope operators, quantitative types, and tentatively, optimal reduction.

A second topic is the intuitionistic variant of Hughes' "proofs without syntax", or "combinatorial proofs". An evolution of proof nets, they are closely related to game semantics and likewise live on the boundary of syntax and semantics. Normalization for intuitionistic combinatorial proofs faces what is essentially the problem of variable capture, not as a small nuisance but as the main obstacle circumscribing the design possibilities for a reduction mechanism. Our solution, by Curry–Howard, then relates to known practical solutions: lambda-lifting, supercombinators, and closed reduction.

Both these topics operate in the traditional space of the Curry–Howard correspondence, where constructions in proof theory have direct computational analogues. The third topic, by contrast, invites us to revisit the foundations of the correspondence. The recent Functional Machine Calculus (FMC), like Levy's call–by–push–value (CBPV) before it, creates a sharp distinction between a computation with a certain outcome, and the outcome itself. And like CBPV, it embeds both the call–by–name and call–by–value (simply typed) lambda-calculus, via different encodings. We have, then, instead of a clear correspondence, two distinct mappings from logic onto computation. Further, unlike CBPV, where computations and values are mediated at the type level by abstract functors, FMC types form a (mostly) straightforward intuitionistic logic. The typed FMC thus presents us with an intriguing question: what is its logical meaning?

An Optimized Amplicon Sequencing Approach to Estimating Lineage Abundances in Viral Metagenomes

Jasper van Bemmelen[1], Davida S. Smyth[2] and Jasmijn A. Baaijens[1,3]

[1] Intelligent Systems Department, Delft University of Technology,
The Netherlands
[2] Texas A&M University San Antonio, USA
[3] Department of Biomedical Informatics, Harvard Medical School, USA
j.a.baaijens@tudelft.nl

During the COVID-19 pandemic, it has become apparent that wastewater surveillance is an effective and cost-efficient way of monitoring viral spread and evolution [1–3]. The computational challenges involved originate in the more general problem of viral metagenomics, where the task is to characterize and estimate relative abundance of different, closely related viral lineages in a given sample. These lineages are not defined by a single genome sequence, but rather consist of groups of closely related sequences with a common ancestor. With genome databases growing ever larger—currently over 10 million sequences for SARS-CoV-2 in GISAID [4]—any approach towards solving (part of) this problem needs to be highly efficient.

Since metagenomic samples typically contain genetic material from a wide variety of microbial species, analyzing a specific virus of interest is done through *targeted amplification* prior to genome sequencing. Genomic material from the virus of interest is copied to high quantities, enabling targeted genome analysis. This requires *primer sequences*: short nucleotide sequences that form the starting point for amplification through DNA synthesis. As such, primer sequences are designed based on a known genome sequence of interest and define the region to be amplified, also referred to as the *amplicon*. Choosing appropriate primer sequences is a delicate task for which various tools have been proposed given a genomic region of interest [5–9]. In practice, a frequently used approach is to design primers such that the resulting amplicons cover the entire genome [7, 10]; for example, the ARTIC primers for whole genome SARS-CoV-2 amplification have been used for sequencing experiments throughout the pandemic [11].

Whole genome amplification, however, is an expensive approach for the purpose of characterizing lineages and estimating relative abundance. Instead, one could first answer the question: which region(s) are most informative in distinguishing between lineages? While this can be determined easily from available sequence databases, it is crucial to select only regions which can be amplified efficiently, using only a small set of primers. In other words, the computational challenge that we address here is to find regions of maximal divergence between lineages such that there is little divergence in the flanking regions (where the primers should bind universally).

We present an algorithm, AmpliDiff, that solves this problem accurately and efficiently. AmpliDiff identifies discriminatory regions in a given set of genomes and simultaneously finds suitable primers, such that these regions can be amplified. AmpliDiff is based on a Set Cover Problem formulation that we solve using a greedy algorithm. We demonstrate AmpliDiff by computing an optimal selection of amplicons for distinguishing between SARS-CoV-2 genomes and show the effectiveness of the resulting amplicons on simulated sequencing data representing real wastewater samples. While these results are specifically for SARS-CoV-2, AmpliDiff is virus-agnostic and can be applied to find primers to maximally distinguish between sequences in any collection of viral genomes.

References

1. Baaijens, J.A., et al.: Lineage abundance estimation for SARS-CoV-2 in wastewater using transcriptome quantification techniques. Genome Biol. **23**, 236 (2022)
2. Crits-Christoph, A., et al.: Genome sequencing of sewage detects regionally prevalent SARS-CoV-2 variants. mBio **12**(1), e02703-20 (2021)
3. Zulli, A., et al.: Predicting daily COVID-19 case rates from SARS-CoV-2 RNA concentration across a diversity of wastewater catchments. FEMS Microbes **2**, xtab022 (2022)
4. Elbe, S., Buckland-Merrett, G.: Data, disease and diplomacy: GISAID's innovative contribution to global health. Global Chall. **1**, 33–46 (2017)
5. Hysom, D.A., et al.: Skip the alignment: degenerate, multiplex primer and probe design using k-mer matching instead of alignments. PloS One **7**(4), e34560 (2012)
6. Kreer, C., et al.: openprimer for multiplex amplification of highly diverse templates. J. Immun. Methods **480**, 112752 (2020)
7. Quick, J., et al.: Multiplex PCR method for MinION and Illumina sequencing of Zika and other virus genomes directly from clinical samples. Nat. Protoc. **12**(6), 1261–1276 (2017)
8. Untergasser, A., et al.: Primer3—new capabilities and interfaces. Nucleic Acids Res. **40**(15), e115 (2012)
9. Ye, J., et al.: Primer-blast: a tool to design target-specific primers for polymerase chain reaction. BMC Bioinf. **13**(1), 1–11 (2012)
10. Grubaugh, N.D., et al.: An amplicon-based sequencing framework for accurately measuring intrahost virus diversity using PrimalSeq and iVar. Genome Biol. **20**, 8 (2019)
11. Lambisia, A.W., et al.: Optimization of the SARS-CoV-2 ARTIC Network V4 primers and whole genome sequencing protocol. Front. Med. **9**, 836728 (2022)

Contents

Degree Theory

Cupping Computably Enumerable Degrees Simultaneously

Hong Hanh Tran and Guohua Wu$^{(\boxtimes)}$

Division of Mathematical Sciences, School of Physical and Mathematical Sciences,
Nanyang Technological University, 21 Nanyang Link, Singapore 637371, Singapore
{honghanh.tran,guohua}@ntu.edu.sg

Abstract. In this paper, we will construct for each $n \geq 1$, n computably enumerable degrees, $\mathcal{A} = \{\mathbf{a}_1, \cdots, \mathbf{a}_n\}$ say, such that any $n - 1$ degrees in $\mathcal{A}$ can be cupped to $\mathbf{0}'$ by one incomplete computably enumerable degree, and no incomplete c.e. degree can cup all degrees in $\mathcal{A}$ to $\mathbf{0}'$ simultaneously. It generalizes the notion of noncuppable degrees (when $n = 1$). Li, Wu and Yang provided an outline of a proof for $n = 2$. Our main work in this paper is to provide a proof for $n = 3$, where the idea of handling cuppings with more degrees is presented and this idea can be generalized to arbitrary n.

1 Introduction

A c.e. degree $\mathbf{a}$ is called *cuppable* if there is an incomplete c.e. degree $\mathbf{b}$ such that $\mathbf{a} \cup \mathbf{b} = \mathbf{0}'$, and *noncuppable* otherwise. Sacks' Splitting Theorem implies the existence of incomplete cuppable degrees. Yates (unpublished) and Cooper [2] provided the existence of noncuppable degrees. The first publication of non-cuppable degrees was done by D. Miller in [8], where the notion of noncuppable degrees was generalized from $\mathbf{0}'$ to high degrees and a pinball machine construction is developed for the high permission.

Based on the high/low hiearchy, Li, Wu and Zhang [6] proposed a hierarchy of cuppable c.e. degrees $\mathbf{LC}_1 \subseteq \mathbf{LC}_2 \subseteq \mathbf{LC}_3 \subseteq \cdots$, where for each $n \geq 1$, $\mathbf{LC}_n$ denotes the class of low$_n$-cuppable degrees. Here, a c.e. degree $\mathbf{a}$ is called *low$_n$-cuppable* if there is a low$_n$ c.e. degree $\mathbf{b}$ such that $\mathbf{a} \cup \mathbf{b} = \mathbf{0}'$. Li, Wu and Zhang showed that $\mathbf{LC}_1$ is a proper subset of $\mathbf{LC}_2$. Recently, Greenberg, Ng and Wu proved in [4] that there is an incomplete cuppable degree which can only be cupped to $\mathbf{0}'$ by high degrees (in fact, superhigh). This shows that $\cup_n \mathbf{LC}_n$ does not exhaust all of the cuppable degrees, refuting a claim of Li [7] that all cuppable degrees are low$_3$-cuppable. In the same paper, Greenberg, Ng and Wu showed that a c.e. degree is in $\mathbf{LC}_2$ if and only if it is array-computable-cuppable, which, together with the result of Li, Wu and Zhang above, implies a theorem of Downey, Greenberg, Miller and Weber in [3] (low-cuppability implies AC-cuppability) immediately. It left open whether all low$_n$-cuppable degrees are low$_3$-cuppable.

H. H. Tran and G. Wu—Both authors are partially supported by MOE Tier 1 grant RG111/19, Singapore.

In this paper, we will work on another topic on cuppable/noncuppable degrees. For $n \geq 1$, say that $\mathcal{A} = \{\mathbf{a}_1, \cdots, \mathbf{a}_n\}$, where each $\mathbf{a}_i$ is c.e., is $(n-1)$-cuppable, but not n-cuppable if any $n-1$ many degrees in $\mathcal{A}$ can be cupped to $\mathbf{0}'$ by one incomplete computably enumerable degree, and no incomplete c.e. degree can cup all degrees in $\mathcal{A}$ to $\mathbf{0}'$ simultaneously. It generalizes the notion of noncuppable degrees $(n = 1)$. We will prove:

Theorem 1. *For each $n \geq 1$, there is a collection of n c.e. degrees, $\mathbf{a}_1, \cdots, \mathbf{a}_n$ say, which is $(n-1)$-cuppable, but not n-cuppable.*

Li, Wu and Yang provided an outline of a proof for $n = 2$ in [5]. In [1], Bie and Wu provided an alternative construction. In this paper, we will prove Theorem 1 for $n = 3$, whose proof shows the basic idea of handling cuppings with more degrees, for arbitrary n.

Our notation and terminology are quite standard and generally follow Soare [9]. A parameter p is defined to be fresh at a stage s if $p > s$ and p is the least number not mentioned so far in the construction.

2   Proof of Theorem 1

To prove Theorem 1 for $n = 3$, we will construct incomplete c.e. degrees $\mathbf{a}, \mathbf{b}, \mathbf{c}$, $\mathbf{e}, \mathbf{f}, \mathbf{g}$ satisfying the following properties:

(i) $\mathbf{a} \cup \mathbf{e} = \mathbf{b} \cup \mathbf{e} = \mathbf{b} \cup \mathbf{f} = \mathbf{c} \cup \mathbf{f} = \mathbf{c} \cup \mathbf{g} = \mathbf{a} \cup \mathbf{g} = \mathbf{0}'$.
(ii) No incomplete c.e. degree can cup $\mathbf{a}, \mathbf{b}, \mathbf{c}$ to $\mathbf{0}'$ simultaneously, i.e., for any c.e. degree $\mathbf{w}$, $\mathbf{a} \cup \mathbf{w} = \mathbf{b} \cup \mathbf{w} = \mathbf{c} \cup \mathbf{w} = \mathbf{0}'$ only when $\mathbf{w} = \mathbf{0}'$.

The property (ii) is obtained by applying directly the technique in [1]. However, unlike the case for $n = 2$, the p.c. functionals constructed for the coding of $\mathbf{0}'$ in (i) are not independent. This is a crucial feature for the constructions for $n \geq 3$.

3   Requirements and Strategies

We will construct c.e. sets A, B, C, D, E, F, G, L and partial computable functionals $\Gamma_1, \Gamma_2, \Omega_1, \Omega_2$ and $\Delta_1, \Delta_2, \Theta_{\langle i,e_1,e_2,e_3 \rangle}$, $i, e_1, e_2, e_3 \in \omega$, such that the following requirements are satisfied:

$\mathcal{S} : \Gamma_1^{A \oplus E} = \Gamma_2^{B \oplus E} = \Omega_1^{B \oplus F} = \Omega_2^{C \oplus F} = \Delta_1^{C \oplus G} = \Delta_2^{A \oplus G} = K,$
$\mathcal{P}_e : \Phi_e^E \neq D,$
$\mathcal{Q}_e : \Phi_e^F \neq D,$
$\mathcal{R}_e : \Phi_e^G \neq D,$
$\mathcal{N}_{\langle i,e_1,e_2,e_3 \rangle} : \Phi_{e_1}^{A \oplus W_i} = \Phi_{e_2}^{B \oplus W_i} = \Phi_{e_3}^{C \oplus W_i} = K \oplus L \Rightarrow K = \Theta_{\langle i,e_1,e_2,e_3 \rangle}^{W_i}.$

Here, K is a fixed complete c.e. set, with an effective enumeration $\{k_s : s \in \omega\}$, where k_s is the number entering K at stage s. Denote $\{k_s : s \leq t\}$ as K_t.

Let $\{\Phi_e : e \in \omega\}$ be an effective enumeration of partial computable functionals, and $\{W_i : i \in \omega\}$ be an effective enumeration of computably enumerable sets.

The $\mathcal{P}, \mathcal{Q}$ and $\mathcal{R}$-requirements ensure that E, F, G are incomplete. Thus, these requirements, together with the requirement $\mathcal{S}$, show that any two of $\mathbf{a}, \mathbf{b}, \mathbf{c}$, degrees of A, B, C, are 2-cuppable. The $\mathcal{N}$-requirements ensure that these three degrees are not 3-cuppable.

In the following, we describe how to satisfy these requirements. The $\mathcal{S}$-strategy has the highest priority and will not to put on the construction tree. All $\mathcal{P}, \mathcal{Q}, \mathcal{R}, \mathcal{N}$-strategies will be processed on a priority tree.

3.1   The $\mathcal{S}$-Strategy

We will construct partial computable functionals $\Gamma_i, \Delta_i, \Omega_i, i = 1, 2$, so that they will code K into the corresponding sets. These p.c. functionals are defined at the beginning of each stage.

The p.c. functional Γ_1 is defined as follows.

(i) If $\Gamma_1^{A \oplus E}(n) \downarrow \neq K(n)$, put $\gamma_1(n)$ into E to undefine $\Gamma_1^{A \oplus E}(n)$.
(ii) Otherwise, for the least number n such that $\Gamma_1^{A \oplus E}(n) \uparrow$, define $\Gamma_1^{A \oplus E}(n) = K(n)$ with use $\gamma_1(n)$ as a fresh large number.

The construction of $\Gamma_2, \Delta_1, \Delta_2, \Omega_1, \Omega_2$ proceeds in exactly the same manner, with numbers being enumerated into the corresponding sets to undefine the related computations.

Note that the constructions of $\Gamma_1^{A \oplus E}$ and $\Gamma_2^{B \oplus E}$ may interact with each other, e.g., a computation $\Gamma_1^{A \oplus E}(n)$ can be undefined by the enumeration of γ_2-uses into E. To avoid such potential problems from happening, we define these functionals in a synchronous way, i.e. we will define $\Gamma_1^{A \oplus E}(n)$ only if all computations $\Gamma_1^{A \oplus E}(n-1), \Gamma_2^{B \oplus E}(n-1), \Omega_1^{B \oplus F}(n-1), \Omega_2^{C \oplus F}(n-1), \Delta_1^{C \oplus G}(n-1)$ and $\Delta_2^{A \oplus G}(n-1)$ have been already defined, and when we define $\Gamma_1^{A \oplus E}(n)$, we also define $\Gamma_2^{B \oplus E}(n), \Omega_1^{B \oplus F}(n), \Omega_2^{C \oplus F}(n), \Delta_1^{C \oplus G}(n)$ and $\Delta_2^{A \oplus G}(n)$. Thus, if $\gamma_1(n)$ is defined at stage s, and $\gamma_2(m)[s]$ is enumerated into E at this stage, where $m > n$, then as $\gamma_1(n)[s] < \gamma_2(m)[s]$, such an enumeration at stage s will not undefine $\Gamma_1^{A \oplus E}(n)$.

The $\mathcal{S}$-strategy only puts numbers into E, F and G, and in the construction, we will have other strategies involved in the definition of these p.c. functionals, as otherwise, K will be coded into E, F, G, making them complete, which will not be true, if we satisfy all the $\mathcal{P}, \mathcal{Q}, \mathcal{R}$-requirements.

Below we give more detail of the construction of Γ_1 and the use γ_1. The construction of other functionals and use-functions works in the same manner.

(1) If $\Gamma_1^{A \oplus E}(n)$ is defined at stage s, then $\gamma_1(n)[s]$ is a fresh number larger than all numbers being used by stage s. In particular, $\gamma_1(n)[s] \notin A_s \cup E_s$.

(2) If $\gamma_1(n)$ has definition at stage s, then for $m < n$, $\gamma_1(m)$ is defined at stage s with $\gamma_1(m)[s] < \gamma_1(n)[s]$.

(3) If $\Gamma_1^{A \oplus E}(n)[s] \downarrow$ and n enters K at stage $s + 1$, then we will force a change of E or A below $\gamma_1(n)[s]$ to undefine $\Gamma_1^{A \oplus E}(n)$.

(4) At stage s, $\Gamma_1^{A \oplus E}(n)$ is undefined iff there is a number $y \leq \gamma_1(n)[s]$ which enters E or A.

Clearly, if (1)–(4) are satisfied and $\Gamma_1^{A \oplus E}$ is total, then $\Gamma_1^{A \oplus E}$ computes K correctly.

3.2   The $\mathcal{P}, \mathcal{Q}, \mathcal{R}$-Strategies

The $\mathcal{P}, \mathcal{Q}, \mathcal{R}$-strategies work in the same manner and we will describe below how a $\mathcal{P}$-strategy, P_e say, works. We denote this strategy by α, a node on the priority tree, which processes as follows.

P1. Pick a killing point k as fresh. The number k is also called a threshold in other papers.

Let $m := 0$. Whenever $n \leq k$ enters K, increase the value of m by 1 and go to P2.

We will say that α is reset when K changes on numbers less than or equal to k. When this happens, we will say that α is reset and we will keep k the same, and cancel all other parameters of α. As k is fixed, such a process of resetting will happen at most $k + 1$ times. We use m to count the number of times of resetting.

P2. Pick a fresh witness $x_m > k$.

P3. Wait for $\Phi_e^E(x_m)[s] \downarrow = 0$.

P4. Enumerate $\gamma_1(k)[s]$ into A, $\gamma_2(k)[s]$ into B, and x_m into D, and stop.

Here, if $\Phi_e^E(x) \downarrow = 0$ at stage s, we put $\gamma_1(k)[s]$ into A and $\gamma_2(k)[s]$ into B so that $\Gamma_1^{A \oplus E}(n), \Gamma_2^{B \oplus E}(n)$, $n \geq k$, are undefined, and this will lift the use of new definition of $\gamma_1(n), \gamma_2(n)$, $n \geq k$, bigger than $\varphi_e(x_m)[s]$. In other words, the computation can be changed only when some small number $m \leq k$ enters K and $\mathcal{S}$ puts $\gamma_1(n), \gamma_2(n)$ into E, in which case, the witness x is redefined as a fresh number. As k is fixed, there is a stage t after which K has no more changes below k and x becomes fixed, and the requirement P_e is satisfied as usual.

The strategy α has two outcomes, which are both finitary.

w: wait at P3 forever for some $m \leq k$. In this case, $D(x_m) = 0 \neq \Phi_e^E(x_m)$, as $\Phi_e^E(x_m)$ does not converge to 0.

s: stop at P4 forever for some $m \leq k$. In this case, K does not change below k after a stage s_0 and $\Phi_e^E(x_m) \downarrow = 0 \neq D(x_m) = 1$.

3.3   The $\mathcal{N}$-Strategies

Fix an $N_{\langle i,e_1,e_2,e_3 \rangle}$-strategy, β say, a node on the priority tree. We omit the subscript here for simplicity. We will construct a partial computable functional Θ_β, or Θ for short, such that if $\Phi_{e_1}^{A \oplus W_i} = \Phi_{e_2}^{B \oplus W_i} = \Phi_{e_3}^{C \oplus W_i} = K \oplus L$, then $\Theta_\beta^{W_i}$ is total and computes K correctly.

The *length of agreement* at stage s, $l(\beta, s)$, is defined as

$$\max\{x < s : \forall y \le x [\Phi_{e_1}^{A \oplus W_i}(y)[s] = \Phi_{e_2}^{B \oplus W_i}(y)[s] = \Phi_{e_3}^{C \oplus W_i}(y)[s] = K_s \oplus L_s(y)]\}.$$

A stage s is called β-*expansionary* if $s = 0$ or $l(\beta, s) > l(\beta, t)$ for all β-stages $t < s$. We also let $u(\beta, x)[s] = \max\left\{\varphi_{e_1}^{A \oplus W_i}(x)[s], \varphi_{e_2}^{B \oplus W_i}(x)[s], \varphi_{e_3}^{C \oplus W_i}(x)[s]\right\}$.

We define $\Theta_\beta^{W_i}$ when the length of agreement increases: at a β-expansionary stage s, if p is the least number such that $\Theta_\beta^{W_i}(p)$ is not defined and $2p + 1 < l(\beta, s)$, then we set $\Theta_\beta^{W_i}(p)[s] = K_s(p)$ with use $\theta_\beta(p)[s]$ as fresh. This computation can be undefined only when W_i changes below $u(\beta, 2p+1)[s]$. Therefore, if p enters K after stage s, we would like to force W_i to change below $u(\beta, 2p+1)[s]$ to undefine $\Theta_\beta^{W_i}(p)$.

The possible outcomes of β are i (for infinitely many β-expansionary stages) and f (for finitely many β-expansionary stages). If β has outcome i, we need to ensure that we will have infinitely many times to extend the definition of $\Theta_\beta^{W_i}$ such that if $\Phi_{e_1}^{A \oplus W_i} = \Phi_{e_2}^{B \oplus W_i} = \Phi_{e_3}^{C \oplus W_i} = K \oplus L$, then $\Theta_\beta^{W_i}$ is total and computes K correctly. If β has outcome f, then $\mathcal{N}$ is satisfied.

3.4   Interactions Between $\mathcal{N}$-Strategies and $\mathcal{P}, \mathcal{Q}, \mathcal{R}$-Strategies

We now consider interactions between $\mathcal{N}$-strategies and $\mathcal{P}, \mathcal{Q}, \mathcal{R}$-strategies. Suppose that $\Theta_\beta^{W_i}(p)$ is defined at a β-expansionary stage s_1, as $K_{s_1}(p) = 0$, with use $\theta_\beta(p)[s_1] > u(\beta, 2p + 1)[s_1]$ (so $l(\beta, s_1) > 2p + 1$). Suppose that W_i has no change below $\theta_\beta(p)[s_1]$ afterwards. A general situation is that the $\mathcal{P}, \mathcal{Q}, \mathcal{R}$-strategies below the outcome i can put numbers into A, B, C, lifting $u(\beta, 2p)$ to large numbers so that at a β-expansionary stage $s_2 > s_1$, we have

$$\Phi_{e_1}^{A \oplus W_i}(2p)[s_2] = \Phi_{e_2}^{B \oplus W_i}(2p)[s_2] = \Phi_{e_3}^{C \oplus W_i}(2p)[s_2] = K_{s_2} \oplus L_{s_2}(2p) = 0.$$

with new use $u(\beta, 2p)[s_2] > \theta_\beta(p)[s_1] > u(\beta, 2p + 1)[s_1]$. Without loss of generality, suppose that p enters K later and W_i changes below $u(\beta, 2p)[s_2]$, leading to

$$\Phi_{e_1}^{A \oplus W_i}(2p)[s_3] = \Phi_{e_2}^{B \oplus W_i}(2p)[s_3] = \Phi_{e_3}^{C \oplus W_i}(2p)[s_3] = K_{s_2} \oplus L_{s_3}(2p) = 1$$

at a further β-expansionary stage $s_3 > s_2$. As $\Theta_\beta^{W_i}(p)$ is still defined as 0, we have $\Theta_\beta^{W_i}(p) \ne K(p)$ and β fails to satisfy the corresponding $\mathcal{N}$-requirement.

Here is an idea to get around of this obstacle. Roughly speaking, when a $\mathcal{P}$-strategy (same for $\mathcal{Q}$-strategies and $\mathcal{R}$-strategies) below β's outcome i puts numbers below $u(\beta, 2p) < \theta_\beta(p)$ into A and B, it also puts an (attached) number into L to force W_i to change below $\theta_\beta(p)$ to undefine $\Theta_\beta^{W_i}(p)$ first. That is, when a $\mathcal{P}$-strategy α below outcome i picks a witness x at stage s_0, α also picks an unattached number $z \notin L$. Say that a stage $s > s_0$ is β-expansionary, we require that $l(\beta, s)$ is also bigger than $2z + 1$ and when we define $\Theta_\beta^{W_i}(p)$ at stage s, we let $\theta(p)[s] > \max\{u(\beta, 2z + 1)[s], u(\beta, 2p + 1)[s]\}$. This delays the construction a little bit but it makes no difference if there are infinitely many β-expansionary stages. If at a β-expansionary stage $s_1 > s_0$, α puts number $\gamma_1(k)[s_1]$ into A and $\gamma_2(k)[s_1]$ into B, it also puts z into L. Thus, if we see a further β-expansionary stage s_2, W_i must have changes below $\theta_\beta(p)[s]$ by stage s_2 and $\Theta_\beta^{W_i}(p)$ is undefined at stage s_2, as C has no change below $u(\beta, 2z + 1)$, and the change of computation $\Phi_{e_3}^{C \oplus W_i}(2z + 1)$ is because of the change of W_i below $u(\beta, 2z + 1)$.

Note that when α acts, all strategies with lower priorities are initialized. A nontrivial case is that on the construction tree, α assumes the infinitary outcome i of an $\mathcal{N}$-strategy β, and another strategy, a $\mathcal{Q}$-strategy α' say, is between β and α. Suppose that after α's enumeration of $\gamma_1(k)[s_1]$ into A, and $\gamma_2(k)[s_1]$ into B, at stage s_1, as z is enumerated into L at this stage. Thus, at the first β-expansionary stage $s_2 > s_1$, we will have, as discussed above, a small change of W_i, undefining those $\Theta_\beta^{W_i}(p)$ which are defined after stage s. On the other hand, at stage s_2, β also extends the definition of $\Theta_{\beta_1}^{W_i}(q)$ for more arguments q. Suppose that at a stage $s_3 \geq s_2$, α' acts and enumerates its witness into L and the corresponding ω-uses into B and C respectively. These are enumerations into B and C, not A. Note that the attached number $z(\alpha')$ is already defined when α selects $k(\alpha)$, and $x(\alpha), z(\alpha)$. Suppose that $s_4 > s_3$ is the next β-expansionary stage, then by stage s_4, we should have a small change of W_i below the use $\theta_\beta(q)$, undefining all those $\Theta_{\beta_1}^{W_i}(q)$ being defined after $z(\alpha')$ is selected, including those defined at stage s_2 of course.

We now need to show that for a fixed p, $\Theta_{\beta_1}^{W_i}(p)$ can be undefined by $\mathcal{P}, \mathcal{Q}, \mathcal{R}$-strategies at most finitely often. It is indeed clear. Suppose that s^* is the first stage at which β defines $\Theta_{\beta_1}^{W_i}(p)$. Then $\Theta_{\beta_1}^{W_i}(p)$ can be undefined only by $\mathcal{P}, \mathcal{Q}, \mathcal{R}$-strategies being accessible by stage s^*, and we have only finitely many such strategies.

The interactions between a $\mathcal{P}$-strategy with more than one $\mathcal{N}$-strategy is more or less the same as the interactions between one $\mathcal{P}$-strategy and one $\mathcal{N}$. Without loss of generality, we assume that β_1, β_2 are $\mathcal{N}$-strategies with priority given as

$$\beta_1 \widehat{\ } i \prec \beta_2 \widehat{\ } i \prec \alpha.$$

Then when α chooses a witness $x(\alpha)$, α also chooses attached numbers $z(\alpha)$ at stage s say, we require that stage s' is β_i-expansionary stage, if $l(\beta_i, s')$ exceeds all $l(\beta_i, t)$, t a β_i-stage, and also $2z(\alpha) + 1$. Recall that k, the killing point of α, is selected earlier, before the selection of x. Then, after α's enumeration of $\gamma_1(k)[s_1]$ into A, and $\gamma_2(k)[s_1]$ into B, at stage s_1, as $z(\alpha)$ is enumerated into L at this stage, at the first β_1-expansionary stage $s_2 > s_1$, we will have, as discussed above, a small change of W_{i_1}, undefining those $\Theta_{\beta_1}^{W_{i_1}}(p)$ which are defined after stage s. On the other hand, at stage s_2, β_1 also extends the definition of $\Theta_{\beta_1}^{W_{i_1}}(q)$ for more arguments q. Note that β_1 takes outcome i at stage s_2. Suppose that $s_3 \geq s_2$ is the first β_2-expansionary stage after stage s_1, then by stage s_3, W_{i_2} should have a small change to undefine $\Theta_{\beta_2}^{W_{i_2}}(p)$ which are defined after stage s. This shows that the enumeration of $z(\alpha)$ into L is enough to force W_{i_1} and W_{i_2} to have changes on small numbers by the first β_1 and β_2-expansionary stages respectively.

The discussion above can be generalized to several $\mathcal{N}$-strategies in an obvious way.

We are now ready to describe the full construction.

4   The Construction

We first give an effective listing of all requirements as follows:

$$\mathcal{S} < \mathcal{P}_0 < \mathcal{Q}_0 < \mathcal{R}_0 < \mathcal{N}_0 < \mathcal{P}_1 < \mathcal{Q}_1 < \mathcal{R}_1 < \mathcal{N}_1 < \cdots$$

$$< \mathcal{P}_n < \mathcal{Q}_n < \mathcal{R}_n < \mathcal{N}_n < \cdots .$$

Here $\mathcal{N}_n$ is just the requirement $\mathcal{N}_{\langle i,e_1,e_2,e_3 \rangle}$, i.e., n is the Gödel number of the 4-tuple (i, e_1, e_2, e_3). We say that a requirement $\mathcal{X}$ has priority higher than a requirement $\mathcal{Y}$, if $\mathcal{X}$ is in the front of $\mathcal{Y}$ in the list above. Thus, $\mathcal{S}$ has the highest priority.

The construction tree T will be the binary tree, and we will allocate all requirements, except $\mathcal{S}$, on T, recursively. $\mathcal{S}$ is a global requirement and will not put it on T. We allocate $\mathcal{P}_0$ to the root λ of T. Having allocating a requirement $\mathcal{X}$ to a node σ on T, σ has two outcomes, $s < w$, if $\mathcal{X}$ is a $\mathcal{P}$- or a $\mathcal{Q}$- or an $\mathcal{R}$-requirement, $i < f$, if $\mathcal{X}$ is an $\mathcal{N}$-requirement. For any outcome o of σ, we allocate the next requirement to the node $\sigma^\frown o$.

When a node is allocated with a $\mathcal{P}$- or $\mathcal{Q}$- or $\mathcal{R}$-requirement, we just denote this node as α. α has parameters $k(\alpha), m(\alpha), x(\alpha)$ and $z(\alpha)$, corresponding to its killing point k, counter m, witness x and attached number z, respectively. When a node is allocated with a $\mathcal{N}$-requirement, we just denote it as β. β has a parameter $l(\beta, s)$, denoting the length of agreement associated to β at stage s.

Construction:

Stage 0. Let all constructed sets be empty and let TP_0 be the root λ of the construction tree T.

Stage $s + 1$.

(a) The $\mathcal{S}$-strategy implements in turn steps to rectify and extend the definitions $\Gamma_1^{A \oplus E}, \Gamma_2^{B \oplus E}, \Omega_1^{B \oplus F}, \Omega_2^{C \oplus F}, \Delta_1^{C \oplus G}$ and $\Delta_2^{A \oplus G}$. For the rectification, the current uses are enumerated into E, F, G correspondingly. For the extension, the uses are selected as fresh numbers.

(b) Let k_{s+1} be the number entering K at this stage. Find a strategy α (with highest priority) with $k_{s+1} \leq k(\alpha)$ and declare that α is reset at stage $s+1$. All strategies with priority lower priority are initialized.

(c) Compute the current true path TP_{s+1} (as the longest accessible node): Start with λ. Suppose that τ is reached. If τ is of length $s+1$, set $\tau = TP_{s+1}$. Otherwise, find the immediate successor of τ on TP_{s+1} as follows. There are four cases.

Case 1. $\tau = \alpha$ is a $\mathcal{P}_e$-strategy. Run the following $\mathcal{P}$-program.

$\quad \alpha 1$. If $k(\alpha)$ has no definition, define it as a fresh number, and go to $\alpha 2$.

$\quad \alpha 2$. If $x(\alpha)$ and $z(\alpha)$ has no definition, then

$\qquad$ select $x(\alpha)$ and $z(\alpha)$ as fresh numbers and let $TP_{s+1} = \alpha$. Initialise all lower priority strategies and go the the next stage.

$\qquad$ Otherwise, go to $\alpha 3$.

$\quad \alpha 3$. All parameters are defined.

$\qquad *$ if $\Phi_e^E(x(\alpha))[s+1] \downarrow = 0$ and $z(\alpha) \in L$, then let $\alpha ^\frown s \preceq TP_{s+1}$;

$\qquad *$ if $\Phi_e^E(x(\alpha))[s+1] \downarrow = 0$ and $z(\alpha) \notin L$, then go to $\alpha 4$;

$\qquad *$ otherwise, let $\alpha ^\frown w \preceq TP_{s+1}$.

$\quad \alpha 4$. Do the following:

$\qquad *$ put $x(\alpha)$ into D, $z(\alpha)$ into L, $\gamma_1(k(\alpha))[s+1]$ into A and $\gamma_2(k(\alpha))[s+1]$ into B;

$\qquad *$ let $TP_{s+1} = \alpha$;

$\qquad *$ initialise all lower priority strategies and go the next stage.

τ works exactly the same as above if τ is a $\mathcal{Q}_e$-strategy or an $\mathcal{R}_e$-strategy, but with sets and p.c. functionals changed accordingly.

Case 2. $\tau = \beta$ is an $\mathcal{N}_e$-strategy, where $e = \langle i, e_1, e_2, e_3 \rangle$. If $s+1$ is a β-expansionary stage, then extend the definition of $\Theta_\beta^{W_i}$ and let $\beta ^\frown i \preceq TP_{s+1}$. Otherwise, let $\beta ^\frown f \preceq TP_{s+1}$.

5 Verification

We let $TP = \liminf_{s \to \infty} TP_s$. We can prove the following by induction on $\tau \prec TP$.

Lemma 1. *For each node $\tau \prec TP$,*

(i) *There is a stage s_0 such that τ is not initialised after s_0, and for each stage $t \geq s_0$, either $\tau \prec TP_t$ or $\tau < TP_t$, and that no node to the left of τ is accessible after stage s_0.*

(ii) *The node τ is accessible at infinitely many stages, i.e. τ can be accessible infinitely many times.*

(iii) *If τ is a P, Q, R-strategy, then there is a stage after which τ has no more actions.*

(iv) *τ has a unique outcome o such that $\tau ^\frown o \prec TP$.*

Proof. We prove the lemma by induction on the length of $\tau \prec TP$.

For $\tau = \lambda \prec TP$, clearly, λ is never initialized after stage 0 and $\lambda \preceq TP_s$ for any $s \geq 0$. So, (i) and (ii) are satisfied.

As being assigned the requirement $\mathcal{P}_0$ with the highest priority on the tree, from the construction, λ chooses its killing point $k = k(\lambda)$, witness $x(\lambda)$ and attached number $z(\lambda)$ at stage 1. Since λ is never initialized, the killing point k never changes. Other parameters $x(\lambda)$ and $z(\lambda)$ are reset only when a number $n \leq k(\lambda)$ enters K, and this may happen at most $k + 1$ times. Hence, there is a stage $s \geq 1$ after which no number $n \leq k$ enters K, and $x(\lambda), z(\lambda)$ are never reset. If at stage $s_0 \geq s$, $\Phi_0^E(x(\lambda))[s_0] \downarrow = 0$, then λ acts following step $\alpha 3$ of the $\mathcal{P}$-program and has outcome $o = s$. Clearly, λ has no more actions after stage s_0, and $\lambda^\frown o \preceq TP_t$ for any stage $t > s_0$. In this case, s is the unique outcome of λ such that $\lambda^\frown s \prec TP$. If such a stage s_0 doesn't exist, then λ never acts after stage s, it has unique outcome $o = w$, and $\lambda^\frown w \preceq TP_t$ for every $t \geq s$. In this case, $\lambda^\frown w \prec TP$. Thus, in both cases, (iii) and (iv) hold for λ.

Suppose that the nodes $\lambda = \tau_0 \prec \tau_1 \prec \cdots \prec \tau_n \prec TP$ satisfy (i)-(iv), where $\tau_{i+1} = \tau_i^\frown o_i$ with $o_i \in \Lambda$ is the unique outcome of τ_i satisfying (iv) for each $0 \leq i \leq n$. We will prove that $\tau_{n+1} = \tau_n^\frown o_n$ also satisfies (i)-(iv).

Let s be the first stage such that τ_{n+1} is accessible at s and after stage s,

(a) τ_n is never initialized and no node to the left of τ_n is accessible;
(b) no $\mathcal{P}, \mathcal{Q}, \mathcal{R}$-strategy $\tau \preceq \tau_n$ takes further actions.

Clearly, τ_{n+1} is not initialized after stage s and satisfies (i) and (ii). In the following, we verify the properties (iii) and (iv) for τ_{n+1}. There are two cases.

Case 1. τ_{n+1} is a $\mathcal{P}, \mathcal{Q}, \mathcal{R}$-strategy. Without loss of generality, suppose that τ_{n+1} is a $\mathcal{P}_e$-strategy α. Let s^+ be the first α-stage after stage s. If the parameters $k(\alpha)$, $x(\alpha)$, and $z(\alpha)$ has not been chosen at stage s, then at stage s^+, they will be assigned fresh numbers. Since α is never initialized after stage s, the killing point $k(\alpha) = k(\alpha)[s^+]$ will never be changed. Other parameters, $x(\alpha)$ and $z(\alpha)$ may be reset at most $k(\alpha) + 1$ times, when a number $m \leq k(\alpha)$ enters K. Therefore, there is a stage $s_0 \geq s^+$ after which that these parameters are never reset. There are two possibilities as follows. If at stage $s_1 \geq s_0$, $\Phi_e^E(x(\alpha))[s_1] \downarrow = 0$, then α follows step $\alpha 3$ in the $\mathcal{P}$-program. It has outcome $o = s$ and will never act after stage s_1. For any α-stage $t \geq s_1$, $\alpha^\frown s \preceq TP_t$. As (i) and (ii) hold for τ_n, for any stage $t \geq s_1$, either $\alpha^\frown s \preceq TP_t$ or $\alpha^\frown s < TP_t$, and (ii) holds for $\alpha^\frown s$. In this case, $\alpha^\frown s \prec TP$. Otherwise, such a stage s_1 doesn't exist, α has a unique outcome $o = w$ and never acts after stage s_0. Clearly, $\alpha^\frown o \preceq TP_t$ for any α-stage $t > s_0$. More over, for any stage $t \geq s_0$, either $\alpha^\frown w \preceq TP_t$ or $\alpha^\frown w < TP_t$. In this case, $\alpha^\frown w \prec TP$. Thus, in both cases, (iii) and (iv) hold for α.

Case 2. τ_{n+1} is an $\mathcal{N}_e$-strategy β. Then β is not initialized after stage s. There are two possibilities.

- β has a unique outcome f. For any β-stage $t > s$, $\beta^\frown f \prec TP_t$. Since τ_n satisfies (i) and (ii), for any stage $t \geq s$, either $\beta^\frown f \preceq TP_t$ or $\beta^\frown f < TP_t$. In this case, $\beta^\frown f \prec TP$.

- β reaches outcome i at infinitely many β-stages after stage s. Let $t_0 \geq s$ be the first stage that $\beta^\frown i$ is accessible, we have that $\beta^\frown i \preceq TP_t$ for any β-expansionary stage $t \geq t_0$ and for any $t > t_0$ such that $\beta^\frown i$ is not accessible, $\beta^\frown i < TP_t$. In this case, $\beta^\frown i \prec TP$.

Thus, TP exists. We can now show in Lemma 2 that every strategy τ on TP satisfies the corresponding requirement. Furthermore, we can show in Lemma 3 that $\Gamma_1^{A \oplus E}$, $\Gamma_2^{B \oplus E}$, $\Omega_1^{B \oplus F}$, $\Omega_2^{C \oplus F}$, $\Delta_1^{C \oplus G}$, $\Delta_2^{A \oplus G}$ are all total and computes K correctly and hence the requirement $\mathcal{S}$ is satisfied.

Lemma 2. *Every strategy $\tau \prec TP$ satisfies the corresponding requirement.*

Proof. Let τ of length e be a node on the true path TP. From Lemma 1, let o be the unique outcome of α such that $\alpha^\frown o \prec TP$ and s be a τ-stage s after which

(a) τ is never initialized, and hence, no node to the left of τ is accessible;

(b) no $\mathcal{P}, \mathcal{Q}, \mathcal{R}$-strategy $\alpha \preceq \tau$ takes further actions.

We consider two cases: τ is a $\mathcal{P}, \mathcal{Q}, \mathcal{R}$-strategy, say a $\mathcal{P}_e$-strategy α (Case 1), and τ is an $\mathcal{N}_e$-strategy β (Case 2). In the latter case, $e = \langle i, e_1, e_2, e_3 \rangle$.

Case 1. τ is a $\mathcal{P}_e$-strategy α. Let $s_0 \geq s$ be the smallest stage at which $\alpha^\frown o$ is accessible. Since no $\mathcal{P}, \mathcal{Q}, \mathcal{R}$-strategy $\alpha \preceq \tau$ takes further actions after stage s, the parameters $k(\alpha), x(\alpha), z(\alpha)$ have been already chosen at stage s_0. Moreover, no number $n \leq k(\alpha)$ enters K after stage s_0, and hence, these parameters will never reset. If $o = w$, i.e. $\alpha^\frown w \prec TP$, then $\Phi_e^E(x(\alpha)) \neq 0 = D(x(\alpha))$. Otherwise, $o = s$, i.e. $\alpha^\frown s \prec TP$, then α has already acted following the step $\alpha 3$ of the program $\mathcal{P}$ by the end of stage s_0. We have, $\Phi_e^E(x(\alpha)) \downarrow= 0 \neq 1 = D(x(\alpha))$. In both cases, $\mathcal{P}, \mathcal{Q}, \mathcal{R}_e$ is satisfied via α.

Case 2. τ is an $\mathcal{N}_e$-strategy β. There are two possibilities. If $o = f$, i.e. there are at most finitely many β-expansionary stages, then $\Phi_{e_1}^{A \oplus W_i} = \Phi_{e_2}^{B \oplus W_i} = \Phi_{e_3}^{C \oplus W_i} = K \oplus L$ cannot be true, and hence, $\mathcal{N}_e$ is satisfied via β vacuously. Otherwise, $o = i$ and there are infinitely many β-expansionary stages. Suppose that $\Phi_{e_1}^{A \oplus W_i} = \Phi_{e_2}^{B \oplus W_i} = \Phi_{e_3}^{C \oplus W_i} = K \oplus L$. In the following, we can prove by induction on p that for any $p \in \omega$, $\Theta_\beta^{W_e}(p) \downarrow= K(p)$, i.e. the function $\Theta_\beta^{W_e}$ is total and computes K correctly, and therefore $\mathcal{N}_e$ is satisfied via β. Without loss of generality, suppose that s is the first stage after which β is never initialized. Consider $p = 0$. Let $s' > s$ be the next β-expansionary stage after stage s, i.e. $\beta^\frown i \preceq TP_{s'}$ and s' is the first stage at which $\beta^\frown i$ is accessible. At stage s', we define $\Theta_\beta^{W_i}(0)[s'] = K_{s'}(0)$ with fresh use $\theta_\beta(0)[s']$ such that $\theta_\beta(0)[s'] > u(\beta, 1)[s']$. If 0 never enters K after stage s', then $\Theta_\beta^{W_e}(0) = \Theta_\beta^{W_i}(0)[s'] = K_{s'}(0) = K(0)$. Otherwise, suppose that 0 enters K at stage $t > s'$. Let s_1 be the least β-expansionary stage such that $s_1 \geq t$. We have

(1) $\Phi_{e_1}^{A\oplus W_i}(0)[s'] = \Phi_{e_2}^{B\oplus W_i}(0)[s'] = \Phi_{e_3}^{C\oplus W_i}(0)[s'] = K_{s'} \oplus L_{s'}(0) = K_{s'}(0) = 0$, and

(2) $\Phi_{e_1}^{A\oplus W_i}(0)[s_1] = \Phi_{e_2}^{B\oplus W_i}(0)[s_1] = \Phi_{e_3}^{C\oplus W_i}(0)[s_1] = K_{s_1} \oplus L_{s_1}(0) = K_{s_1}(0) = K_t(0) = 1$.

Note that

(i) any $\mathcal{P}, \mathcal{Q}, \mathcal{R}$-strategy $\alpha \succeq \beta^\frown i$ has parameters larger than $\theta_\beta(0)[s']$;

(ii) all parameters chosen by $\mathcal{P}, \mathcal{Q}, \mathcal{R}$-strategies to the right of $\beta^\frown i$ after stage s' are larger than $\theta_\beta(0)[s']$;

(iii) all $\mathcal{P}, \mathcal{Q}, \mathcal{R}$-strategies which are to the right of $\beta^\frown i$ and were accessible before stage s', have been already cancelled by the end of stage s';

(iv) no strategy to the left of $\beta^\frown i$ is accessible after stage s';

(v) no $\mathcal{P}, \mathcal{Q}, \mathcal{R}$-strategy $\alpha \prec \beta$ take actions after stage s'.

Therefore, no $\mathcal{P}, \mathcal{Q}, \mathcal{R}$-strategy enumerates numbers below $\theta_\beta(0)[s']$ into A, B, C and L after stage s', and hence, equation (2) is obtained at stage s_1 because W_i has changed below $u_\beta(0)[s'] \le u(\beta, 1)[s'] < \theta_\beta(0)[s']$. This change on W_i allows $\Theta_\beta^{W_i}(0)[s']$ to be undefined, and at stage s_1, we can define $\Theta_\beta^{W_i}(0)[s_1] = K_{s_1}(0) = 1$. This computation remains correct, i.e. $\Theta_\beta^{W_i}(0) = \Theta_\beta^{W_i}(0)[s_1] = K(0) = 1$.

Suppose that $\Theta_\beta^{W_i}(q)$ is eventually defined such that $\Theta_\beta^{W_i}(q) = K(q)$ for every $q \le p - 1$. We will prove that $\Theta_\beta^{W_i}(p) \downarrow= K(p)$. Let $s_0 \ge s$ be the β-expansionary stage at which $\Theta_\beta^{W_i}(p-1)[s_0]$ has been defined and

$$\Theta_\beta^{W_i}(p-1) = \Theta_\beta^{W_i}(p-1)[s_0] = K_{s_0}(p-1) = K(p-1).$$

At stage s_0, $\Theta_\beta^{W_i}(p)$ has not been defined yet. Let s_1 be the least β-expansionary stage after s_0 such that $l(\beta, s_1) > 2p + 1$. At stage s_1, we define $\Theta_\beta^{W_i}(p)[s_1] = K_{s_1}(p)$ with a fresh use $\theta_\beta(p)[s_1] > u_\beta(l(\beta, s_1))[s_1]$. If p never enters K after stage s_1, then $\Theta_\beta^{W_i}(p) = \Theta_\beta^{W_i}(p)[s_1] = K_{s_1}(p) = K(p) = 0$. Otherwise, suppose that p enters K at stage $\bar{s} > s_1$. Let s_2 be the least β-expansionary stages such that $s_1 < \bar{s} \le s_2$. We will show in the following that at the beginning of stage s_3, W_i has changed below $\theta(\beta, p)[s_1]$, allowing $\Theta_\beta^{W_i}(p)$ to be undefined. Indeed, we have that

(3) $\Phi_{e_1}^{A\oplus W_i}(2p)[s_1] = \Phi_{e_2}^{B\oplus W_i}(2p)[s_1] = \Phi_{e_3}^{C\oplus W_i}(2p)[s_1] = K_{s_1} \oplus L_{s_1}(2p) = K_{s_1}(p) = 0$, and

(4) $\Phi_{e_1}^{A\oplus W_i}(2p)[s_2] = \Phi_{e_2}^{B\oplus W_i}(2p)[s_2] = \Phi_{e_3}^{C\oplus W_i}(2p)[s_2] = K_{s_2} \oplus L_{s_2}(2p) = K_{s_2}(p) = K_{\bar{s}}(p) = 1$.

If no $\mathcal{P}, \mathcal{Q}, \mathcal{R}$-strategy $\alpha \succeq \beta^\frown i$ puts numbers less than $u(\beta, l(\beta, s_1))[s_1] > u(\beta, 2p)[s_1]$ into A, B or C during β-expansionary stages between s_1 and s_2, then equation (4) is obtained at stage s_2 only because W_i has changed below $u_\beta(2p)[s_1] < u_\beta(l(\beta, s_1))[s_1] < \theta_\beta(p)[s_1]$. Otherwise, without loss of generality, let t ($s_1 \le t < s_2$) be the least β-expansionary stage at which a $\mathcal{P}, \mathcal{Q}, \mathcal{R}$-strategy, say a $\mathcal{P}$-strategy

$\alpha \succeq \beta \frown i$ puts numbers below $u_\beta(l(\beta, s_1))[s_1]$ into A and B. Clearly, all α's parameters $k(\alpha)$, $x(\alpha)$, and $z(\alpha)$ were chosen before stage s_1. Hence, $2z(\alpha) + 1 < l(\beta, s_1)$ and $u_\beta(2z(\alpha) + 1)[s_1] < \theta_\beta(p)[s_1]$. At stage t, when putting $\gamma_1(k(\alpha))[t]$ and $\gamma_2(k(\alpha))[t]$ into A and B, respectively, α also puts $z(\alpha)$ (or z for short) into L. Let t_1 be the next β-expansionary stage after t. Note that $t < t_1 \le s_2$ and

(5) $\Phi_{e_1}^{A \oplus W_i}(2z + 1)[s_1] = \Phi_{e_2}^{B \oplus W_i}(2z + 1)[s_1] = \Phi_{e_3}^{C \oplus W_i}(2z + 1)[s_1] = K_{s_1} \oplus L_{s_1}(2z + 1) = L_{s_1}(z) = 0$, and

(6) $\Phi_{e_1}^{A \oplus W_i}(2z + 1)[t_1] = \Phi_{e_2}^{B \oplus W_i}(2z + 1)[t_1] = \Phi_{e_3}^{C \oplus W_i}(2z + 1)[t_1] = K_{t_1} \oplus L_{t_1}(2z + 1) = L_{t_1}(z) = 1$.

By the choice of stage t, from stage s_1 to stage t, no number less than $u(\beta, l(\beta, s_1))[s_1]$ is enumerated into C. Moreover, every strategy $\tau \ge \alpha$ is initialized at the end of stage t, and no $\mathcal{P}, \mathcal{Q}, \mathcal{R}$-strategy $\alpha' \le \alpha$ acts during stages between t and t_1. Therefore, from stage s_1 to stage t_1, no number less than $u(\beta, l(\beta, s_1))[s_1]$ enters C. Hence, the equation (6) is obtained because at the beginning of stage s_2, W_i has changed below $u(\beta, 2z + 1)[s_1] \le u(\beta, l(\beta, s_1))[s_1] < \theta_\beta(p)[s_1]$.

Thus, at stage s_2, we can define $\Theta_\beta^{W_i}(p)[s_2] = K_{s_2}(p) = 1$, and this computation remains correct, i.e. $\Theta_\beta^{W_i}(p) = \Theta_\beta^{W_i}(p)[s_2] = 1 = K(p)$.

Lemma 3. *The requirement S is satisfied.*

Proof. We prove it by induction that for any $n \in \omega$, $i = 1, 2$,

(7) $\Gamma_1^{A \oplus E}(n) = \Gamma_2^{B \oplus E}(n) = \Omega_1^{B \oplus F}(n) = \Omega_2^{C \oplus F}(n) = \Delta_1^{C \oplus G}(n) = \Delta_2^{A \oplus G}(n) = K(n)$.

For $n = 0$, at stage 1 of the construction, we define for $i = 1, 2$:

$\Gamma_1^{A \oplus E}(n) = \Gamma_2^{B \oplus E}(0)[1] = \Omega_1^{B \oplus F}(0)[1] = \Omega_2^{C \oplus F}(0)[1] = \Delta_1^{C \oplus G}(0)[1] = \Delta_2^{A \oplus G}(0)[1] = K_1(0)$.

All parameters of $\mathcal{P}, \mathcal{Q}, \mathcal{R}$-strategies are chosen as fresh numbers greater than 0, and hence, these computations will be unchanged and equal to $K(0)$, unless 0 enters K at a stage $s > 1$. If the latter happens, at the beginning of stage s, we follow step (a) of the construction to redefine for $i = 1, 2$:

$\Gamma_1^{A \oplus E}(0)[s] = \Gamma_2^{B \oplus E}(0)[s] = \Omega_1^{B \oplus F}(0)[s] = \Omega_2^{C \oplus F}(0)[s] = \Delta_1^{C \oplus G}(0)[s] = \Delta_2^{A \oplus G}(0)[s] = K_s(0) = 1$,

with fresh uses. These new computations remain unchanged and compute $K(0)$ correctly.

Assuming (7) holds for all $m < n$. In the following, we prove it also holds for n. Let s be the first stage at which $\Gamma_1^{A \oplus E}(m), \Gamma_2^{B \oplus E}(m), \Omega_1^{B \oplus F}(m), \Omega_2^{C \oplus F}(m), \Delta_1^{C \oplus G}(m), \Delta_2^{A \oplus G}(m)$ are all defined and compute $K(m)$ correctly for every $m \le n - 1$. The followings are obtained from the construction and Lemma 1:

(i) After stage s, all uses $\gamma_i(m)[s]$, $\omega_i(m)[s]$, $\delta_i(m)[s]$, $i = 1, 2$, are never change for every $m < n$.

(ii) Any $\mathcal{P}, \mathcal{Q}, \mathcal{R}$-strategy which puts numbers into A, B or C after stage s has killing point greater than $n - 1$.

(iii) By the beginning of stage $s+1$, all uses $\gamma_i(n)[s+1]$, $\omega_i(n)[s+1]$, $\delta_i(n)[s+1]$, $i = 1, 2$, have been defined. Let M be the set of these uses.

(iv) If a γ, ω, δ-use at $q \geq n$ has definition by the end of stage s, then it has been actually defined before stage s. Let U be the set of all such γ, ω, δ-uses and $p \geq n$ be the largest such q.

Without loss of generality, we assume that $K_{s+1}(n) = K(n)$ (otherwise, if n enters K at a stage $s' > s+1$ then at the beginning of stage s', all uses in M are reset as fresh numbers, and we can consider stage s' instead).

At the beginning of stage $s+1$, if a γ, δ, ω-use at n, say $\gamma_1(n)[s+1]$, is defined, then it is greater than $\max U$. Therefore, a γ, ω, δ-use u in M is undefined after stage $s+1$ only when a γ, ω, δ-use $u' \leq u$ in $U \cup M$ is enumerated into the corresponding oracle via

(a) rectification actions of S when a number $n < x \leq p$ enters K after stage $s+1$;

(b) or actions of putting numbers into A, B or C of a $\mathcal{P}, \mathcal{Q}, \mathcal{R}$-strategy with the killing point $n \leq k \leq p$.

If at a stage $t_0 > s+1$, (a) or (b) happens, then all affected γ, δ, ω-uses at n are reset as fresh numbers by the beginning of stage $t_0 + 1$. Since $U \cup M$ is finite, the γ, δ, ω-uses at n can only be undefined at most finitely many times. Therefore, there is a stage $t \geq s+1$ such that all uses $\gamma_i(n)[t]$, $\omega_i(n)[t]$, $\delta_i(n)[t]$ $(i = 1, 2)$ are defined and from stage t onwards,

– there is no $n \leq k \leq p$ entering K,
– there is no $\mathcal{P}, \mathcal{Q}, \mathcal{R}$-strategy with killing point $n \leq k \leq p$ putting numbers into A, B or C.

Thus, the Γ, Ω, Δ-computations at n are unchanged from stage t onwards and compute $K(n)$ correctly, and so, (7) holds for n.

This completes the proof of Theorem 1.

6   Discussion

We now discuss the generalization of Theorem 1 to $n > 3$, which involves a construction of n c.e sets $A_1, \cdots, A_n$, satisfying for every $1 \leq k, l \leq n$, $e, r = \langle i, e_1, \cdots, e_n \rangle \in \omega$, the following requirements:

$\mathcal{S}_{k,l} : \Gamma_{kl}^{A_k \oplus E_l} = K$, for each pair (k, l), with $1 \leq k \neq l \leq n$.

$\mathcal{P}_{e,l} : \Phi_e^{E_l} \neq D$,

$\mathcal{N}_r : \Phi_{e_1}^{A_1 \oplus W_i} = \cdots = \Phi_{e_n}^{A_n \oplus W_i} = K \oplus L \Rightarrow K = \Theta_r^{W_i}$.

The strategies to satisfy $\mathcal{S}_{k,l}, \mathcal{P}_{e,l}, \mathcal{N}_r$-requirements are analogous to the $\mathcal{S}, \mathcal{P}, \mathcal{N}$-strategies described previously. In particular, each function $\Gamma_{kl}^{A_k \oplus E_l}$ is defined in the same manner as $\Gamma_1^{A \oplus E}$, where numbers will be enumerated into E_l, to undefine $\Gamma_{kl}^{A_k \oplus E_l}$-computations. Such actions may cause interactions among the constructions of the functions $\Gamma_{kl_0}^{A_k \oplus E_{l_0}}$, $1 \le k \le n$, $k \ne l_0$, for some $1 \le l_0 \le n$. Additionally, the construction of p.c. functionals Γ_{kl} also involves $\mathcal{P}_{e,l}$-strategies, which may put numbers into A_k's, raising interactions among all Γ_{kl}-functionals. To overcome such problems, using the same idea as the $\mathcal{S}$-strategy described in the proof of Theorem [1], we also define all Γ_{lk}-functionals in a synchronous way: at a stage s, a computation $\Gamma_{k_0 l_0}^{A_{k_0} \oplus E_{l_0}}(n)$ is defined only if $\Gamma_{kl}^{A_k \oplus E_l}(n-1)$ has already been defined for every $1 \le k \ne l \le n$.

A $\mathcal{P}_{e,l}$-strategy is analogous to the $\mathcal{P}_e$-strategy α, but with numbers are put into A_k (for every $1 \le k \le n, k \ne l$) correspondingly to lift the γ_{kl}-uses beyond a φ_e-use. Finally, an $\mathcal{N}_r$-strategy works in the same way as the previous $\mathcal{N}_{\langle i, e_1, e_2, e_3 \rangle}$-strategy β does.

References

1. Bie, R., Wu, G.: A minimal pair in the quotient structure $M/NCup$. In: Cooper, S.B., Löwe, B., Sorbi, A. (eds.) CiE 2007. LNCS, vol. 4497, pp. 53–62. Springer, Heidelberg (2007). https://doi.org/10.1007/978-3-540-73001-9_6
2. Cooper, S.B.: On a theorem of C. E. M. Yates. Handwritten Notes (1974)
3. Downey, R., Greenberg, N., Miller, J.S., Weber, R.: Prompt simplicity, array computability and cupping. Computational Prospects of Infinity. Part II. Presented Talks, Lecture Notes Series, vol. 15, pp. 59–77. World Scientific Publishing, Hackensack (2008)
4. Greenberg, N., Ng, K.M., Wu, G.: Cupping and jump classes in the computably enumerable degrees. J. Symbolic Logic **85**(4), 1499–1545 (2020)
5. Li, A., Wu, G., Yang, Y.: On the quotient structure of computably enumerable degrees modulo the noncuppable ideal. In: Cai, J.-Y., Cooper, S.B., Li, A. (eds.) TAMC 2006. LNCS, vol. 3959, pp. 731–736. Springer, Heidelberg (2006). https://doi.org/10.1007/11750321_69
6. Li, A., Wu, G., Zhang, Z.: A hierarchy for cuppable degrees. Illinois J. Math. **44**(3), 619–632 (2000)
7. Li, A.: A hierarchy characterisation of cuppable degrees. University of Leeds, Dept. of Pure Math., 2001, Preprint series, No. 1, 21 pp (2001)
8. Miller, D.P.: High recursively enumerable degrees and the anti-cupping properties. Logic Year 1979–80, Lecture Notes in Math., vol. 859, pp. 230–235 (1981)
9. Soare, R.I.: Recursively Enumerable Sets and Degrees. Perspectives in Mathematical Logic. Springer, Heidelberg (1987)

The Relationship Between Local and Global Structure in the Enumeration Degrees

Mariya I. Soskova$^{(\boxtimes)}$ (iD)

University of Wisconsin–Madiosn, 480 Lincoln Dr, Madison, WI 537206, USA
soskova@wisc.edu
https://people.math.wisc.edu/~soskova/

Abstract. We discuss core ideas in degree theory including biinterpretability, automorphisms, and definability. We focus on the Turing degrees $\mathcal{D}_T$, the enumeration degrees $\mathcal{D}_e$, as well as their local substructures $\mathcal{D}_T(\leq \mathbf{0}'_T)$ and $\mathcal{D}_e(\leq \mathbf{0}'_e)$.

Keywords: enumeration degrees · automorphism base · definability

1 Introduction

This is the extended abstract of my talk for the special session on Degree Theory at the conference CiE 2023 "Unity of Logic and Computation". It is a privilege to indulge in talking about pure degree theory, as the subject has fallen out of fashion. Yet, it is my favorite part of computability theory and I have decided to talk about older joint work with Slaman [9] that, I believe, reveals intrinsic beauty in the subject and leads to fascinating remaining open questions. The talk will cover topics such as the biinterpretability conjecture, the automorphism problem, and definability, focused on the enumeration degrees, rather than the more traditionally studied Turing degrees. The enumeration degrees can be viewed as an extension of the Turing degrees, in which we have enough additional structure to reveal certain phenomena that remain hidden in the Turing degrees. In particular, we will discuss a strong relationship between the local and global structure of the enumeration degrees.

2 Biinterpretability and Automorphisms

From one's first encounter with the Turing degrees and Post's theorem, one knows that there is a deep relationship between the Turing degrees and arithmetic. Simpson [8] proved that the first order theory of the Turing degrees is computably isomorphic to the theory of second-order arithmetic. One way to prove this following Slaman and Woodin [11] is to show that one can encode models of arithmetic within the degree structure: there are formulas $\varphi_{\mathbb{N}}$, φ_+, φ_*, and φ_X in the language of partial orders, such that for every set of natural numbers C there are finitely many parameters $\overline{\mathbf{p}} \in \mathcal{D}_T^{<\omega}$ so that the set of degrees that

G. Della Vedova et al. (Eds.): CiE 2023, LNCS 13967, pp. 17–22, 2023.
https://doi.org/10.1007/978-3-031-36978-0_2

18   M. I. Soskova

satisfy the formulas above with parameters $\overline{\mathbf{p}}$ give a copy of the structure of first order arithmetic with a predicate for C. Thus we can transfer statements in the language of second order arithmetic into degree theoretic statements, replacing quantification over sets with quantification over parameters.

Slaman and Woodin conjectured that the relationship between the structure of the Turing degrees and second-order arithmetic is even stronger. Their *biinterpretability conjecture* states that the relation on $\mathcal{D}_T$ that is true of $\overline{\mathbf{p}}$ and $\mathbf{c}$ if and only if $\overline{\mathbf{p}}$ code a model of arithmetic with a predicate for a set C and $\deg_T(C) = \mathbf{c}$ is first order definable in $\mathcal{D}_T$. In other words, not only does the structure of the Turing degrees have an internal understanding of second order arithmetic, but it also understand precisely how the sets in that model correspond to its degrees. Slaman and Woodin [11] showed that their Biinterpretability conjecture is equivalent to a long standing open problem in degree theory—the *automorphism problem*:

Question 1. Are there any nontrivial automorphisms of the Turing degrees?

In the open questions session held at the IMS meeting in Singapore in 2011, Slaman identified this question as the most important question left open in Degree Theory.

Slaman and Woodin [11] make significant progress towards a solution to this question. They showed that their biinterpretability conjecture is true if you allow the use of finitely many parameters, that the automorphism group of the Turing degrees is countable and that every member has an arithmetically definable presentation. Their proof is complicated, combining meta-mathematical set theoretic techniques with purely computability theoretic proofs. At the heart is a theorem about *automorphism bases* of the Turing degrees:

Definition 1. *An* automorphism base *for a structure $\mathcal{A}$ with domain A is a set $B \subseteq A$, such that if π is an automorphism that fixes every member of B, i.e. $\pi(\mathbf{x}) = \mathbf{x}$ for all $\mathbf{x} \in B$, then π is the identity.*

Theorem 1. *There is a Turing degree $\mathbf{g} \leq \mathbf{0}_T^{(5)}$ such that $\{\mathbf{g}\}$ is an automorphism base for $\mathcal{D}_T$.*

A lot of work in Degree Theory has been devoted to understanding local substructures. Typically these are countable substructures whose elements have low arithmetic complexity. Local structures are connected to first order arithmetic. Shore [7] proved that the theory of $\mathcal{D}_T(\leq \mathbf{0}_T')$, the structure consisting of all Δ_2^0 Turing degrees, is computably isomorphic to first order arithmetic. Slaman and Harrington (see [5]) prove the same for the theory of $\mathcal{R}$, the c.e. Turing degrees. Once again, this can be shown by coding the standard model of arithmetic via finitely many parameters. In fact, in both cases it can be shown that one can define such a model without parameters. The Biinterpretability conjecture can be formulated in the local setting as well.

Definition 2. *Let $\mathcal{Z}$ be a class of degrees in a degree structure $\mathcal{D}$, represented by a sequence $\{Z_i\}_{i<\omega}$, i.e. $\mathcal{Z} = \{d(Z_i) \mid i \in \omega\}$. We say that $\overline{\mathbf{p}} \in \mathcal{D}^{<\omega}$ define* *an indexing of $\mathcal{Z}$ with respect to the sequence $\{Z_i\}_{i<\omega}$, if they define a standard model of arithmetic $\mathcal{M}$ and a function $\varphi : \mathbb{N}^{\mathcal{M}} \to \mathcal{D}$, such that $\varphi(i^{\mathcal{M}}) = d(Z_i)$.*

If $\mathcal{D}$ is a countable structure then $\mathcal{D}$ itself can be represented by a sequence $\{Z_i\}_{i<\omega}$. If $\overline{\mathbf{p}}$ define an indexing of $\mathcal{D}$ then the degrees in $\overline{\mathbf{p}}$ form an automorphism base for $\mathcal{D}$. Indeed, if π is an automorphism of $\mathcal{D}$ that fixes every degree in $\overline{\mathbf{p}}$ then π fixes the degrees that represent the natural numbers in the model $\mathcal{M}$ coded by $\overline{\mathbf{p}}$, and hence by the definability of φ from $\overline{\mathbf{p}}$ it also fixes for every i the degree $\varphi(i^{\mathcal{M}})$. The biinterpretability conjecture for a countable local structure $\mathcal{D} = \{d(Z_i) \mid i \in \omega\}$ is the statement "There is a definable (without parameters) indexing of $\mathcal{D}$". In this case, as well, biinterpretability is equivalent to rigidity for the local structure, i.e. it is equivalent to the lack of non-trivial automorphisms.

Slaman and Woodin [12] showed that in $\mathcal{D}_T(\le \mathbf{0}_T')$ there is an indexing of the c.e. degrees (with respect to the standard enumeration of all c.e. sets $\{W_e\}_{e<\omega}$) which is definable from parameters. Building on this result, Slaman and Soskova [10] show the existence of finitely many parameters in $\mathcal{D}_T(\le \mathbf{0}_T')$ that define an indexing of the Δ_2^0 degrees. As a corollary, we obtain that, $\mathcal{D}_T(\le \mathbf{0}_T')$ has at most countably many automorphisms as well and that the biinterpretability conjecture for $\mathcal{D}_T(\le \mathbf{0}_T')$ is true modulo finitely many parameters.

3   The Enumeration Degrees

We will focus on an extension of the Turing degrees, the structure of the enumeration degrees, $\mathcal{D}_e$. This structure arises from the relation *enumeration reducibility*, introduced by Friedberg and Rogers [3] in 1959.

Definition 3 (Friedberg and Rogers [3]). *A set A is enumeration reducible to a set B (denoted by $A \le_e B$) if there is a c.e. set Φ, such that*

$$A = \Phi(B) = \{n : \exists u(\langle n, u \rangle \in \Phi \ \& \ D_u \subseteq B)\},$$

where D_u denotes the finite set with code (canonical index) u under the standard coding of finite sets.

A set A is *enumeration equivalent* to a set B (denoted by $A \equiv_e B$) if $A \le_e B$ and $B \le_e A$. The equivalence class of A under the relation $\equiv_e$ is the *enumeration degree* $d_e(A)$ of A. The enumeration degrees are ordered by $d_e(A) \le d_e(B)$ if and only if $A \le_e B$. The least element in this ordering is $\mathbf{0}_e = d_e(\emptyset)$, the set of all c.e. sets. We define a least upper bound operation by setting $d_e(A) \vee d_e(B) = d_e(A \oplus B)$. The enumeration jump of a set A was defined by Cooper [2], as $K_A \oplus \overline{K_A}$, where $K_A = \{\langle e, x\rangle \mid x \in \Phi_e(A)\}$. The enumeration jump of the degree of A is $d_e(A)' = d_e(K_A \oplus \overline{K_A})$. Thus the structure of the enumeration degrees $\langle \mathcal{D}_e, \le, \vee, ', \mathbf{0}_e \rangle$ is an upper semi-lattice with least element and a jump operation.

Enumeration reducibility is close to Turing reducibility in the spectrum of relative definability. It was introduced to capture the notion of relative computability of partial functions. Turing reducibility can be expressed via enumeration reducibility, namely $A \leq_T B$ if and only if $A \oplus \overline{A} \leq_e B \oplus \overline{B}$, and so the Turing degrees have a natural isomorphic copy in $\mathcal{D}_e$, *the total enumeration degrees*. The standard embedding of $\mathcal{D}_T$ into $\mathcal{D}_e$ mapping $d_T(A)$ to $d_e(A \oplus \overline{A})$ preserves the order, least upper bound and jump operator. Selman [6] showed a reverse connection: every enumeration degree is completely determined by the set of total enumeration degrees above it.

Theorem 2 (Selman [6]). $A \leq_e B$ *if for all* X *if* $B \leq_e X \oplus \overline{X}$ *then* $A \leq_e X \oplus \overline{X}$

Thus the total enumeration degrees are an automorphism base for the enumeration degrees. We can transfer fact about the automorphisms of Turing degrees to the enumeration degrees through the standard embedding. Theorem 1 for examples translates to:

Corollary 1. *There is a total enumeration degree* $\mathbf{g} \leq \mathbf{0}_e^{(5)}$ *such that* $\{\mathbf{g}\}$ *is an automorphism base for the structure of the enumeration degrees.*

One particular aspect of the structure of the enumeration degrees that makes it a favorable context to work in is that several nontrivial relations on the degree structure have natural order theoretic definition. It is precisely this definability phenomenon that will be exploited in this work. We list these results below:

Theorem 3 (Kalimullin [4]). *The enumeration jump operator is first order definable in* $\mathcal{D}_e$.

Theorem 4 (Cai, Ganchev, Lempp, Miller and Soskova [1]). *The set of total enumeration degrees is first order definable in* $\mathcal{D}_e$.

Recall that for Turing degrees $\mathbf{a}$ and $\mathbf{b}$, we say that $\mathbf{a}$ is *c.e. in* $\mathbf{b}$ if there are sets $A \in \mathbf{a}$ and $B \in \mathbf{b}$, such that A is c.e. in B.

Theorem 5 (Cai, Ganchev, Lempp, Miller and Soskova [1]). *The image of the relation "c.e. in" under the standard embedding of* $\mathcal{D}_T$ *in* $\mathcal{D}_e$ *is first-order definable in the structure of the enumeration degrees.*

4 The Coding Method

Theorem 2 and Theorem 4 together provide an important relationship between the automorphism problems of $\mathcal{D}_T$ and $\mathcal{D}_e$: since $\mathcal{D}_T$ has a first order definable copy in $\mathcal{D}_e$ which is also an automorphism base for $\mathcal{D}_e$, we have that a nontrivial automorphism of $\mathcal{D}_e$ would give rise to a nontrivial automorphism of $\mathcal{D}_T$.

Using the method presented here we will strengthen this relationship further. The local structure of the enumeration degrees, denoted by $\mathcal{D}_e(\leq \mathbf{0}_e')$, consists of the enumeration degrees of Σ_2^0 sets. Our main theorem is as follows

Theorem 6 (Slaman, Soskova [9]). *Let $\mathcal{L}$ be any of the local structures $\mathcal{R}$, $\mathcal{D}_T(\leq \mathbf{0}'_T)$, or $\mathcal{D}_e(\leq \mathbf{0}'_e)$. The rigidity of $\mathcal{L}$ implies the rigidity of $\mathcal{D}_e$.*

Recall, Slaman and Woodin's [12] result in $\mathcal{D}_T(\leq \mathbf{0}'_T)$ there is an indexing of the c.e. degrees (with respect to the standard enumeration of all c.e. sets $\{W_e\}_{e<\omega}$) which is definable from parameters. The c.e. Turing degrees are mapped to the Π^0_1 enumeration degrees under the standard embedding. Transferring Slaman and Woodin's result to the enumeration degrees we have the following:

Corollary 2. *There are finitely many total parameters in $\mathcal{D}_e(\leq \mathbf{0}'_e)$ that define an indexing of the Π^0_1 enumeration degrees with respect to the sequence $\{\overline{W}_e\}_{e<\omega}$.*

An indexing of the Π^0_1 enumeration degrees with respect to the sequence $\{\overline{W}_e\}_{e<\omega}$ will be called *a basic indexing*. Parameters that define a basic indexing will be called *basic indexing parameters*.

Slaman and Soskova [9] prove the following sequence of results, each building on top of the previous one:

1. Every set of basic indexing parameters defines an indexing of the total degrees in the interval $[\mathbf{0}_e, \mathbf{0}'_e]$.
2. Every set of basic indexing parameters defines an indexing of the total degrees that are c.e. in and above some total degree in the interval $[\mathbf{0}_e, \mathbf{0}'_e]$.
3. Every set of basic indexing parameters defines an indexing of the total degrees in the union of all intervals $[\mathbf{x}, \mathbf{x}']$, where $\mathbf{x}$ is a total enumeration degree below $\mathbf{0}'_e$.
4. Every set of basic indexing parameters defines an indexing of the interval $[\mathbf{0}_e, \mathbf{0}''_e]$.

The first three steps have a definability component: The first step relies on the definability of the total enumeration degrees. The second on the definability of the (image of the) relation "c.e. in", the third on the definability of the jump operator. In addition, each step has a purely degree theoretic component, a structural property proved using the priority method or using forcing.

These steps can be iterated to show that

Theorem 7 (Slaman, Soskova [9]). *Every set of basic indexing parameters defines an indexing of the total degrees in the interval $[\mathbf{0}_e, \mathbf{0}_e^{(n)}]$.*

In particular, when $n = 5$ we see that any set of basic indexing parameters determines the total enumeration degrees below $\mathbf{0}_e^{(5)}$. By Corollary 1 this is an automorphism base for the enumeration degrees.

5   Open Questions

Some interesting open questions remain. Of course, whether any of the local structures has a non-trivial automorphism is a long-standing open problem, perhaps still out of our reach. But, here is something that remain unclear from this analysis that feels more approachable. We know that finitely many parameters below $\mathbf{0}'_e$ determine the position of every other enumeration degree. This means that they determine, in particular, every other Σ_2^0 enumeration degree. But the way that this works requires us to step outside the local structure. Can we achieve that by just staying inside $\mathcal{D}_e(\leq \mathbf{0}'_e)$?

Question 2 Is there an indexing of the Σ_2^0 enumeration degrees that is definable (with parameters) in $\mathcal{D}_e(\leq \mathbf{0}'_e)$?

On the flip side, we may ask whether we needed the larger context of the enumeration degrees to capture the interaction between local and global structure. Notice that we mainly stay within the total degrees, but we use the definability of three relations, which requires us to step outside the total degrees. Is this necessary?

Question 3 Does the rigidity of $\mathcal{D}_T(\leq \mathbf{0}'_T)$ or $\mathcal{R}$ imply the rigidity of $\mathcal{D}_T$?

Acknowledgements. The author is supported by NSF Grant No. DMS-1762648 and NSF Grant No. DMS-2053848.

References

1. Cai, M., Ganchev, H.A., Lempp, S., Miller, J.S., Soskova, M.I.: Defining totality in the enumeration degrees, to appear in J. Amer. Math. Soc
2. Cooper, S.B.: Partial degrees and the density problem. Part 2: the enumeration degrees of the Σ_2 sets are dense. J. Symbolic Logic **49**, 503–513 (1984)
3. Friedberg, R.M., Rogers Jr., H.: Reducibility and completeness for sets of integers, Z. Math. Logik Grundlag. Math. **5**, 117–125 (1959)
4. Kalimullin, I.S.: Definability of the jump operator in the enumeration degrees. J. Math. Log. **3**(2), 257–267 (2003)
5. Nies, A., Shore, R.A., Slaman, T.A.: Definability in the recursively enumerable degrees. Bull. Symbolic Logic **2**(4), 392–404 (1996)
6. Selman, A.L.: Arithmetical reducibilities I. Z. Math. Logik Grundlag. Math. **17**, 335–350 (1971)
7. Shore, R.A.: The theory of the degrees below $0'$. J. London Math. Soc **24**, 1–14 (1981)
8. Simpson, S.G.: First-order theory of the degrees of recursive unsolvability. Ann. of Math. (2), **105**(1), 121–139 (1977)
9. Slaman, T.A., Soskova, M.I.: The enumeration degrees: local and global structural interactions, Foundations of mathematics. Contemp. Math., (Amer. Math. Soc., Providence, RI), **690**, 31–67 (2017)
10. Slaman, T.A., Soskova, M.I.: The Δ_2^0 Turing degrees: automorphisms and definability. Trans. Amer. Math. Soc. **370**(2), 1351–1375 (2018)
11. Slaman, T.A., Hugh Woodin, W.: Definability in degree structures (2005). preprint http://math.berkeley.edu/slaman/talks/sw.pdf
12. Slaman, T.A., Hugh Woodin, W.: Definability in the Turing degrees. Illinois J. Math. **30**(2), 320–334 (1986)

Direct Construction of Scott Ideals

Russell Miller[1,2(✉)]

[1] Queens College, 65-30 Kissena Blvd., Queens, NY 11367, U.S.A.
Russell.Miller@qc.cuny.edu
[2] C.U.N.Y. Graduate Center, 365 Fifth Avenue, New York, NY 10016, U.S.A.

Abstract. A Scott ideal is an ideal $\mathcal{I}$ in the Turing degrees, closed downwards and under join, such that for every degree d in $\mathcal{I}$, there is another degree in $\mathcal{I}$ that is a PA-degree relative to d. It is known that, for every Turing degree d, there is a Scott ideal containing d in which every degree is low relative to d (with jump Turing-reducible to d'). We give a construction of such an ideal $\mathcal{I}_d$, uniform in a given set $D \in d$, using the Uniform Low Basis Theorem of Brattka, de Brecht, and Pauly. The primary contribution of this article may be the questions posed at the end about the monotonicity of this construction.

Keywords: computability theory · PA-degree · Π^0_1-class · Scott ideal · Turing degree · Turing reducibility · Uniform Low Basis Theorem

1 Introduction

Finite-branching trees are ubiquitous in mathematical logic. They arise as soon as one begins to consider the completions of a consistent theory. For a consistent, decidable axiom set, such as the axioms **PA** for Peano arithmetic, the complete consistent extensions of the axiom set correspond bijectively to the (infinite) paths through a decidable subtree of the complete binary tree $2^{<\omega}$.

From the Incompleteness Theorem of Gödel, we immediately realize that the subtree above, despite all its decidability, has no computable path. Kreisel remarked that the Halting Problem $\emptyset'$ must be able to compute some path through each such tree. Shoenfield went further in [8], proving that every such tree contains a path whose Turing degree lies strictly below the degree $\mathbf{0}'$ of $\emptyset'$. But it was Jockusch and Soare who claimed the sharpest result, as their Low Basis Theorem in [3] established that every such tree has an infinite path of *low* Turing degree d, i.e., with jump $d' = \mathbf{0}'$. Such a path is "almost" computable, in the sense that its relativization of the Halting Problem is no more complicated than the actual Halting Problem.

The paths through the tree described above for the axiom set **PA** came to be called the **PA**-*degrees*, the Turing degrees of complete consistent extensions of

---

R. Miller—The author was partially supported by Grant #581896 from the Simons Foundation and by the City University of New York PSC-CUNY Research Award Program. The composition of this article was aided by useful conversations with Emma Dinowitz.

G. Della Vedova et al. (Eds.): CiE 2023, LNCS 13967, pp. 23–34, 2023.
https://doi.org/10.1007/978-3-031-36978-0_3

PA. It turns out that these are precisely the degrees capable of computing some path through every decidable infinite subtree of $2^{<\omega}$. In turn, the term "**PA** degree" was relativized: for an arbitrary degree a, a degree d is **PA** *relative to* a if d computes a path through every a-computable infinite subtree of $2^{<\omega}$. (Equivalently, d computes a path through every a-computable infinite finite-branching tree whose branching function is a-computable.) The results of [3] relativize to show that for every Turing degree a, there is a degree d that is both **PA** relative to a and low relative to a, that is, with $a' = d'$. (Necessarily $a < d$ for every d that is **PA** relative to a. Here the relations $<$ and $\leq$ on degrees always denote Turing reducibility.)

More recently, in 2012, Brattka, de Brecht, and Pauly gave a uniform version of the Low Basis Theorem, constructing a Turing functional Γ such that, for every $A \subseteq \omega$, $\Gamma^A(n, s)$ computes a function on ω^2 whose limit, as $s \to \infty$, is the characteristic function of the jump of a set D of **PA**-degree relative to A. Thus D itself must be low relative to A, as A' allows one to compute D'.

Our purpose in this abstract is to apply the Uniform Low Basis Theorem (Theorem 2 below) to give a uniform construction of Scott ideals, a well-known concept in reverse mathematics that we introduce in Sect. 3. As we will explain in Sect. 4, however, our ultimate goal is not related to reverse math, but rather to the absolute Galois group of the rational numbers. In light of this goal, two open questions naturally arise, to be described (but not answered) in that section. We view these questions as important and challenging. Quite possibly the questions themselves are the most important items in this abstract. The technical constructions preceding them require attention but follow a predictable path and lead to results that will not seem foreign or unusual.

2   Constructing PA Degrees Uniformly

For the degree $\mathbf{0}$, the tree described above, whose paths are the complete extensions of **PA**, has the property that the degrees of paths through that tree are precisely the **PA** degrees relative to $\mathbf{0}$. The first result here, which is well-known, relativizes this statement to an arbitrary degree a and says that such a tree can be created uniformly in a set $A \in a$.

Theorem 1. *There is a computable relation $R \subseteq \omega \times 2^{<\omega} \times 2^{\omega}$ such that, for every $A \in 2^{\omega}$, the set*

$$\{\sigma \in 2^{<\omega} : (\forall m, n \leq |\sigma|) R(n, \sigma{\restriction}m, A)\}$$

forms an A-computable subtree $T_A \subseteq 2^{<\omega}$ such that, for every degree c,

$$c \text{ is PA relative to } A \iff c \text{ computes a path through } T_A.$$

Moreover, since T_A is computable uniformly from A, there is a computable total injective function $h : \omega \to \omega$ such that, for every A, h is a 1-reduction from the jump $(T_A)'$ to the jump A'.

T_A is built so that its paths are the consistent completions of the axiom set **PA** augmented by axioms saying $f = \chi_A$, in the language of **PA** with a unary function symbol f adjoined. If Υ is the Turing functional such that $T_A = \Upsilon^A$, then the function h, on input e, outputs the code number of the Turing functional $\Phi_{h(e)}$ such that

$$\Phi^C_{h(e)}(x) = \Phi^{\Upsilon^C}_e(e).$$

Thus, for arbitrary sets A,

$$h(e) \in A' \iff \Phi^A_{h(e)}(h(e))\downarrow \iff \Phi^{\Upsilon^A}_e(e)\downarrow \iff \Phi^{T_A}_e(e)\downarrow \iff e \in (T_A)'.$$

Theorem 2 (Uniform Low Basis Theorem: Thm. 8.3 in [1]). *There exists a Turing functional Γ such that, for every set $A \subseteq \omega$, Γ^A is total and there exists a set P_A, of **PA** degree relative to A, such that*

$$(\forall n) \lim_s \Gamma^A(n, s) = \chi_{(P_A)'}(n),$$

The set P_A may be viewed as a path through the universal A-computable subtree T_A of $2^{<\omega}$. This path is *low relative to T*, meaning that $(P_A)' \leq_T A'$, as its jump $(P_A)'$ is the limit of an A-computable function. The original Low Basis Theorem of Jockusch and Soare [3], relativized to A, proved the existence of such a path. Brattka, de Brecht, and Pauly showed that the jump of P_A can be approximated uniformly using a A-oracle.

With this, for an arbitrary set A, we will define an infinite sequence $A = A_0 <_T A_1 <_T A_2 <_T \cdots$ of subsets of ω such that:

- For every $n \in \omega$, $\deg A_{n+1}$ is a PA degree relative to A_n; and
- There exists an A-computable function M, which we will call a *master function*, such that

$$(\forall n)(\forall x) \lim_{s \to \infty} M(n, x, s) = \begin{cases} 1, \text{ if } x \in A'_n \\ 0, \text{ if } x \notin A'_n. \end{cases}$$

The first condition automatically implies $A_{n+1} \not\leq_T A_n$. The second condition yields a uniform-limit result for the sets A_n themselves, using the following easy lemma.

Lemma 1. *There is a computable total function f such that, for every $C \subseteq \omega$, f is a 1-reduction from C to C'.*

Proof. Define $f(n)$ to be the index e of the functional Φ_e given by

$$\Phi^B_e(x) = \begin{cases} 0, \text{ if } n \in B; \\ \uparrow, \text{ if not.} \end{cases} \qquad \square$$

Thus, uniformly for all n and x, $A_n(x) = \lim_s M(n, f(x), s)$. However, the uniform computation of the jumps A'_n is substantially stronger than this. One might say that the sets A_n are *uniformly low*, as their jumps are uniformly limit-computable in A (or equivalently, uniformly A'-computable).

Our sequence is readily defined. It begins with $A_0 = A$. Next, given A_n, we define T_n to be the tree T_{A_n} as given in Theorem 1, which shows that T_n may be computed uniformly from A_n. Then Theorem 2 yields a path $P_{n+1} = P_{T_n}$ through this tree T_n. By Theorem 1, the Turing degree of P_{n+1} is a PA degree relative to A_n, and we define $A_{n+1} = P_{n+1}$.

The sequence $\{A_n\}_{n \in \omega}$ will instantiate the following Proposition.

Proposition 1. *For arbitrary $A \subseteq \omega$, there exists a strictly ascending sequence $\{A_n\}_{n \in \omega}$ of subsets of ω, all low relative to A, with $A_0 = A$ and such that every A_{n+1} has PA degree relative to A_n, and an A'-computable master function M such that $M(n, x) = \chi_{A'_n}(x)$ for all n and x.*

Proof. We use the sets A_n defined above. Since A_{n+1} is a PA degree relative to A_n, we immediately have $A_n <_T A_{n+1}$. (The reduction $A_n \leq_T A_{n+1}$ follows by considering a single fixed index e such that Φ_e^B defines the subtree of $2^{<\omega}$ whose nodes are just the initial segments of B. The path P_{n+1} computes a path through the tree Φ_e^A, hence computes A_n; and since the same index e works for every n, this reduction is uniform in n.)

Next we show how to compute the required master function $M(n, x)$. Of course, since $A_0 = A$, we begin with $M(0, x) = \chi_{A'}(x)$. Assuming by induction on n that, with the A'-oracle, we have computed $M(n, x) = \chi_{A'_n}(x)$ for all x, we now address $(A_{n+1})' = (P_{n+1})'$. Recall from Theorem 1 that for the tree $T_n = T_{A_n}$, there is a computable 1-reduction h from $(T_n)'$ to $(A_n)'$. Moreover, by Theorem 2, the jump $(P_{n+1})' = (P_{T_n})'$ is given by $\lim_s \Gamma^{T_n}(x, s)$. Therefore

$$x \in (A_{n+1})' \iff \lim_s \Gamma^{T_n}(x, s) = 1.$$

We search for a number s_0 such that $(\forall s \geq s_0)\Gamma^{T_n}(x, s) = \Gamma^{T_n}(x, s_0)$. For each s_0, this is a question about the membership in $(T_n)'$ of a particular index $g(s_0)$ (computable from s_0 uniformly in x and n). The function h allows us to convert this question into the question of membership of $h(g(s_0))$ in $(A_n)'$, which we can compute with our oracle, by inductive hypothesis. Moreover, $\lim_s \Gamma^{T_n}(x, s)$ exists, so eventually we find such an s_0, and when we do, we define $M(n, x) = \Gamma^{T_n}(x, s_0)$. Thus $M(n + 1, x) = \chi_{(A_{n+1})'}(x)$ as desired. $\square$

3   Defining Scott Ideals

Proposition 1 allows us to build Scott ideals uniformly. We recall the relevant definition. (Certain applications of it will be discussed briefly in Sect. 4.)

Definition 1. *A nonempty set $\mathcal{I}$ of Turing degrees is a* Turing ideal *if it is closed downward under Turing reducibility $\leq$ and also under the finite join operation. A Turing ideal $\mathcal{I}$ is a* Scott ideal *if it has the additional property that, for every $\mathbf{a} \in \mathcal{I}$, $\mathcal{I}$ also contains a* **PA-degree** *relative to $\mathbf{a}$.*

The most common Turing ideals are the *principal ideals* $\{\mathbf{d} : \mathbf{d} \leq \mathbf{c}\}$ defined by any single degree $\mathbf{c}$. These are not Scott ideals, however, as they contain $\mathbf{c}$

but no degree $> c$ and consequently no degree **PA** relative to c. The natural strategy for building a Scott ideal $\mathcal{I}$ (especially if one wants $\mathcal{I}$ to be countable) is to start with a degree a and close under the condition of Definition 1, adjoining to $\mathcal{I}$ some degree a_1 **PA** relative to a, then another degree a_2 **PA** relative to a_1, and so on. (Of course, when adjoining a_n, we also adjoin all degrees $\leq a_n$.) Proposition 1 shows exactly how to do this effectively, while keeping each a_n as small in the Turing hierarchy as possible. Indeed, since each a_{n+1} is low relative to a_n, we have $a'_{n+1} \leq a'_n \leq \cdots \leq a'_1 \leq a'$, so the entire ideal stays very close to the starting point a.

The point of the upcoming Theorem 4 is to give a cleaner definition of the Scott ideal than the foregoing. The concept of an *exact pair* of Turing degrees appears in Theorem 3 in Spector's article [12], which in turn cites the article [4] by Kleene and Post. Rephrased in the language of the textbook [11], it states that every strictly ascending sequence of Turing degrees (under Turing reducibility $\leq$) has an exact pair.

Theorem 3 (Kleene-Post-Spector; see Theorem VI.4.2 in [11]). *For every sequence $\{a_n\}_{n \in \omega}$ of Turing degrees with $a_n < a_{n+1}$ for all n, there exist upper bounds b and c (called an* exact pair *for the sequence) such that*

$$(\forall d) \; [[d \leq b \;\&\; d \leq c] \iff [\exists n \; d \leq a_n]].$$

We wish to apply Theorem 3 to the sequence of degrees a_n of the sets A_n produced by Proposition 1 above, taking advantage of the specific properties of that sequence. Recall that every degree a_n from that sequence is low relative to the given set A of degree a, with $a'_n = a'$. Moreover, we have a single uniform computable approximation of their jumps. In Proposition 1, the master function was given as an A'-computable function $M(n, x)$. Here we use the equivalent formulation of an A-computable master function $M(n, x, s)$, with $\chi_{(A_n)'}(x) = \lim_{s \to \infty} M(n, x, s)$ for all n and x. (This is better adapted to our construction in Theorem 4 below, whereas the A'-computable version simplified the proof of Proposition 1.) On the other hand, every A_{n+1} computes a path through the universal strongly-A_n-computable subtree T_n of $2^{<\omega}$, and so $A_{n+1} \not\leq_T A_n$. We noted earlier that $A_n \leq_T A_{n+1}$ uniformly in n, so the sequence of degrees $\{a_n\}$ is indeed strictly ascending, allowing us to apply the following theorem to it.

Theorem 4 (Low exact pairs for uniform low ascending sequences). *For every strictly ascending sequence $\{A_n\}_{n \in \omega}$ of subsets of ω such that the reductions $A_n \leq_T A_{n+1}$ are computable uniformly in n, and for every master function M with $\lim_{s \to \infty} M(n, x, s) = \chi_{A'_n}(x)$ for all n and x, there exist subsets B and C of ω that form an exact pair for the sequence $\{A_n\}$ and whose join is low relative to M (i.e., $(B \oplus C)' \leq_T M'$).*

Proof. We give the proof under the assumption that A_0 and M are computable. Relativizing to an arbitrary A_0 and an A_0-computable M is trivial. In our construction, $S =^* T$ denotes that the symmetric difference of the sets S and T is finite, while $S^{[n]} = \{m \in \omega : \langle n, m \rangle \in S\}$ is the n-th "column" of the set S, when the subset S of ω is viewed as a two-dimensional array using a computable bijection $\langle \cdot, \cdot \rangle$ from ω^2 onto ω. This and other standard notation comes from [11], in which Theorem VI.4.2 is a non-effective version of the proof given here. We use requirements similar to those there, for all i, j, and n, along with our lowness requirements for all e:

$$\mathcal{T}_n^B : B^{[n]} =^* A_n.$$
$$\mathcal{T}_n^C : C^{[n]} =^* A_n.$$
$$\mathcal{L}_e : \text{if } (\exists^\infty s) \, \Phi_{e,s}^{\beta_s \oplus \gamma_s}(e)\downarrow, \text{ then } \Phi_e^{B \oplus C}(e)\downarrow.$$
$$\mathcal{R}_{\langle i,j \rangle} : \text{if } \Phi_i^B = \Phi_j^C \text{ and both are total, then } (\exists n) \, \Phi_i^B \leq_T A_n.$$

In the last of these, β_s and γ_s are the s-th finite strings in the computable approximations $\{\beta_s\}_{s \in \omega}$ and $\{\gamma_s\}_{s \in \omega}$ that we will build, with $B = \lim_s \beta_s$ and $C = \lim_s \gamma_s$. It is well known that, if all of these $\mathcal{L}$-requirements are satisfied, then $(B \oplus C)$ will indeed be a low set. The $\mathcal{R}$-requirements will establish that every set computable both from B and from C will be computable from some A_n, while the $\mathcal{T}$-requirements yield the converse, that every A_n is both B-computable and C-computable. Each $\mathcal{T}_n^B$ is given priority over $\mathcal{T}_n^C$, which has priority over $\mathcal{L}_n$, which has priority over $\mathcal{R}_n$, and all of these have priority over $\mathcal{T}_{n+1}^B$.

(The original result of Spector, Theorem 3 in [12], is somewhat effective, noting that both B and C lie strictly below the jump $(\oplus_n A_n)'$ of the infinite join of the sets A_n. This also holds of the construction in [11], although it goes unmentioned there. The construction of [11] is somewhat easier to imitate, so we adapt it here. The new result here in Theorem 4 is the lowness of $(B \oplus C)$, which will follow from the new assumption of uniform lowness of the sets A_n.)

As is common, each requirement $\mathcal{L}_e$ may impose a *restraint* $l(e,s)$ at each stage $s \geq e$. This will mean that only requirements of higher priority than $\mathcal{L}_e$ may move elements $< l(e,s)$ into or out of $(\beta_s \oplus \gamma_s)$ at stage $s+1$. Likewise, a requirement $\mathcal{R}_k = \mathcal{R}_{\langle i,j \rangle}$ may impose a restraint $r(k,s)$ at that stage, which must be similarly respected by all lower-priority requirements. The restraint $l(e,s)$ will help ensure that $\Phi_e^{B \oplus C}(e)\downarrow$, once convergence has occurred at a finite stage. The restraint $r(k,s)$ will help preserve computations $\Phi_i^B(x)\downarrow \neq \Phi_j^C(x)\downarrow$, once they have been seen to occur at a finite stage.

At stage 0, all restraints are set with $l(e,0) = r(k,0) = 0$, and β_0 and γ_0 are both the empty string. It is convenient to consider every requirement to be *initialized* at this stage. (Each time a requirement is injured, it will be re-initialized.)

At each stage $s+1$ of the construction, we first consider the $\mathcal{L}$-requirements. For each $e \leq s$, we check whether the computation $\Phi_{e,s}^{\beta_s \oplus \gamma_s}(e)$ halts. If it does halt, let u be the use of this computation (i.e., the greatest cell on the oracle tape that is read by the machine during the computation), and set $l(e,s+1) = \lfloor \frac{u+1}{2} \rfloor$. This will cause our procedure to protect the first u bits of $\beta_s \oplus \gamma_s$, with priority e. We do this independently for every $e \leq s$; newly chosen restraints are *not* considered to have injured lower-priority requirements, so no requirements are initialized at this point.

Next we check which $\mathcal{R}$-requirements *need attention*. To determine whether $\mathcal{R}_k$ needs attention at stage $s+1$, with $k = \langle i,j \rangle$, let e_{ks} be the code number of a program which uses an A_n-oracle to search for strings σ and τ in $2^{<\omega}$ and $t, y \in \omega$ such that all of the following hold.

1. For all $k' \leq k$ and all $\langle k', m \rangle$ with $r(k', s) \leq \langle k', m \rangle < |\sigma|$, $\sigma(\langle k', m \rangle) = A_{k'}(m)$. (Notice that checking this requires an A_k-oracle, along with the uniform reductions $A_{k'} \leq_T A_k$ for all $k' < k$.)
2. For all $k' \leq k$ and all $\langle k', m \rangle$ with $r(k', s) \leq \langle k', m \rangle < |\tau|$, $\tau(\langle k', m \rangle) = A_{k'}(m)$. (Again this requires an A_k-oracle.)
3. $(\forall e \leq k)(\forall x < l(e, s+1))\, [\sigma(x) = \beta_s(x) \ \& \ \tau(x) = \gamma_s(x)]$.
4. $(\forall k' < k)(\forall x < r(k', s))\, [\sigma(x) = \beta_s(x) \ \& \ \tau(x) = \gamma_s(x)]$.
5. $\Phi^\sigma_{i,t}(y)\downarrow \ \neq \Phi^\tau_{j,t}(y)\downarrow$.

The first of these says that setting $\beta_{s+1} = \sigma$ would not injure the higher-priority $\mathcal{T}_B$ requirements, and the next one says that setting $\gamma_{s+1} = \tau$ would not injure the higher-priority $\mathcal{T}_C$ requirements. Items (3) and (4) say that doing this would not injure any higher-priority $\mathcal{L}$- or $\mathcal{R}$-requirements, and the last item says that doing it would satisfy $\mathcal{R}_k$ (provided $\beta_{s+1} \oplus \gamma_{s+1}$ is preserved thereafter).

If $M(n, e_{ks}, s) = 0$, then our master function currently guesses that there are no such σ and τ, and so $\mathcal{R}_k$ does not need attention at stage $s+1$. Also, if $\mathcal{R}_k$ has received attention at a previous stage and has not been injured since that stage, then it does not need attention now. (In this case, taking $\sigma = \beta_s$ and $\tau = \gamma_s$ satisfies all these conditions!) Otherwise, with $M(n, e_{ks}, s) = 1$, we search either until we find (σ, τ, y, t) satisfying all of these conditions, or until we reach a stage $s' > s$ at which $M(n, e_{ks}, s') = 0$. If we first find such a stage s', then the master function's current guess is later superseded and $\mathcal{R}_k$ does not need attention at stage $s+1$; but if we first find the tuple (σ, τ, y, t), then it does need attention. (Notice that one or the other of these must occur, because if $\lim_{s'} M(n, e_{ks}, s') = 1$, then $e_{ks} \in (A_n)'$, meaning that the search must terminate with the discovery of a tuple (σ, τ, y, t).)

If there is no $k \leq s$ for which $\mathcal{R}_k$ needs attention at this stage, then for the pair $\langle n, m \rangle = |\beta_s|$, we define $\beta_{s+1} = \beta_s {}^\frown(A_n(m))$, extending β_s by a single bit which is either 1 or 0 according to whether $m \in A_n$ or not. Thus this last bit agrees with the requirement $\mathcal{T}^B_n$. Likewise, for $\langle n', m' \rangle = |\gamma_s|$, we define $\gamma_{s+1} = \gamma_s {}^\frown(A_{n'}(m'))$, as demanded by $\mathcal{T}^C_{n'}$. In this case all restraints are preserved: $l(e, s+1) = l(e, s)$ and $r(k, s+1) = r(k, s)$.

If there exists a $k = \langle i,j \rangle \leq s$ such that $\mathcal{R}_k$ needs attention at stage $s+1$, then for the least such k, we find the (least) tuple (σ, τ, y, t) that satisfies all five conditions and define

$$\beta_{s+1}(x) = \begin{cases} \sigma(x), & \text{if } x < |\sigma|; \\ \beta_s(x), & \text{if } |\sigma| \leq x < |\beta_s|; \\ A_n(m), & \text{if } |\sigma| \leq |\beta_s| = x = \langle n, m \rangle \end{cases}$$

and

$$\gamma_{s+1}(x) = \begin{cases} \tau(x), & \text{if } x < |\tau|; \\ \gamma_s(x), & \text{if } |\tau| \leq x < |\gamma_s|; \\ A_n(m), & \text{if } |\tau| \leq |\gamma_s| = x = \langle n, m \rangle. \end{cases}$$

Thus $\sigma \sqsubseteq \beta_{s+1}$ and $\tau \sqsubseteq \gamma_{s+1}$, and we have filled in bits as needed to ensure $|\beta_{s+1}| > |\beta_s|$ and $|\gamma_{s+1}| > |\gamma_s|$. For every $e > k$, both $\mathcal{R}_e$ and $\mathcal{L}_e$ are initialized at this stage, with $l(e, s+1) = r(e, s+1) = 0$. We keep $l(e, s+1) = l(e, s)$ for all $e \leq k$ and $r(e, s+1) = r(e, s)$ for every $e < k$. For $\mathcal{R}_k$ itself, we define $r(k, s+1) = \max(|\sigma|, |\tau|)$, which is sufficiently long to protect both of the computations $\Phi_{i,t}^{\beta_{s+1}}(y)$ and $\Phi_{j,t}^{\gamma_{s+1}}(y)$ in Condition (5). $\mathcal{R}_k$ is said to have *received attention* at this stage.

This completes stage $s+1$. We will define $B = \lim_s \beta_s$ and $C = \lim_s \gamma_s$ once we have shown that these limits actually exist. To see that $\lim_s \beta_s$ exists, observe first that in our construction, $|\beta_{s+1}| > |\beta_s|$ for all s, and second that the only situation in the construction that can cause an incompatibility in these strings (with $\beta_{s+1} \not\sqsupseteq \beta_s$) is when a requirement $\mathcal{R}_k$ receives attention. Fix an arbitrary $x \in \omega$ and consider the first stage s_0 at which some requirement $\mathcal{R}_{k_0} = \mathcal{R}_{\langle i,j \rangle}$ causes $\beta_{s_0-1}(x) \neq \beta_{s_0}(x)$. At this stage, $\mathcal{R}_{k_0}$ becomes satisfied; the only reason why it might act again is if it is subsequently injured, and the only requirements that can injure it are higher-priority $\mathcal{R}$-requirements (as no other requirements can alter $\beta_s \restriction r(k, s_0)$ or $\gamma_s \restriction r(k, s_0)$). But when a higher-priority requirement $\mathcal{R}_{k_1}$ acts at a stage $s_1 > s_0$, it defines β_{s_1} with length $> |\beta_{s_0}|$. Therefore, after stage s_1, only requirements of higher priority than $\mathcal{R}_{k_1}$ can redefine $\beta_s(x)$. Continuing by induction, we see that $\beta_s(x)$ may be redefined at most k_0-many times after stage s_0, so eventually it stabilizes. Thus $\lim_s \beta_s(x)$ always exists, as does $\lim_s \gamma_s(x)$ by the same argument, so B and C are indeed well-defined.

It remains to show that this B and C satisfy our requirements and consequently instantiate the theorem. We argue by induction on the priority of the requirements, starting with $\mathcal{T}_0^B$ and proving that each one is satisfied, that it only receives attention at finitely many stages, and that any relevant restraints $l(e, s)$ or $r(k, s)$ stabilize at finite values as $s \to \infty$.

For a requirement $\mathcal{T}_n^B$, notice first that whenever β_s is extended by one bit to β_{s+1} (at stages $s+1$ at which no $\mathcal{R}$-requirement needs attention), the new bit is always defined to satisfy the (only) relevant $\mathcal{T}^B$-requirement. The only other way that bits in β_{s+1} can be redefined or newly defined is if a requirement $\mathcal{R}_k$ receives attention. By inductive hypothesis there is a stage s_0 after which no higher-priority requirement acts again. But if $k \geq n$, then Condition (4) ensures that the relevant string σ must match β_s on $\omega^{[n]} \cap \{0, 1, \ldots, r(n, s) - 1\}$, while Condition (1) ensures that σ must match A_n on the rest of the column $\omega^{[n]}$ (up to $|\sigma|$). Thus, after stage s_0, no further extension of β_s will cause any more disagreements between A_n and $B^{[n]}$, and no bit in $\beta_s \restriction \omega^{[n]}$ will ever be redefined again once it has entered $\mathrm{dom}(\beta_s)$ for some s. Thus $\mathcal{T}_n^B$ is satisfied. A parallel argument shows that $\mathcal{T}_n^C$ is also satisfied.

For the requirement $\mathcal{L}_e$, we again fix a stage s_0 after which no higher-priority requirement than $\mathcal{L}_e$ receives attention. Assume that there are indeed infinitely many stages s at which $\Phi_{e,s}^{\beta_s \oplus \gamma_s}(e) \downarrow$, and fix the first such stage $s_1 > s_0$. The construction therefore sets $l(e, s_1 + 1) = \lfloor \frac{u+1}{2} \rfloor$, where u is the use of the computation $\Phi_{e,s_1}^{\beta_{s_1} \oplus \gamma_{s_1}}(e)$. Only $\mathcal{R}$-requirements could possibly cause $\beta_s \restriction l(e, s_1) \neq \beta_{s_1} \restriction l(e, s_1)$ at subsequent stages s, and by inductive hypothesis no higher-priority $\mathcal{R}$-requirements ever do so. But whenever an $\mathcal{R}_k$ with $k \geq e$ redefines $\beta_{s+1} \oplus \gamma_{s+1}$ to equal some new $\sigma \oplus \tau$ incompatible with $\beta_s \oplus \gamma_s$, Condition (3) forces it to choose them so that $\sigma \upharpoonright l(e, s+1) = \beta_s \upharpoonright l(e, s+1)$ and $\tau \upharpoonright l(e, s+1) = \gamma_s \upharpoonright l(e, s+1)$. Therefore the computation $\Phi_{e,s_1}^{\beta_{s_1} \oplus \gamma_{s_1}}(e)$ is preserved at all subsequent stages, and so $\Phi_e^{B \oplus C}(e) \downarrow$, satisfying $\mathcal{L}_e$. Moreover, $\mathcal{L}_e$ never again redefines $l(e, s+1)$, as the current $l(e, s_1 + 1)$ preserves the convergence.

Finally, consider a requirement $\mathcal{R}_k = \mathcal{R}_{\langle i,j \rangle}$, and suppose that $\Phi_i^B = \Phi_j^C = f$ is a total function from ω to $\{0, 1\}$. We fix a stage s_0 after which no higher-priority requirement acts again, and give a program Ψ^{A_k} for computing f from an A_k-oracle. (Here k is in fact the index $\langle i, j \rangle$ of the requirement.) Ψ^{A_k} begins with finitely much information: the stage s_0 and the strings β_{s_0} and γ_{s_0}. On input y, it searches for either a string σ or a string τ that satisfy all of the Conditions (1)-(4) (as listed on page 7) relevant to itself and such that either $\Phi_i^\sigma(y)$ or $\Phi_j^\tau(y)$ converges. (For a σ, Condition (2) is irrelevant, as is (1) for a τ; also, only half of (3) and (4) is relevant to either.) Whichever of those two programs halts, Ψ^{A_k} outputs that value, claiming that it must be the value of $f(y)$. (Notice that we did need the oracle A_k here, in order to verify satisfaction of Conditions (1) and (2).)

We remark first that Ψ^{A_k} does indeed compute a total function. After all, $\Phi_i^B(y)$ halts, using some finite initial segment $B \upharpoonright u$ of its oracle B, as does $\Phi_j^C(y)$ using some $C \upharpoonright u$. But every extension of $\beta_{s_0} \oplus \gamma_{s_0}$ to a subsequent $\beta_s \oplus \gamma_s$ in our construction must have satisfied all of Conditions (1)-(4), because no requirement of lower priority than $\mathcal{R}_k$ ever acted again. (One-bit extensions, at stages when no $\mathcal{R}_{k'}$ needed attention, also satisfy those conditions.) Therefore, if it does not find some other σ or τ first, Ψ^{A_k} will eventually find some $\beta_s \supseteq B \upharpoonright u$ or some $\gamma_s \supseteq C \upharpoonright u$ which satisfy the conditions, and it will output $\Phi_i^B(y)$ or $\Phi_j^C(y)$ accordingly. In this case, those are both the correct value $f(y)$ that we wanted it to output. It remains to show that, even if it found some other σ or τ first, Ψ^{A_k} still outputs the correct value $f(y)$.

So suppose that there is some σ (say) which satisfied all the relevant conditions and had $\Phi_i^\sigma(y) \downarrow$, thus producing our value $\Psi^{A_k}(y)$. If $\Psi^{A_k}(y) \neq f(y)$, then $\Phi_i^\sigma(y) \neq \Phi_i^B(y)$. Let $C \upharpoonright u$ be the initial segment used here, and find an $s_1 > s_0$ such that $\gamma_s \upharpoonright u = C \upharpoonright u$ for all $s \geq s_1$. We claim now that at all stages $s + 1 > s_1$, $\mathcal{R}_k$'s need for attention was witnessed by some finite σ_1 extending the given σ, by $\tau = \gamma_{s+1}$, and by the given y and $t = s$. Indeed $\Phi_i^{\sigma_1}(y) \downarrow \neq \Phi_j^\tau(y) \downarrow$, satisfying (5), and the satisfaction of all the other conditions follows from their satisfaction by σ and by γ_{s+1}. Since this held at all stages $> s_1$, the program $\Phi_{e_{ks}}^{A_k}$ halts on every input, making $e_{ks} \in (A_n)'$. But $M(n, e_{ks}, t)$ approximates $(A_k)'$, so at a sufficiently large stage t it will have $M(n, e_{ks}, t) = 1$, and at this stage $\mathcal{R}_k$ needed attention. By the choice of s_0, no higher-priority $\mathcal{R}_{k'}$ needed attention at that stage, so $\mathcal{R}_k$ will have received attention at that stage, with $\beta_{t+1} \supseteq \sigma_1$ and $\gamma_{t+1} \supseteq \tau$. Since $\mathcal{R}_k$ is never injured again, the halting computations $\Phi_i^{\beta_{t+1}}(y)$ and $\Phi_j^{\gamma_{t+1}}(y)$ will have been preserved forever after, contradicting the hypothesis that $\Phi_i^B = \Phi_j^C$. A symmetric argument shows that no τ can have caused $\Psi^{A_k}(y)$

to output an incorrect value, so indeed $f = \Psi^{A_k}$. This shows that $f \leq_T A_k$ as required, and completes the proof.   □

Corollary 1. *For each Turing degree $\boldsymbol{a}$, let $\boldsymbol{a} = \boldsymbol{a}_0 < \boldsymbol{a}_1 < \cdots$ be the sequence of degrees defined by Proposition 1, and let $\mathcal{I}_{\boldsymbol{a}} = \{\boldsymbol{d} : (\exists n)\ \boldsymbol{d} \leq \boldsymbol{a}_n\}$ be the corresponding Scott ideal. Then $\mathcal{I}_{\boldsymbol{a}}$ is the intersection of the two lower cones*

$$\mathcal{I}_{\boldsymbol{a}} = \{\boldsymbol{d} : \boldsymbol{d} \leq \boldsymbol{b}\ \&\ \boldsymbol{d} \leq \boldsymbol{c}\},$$

with $\boldsymbol{b}$ and $\boldsymbol{c}$ defined as in Theorem 4 (hence with jumps limit-computable in $\boldsymbol{a}$, uniformly in the given $A \in \boldsymbol{a}$).   □

4   Applications and Questions

The first use of Scott ideals that will spring to the minds of many readers is the creation of ω-models of the axiom system **WKL$_0$**. It is well-known that Scott ideals yield models for this system: given a Scott ideal $\mathcal{I}$, just take the model of second-order arithmetic with standard first-order part and containing those subsets of ω whose Turing degrees lie in $\mathcal{I}$. Theorem 4 offers a uniform method of producing such models.

However, the existence of such models of **WKL$_0$** has long been known (see [2,9], among other sources, for background), and the present author cannot see that the uniformity here adds anything significant to our understanding of those models. The motivation for the work in this article was different. The author's original purpose in establishing Theorem 4 was to use the sets B and C constructed there to define the subgroup

$$G_{BC} = \{f \in \mathrm{Aut}(\overline{\mathbb{Q}}) : f \leq_T B\ \&\ f \leq_T C\}$$

of the absolute Galois group $\mathrm{Gal}(\overline{\mathbb{Q}}/\mathbb{Q})$ of the field $\mathbb{Q}$ of rational numbers – or equivalently, the automorphism group $\mathrm{Aut}(\overline{\mathbb{Q}})$ of the algebraic closure $\overline{\mathbb{Q}}$. Here we have fixed a computable presentation $\overline{\mathbb{Q}}$ of this algebraic closure. (In fact, $\overline{\mathbb{Q}}$ is computably categorical, so the specific choice of presentation is irrelevant.) In some respects this work follows and expands upon that in [5,6,10].

Elements of $\mathrm{Aut}(\overline{\mathbb{Q}})$, expressed as permutations of $\overline{\mathbb{Q}}$, are readily viewed as paths through a finite-branching tree T, which can be computably presented and has computable branching. The subgroup G_{BC} has the further property that, whenever a computable infinite subtree of T is computed using finitely many elements $f_1, \ldots, f_n$ of G_{BC} as parameters, that subtree will contain a path that also lies in G_{BC}. (Recall that the intersection of the lower cones below B and C has the property that, for every D in this intersection, the intersection also contains a set E having PA degree relative to D. With $D = f_1 \oplus \cdots \oplus f_n$, the corresponding E will compute the desired path.)

In forthcoming work [7], the author has shown the following.

Theorem 5. *For every Scott ideal $\mathcal{I}$ in the Turing degrees, the set*

$$\mathrm{Aut}_I(\overline{\mathbb{Q}}) = \{f \in \mathrm{Aut}(\overline{\mathbb{Q}}) : \deg f \in \mathcal{I}\}$$

forms a subgroup of $\mathrm{Aut}(\overline{\mathbb{Q}})$ that is elementary for Σ_1 and Π_1 formulas and also for all positive formulas (i.e., prenex formulas in the language of fields that do not use the negation connective).

This elementarity has been extended to a further class of Σ_2 formulas, and might yet turn out to hold for more complicated formulas (allowing negation) as well. On the other hand, it is conjectured that the subgroups $\mathrm{Aut}_d(\overline{\mathbb{Q}}) = \{f \in \mathrm{Aut}(\overline{\mathbb{Q}}) : \deg f \leq d\}$ defined by principal Turing ideals may not be elementary to the same extent.

The group $\mathrm{Aut}(\overline{\mathbb{Q}})$ is naturally viewed as a profinite group: an inverse limit of finite groups, namely the Galois groups of number fields over $\mathbb{Q}$. It is hoped here that it may turn out to be productive to view $\mathrm{Aut}(\overline{\mathbb{Q}})$ simultaneously as a direct limit. The subgroups $\mathrm{Aut}_I(\overline{\mathbb{Q}})$ of the form above, under inclusion, do form a directed system whose direct limit is $\mathrm{Aut}(\overline{\mathbb{Q}})$. So also do the subgroups $\mathrm{Aut}_d(\overline{\mathbb{Q}})$, as d ranges over all Turing degrees, but using subgroups of greater elementarity appears to be a more promising path. On the other hand, for the subgroups $\mathrm{Aut}_d(\overline{\mathbb{Q}})$, the directed system is well-known: it is simply the set of all degrees under Turing reducibility $\leq$, as $\mathrm{Aut}_c(\overline{\mathbb{Q}}) \subseteq \mathrm{Aut}_d(\overline{\mathbb{Q}})$ just if $c \leq d$.

For the subgroups given by Scott ideals, it is natural to use the specific Scott ideals $\mathcal{I}_a$ constructed above. Clearly, under inclusion, these too form a directed system with direct limit $\mathrm{Aut}(\overline{\mathbb{Q}})$. However, the inclusion relation here seems substantially more complicated. It will be clear, first of all, that distinct degrees a and $\tilde{a}$ may yield equal Scott ideals $\mathcal{I}_a = \mathcal{I}_{\tilde{a}}$: just run the procedure from Theorem 4 on a set $A \in a$, and let $\tilde{A}$ be the set A_1 produced by that procedure, so that $\mathcal{I}_{\tilde{a}}$ is defined by the increasing sequence $a_1 < a_2 < \cdots$.

The surprising aspect of this problem, however, is the question of whether Theorem 4 is monotonic at all.

Definition 2. *An operator F on Turing degrees (mapping each d to a Turing degree $F(d)$) is* monotonic *if*

$$(\forall c)(\forall d)\ [c \leq d \implies F(c) \leq F(d)].$$

An operator G mapping Turing degrees to ideals (or other sets of degrees) is monotonic *if*
$$(\forall c)(\forall d)\ [c \leq d \implies G(c) \subseteq G(d)].$$

The operator U defined using the functional Γ in the Uniform Low Basis Theorem, mapping each a to some degree **PA** relative to a, is of the first type here, while the map $a \mapsto \mathcal{I}_a$ is of the second type. It is an open question (to this author's knowledge) whether either of these operators is monotonic in the sense above. The question may startle many readers, who would have assumed (as the author did at first!) that constructions such as that in the Uniform Low Basis Theorem automatically respect Turing reducibility. Recall, however, that for each a, there are a wide variety of degrees **PA** relative to a: indeed, even among those low relative to a, there are pairs of degrees, both **PA** relative to a, whose greatest lower bound under $\leq$ is a itself. Of course, when $a \leq \tilde{a}$, the degree $U(\tilde{a})$, being **PA** relative to $\tilde{a}$, computes a path through every a-computable infinite subtree of $2^{<\omega}$, hence is **PA** relative to $\boldsymbol{a}$ as well – but this does not ensure that $U(\boldsymbol{a})$ will lie below $U(\tilde{\boldsymbol{a}})$. For addressing the possibility of using the groups $\mathrm{Aut}_{I_a}(\overline{\mathbb{Q}})$ to form a directed system with recognizable inclusions, therefore, it would be highly useful to have answers to the following questions about monotonicity.

Question 1. Does the Uniform Low Basis Theorem hold monotonically? That is, does there exist a Turing functional Φ with all of the following properties?

- For every $A \subseteq \omega$, Φ^A is total with $(\forall n) \lim_s \Phi^A(n,s) = \chi_{(P_A)'}(n)$ for the jump $(P_A)'$ of some set P_A that is **PA** relative to A (as in the Uniform Low Basis Theorem); and
- When $A \leq_T B$, the sets P_A and P_B defined as above by Φ satisfy $P_A \leq_T P_B$ (or equivalently, $(P_A)' \leq_1 (P_B)'$).

Question 2. Can we produce low Scott ideals monotonically? That is, do there exist Turing functionals Θ and Γ with all of the following properties?

- For every $A \subseteq \omega$, Θ^A and Γ^A are both total with

$$(\forall n) \, [\lim_s \Theta^A(n,s) = \chi_{(B_A)'}(n) \, \& \, \lim_s \Gamma^A(n,s) = \chi_{(C_A)'}(n)$$

for the jumps $(B_A)'$ and $(C_A)'$ of some sets B_A and C_A such that the set $\{\boldsymbol{d} : \boldsymbol{d} \leq \deg B_A \, \& \, \boldsymbol{d} \leq \deg C_A\}$ is a Scott ideal containing $\deg A$; and
- When $A \leq_T \tilde{A}$, the sets B_A, C_A, $B_{\tilde{A}}$, and $C_{\tilde{A}}$ defined by Θ and Γ satisfy

$$(\forall \boldsymbol{d}) \, [(\boldsymbol{d} \leq \deg B_A \, \& \, \boldsymbol{d} \leq \deg C_A) \implies (\boldsymbol{d} \leq \deg B_{\tilde{A}} \, \& \, \boldsymbol{d} \leq \deg C_{\tilde{A}})].$$

A positive answer to Question 1 would yield a positive answer to Question 2, by applying the procedure from Theorem 4 to the functional Φ in Question 1.

References

1. Brattka, V., de Brecht, M., Pauly, A.: Closed choice and a uniform low basis theorem. Ann. Pure Appl. Logic **163**(8), 986–1008 (2012)
2. Hirschfeldt, D.R.: Slicing the Truth: On the Computable and Reverse Mathematics of Combinatorial Principles, Lecture Notes Series, Institute for Mathematical Sciences, National Univ. of Singapore, vol. 28. World Scientific, Singapore (2014)
3. Jockusch, C.G., Soare, R.I.: Π_1^0-classes and degrees of theories. Trans. Am. Math. Soc. **173**, 33–56 (1972)
4. Kleene, S.C., Post, E.L.: The upper semi-lattice of degrees of recursive unsolvability. Ann. Math. **59**(3), 379–407 (1954)
5. La Roche, P.: Effective Galois theory. J. Symb. Log. **46**(2), 385–392 (1981)
6. Metakides, G., Nerode, A.: Effective content of field theory. Ann. Math. Log. **17**, 289–320 (1979)
7. Miller, R.: Computability and the absolute Galois group of $\mathbb{Q}$, to appear
8. Shoenfield, J.R.: Degrees of models. J. Symb. Log. **25**, 233–237 (1960)
9. Simpson, S.G.: Subsystems of Second-Order Arithmetic, 2nd edn. Cambridge University Press, Cambridge (2010)
10. Smith, R.L.: Effective aspects of profinite groups. J. Symb. Log. **46**(4), 851–863 (1981)
11. Soare, R.I.: Recursively Enumerable Sets and Degrees. Springer, New York (1987)
12. Spector, C.: On degrees of recursive unsolvability. Ann. Math. **64**(3), 581–592 (1956)

Proof Theory

The Non-normal Abyss in Kleene's Computability Theory

Sam Sanders[(✉)]

Department of Philosophy II, RUB, Bochum, Germany
sasander@me.com
https://sasander.wixsite.com/academic

Abstract. Kleene's computability theory based on his S1-S9 computation schemes constitutes a model for *computing with objects of any finite type* and extends Turing's 'machine model' which formalises *computing with real numbers*. A fundamental distinction in Kleene's framework is between *normal* and *non-normal* functionals where the former compute the associated *Kleene quantifier* $\exists^n$ and the latter do not. Historically, the focus was on normal functionals, but recently new non-normal functionals have been studied, based on well-known theorems like the *uncountability of the reals*. These new non-normal functionals are fundamentally different from historical examples like Tait's fan functional: the latter is computable from $\exists^2$ while the former are only computable in $\exists^3$. While there is a great divide separating $\exists^2$ and $\exists^3$, we identify certain closely related non-normal functionals that fall on different sides of this abyss. Our examples are based on mainstream mathematical notions, like *quasi-continuity*, *Baire classes*, and *semi-continuity*.

1 Introduction

1.1 Motivation and Overview

Computability theory is a discipline in the intersection of theoretical computer science and mathematical logic where the fundamental question is as follows:

given two mathematical objects X and Y, does X compute Y in principle?

In the case where X and Y are real numbers, Turing's famous 'machine' model ([31]) is the standard approach to this question, i.e. 'computation' is interpreted in the sense of Turing machines. To formalise computation involving (total) abstract objects, like functions on the real numbers or well-orderings of the reals, Kleene introduced his S1-S9 computation schemes in [13]. Dag Normann and the author have recently introduced ([25]) a version of the lambda calculus involving fixed point operators that exactly captures S1-S9 and accommodates

This research was supported by the *Deutsche Forschungsgemeinschaft* (DFG) (grant nr. SA3418/1-1) and the *Klaus Tschira Boost Fund* (grant nr. GSO/KT 43).

G. Della Vedova et al. (Eds.): CiE 2023, LNCS 13967, pp. 37–49, 2023.
https://doi.org/10.1007/978-3-031-36978-0_4

partial objects. Henceforth, any reference to computability is to be understood in Kleene's framework and (if relevant) the extension from [25].

A fundamental distinction in Kleene's framework is between *normal* and *non-normal* functionals where the former compute the associated *Kleene quantifier* $\exists^n$ and the latter do not (see Sect. 1.2). Historically, the focus was on normal functionals in that only few examples of *natural* non-normal functionals were even known. The first such example was Tait's *fan functional*, which computes a modulus of uniform continuity on input a continuous function on $2^{\mathbb{N}}$ ([27]).

Recently, Dag Normann and the author have identified *new* non-normal functionals based on mainstream theorems like e.g. the *Heine-Borel theorem*, the *Jordan decomposition theorem*, and the *uncountability of* $\mathbb{R}$ ([19–21,23–25]). These non-normal functionals are *very different* as follows: Tait's fan functional is computable in $\exists^2$, making it rather tame; by contrast the following non-normal operation is not computable in any S_k^2, where the latter decides Π_k^1-formulas.

$$\text{Given } Y : [0,1] \to \mathbb{N}, find\ x, y \in \mathbb{R} \text{ such that } x \neq_{\mathbb{R}} y \text{ and } Y(x) =_{\mathbb{N}} Y(y). \quad (1)$$

Clearly, this operation witnesses the basic fact there is no injection from the unit interval to the naturals. The operation in (1) *can* be performed by $\exists^3$, which follows from some of the many proofs that $\mathbb{R}$ is uncountable. Essentially all the non-normal functionals studied in [19–21,23–25] compute the operation in (1), or some equally hard variation.

In light of the previous, there are two classes of non-normal functionals: those computable in $\exists^2$, like Tait's fan functional, and those computable **only** from $\exists^3$, like the operation in (1). Given the difference in computational power between $\exists^2$ and $\exists^3$, there would seem to be a great divide between these two classes. In this paper, we identify certain *closely related* non-normal functionals that fall on different sides of this abyss. In particular, we obtain the following results.

- Basic operations (finding a point of continuity or the supremum) on *quasi-continuous* functions can be done using $\exists^2$; the same operations on the closely related *cliquish* functions are only computable in $\exists^3$ (Sect. 2).
- Finding the supremum of *Baire 2* functions requires $\exists^3$; the same operation is computable in S^2 for *effectively* Baire 2 functions (Sect. 3).
- Basic operations (finding a point of continuity or the supremum) on *semi-continuous* functions require $\exists^3$, even if we assume an oscillation function (Definition 4); the same operations are computable in $\exists^2$ if we assume a 'modulus of semi-continuity' (Sect. 4).

Finally, we briefly sketch Kleene's framework in Sect. 1.2.1. Required axioms and definitions are introduced in Sects. 1.2.2 and 1.2.3.

1.2   Preliminaries and Definitions

We briefly introduce Kleene's *higher-order computability theory* in Sect. 1.2.1. We introduce some essential axioms (Sect. 1.2.2) and definitions (Sect. 1.2.3). A full introduction may be found in e.g. [24, §2] or [17]. Since Kleene's computability theory borrows heavily from type theory, we shall often use common notations from the latter; for instance, the natural numbers are type 0 objects, denoted n^0 or $n \in \mathbb{N}$. Similarly, elements of Baire space are type 1 objects, denoted $f \in \mathbb{N}^{\mathbb{N}}$ or f^1. Mappings from Baire space $\mathbb{N}^{\mathbb{N}}$ to $\mathbb{N}$ are denoted $Y : \mathbb{N}^{\mathbb{N}} \to \mathbb{N}$ or Y^2. An overview of this kind of notations can be found in e.g. [17,25].

1.2.1 Kleene's Computability Theory

Our main results are in computability theory and we make our notion of 'computability' precise as follows.

(I) We adopt ZFC, i.e. Zermelo-Fraenkel set theory with the Axiom of Choice, as the official metatheory for all results, unless explicitly stated otherwise.

(II) We adopt Kleene's notion of *higher-order computation* as given by his nine clauses S1-S9 (see [17, Ch. 5] or [13]) as our official notion of 'computable' involving total objects.

We mention that S1-S8 are rather basic and merely introduce a kind of higher-order primitive with higher-order parameters. The real power comes from S9, which essentially hard-codes the *recursion theorem* for S1-S9-computability in an ad hoc way. By contrast, the recursion theorem for Turing machines is derived from first principles in [30].

On a historical note, it is part of the folklore of computability theory that many have tried (and failed) to formulate models of computation for objects of all finite types and in which one derives the recursion theorem in a natural way. For this reason, Kleene ultimately introduced S1-S9, which were initially criticised for their aforementioned ad hoc nature, but eventually received general acceptance. Now, Dag Normann and the author have introduced a new computational model based on the lambda calculus in [25] with the following properties:

- S1-S8 is included while the 'ad hoc' scheme S9 is replaced by more natural (least) fixed point operators,
- the new model exactly captures S1-S9 computability for total objects,
- the new model accommodates 'computing with partial objects',
- the new model is more modular than S1-S9 in that sub-models are readily obtained by leaving out certain fixed point operators.

We refer to [17,25] for a thorough overview of higher-order computability theory. We do mention the distinction between 'normal' and 'non-normal' functionals based on the following definition from [17],§5.4. We only make use of $\exists^n$ for $n = 2, 3$, as defined in Sect. 1.2.2.

Definition 1. For $n \geq 2$, a functional of type n is called *normal* if it computes Kleene's quantifier $\exists^n$ following S1-S9, and *non-normal* otherwise.

It is a historical fact that higher-order computability theory, based on Kleene's S1-S9 schemes, has focused primarily on the world of *normal* functionals; this opinion can be found [17, §5.4]. Nonetheless, we have previously studied the computational properties of new *non-normal* functionals, namely those that compute the objects claimed to exist by:

– covering theorems due to Heine-Borel, Vitali, and Lindelöf ([20]),
– the Baire category theorem ([19]),
– local-global principles like *Pincherle's theorem* ([20]),
– weak fragments of the Axiom of (countable) Choice ([21]),
– the Jordan decomposition theorem and related results ([23,25]),
– the uncountability of $\mathbb{R}$ ([22,24]).

Finally, the first example of a non-computable non-normal functional, Tait's fan functional ([27]), is rather tame: it is computable in $\exists^2$. By contrast, the functionals based on the previous list, including the operation (1) from Sect. 1.1, are computable in $\exists^3$ but not computable in any S_k^2, where the later decides Π_k^1-formulas (see Sect. 1.2.2 for details).

1.2.2 Some Comprehension Functionals

In Turing-style computability theory, computational hardness is measured in terms of where the oracle set fits in the well-known comprehension hierarchy. For this reason, we introduce some axioms and functionals related to *higher-order comprehension* in this section. We are mostly dealing with *conventional* comprehension here, i.e. only parameters over $\mathbb{N}$ and $\mathbb{N}^{\mathbb{N}}$ are allowed in formula classes like Π_k^1 and Σ_k^1.

First of all, the functional φ^2, also called *Kleene's quantifier* $\exists^2$, as in $(\exists^2)$ is discontinuous[1] at $f = 11\ldots$; in fact, $\exists^2$ is (computationally) equivalent to the existence of $F : \mathbb{R} \to \mathbb{R}$ such that $F(x) = 1$ if $x >_{\mathbb{R}} 0$, and 0 otherwise via Grilliot's trick (see [15, §3]).

$$(\exists \varphi^2 \leq_2 1)(\forall f^1)\big[(\exists n)(f(n) = 0) \leftrightarrow \varphi(f) = 0\big]. \qquad (\exists^2)$$

Related to $(\exists^2)$, the functional μ^2 in (μ^2) is called *Feferman's μ* ([1]).

$$(\exists \mu^2)(\forall f^1)\big([(\exists n)(f(n) = 0) \to [f(\mu(f)) = 0 \wedge (\forall i < \mu(f))(f(i) \neq 0)] \qquad (\mu^2)$$
$$\wedge\,[(\forall n)(f(n) \neq 0) \to \mu(f) = 0]\big).$$

We have $(\exists^2) \leftrightarrow (\mu^2)$ over Kohlenbach's base theory ([15]), while $\exists^2$ and μ^2 are also computationally equivalent. Hilbert and Bernays formalise considerable swaths of mathematics using only μ^2 in [10, Supplement IV].

Secondly, the functional S^2 in (S^2) is called *the Suslin functional* ([15]).

$$(\exists \mathsf{S}^2 \leq_2 1)(\forall f^1)\big[(\exists g^1)(\forall n^0)(f(\bar{g}n) = 0) \leftrightarrow \mathsf{S}(f) = 0\big]. \qquad (\mathsf{S}^2)$$

By definition, the Suslin functional S^2 can decide whether a Σ_1^1-formula as in the left-hand side of (S^2) is true or false. We similarly define the functional S_k^2 which decides the truth or falsity of Σ_k^1-formulas. We note that the Feferman-Sieg operators ν_n from [7],p. 129 are essentially S_n^2 strengthened to return a witness (if existant) to the Σ_n^1-formula at hand.

Thirdly, the following functional E^3 clearly computes $\exists^2$ and S_k^2 for any $k \in \mathbb{N}$:

$$(\exists E^3 \leq_3 1)(\forall Y^2)\big[(\exists f^1)(Y(f) = 0) \leftrightarrow E(Y) = 0\big]. \qquad (\exists^3)$$

---

[1] Note that $\varphi(11\ldots) = 1$ and $\varphi(g) = 0$ for $g \neq_1 11\ldots$ by the definition of $(\exists^2)$, i.e. $\lambda f.\varphi(f)$ is discontinuous at $f = 11\ldots$ in the usual 'epsilon-delta' sense.

The functional from ($\exists^3$) is also called *Kleene's quantifier* $\exists^3$, and we use the same -by now obvious- convention for other functionals. Hilbert and Bernays introduce a functional ν^3 in [10, Supplement IV], and the latter is essentially $\exists^3$ which also provides a witness like the aforementioned functional ν_n does.

In conclusion, the operation (1) from Sect. 1.1 is computable in $\exists^3$ but not in any S_k^2, as established in [22]. Many non-normal functionals exhibit the same 'computational hardness' and we merely view this as support for the development of a separate scale for classifying non-normal functionals.

1.2.3   Some Definitions

We introduce some definitions needed in the below, mostly stemming from mainstream mathematics. We note that subsets of $\mathbb{R}$ are given by their characteristic functions (Definition 2), where the latter are common in measure and probability theory.

First of all, we make use the usual definition of (open) set, where $B(x, r)$ is the open ball with radius $r > 0$ centred at $x \in \mathbb{R}$.

Definition 2. [Set]

- Subsets A of $\mathbb{R}$ are given by their characteristic function $F_A : \mathbb{R} \to \{0, 1\}$, i.e. we write $x \in A$ for $F_A(x) = 1$ for all $x \in \mathbb{R}$.
- We write '$A \subset B$' if we have $F_A(x) \le F_B(x)$ for all $x \in \mathbb{R}$.
- A subset $O \subset \mathbb{R}$ is *open* in case $x \in O$ implies that there is $k \in \mathbb{N}$ such that $B(x, \frac{1}{2^k}) \subset O$.
- A subset $C \subset \mathbb{R}$ is *closed* if the complement $\mathbb{R} \setminus C$ is open.

No computational data/additional representation is assumed in the previous definition. As established in [23,25], one readily comes across closed sets in basic real analysis (Fourier series) that come with no additional representation.

Secondly, the following sets are often crucial in proofs in real analysis.

Definition 3. The sets C_f and D_f respectively gather the points where $f : \mathbb{R} \to \mathbb{R}$ is continuous and discontinuous.

One problem with C_f, D_f is that the definition of continuity involves quantifiers over $\mathbb{R}$. In general, deciding whether a given $\mathbb{R} \to \mathbb{R}$-function is continuous at a given real, is as hard as $\exists^3$ from Sect. 1.2.2. For these reasons, the sets C_f, D_f do exist in general, but are not computable in e.g. $\exists^2$. We show that for quasi-continuous and semi-continuous functions, these sets are definable in $\exists^2$.

Thirdly, to define C_f using $\exists^2$, one can also (additionally) assume the existence of the oscillation function $\mathrm{osc}_f : \mathbb{R} \to \mathbb{R}$ as in Definition 4. Indeed, the continuity of f as $x \in \mathbb{R}$ is then equivalent to the *arithmetical* formula $\mathrm{osc}_f(x) =_{\mathbb{R}} 0$.

Definition 4. [Oscillation function] For any $f : \mathbb{R} \to \mathbb{R}$, the associated *oscillation functions* are defined as follows: $\mathrm{osc}_f([a, b]) := \sup_{x \in [a,b]} f(x) - \inf_{x \in [a,b]} f(x)$ and $\mathrm{osc}_f(x) := \lim_{k \to \infty} \mathrm{osc}_f(B(x, \frac{1}{2^k}))$.

We note that Riemann and Hankel already considered the notion of oscillation in the context of Riemann integration ([9, 28]).

2   Quasi-continuity and Related Notions

We study the notion of *quasi-continuity* and the closely related concept of *cliquishness*, as in Definition 5. As discussed below, the latter is essentially the closure of the former under sums. Nonetheless, basic properties concerning quasi-continuity give rise to functionals computable in $\exists^2$ while the same functionals generalised to cliquish functions are not computable in any S_k^2 by Theorem 8.

First of all, Definition 5 has some historical background: Baire has shown that separately continuous $\mathbb{R}^2 \to \mathbb{R}$ are *quasi-continuous* in one variable; he mentions in [2, p. 95] that the latter notion (without naming it) was suggested by Volterra.

Definition 5. For $f : [0,1] \to \mathbb{R}$, we have the following definitions:

- f is *quasi-continuous* at $x_0 \in [0,1]$ if for $\epsilon > 0$ and any open neighbourhood U of x_0, there is non-empty open $G \subset U$ with $(\forall x \in G)(|f(x_0) - f(x)| < \varepsilon)$.
- f is *cliquish* at $x_0 \in [0,1]$ if for $\epsilon > 0$ and any open neighbourhood U of x_0, there is a non-empty open $G \subset U$ with $(\forall y, z \in G)(|f(y) - f(z)| < \varepsilon)$.

These notions have nice technical and conceptual properties, as follows.

- The class of cliquish functions is exactly the class of sums of quasi-continuous functions ([5,6,18]). In particular, cliquish functions are closed under sums while quasi-continuous ones are not.
- The pointwise limit (if it exists) of quasi-continuous functions, is always cliquish ([11, Cor. 2.5.2]).
- The set C_f is dense in $\mathbb{R}$ if and only if $f : \mathbb{R} \to \mathbb{R}$ is cliquish (see [5,8]); the former notion was called *pointwise discontinuous* by Hankel (1870, [9]).

Moreover, quasi-continuous functions can be quite 'wild': if $\mathfrak{c}$ is the cardinality of $\mathbb{R}$, there are $2^{\mathfrak{c}}$ non-measurable quasi-continuous $[0,1] \to \mathbb{R}$-functions and $2^{\mathfrak{c}}$ measurable quasi-continuous $[0,1] \to [0,1]$-functions (see [12]).

Secondly, we show that $\exists^2$ suffices to witness basic properties of quasi-continuous functions. Hence, the associated functionals fall in the same class as Tait's fan functional. We call a set 'RM-open' if it is given via an RM-code (see [29, II.5.6]), i.e. a sequence of rational open balls.

Theorem 6. *For quasi-continuous $f : [0,1] \to \mathbb{R}$, we have the following:*

- *the set C_f is definable using $\exists^2$ and the latter computes some $x \in C_f$,*
- *there is a sequence $(O_n)_{n \in \mathbb{N}}$ of RM-open sets, definable in $\exists^2$, such that $C_f = \cap_{n \in \mathbb{N}} O_n$,*
- *the oscillation function $\mathrm{osc}_f : [0,1] \to \mathbb{R}$ is computable in $\exists^2$.*
- *the supremum $\sup_{x \in [p,q]} f(x)$ is computable in $\exists^2$ for any $p, q \in \mathbb{Q} \cap [0,1]$.*

Proof. Fix quasi-continuous $f : [0,1] \to \mathbb{R}$ and use $\exists^2$ to define $x \in O_m$ in case

$$(\exists N_0 \in \mathbb{N})(\forall q, r \in B(x, \tfrac{1}{2^{N_0}}) \cap \mathbb{Q})(|f(q) - f(r)| \leq \tfrac{1}{2^m}). \tag{2}$$

By (the definition of) quasi-continuity, the formula (2) is equivalent to

$$(\exists N_1 \in \mathbb{N})(\forall w, z \in B(x, \tfrac{1}{2^{N_1}}))(|f(w) - f(z)| \leq \tfrac{1}{2^m}), \tag{3}$$

where we note that the equivalence remains valid if $N_0 = N_1$ in (2) and (3). Now apply μ^2 to (2) to obtain $G : ([0,1] \times \mathbb{N}) \to \mathbb{N}$ such that for all $x \in [0,1]$ and $m \in \mathbb{N}$, we have

$$x \in O_m \to (\forall w, z \in B(x, \tfrac{1}{2^{G(x,m)}}))(|f(w) - f(z)| \leq \tfrac{1}{2^m}).$$

Hence, $x \in O_m \to B(x, \tfrac{1}{2^{G(x,m)}}) \subset O_m$, witnessing that O_m is open. Clearly, we also have $O_m = \cup_{q \in \mathbb{Q}} B(q, \tfrac{1}{2^{G(q,m)}})$, i.e. we also have an RM-representation of O_m. To find a point $x \in C_f = \cap_{m \in \mathbb{N}} O_m$, the proof of the Baire category theorem for RM-representations is effective by [29, II.5.8], and the first two items are done.

For the final two items, note that $\sup_{x \in [p,q]} f(x)$ equals $\sup_{x \in [p,q] \cap \mathbb{Q}} f(x)$ due to the definition of quasi-continuity. In particular, in the usual interval-halving procedure for finding the supremum, one can equivalently replace '$(\exists x \in [0,1])(f(x) > y)$' by '$(\exists q \in [0,1] \cap \mathbb{Q})(f(q) > y)$' in light of the definition of quasi-continuity. The same holds for infima and the oscillation function $\mathrm{osc}_f : [0,1] \to \mathbb{R}$ is therefore also computable in $\exists^2$.   □

Thirdly, despite their close connection and Theorem 6, basic properties of cliquish functions give rise to functionals that are *hard* to compute in terms of comprehension functionals by Theorem 8. To this end, we need the following definition from [25], which also witnesses that the unit interval is uncountable.

Definition 7. Any $\Phi : ((\mathbb{R} \to \{0,1\}) \times (\mathbb{R} \to \mathbb{N})) \to \mathbb{R}$ is called a *Cantor realiser* in case $\Phi(A, Y) \notin A$ for non-empty $A \subset [0,1]$ and $Y : [0,1] \to \mathbb{N}$ injective on A.

As shown in [23], no Cantor realiser is computable in any S_k^2, even if we require a bijection (rather than an injection). We have the following result.

Theorem 8. *The following functionals are not computable in any S_k^2:*

- *any functional $\Phi : (\mathbb{R} \to \mathbb{R}) \to \mathbb{R}$ such that for all cliquish $f : [0,1] \to [0,1]$, we have $\Phi(f) \in C_f$.*
- *any functional $\Psi : (\mathbb{R} \to \mathbb{R}) \to (\mathbb{R}^2 \to \mathbb{R})$ such that for all cliquish $f : [0,1] \to [0,1]$, we have $\Psi(f, p, q) = \sup_{x \in [p,q]} f(x)$ for $p, q \in [0,1]$.*
- *any functional $\zeta : (\mathbb{R} \to \mathbb{R}) \to ((\mathbb{N} \times \mathbb{N}) \to \mathbb{Q}^2)$ such that for all cliquish $f : [0,1] \to [0,1]$ and any $n, m \in \mathbb{N}$, $\zeta(f, m, n)$ is an open interval such that $C_f = \cap_{n \in \mathbb{N}} (\cup_{m \in \mathbb{N}} \zeta(f, m, n))$.*

In particular, each of these functionals computes a Cantor realiser (given $\exists^2$).

Proof. Fix $A \subset [0,1]$ and $Y : [0,1] \to \mathbb{N}$ injective on A. Now define the following function $f : [0,1] \to \mathbb{R}$, for any $x \in [0,1]$, as follows:

$$f(x) := \begin{cases} \frac{1}{2^{Y(x)+1}} & \text{in case } x \in A \\ 0 & \text{otherwise} \end{cases}. \tag{4}$$

By definition, for any $\varepsilon > 0$, there are only finitely many $x \in A$ such that $f(x) > \varepsilon$ for $i \leq k$. This readily implies that f is *cliquish* at any $x \in [0,1]$ and *continuous* at any $y \notin A$. Now let Φ be as in the first item and note that $\Phi(f) \in C_f$ implies that $\Phi(f) \notin A$, as required for a Cantor realiser.

For the second item, let Ψ be as in the latter and consider $\Psi(f,0,1)$, which has the form $\frac{1}{2^{n_0+1}} = f(y_0)$ for some $y_0 \in [0,1]$ and $n_0 \in \mathbb{N}$. Now check whether $\Psi(f,0,\frac{1}{2}) = \Psi(f,0,1)$ to decide if $y_0 \in [0,\frac{1}{2}]$ or not. Hence, we know the first bit of the binary representation of y_0. Repeating this process, we can *compute* y_0, and similarly obtain an enumeration of A. With this enumeration, we can compute $z \notin A$ following [29, II.4.9], as required for a Cantor realiser.

For the third item, to find a point $x \in C_f = \bigcap_{n \in \mathbb{N}} (\cup_{m \in \mathbb{N}} \zeta(f,m,n))$, the proof of the Baire category theorem for RM-representations is effective by [29], II.5.8, and the first item provides a Cantor realiser.   □

3   The First and Second Baire Classes

We study the notion of *Baire 1* function and the closely related concept of (effectively) *Baire 2* function, as in Definition 9. Nonetheless, basic properties of Baire 1 functions give rise to functionals computable in $\exists^2$ while the same functionals generalised to Baire 2 are not computable in any S_k^2. Properties of *effectively* Baire 2 functions are still computable by the Suslin functional S^2.

First of all, after introducing the Baire classes, Baire notes that Baire 2 functions can be *represented* by repeated limits as in (5) (see [2, p. 69]). Given $\exists^2$, effectively Baire 2 functions are essentially the representation of Baire 2 functions used in second-order arithmetic ([3]).

Definition 9. For $f : [0,1] \to \mathbb{R}$, we have the following definitions:

- f is *Baire 1* if it is the pointwise limit of a sequence of continuous functions.
- f is *Baire 2* if it is the pointwise limit of a sequence of Baire 1 functions.
- f is *effectively Baire 2* if there is a double sequence $(f_{n,m})_{n,m \in \mathbb{N}}$ of continuous functions on $[0,1]$ such that

$$f(x) =_{\mathbb{R}} \lim_{n \to \infty} \lim_{m \to \infty} f_{n,m}(x) \text{ for all } x \in [0,1]. \tag{5}$$

Secondly, the following theorem -together with Theorem 11- shows there is a great divide in terms of computability theoretic properties for Baire 2 functions and representations. Note that for effectively Baire 2 functions, we assume the associated (double) sequence is an input for the algorithm.

Theorem 10. *For effectively Baire 2* $f : [0,1] \to [0,1]$, *the supremum* $\sup_{x \in [p,q]} f(x)$ *is computable in* S^2 *for any* $p,q \in \mathbb{Q} \cap [0,1]$.

Proof. Let $(f_{n,m})$ be a double sequence as in (5). By the definition of repeated limit, the formula $(\exists x \in [0,1])(f(x) > q)$ is equivalent to

$$(\exists y \in [0,1], l \in \mathbb{N})(\exists N \in \mathbb{N})(\forall n \geq N)(\exists M \in \mathbb{N})(\forall m \geq M)(f_{n,m}(y) \geq q + \tfrac{1}{2^l}),$$

which is equivalent to a Σ_1^1-formula upon replacing $f_{n,m}$ by RM-codes codes for continuous functions. Note that $\exists^2$ computes such codes (uniformly) by [14, §4] (for Baire space) and [26, §2.2] (for $\mathbb{R}$). In light of the above equivalence, S^2 can decide $(\exists x \in [0,1])(f(x) > q)$ and hence compute the required suprema.   □

By the results in [26, §2.3.1], $\exists^2$ can compute the supremum of a bounded Baire 1 function. One could explore similar results for sub-classes.

Thirdly, we have the following theorem. Note that for Baire 2 functions, we assume the associated sequence of Baire 1 functions is an input for the algorithm.

Theorem 11. *The following functionals are not computable in any S_k^2:*

- *any functional $\Phi : (\mathbb{R} \to \mathbb{R}) \to (\mathbb{R}^2 \to \mathbb{R})$ such that for Baire 2 $f : [0,1] \to [0,1]$, we have $\Phi(f,p,q) = \sup_{x \in [p,q]} f(x)$ for $p,q \in [0,1]$.*
- *any functional $\Psi : (\mathbb{R} \to \mathbb{R}) \to (\mathbb{N}^2 \to (\mathbb{R} \to \mathbb{R}))$ such that for Baire 2 $f : [0,1] \to [0,1]$, the double sequence $(\Psi(f,n,m))_{n,m \in \mathbb{N}}$ satisfies (5).*

In particular, each of these functionals computes a Cantor realiser (given S^2).

Proof. For the first item, f as in (4) is Baire 2. Indeed, consider the following

$$f_n(x) := \begin{cases} \frac{1}{2^{Y(x)+1}} & \text{in case } x \in A \wedge Y(x) \leq n \\ 0 & \text{otherwise} \end{cases}, \tag{6}$$

which has only got at most $n+1$ points of discontinuity, i.e. f_n is definitely Baire 1. We trivially have $\lim_{n \to \infty} f_n(x) = f(x)$ for $x \in [0,1]$. For the second item, combine the results for the first item with Theorem 10.   □

4   Semi-continuity

We study the notion of *upper and lower semi-continuity* due to Baire ([2]). Curiously, we *can* define C_f for a usco $f : [0,1] \to \mathbb{R}$ using $\exists^2$, but computing an $x \in C_f$ is *not* possible via any S_k^2 (see Theorems 13 and 14), even assuming an oscillation function. Requiring a 'modulus of semi-continuity' (see Definition 12), $\exists^2$ can compute some $x \in C_f$ (Theorem 15). However, while a modulus of *continuity* is computable in $\exists^2$, a modulus of *semi-continuity* is not computable in any S_k^2 by Corollary 16.

First of all, we use the following standard definitions.

Definition 12 [Semi-continuity]. For $f : [0,1] \to \mathbb{R}$, we have the following:

- f is *upper semi-continuous* (usco) at $x_0 \in [0,1]$ if for any $y > f(x_0)$, there is $N \in \mathbb{N}$ such that for all $z \in B(x, \frac{1}{2^N})$, we have $f(z) < y$,
- f is *lower semi-continuous* (lsco) at $x_0 \in [0,1]$ if for any $y < f(x_0)$, there is $N \in \mathbb{N}$ such that for all $z \in B(x, \frac{1}{2^N})$, we have $f(z) > y$,

– a *modulus of usco* for f is any function $\Psi : [0,1] \to \mathbb{R}^+$ such that :

$$(\forall k \in \mathbb{N})(\forall y \in B(x, \Psi(x,k)))(f(y) < f(x) + \tfrac{1}{2^k}).$$

We also refer to Ψ as a 'usco modulus'.

Secondly, we have the following theorem.

Theorem 13. *For usco* $f : [0,1] \to \mathbb{R}$, *the set* C_f *is definable using* $\exists^2$.

Proof. First of all, it is a matter of definitions to show the equivalence between '$g : \mathbb{R} \to \mathbb{R}$ is continuous at $x \in \mathbb{R}$' and '$g : \mathbb{R} \to \mathbb{R}$ is usco and lsco at $x \in \mathbb{R}$'. Then, for usco $f : [0,1] \to \mathbb{R}$, 'f is discontinuous at $x \in [0,1]$' is equivalent to

$$(\exists l \in \mathbb{N})(\forall k \in \mathbb{N})(\exists y \in B(x, \tfrac{1}{2^k})(f(y) \le f(x) - \tfrac{1}{2^l}), \tag{7}$$

which expresses that f is not lsco at $x \in [0,1]$. Now, (7) is equivalent to

$$(\exists l \in \mathbb{N})(\forall k \in \mathbb{N})(\underline{\exists r \in B(x, \tfrac{1}{2^k}) \cap \mathbb{Q}})(f(r) \le f(x) - \tfrac{1}{2^l}), \tag{8}$$

where in particular the underlined quantifier in (8) has rational range due to f being usco. Since (8) is arithmetical, $\exists^2$ allows us to define D_f (and C_f). □

Thirdly, we have the following theorem showing that while C_f is definable using $\exists^2$, the latter cannot compute any $x \in C_f$ (and the same for any S_k^2), even if we assume an oscillation function (see Definition 4).

Theorem 14. *Theorem 8 remains correct if we replace 'cliquish' by 'usco' or 'usco with an oscillation function'.*

Proof. The function f from (4) is usco, which follows from the observation that for any $\varepsilon > 0$, there are only finitely many $x \in A$ such that $f(x) > \varepsilon$ for $i \le k$. Now repeat the proof of Theorem 8 for usco functions. One readily proves that f equals osc_f, i.e. f is its own oscillation function. □

To our genuine surprise, functions that are their own oscillation function are studied in the mathematical literature ([16]). Moreover, there is no contradiction between Theorems 10 and 14 as follows: while usco functions are Baire 1, Theorem 14 does not assume a Baire 1 (or effectively Baire 2) representation is given as an input, while of course Theorem 10 does.

Fourth, we now show that given a modulus of usco, we can find points of continuity of usco functions using $\exists^2$.

Theorem 15. *For usco* $f : [0,1] \to \mathbb{R}$ *with a modulus* $\Psi : [0,1] \to \mathbb{R}^+$, *a real* $x \in C_f$ *can be computed by* $\exists^2$.

Proof. Fix usco $f : [0,1] \to \mathbb{R}$ with modulus $\Psi : [0,1] \to \mathbb{R}^+$ and note that for $x \in [0,1]$ and $q \in \mathbb{Q}$, we have by definition that:

$$(\exists N \in \mathbb{N})(\forall z \in B(x, \tfrac{1}{2^N}))(f(z) \geq q) \leftrightarrow \underline{(\exists M \in \mathbb{N})(\forall r \in B(x, \tfrac{1}{2^M}) \cap \mathbb{Q})(f(r) \geq q)},$$

where we abbreviate the right-hand side (arithmetical) formula by $A(x,q)$. We note that the above equivalence even goes through for $N = M$. Define $O_q := \{x \in [0,1] : f(x) < q \vee A(x,q)\}$ using $\exists^2$ and note that $D_q := [0,1] \setminus O_q$ is closed and (by definition) nowhere dense.

Next, we show that $D_f \subset \cup_{q \in \mathbb{Q}} D_q$. Indeed, in case $x_0 \in D_f$, f cannot be lsco at $x_0 \in [0,1]$, i.e. we have

$$(\exists l \in \mathbb{N})(\forall N \in \mathbb{N})(\exists z \in B(x_0, \tfrac{1}{2^N}))(f(z) \leq f(x_0) - \tfrac{1}{2^l}). \tag{9}$$

Let l_0 be as in (9) and consider $q_0 \in \mathbb{Q}$ such that $f(x_0) > q_0 > f(x_0) - \tfrac{1}{2^{l_0}}$. By definition, $f(x_0) \geq q_0$ and $\neg A(x_0, q_0)$, i.e. $x_0 \in D_{q_0}$ as required.

Finally, define $Y(x)$ as $\Psi(x, k_0)$ in case k_0 is the least $k \in \mathbb{N}$ with $f(x) + \tfrac{1}{2^k} \leq q$ (if such exists), and zero otherwise. In case $x \in O_q \wedge f(x) < q$, then $B(x, Y(x)) \subset O_q$. In case $x \in O_q \wedge A(x,q)$, then μ^2 can find M_0, the least $M \in \mathbb{N}$ as in $A(x,q)$, which is such that $B(x, \tfrac{1}{2^{M_0}}) \subset O_q$. Hence, in case $x \in O_q$, we can compute (using μ^2) some ball around x completely within O_q. The latter kind of representation of open sets is called the *R2-representation* in [19]. Now, the Baire category theorem implies that there exists $y \in \cup_{q \in \mathbb{Q}} O_q$, which satisfies $y \notin D_f$ by the previous paragraph. By [19, Theorem 7.10], $\exists^2$ can compute such $y \in \cup_{q \in \mathbb{Q}} O_q$, thanks to the R2-representation of open sets. Essentially, the well-known constructive proof goes through (see e.g. [4, p. 87]) and one uses the R2-representation to avoid the use of the (countable) Axiom of Choice. $\square$

The following corollary should be contrasted with the fact that a modulus of continuity for real functions is computable from $\exists^2$.

Corollary 16. *The following functional is not computable in any S_k^2:*

any functional $\Phi : (\mathbb{R} \to \mathbb{R}) \to ((\mathbb{R} \times \mathbb{N}) \to \mathbb{R})$ such that $\Phi(f)$ is a usco modulus for usco $f : [0,1] \to [0,1]$.

Proof. Combine Theorems 14 and 15. $\square$

Acknowledgement. We thank Anil Nerode for his valuable advice and discussions related to this topic.

References

1. Avigad, J., Feferman, S.: Gödel's functional ("Dialectic") interpretation, handbook of proof theory. Stud. Logic Found. Math. **137**, 337–405 (1998)
2. Baire, R.: Sur les fonctions de variables réelles. Annali di Matematica Pura ed Applicata (1898-1922) **3**(1), 1–123 (1899). https://doi.org/10.1007/BF02419243

3. Barrett, J.M., Downey, R.G., Greenberg, N.: Cousin's lemma in second-order arithmetic. Preprint, arxiv: https://arxiv.org/abs/2105.02975 (2021)
4. Bishop, E.: Foundations of constructive analysis. McGraw-Hill (1967)
5. Borsík, J., Doboš, J.: A note on real cliquish functions, Real Anal. Exchange 18(1), 139–145 (1992/93)
6. Borsík, J.: Sums of quasicontinuous functions defined on pseudometrizable spaces. Real Anal. Exchange 22(1), 328–337 (1996/97)
7. Buchholz, W., Feferman, S., Pohlers, W., Sieg, W.: Iterated Inductive Definitions and Subsystems of Analysis: Recent Proof-Theoretical Studies. LNM, vol. 897. Springer, Heidelberg (1981). https://doi.org/10.1007/BFb0091894
8. Doboš, J., Šalát, T.: Cliquish functions, Riemann integrable functions and quasi-uniform convergence. Acta Math. Univ. Comenian. 40(41), 219–223 (1982)
9. Hankel, H.: Untersuchungen über die unendlich oft oscillirenden und unstetigen Functionen., Ludwig Friedrich Fues (1870)
10. Hilbert, D., Bernays, P.: Grundlagen der Mathematik. II, Zweite Auflage. Die Grundlehren der mathematischen Wissenschaften, Band 50, Springer (1970). https://doi.org/10.1007/978-3-642-86896-2
11. Holá, L., Holý, D., Moors, W.: USCO and quasicontinuous mappings, vol. 81, De Gruyter (2021)
12. Holá, Ľ.: There are $2^{\mathfrak{c}}$ quasicontinuous non Borel functions on uncountable Polish space, Results Math. 76, no. 3, Paper No. 126, 11 (2021)
13. Kleene, S.C.: Recursive functionals and quantifiers of finite types I. Trans. Amer. Math. Soc. 91, 1–52 (1959)
14. Kohlenbach, U.: Foundational and mathematical uses of higher types, Reflections on the foundations of mathematics, Lect. Notes Log., vol. 15, ASL, pp. 92–116 (2002)
15. _____, Higher order reverse mathematics, reverse mathematics. Lect. Notes Log., vol. 21. ASL 2005, 281–295 (2001)
16. Kostyrko, P.: Some properties of oscillation. Math. Slovaca 30, 157–162 (1980)
17. Longley, J., Normann, D.: Higher-order Computability. Springer, Theory and Applications of Computability (2015)
18. Maliszewski, A.: On the products of bounded Darboux Baire one functions. J. Appl. Anal. 5(2), 171–185 (1999)
19. Normann, D.: Sanders, S.: Open sets in reverse mathematics and computability theory. J. Logic Comput. 30(8), 40 (2020)
20. _____, Pincherle's theorem in reverse mathematics and computability theory. Ann. Pure Appl. Logic 171, no. 5, 102788, 41 (2020)
21. _____, The axiom of choice in computability theory and reverse mathematics. J. Logic Comput. 31(1), 297–325 (2021)
22. _____, On robust theorems due to Bolzano, Weierstrass, and Cantor in Reverse Mathematics. J. Symbolic Logic, 51 (2022). https://doi.org/10.1017/jsl.2022.71
23. _____, Betwixt Turing and Kleene, Lecture Notes in Computer Science 13137, pp. 236–252. Springer (2022)
24. _____, On the uncountability of R. J. Symb. Logic 87(4), 1474–1521 (2022)
25. _____, On the computational properties of basic mathematical notions. J. Logic Comput. 32(8), 1747–1795 (2022)
26. _____, The Biggest Five of Reverse Mathematics, Submitted, 39 (2023). arxiv: https://arxiv.org/abs/2212.00489
27. Normann, D., Tait, W.: On the computability of the fan functional. In: Jäger, G., Sieg, W. (eds.) Feferman on Foundations. OCL, vol. 13, pp. 57–69. Springer, Cham (2017). https://doi.org/10.1007/978-3-319-63334-3_3

28. Riemann, B., Clive Baker, R., Christenson, C.O., Orde, H.: Bernhard Riemann: Collected Works. Kendrick Press, Heber City (2004)
29. Stephen, G.: Simpson, Subsystems of Second Order Arithmetic, 2nd edn. Perspectives in Logic, CUP (2009)
30. Soare, R.I.: Recursively enumerable sets and degrees, Perspectives in Mathematical Logic. Springer (1987)
31. Turing, A.: On computable numbers, with an application to the Entscheidungsproblem. Proc. London Math. Soc. **42**, 230–265 (1936)

A Constructive Picture of Noetherian Conditions and Well Quasi-orders

Gabriele Buriola[1]([✉])(ID), Peter Schuster[1](ID), and Ingo Blechschmidt[2](ID)

[1] Università di Verona, Strada le Grazie 15, 37134 Verona, Italy
{gabriele.buriola,peter.schuster}@univr.it
[2] Universität Augsburg, Universitätsstr. 14, 86159 Augsburg, Germany
ingo.blechschmidt@math.uni-augsburg.de

Abstract. From a constructive perspective the many notions of Noetherianity and well quasi-order form a rich landscape, which we here explore. Besides the well-studied conditions about sequences, we include the finite basis property of the original Higman lemma, trying a first joint analysis of Noetherianity and well quasi-order in the spirit of reverse mathematics with intuitionistic logic. Applying a topological semantics for intuitionistic logic, we settle a conjecture by Ray Mines; moreover, by the realizability topos of infinite-time Turing machines, we separate the ascending chain condition with finite generation from the one without.

Keywords: Constructive mathematics · chain conditions · well quasi-order · finite generation · inductive definition

MS Classification 2020: 03F65 (06A07 06A11 13E05)

1 Introduction

This article analyses from an intuitionistic point of view the main definitions for *well quasi-orders*, wqo, present in the literature together with the related constructively viable concepts of Noetherian ring. Despite being all equivalent to each other in the classical setting, their constructive contents are different, as has already been proved in reverse mathematics [10,25,26]. Our goal is to carry out a first joint analysis of Noetherianity and wqo, in such a way that the rich literature of the former can be usefully applied to the latter. We thus aim for a more comprehensive picture of partial and quasi-order properties in the spirit of intuitionistic and constructive reverse mathematics [22,28,42].

Given the intuitionistic setting of this work, we do not use the law of excluded middle nor do we assume that order relations are decidable. Moreover, by *finite set* we will always mean "finitely enumerable"; so a set A is finite if there exists a natural number n such that all the elements of A can be listed as $a_1, \ldots, a_n$, possibly with repetitions. This work could be formalized in IZF [15] or in the internal language of elementary toposes [24].

The paper consists of two main sections. In the first one, devoted to properly collocate Noetherianity in an intuitionistic framework, different definitions of

G. Della Vedova et al. (Eds.): CiE 2023, LNCS 13967, pp. 50–62, 2023.
https://doi.org/10.1007/978-3-031-36978-0_5

Noetherianity are treated, establishing their constructive nature and separating two classically (but not intuitionistically) equivalent ascending chain conditions. In the second, after having constructively analysed the most widespread definitions of wqo's, the proof-theoretic relations of the intuitionistically sensible ones are explored together with a subset closure property. We conclude by briefly outlining open problems and future work.

2   Noetherian chain conditions

The concept of a Noetherian ring or module is ubiquitous in abstract algebra. Not least for its important role in computational algebra, e.g., for the termination of Buchberger's algorithm, Noetherianity has been studied also in constructive algebra [27,34,36] up to Gröbner bases [14,43]. The initial challenge for the latter setting was that, with intuitionistic logic, only the trivial ring can be proved Noetherian according to the classical definitions.

Yet many constructively sensible definitions are present in the literature. We start off with the one given by Richman [34] and Seidenberg [36] reworking an idea of Tennenbaum's [40], and with how it differs from the classical concept.

Definition 2.1. *A commutative ring R has the property*

1. FBP (finite basis property) *if every ideal of R is finitely generated;*
2. $\text{ACC}^{(\text{fg})}$ *if in R every ascending chain of (finitely generated) ideals $I_1 \subseteq I_2 \subseteq \ldots$ stabilizes in that there exists an index n such that $I_n = I_{n+1} = \ldots$;*
3. $\text{ACC}_0^{(\text{fg})}$ *if in R every ascending chain of (finitely generated) ideals $I_1 \subseteq I_2 \subseteq \ldots$ stalls in that there exists an index n such that $I_n = I_{n+1}$.*

The above definitions can be schematized as follows:

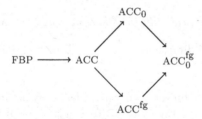

The classical *ascending chain condition* due to Noether is ACC, whereas ACC_0^{fg} is Richman's and Seidenberg's constructive substitute [34,36], thus often dubbed *RS-Noetherian*. The latter was motivated by the observation that ACC and ACC^{fg} cannot be verified with intuitionistic logic but for the trivial ring [16,34].

While the Noetherian conditions listed in Definition 2.1 are classically equivalent, their known constructive relations are displayed in the figure above, and we conjecture that none of the implications can be reversed. We now show that the hybrid condition ACC_0—referring to arbitrary ideals but requiring only stalling, not stabilizing—is not constructively sensible, thus settling an issue raised by the late Ray Mines.[1]

---

[1] Personal communication by Hajime Ishihara, January 2023.

Proposition 2.2. *The field with two elements satisfies the condition* ACC_0 *if and only if every increasing sequence of truth values stalls; but there are topological models which falsify this principle.*

Proof. In classical logic, a sequence $(\Psi_i)_{i \in \mathbb{N}}$ of truth values which is "increasing", in that $\Psi_i \Rightarrow \Psi_{i+1}$ for all $i \in \mathbb{N}$, always *stalls*: There always exists a number n such that $\Psi_n \Leftrightarrow \Psi_{n+1}$. Indeed, if $\neg\Psi_2$, then $\Psi_2 \Rightarrow \Psi_1$, and if Ψ_2, then $\Psi_3 \Rightarrow \Psi_2$.

In the topological model of intuitionistic logic given by the Heyting algebra of opens in the real line, the ascending sequence $((-n, n))_{n \in \mathbb{N}}$ does not stall (for topological models see, e.g., [39, Section 4]). The intervals $(-n, n)$ are the truth values of the sentences "$|\xi| < n$", where ξ is the generic real number of the topological model (the identity function $\mathbb{R} \to \mathbb{R}$).

In contrast, if the field $\mathbb{F}_2 = \{0, 1\}$ with two elements validates ACC_0, then every increasing sequence $(\Psi_i)_i$ of truth values does stall. We build the ascending chain of ideals $\mathfrak{a}_1 \subseteq \mathfrak{a}_2 \subseteq \ldots$ where $\mathfrak{a}_i = \{x \in \mathbb{F}_2 \mid x = 0 \vee \Psi_i\}$. By ACC_0, this sequence stalls, that is there exists a number $\bar{n}$ such that $\mathfrak{a}_{\bar{n}} = \mathfrak{a}_{\bar{n}+1}$; hence $1 \in \mathfrak{a}_{\bar{n}+1} \Rightarrow 1 \in \mathfrak{a}_{\bar{n}}$ and thus, by definition of these ideals, $\Psi_{\bar{n}+1} \Rightarrow \Psi_{\bar{n}}$.

The converse direction rests on the fact that two ideals $\mathfrak{a}, \mathfrak{a}' \subseteq \mathbb{F}_2$ are equal iff the truth values of $1 \in \mathfrak{a}$ and $1 \in \mathfrak{a}'$ agree. |

Our next result is a source of countermodels for the converse of the implication $\mathrm{ACC}^{\mathrm{fg}} \Rightarrow \mathrm{ACC}_0^{\mathrm{fg}}$: The field with two elements verifies $\mathrm{ACC}_0^{\mathrm{fg}}$, but models of constructive mathematics which falsify Bishop's *limited principle of omniscience* (LPO) abound. We take this principle to mean that every infinite descending binary sequence $\mathbb{N} \to \mathbb{B}$ is either constantly one or contains a zero. For instance, LPO is falsified in the effective topos (see [9, Section 4.2] for a survey and the references [4, 21, 29, 32]).

Proposition 2.3. *The field with two elements validates* $\mathrm{ACC}^{\mathrm{fg}}$ *iff* LPO *holds.*

Proof. For the "only if" direction, let $\alpha : \mathbb{N} \to \mathbb{B}$ be an infinite descending binary sequence. Then the family $(\mathfrak{a}_n)_{n \in \mathbb{N}}$ given by $\mathfrak{a}_n := (1 - \alpha(0), \ldots, 1 - \alpha(n)) \subseteq \mathbb{F}_2$ (where we identify the two elements of $\mathbb{B}$ with the zero and unit element of $\mathbb{F}_2$) is an ascending sequence of finitely generated ideals. By assumption, this sequence stabilizes at some index n. Either $\mathfrak{a}_n = (0)$ or $\mathfrak{a}_n = (1)$. If the former, then α is constantly one. If the latter, then α has a zero among the terms 0 to n.

The "if" direction follows from the observation that every finitely generated ideal of $\mathbb{F}_2$ is either (0) or (1).   ⊣

Bauer [5] first considered the variant of the effective topos which is built using the infinite-time Turing machines of Hamkins, Kidder and Lewis [19]. This topos provides a countermodel for the reversal of the implication $\mathrm{ACC} \Rightarrow \mathrm{ACC}^{\mathrm{fg}}$; for background on realizability toposes, we refer to [29].

Proposition 2.4. *In the realizability topos corresponding to infinite-time Turing machines, the field with two elements validates* $\mathrm{ACC}^{\mathrm{fg}}$ *but not* ACC.

Proof. This realizability topos is known to validate the limited principle of omniscience [5], so its field with two elements validates ACC^{fg} by Proposition 2.3. Assuming that it also validates ACC, we obtain a contradiction as follows, arguing internally to the topos.

If M is any infinite-time Turing machine, then because the ascending chain

$$\{x \in \mathbb{F}_2 \,|\, x = 0 \vee (M \text{ halts on at least one of the inputs } 0, \dots, n)\}$$

stabilizes, there is a number $n_M \in \mathbb{N}$ such that M halts on at least one of the inputs $0, \dots, n_M$ iff there is at least one input $k \geqslant n_M$ on which it terminates. By countable choice (available in the topos even if it is not on the meta level), we obtain a map $M \mapsto n_M$ and an infinite-time Turing machine E computing this map.

The following description then defines a self-referencing machine P defeating E: "Read a number n as input. Simulate E on input P. Compare n with n_P. If $n > n_P$, then terminate. Else go into an infinite loop." (The self-reference is resolved by Kleene's second recursion theorem, whose textbook proof carries over step for step to infinite-time Turing machines.) This machine terminates on input $n_P + 1$, but does not terminate on any of the inputs $0, \dots, n_P$.   ⊣

Topological countermodels for the reversal of the implication $\text{ACC} \Rightarrow \text{ACC}^{\text{fg}}$ also exist; for the required background, we refer to [39, Section 4] and to [8].

Proposition 2.5. *In the topological model over the real line, there is a ring validating ACC^{fg} but not ACC_0 (hence also not ACC).*

Proof. Let M be the subset, internally speaking, of the naturals which contains n with truth value the open interval $(-1/n, 1/n)$ as in [6, Example 2]. The polynomial ring $\mathbb{Z}[M]$ over this set validates ACC^{fg} but not ACC. It validates ACC^{fg} because, due to connectedness of open intervals, a finitely generated sheaf of ideals over an open interval is globally generated over every slightly smaller open interval. It falsifies ACC, and also ACC_0, because the sequence of ideals generated by $M \cap \downarrow(n)$ neither stabilizes nor stalls.

Beyond RS-Noetherianity, in these notes we consider five other constructive versions of Noetherianity, namely: *ML-Noetherianity*, proposed by Martin-Löf (from whom the letters ML are derived) and applied by Jacobsson and Löfwall [23]; *strong Noetherianity*, developed by Perdry [30]; *inductive Noetherianity*, considered by Coquand, Lombardi and Persson [11–13]; and *tree Noetherianity* and *processly Noetherianity*, tailored for nondeterministic algorithms and originally proposed by Richman [35] respectively the third author [7, Section 3.9]. For some of the above definitions we need the following auxiliary properties:

Definition 2.6. *Let $(E, \leqslant)$ be a partial order.*

1. *By "$x < y$", we mean $x \leqslant y \wedge \neg(x = y)$.*
2. *A subset $H \subseteq E$ is hereditary iff $\forall (x \in E). (\{y \,|\, y < x\} \subseteq H \Rightarrow x \in H)$.*
3. *The poset E is hereditarily well-founded, hwf, if the only hereditary subset H of E is $H = E$.*

4. *The poset E is a* well-order *iff it is a hereditarily well-founded linear order.*[2]
5. *An* ascending tree *with values in E is a family* $(x_i)_{i \in I}$ *of elements of E such that I is a tree (in the sense of [35, Section 1]) and such that $j < k$ in I implies $x_j \leqslant x_k$. Such a tree* stalls *iff there are indices $j < k$ such that $x_j = x_k$.*
6. *An* ascending process *with values in E consists of an initial value $x_0 \in E$ and a function $f \colon E \to \mathcal{P}(E)$ such that for every $x \in E$ and every $y \in f(x)$, $x \leqslant y$, and: (1) the set $f(x_0)$ is inhabited; (2) for every number n and for all elements $x_1, \ldots, x_n$ such that $x_{i+1} \in f(x_i)$ for $i = 0, \ldots, n-1$, the set $f(x_{n+1})$ is inhabited. Such a process* stalls *iff there exists a number n and elements $x_1, \ldots x_n$ such that $x_{i+1} \in f(x_i)$ for $i = 0, \ldots, n-1$ and such that $x_n \in f(x_n)$.*
7. *For a predicate P on ascending finite lists of elements of E, we inductively generate the predicate "$P \mid \sigma$" (pronounced "P bars σ") by the following clauses:*
   (a) *If $P(\sigma)$, then $P \mid \sigma$.*
   (b) *If $P \mid \sigma x$ for all elements $x \in E$ such that $x \geqslant \sigma$, then $P \mid \sigma$.*
   Here and in the following, by "$x \geqslant \sigma$" we mean that $x \geqslant y$ for all terms y of σ.

Part 7 of Definition 2.6 is to be read with generalized inductive definitions [1–3,33]. The statement "$P \mid [\,]$" expresses the following induction principle: If Q is a predicate on ascending finite lists of elements of E such that

1. if $P(\sigma)$, then $Q(\sigma)$, and
2. if $Q(\sigma x)$ for all $x \geqslant E$ such that $x \geqslant \sigma$, then $Q(\sigma)$,

then $Q([\,])$.

As, e.g., in [31] we now consider Noetherian conditions for arbitrary partial orders, not necessarily stemming from ideals of commutative rings.

Definition 2.7. *A partial order $(E, \leqslant)$ is*

1. Noetherian *iff for every ascending chain $e_1 \leqslant e_2 \leqslant \ldots$ in E there exists a number n such that $e_n = e_{n+1} = e_{n+2} = \ldots$;*
2. RS-Noetherian *iff for every ascending chain $e_1 \leqslant e_2 \leqslant \ldots$ in E there exists a number n such that $e_n = e_{n+1}$;*
3. ML-Noetherian *if the reverse order $(E, \geqslant)$ is hereditarily well-founded;*
4. strongly Noetherian *iff there exists a well-order W and a map $\varphi \colon E \to W$ which is strictly descending: that is, $e < f \Rightarrow \varphi(f) < \varphi(e)$;*
5. processly Noetherian *iff every ascending process with values in E stalls;*
6. tree Noetherian *iff every ascending tree with values in E stalls;*
7. inductively Noetherian *iff* Stalls $\mid [\,]$*, where* Stalls(σ) *expresses that the ascending finite list σ of elements of E contains repeated terms.*

Consequently, a ring is Noetherian (resp. RS-Noetherian, ...) if the partially ordered set of its finitely generated ideals is Noetherian (resp. RS-Noetherian, ...). Although we will focus on the applications of these definitions in the specific

---

[2] By a well-order we thus always mean a linear order which is *hereditarily* well-founded.

case of the family of closed subsets of a well quasi-order, further abstract developments are possible [31]. The tree and the process condition are equivalent [7, p. 36].

A first analysis unveils quite a complex picture of relations between these notions. For instance, inductive Noetherian implies ML-Noetherian, but ML-Noetherian implies RS-Noetherian only in the case that equality of comparable elements is decidable. On the other hand, inductive Noetherian implies RS-Noetherian also without any decidability condition. Hence the conditions seem not fit into a linear hierarchy. The picture is clarified when we introduce a classically equivalent but constructively stronger relation $\leqslant'$ derived from $\leqslant$: $x \leqslant' y$ iff $x = y \vee x < y$. We then obtain the following two-dimensional picture.

Theorem 2.8. *Let $(E, \leqslant)$ be a partial order. Let E' be the partial order with the same underlying set as E but with $\leqslant'$ as ordering relation. Then:*

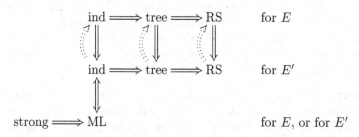

The *dotted implications hold if equality of comparable elements is decidable for E, that is if $x \leqslant y \Rightarrow (x = y \vee x < y)$; in this case $\leqslant$ and $\leqslant'$ agree.*

Proof. The conditions "strong" and "ML" are equivalent for E and E' because these only refer to the induced strict orders, and $<$ and $<'$ coincide.

"*Ind implies tree*": For ascending finite lists σ of elements of E, we define the predicate $P(\sigma)$ stating that every ascending tree $(x_i)_{i \in I}$ with a path in which all terms of σ occur stalls. We verify $P([\,])$ by induction.

1. If σ is a list containing repeated terms, then trivially $P(\sigma)$.
2. Assume that $P(\sigma a)$ holds for all $a \geqslant \sigma$. Let $(x_i)_{i \in I}$ be an ascending tree containing a path in which all terms of σ occur. By the tree condition, this path can be enlarged to a path containing a further term a. Hence $(x_i)_{i \in I}$ is an ascending tree which has a path containing all terms of σa and hence stalls by $P(\sigma a)$.

"*Tree implies RS*": Every ascending sequence is also an ascending tree.
"*Strong implies ML*": [30, p. 517].
"*Ind for E' implies ML*": For ascending finite lists σ of elements of E', we define the predicate $P(\sigma)$ stating that:

For every hereditary subset $H \subseteq E'$ and for every element $x \in E'$, if the list σx is ascending and does not contain repeated terms, then $x \in H$.

Using the induction principle available by the assumption that E' is inductively Noetherian, we will verify $P([\,])$, thereby validating that E' is ML-Noetherian.

1. If σ is a list containing repeated terms, then $P(\sigma)$ by ex falsum quodlibet.
2. Assume that $P(\sigma x)$ holds for all $x \in E'$ such that σx is ascending. Let $H \subseteq E'$ be a hereditary subset and let $x \in E'$ be an element such that σx is an ascending list without repeated terms. To verify that $x \in H$, we show that $y \in H$ for every element $y > x$. This follows from $P(\sigma x)$, for the list $\sigma x y$ is ascending and without repeated terms.

"ML implies ind for E'": Let P be a property of finite ascending lists of elements of E' such that (1) $\mathrm{Stalls}(\sigma) \Rightarrow P(\sigma)$ and such that (2) $(\forall (x \geqslant' \sigma).\, P(\sigma x)) \Rightarrow P(\sigma)$. To verify that $P(\sigma)$ for all σ, we verify that the set $H := \{x \in E \mid \forall (\sigma \leqslant' x).\, P(\sigma x)\}$ is hereditary.

So let an element $x \in E$ be given and assume that all elements strictly larger than x are contained in H. Let σ be an ascending list such that σx is also an ascending list. We verify $P(\sigma x)$ by making use of property (2).

So let $y \geqslant' x$ be given. Hence either $y = x$ or $y > x$. In the first case, we have $\mathrm{Stalls}(\sigma x y)$ and hence $P(\sigma x y)$ by property (1). In the second case, we have $P((\sigma x)y)$ by $y \in H$.   ⊣

We conjecture that none of the solid implications can be constructively reversed. The question whether "strong $\Rightarrow$ ML" could be reversed is already raised in [31, p. 123]. Blass gave an example falsifying "RS $\Rightarrow$ ML" in a topological model [6, Example 2]; his example also falsifies "tree $\Rightarrow$ ML". Because there the ordering relation is decidable, there is no difference between ML and inductive Noetherian.

On the ML condition, which for important applications like the Hilbert basis theorem requires that equality of comparable elements is decidable, Richman writes [35]: "This seems necessary and is reasonable for a theory that emphasizes strict inclusion of ideals. I have yet to learn to love this approach although I have tried, off and on, for many years." With his proposed ascending tree condition he can indeed do without decidability assumptions; however, for his version of the Hilbert basis theorem he still requires an additional coherence assumption.

The cleanest form of the Hilbert basis theorem is instead obtained for inductive Noetherian: If R is inductively Noetherian, then so is $R[X]$ [13, Corollary 16]. Our Theorem 2.8 puts this state of affairs into a wider context: The tree condition is already on the right track because it uses $\leqslant$ instead of $\leqslant'$. On the other hand, it is slightly too weak—the ML condition is better from this point of view. Since ML is just inductive Noetherian for $\leqslant'$, the resolution is to use inductive Noetherian, but for $\leqslant$; that is, the Noetherian condition of Coquand and Persson.

3   Well Quasi-Orders

Definition 3.1. *A quasi-order (for short, qo) $(Q, \leqslant_Q)$ is a set Q with a reflexive and transitive relation $\leqslant_Q$.*

By moving from partial orders to quasi-orders one leaves out the antisymmetry requirement. For what concerns notation, we omit the subscript Q from the qo when there is no ambiguity; moreover, we sometimes write just Q for a qo if the relation over it is clear from the context. A *linear* qo $\leqslant$ is one for which any two given elements are *comparable*: that is, $p \leqslant q \vee q \leqslant p$.

We abbreviate as follows: $p < q$ is a shorthand for $p \leqslant q \wedge q \not\leqslant p$;[3] $p \geqslant q$ stands for $q \leqslant p$; $\perp$ denotes *incomparability*, i.e., $q \perp p$ iff $q \not\leqslant p \wedge p \not\leqslant q$; and $\sim$ denotes *equivalent* elements, i.e., $p \sim q$ iff $p \leqslant q \wedge q \leqslant p$. Notice that if $(Q, \leqslant_Q)$ is a qo, then the quotient set $Q/\sim$ with the relation induced by $\leqslant_Q$ is a partial order.

Definition 3.2. *For every quasi-order* $(Q, \leqslant)$,

- *the* closure *of a subset B of Q is* $\uparrow B = \{q \in Q \mid \exists (b \in B)\, b \leqslant q\}$;
- *a subset of Q is* closed *if it equals its own closure, and* finitely generated *if it is the closure of a finite set;*
- *a* sequence $(q_k)_k$ *(of elements) in Q is a total function from $\mathbb{N}$ to Q;*
- *an* antichain *in Q is a sequence $(q_k)_k$ in Q such that $q_i \perp q_j$ whenever $i \neq j$;*
- *an* extension *of $(Q, \leqslant)$ is a qo $\preccurlyeq$ on Q extending $\leqslant$ in the sense that $p \leqslant q \Rightarrow p \preccurlyeq q$ and $p \preccurlyeq q \wedge q \preccurlyeq p \Rightarrow p \sim q$.*

The weak antisymmetry requirement on extensions ensures that there is a canonical bijection between the linear extensions of Q as a qo and the linear partial orders on $Q/\sim$ which contain $\leqslant$. This last definition, as well as some of the next ones regarding well quasi-orders (e.g., wqo(set) or wqo(anti)), are adopted from the context of reverse mathematics, where a thorough analysis of wqo's has already been done [10, 25, 26]. We take the opportunity to briefly recall that the reverse mathematics programme is using *classical* logic to calibrate mathematical statements having as benchmark suitable existential axioms. A standard reference for reverse mathematics is [38].

We consider now the main definitions of a *well quasi-order*, wqo, we could find in literature, together with others coming from the foregoing reflections on constructive Noetherianity. Except for the first two ones, which are only about well-foundedness, all of them are equivalent with classical logic [20, Theorem 2.1], see also [18, Lemma 2.4].

Definition 3.3. *A quasi-order* $(Q, \leqslant)$ *is*

1. well-founded, wf, *if, for every descending chain $q_0 \geqslant q_1 \geqslant \ldots$ in Q there are $i < j$ such that $q_i \leqslant q_j$ and thus $q_i \sim q_j$;[4] in this sense every strictly descending chain in Q is finite [see also Definition 2.6];*
2. sequentially well-founded, wf(set), *if every descending chain $q_1 \geqslant q_2 \geqslant \ldots$ in Q has an infinite subsequence of equivalent elements, i.e., there are indices $k_0 < k_1 < \ldots$ such that $q_{k_i} \leqslant q_{k_j}$ and thus $q_{k_i} \sim q_{k_j}$ whenever $i < j$;*

---

[3] Definition 2.6(1) is not appropriate for quasi-orders which are not antisymmetric. One could have $p \leqslant q \wedge q \leqslant p$, although $p \neq q$; obtaining, following Definition 2.6(1), $p < q \wedge q < p$, which is commonly unwanted.

[4] By transitivity, an equivalent condition is that there is an index i such that $q_i \leqslant q_{i+1}$. We are grateful to one of the reviewers for pointing this out.

3. *a* well quasi-order, wqo, *if for every sequence* $(q_k)_k$ *in* Q *there are* $i < j$ *such that* $q_i \leqslant q_j$;

4. *a* sequentially well quasi-order, wqo(set), *if every sequence* $(q_k)_k$ *in* Q *has an infinite ascending subsequence, i.e., there are indices* $k_0 < k_1 < \dots$ *such that* $q_{k_i} \leqslant q_{k_j}$ *whenever* $i < j$;

5. *an* antichain well quasi-order, wqo(anti), *if* Q *is well-founded and if, for every sequence* $(q_k)_k$ *of equal or incomparable elements, there exist* $i < j$ *such that* $q_i = q_j$; *namely every strictly descending chain and every antichain are finite;*

6. *an* extensional well quasi-order, wqo(ext), *if every linear extension* $\preccurlyeq$ *of* $\leqslant$ *is well-founded;*

7. wqo(fbp) *if* Q *has the* finite basis property, *i.e., every closed subset is finitely generated;*

8. wqo(acc) *if the set of closed subsets is Noetherian;*

9. wqo(RS), wqo(ML), wqo(str), wqo(ind), wqo(prc) *if the set of finitely generated closed subsets is RS-Noetherian (resp. ML, strong, inductively, processly).*

Remark 3.4.

1. For quasi-orders, we have the following implications:
   (a) wf(set) implies wf, and wqo(set) implies wqo;
   (b) wqo(set) implies wf(set), and wqo implies wf.
2. Let $(E, \leqslant)$ be a *partial* order,
   (a) $(E, \leqslant)$ is well-founded iff $(E, \geqslant)$ is RS-Noetherian;
   (b) $(E, \leqslant)$ is sequentially well-founded iff $(E, \geqslant)$ is Noetherian;
   (c) $(E, \leqslant)$ is hereditarily well-founded iff $(E, \geqslant)$ is ML-Noetherian.

At least two of the above definitions are worth some further remarks. By Theorem 2.8, hereditarily well-founded implies well-founded, but not the other way round [6, Example 2]. While wqo(anti) is commonly found as the negative statement "there is no infinite strictly descending chain nor any infinite antichain", we propose a constructively suitable and to some extent positive version.

Theorem 3.5. *The conditions* wqo(set), wf(set), wqo(fbp) *and* wqo(acc) *are constructively bland already for partial orders.*

Proof. Endow $\mathbb{B} = \{0, 1\}$ with the partial order $0 \leqslant 1$. While there is a Brouwerian counterexample to $\mathbb{B}$ being wqo(set) [41], we show that if $\mathbb{B}$ is wf(set), then LPO holds. To this end let $a_0 \geqslant a_1 \geqslant \dots$ in $\mathbb{B}$. If there are $k_0 < k_1 < \dots$ such that $a_{k_0} \leqslant a_{k_1} \leqslant \dots$ too, then actually $a_{k_0} = a_{k_1} = \dots$ Now if $a_{k_0} = 1$, then $a_i = 1$ for all i, simply because $i \leqslant k_i$ for every i.

We next show that if $\mathbb{B}$ is wqo(fbp), then the law of excluded middle (LEM) holds. To do so, we carry over from rings to orders the argument that LEM follows from "every ideal of the two-element field $\mathbb{F}_2$ is finitely generated". Let φ be a truth value. We resort to the "fishy set" $F_\varphi := \{x \in \mathbb{B} \mid (x = 0 \wedge \varphi) \vee x = 1\}$ and suppose that $\uparrow F_\varphi = \uparrow \{b_1, \dots, b_n\}$. Now if $b_i = 1$ for all i, then $F_\varphi \subseteq \uparrow F_\varphi =$

$\uparrow\{1\} = \{1\}$ and thus $0 \notin F_\varphi$, which is to say that $\neg\varphi$; if $b_i = 0$ for some i, then $0 \in \uparrow F_\varphi$, that is, $p \leqslant 0$ for some p in F_φ, which means $0 \in F_\varphi$ and thus φ.[5]

Finally, LPO follows from $\mathbb{B}$ being wqo(acc) along the route to LPO from "the two-element field $\mathbb{F}_2$ is Noetherian" [16].[6] $\dashv$

We now analyse the implications among the constructively sensible conditions wqo, wqo(anti), wqo(ext), wqo(RS), wqo(ML) and wqo(str); for wqo see, e.g., [37]

Theorem 3.6. *The following implications hold:*

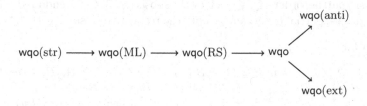

Proof. For what concerns the first two implications they are consequence of Theorem 2.8; so let us focus on the last three.

"wqo(RS) $\Rightarrow$ wqo" Let Q be a qo. For every infinite sequence $q_0, q_1, \ldots$ in Q consider the ascending chain of closed subsets $\uparrow\{q_0\} \subseteq \uparrow\{q_0, q_1\} \subseteq \ldots$. If Q is wqo(RS), then there is n such that $\uparrow\{q_0, \ldots, q_n\} = \uparrow\{q_0, \ldots, q_n, q_{n+1}\}$; thus $q_{n+1} \in \uparrow\{q_0, \ldots, q_n\}$ and there exists $i \in \{0, \ldots, n\}$ such that $q_i \leqslant q_{n+1}$.

"wqo $\Rightarrow$ wqo(anti)" Notice first that every wqo is well-founded. If $q_0, q_1, \ldots$ is an infinite sequence in a wqo Q such that any given q_i and q_j are equal or incomparable, then there are $i < j$ such that $q_i \leqslant q_j$ and thus $q_i = q_j$.

"wqo $\Rightarrow$ wqo(ext)" Let $(Q, \leqslant)$ be a wqo, and $(Q, \preccurlyeq)$ a linear extension (in fact any extension whatsoever would do [18, Lemma 2.4]). Given any $\preccurlyeq$-descending chain $q_0 \succcurlyeq q_1 \succcurlyeq q_2 \succcurlyeq \ldots$, since $\leqslant$ is wqo, there are $i < j$ such that $q_i \leqslant q_j$ and thus $q_i \preccurlyeq q_j$. By transitivity, $q_i \succcurlyeq q_j$; whence $q_i \sim q_j$, i.e., $\preccurlyeq$ is wf. $\dashv$

Remark 3.7. There is a certain similarity between the constructive implications and the implications over RCA$_0$[7] which, regarding wqo(set), wqo, wqo(anti) and wqo(ext), depicted below, where no other implications hold [26, Theorem 2.9]. Differently from reverse mathematics (where there are counterexamples to each direction), we do not know which relation, if any, holds constructively between wqo(anti) and wqo(ext); the correspondence between RCA$_0$ and constructive mathematics (see Footnote 7) may suggest a likewise incomparable situation.

---

[5] While we generally work in IZF, in CZF we would get LEM only for formulas φ of set theory which are *restricted*: that is, every bound variable x occurring in φ ranges over a set as in $\forall x \in y$ and $\exists x \in y$. By this restriction F_φ would be a set also in CZF where the separation axiom scheme is limited to restricted formulas.

[6] Similarly one could consider something like wqo(acc^{fg}) or wqo(acc$_0$).

[7] RCA$_0$ is the weakest of five main systems in reverse mathematics and roughly corresponds to effectively computable mathematics [38], see also [17].

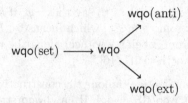

We conclude with a study of the closure properties of wqo's under subsets; for the argument's sake, we include some constructively bland concepts. Given any quasi-/partial order $(Q, \leqslant)$, let every subset $P \subseteq Q$ be endowed with the induced quasi-/partial order, and denote the respective closures with $\uparrow_Q$ and $\uparrow_P$.

Lemma 3.8.

1. Let $(Q, \leqslant)$ be a qo, and $P \subseteq Q$. If $B \subseteq P$, then $\uparrow_P B = P \cap \uparrow_Q B$. In particular, $B_1 \subseteq B_2 \Leftrightarrow \uparrow_Q B_1 \subseteq \uparrow_Q B_2$ for all closed subsets B_1, B_2 of P.
2. If a partial order $(E, \leqslant)$ is hwf, then $(E_0, \leqslant)$ is hwf for every subset $E_0 \subseteq E$.

Proof. As for item 2, let $H_0 \subseteq E_0$ be hereditary. Then $H = \{x \in E \mid x \in E_0 \Rightarrow x \in H_0\}$ is a hereditary subset of E such that $H_0 = E_0 \Leftrightarrow H - E$.   ⊣

Proposition 3.9. Let $\mathcal{P}$ be any of the properties wf, wf(set), wqo, wqo(set), wqo(anti), wqo(acc), wqo(RS), wqo(ML), wqo(str). If the qo $(Q, \leqslant)$ has property $\mathcal{P}$ and $P \subseteq Q$, then $(P, \leqslant)$ has property $\mathcal{P}$.

Proof. While the cases wf, wf(set), wqo, wqo(set) and wqo(anti) are straightforward, the cases wqo(acc) and wqo(RS) follow from Lemma 3.8. As for wqo(ML) and wqo(str), let $\mathcal{F}_P$ and $\mathcal{F}_Q$ consist of the finitely generated closed subsets of P and Q. The map $\mathcal{F}_P \to \mathcal{F}_Q$ with $B \mapsto \uparrow_Q B$ is strictly increasing (Lemma 3.8). In particular, if $\mathcal{F}_Q$ is hwf, then so is $\mathcal{F}_P$ [27, Chapter I, Theorem 6.2].   ⊣

Future Work

In Proposition 3.9, we left out wqo(ext) on purpose: this is an open problem just as it is in reverse mathematics over RCA_0 [26, Question 2.15]. Several other closure conditions equally deserve attention from a constructive angle, e.g., preservation of wqo under products. A deeper analysis would further call for a thorough distinction between a well-order as in Definition 2.6, i.e., a *hereditarily* well-founded linear order, and a well-order in the customary understanding: that is, a linear order which is well-founded in the sense of Definition 3.3. Finally, a few implications related to Definition 2.1 and Theorem 2.8 ought to be considered.

References

1. Aczel, P.: An introduction to inductive definitions. In: Barwise, J. (ed.) Handbook of Mathematical Logic, Stud. Logic Found. Math., vol. 90, pp. 739–782. North-Holland (1977)

2. Aczel, P., Rathjen, M.: Notes on constructive set theory. Tech. rep., Institut Mittag-Leffler (2000), report No. 40
3. Aczel, P., Rathjen, M.: Constructive Set Theory (2010), book draft
4. Bauer, A.: Realizability as the connection between computable and constructive mathematics (2005). http://math.andrej.com/asset/data/c2c.pdf
5. Bauer, A.: An injection from the Baire space to natural numbers. Math. Struct. Comput. Sci. **25**(7), 1484–1489 (2015)
6. Blass, A.: Well-ordering and induction in intuitionistic logic and topoi. In: Kueker, D., Lopez-Escobar, F., Smith, C. (eds.) Math. Logic Theor. Comput. Sci. Taylor & Francis Group, United Kingdom (1986)
7. Blechschmidt, I.: Using the internal language of toposes in algebraic geometry. Ph.D. thesis, University of Augsburg (2017). https://arxiv.org/abs/2111.03685
8. Blechschmidt, I.: Generalized spaces for constructive algebra. In: Mainzer, K., Schuster, P., Schwichtenberg, H., (eds.) Proof and Computation II, pp. 99–187. World Scientific (2021)
9. Blechschmidt, I.: Exploring mathematical objects from custom-tailored mathematical universes. In: Oliveri, G., Ternullo, C., Boscolo, S. (eds.) Objects, structures, and logics: FilMat studies in the philosophy of mathematics. Springer (2022). https://doi.org/10.1007/978-3-030-84706-7_4
10. Cholak, P., Marcone, A., Solomon, R.: Reverse mathematics and the equivalence of definitions for well and better quasi-orders. JSL **66**(1), 683–55 (2004)
11. Coquand, T.: Notions invariant by change of basis (2001)
12. Coquand, T., Lombardi, H.: Krull's Principal Ideal Theorem. Tech. Rep. 30, Institut Mittag-Leffler (2000/2001)
13. Coquand, T., Persson, H.: Gröbner bases in type theory. In: Altenkirch, T., Reus, B., Naraschewski, W. (eds.) TYPES 1998: Types for Proofs and Programs. Lecture Notes in Comput. Sci., vol. 1657, pp. 33–46. Springer (1999)
14. Cox, D.A., Little, J., O'Shea, D.: Ideals, Varieties, and Algorithms. UTM, Springer, Cham (2015). https://doi.org/10.1007/978-3-319-16721-3
15. Crosilla, L.: Set theory: constructive and intuitionistic ZF. In: Zalta, E. (ed.) The Stanford Encyclopedia of Philosophy. Metaphysics Research Lab (2015)
16. Crosilla, L., Schuster, P.: Finite Methods in Mathematical Practice. In: Link, G. (ed.) Formalism and Beyond, pp. 351–410. De Gruyter (2014)
17. Downey, R., Hirschfeldt, D., Lempp, S., Solomon, R.: Computability-theoretic and proof-theoretic aspects of partial and linear orderings. Israel J. Math. **138**(1), 271–289 (2003)
18. Gallier, J.: What's so special about Kruskal's theorem and the ordinal Γ_0? A survey of some results in proof theory. Ann. Pure Appl. Logic **53**(3), 199–260 (1991)
19. Hamkins, J., Lewis, A.: Infinite time turing machines. J. Symbolic Logic **65**(2), 567–604 (2000)
20. Higman, G.: Ordering by divisibility in abstract algebras. Proc. London Math. Soc. **3**(2), 326–336 (1952)
21. Hyland, M.: The effective topos. In: Troelstra, A.S., van Dalen, D. (eds.) The L. E. J. Brouwer Centenary Symposium, pp. 165–216. North-Holland (1982)
22. Ishihara, H.: Reverse mathematics in Bishop's constructive mathematics. Philosophia scientiae (CS 6), 43–59 (2006)
23. Jacobsson, C., Löfwall, C.: Standard bases for general coefficient rings and a new constructive proof of Hilbert's basis theorem. J. Symbolic Comput. **12**(3), 337–371 (1991)

24. Maietti, M.: Modular correspondence between dependent type theories and categories including pretopoi and topoi. Math. Struct. Comput. Sci. **15**(6), 1089–1149 (2005)
25. Marcone, A.: WQO and BQO theory in subsystems of second order arithmetic. In: Simpson, S.G. (ed.) Reverse Mathematics 2001. vol. 21, pp. 303–330 (2005)
26. Marcone, A.: The reverse mathematics of WQOs and BQOs. In: Schuster, P., Seisenberger, M., Weiermann, A. (eds.) Well-Quasi Orders in Computation, Logic, Language and Reasoning, pp. 189–219. Springer International Publishing, Cham (2020)
27. Mines, R., Richman, F., Ruitenburg, W.: A Course in Constructive Algebra. Universitext, Springer, New York (2012). https://doi.org/10.1007/978-1-4419-8640-5
28. Nemoto, T., Kentaro, S.: A marriage of Brouwser's intuitionism and Hilbert's finitism I: arithmetic. J. Symbolic Logic **87**(2), 437–497 (2022)
29. van Oosten, J.: Realizability: an introduction to its categorical Side, Stud. Logic Found. Math., vol. 152. Elsevier (2008)
30. Perdry, H.: Strongly Noetherian rings and constructive ideal theory. J. Symb. Comput. **37**(4), 511–535 (2004)
31. Perdry, H., Schuster, P.: Noetherian orders. Math. Struct. Comput. Sci. **21**(1), 111–124 (2011)
32. Phoa, W.: An introduction to fibrations, topos theory, the effective topos and modest sets. University of Edinburgh, Tech. rep. (1992)
33. Rathjen, M.: Generalized inductive definitions in constructive set theory. In: Crosilla, L., Schuster, P. (eds.) From Sets and Types to Topology and Analysis, Oxford Logic Guides, vol. 48, chap. 16. Clarendon Press (2005)
34. Richman, F.: Constructive aspects of Noetherian rings. Proc. Am. Math. Soc. **44**(2), 436–441 (1974)
35. Richman, F.: The ascending tree condition: constructive algebra without countable choice. Commun. Algebra **31**(4), 1993–2002 (2003)
36. Seidenberg, A.: What is Noetherian? Rendiconti del Seminario matematico e fisico di Milano **44**(1), 55–61 (1974)
37. Seisenberger, M.: An inductive version of Nash-Williams' minimal-bad-sequence argument for Higman's lemma. In: Callaghan, P., Luo, Z., McKinna, J., Pollack, R., Pollack, R. (eds.) TYPES 2000. LNCS, vol. 2277, pp. 233–242. Springer, Heidelberg (2002). https://doi.org/10.1007/3-540-45842-5_15
38. Simpson, S.: Subsystems of Second Order Arithmetic Perspectives in Logic, 2nd edn. Cambridge University Press, Cambridge (2009)
39. Streicher, T.: Introduction to Constructive Logic and Mathematics (2001)
40. Tennenbaum, J.: A constructive version of Hilbert's basis theorem. Ph.D. thesis, University of California, San Diego, California (1973)
41. Veldman, W.: An intuitionistic proof of Kruskal's theorem. Arch. Math. Logic **43**(2), 215–264 (2004)
42. Veldman, W.: Brouwer's fan theorem as an axiom and as a contrast to Kleene's alternative. Arch. Math. Logic **53**, 621–693 (2014)
43. Yengui, I.: Detailed solutions to the exercises. In: Constructive Commutative Algebra. LNM, vol. 2138, pp. 221–253. Springer, Cham (2015). https://doi.org/10.1007/978-3-319-19494-3_6

Computability

Symmetry for Transfinite Computability

Lorenzo Galeotti[1]([✉]), Ethan S. Lewis[2], and Benedikt Löwe[3,4,5]([✉])

[1] Amsterdam University College, Postbus 94160, 1090 Amsterdam, The Netherlands
l.galeotti@uva.nl
[2] 1179 W 1200 S, Springville 84663, USA
[3] Institute for Logic, Language and Computation, Universiteit van Amsterdam,
Postbus 94242, 1090 Amsterdam, The Netherlands
b.loewe@uva.nl
[4] Fachbereich Mathematik, Universität Hamburg,
Bundesstrasse 55, 20146 Hamburg, Germany
[5] Department of Pure Mathematics and Mathematical Statistics, Churchill College,
Lucy Cavendish College, St. Edmund's College, University of Cambridge,
Storey's Way, Cambridge CB3 0DS, England

Abstract. Finite Turing computation has a fundamental symmetry between inputs, outputs, programs, time, and storage space. Standard models of transfinite computation break this symmetry; we consider ways to recover it and study the resulting model of computation. Whether this model exhibits the same symmetry as finite Turing computation is independent of von Neumann-Gödel-Bernays class theory: it holds if and only if the universe is constructible from a set of ordinals.

1 Introduction

A fundamental feature of the theory of computation is that the constituents of computability, viz. in-/output, programs, time, and storage space can be considered to be the same type of object: natural numbers (if necessary, via coding). A Turing machine receives a finite string of symbols as input, has a finite string of symbols as its program, and produces a finite string of symbols as output. Moreover, both its tape and its time flow are indexed by natural numbers. Hence, since finite strings of symbols can be coded as a natural number, all these objects are of the same type.

We shall refer to this feature as *symmetry*. Various aspects of symmetry permeate the general theory of computation: the symmetry between inputs and programs is the reason for the *software principle* (the existence of universal machines) and the *s-m-n* Theorem; the symmetry between programs and time underlies the zigzag method that allows us to parallelise infinitely many computations into one by identifying the cartesian product of the program space and time with $\mathbb{N} \times \mathbb{N}$ and using Cantor's zigzag function.

The oldest model of transfinite computation is the model called *Hamkins-Kidder machines* or *Infinite Time Turing Machines* (ITTM), defined in [9]. These machines have a *storage space* of order type ω, but allow computation

G. Della Vedova et al. (Eds.): CiE 2023, LNCS 13967, pp. 65–76, 2023.
https://doi.org/10.1007/978-3-031-36978-0_6

to be of arbitrary transfinite ordinal length, thereby breaking the symmetry between time and space. This asymmetry makes their complexity theory vastly different from ordinary complexity theory, as discussed in [5, 11, 17, 20, 23, 24].

In [13, 14], Koepke symmetrised Hamkins-Kidder machines and defined what is now known as *Koepke machines* or *Ordinal Turing Machines*: Koepke machines have a class-sized tape indexed by ordinals and run through ordinal time, thereby re-establishing the symmetry between time and storage space.[1] However, Koepke machines do not have the full symmetry that we find in finite Turing computation: while time and storage space are represented by arbitrary ordinals, programs are still finite objects.

In this paper, we shall provide a general framework for models of computation and computability that allows us to phrase the quest for symmetry in abstract terms; this is done in Sect. 3. In this framework, we shall define the relevant models of computability, i.e., ordinary Turing computability, Hamkins-Kidder computability, Koepke computability, and our new notion called *symmetric computability* in Sect. 4. We study basic properties of symmetric computability in Sect. 5, and finally show that the full symmetry of symmetric computability cannot be proved in von Neumann-Gödel-Bernays class theory (NBGC) in Sect. 6: symmetry holds if and only if the universe is constructible from a set of ordinals.

This paper contains results from the second author's Master's thesis [16] written under the supervision of the first and the third author. These results are cited in [2, 3, 8] and [1, Exercise 3.9.7].

2   Class Theories

In this paper, we work in *von Neumann-Gödel-Bernays class theory*.[2] The language is the usual language of set theory $\mathcal{L}_\in$ with a single binary relation symbol $\in$. We define a unary predicate $\mathrm{set}(x) := \exists y(x \in y)$. Using this predicate, we can define the two *set quantifiers* $\exists^{\mathrm{set}} x \varphi := \exists x(\mathrm{set}(x) \wedge \varphi)$ and $\forall^{\mathrm{set}} x \varphi := \forall x(\mathrm{set}(x) \to \varphi)$. A formula is called *set theoretic* if all of its quantifiers are set quantifiers. In this context we denote by AC the *axiom of choice* for sets, i.e., the statement that "Every set x of non-empty sets has a choice function" and contrast it with the axiom of *Global Choice*, which is the statement "There is a global choice class function". We write NBG for von Neumann-Gödel-Bernays class theory without the axiom of Global Choice [12, p. 70: Axioms A–D] and NBGC for the theory obtained from NBG by adding the axiom of Global Choice [12, p. 70: Axioms A–E]. It is a well-known result due to Easton that if NBG is consistent, then NBG + AC does not prove the axiom of Global Choice (cf., e.g., [6, Theorem 3.1]).

We can transform a formula φ in the language $\mathcal{L}_\in$ into a set theoretic formula φ^{set} by recursively replacing all quantifiers with the corresponding set quantifiers.

---

[1] Carl argues in [1, Chapter 9] that Koepke machines are the natural infinitary analogue for finitary computation and complexity theory and this was explored in detail in [4].

[2] For more details, cf., e.g., [18, Chapter 4].

This allows us to formulate the famous *conservativity theorem for* NBGC (cf., e.g., [6, Corollary 4.1 & Theorem 4.2]):[3]

Theorem 1. If φ is a sentence in $\mathcal{L}_\in$, then ZFC $\vdash \varphi$ if and only if NBGC $\vdash \varphi^{\mathrm{set}}$ if and only if NBG + AC $\vdash \varphi^{\mathrm{set}}$.

We define the *axiom of constructibility from a set of ordinals* as the statement "there is a set of ordinals x such that V=L[x]". This is a set theoretic sentence that is well-known to be independent of the axioms of ZFC. It implies the axiom of Global Choice; therefore, Theorem 1 implies the following result.

Theorem 2. If NBGC is consistent, then NBGC does not prove nor disprove the axiom of constructibility from a set of ordinals.

3 The General Framework of Turing Computation and Computability

We shall frame our discussion of symmetry in a context that makes the relevant models of computability special cases of a general framework. We denote the class of all ordinals by Ord and refer to the class V of all sets as potential programs for the machines in our framework. All models of computation in this paper will be variants of Turing machines: they have a single class-length tape indexed by ordinals,[4] a read/write head that moves on the tape according to a program. We fix a finite alphabet Σ with at least two elements **0** and **1** for the remainder of the paper.[5]

Turing Hardware and Computations. At the highest level of abstraction, we deal with the *Turing hardware:* the *tape* and the *head*, including the description of how they work. We assume that the tape is always indexed by ordinals, split into discrete *cells* in which a symbol from Σ can be written; also, we assume that time is considered as discrete points in time, indexed by ordinals, and that at each point in time, the head is located at one of the cells; finally, we assume that we have a discrete set of *states*, indexed by ordinals.

For classes X and Y, we write $f : X \dashrightarrow Y$ for "f is a class function with $\mathrm{dom}(f) \subseteq X$ and $\mathrm{ran}(f) \subseteq Y$" and $f(x)\downarrow$ if and only if $x \in \mathrm{dom}(f)$ and $f(x)\uparrow$ otherwise. We represent the tape content by arbitrary partial class functions

---

[3] We refer the reader to [6, p. 242] and [7, p. 381] for more information on the history of this theorem.

[4] For most models of computability, the number of tapes does not matter; however, in the case of Hamkins-Kidder machines, 1-tape machines and 3-tape machines differ (cf. [10]). Since we do not discuss Hamkins-Kidder machines in detail, this is immaterial for our context. .

[5] As one of the referees pointed out, the requirement that the alphabet is finite could be seen as yet another failure of symmetry. Our notion of *symmetric computability* as discussed in Sects. 5 & 6 is equivalent to the same notion where the alphabet Σ is allowed to be of arbitrary ordinal size.

from Ord to Σ; we write $\Sigma^{(\mathrm{Ord})}$ for the class of these objects. We shall consider a number of relevant subclasses of this class: $\Sigma^{<\mathrm{Ord}} := \{x \in \Sigma^{(\mathrm{Ord})} ; \mathrm{dom}(x) \in \mathrm{Ord}\}$, $\Sigma^{\mathrm{FS}} := \{x \in \Sigma^{(\mathrm{Ord})} ; \mathrm{dom}(x) \text{ is finite}\}$, $\Sigma^{\omega} := \{x \in \Sigma^{(\mathrm{Ord})} ; \mathrm{dom}(x) = \omega\}$, $\Sigma^* = \Sigma^{<\omega} := \{x \in \Sigma^{(\mathrm{Ord})} ; \mathrm{dom}(x) \in \omega\}$, and $\Sigma^{\mathrm{O}} := \{x \in \Sigma^{(\mathrm{Ord})} ; |\mathrm{dom}(x)| = 1 \text{ and } \mathrm{ran}(x) = \{\mathbf{0}\}\}$.

The classes Σ^{O} and Σ^{FS} are our representations of the classes Ord and Ord$^{<\omega}$, respectively. The classes Ord and Σ^{O} have a canonical bijection; the classes Σ^{FS} and Ord$^{<\omega}$ can be identified via the Gödel pairing function.[6] Furthermore, the Gödel pairing function yields a definable bijection between Ord and Ord$^{<\omega}$ and a bijection $(w, v) \mapsto w * v : \Sigma^{<\mathrm{Ord}} \times \Sigma^{<\mathrm{Ord}} \to \Sigma^{<\mathrm{Ord}}$ identifying pairs of words as single words.

A *snapshot* of the machine consists of the tape content, a state, and a position of the head, i.e., a tuple from Snap $:= \Sigma^{(\mathrm{Ord})} \times \mathrm{Ord} \times \mathrm{Ord}$.

The behaviour of the head is governed by the *transition rule*, a class function that describes what the head will do given its past behaviour and a program p. For now, we still allow all sets to be programs (we consider the further specification of what a program is to be part of the *software*). Consequently, a transition function is a class function $T : \mathrm{Snap}^{<\mathrm{Ord}} \times V \to \mathrm{Snap}$. Once a transition function T is fixed, given a program p and a snapshot $s = (x, \alpha, \beta)$, we define an ordinal-length sequence of snapshots by recursion: $C_{p,s}(0) := s$, and $C_{p,s}(\gamma) := T(C_{p,s} \restriction \gamma, p)$ for $\gamma > 0$. We shall call this *the computation of program p with initial snapshot s*.

In this paper, we shall only consider two different transition functions, the *finite transition function* T_{f}, which is used by ordinary Turing machines and Hamkins-Kidder machines, and the *set-sized transition function* T_{s}, which is used by Koepke machines (for definitions, cf. Sect. 4).

Turing Software. A *model of computation* consists of hardware (i.e., a transition function T) and a class of programs P that can be used for computing. Specifying the class of programs identifies which of the computations are computations according to a program in P.

In this paper, we shall only consider two classes of programs, the class of *finite programs* P_{f} and the class of *set-sized programs* P_{s} (for definitions, cf. Sect. 4).

Computability. A model of computation determines a class of computations, but does not yet tell us what they do. To illustrate this, consider the ordinary notion of Turing computation: for each program and snapshot, we get an infinite sequence of snapshots, but there are many ways to interpret this infinite sequence. Following Turing's original seminal definition [21, § 2], we designate *start* and *halt states*, give a definition of *halting computations* and then interpret the computation as producing a partial function (for definitions, cf. Sect. 4).

Abstractly, we say that an *interpretation* consists of a partial class function I that assigns to a transition function T and each program $p \in P$ a partial function $I(T, p) : \Sigma^{(\mathrm{Ord})} \dashrightarrow \Sigma^{(\mathrm{Ord})}$ and a class $D \subseteq \Sigma^{(\mathrm{Ord})}$ called the *domain* of the interpretation. A *model of computability* is a model of computation (i.e., a

---

[6] The Gödel pairing function is an absolutely definable class bijection between Ord and Ord^2; cf. [12, pp. 30–31].

transition function T and a class of programs P) together with an interpretation. We say that $f : D \dashrightarrow D$ is *computable* according to this model of computability if there is a $p \in P$ such that $f = I(T, p) \restriction D$.

Note that for a given model of computation and a fixed interpretation function, there is some freedom to choose D. E.g., usually, for ordinary Turing computations with the usual textbook interpretation, we let $D = \Sigma^*$ and thus, computability is a property of partial functions $f : \Sigma^* \dashrightarrow \Sigma^*$. However, we could consider $D = \Sigma^\omega$, i.e., letting the Turing machine operate on arbitrary tape contents of length ω, obtaining a different model of computability.[7] On the other hand, if you fix the model of computation and the type of interpretation function, D cannot be chosen entirely freely: the class D needs to be closed under the operations $I(T, p)$ for $p \in P$. E.g., if our model of computation is Koepke machines with the usual interpretation, we cannot choose $D = \Sigma^*$ or even $D = \Sigma^\omega$ since there are programs with which a Koepke machine would produce an output that is not in D anymore.

In this paper, we shall consider two types of interpretation function, the *finite interpretation* I_f and the *set-sized interpretation* I_s (for definitions, cf. Sect. 4).

4   Concrete Models of Computation

Programs. We fix a set of three *motion tokens* MT $:= \{\blacktriangleleft, \blacktriangledown, \blacktriangleright\}$ that represent the instructions for the head movements ("move left", "do nothing", and "move right") and use **m** as a variable for motion tokens. Among the states (indexed by ordinals), we single out three particular states: the *start state* indexed by 0, the *halt state* indexed by 1, and the *limit state* indexed by 2. We write $\Sigma_o := \Sigma \cup \{o\}$ where o is a special symbol representing an empty cell. All of our programs will be partial functions $p : \mathrm{Ord} \times \Sigma_o \dashrightarrow \mathrm{Ord} \times \Sigma_o \times \mathrm{MT}$. We call a program *finite* if its domain is finite and *set-sized* if its domain is a set. The classes of finite and set-sized programs are denoted by P_f and P_s, respectively.

Via the canonical identification of the classes Ord, Ord $\times \Sigma_o$, and Ord $\times \Sigma_o \times$ MT, we can encode programs as elements of $\Sigma^{(\mathrm{Ord})}$. Under our encoding, we identify P_f with the class Σ^{FS} and P_s with the class $\Sigma^{<\mathrm{Ord}}$.

Transition Functions. Given a program p, we shall now define the transition functions T_f ("finite transition function") and T_s ("set-sized transition function"). They are identical on sequences of successor length and coincide there with the ordinary transition function defined by Turing for his machines; they differ for sequences of limit length.

If $s = (s_\xi ; \xi < \gamma + 1)$ is a sequence of snapshots of successor length, the transition function will only depend on $s_\gamma = (x, \alpha, \beta)$, the final snapshot in the list where

---

[7] This is a curious model of computability that exhibits a discrepancy between 1-tape and 3-tape machines (cf. Footnote 4): since only finitely many cells are changed in halting computations, for 1-tape machines the identity function is computable and constant functions are not; in contrast, for 3-tape machines constant functions with value $w \in \Sigma^*$ are computable, but other constant functions or the identity function are not..

$x \in \Sigma^{(\text{Ord})}$ is the tape content at time γ, α is the state at time γ, and β is the location of the head at time γ. If $p(\alpha, x(\beta))$ is undefined, we let $T(s) := s_\gamma$; otherwise, let $p(\alpha, x(\beta)) = (\delta, \sigma, \mathbf{m})$. Then $T(s) = (y, \alpha^*, \beta^*)$ where $\alpha^* := \delta$,

$$y(\eta) := \begin{cases} x(\eta) & \text{if } \eta \neq \beta, \\ \sigma & \text{if } \eta = \beta, \end{cases} \quad \text{and} \quad \beta^* := \begin{cases} \beta - 1 & \text{if } \mathbf{m} = \blacktriangleleft \text{ and } \beta \text{ is a successor,} \\ 0 & \text{if } \mathbf{m} = \blacktriangleleft \text{ and } \beta \text{ is a limit,} \\ \beta + 1 & \text{if } \mathbf{m} = \blacktriangleright, \\ \beta & \text{if } \mathbf{m} = \blacktriangledown. \end{cases}$$

If $s = (s_\xi \,;\, \xi < \lambda)$ with $s_\xi = (x_\xi, \alpha_\xi, \beta_\xi)$ is a sequence of snapshots of limit length λ, the two transition functions agree in their definition of the tape content, but disagree in their treatment of the head position and state. Let us write $T_{\text{f}}(s) = (y, \alpha_{\text{f}}, \beta_{\text{f}})$ and $T_{\text{s}}(s) = (y, \alpha_{\text{s}}, \beta_{\text{s}})$. For the tape content, we assume that we have a total ordering on Σ and define $y(\eta) := \liminf\{x_\xi(\eta) \,;\, \xi < \lambda\}$.

The finite transition function T_{f} moves the head to cell 0, moves to the limit state (indexed by 2), i.e., $\alpha_{\text{f}} := 2$ and $\beta_{\text{f}} := 0$. Note that in any computation using the finite transition function, the head will never reach a cell indexed by an infinite ordinal.

The set-sized transition function T_{s} moves both the head and the cell to the *inferior limit* of the ordinals occurring in the sequence, i.e., $\alpha_{\text{s}} := \liminf\{\alpha_\xi \,;\, \xi < \lambda\}$ and $\beta_{\text{s}} := \liminf\{\beta_\xi \,;\, \xi < \lambda \ \wedge \ \alpha_\xi = \alpha_{\text{s}}\}$.

Interpretations. We define our two interpretation functions uniformly for arbitrary tape contents $x \in \Sigma^{(\text{Ord})}$. Both interpretations take a tape content x and a program p, define the initial snapshot $s := (x, 0, 0)$, and produce the computation $C_{p,s}$ of program p with initial snapshot s.

The *finite interpretation* I_{f} considers a computation as *halting* if there is a natural number n such that the state of $C_{p,s}(n)$ is 1 (i.e., the halting state); the *set-sized interpretation* I_{s} considers a computation as *halting* if there is an ordinal α such that the state of $C_{p,s}(\alpha)$ is 1. If it exists, the smallest such number is called the *halting time* of the computation. This implicitly defines the time considered by these models of computability: in general, we say that the *time relevant for a model of computability* is the supremum of its halting times. This is at most ω for models with the finite interpretation and at most Ord for models with the set-sized interpretation. We let $\Omega \subseteq D$ be a subclass that is identified with the time relevant of the model, e.g., $\Omega = \Sigma^{\text{O}}$ if the relevant time is Ord.

If a computation is halting, we say that the tape content at its halting time is the *output* of the computation. Finally, for $I = I_{\text{f}}$ or $I = I_{\text{s}}$ and the appropriate notion of halting, we let $I(T, p)(x) := y$ if $C_{p,s}$ is halting and y is its output, and $I(T, p)(x)\!\uparrow$ otherwise.

Models of Computability. Using our finite specifications T_{f}, P_{f}, and I_{f} and our set-sized specifications T_{s}, P_{s}, and I_{s}, we can now recover the known models of computability (and a new one) as special cases.

First observe that if the transition function is finite, then any tape content beyond the cells indexed by natural numbers will be immaterial for the computation since the head never moves to these cells. Hence, the relevant input domain has to be Σ^* or Σ^ω. Moreover, if the interpretation function is finite, then all computations that go on to ω or beyond will be disregarded in the interpretation. Therefore, we can assume without loss of generality that the transition function is finite as well. This leads to the models of computability listed in Table 1.

Table 1. The considered models of computability

	Transition	Programs	Interpretation	In-/Output	
(a)	Finite	Finite	Finite	Σ^*	ordinary Turing machines
(b)	Finite	Finite	Set-sized	Σ^ω	Hamkins-Kidder machines
(c)	Set-sized	Finite	Set-sized	$\Sigma^{<\mathrm{Ord}}$	Koepke machines
(d)	Set-sized	Set-sized	Set-sized	$\Sigma^{<\mathrm{Ord}}$	symmetric machines; cf. Sect. 5

We briefly discuss the choice of in-/output for the described models:

Table 1 (a). Since the transition function is finite, only Σ^* and Σ^ω make sense as choice of in-/output. However, since the interpretation is also finite, no halting computation will ever be able to read an entire infinite tape. Therefore Σ^* is the natural choice for in-/output. Choosing Σ^ω leads to the model of computability discussed in Footnote 7. The time relevant for this model of computation is ω.

Table 1 (b). Similarly in this case, the finite transition function means that we can only choose Σ^* or Σ^ω as input; however, Σ^* is not closed under the operation of the interpretation (a Hamkins-Kidder machine can fill the entire tape and then halt). Therefore, Σ^ω is the only remaining natural choice. The time relevant for Hamkins-Kidder machines has been investigated in [9,22].

Table 1 (c). In analogy to the argument given for line (a), a halting Koepke machine will only consider a set of cells on the tape. Thus, the natural choice of in-/output is $\Sigma^{<\mathrm{Ord}}$. Similarly to (a), it makes sense to consider $D = \Sigma^{(\mathrm{Ord})}$ in which case the discussion of Footnote 7 applies. The time relevant for Koepke computability is the class Ord of all ordinals. If $p \in \Sigma^{<\mathrm{Ord}}$, we say that a partial function $f : \Sigma^{<\mathrm{Ord}} \dashrightarrow \Sigma^{<\mathrm{Ord}}$ is *Koepke computable with parameter p* if the partial function $p * w \mapsto f(w)$ is Koepke computable. We shall prove in Proposition 4 that this notion is equivalent to the new notion introduced in line (d).

Table 1 (d). The notion of computability introduced in line (d), called *symmetric computability*, corrects the lack of symmetry for transfinite computability. In this model, time, space, and programs are all transfinite. The time relevant for symmetric computability is the class Ord of all ordinals.

5   Symmetric Machines

In Table 1, we defined the *model of symmetric computability* to be given by the set-sized transition function, set-sized programs, and the set-sized interpretation, using $\Sigma^{<\mathrm{Ord}}$ as input and output. We call the corresponding model of computation *symmetric machines*. In contrast to Hamkins-Kidder machines (which have considerably more time than space) and Koepke machines (whose programs are tiny compared to the time and space they have available), symmetric machines have set-sized time, space, and programs. They are the model of computability that systematically replaces the word "finite" in ordinary Turing computation with "set-sized".

Proposition 3. If $f : \Sigma^{<\mathrm{Ord}} \dashrightarrow \Sigma^{<\mathrm{Ord}}$ is a set, then f is symmetrically computable.

Proof sketch. Clearly, if $x \in \Sigma^{<\mathrm{Ord}}$, there is a set-sized program p that produces x upon empty input (just explicitly specify the values of x).

Since f is a set, find some ξ and $\Sigma^{(\xi)} := \{w \in \Sigma^{(\mathrm{Ord})} ; \operatorname{dom}(w) \subseteq \xi\}$ such that both $\operatorname{dom}(f) \subseteq \Sigma^{(\xi)}$ and $\operatorname{ran}(f) \subseteq \Sigma^{(\xi)}$. By AC, let g be a bijection between some ordinal λ and $\Sigma^{(\xi)}$. We define $x_f : \lambda \cdot \xi \cdot 2 \dashrightarrow \Sigma$ by letting $x_f(\alpha, \beta, 0) := g(\alpha)(\beta)$ and $x_f(\alpha, \beta, 1) := f(g(\alpha))(\beta)$.

Now find a program that writes x_f on the tape. Upon input $w \in \Sigma^{(\xi)}$, we can now determine $f(w)$ as follows: search through the 0-components of x_f until you find w; when you found w at index α, output $\{(\beta, x_f(\alpha, \beta, 1)) ; \beta < \xi\}$.   Q.E.D.

Proposition 4. A partial function $f : \Sigma^{<\mathrm{Ord}} \dashrightarrow \Sigma^{<\mathrm{Ord}}$ is symmetrically computable if and only if there is a $p \in \Sigma^{<\mathrm{Ord}}$ such that f is Koepke computable in parameter p.

Proof sketch. By Proposition 3, any parameter p is symmetrically computable.

Therefore, if f is Koepke computable in parameter p, it is symmetrically computable as follows: upon input w, first compute p, then $w * p$, then $f(p * w)$.

For the other direction, observe that in terms of hardware and interpretation, Koepke machines are just symmetric machines. Therefore, the universal Koepke machine is also a universal symmetric machine, i.e., there is a Koepke machine u such that for all set-sized programs p and all $w \in \Sigma^{<\mathrm{Ord}}$, we have

$$I_{\mathrm{s}}(T_{\mathrm{s}}, u)(p * w) = I_{\mathrm{s}}(T_{\mathrm{s}}, p)(w).$$

Thus, if a partial function f is symmetrically computed by a program p, it is Koepke computable with parameter p.   Q.E.D.

As usual, we can define the *halting problem* by

$$K := \{v * w \in \Sigma^{<\mathrm{Ord}} ; I_{\mathrm{s}}(T_{\mathrm{s}}, v)(w){\downarrow}\}$$

(where v is interpreted as a set-sized program). The usual proof shows that K is not symmetrically computable.

We shall now have a closer look at the symmetry properties for symmetric computability and ask whether it is the precise analogue of the symmetry exhibited by ordinary Turing computability. For ordinary Turing machines, time and space are indexed by natural numbers; however, programs and in-/output are not *prima facie* natural numbers; they are finite sequences of elements of a finite set, i.e., via some encoding elements of Σ^*. In this case, the symmetry is given by the fact that there is a computable encoding function that identifies Σ^* and ω. Via such an encoding, we can see all four different parameters of the model of computability as the same type of object.

In the case of symmetric computation, the word "finite" is systematically replaced by "set-sized". This means that both time and space are indexed by ordinals and programs and in-/outputs are (up to encoding) elements of $\Sigma^{<\mathrm{Ord}}$. Alas, in general, we cannot identify $\Sigma^{<\mathrm{Ord}}$ and Ord: The encodings between the classes Ord, $\mathrm{Ord}^{<\omega}$, Σ^{O}, and Σ^{FS} mentioned in Sect. 3 can be performed by Koepke machines (see, e.g., [13, Section 4]), but the class $\Sigma^{<\mathrm{Ord}}$ is a very different type of object: among other things, it contains the entire Cantor space (functions $f : \omega \to \Sigma$). As a consequence, any computable encoding of elements $\Sigma^{<\mathrm{Ord}}$ as ordinals would yield a computable wellordering of the reals and thus, the existence of such a class function cannot be proved without additional set theoretic assumptions.

6   The Symmetry Condition

We give definitions of the notions of *semidecidability* and *computable enumerability* within our abstract framework. For the model of ordinary Turing computability, these definitions coincide with the usual definitions.

Definition 5. Suppose that a model of computability is given by a transition function T, a class of programs P, and an interpretation I with domain class D. Let $A \subseteq D$ be a non-empty class and let ψ_A be a function such that $\psi_A(w) = \mathbf{0}$ if $w \in A$ and $\psi_A(w)\uparrow$ otherwise (the *pseudocharacteristic function*). Then A is called *semidecidable* if ψ_A is computable. Fixing some $\Omega \subseteq D$ representing the relevant time of the model, we say that A is *computably enumerable* if there is a program $p \in P$ such that $A = \{I(T,p)(w)\,;\, w \in \Omega\}$.

Theorem 6 (Folklore). For the model of ordinary Turing computability and any non-empty set $A \subseteq \Sigma^*$, the following hold:

  (i) the set A is semidecidable if and only if it is the range of a partial computable function $f : \Sigma^* \dashrightarrow \Sigma^*$ and
 (ii) the set A is computably enumerable if and only if it is semidecidable.

The equivalence (i) is a classical textbook argument [19, Theorem V]; in equivalence (ii), the forwards direction is a trivial consequence of (i) and the backwards direction uses the computable bijection between Σ^* and the relevant time ω. Therefore, adapting this proof to the case of symmetric computability will preserve the equivalence (i) and the forwards direction of (ii).

Theorem 7. For the model of symmetric computability and any non-empty class $A \subseteq \Sigma^{<\mathrm{Ord}}$, the following hold:

(i) the class A is semidecidable if and only if it is the range of a computable class function $f : \Sigma^{<\mathrm{Ord}} \dashrightarrow \Sigma^{<\mathrm{Ord}}$ and

(ii) if the class A is computably enumerable, then it is semidecidable.

In comparison to Theorem 6, the converse of (ii) is missing in Theorem 7; it turns out that this difference is crucial for our quest for the desired symmetry from Sect. 5. We write SC for the statement "the class $\Sigma^{<\mathrm{Ord}}$ is symmetrically computably enumerable", call this the *symmetry condition*, and note that it is a set theoretic sentence in the sense of Sect. 2.

Proposition 8. The symmetry condition SC is equivalent to the statement "every symmetrically semi-decidable class is symmetrically computably enumerable".

Proof sketch. Clearly, $\Sigma^{<\mathrm{Ord}}$ is semi-decidable whence "$\Leftarrow$" is obvious. For "$\Rightarrow$", let $g : \Sigma^{O} \to \Sigma^{<\mathrm{Ord}}$ be a computable enumeration and A be any semi-decidable class. By Theorem 7, we have a computable surjection $f : \Sigma^{<\mathrm{Ord}} \to A$. Then $f \circ g$ enumerates A. $\hfill$ Q.E.D.

The symmetry condition expresses that the classes $\Sigma^{<\mathrm{Ord}}$ and Ord can be identified via the computable listing provided by SC. Therefore, assuming SC, time, space, programs, and in-/outputs can be considered the same type of object, and the model of symmetric computability has the symmetry exhibited by ordinary Turing computability.

We shall now see that SC is independent from NBG and characterise under which circumstances SC holds. A crucial ingredient to prove our characterisation is the following result which is a straightforward relativisation of [13, Theorem 6.2].

Theorem 9 (Koepke). Let x be a set of ordinals. Then any $w \in \Sigma^{<\mathrm{Ord}}$ is in $L[x]$ if and only if there is a finite program p and $v \in \Sigma^{O}$ such that the Koepke computation of p with input v and parameter x halts and produces the output w.

Proof sketch. The backwards direction follows from the fact that a Koepke computation from a parameter x is absolutely defined. Thus, if a Koepke machine produces the output w upon input $x * v$, then w lies in every model containing both x and v. Since $v \in \Sigma^{O} \subseteq L[x]$, we have $w \in L[x]$. For the forwards direction, assume $w \in L[x]$ and let α be an exponentially closed ordinal such that $w \in L_{\alpha}[x]$. Then by [15, Theorem 7 (a)], w is α-Koepke computable, and thus Koepke computable from the parameter α, i.e., Koepke computable from a parameter in $\Sigma^{O} \subseteq \Sigma^{\mathrm{FS}}$. $\hfill$ Q.E.D.

Lemma 10. *If x is a set of ordinals and $\Sigma^{<\mathrm{Ord}} \subseteq L[x]$, then $V = L[x]$.*

Proof sketch. Assume that $\Sigma^{<\mathrm{Ord}} \subseteq L[x]$. Assume by contradiction that $V \neq L[x]$. Let A be an $\in$-minimal set not in $L[x]$, i.e., $A \notin L[x]$, but $A \subseteq L[x]$. There is a bijection $G : \mathrm{Ord} \to L[x]$ definable from x, (cf., e.g., [12, p. 193]). Define w with $\mathrm{ran}(w) \subseteq \{0\}$ such that $w(\alpha)\downarrow$ if and only if $G(\alpha) \in A$; then $w \in \Sigma^{<\mathrm{Ord}} \subseteq L[x]$. But then $A = \{G(\alpha) \in L[x]; w(\alpha)\downarrow\}$ and therefore $A \in L[x]$. $\hfill$ Q.E.D.

Theorem 11. The symmetry condition SC holds if and only if the universe is constructible from a set of ordinals.

Proof sketch. For the implication from right to left, use the (computable) Gödel pairing function to get a computable bijection $C : \Sigma^O \to \Sigma^O \times \Sigma^{FS}$ and identify the finite programs with Σ^{FS}. If $u \in \Sigma^O$, let $C(u) = (v, p)$, and let $F(u)$ be the result of running the finite program p on input v. By Theorem 9, F enumerates $\Sigma^{<Ord}$.

For the implication from left to right, assume SC. Let p be the program of the computable enumeration of $\Sigma^{<Ord}$ (which can be encoded as a set of ordinals). By Lemma 10, it is enough to show that $\Sigma^{<Ord} \subseteq L[p]$. But this follows from the fact that p defines a class surjection from Ord onto $\Sigma^{<Ord}$.   Q.E.D.

It follows from Theorems 2 & 11 that SC is independent from NBGC. We note that in the special case of V=L, Koepke computability and symmetric computability are equivalent (cf. [1, Exercise 3.9.7 (d)]); however, if we take any nonconstructible set of ordinals z, then $L[z]$ is a model of SC by Theorem 11, the set z is symmetrically computable (by Proposition 3), but not Koepke computable by Theorem 9 (letting $x = \varnothing$). Therefore, the two models of computability are different. This also answers [16, Question 5.12] about separating the stronger versions SC_κ ("$\Sigma^{<Ord}$ is computably enumerable by a program of size $<\kappa$"): e.g., if x is a non-constructible real, then $SC_{\aleph_1}$ holds in $L[x]$, but not $SC_{\aleph_0}$.

References

1. Carl, M.: Ordinal Computability. An Introduction to Infinitary Machines. De Gruyter Series in Logic and Its Applications, vol. 9. De Gruyter (2019)
2. Carl, M.: Space-bounded OTMs and REG$^\infty$. Computability **11**, 41–56 (2022)
3. Carl, M., Galeotti, L., Paßmann, R.: Realisability for infinitary intuitionistic set theory. Ann. Pure Appl. Log. **174**(6), 103259 (2023)
4. Carl, M., Löwe, B., Rin, B.G.: Koepke machines and satisfiability for infinitary propositional languages. In: Kari, J., Manea, F., Petre, I. (eds.) CiE 2017. LNCS, vol. 10307, pp. 187–197. Springer, Cham (2017). https://doi.org/10.1007/978-3-319-58741-7_19
5. Deolalikar, V., Hamkins, J.D., Schindler, R.: **P** ≠ **NP** ∩ **co-NP** for infinite time Turing machines. J. Log. Comput. **15**(5), 577–592 (2005)
6. Felgner, U.: Choice functions on sets and classes. In: Müller, G.H. (ed.) Sets and Classes: On The Work by Paul Bernays. Studies in Logic and the Foundations of Mathematics, vol. 84, pp. 217–255. Elsevier (1976)
7. Ferreirós, J.: Labyrinth of Thought: A History of Set Theory and Its Role in Modern Mathematics. Birkhäuser, Basel (2007)
8. Galeotti, L.: Surreal blum-shub-smale machines. In: Manea, F., Martin, B., Paulusma, D., Primiero, G. (eds.) CiE 2019. LNCS, vol. 11558, pp. 13–24. Springer, Cham (2019). https://doi.org/10.1007/978-3-030-22996-2_2
9. Hamkins, J.D., Lewis, A.: Infinite time Turing machines. J. Symb. Log. **65**(2), 567–604 (2000)
10. Hamkins, J.D., Seabold, D.E.: Infinite time Turing machines with only one tape. Math. Log. Q. **47**(2), 271–287 (2001)

11. Hamkins, J.D., Welch, P.D.: $\mathbf{P}^f \neq \mathbf{NP}^f$ for almost all f. Math. Log. Q. **49**(5), 536–540 (2003)

12. Jech, T.S.: Set Theory. Springer Monographs in Mathematics, 3rd millenium edn. Springer, Heidelberg (2003). https://doi.org/10.1007/3-540-44761-X

13. Koepke, P.: Turing computations on ordinals. Bull. Symb. Log. **11**(3), 377–397 (2005)

14. Koepke, P.: Ordinal computability. In: Ambos-Spies, K., Löwe, B., Merkle, W. (eds.) CiE 2009. LNCS, vol. 5635, pp. 280–289. Springer, Heidelberg (2009). https://doi.org/10.1007/978-3-642-03073-4_29

15. Koepke, P., Seyfferth, B.: Ordinal machines and admissible recursion theory. Ann. Pure Appl. Log. **160**(3), 310–318 (2009)

16. Lewis, E.S.: Computation with infinite programs. Master's thesis, Universiteit van Amsterdam (2018). ILLC Publications MoL-2018-14

17. Löwe, B.: Space bounds for infinitary computation. In: Beckmann, A., Berger, U., Löwe, B., Tucker, J.V. (eds.) CiE 2006. LNCS, vol. 3988, pp. 319–329. Springer, Heidelberg (2006). https://doi.org/10.1007/11780342_34

18. Mendelson, E.: Introduction to Mathematical Logic. Textbooks in Mathematics, 6 edn. CRC Press (2015)

19. Rogers, H.: Theory of Recursive Functions and Effective Computability. MIT Press (1987)

20. Schindler, R., $\mathbf{P} \neq \mathbf{NP}$ for infinite time Turing machines. Monatsh. Math. **139**, 335–340 (2003)

21. Turing, A.M.: On computable numbers, with an application to the Entscheidungsproblem. Proc. Lond. Math. Soc. **42**, 230–265 (1937)

22. Welch, P.D.: Characteristics of discrete transfinite time Turing machine models: halting times, stabilization times, and normal form theorems. Theor. Comput. Sci. **410**, 426–442 (2009)

23. Winter, J.: Space complexity in infinite time Turing machines. Master's thesis, Universiteit van Amsterdam (2007). ILLC Publications MoL-2007-14

24. Winter, J.: Is $\mathbf{P} = \mathbf{PSPACE}$ for infinite time Turing machines? In: Archibald, M., Brattka, V., Goranko, V., Löwe, B. (eds.) ILC 2007. LNCS (LNAI), vol. 5489, pp. 126–137. Springer, Heidelberg (2009). https://doi.org/10.1007/978-3-642-03092-5_10

All Melodies Are Lost – Recognizability for Weak and Strong α-Register Machines

Merlin Carl[(✉)]

Europa-Universität Flensburg, Flensburg, Germany
merlin.carl@uni-flensburg.de

Abstract. For exponentially closed ordinals α, we consider recognizability of constructible subsets of α for weak and strong α-register machines (α-(w)ITRMs) with parameters and their distribution in the constructible hierarchy. In particular, we show that, for class many values of α, the sets of α-wITRM-computable and α-wITRM-recognizable subsets of α are both non-empty, but disjoint, and, also for class many values of α, the set of α-wITRM-recognizable subsets of α is empty. (We thank our three anonymous referees for their valuable comments.)

Keywords: Ordinal Computability · Infinite Time Register Machines · Recognizability · Definability · Constructibility

1 Introduction

Associated with each model of computation are a concept of explicit definability – called computability – which concerns the ability of the machine to produce a certain object "from scratch", and another one of implicit definability, which concerns the ability of the machine to decide whether or not an object given in the oracle is equal to a certain x; in ordinal computability, the latter is known as "recognizability". For many models of ordinal computability, the "lost melody phenomenon" occurs, which means that there are objects which are recognizable, but not computable; this phenomenon was first discovered (and named) for Infinite Time Turing machines in Hamkins and Lewis [12]. Recognizability has been studied in detail for ITTMs and Koepke's weak and strong Infinite Time Register Machines ((w)ITRMs) in [6–8,12] and for Ordinal Turing Machines (OTMs) in [4]. In [6], we considered recognizability by α-ITRMs. All of these works concerned real numbers, i.e., subsets of ω. This has the advantage that the recognizability strength of different models becomes comparable.

However, the natural domain of computation for α-(w)ITRMs are clearly subsets of α, not just subsets of ω. (By analogy, the computability strength of these models is studied in terms of subsets of α, not of ω.) Since, for some models of transfinite computability, already the recognizable subsets of ω can, depending on the set-theoretic background, go far beyond L (see [4]), it is hardly surprising that the same happens in the more general case. However, interesting phenomena also arise under the assumption $V = L$. This paper studies the recognizability

G. Della Vedova et al. (Eds.): CiE 2023, LNCS 13967, pp. 77–88, 2023.
https://doi.org/10.1007/978-3-031-36978-0_7

strength of weak and strong α-register machines with respect to constructible subsets of α. While α-ITRMs behave rather similarly to ITRMs, α-wITRMs show a rather interesting behaviour. In particular, while the computable sets are included in the recognizable sets for all models studied so far, we will below show that, for class many values of α, the sets of α-wITRM-computable and α-wITRM-recognizable subsets of α are both non-empty and disjoint, while for other values of α, the set of α-wITRM-recognizable subsets of α is empty.

2 Preliminaries

In the following, α will denote an exponentially closed ordinal, unless explicitly stated otherwise. We briefly describe α-ITRMs and α-wITRMs, which were originally introduced by Koepke in [15]; full definitions can also be found in [3].

α-register machines use some $k \in \omega$ many registers for storing one ordinal strictly less than α each. Programs for α-(w)ITRMs are just programs for classical register machines as introduced in Cutland [10]. When we write something like "α-wITRM-program", we really mean that the program is intended to be run on an α-wITRM. Oracles for α-register machines are subsets x of α. Given a register index $j \in \omega$, the oracle command $O(j)$ takes the content of the j-th register, say ι, and then writes 1 to the jth register when $\iota \in x$ and otherwise 0.

Infinitary register computations are now defined by recursion along the ordinals, carrying out commands at successor stages and taking inferior limits at limit stages both for register contents and the active program line.

A difficulty arises when this limit is equal to α, and this can be solved in two ways: Either one regards the computation as undefined, thus obtaining "weak" or "unresetting" α-register machines, called α-wITRMs, or one resets the contents of the overflowing registers to 0, which yields "resetting" or "strong" α-register machines, called α-ITRMs. An important standard observation about α-(w)ITRM-computations is the following:

Definition 1. *In an α-(w)ITRM-computation, a "strong loop" is a pair (ι, ξ) of ordinals such that the computation states – i.e., the active program line and the register contents – at times ι and ξ are identical and such that, for every time in between, the computation states were in each component greater than or equal to these states.*

It is easy to see from the liminf-rule that a strong loop will be repeated forever.

Theorem 1 (Cf. [3], generalizing [16], Lemma 3). *An α-ITRM-program either halts or runs into a strong loop. An α-wITRM-program either halts, runs into a strong loop or is undefined due to a register overflow.*

We denote by χ_x the characteristic function of a set $x \subseteq \alpha$.

Definition 2. *A set $x \subseteq \alpha$ is α-(w)ITRM-computable if and only if there is an α-(w)ITRM-program P such that, for each $\iota < \alpha$, $P(\iota) \downarrow = \chi_x(\iota)$.*

Definition 3. *1. For $X \subseteq \mathfrak{P}(\alpha)$, let us denote by χ_X the characteristic function of X in $\mathfrak{P}(\alpha)$.*

2. A set $X \subseteq \mathfrak{P}(\alpha)$ is α-(w)ITRM-semi-decidable if and only if there are an α-(w)ITRM-program P and some $\xi < \alpha$ such that, for all $y \subseteq \alpha$, $P^y(\xi) \downarrow$ if and only if $y \in X$. In the case of α-wITRMs, we demand that the computations $P^y(\xi)$ for $y \notin X$ do not halt, but are still defined.

3. X is called α-(w)ITRM-co-semi-decidable if and only if $\mathfrak{P}(\alpha) \setminus X$ is α-(w)ITRM-semi-decidable.

4. If X is both α-(w)ITRM-semi-decidable and α-(w)ITRM-co-semi-decidable, i.e., if there is an α-(w)ITRM-program P and some $\xi < \alpha$ such that $P^y(\xi) \downarrow = \chi_X(y)$ for all $y \subseteq \alpha$, we call X α-(w)ITRM-decidable.

5. If there are an α-wITRM-program P and some $\xi < \alpha$ such that $P^y(\xi) \downarrow$ for all $y \in X$ and, for all $y \notin X$, $P^y(\xi)$ is either undefined or diverges, we call X "weakly α-wITRM-semi-decidable". The concept of weak α-wITRM-co-semidecidability and of α-wITRM-decidability are now defined in the obvious way.

Definition 4. *Let $x \subseteq \alpha$.*

1. x is called α-(w)ITRM-recognizable if and only if $\{x\}$ is α-(w)ITRM-decidable.

2. x is called α-(w)ITRM-semirecognizable if and only if $\{x\}$ is α-(w)ITRM-semidecidable.

3. x is called α-(w)ITRM-cosemirecognizable if and only if $\{x\}$ is α-(w)ITRM-co-semi-decidable.

The weak versions of α-wITRM-semirecognizability and α-wITRM-co-semi-recognizability are defined in the obvious way.[1]

We fix a standard convenient encoding of sets as subsets of α (cf, e.g., [5] or [3], Def. 2.3.18):

Definition 5. *Let α be exponentially closed, X a transitive set with $\alpha \subseteq X$, and let $f : \alpha \to X$ be bijective such that, for all $\iota < \alpha$, we have $f(\omega\iota) = \iota$. Then $c_f(X, \in) := \{p(\iota, \xi) : \iota, \xi < \alpha \wedge f(\iota) E f(\xi)\}$ is called a "nice" α-code for X, where p is the Cantor pairing function for ordinals.*

When proving that certain subsets of α are not computable, it is often convenient to recall from the folklore that, by a straightforward diagonalization argument, no L-level can contain a nice code for itself:

Lemma 1. *Let $\beta < \alpha$. Then L_α does not contain a nice β-code for L_α.*

We recall a standard definition and two observations.

Definition 6. *For $\alpha \in \text{On}$, σ_α is the first stable ordinal above α, that is, the smallest ordinal $\beta > \alpha$ such that $L_\beta \prec_{\Sigma_1} L$.*

---

[1] For ITRMs, it is known that decidability, semidecidability and co-semi-decidability, and hence also recognizability, semirecognizability and cosemirecognizability coincide. However, we do not know this for α-ITRMs.

Lemma 2. *1. For an ordinal α, σ_α is the supremum of all ordinals β such that, for some $\in$-formula ϕ and some $\xi < \alpha$, β is minimal with the property $L_\beta \models \phi(\xi)$.*
2. If α and β are ordinals such that $\beta \in [\alpha, \sigma_\alpha)$, then $\sigma_\beta = \sigma_\alpha$.

Proof. (1) is a variant of Theorem 7.8 of Barwise [1], (2) follows easily by fine-structure.

Definition 7. *(Cf. [3], p. 34) An ordinal α is called α-(w)ITRM-singular if and only if there are an α-(w)ITRM-program P and an ordinal $\xi < \alpha$ such that, for some $\beta < \alpha$, P computes a cofinal function $f : \beta \to \alpha$ in the parameter ξ.*

We will make use of the following result of Boolos:

Lemma 3. *([2], Theorem 1') There is a parameter-free $\in$-formula ϕ such that, for a transitive set X, we have $X \models \phi$ if and only if X is of the form L_α for some ordinal α. We will call this sentence "I am an L-level" from now on.*

3 α-ITRMs

In this section, we will consider recognizability of subsets of α for α-ITRMs. In particular, we will prove that lost melodies exist for all exponentially closed α.
We recall the following theorem from [5].[2]

Theorem 2. *For every α, there is an ordinal $\gamma =: \beta(\alpha)$ such that $x \subseteq \alpha$ is α-ITRM-computable if and only if $x \in L_\gamma$. Moreover, γ is smaller than the next Σ_2-admissible ordinal after α. If $L_\alpha \models ZF^-$, then $\gamma = \alpha + 1$.*

It was shown in [5] that, for α ITRM-singular, there is a lost melody for α-ITRMs, namely the halting set (encoded as a subset of α). We start by showing that the extra condition is in fact unnecessary and that there are constructible lost melodies for all exponentially closed ordinals α.[3]

Lemma 4. *Let α be exponentially closed.*

1. *If α is not a regular cardinal in L, then there are a constructible set $s \subseteq \alpha$ and a program $P_{\alpha-WO}$ such that, for all $x \subseteq \alpha$, $P_{\alpha-WO}^{x \oplus s} \downarrow = 1$ if and only if x codes a well-ordering, and otherwise, $P_{\alpha-WO}^{x \oplus s} \downarrow = 0$.*
2. *([3], Exercise 2.3.26) If $\alpha = \omega$ or $cf^V(\alpha) > \omega$, then there is such a program $P_{\alpha-WO}$ that works in the empty oracle.*

---

[2] ZF^- denotes Zermelo-Fraenkel set theory without the power set axiom; see [11] for a discussion of the axiomatizations. An ordinal α is Σ_2-admissible if and only if $L_\alpha \models \Sigma_2$-KP.

[3] The condition of exponential closure is a technical convenience; it allows us, for example, to carry out halting algorithms after each other or run nested loops of algorithms without caring for possible register overflows. We conjecture that dropping this condition would not substantially change most of the results, but merely lead to more cumbersome arguments.

We also recall the following generalization of results by Koepke and Seyfferth [17], which is Theorem 2.3.28(iii) of [3].

Lemma 5. *For every exponentially closed α and any $n \in \omega$, there are $s \subseteq \alpha$ and an α-ITRM-program $P_{\alpha-ntruth}$ such that, for every formula ϕ that starts with n quantifier alternations, followed by a quantifier-free formula and every $x \subseteq \alpha$, $P_{\alpha-ntruth}^{x \oplus s}(\phi, x) \downarrow = 1$ if and only if ϕ holds in the structure coded by x, and otherwise, $P_{\alpha-ntruth}^{x \oplus s} \downarrow = 0$.*

Theorem 3. *For every exponentially closed α, there is a lost melody for α-ITRMs, i.e., a set $x \subseteq \alpha$ such that x is α-ITRM-recognizable, but not α-ITRM-computable.*

Proof. By Theorem 2, every α-ITRM-computable $x \subseteq \alpha$ will be an element of $L_{\beta(\alpha)}$. It thus suffices to find a recognizable subset of α that is not contained in $L_{\beta(\alpha)}$. To this end, we define a (particularly) nice α-code c for an L-level L_β with $\beta \geq \beta(\alpha)$ and then use Lemma 1.

We split the proof into two cases, depending on whether or not α is a regular cardinal in L.

Case 1: α *is not a regular cardinal in L.*

Recall from Theorem 2 that $\beta(\alpha) < \delta$, where δ is the smallest Σ_2-admissible ordinal strictly larger than α. We consider the $<_L$-minimal nice α-code c for L_δ in which additionally α is coded by 1. By fine-structure, L_δ is the Σ_2-Skolem hull of $\alpha + 1$ in itself, so a bijection $f : \alpha \to L_\delta$ is definable over L_δ and thus, we have $c \in L_{\delta+1}$. This means that $c = \{\iota < \alpha : L_\delta \models \phi(\rho, \iota)\}$ for some $\rho < \delta$ and some $\in$-formula ϕ; pick ρ minimal with this property. In c, let ρ be coded by $\rho' < \alpha$. By Lemma 1, we have $c \notin L_\delta$, and thus, c is not α-ITRM-computable.

We claim that c is α-ITRM-recognizable in the parameter ρ'. To see this, let $x \subseteq \alpha$ be given in the oracle; we need to determine whether $x = c$.

We can check as in Case 2 below that, in x, each $\iota < \alpha$ is coded by $\omega\iota$ while 1 codes α. By Lemma 4, we can check whether x codes a well-founded structure (X, E). By Lemma 5, we can check whether (X, E) is a model of "I am an L-level" and of Σ_2-collection. If any of these checks fails, we halt with output 0. Otherwise, we know that x codes a Σ_2-admissible L-level L_γ with $\gamma > \alpha$, i.e., $\gamma \geq \delta$.

To see whether $\gamma = \delta$, we again use the algorithm from Lemma 5 to check whether (X, E) contains a Σ_2-admissible L-level L_ξ with $\xi > \alpha$. If so, we have $\gamma > \delta$ and halt with output 0. Otherwise, we know that x codes L_δ, and it remains to see that x is the "right" code. By searching through α, we can check if ρ' codes an ordinal ξ in the sense of x and whether ξ is minimal such that $\{\iota < \alpha : L_\delta \models \phi(\iota, \xi)\}$ has these properties; if not, we halt with output 0. Otherwise, we use Lemma 5 once more to run though α and check, for every $\iota < \alpha$, whether $\iota \in x$ holds if and only if $L_\delta \models \phi(\iota, \rho)$ (recall that, at this point, we are guaranteed that L_δ is coded by c and we also know that, in x, ρ is coded by ρ'). If this is the case, we halt with output 1; otherwise, we halt with output 0.

Case 2:[4] α is a regular cardinal in L. In this case, we have $L_\alpha \models \text{ZF}^-$, and so it follows from Theorem 2 that the α-ITRM-computable subsets of α are exactly those in $L_{\alpha+1}$. By Lemma 1, it suffices to show that there is an α-ITRM-recognizable nice α-code for $L_{\alpha+1}$. Let c be the $<_L$-minimal nice α-code for $L_{\alpha+1}$ in which additionally α is coded by 1. It is not hard to see that such a code occurs in $L_{\alpha+2}$ and is thus definable over $L_{\alpha+1}$, say by the formula ϕ in the parameter $\rho < \alpha$.[5] Let $f : \alpha \to L_{\alpha+1}$ be the corresponding bijection (so that $f(\omega\rho) = \rho$). We claim that c is α-ITRM-recognizable in the parameter $\zeta := \omega\rho$.

To see this, let $d \subseteq \alpha$ be given in the oracle. We start by checking whether, for each $\iota < \alpha$, we have $p(\xi, \omega\iota) \in d$ if and only if ξ is of the form $\omega\xi'$ with $\xi' < \iota$, which is easily done by searching through α. If not, we halt with output 0. Otherwise, we know that $\omega\iota$ codes ι, for $\iota < \alpha$. Next, we check whether $p(\xi, 1) \in d$ if and only if ξ is of the form $\omega\xi'$ with $\xi' < \alpha$, which is again easy. If not, we halt with output 0; otherwise, we know that 1 codes α.

Using bounded truth predicate evaluation from Lemma 5, we can now run through α and check, for each $\iota < \alpha$, whether the $\in$-structure coded by d believes that ι codes an ordinal if and only if ι is either 1 or a limit ordinal. If not, we halt with output 0; otherwise, we know that the set of ordinals coded by d is equal to $\alpha + 1$.

Again using bounded truth predicate evaluation, we check whether the structure coded by d is a model of the sentence "I am an L-level". If not, we halt with output 0. Otherwise, we know that d codes $L_{\alpha+1}$, and it remains to check that d is the "right" code.

Running through α and using ζ and bounded truth predicate evaluation once more, we can now check, for each $\iota < \alpha$, whether $L_\alpha \models \phi(\rho, \iota)$ if and only if $\iota \in d$. If not, we halt with output 0. Otherwise, we have $d = c$, and we halt with output 1.

Definition 8. *Denote by $\rho(\alpha)$ the supremum of the set of ordinals β for which $L_{\beta+1} \setminus L_\beta$ contains an α-ITRM-recognizable subset of α. Similarly, we write $\rho^w(\alpha)$ for the analogous concept for α-wITRMs.*

Moreover, denote by $\theta(\alpha)$ and $\theta^w(\alpha)$ the suprema of ordinals with an α-ITRM-computable and an α-wITRM-computable α-code, respectively.

Remark 1. It was shown in [5] that $\theta(\alpha) = \beta(\alpha)$ if and only if $L_\alpha \not\models \text{ZF}^-$.

The only property of $\alpha + 1$ used in the argument for the existence of a recognizable nice α-code for $L_{\alpha+1}$ is the existence of an α-ITRM-computable α-code for it. The same argument hence yields:

Corollary 1. *If β has an α-ITRM-computable α-code, then L_β has an α-ITRM-recognizable α-code. In particular, we have $\rho(\alpha) \geq \theta(\alpha)$.*

---

[4] This case uses ideas similar to those used for proving the lost melody theorem for infinite time Blum-Shub-Smale machines, see [9].
[5] Note that α itself is definable in $L_{\alpha+1}$ without parameters.

It is shown in [6] that $\rho^w(\omega) = \beta^w(\omega)$. We currently do not know whether $\rho(\alpha) = \beta(\alpha)$ for any exponentially closed α (it is known to be false for $\alpha = \omega$). However, we can also get more precise information about their distribution:[6]

Theorem 4. *Let α be exponentially closed and not a regular cardinal in L.*

1. *(Cf. [7], Theorem 27(i)) The constructible α-ITRM-recognizable subsets of α are contained in L_{σ_α}.*
2. *(Cf. [7], Theorem 27(ii)) σ_α is minimal with this property. Thus $\rho(\alpha) = \sigma_\alpha$.*
3. *(Cf. [7], Theorem 27(iii)) For any $\delta < \sigma_\alpha$, there is a "gap" of length $\geq \delta$ in the α-ITRM-recognizables; that is, there are ordinals β, γ, η such that $\beta + \delta \leq \gamma < \eta$, $L_\gamma \setminus L_\beta$ contains no α-ITRM-recognizable subsets of α, $L_\eta \setminus L_\gamma$ does contain an α-ITRM-recognizable subset of α, and for cofinally in γ many ξ, we have $(L_{\xi+1} \setminus L_\xi) \cap \mathfrak{P}(\alpha) \neq \emptyset$ (we will call such an ordinal ξ an α-index).*

Proof. The proofs are adaptations of those given for ITRMs in [7].

1. Let P be an α-ITRM-program that recognizes a constructible set $X \subseteq \alpha$ in the parameter $\zeta < \alpha$. The statement "There is $Y \subseteq \alpha$ such that $P^Y(\zeta) \downarrow = 1$" is Σ_1 in the parameters ζ and α. Let us write this statement as $\exists x, c\phi(x, c)$, where $\phi(x, c)$ is the Δ_0-statement "c is a halting computation of P in the oracle x with output 1". By assumption, this statement is true in L. Thus, by definition of $\sigma_{\alpha+1}$, it holds in $L_{\sigma_{\alpha+1}}$. So there are $x, c \in L_{\sigma_{\alpha+1}}$ such that $\phi(x, c)$. Since computations are absolute between transitive $\in$-structures, c is actually such a computation, so we must have $x = X$, so that $X \in L_{\sigma_{\alpha+1}}$. By Lemma 2(2), we have $\sigma_\alpha = \sigma_{\alpha+1}$, so $X \in L_{\sigma_\alpha}$.
2. Let $\beta < \sigma_\alpha$. We will show that there is an α-ITRM-recognizable subset of α that is not contained in L_β. To this end, pick, by definition of L_{σ_α}, an ordinal $\gamma \in (\beta, \sigma_\alpha)$ such that, for some Σ_1-statement $\phi(\rho)$ with parameter $\rho \in \alpha$, we have $L_\gamma \models \phi(\rho)$ and γ is minimal with this property. By acceptability of the L-hierarchy (cf. Boolos, [2], p. 147), $L_{\gamma+1}$ then contains an α-code for L_γ. It is then not hard to see that $L_{\gamma+1}$ also contains a nice α-code for L_γ. Let c be the $<_L$-minimal nice α-code for L_γ. Using the ability of α-ITRMs for ITRM-singular α to check α-codes for well-foundedness and to evaluate truth predicates in structures encoded by such codes, one can now imitate the argument for Theorem 3 above to see that c is α-ITRM-recognizable.
3. Pick $\beta > \sigma_\alpha$, along with a limit λ of α-indices greater than $\beta + \delta$ which is at the same time Σ_2-admissible. Then L_λ is a model of the statement $\psi(\alpha, \delta)$, which is "There is an ordinal β such that $\beta + \delta$ exists and all α-ITRM-recognizable subsets of α are contained in L_β", and also of "There are cofinally many α-indices". Thus, the statement that there exists an L-level with these properties is true in L; moreover, it is easily seen to be Σ_1 in the parameters α and δ. Consequently, it will be true in $L_{\sigma_{\alpha+1}}$, and hence in L_{σ_α}. Hence, there is a Σ_2-admissible ordinal $\lambda \in L_{\sigma_\alpha}$ which is a limit of α-indices and believes $\psi(\alpha, \delta)$. Pick a witness β for this statement. Assume

---

[6] The following results are analogues for ITRM-singular α of results obtained in [7] for $\alpha = \omega$.

for a contradiction that some element X of $(L_\lambda \setminus L_\beta) \cap \mathfrak{P}(\alpha)$ is α-ITRM-recognizable, say by the program P. It follows from [5], Theorem 46 by the Σ_2-admissibility of λ that P^Y will either halt or run into a strong loop by time λ for all $Y \in L_\lambda \cap \mathfrak{P}(\alpha)$. If the latter option were true for any such Y, then P^Y would actually be looping and hence P could not recognize X. Thus P^Y halts in less than λ many steps for all $Y \in L_\lambda$. Since L_λ does not believe X to be recognizable by P, we either must have $P^X \downarrow = 0$ or $P^Y \downarrow = 1$ for some $Y \in L_\lambda \cap \mathfrak{P}(\alpha)$ different from X. But both options contradict the assumption that P recognizes X by absoluteness of computations.

The Jensen-Karp-theorem ([13], section 5) states that Σ_1-statements are absolute between V_α and L_α when α is a limit or admissible ordinals. From this, and the fact that $\beta^x(\omega) = \omega_\omega^{\mathrm{CK},x}$ for all $x \subseteq \omega$ (Koepke, [15]) one obtains that, when x is ω-ITRM-recognizable, then $x \in L_{\omega_\omega^{\mathrm{CK},x}}$ ([8]). It is then natural to ask whether we have in general that $x \in L_{\beta^x(\alpha)}$ when $x \subseteq \alpha$ is α-ITRM-recognizable. We note here that Theorem 4 implies this to be false:

Corollary 2. *If α is a regular cardinal in V, then there are α-ITRM-recognizable constructible sets $x \subseteq \alpha$ such that $x \notin L_{\beta^x(\alpha)}$.*

Proof. By [3], Corollary 3.4.15, we have $\beta^x(\alpha) = \alpha^\omega$ when α is a regular cardinal. On the other hand, by Theorem 4(2), there are cofinally in σ_α many γ such that $L_{\gamma+1} \setminus L_\gamma$ contains an α-ITRM-recognizable subsets of α, while, clearly, $\sigma_\alpha > \alpha^\omega$.

4 α-WITRMs

We now consider recognizability for unresetting α-register machines.

A convenient feature of α-ITRMs is their ability to "search through α", i.e., count upwards in some register from 0 on until it overflows, thus making it possible to check each element of α for a certain property. For unresetting machines, this obvious strategy is not available: Counting upwards in some register would lead to an overflow of that register at time α, which results in the computation being undefined. In some cases, however, such a search is still possible. This motivates the next definition.

Definition 9. *An ordinal α is wITRM-searchable if and only if there is a halting α-wITRM-program P such that the first register used by P contains each element of α at least once before P stops. If such a program exists in the oracle $x \subseteq \alpha$, we call α wITRM-searchable in x.*

Based on the results in [5], we can give a full characterization of the wITRM-searchable ordinals. To this end, we recall from [[5], Definition 53] that an ordinal is called "u-weak" if and only if any halting α-wITRM in the empty input halts in less than α many steps. By [5], Theorem 46, all Π_3-reflecting ordinals (and hence, in particular, all Σ_2-admissible ordinals) are u-weak. Moreover, the following was proved in [5]:

Theorem 5 ([5], Theorem 54 and 56). *An ordinal is u-weak if and only if it is admissible and not wITRM-singular.*

Lemma 6. *An ordinal α is wITRM-searchable if and only if it is not u-weak.*

Proof. Suppose first that α is wITRM-searchable, and let P be an α-wITRM-program that halts after writing each element of α to the first register R_1 at least once. Consider the slightly modified program P' that runs P but, whenever the content of R_1 changes, uses a separate register to count from 0 upwards to the content of R_1. Clearly, P' will run for at least α many steps before halting, so that α is not u-weak.

On the other hand, suppose that α is not u-weak. Thus, α is not admissible or wITRM-singular. In the latter case, it is immediate from the definition of wITRM-singularity that there is an α-wITRM-computable cofinal function $f :$ $\beta \to \alpha$ for some $\beta < \alpha$, in the former case, this is shown in [[5], Theorem 56]. For simplicity, let us assume without loss of generality that f is increasing. Consider the following algorithm, which works in the parameter β: Use some register R_2 to run through β. For each $\iota < \beta$, compute $f(\iota)$ and $f(\iota + 1)$ and store them in R_3 and R_4. Copy the content of R_3 to R_1 and use R_1 to count upwards until one reaches the content of R_4. After that, reset the contents of R_1, R_3 and R_4 to 0 and increase the content of R_2 by 1. If R_2 contains β, halt. It is easy to see that, in this way, R_1 will contain every ordinal less than α at least once before halting.

It was shown in [6], Corollary 9 (see also [3], Corollary 4.2.20) to follow from Kreisel's basis theorem that there are no lost melodies for ω-wITRMs.

If α is an uncountable regular cardinal in L, then the lost melody theorem fails for α-wITRMs for rather drastic reasons:[7]

Corollary 3. *1. If α is u-weak, then no α-wITRM-computable subset of α is α-wITRM-recognizable.*
2. If α is a regular cardinal in L, then there are no constructible α-wITRM-recognizable subsets of α.

Proof. 1. Suppose for a contradiction that α is u-weak and that $L \ni x \subseteq \alpha$ is recognized by the α-wITRM-program P in the parameter $\rho < \alpha$. In particular, this means that P^x halts in $\tau < \alpha$ many steps. Since the basic command set for α-wITRMs allows a register content to increase at most by 1 in each step, all register contents generated by P during this computation will be smaller than $\rho + \tau$. Since α is indecomposable, we have $\rho + \tau < \alpha$. In particular, the oracle command can only be applied to the first $\rho + \tau$ many bits of x. Consequently, if we flip the $(\rho + \tau + 1)$th bit of x to obtain $\tilde{x}$, we shall have $P^{\tilde{x}}(\rho) \downarrow = 1$ and $\tilde{x} \neq x$, contradicting the assumption that P recognizes x in the parameter ρ.

---

[7] This will be further generalized in Lemma 9 below.

2. If α is a regular cardinal in L, then it is in particular Σ_2^x-admissible for any constructible set $x \subseteq \alpha$. It is shown in [[3], Lemma 3.4.10(ii)] that this implies that, for every $x \subseteq \alpha$ and any α-wITRM-program P, P^x will either halt in $< \alpha$ many steps or not at all. Now argue as for (1).

We recall some results from [3], which in turn are generalizations of results from Koepke [14] (pp. 261f).

Lemma 7. *(Cf. [3], pp. 40–41, generalizing [14], p. 261f.) Let α be exponentially closed, $\beta < \alpha$ and c a nice β-code for a (transitive) $\in$-structure $S \supseteq \alpha$ via some bijection $f : \beta \to S$.*

Then there is an α-wITRM-program P_{decode} such that, for every $\iota < \beta$ such that $f(\omega\iota) \in \alpha$, $P_{decode}^c(\omega\iota, \beta)$ halts with output $f(\omega\iota)$, i.e., with output ι.

Lemma 8. *Let α be an exponentially closed ordinal such that, for some $\beta > \omega$, we have $\beta < \alpha < \sigma_\beta$. Then there is a lost melody for α-wITRMs.*

Proof. By Lemma 2(2), we have $\sigma_\alpha = \sigma_\beta$.

The statement "There is an ordinal τ such that every α-wITRM-program in every parameter $\rho < \alpha$ either halts, loops or overflows by time τ" is Σ_1 (since computations of length $< \tau$ are contained in L_τ) and thus, since such τ exists, it is $< \sigma_\alpha$.

By fine-structure, L_{σ_β} contains a bijection $f : \beta \to \alpha$. Pick $\gamma \in (\tau, \sigma_\beta)$ such that $f \in L_\gamma$, and for some $\rho \in \beta$ and some $\in$-formula ϕ, γ is minimal with the property $L_\gamma \models \phi(\rho)$. Let c be the $<_L$-minimal nice β-code for L_γ and let $\iota < \beta$ be the ordinal that codes f in the sense of c. By the techniques discussed in section 3, c is β-ITRM-recognizable in the parameter ρ.

We claim that c is α-wITRM-recognizable (as a subset of α) in the parameters β, ρ and ι. Thus, let a set $d \subseteq \alpha$ be given in the oracle.

First, use the parameter β to simulate a β-ITRM-program that recognizes c (as a subset of β) on an α-wITRM and run this program on $d \cap \beta$. If the program returns 0, we halt with output 0.

Otherwise, we know that the first β many bits of d are correct and it remains to check that d contains no elements that are greater than or equal to β.

Using the parameter ι and the program P_{decode} from Lemma 7, we can compute the bijection $f : \beta \to \alpha$ as follows: Given $\xi < \beta$, search through c to find the (unique) element of the form $p(p(\omega\xi, \zeta), \iota)$. Then run $P_{decode}^c(\zeta, \beta)$.

Using f, we can now run through β and check, for every $\xi \in \beta$, whether $f(\xi) \geq \beta$ and whether $f(\xi) \in c$. If the answer is positive for some $\xi \in \beta$, we halt with output 0. Otherwise, we halt with output 1.

We note the following amusing consequence which yields examples of a definability concept for which the sets of explicitly and implicitly definable objects are disjoint:

Corollary 4. *If α is Π_3-reflecting and $\alpha \in (\beta, \sigma_\beta)$ for some ordinal β,[8] then the set of α-wITRM-computable subsets of α and the set of constructible α-wITRM-recognizable subsets of α are (both non-empty, but) disjoint.*

---

[8] Note that, for example, the first Π_3-reflecting ordinal has this property.

Proof. Immediate from Lemma 8 and Corollary 3.[9]

It thus remains to consider the cases where α is of the form σ_β (note that limits of stable ordinals are themselves stable, see, e.g., [1], Corollary 7.9) (which generalizes the case of regular cardinals in L).

Lemma 9. *If α is of the form σ_β for some ordinal β, then there are no α-wITRM-recognizable constructible subsets of α (and thus no lost melodies for α-wITRMs).*

Proof. Let us first assume that $\alpha = \sigma_\beta$ for some $\beta \in$ On. Suppose for a contradiction that $x \subseteq \alpha$ is α-wITRM-recognizable by the program P in the parameter $\rho < \alpha$. Thus, L believes that there are a set $x \subseteq \alpha$ and a halting α-wITRM-computation of $P^x(\rho)$ with output 1. In particular, L believes that there are a set $x \subseteq$ On and a halting ORM-computation of $P^x(\rho)$ with output 1, which is a Σ_1-formula in the parameter ρ. By definition of σ_β, and the fact that $\rho \in L_{\rho_\beta}$ (see Lemma 2(2) above), the same holds in L_{σ_β}. Since computations are absolute between transitive $\in$-structures, L_{σ_β} contains a set x of ordinals and a halting ORM-computation P^x with output 1. Let δ be the length of this computation. Then $\delta < \alpha$. Consequently, this computation cannot generate register contents $\geq \alpha$ and is thus actually a σ-wITRM-computation. During this computation, at most the first δ many bits of x can be considered. It follows that both $P^{(x \cap \delta)}(\rho)$ and $P^{(x \cap \delta) \cup (\delta+1)}(\rho)$ halt in δ many steps with output 1 without generating register contents $\geq \alpha$; thus, we have found two different oracles y for which the α-wITRM-computation $P^y(\rho)$ halts with output 1, a contradiction to the assumption that P recognizes x in the oracle y. If α is a limit of ordinals of the form σ_β, pick $\beta \in$ On large enough such that $\rho \in \sigma_\beta$ and repeat the above argument.

This settles the question whether lost melodies exist for α-wITRMs for all exponentially closed values of α.

Corollary 5. *If α is of the form σ_β for some ordinal β, then there are no (weakly) α-wITRM-semi-recognizable and no α-wITRM-co-semi-recognizable constructible subsets of α.*

Proof. This works by the same argument as Lemma 9, noting that "There is x such that $P^x(\rho)$ halts" is a Σ_1-formula and that "There is x such that $P^x(\rho)$ does not halt (but is defined)" is equivalent to "There is x such that there is a strong loop in the computation of $P^x(\rho)$", which is again Σ_1.

For weak α-wITRM-co-semi-recognizability, however, things are different:

Proposition 1. *For all α, each α-wITRM-computable subset $x \subseteq \alpha$ is also weakly α-wITRM-co-semi-recognizable.*

---

[9] Recall that, by Theorem 46 of [3], every Π_3-reflecting ordinal is u-weak.

Proof. Let $x \subseteq \alpha$ be α-wITRM-computable, and pick a program P and an ordinal $\xi < \alpha$ such that P computes x in the parameter ξ. Let Q be the program that, for each $\iota < \alpha$, stored in some register R, computes $P(\iota, \xi)$ and compares the output to the ι-th bit of the oracle. If they agree, Q continues with $\iota + 1$; otherwise, Q halts. Clearly, R will overflow at time α if and only if the oracle is equal to x, and otherwise, Q will halt.

References

1. Barwise, J.: Admissible Sets and Structures, An Approach to Definability Theory. Cambridge University Press, Cambridge (2016)
2. Boolos. G.: On the Semantics of the Constructible Levels. Zeitschrift für mathematische Logik und Grundlagen der Mathematik, vol. 18 (1970)
3. Carl, M.: Ordinal Computability. De Gruyter, An Introduction to Infinitary Machines (2019)
4. Carl, M., Schlicht, P., Welch, P.: Recognizable sets and Woodin cardinals: computation beyond the constructible universe. Ann. Pure Appl. Logic **169**, (2015)
5. Carl, M.: Taming Koepke's Zoo II: Register Machines. Ann. Pure Appl. Logic, **173**(3) (2021)
6. Carl. M., The lost melody phenomenon. In: Geschke, S., et al. (eds.) Infinity, Computability and Metamathematics. Festschrift Celebrating the 60th Birthdays of Peter Koepke and Philip Welch. College Publications, London (2014)
7. Carl, M.: The distribution of ITRM-recognizable reals. Ann. Pure Applied Logic **165**(9) (2012)
8. Carl, M.: Optimal results on recognizability for infinite time register machines. J. Symb. Logic **80**(4) (2015)
9. Carl, M.: The lost melody theorem for infinite time Blum-Shub-Smale machines. In: de Mol, L., et al., (eds.). Connecting with Computability, 17th Conference on Computability in Europe, CiE 2021. (2021)
10. Cutland, N.: Computability, An Introduction to Recursive Function Theory. Cambridge University Press, Cambridge (1980)
11. Gitman, V., Hamkins, J., Johnstone, T.: What is the theory ZFC without power set? Math. Logic Q. **62**(4) (2011)
12. Hamkins, J., Lewis, A.: Infinite time turing machines. J. Symb. Logic **65**(2) (1998)
13. Jensen, R., Karp, C.: Primitive recursive set functions. In: Axiomatic Set Theory, Amer. Math. Soc., 143–176 (1967)
14. Koepke, P.: Infinite time register machines. In: Beckmann, A., et al., (eds.) Logical Approaches to Computational Barriers. Second Conference on Computability in Europe, CiE 2006 (2006)
15. Koepke, P.: Ordinal computability. In: Ambos-Spies, K., et al., (eds.) Mathematical Theory and Computational Practice. 5th Conference on Computability in Europe, CiE 2009 (2009)
16. Koepke, P., Miller, R.: An enhanced theory of infinite time register machines. In: Beckmann, A., et al., (eds.) Logic and Theory of Algorithms. 4th Conference on Computaiblity in Europe, CiE 2008 (2008)
17. Koepke, P., Seyfferth, B.: Ordinal machines and admissible recursion theory. Ann. Pure Appl. Logic **160**(3) (2009)
18. Koepke, P., Siders, R.: Register computations on ordinals. Arch. Math. Logic **47**(6) (2008)

De Groot Duality for Represented Spaces

Takayuki Kihara[1,2] and Arno Pauly[1,2(✉)]

[1] Department of Mathematical Informatics, Nagoya University, Nagoya, Japan
kihara@i.nagoya-u.ac.jp, Arno.Pauly@gmail.com
[2] School of Mathematics and Computer Science, Swansea University, Swansea, UK

Abstract. We explore de Groot duality in the setting of represented spaces. The de Groot dual of a space is the space of closures of its singletons, with the representation inherited from the hyperspace of closed subsets. This yields an elegant duality, in particular between Hausdorff spaces and compact T_1-spaces. As an application of the concept, we study the point degree spectrum of the dual of Baire space, and show that it is, in a formal sense, far from being countably-based.

1 Introduction

In this article, through the theory of represented spaces and higher type computability, we give a unified treatment of the studies of Π_1^0 *singletons* in classical computability theory [8, Definition XII.2.13] and *de Groot duality* in general topology [3, Section 9.1.2]. The former notion has been associated with *implicit definability* in classical logic [8, Definition XII.2.13]; hence, this unified treatment gives de Groot duality a new interpretation: the duality of "explicit" and "implicit". Conversely, the pure topological aspect of the latter also provides a renewed understanding of Π_1^0 singletons. By exploring these notions, in this article, we see an elegant duality between Hausdorff spaces and compact T_1-spaces.

Formally, we introduce the de Groot dual of a represented space. Recall that for any represented space $\mathbf{X}$, we obtain the represented space $\mathcal{A}(\mathbf{X})$ of closed subsets by identifying a set with the characteristic function of its complement into Sierpiński space.

Definition 1. *For a represented space* $\mathbf{X}$, *let* $\mathbf{X}^d$ *denote the space* $\{\overline{\{x\}} \mid x \in \mathbf{X}\} \subseteq \mathcal{A}(\mathbf{X})$. *We call* $\mathbf{X}^d$ *the* de Groot dual *of* $\mathbf{X}$.

Example 2. Computable points in $(\mathbb{N}^{\mathbb{N}})^d$ are exactly Π_1^0 singletons in $\mathbb{N}^{\mathbb{N}}$.

Usually, we are only interested in T_0 represented spaces, and we will assume spaces to be T_0 throughout the rest of the paper[1]. The T_0-property is equivalent to $x \mapsto \overline{\{x\}} : \mathbf{X} \to \mathbf{X}^d$ being a bijection, and we can thus treat $\mathbf{X}$ and $\mathbf{X}^d$ to have the same underlying set. The de Groot dual is particularly well-behaved when

---

[1] The de Groot dual of a space is the same as the de Groot dual of its T_0-quotient anyway.

G. Della Vedova et al. (Eds.): CiE 2023, LNCS 13967, pp. 89–101, 2023.
https://doi.org/10.1007/978-3-031-36978-0_8

we restrict our attention further to T_1-spaces, where points are already closed. A primary appeal of the dual is that for T_1-spaces, it interchanges Hausdorff and compact spaces. We summarize the properties of de Groot duality for T_1-spaces in Theorem 3 in Sect. 2.

While the de Groot dual has a natural definition in the setting of represented spaces, the concept is originally from topology [4]; see [3, Section 9.1.2]. For a topological space $\mathcal{X}$, its *de Groot dual* is the topology on $\mathcal{X}$ generated by complements of saturated compact subsets of $\mathcal{X}$. It is no surprise to have an analogy between concepts for represented spaces and topological spaces [2,9]; and each represented space naturally comes equipped with a topology. Often, these concepts align (only) up to sequentialization. We leave the study of the precise relation of de Groot duality for represented spaces and for topological spaces for future work.

1.1   Preliminaries

We briefly recap some preliminaries, and refer to [9] for more details. A *represented space* is a set X equipped with a partial surjection $\delta_X \colon \subseteq \mathbb{N}^{\mathbb{N}} \to X$. If $\delta_X(p) = x$ then we say that p is a name of x. A point $x \in \mathbf{X}$ is computable if it has a computable name. A function $f \colon \mathbf{X} \to \mathbf{Y}$ is continuous (computable, resp.) if there exists a continuous (computable, resp.) function which, given a name of $x \in \mathbf{X}$, returns a name of $f(x) \in \mathbf{Y}$. We write $\mathbf{X} \simeq \mathbf{Y}$ if $\mathbf{X}$ is computably isomorphic to $\mathbf{Y}$. One of the remarkable properties of the category of represented spaces and continuous (computable) functions is that it is cartesian closed.

We denote the represented *Sierpiński space* by $\mathbb{S}$, which consists of a closed point $\bot$ (whose name is $000\ldots$) and an open point $\top$ (whose names are other sequences). A subset A of a represented space $\mathbf{X}$ is *open* if its characteristic map $\chi_A \colon \mathbf{X} \to \mathbb{S}$ is continuous. Identifying a subset with its characteristic map, the represented hyperspace $\mathcal{O}(\mathbf{X})$ of all open subsets of $\mathbf{X}$ can be defined by the exponential $\mathbb{S}^{\mathbf{X}}$. In a similar way, the represented hyperspace $\mathcal{A}(\mathbf{X})$ of all closed sets can also be defined. As a subspace of a represented space is also represented, the de Groot dual $\mathbf{X}^{\mathsf{d}} \subseteq \mathcal{A}(\mathbf{X})$ can also be treated as a represented space. If there is no risk of confusion, a point $\overline{\{x\}}$ in the de Groot dual $\mathbf{X}^{\mathsf{d}}$ is simply written as x. Formally, this is justified by defining a dual name of x as an $\mathbf{X}^{\mathsf{d}}$-name of $\overline{\{x\}}$.

Given $x \in \mathbf{X}$, let $\kappa_{\mathbf{X}}(x)$ be the neighborhood filter of x; that is, $\{U \in \mathcal{O}(\mathbf{X}) : x \in U\}$. Note that $\kappa_{\mathbf{X}} \colon \mathbf{X} \to \mathcal{O}\mathcal{O}(\mathbf{X})$ is always well-defined and computable, since $\kappa_{\mathbf{X}}$ is obtained as currying of the evaluation map $\in \colon X \times \mathcal{O}(\mathbf{X}) \to \mathbb{S}$. A space $\mathbf{X}$ is *computably admissible* if $\kappa_{\mathbf{X}}$ has a partial computable left-inverse. The image $\mathbf{X}_{\kappa}$ of $\kappa_{\mathbf{X}}$ is called the *admissibilification* of $\mathbf{X}$. Note that $\mathbf{X}$ is computably admissible iff $\kappa_{\mathbf{X}}$ is a computable isomorphism between $\mathbf{X}$ and $\mathbf{X}_{\kappa}$.

A space $\mathbf{X}$ is *computably compact* if $\forall_{\mathbf{X}} \colon \mathcal{O}(\mathbf{X}) \to \mathbb{S}$ is computable, where $\forall_{\mathbf{X}}(U) = \top$ iff $U = X$. Equivalently, $\{U \in \mathcal{O}(\mathbf{X}) : \mathbf{U} = \mathbf{X}\}$ is a computable point in $\mathcal{O}\mathcal{O}(\mathbf{X})$. A space $\mathbf{X}$ is *computably Hausdorff* if $\neq \colon \mathbf{X} \times \mathbf{X} \to \mathbb{S}$ is computable. A space $\mathbf{X}$ is T_1 if, for any $x \in \mathbf{X}$, $\neq_x \colon \mathbf{X} \to \mathbb{S}$ defined by $\neq_x(y) = (x \neq y)$ is continuous; that is, $\{x\} \in \mathcal{A}(\mathbf{X})$. A space $\mathbf{X}$ is T_0 if $\kappa_{\mathbf{X}}$ has a partial left-inverse.

Note that these notions are defined for a represented space (not necessarily a topological space), although, of course, a represented space can always be equipped with its quotient topology.

2 Duality for T_1 Represented Spaces

If we restrict to T_1 spaces, the de Groot dual of $\mathbf{X}$ is simply the space of closed singletons of $\mathbf{X}$, with the subspace representation inherited from $\mathcal{A}(\mathbf{X})$. It is in this setting that the dual exhibits very elegant properties, and in particular becomes a duality between Hausdorffness and compactness. The following theorem lays out how the duality works. The proofs of its claims are spread throughout Subsect. 2 below. The requirement for the space and or its dual to contain one or two computable points are used only for a few of the implications. We do not know whether these requirements are needed, but having some computable points seems like a sufficiently innocent restriction.

Theorem 3. *Let $\mathbf{X}$ be computably admissible and T_1, and let $\mathbf{X}$ and $\mathbf{X}^d$ each contain two computable points. Then:*

1. $\mathrm{id} : \mathbf{X} \to \mathbf{X}^{dd}$ *is computable.*
2. $\mathbf{X}^d \cong \mathbf{X}^{ddd}$.
3. *The following are equivalent:*
   (a) $\mathbf{X}$ *is computably Hausdorff.*
   (b) $\mathbf{X}$ *is computably Hausdorff and $\mathbf{X} \cong \mathbf{X}^{dd}$.*
   (c) $\mathbf{X}^{dd}$ *is computably Hausdorff.*
   (d) $\mathbf{X}^d$ *is computably compact.*
   (e) $\mathrm{id} : \mathbf{X} \to \mathbf{X}^d$ *is computable.*
   (f) $\mathrm{id} : \mathbf{X}^{dd} \to \mathbf{X}^d$ *is computable.*
4. *The following are equivalent:*
   (a) $\mathbf{X}$ *is computably compact.*
   (b) $\mathbf{X}^{dd}$ *is computably compact.*
   (c) $\mathbf{X}^d$ *is computably Hausdorff.*
   (d) $\mathrm{id} : \mathbf{X}^d \to \mathbf{X}$ *is computable.*
   (e) $\mathrm{id} : \mathbf{X}^d \to \mathbf{X}^{dd}$ *is computable.*
5. *The following are equivalent:*
   (a) $\mathbf{X}$ *is computably compact and computably Hausdorff.*
   (b) $\mathbf{X} \cong \mathbf{X}^d$.

The item (5) can be thought of as a computable version of [7, Example 4.1]. While the situation of Hausdorffness and compactness are mostly symmetrical in our main theorem, there is a notable absence: For computably compact $\mathbf{X}$ we cannot conclude that $\mathbf{X} \cong \mathbf{X}^{dd}$. An example for this is exhibited in Sect. 4.

Proofs of the Basics. We proceed to prove the various components of Theorem 3. Most of the proofs are presented by crystal-clear arguments based on higher type computability. These seem to fit well with synthetic topology [2], with the exception of the proofs of Propositions 8 and 16 and Lemma 14.

Throughout this section, the space $\mathbf{X}$ is assumed to be T_1 without this being necessarily stated explicitly.

Observation 4. *The map* $\neq : \mathbf{X} \times \mathbf{X}^d \to \mathbb{S}$ *is computable.*

Proof. As $\mathcal{A}(\mathbf{X}) \simeq \mathbb{S}^{\mathbf{X}}$, the non-membership relation $\notin : \mathbf{X} \times \mathcal{A}(\mathbf{X}) \to \mathbb{S}$ is exactly the evaluation map, so it is computable. For $x, y \in X$, note that $x \notin \{y\}$ iff $x \neq y$. Thus, the non-membership relation $\notin$ restricted to $\mathbf{X} \times \mathbf{X}^d$ is exactly the non-equality relation $\neq$ via the identification of $\{y\}$ with $y \in \mathbf{X}^d$. Therefore, $\neq : \mathbf{X} \times \mathbf{X}^d \to \mathbb{S}$ is computable. $\qquad\square$

Corollary 5. *1.* $\mathbf{X}^d$ *is* T_1 *(and thus* $\mathbf{X}^{dd}$ *is well-defined).*
2. id $: \mathbf{X} \to \mathbf{X}^{dd}$ *is computable.*

Proof. For (1), currying the function $\neq$ in Observation 4 yields the function $x \mapsto X \setminus \{x\} : \mathbf{X} \to \mathcal{O}(\mathbf{X}^d)$. In particular, $X \setminus \{x\}$ is open in $\mathbf{X}^d$, which means that $\mathbf{X}^d$ is T_1. For (2), as currying preserves computability, the above function is computable, and an $\mathcal{O}(\mathbf{X}^d)$-name of $X \setminus \{x\}$ is exactly an $\mathbf{X}^{dd}$-name of x. $\qquad\square$

The following is essentially just a rephrasing of the definition of being computably Hausdorff:

Observation 6. id $: \mathbf{X} \to \mathbf{X}^d$ *is computable iff* $\mathbf{X}$ *is computably Hausdorff.*

Proof. As in Corollary 5, one can see that id$: \mathbf{X} \to \mathbf{X}^d$ is computable iff $\neq : X \times X \to \mathbb{S}$ is computable, which means that $\mathbf{X}$ is computably Hausdorff. $\qquad\square$

The Connection to Unique Closed Choice. The map id$: \mathbf{X}^d \to \mathbf{X}$ is just another perspective on the principle of *unique closed choice* $\mathrm{UC}_{\mathbf{X}}$ studied in [1], which is formally a partial function $\mathrm{UC}_{\mathbf{X}} : \subseteq \mathcal{A}(\mathbf{X}) \to \mathbf{X}$, whose domain is the set of all closed singletons, and $\mathrm{UC}_{\mathbf{X}}(\{a\}) = a$ for any $a \in X$. In particular, id$: \mathbf{X}^d \to \mathbf{X}$ is computable iff $\mathrm{UC}_{\mathbf{X}}$ is computable. More or less by the definition of admissibility, we find that $\mathrm{UC}_{\mathbf{X}}$ is computable for a computably compact computably admissible space:

Observation 7

1. If $\mathbf{X}$ *is computably compact and computably admissible, then* id$: \mathbf{X}^d \to \mathbf{X}$ *is computable.*
2. If $\mathbf{X}$ *is computably compact, then* $\mathbf{X}^d$ *is computably Hausdorff.*

Proof. (1) A name of a given $x \in \mathbf{X}^d$ is also a name of $X \setminus \{x\} \in \mathcal{O}(\mathbf{X})$. By computable compactness, given $U \in \mathcal{O}(\mathbf{X})$, one can semidecide if $(X \setminus \{x\}) \cup U =$

X, which is true iff $x \in U$. By computable admissibility, this yields an $\mathbf{X}$-name of x.

(2) Names of $x, y \in \mathbf{X}^d$ are also names of $X \setminus \{x\}, X \setminus \{y\} \in \mathcal{O}(\mathbf{X})$. By computable compactness, one can semidecide if $(X \setminus \{x\}) \cup (X \setminus \{y\}) = X$, which is true iff $x \neq y$. This shows that $\neq \colon \mathbf{X}^d \times \mathbf{X}^d \to \mathbb{S}$ is computable. Consequently, $\mathbf{X}^d$ is computably Hausdorff.   □

Observation 7 (1) generalizes the classical observation that a Π_1^0 singleton in Cantor space is computable [8, Exercise XII.2.15 (c)] (whose uniform version is given in [1, Corollary 6.4] in the context of a unique closed choice).

Interestingly, we also have a converse direction, which gives a topological interpretation of the classical observation that a Π_1^0 singleton in Baire space (which is non-compact) is not necessarily computable [8, Exercise XII.2.15 (d)]. The statement can be described using the Weihrauch degree of $\mathrm{UC}_\mathbf{X} \colon \{a\} \mapsto a$. That $1 \leq_W \mathrm{UC}_\mathbf{X}$ means that $\mathrm{UC}_\mathbf{X}$ has a computable instance $\{a\} \in \mathcal{A}(\mathbf{X})$. That $\mathrm{UC}_\mathbf{X} \leq_W 1$ just means that $\mathrm{UC}_\mathbf{X}$ is computable.

Proposition 8. *If* $\mathrm{UC}_\mathbf{X} \equiv_W 1$, *then* $\mathbf{X}$ *is computably compact.*

Before we begin the proof, let us make a technical comment. For $A, B \in \mathcal{O}(\mathbf{X})$, one can see that $A \subseteq B$ iff $A \leq_{\mathcal{O}(\mathbf{X})} B$; that is, A is contained in the closure of $\{B\}$ in $\mathcal{O}(X)$. In fact, the standard representation of the function space $\mathcal{O}(\mathbf{X}) \simeq \mathbb{S}^\mathbf{X}$ gives us even a better property: If $A \subseteq B$ then the set of names of A is included in the closure of the set of names of B; that is, any neighborhood of a name of A contains a name of B.

Proof (Proposition 8). To prove that $\mathbf{X}$ is computably compact, we need to prove that given some $U \in \mathcal{O}(\mathbf{X})$ we can recognize if $U = X$. To do this, we compute $U^a := \{a\} \cup (X \setminus U) \in \mathcal{A}(\mathbf{X})$, and attempt to semidecide $\mathrm{UC}_\mathbf{X}(U^a) \in U?$. If we get a positive answer, we conclude that $U = X$. Note that since U^a is not necessarily in the domain of $\mathrm{UC}_\mathbf{X}$, this is not a well-typed expression - we just run it as a partial algorithm to the best of our ability.

For correctness of this algorithm, first consider the case that $X = U$. Then $U^a = \{a\}$, and thus $\mathrm{UC}_\mathbf{X}(U^a)$ is well-defined and returns a, and $a \in U = X$ is going to be recognized as true. Next, we consider the case that $U = X \setminus \{a\}$. Again, we have that $U^a = \{a\}$, and $\mathrm{UC}_\mathbf{X}(U^a) = a$, but as $a \notin U$, we will not answer *yes*. Finally, we consider the case where there exists some $b \neq a$ with $b \notin U$. Since $\{b\} \subseteq U^a \in \mathcal{A}(\mathbf{X})$, the name for U^a we compute can change arbitrarily late to be a name for $\{b\}$ instead; that is, any finite prefix of a name of U^a can be extended to a name of $\{b\}$. While the computation $\mathrm{UC}_\mathbf{X}(U^a)$ has no need to output anything, it must not output a prefix which cannot be extended to a name for b. But if a prefix returned by $\mathrm{UC}_\mathbf{X}(U^a)$ is sufficient to confirm membership of the potential output in U, it is inconsistent with a name for b, as $b \notin U$. Thus, this case cannot lead to an erroneous positive answer.   □

Corollary 9. *If* id $\colon \mathbf{X}^d \to \mathbf{X}$ *is computable and* $\mathbf{X}^d$ *contains a computable point, then* $\mathbf{X}$ *is computably compact.*

Proof. Just note that id: $\mathbf{X}^\mathsf{d} \to \mathbf{X}$ is computable iff $\mathrm{UC}_\mathbf{X} \leq_\mathrm{W} \mathbf{1}$, and $\mathbf{X}^\mathsf{d}$ contains a computable point iff $\mathbf{1} \leq_\mathrm{W} \mathrm{UC}_\mathbf{X}$. Then the assertion follows from Proposition 8.   □

Corollary 10. *Let* $\mathbf{X}$ *contain a computable point. Then the following are equivalent:*

1. id : $\mathbf{X} \to \mathbf{X}^\mathsf{d}$ *and* id : $\mathbf{X}^\mathsf{d} \to \mathbf{X}$ *are both computable.*
2. $\mathbf{X}$ *is computably admissible, computably compact and computably Hausdorff.*

Proof. The direction from (2) to (1) follows from Observations 6 and 7 (1). For the direction from (1) to (2), Observation 6 and Corollary 9 show that $\mathbf{X}$ is computably compact and computably Hausdorff. It remains to show that $\mathbf{X}$ is computably admissible. Let $\mathrm{ev}_x \colon \mathcal{O}(\mathbf{X}) \to \mathbb{S}$ defined by $\mathrm{ev}_x(U) = (x \in U)$ be given. As $y \mapsto X \setminus \{y\} \colon \mathbf{X}^\mathsf{d} \to \mathcal{O}(\mathbf{X})$ is a computable embedding, the function $y \mapsto \mathrm{ev}_x(X \setminus \{y\}) \colon \mathbf{X}^d \to \mathbb{S}$ is also computable. Note that $\mathrm{ev}_x(X \setminus \{y\}) = \top$ iff $x \neq y$, so this yields a name of $X \setminus \{x\} \in \mathcal{O}(\mathbf{X}^\mathsf{d})$, which is exactly an $\mathbf{X}^{\mathsf{dd}}$-name of x. This shows that $\mathrm{ev}_x \mapsto x \colon \subseteq \mathcal{OO}(\mathbf{X}) \to \mathbf{X}^{\mathsf{dd}}$ is always computable. By using our assumption (1) twice, we see that id: $\mathbf{X}^{\mathsf{dd}} \to \mathbf{X}$ is computable, so we conclude that $\mathbf{X}$ is computably admissible.   □

More on Hausdorffness

Proposition 11. *If* $\mathbf{X}$ *is computably Hausdorff, then* id: $\mathbf{X}^{\mathsf{dd}} \to \mathbf{X}^\mathsf{d}$ *is computable.*

Proof. By Observation 4, $\neq \colon \mathbf{X}^\mathsf{d} \times \mathbf{X}^{\mathsf{dd}} \to \mathbb{S}$ is computable. Since $\mathbf{X}$ is computably Hausdorff, by Observation 6, id: $\mathbf{X} \to \mathbf{X}^\mathsf{d}$ is computable, so $\neq \colon \mathbf{X} \times \mathbf{X}^{\mathsf{dd}} \to \mathbb{S}$ is computable. By currying, the function $x \mapsto X \setminus \{x\} \colon \mathbf{X}^{\mathsf{dd}} \to \mathcal{O}(\mathbf{X})$ is computable, which means that id: $\mathbf{X}^{\mathsf{dd}} \to \mathbf{X}^\mathsf{d}$ is computable.   □

Corollary 12. *Let* $\mathbf{X}$ *be computably Hausdorff and contain a computable point. Then* $\mathbf{X}^\mathsf{d}$ *is computably compact.*

Proof. By Proposition 11 and Corollary 9 (applied to $\mathbf{X}^\mathsf{d}$ rather than $\mathbf{X}$). Note that by Corollary 5 (2), we obtain a computable point in $\mathbf{X}^{\mathsf{dd}}$ from the one we have in $\mathbf{X}$.   □

Corollary 13. *If* $\mathbf{X}^\mathsf{d}$ *is computably compact, then* $\mathbf{X}$ *is computably Hausdorff.*

Proof. By Observation 7 (2), if $\mathbf{X}^\mathsf{d}$ is computably compact, then $\mathbf{X}^{\mathsf{dd}}$ is computably Hausdorff. By Corollary 5, id: $\mathbf{X} \to \mathbf{X}^{\mathsf{dd}}$ is computable, so $\mathbf{X}$ admits a computable injection into a computable Hausdorff space, and is thus itself computably Hausdorff.   □

Lemma 14. *Let* $\mathbf{X}^\mathsf{d}$ *contain two computable points and let* $\mathbf{X}$ *be computably admissible. Then* id : $(\mathbf{X}^\mathsf{d} \wedge \mathbf{X}^{\mathsf{dd}}) \to \mathbf{X}$ *is computable.*

Proof. We are given $\{x\} \in \mathbf{X}^d$ and $\{\{x\}\} \in \mathbf{X}^{dd}$ and seek to compute $x \in \mathbf{X}$. As $\mathbf{X}$ is computably admissible, we can equivalently seek to semidecide whether $x \in U$ for given $U \in \mathcal{O}(\mathbf{X})$. In addition, we have access to computable $\{y\}, \{z\} \in \mathbf{X}^d$ with $y \neq z$.

We can compute $A_y = \{y\} \cup (\{x\} \cap (X \setminus U))$ and $A_z = \{z\} \cup (\{x\} \cap (X \setminus U))$ as elements of $\mathcal{A}(\mathbf{X})$. While A_y and A_z may fail to be singletons, and thus the queries $A_y \in \{\{x\}\}$? and $A_z \in \{\{x\}\}$? are not necessarily well-typed, we can attempt the computations anyway. If either of them yields a *no*-answer, we have confirmed that $x \in U$.

To see this, first consider the case where $x \in U$. Then $A_y = \{y\}$ and $A_z = \{z\}$, thus our queries are well-typed. Moreover, since $y \neq z$, at least one of $x \neq y$ and $x \neq z$ must be true. The corresponding query will yield *no*, and we thus answer correctly.

Now consider the case where $x \notin U$. Then $A_y = \{x, y\}$ and $A_z = \{x, z\}$. Our names for A_y and A_z thus can change arbitrarily late to become a name for $\{x\}$ instead. While the computations $A_y \in \{\{x\}\}$? and $A_z \in \{\{x\}\}$? may be ill-typed, they must not produce output inconsistent with returning a positive answer for $\{x\} \in \{\{x\}\}$?. Thus, we will not receive a *no*-answer, and hence not answer incorrectly. $\qquad\square$

Corollary 15. *Let $\mathbf{X}$ be computably Hausdorff, computably admissible and contain two computable points. Then $\mathbf{X} \cong \mathbf{X}^{dd}$.*

Proof. Computability of $\mathrm{id} : \mathbf{X} \to \mathbf{X}^{dd}$ is available without assumptions (Corollary 5). For the converse direction, note that given $\{\{x\}\} \in \mathbf{X}^{dd}$ we can first invoke Proposition 11 (since $\mathbf{X}$ is assumed to be computably Hausdorff) to obtain $\{x\} \in \mathbf{X}^d$. We then use Lemma 14 to get $x \in \mathbf{X}$. Note that since $\mathbf{X}$ is computably Hausdorff, having two computable points in $\mathbf{X}$ yields two computable points in $\mathbf{X}^d$ by Observation 6. $\qquad\square$

Note that combining Observation 6 and Corollaries 9 and 15 yields the effectivization of [7, Example 4.2].

Proposition 16. *If $\mathbf{X}^d$ contains two computable points and is computably Hausdorff, then $\mathbf{X}$ is computably compact.*

Proof. Let $\{a\}, \{b\} \in \mathbf{X}^d$, $a \neq b$, be the computable points available to us. To show that $\mathbf{X}$ is computably compact, we show that we can, given $A \in \mathcal{A}(\mathbf{X})$, recognize if $A = \emptyset$. That $\mathbf{X}^d$ is computably Hausdorff means we have available to us a computable map isNotEqual : $\mathbf{X}^d \times \mathbf{X}^d \to \mathbb{S}$. We attempt the computation isNotEqual($\{a\} \cup A, \{b\} \cup A$), and claim that the answer to this correctly identifies whether $A = \emptyset$.

If $A = \emptyset$, we are computing isNotEqual($\{a\}, \{b\}$), which has to answer *yes*. If $A \neq \emptyset$, then isNotEqual($\{a\} \cup A, \{b\} \cup A$) is not well-typed. Consider some $c \in A$. Then names for both $\{a\} \cup A$ and $\{b\} \cup A$ can change arbitrarily late to be a name for $\{c\}$ instead. Thus, the computation of isNotEqual($\{a\} \cup A, \{b\} \cup A$) must never output anything that would be inconsistent with isNotEqual($\{c\}, \{c\}$), i.e., it must never answer *yes*. We thus obtain the desired behaviour. $\qquad\square$

Iterated Duality. The following observation is straightforward for T_1-spaces, but false in general (see Example 27 below).

Observation 17. *If $f : \mathbf{X} \to \mathbf{Y}$ is a computable bijection, then $f^{-1} : \mathbf{Y}^d \to \mathbf{X}^d$ is well-defined and computable.*

For the topological de Groot dual, Kovár has shown that taking iterated duals will yield at most four distinct topological spaces [7]. For T_1 represented spaces, the iterated dual will only yield at most three distinct represented spaces, with an argument that is similar to but simpler than the one by Kovár. We will see later an example showing that $\mathbf{X}, \mathbf{X}^d$ and $\mathbf{X}^{dd}$ can indeed be three non-isomorphic represented spaces (Sect. 4).

Corollary 18. $\mathbf{X}^d \cong \mathbf{X}^{ddd}$.

Proof. That id $: \mathbf{X}^d \to \mathbf{X}^{ddd}$ is computable is just a consequence of Corollary 5. To get the computability of id $: \mathbf{X}^{ddd} \to \mathbf{X}^d$, we apply Observation 17 to id $: \mathbf{X} \to \mathbf{X}^{dd}$ from Corollary 5.   □

Corollary 19. *Let $\mathbf{X}$ contain two computable points. Then $\mathbf{X}^{dd}$ is computably Hausdorff iff $\mathbf{X}$ is.*

Proof. If $\mathbf{X}$ is computably Hausdorff, so is its admissibilification $\mathbf{X}_\kappa$, and they have the same dual. Corollary 15 then yields $\mathbf{X}_\kappa \cong \mathbf{X}^{dd}$, so the latter is computably Hausdorff.

Conversely, if $\mathbf{X}^{dd}$ is computably Hausdorff, then by Corollary 12, $\mathbf{X}^{ddd}$ is computably compact (we can lift a computable point from $\mathbf{X}$ to $\mathbf{X}^{dd}$ by Corollary 5). Since $\mathbf{X}^d \cong \mathbf{X}^{ddd}$ by Corollary 18, $\mathbf{X}^d$ is computably compact. Then Corollary 13 shows that $\mathbf{X}$ is computably Hausdorff.   □

Let us confirm that the above completes the proof of Theorem 3. The item (1) follows from Corollary 5 (2). The item (2) follows from Corollary 18. For the item (3), (a)→(b): Corollary 15. (b)→(c): trivial. (a)↔(c): Corollary 19. (a)↔(d): Corollaries 12 and 13. (a)↔(e): Observation 6. (a)→(f): Proposition 11. (f)→(e): Theorem 3 (1). For the item (4), (a)↔(c): Observation 7 (2) and Proposition 16. (b)↔(c)↔(e): Apply Theorem 3 (3) (d)↔(a)↔(e) to $\mathbf{X}^d$. (a)↔(d): Observation 7 (1) and Corollary 9. The item (5) follows from Corollary 10.

3   Duality for Non-T_1 Represented Spaces

Notation. We now leave behind the tacit restriction to T_1-spaces. We recap some basic notions we will need for our discussion here. For a represented space $\mathbf{X}$, we shall write $\leq_\mathbf{X}$ for its specialization preorder; which is defined as $x \leq_\mathbf{X} y$ iff every open containing x also contains y. Equivalently, $\overline{\{x\}} \subseteq \overline{\{y\}}$. A set $A \subseteq X$ is *saturated* if it is an intersection of open sets. The saturation of a set A is $\uparrow A := \bigcap_{\{U \in \mathcal{O}(\mathbf{X}) | A \subseteq U\}} U$. Note that the saturation of a compact set is also compact since an open cover of A always covers the saturation $\uparrow A$. If we consider only singletons, the topological closure corresponds to the $\leq_{\mathbf{X}}$-downward closure, and the saturation corresponds to the $\leq_{\mathbf{X}}$-upward closure.

One can see that the de Groot dual inverts the specialization preorder; that is, $x \leq_{\mathbf{X}^d} y$ iff $y \leq_{\mathbf{X}} x$. In particular, $\mathbf{X}$ is T_1 iff $\mathbf{X}^d$ is T_1. Thus, the sequences of iterated duals of T_1 and non-T_1 spaces never intersect. Recall that, for T_0-case, the map $x \mapsto \overline{\{x\}} = \downarrow x$ is bijective, so one can think of an underlying set of $\mathbf{X}^d$ as X by identifying $\overline{\{x\}}$ with x. Hereafter, we assume that a represented space $\mathbf{X}$ is always T_0.

Iterated Duality for Non-T_1 Represented Spaces. Below we observe that the iteration sequence of the de Groot dual of a represented space terminates in at most three steps, even if we start from a non-T_1 space. This contrasts with the existence of a topological space whose iterated dual sequence does not terminate in at three steps [7].

Theorem 20. $\mathbf{X}^{ddd} \simeq \mathbf{X}^d$ for any represented T_0-space $\mathbf{X}$.

To see this, we first see the following analogue of Observation 4.

Observation 21. The map $\nleq_{\mathbf{X}} \colon \mathbf{X} \times \mathbf{X}^d \to \mathbb{S}$ is computable.

Proof. As $\mathcal{A}(\mathbf{X}) \simeq \mathbb{S}^{\mathbf{X}}$, the non-membership relation $\notin \colon \mathbf{X} \times \mathcal{A}(\mathbf{X}) \to \mathbb{S}$ is exactly the evaluation map, so it is computable. For $x, y \in X$, note that $x \notin \overline{\{y\}}$ iff $x \nleq_{\mathbf{X}} y$. Thus, the non-membership relation $\notin$ restricted to $\mathbf{X} \times \mathbf{X}^d$ is exactly the relation $\nleq_{\mathbf{X}}$ via the identification of $\overline{\{y\}}$ with $y \in \mathbf{X}^d$. Therefore, $\nleq_{\mathbf{X}} \colon \mathbf{X} \times \mathbf{X}^d \to \mathbb{S}$ is computable. $\square$

We see that Corollary 5 (2) also holds for non-T_1 spaces.

Corollary 22. id$\colon \mathbf{X} \to \mathbf{X}^{dd}$ is computable.

Proof. Currying the function $\nleq_{\mathbf{X}}$ in Observation 21 yields the saturation $x \mapsto \uparrow_{\mathbf{X}}\{x\} = \{y \in X : x \leq_{\mathbf{X}} y\} \colon \mathbf{X} \to \mathcal{A}(\mathbf{X}^d)$. Note that an element of $\mathbf{X}^{dd}$ is of the form $\downarrow_{\mathbf{X}^d}\{x\}$, which turns out to be $\uparrow_{\mathbf{X}} \{x\}$ since the de Groot dual inverts the specialization preorder as mentioned above. Hence, the range of the saturation is exactly $\mathbf{X}^{dd}$, so id$\colon \mathbf{X} \to \mathbf{X}^{dd}$ is computable. $\square$

In general, for (non-T_1) topologies σ and τ (on the same underlying set), the condition $\sigma \subseteq \tau$ does not imply $\tau^d \subseteq \sigma^d$, but if σ and τ have the same specialization order, this does hold. Based on this observation, we see the following non-T_1 analogue of Observation 17.

Observation 23 If $f \colon \mathbf{X} \to \mathbf{Y}$ is computable, and $f \colon (X, \leq_{\mathbf{X}}) \to (Y, \leq_{\mathbf{Y}})$ is an order isomorphism, then $f^{-1} \colon \mathbf{Y}^d \to \mathbf{X}^d$ is well-defined and computable.

Proof. Computability of $f \colon \mathbf{X} \to \mathbf{Y}$ implies computability of $f^{-1} \colon \mathcal{A}(\mathbf{Y}) \to \mathcal{A}(\mathbf{X})$ (via computability of $\mathbf{Y}$). For any $y \in Y$, by surjectivity, we have some $x \in X$ such that $f(x) = y$. Since f is an order isomorphism, $x' \leq_{\mathbf{X}} x$ if and only if $f(x') \leq_{\mathbf{Y}} f(x) = y$. This implies that $f^{-1}[\downarrow_{\mathbf{Y}}\{y\}] = \downarrow_{\mathbf{X}}\{x\}$. Hence, $f^{-1} \colon \mathbf{Y}^d \to \mathbf{X}^d$ is well-defined and computable. $\square$

Proof (Theorem 20). That id: $\mathbf{X}^{\mathsf{d}} \to \mathbf{X}^{\mathsf{ddd}}$ is computable is just a consequence of Corollary 22. To get the computability of id: $\mathbf{X}^{\mathsf{ddd}} \to \mathbf{X}^{\mathsf{d}}$, note that $\mathbf{X}$ and $\mathbf{X}^{\mathsf{dd}}$ have the same specialization order since the de Groot dual inverts the specialization preorder as mentioned above. In particular, id: $\mathbf{X} \to \mathbf{X}^{\mathsf{dd}}$ is an order isomorphism. Hence, we just need to apply Observation 23 to id: $\mathbf{X} \to \mathbf{X}^{\mathsf{dd}}$ from Corollary 22.   □

4   Examples

The Cofinite Topology on $\mathbb{N}$. An important example to illustrate the duality between Hausdorff spaces and compact T_1-spaces is the observation that $\mathbb{N}^{\mathsf{d}} = \mathbb{N}_{\mathrm{cof}}$, where $\mathbb{N}_{\mathrm{cof}}$ are the natural numbers equipped with the cofinite topology. We then also have that $(\mathbb{N}_{\mathrm{cof}})^{\mathsf{d}} = \mathbb{N}$.

The Cocylinder Topology on Baire Space. As announced in Sect. 2, we give an example where $\mathbf{X} \simeq \mathbf{X}^{\mathsf{dd}}$ is not necessarily true even if $\mathbf{X}$ is computably compact and T_1.

Definition 24 *The cocylinder topology τ_c on $\mathbb{N}^{\mathbb{N}}$ is generated by co-cylinders $\{X : X \not\succ \sigma\}$ where σ ranges over finite strings. We write $\mathbb{N}_c^{\mathbb{N}} = (\mathbb{N}^{\mathbb{N}}, \tau_c)$.*

The space $\mathbb{N}_c^{\mathbb{N}}$ is second-countable, computably compact and T_1. It is neither Hausdorff nor sober (and thus not stably compact). We see below that $(\mathbb{N}_c^{\mathbb{N}})^{\mathsf{d}} \simeq \mathbb{N}^{\mathbb{N}}$ and thus $(\mathbb{N}_c^{\mathbb{N}})^{\mathsf{dd}} \simeq (\mathbb{N}^{\mathbb{N}})^{\mathsf{d}}$, but $(\mathbb{N}^{\mathbb{N}})^{\mathsf{d}}$ is not second-countable (see Sect. 5), so $(\mathbb{N}_c^{\mathbb{N}})^{\mathsf{dd}} \not\simeq \mathbb{N}_c^{\mathbb{N}}$.

Proposition 25. $(\mathbb{N}_c^{\mathbb{N}})^{\mathsf{d}} \simeq \mathbb{N}^{\mathbb{N}}$

Proof. First note that a name of $x \in \mathbb{N}_c^{\mathbb{N}}$ is an enumeration $(\sigma_n)_{n \in \mathbb{N}}$ of all non-prefixes of x. And, a name of a closed set $A \in \mathcal{A}(\mathbb{N}_c^{\mathbb{N}})$ is a sequence $D = (D_n)_{n \in \mathbb{N}}$ of finite sets D_n of strings such that $x \in A$ iff, for any $n \in \mathbb{N}$, D_n contains a prefix of x. Thus, given an $\mathbb{N}^{\mathbb{N}}$-name of x, by putting D_n to be the singleton $\{x \upharpoonright n\}$, where $x \upharpoonright n$ is the prefix of x of length n, we get a name of $\{x\} \in \mathcal{A}(\mathbb{N}_c^{\mathbb{N}})$. This shows that id: $\mathbb{N}^{\mathbb{N}} \to (\mathbb{N}_c^{\mathbb{N}})^{\mathsf{d}}$ is computable.

Conversely, assume that a name D of a closed set $A \in \mathcal{A}(\mathbb{N}_c^{\mathbb{N}})$ is given. From such a sequence D, one may construct a finite-branching tree whose infinite paths correspond to the elements of A. To see this, we inductively construct a sequence $E = (E_n)_{n \in \mathbb{N}}$ of finite sets of strings as follows: Let E_0 be the singleton consisting of the empty string. Assume that E_n has already been constructed. For each $\sigma \in E_n$, and each $\tau \in D_n$ which is comparable with σ, put the longer of σ and τ into E_{n+1}. By leaving only shorter strings in E_{n+1}, we may assume that elements of E_{n+1} are pairwise incomparable. Note that E_{n+1} is contained in the upward closure of E_n (w.r.t. the prefix order). We claim that $x \in A$ iff E_n has a prefix of x for any $n \in \mathbb{N}$. For the backward direction, note that if E_{n+1} has a prefix of x then so does D_n. For the forward direction, if $x \in A$, one can inductively ensure that E_n contains a prefix of x. By the assumption $x \in A$, D_n also contains a prefix of x, so a prefix of x survives in E_{n+1}.

Now, the downward closure of $\bigcup_{n\in\mathbb{N}} E_n$ yields a finite-branching tree T_E. If A is a singleton $\{x\}$, by the above arguments, one can see that T_E has a unique infinite path x. However, we only have an enumeration of the tree T_E which is not pruned, so it is not straightforward to compute an $\mathbb{N}^\mathbb{N}$-name of the unique path x. To overcome this difficulty, note that only one of the elements of E_n is a prefix of x. If $\sigma \in E_n$ is not a prefix of x, we claim that there exists $m > n$ such that E_m fails to have an extension of σ. Otherwise, for any $m > n$, E_m has an extension τ_m of σ. If $(\tau_m)_{m>n}$ is eventually constant, say τ, then almost all D_m contain an initial segment of τ, so any infinite string extending τ must be a path through T_E, which is impossible. Hence, $(\tau_m)_{m\in\mathbb{N}}$ contains infinitely many different strings in T_E extending σ. Since T_E is finite-branching, König's lemma implies that T_E has an infinite path extending σ, which is again impossible by our assumption. This verifies the claim, which shows that $\sigma \in E_n$ not being a prefix of x is semidecidable. Wait for all but one string in E_n to turn out not to be a prefix of x. Then the last remaining one turns out to be a prefix of x. In this way, we can compute a $\mathbb{N}^\mathbb{N}$-name of the unique path x, which shows that id: $(\mathbb{N}_c^\mathbb{N})^\mathsf{d} \to \mathbb{N}^\mathbb{N}$ is computable. $\qquad\square$

The Lower Reals. The following example shows that we need to distinguish a space being isomorphic to its dual and being equal to its dual: The lower reals and the upper reals are isomorphic (with $x \mapsto -x$ being a computable isomorphism), but not equal (as id $: \mathbb{R}_< \to \mathbb{R}_>$ is not computable).

Proposition 26. $\mathbb{R}_<^\mathsf{d} = \mathbb{R}_>$

The following shows that Observation 17 (about being able to reverse the direction of a computable bijection by taking the dual) does not hold once we move beyond T_1-spaces:

Example 27. id $: \mathbb{R} \to \mathbb{R}_<$ is a computable bijection, yet id $: \mathbb{R}_<^\mathsf{d} \to \mathbb{R}^\mathsf{d}$ is not computable.

5   The Point Degree Spectrum of $(\mathbb{N}^\mathbb{N})^\mathsf{d}$

As an application for de Groot duality, we show that, relative to any oracle, the point degree spectrum of the de Groot dual of $\mathbb{N}^\mathbb{N}$ contains non-enumeration degrees. The point degree spectrum links the study of recursion-theoretic degree structures such as the Medvedev degrees, enumeration degrees and Turing degrees to σ-homeomorphism types of topological spaces [5,6,10].

Let $\mathbf{X}$ and $\mathbf{Y}$ be represented spaces. For $x \in \mathbf{X}$ and $y \in \mathbf{Y}$ we write $y \leq_M x$ if there exists a partial computable function $F \colon \subseteq \mathbf{X} \to \mathbf{Y}$ such that $F(x) = y$; that is, given a name of x, one can effectively find a name of y.

Definition 28. *A non-computable point $x \in \mathbf{X}$ is $\mathbb{S}^\mathbb{N}$-quasi-minimal if for any $y \in \mathbb{S}^\mathbb{N}$, $y \leq_M x$ implies that y is computable.*

As $\mathbb{S}^{\mathbb{N}}$ is a universal second-countable T_0 space, we find that a $\mathbb{S}^{\mathbb{N}}$-quasi-minimal point is $\mathbf{Y}$-quasi-minimal for any second countable space $\mathbf{Y}$. The degrees of points in $\mathbb{S}^{\mathbb{N}}$ are exactly the enumeration degrees, so another perspective on $\mathbb{S}^{\mathbb{N}}$-quasi-minimal points is that they are non-computable points not computing any non-trivial enumeration degree.

Theorem 29. *Relative to any oracle, there are continuum many $\mathbb{S}^{\mathbb{N}}$-quasi-minimal $(\mathbb{N}^{\mathbb{N}})^{\mathsf{d}}$-degrees.*

In the following, we write $x^{\mathbf{X}}$ to emphasize that x is a point in the represented space $\mathbf{X}$. To avert superscript-overload, we will write $\mathcal{E}$ for $\mathbb{S}^{\mathbb{N}}$ and $\mathcal{B}$ for $\mathbb{N}^{\mathbb{N}}$.

Lemma 30. *If $y^{\mathcal{E}} \leq_T x^{\mathcal{B}^{\mathsf{d}}}$, then one of the following must hold:*

1. $y^{\mathcal{E}}$ *is computable.*
2. $x^{\mathcal{B}} \leq_T x^{\mathcal{B}^{\mathsf{d}}} \oplus (\mathbb{N} \setminus y)^{\mathcal{E}}$.

Proof (Theorem 29). Given an oracle z, it is easy to construct a $\mathit{\Pi}_1^0(z)$ singleton $\{x\}$ in $\mathbb{N}^{\mathbb{N}}$ such that $x \not\leq_T z'$ (see [8, Exercises XII.2.14 (d), and XII.2.15 (e)]). Moreover, if $\{x\}$ is such a $\mathit{\Pi}_1^0(z)$, then so is $\{x \oplus z\}$. We will write $x_z := x \oplus z$ where x is constructed from z in this manner.

Now, given an oracle r, consider any $z \geq_T \mathcal{O}^r$, where $\mathcal{O}^r$ is the hyperjump of r, that is, a $\mathit{\Pi}_1^1(r)$-complete subset of $\mathbb{N}$. Then, $\{x_z\}$ is not a $\mathit{\Pi}_1^0(r)$ singleton; otherwise, x_z is Δ_1^1 in r [8, Proposition XII.2.16], and thus $x_z \leq_T \mathcal{O}^r \leq_T z$, a contradiction.

We will show that $(x_z)^{\mathcal{B}^{\mathsf{d}}}$ is $\mathcal{E}$-quasiminimal relative to r. We argued above that $(x_z)^{\mathcal{B}^{\mathsf{d}}}$ is not computable relative to r. Assume that some non-computable $y \in \mathcal{E}$ satisfies $y^{\mathcal{E}} \leq_T (x_z)^{\mathcal{B}^{\mathsf{d}}}$ relative to r. Then it follows by Lemma 30 that $x_z^{\mathcal{B}} \leq_T x_z^{\mathcal{B}^{\mathsf{d}}} \oplus (\mathbb{N} \setminus y)^{\mathcal{E}} \oplus r$. We know that z can compute $x_z^{\mathcal{B}^{\mathsf{d}}}$ and r, and thus also $y^{\mathcal{E}}$. But then z' computes z and $(\mathbb{N} \setminus y)^{\mathcal{E}}$, hence $x_z \leq_T z'$. But we constructed x_z such that $x \not\leq_T z'$, and thus have reached a contradiction. It follows that $(x_z)^{\mathcal{B}^{\mathsf{d}}}$ is $\mathcal{E}$-quasiminimal relative to r. As there are continuum many $z \geq_T \mathcal{O}^r$, and since $z_1 \neq z_2$ implies $x_{z_1} \neq x_{z_2}$, the claim follows. $\square$

Having continuum many $\mathbb{S}^{\mathbb{N}}$-quasi-minimal points has a topological interpretation:

Corollary 31. *For any second-countable T_0 space $\mathcal{Y}$, if $f : (\mathbb{N}^{\mathbb{N}})^{\mathsf{d}} \to \mathcal{Y}$ can be decomposed into countably many continuous functions, then there is a continuum-sized set A such that the image $f[A]$ is countable.*

Proof. Let $f : \mathcal{B}^{\mathsf{d}} \to \mathcal{Y}$ be a σ-continuous function, where $\mathcal{Y}$ is a second-countable T_0 space. Then, via an embedding $\mathcal{Y} \hookrightarrow \mathbb{S}^{\mathbb{N}}$, one can think of f as a σ-continuous function $f : \mathcal{B}^{\mathsf{d}} \to \mathbb{S}^{\mathbb{N}}$. Then, f is σ-computable relative to some oracle r. Note that $f(x) \leq_M x \oplus r$. Let $A \subseteq \mathcal{B}^{\mathsf{d}}$ be the set of all points which are second-countable quasi-minimal relative to r, that is, if $x \in A$ then $f(x)$ is r-computable. Then, since there are only countably many r-computable points in $\mathbb{S}^{\mathbb{N}}$, the range of $f[A]$ is countable as desired. $\square$

The idea of the proof of Theorem 29 is to exploit the difference in computability theoretic strength between explicit and implicit definability. A similar idea has been used in the classical theory of implicit definability (Π_1^0 singletons), so we mention its historical origin to conclude the discussion.

Recall that an object is implicitly definable (in arithmetic) if it is a unique solution of an (arithmetical) predicate; see e.g. Odifreddi [8, Definition XII.2.13]. One of the triggers that made this notion worth studying in logic was, for example, the following observation: Tarski's truth undefinability theorem tells us that arithmetical truth is not explicitly definable in arithmetic; nevertheless, arithmetical truth is known to be implicitly definable in arithmetic. What the latter means is that arithmetical truth is a unique solution of an arithmetical predicate; more precisely, the set of codes of true sentences in first order arithmetic is an arithmetical singleton in $\mathcal{P}(\mathbb{N})$ (see e.g. Odifreddi [8, Definition XII.2.13 and Proposition XII.2.19]).

In this way, implicit definability can often encode powerful information, and in fact, we have used this property to analyze the point degree spectrum of the de Groot dual of $\mathbb{N}^{\mathbb{N}}$.

Acknowledgements. We are grateful to Matthew de Brecht for fruitful discussions. We are also grateful to the anonymous referees for valuable suggestions and comments.

References

1. Brattka, V., de Brecht, M., Pauly, A.: Closed choice and a uniform low basis theorem. Ann. Pure Appl. Logic **163**(8), 986–1008 (2012)
2. Escardó, M.: Synthetic topology: of data types and classical spaces. Electr. Notes Theoret. Comput. Sci. **87**, 21–156 (2004)
3. Goubault-Larrecq, J.: Non-Hausdorff topology and domain theory: Selected topics in point-set topology, New Mathematical Monographs, vol. 22. Cambridge University Press, Cambridge (2013)
4. de Groot, J., Herrlich, H., Strecker, G.E., Wattel, E.: Compactness as an operator. Composit. Math. **21**, 349–375 (1969)
5. Kihara, T., Ng, K.M., Pauly, A.: Enumeration degrees and non-metrizable topology. arXiv:1904.04107 (2019)
6. Kihara, T., Pauly, A.: Point degree spectra of represented spaces. Forum Math. Sigma **10**, e31, 27 (2022)
7. Kovár, M.M.: At most 4 topologies can arise from iterating the de Groot dual. Topology Appl. **130**(2), 175–182 (2003)
8. Odifreddi, P.G.: Classical recursion theory. Vol. II, Studies in Logic and the Foundations of Mathematics, vol. 143. North-Holland Publishing Co., Amsterdam (1999)
9. Pauly, A.: On the topological aspects of the theory of represented spaces. Computability **5**(2), 159–180 (2016)
10. Pauly, A.: Enumeration degrees and topology. In: Manea, F., Miller, R.G., Nowotka, D. (eds.) CiE 2018. LNCS, vol. 10936, pp. 328–337. Springer, Cham (2018). https://doi.org/10.1007/978-3-319-94418-0_33

Algorithmic Randomness

Some Games on Turing Machines and Power from Random Strings

Alexey Milovanov[1,2(✉)] (iD)

[1] HSE University, Moscow, Russian Federation
almas239@gmail.com
[2] Moscow Institute of Physics and Technology, Moscow, Russian Federation

Abstract. Denote by R the set of strings with high Kolmogorov complexity. In [3], the authors presented the idea of using R as an oracle for resource-bounded computation models. This idea was further developed in later works [1,2,5,7]. We prove lower bounds for QP_{tt}^{R} and QP_{sa}^{R}:

- Oblivious NP $\subseteq \mathrm{QP}_{tt}^{R}$;
- Oblivious MA $\subseteq \mathrm{QP}_{sa}^{R}$.

In the above QP means quasi-polynomial-time; "sa" stands for sub-adaptive reduction, which is a new type of reduction that we introduce. This type of reduction is between truth-table reduction and Turing reduction.

Additionally, we establish upper bounds for BPP_{tt}^{R} and P_{sa}^{R} using ideas from [1]:

- $\mathrm{P}_{sa}^{R} \subseteq \mathrm{EXP}$;
- $\mathrm{BPP}_{tt}^{R} \subseteq \mathrm{AEXP}^{\mathrm{poly}}$.

Here $\mathrm{AEXP}^{\mathrm{poly}}$ is defined as the class of languages decidable in exponential time by an alternating Turing machine that switches from an existential to a universal state or vice versa at most polynomial times.

Finally, we examine some games that were originally introduced in [1] and prove their completeness. These results indicate that methods in [1] cannot provide better upper bounds for P^{R}, NP^{R} and P_{tt}^{R} than what is already known.

Introduction

Denote by $\mathrm{K}_U(x)$ the prefix complexity of x with respect to a universal decompressor U—the minimal length of a prefix-free program that outputs x. (For the formal definition and properties of Kolmogorov complexity, see references such as [12] or [10].) Denote by R_U the oracle function that outputs $\mathrm{K}_U(x)$ on input x.

In the sense of computational complexity, how strong is this oracle?[1] In [1–5,7] the following results are proved:

$$\mathrm{EXP}^{\mathrm{NP}} \subseteq \bigcap_U \mathrm{P}^{R_U}, \bigcap_U \mathrm{NP}^{R_U} \subseteq \mathrm{EXPSPACE},$$

---

[1] For the unprepared reader, this may look strange because Kolmogorov complexity is a concept from computability theory, not computational complexity. However, this examination raises interesting questions in areas such as derandomization and interactive proofs within computational complexity.

G. Della Vedova et al. (Eds.): CiE 2023, LNCS 13967, pp. 105–119, 2023.
https://doi.org/10.1007/978-3-031-36978-0_9

$$BPP \subseteq \bigcap_U P_{tt}^{R_U} \subseteq PSPACE,$$

$$NEXP \subseteq \bigcap_U BPP_{tt}^{R_U} \subseteq EXPSPACE.$$

$$H \in \bigcap_U P^{R_U}/poly.$$

Here H is a Halting problem; P_{tt}^A is $\{L : L \leq_{tt}^P A\}$, BPP_{tt}^A is $\{L : L \leq_{tt}^{BPP} A\}$; the intersection (everywhere) is by all universal decompressors U.[2] For convenience, we introduce the abbreviations: $NP^R := \bigcap_U NP^{R_U}$, $P^R := \bigcap_U P^{R_U}$, $P_{tt}^R := \bigcap_U P_{tt}^{R_U}$, $BPP_{tt}^R := \bigcap_U BPP_{tt}^{R_U}$.

In Sect. 1 we prove a lower bound for QP_{tt}^R, where $QP = \bigcup_i Time2^{O(\log^i n)}$. Recall the definition of Oblivious NP [6].

Definition 1. *A language L is in Oblivious NP if there exists a polynomial time verifier V taking an input and a witness, so that: there is a witness for each n of polynomial size, so that for any input of size n,*

  – *if the input is in L, then the verifier accepts on that input and the witness.*
  – *If the input is not in L, then for any witness, the verifier rejects on that input.*

We prove the following theorem.

Theorem 1.
$$Oblivious\ NP \subseteq QP_{tt}^R.$$

Remark 1. In fact, the results in [7] cover this theorem. In Sect. 8.3 of this paper it is proved that $S_2^p \subseteq QP_{tt}^R$.

To define some complexity classes we introduce new types of reductions. Machine M with an oracle access defines a reduction tree, see Fig. 1.

Definition 2. *A machine M with an oracle access is called* strictly sub-adaptive *if for every input string x all nodes in the reduction tree (i.e., all the oracle queries) are different, see Fig. 1.*

The following type of reduction is of greater interest. This is a "mixture" of truth-table and strictly sub-adaptivity reductions.

Definition 3. *A machine M with an oracle access is called* sub-adaptive *if for every input string x the computation of M(x) using an oracle follows these two steps:*

  – *In the first step, M asks non-adaptively several queries to an oracle.*
  – *In the second step M works strictly sub-adaptivity. This means that all oracle queries in the second step (for all sub-trees) are different, see Fig. 2.*

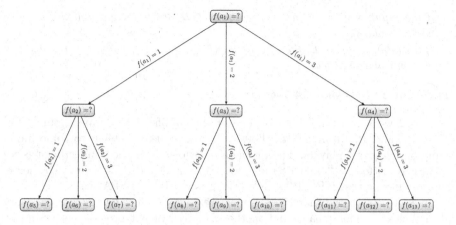

Fig. 1. For strictly sub-adaptivity reduction all nodes are different

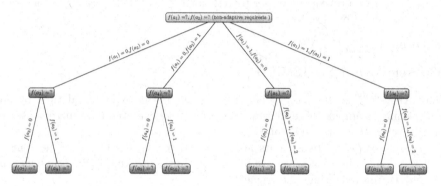

Fig. 2. For sub-adaptive reduction at the second step all queries are different.

This type of reduction is between Turing reduction and tt-reduction. Denote by $P_{sa}^{R_U}$ the class of languages that are recognized in polynomial time by a sub-adaptive Turing machine using oracle function R_U. Denote

$$P_{sa}^R := \bigcap_{\text{universal } U} P_{sa}^{R_U}; \quad QP_{sa}^R := \bigcap_{\text{universal } U} QP_{sa}^{R_U}.$$

For QP_{sa}^R we get some better lower bound than QP_{tt}^R, namely Oblivious MA.

Definition 4. *A language L is in Oblivious MA if there exists a randomized, polynomial time verifier V taking an input and a witness, so that:*
There is a witness for each n of polynomial size, so that for any input of size n,

---

[2] In [2,3] the plain complexity instead of prefix complexity was considered. However, as was mentioned in [1] this change does not affect on the lower bounds for $\bigcap_U NP^{R_U}$, $\bigcap_U P^{R_U}$ and $\bigcap_U P_{tt}^{R_U}$.

– if the input is in L, then the verifier accepts on that input and the witness with probability 1.
– If the input is not in L, then for any witness, the verifier rejects on that input with probability at least $\frac{1}{2}$.

Theorem 2. *Oblivious* $MA \subseteq QP_{sa}^R$.

In Sect. 2 we give a high-level outline of the proofs of the upper bounds for NP^R, P^R and P_{tt}^R from [1]. The idea is to reduce the problem to some finite game between two players. The problem of determining the winner belongs to EXPSPACE (for NP^R and P^R) and to PSPACE (for P_{tt}^R). This fact (by some reasons) means that $NP^R, P^R \subseteq$ EXPSPACE and $P_{tt}^R \subseteq$ PSPACE.

In Sect. 4 we prove that these games are complete for their respective complexity classes. This means that methods in [1] can not provide better upper bounds for P^R, NP^R and P_{tt}^R than known.

In Sect. 3 we prove some upper bounds for P_{sa}^R and BPP_{tt}^R by using the same technique. We prove the following theorems.

Theorem 3. $P_{sa}^R \subseteq EXP$.

Theorem 4. $BPP_{tt}^R \subseteq AEXP^{poly}$.

Here $AEXP^{poly}$ is the class of languages decidable in exponential time by an alternating Turing machine that switches from an existential to a universal state or vice versa at most polynomial times.

Therefore, we get two results about known complexity classes (Theorems 1 and 4) and introduce a new type of reduction, that is presumably strictly between tt- and Turing reductions for oracle R.

1 Lower Bounds for QP_{tt}^R and QP_{sa}^R

Fix some universal U and denote $K(x) = K_U(x)$ and $R = R_U$.[3]

The key ingredient for proving Theorems 1 and 2 is the following fact.

Theorem 5. *For every C there exists a quasi-polynomial in n algorithm using non-adaptively oracle-function R that on input n outputs a quasi-polynomial size list A of strings that contains all strings with length n and Kolmogorov complexity at most $C \log n$.*

Proof. Consider a string x of length n as the truth-table of a function $f_x :$ $\{0,1\}^{\log n} \to \{0,1\}$. In [2] the following connection between $K(x)$ and circuit-complexity of f_x is proved.

---

[3] The results of this section are valid for other types of Kolmogorov complexity (plane complexity, monotone complexity,...) that are equal each other with logarithmic precision.

Theorem 6 ([2]). *For every n and for every string x the function f_x can be computed by a circuit of size $\mathrm{poly}(\mathrm{K}(x) + \log n)$ with access to Halting problem H as oracle.*

Recall that Halting problem can be computed by poly-size circuits with oracle R. Hence, for every x with length n and complexity $O(\log n)$ the function f_x can be computed by a $\mathrm{poly}(\log n)$-size circuit with oracle R.

The required algorithm on input n constructs all $\mathrm{poly}(\log n)$-size circuits with oracle R and computes all truth tables of the resulting functions. Note that all queries to oracle R in this algorithm have length $\mathrm{poly}(\log n)$, so the queries can be done non-adaptively. □

Proof (Proof of Theorem 1). Let L be a string from Oblivious NP. Denote by y the lexicographically first witness for strings of length n. Note that Kolmogorov complexity of y is equal to $O(\log n)$ since y is restored from n in a computable way.

Let x be an input. Run the algorithm from Theorem 5 for $n = |y|$ (the length of y). Since $|y| = \mathrm{poly}(|x|)$ this algorithm works quasi-polynomial in $|x|$ time. Finally, one only needs to query the verifier on every possible witnesses from the list. □

Proof (Proof of Theorem 2). The first step of the proof is the same as in the proof above. It remains to derandomize the verifier. The approach is similar to the proof of $\mathrm{P}^R = \mathrm{BPP}^R$ presented in [2]. The algorithm construct (using oracle R sub-adaptively) a string r with poly-logarithmic length such that $\mathrm{K}(r) = \Omega(|r|)$. This string is then used as a hard-function in the pseudo-random generator from [8,9] to derandomize the verifier.

Give more detailed proof. First we get the list of strings with simple complexity from Theorem 5. This is the first step of sub-adaptive reduction. After this point all queries will be strictly sub-adaptive.

For each string from the list do the following. Let m be a binary string that encodes the previous oracle queries and their answers. First query $\mathrm{K}(m)$.

To maintain sub-adaptivity we will query the oracle only some continuations of word m. It ensures that in the reduction tree nodes from different sub-trees (that corresponds to different values of m) are not intersected.

The aim is to construct a string r of length $2^{\mathrm{poly}(\log n)}$ (here n is the length of input) such that

$$\mathrm{K}(mr) \geq \mathrm{K}(m) + \frac{|r|}{2}. \tag{1}$$

For this we use the following well-known fact in Kolmogorov complexity theory.

Lemma 1 ([12]). *For every string z and for every t there exists a string y of length t such that $\mathrm{K}(zy) \geq \mathrm{K}(z) + t - O(\log t)$.*

From this lemma it follows that we can add to m a suffix of logarithmic length such that the condition (1) holds (as it was done in [2]). We find the lexicographically first such suffix querying the oracle strictly sub-adaptively.

From (1) it follows that $K(r) \geq |r|/2 - O(\log |r|)$. Recall that $|r| = 2^{\text{poly}(\log n)}$. We argue (as it was mentioned in [2]) that the function f_r can not be computed by circuits with oracle R of size less than $|r|^{\varepsilon}$ for some positive ε. For oracle H instead of R it follows from the following theorem.

Theorem 7. *There is a $\delta > 0$ such that for every string r the minimal size of a circuit with oracle H computing f_r is at least $K(r)^{\delta}$.*

As we already mentioned, R can be computed by poly-size circuits with oracle H. Hence, f_r can not be computed by small circuits with oracle R. To derandomize the verifier it remains to use the following pseudo-random generator.

Theorem 8. *([8,9]). For any $\varepsilon > 0$, there exist constants $c, c_0 > 0$ such that the following holds. Let A be a set and $l > 1$ be an integer. Let $f : \{0,1\}^{c \log l} \to \{0,1\}$ be a boolean function that cannot be computed by oracle circuits of size $l^{c\varepsilon}$ with oracle A. Then $G_f : \{0,1\}^{c_0 \log l} \to \{0,1\}^l$ satisfies:*

$$| \Pr_{r \in U_l} [C^A(r) = 1] - \Pr_{x \in U_{c_0 \log l}} [C^A(G_f(x)) = 1]| < 1/l,$$

for any oracle circuit C^A of size at most l.

For x of size $c_0 \log n$, $G_f(x)$ is computable in time polynomial in n given access to f on inputs of length $c \log n$. □

To derandomize the verifier it is enough to use this theorem for $l = 2^{\text{poly}(\log n)}$.

2   The Idea of the Proof for Upper Bounds for Classes Containing Oracle R

Here we give the proof of the following theorem from [1].

Theorem 9. *Let L be a decidable language not in EXPSPACE. Then there exists an optimal prefix-free decompressor D such that L is not polynomially Turing reducible to the corresponding complexity function $K(\cdot) = K_D(\cdot)$.*

In [5] it was shown that P^R and NP^R contain only decidable languages. Together with Theorem 9 it gives that $P^R \subseteq$ EXPSPACE.

This theorem can be reformulated as a game. The main idea is that the function $2^{-K_U(x)}$ defines a universal semi-measure for suitable universal U.

Game Reformulation. Fix some decidable L not in EXPSPACE. Consider the following game with full information. Alice and Bob start with a function $k : \{0,1\}^* \to \mathbb{N}$ defined as $k(x) = 2|x| + c$ where c is large enough constant such that $\sum 2^{-k(x)} \leq 1/4$. At any moment each of the players may decrease the value of the function (replacing this value by some smaller non-negative integer). The cost of this decrease is the increase in $\sum_x 2^{-k(x)}$. There is a total budget for Alice—1/2 and for Bob—1/4; moves that violate the budget restriction are illegal.

The game is infinite; the winner is determined by the limit of the decreasing function k. Namely, Bob wins if L is polynomially Turing reducible to the limit function k, otherwise Alice wins.

Remark 2. We may assume that players alternate or use any other ordering (where each player makes infinitely many moves), since the winner is determined by a limit function and each player may postpone his/her move (this may only save the player's money and make the opponent spend more).

Lemma 2. *If Alice has a computable winning strategy in this game, then the statement of Theorem 9 is true.*

Proof. Let Alice play against the blind strategy of Bob that decreases the values of $k(x)$ until $K(x) + 2$ (the constant 2 is needed not to exceed the budget of $1/4$). This strategy is computable (since the set $\{(x, y)|K(x) \le y\}$ is computable enumerable), so we get a computable sequence of moves if Alice uses her computable strategy against this blind strategy. Therefore the limit function will be upper semi-computable, the corresponding series has sum at most 1 (since the initial function had sum at most $1/4$, and players increase it at most by $3/4$, and the limit function is optimal since Bob guarantees this. On the other hand, there is no reduction since Alice wins in the game.   □

A Series of Requirements. The winning condition in the game is a conjunction of a countable series of requirements: for each machine M there is a requirement "M does not perform a truth table polynomial reduction of L to the limit function k". We can effectively enumerate these requirements: we assume that for each machine some bounding polynomial is declared (as part of its description), and stop the computation when the time bound is reached (giving an arbitrary output). Let M_i be the sequence of the bounded machines; the corresponding requirement "M_i does not reduce L to k" we will also denote by M_i.

How to Deal with One Requirement. For a start, let us consider the simplified case when we have only one requirement (machine) M. Why can Alice win the game in this case? To win the game, Alice should ensure that for some x the output of the reduction machine M on x is different from the true answer $L(x)$ (**true** if x in L, **false** otherwise). Consider some x and let us see what Alice can do to destroy the reduction at this x. The pair M and x defines a reduction tree (see Fig. 1). Since M is a polynomial-time machine the size of the tree is exponential in the length of x. So, there are exponential many strings a_1, $a_2, \ldots a_n$ whose limit values of $k(a_1), \ldots, k(a_n)$ define the output $M(x)$.

We may consider a "local" version of the game that deals only with $a_1, \ldots, a_n$. Initially we have a list of n numbers $(2|a_1| + c, \ldots, 2|a_n| + c)$, Alice and Bob may at any time decrease any of these numbers (paying the corresponding amount, the increase in $2^{-k(a_i)}$), each not exceeding his/her budget $1/4$. Alice wins if she may ensure that the reduction answer for the limit values is different from $L(x)$. If Alice can win in such a game for some x, this is enough: using the winning strategy for the local game, she wins the global game. (She never decreases other values of k, and if Bob does so, he just wastes his budget, since only the values $k(a_i)$ matter.)

We arrive at the main point of the argument where the class EXPSPACE appears: for each x we have a local game between two players who have symmetric rights. For such a game, *either there is a strategy which guarantees that M outputs 0, or there is a strategy that guarantees that M outputs 1.* (We do not say who uses this strategy, since the rules of the game are symmetric, only the winning condition is different for Alice and Bob.) *And one can decide in EXPSPACE which of the two cases happens for a given x.*

Lemma 3. *The language containing all strings x such that there is a winning strategy to get $M(x) = 1$ belongs to EXPSPACE.*

The same is true if we change 1/4 (budget of players) to any other positive constant.

Proof. Recall that the number of strings $a_1, a_2, \ldots, a_n$ is at most exponential in the length of x. Therefore, the total number of steps in this game is also bounded by some exponent. (A player can miss his or her step. However, we assume that a player can do it only if they find the current value of $M(x)$ acceptable.) Hence, this game belongs to EXPSPACE by a standard argument.   □

Since L is *not* in EXPSPACE (by assumption), there is some x for which $L(x)$ is *not* equal to the answer that can be enforced by a strategy. For this x Alice can enforce the answer that is opposite to what L says, so she can win the local game (and the global one, if there were only one requirement). Since L is decidable Alice can effectively find such an x.

Dealing with Many Requirements: The Problem. What are the problems if we try to use the argument explained above against *two* machines (to guarantee that none of them reduces L to k)? There are two problems. First, the sets of strings $a_1, \ldots, a_k$ (the k-values used for both reductions) may intersect, and the change in one local game influences the other. Second, the budget in the global game is shared between the local games, so the strategies in the local games that assume a fixed budget do not work any more.

The solution is to deal with the machines M_i sequentially. Imagine we have two machines M_1 and M_2. First we deal with M_1 as if M_2 did not exist at all. When the game reaches the final stage, we start analyzing the local game for M_2, but use the current values of k as the initial configuration for M_2. It is possible since our argument (about symmetric games and EXPSPACE) does not depend on the initial values of k. The we can treat M_2 in the same way as before (for one machine).

There are two problems with this argument. First, we do not know "when the game reaches the final stage": the blind strategy played by Bob may decrease any value of k at any moment. This is not so bad, since we can restart the actions against the second machine many times (and hope each time that the first game is finished). In the same way one may treat countably many conditions (priority argument).[4]

The second problem, with the common budget, is more serious. It is possible that in the first game (against M_1) Alice wins but uses almost all budget ($1/4$ in our example) while Bob used only a small part of his budget (also $1/4$ in our example). Then, if we use the remaining resources for the second game, it is no more symmetric (and is biased in the wrong direction), so the game argument cannot be used anymore. For two conditions we may allow Alice to use $1/4$ in the first game and (separately) $1/4$ in the second game, while Bob is allowed to use only $1/4$ in total, and this almost saves the argument: it is OK that Alice uses $1/4 + 1/4 = 1/2$ in total. The only remaining problem is that the second game is restarted many times (when a new move is made by Bob in the first game), and if $1/4$ is allocated for each restart, then the total spending of Alice is unlimited. What can be done?

An Economical Way to Deal with One Requirement. To solve these problems, we modify the argument for one requirement. Assume that some small ε is chosen, and we consider a symmetric local game where both players are allowed to spend at most ε. Alice chooses some x where the EXPSPACE-prediction of the outcome of this ε-bounded game differs from L, and uses the winning strategy to play with Bob. However, Bob does not know that his spending is bounded by ε, and may—instead of losing the game—spend more. Then the game is abandoned, and new game (again with symmetric bound ε, with new x where L differs from EXPSPACE-set) is started. The main advantage of this approach is that *when the game is stopped, Bob spends more than Alice since it was him who increased the ε-bound.*

Therefore, if Alice repeats this procedure, Bob will be the first who violated the global spending limit $1/4$. (We assume here that ε is a negative power of 2, so $1/4$ is a multiple of ε and there is no last game with reduced budget.) So this approach works for one requirement. This is not directly useful (since we know how to deal with one requirement anyway) but this improvement is important when we combine strategies against different reductions.

Final Argument. The Alice's strategy in the global game is the priority-type combination of the economical strategies described in the previous section. We assume that Bob's budget in the global game is $1/4$, while Alice's budget is $1/2$, so she has some reserve of size $1/4$. (This increase in Alice's budget is not important in the global game as we have discussed.) This reserve is split into

---

[4] Imagine a knight who deals with infinitely many dragons; each dragon has only finitely many lives (but the number is unknown); moreover, when the knight hits ith dragon, all subsequent dragons are replaced with fresh instances. Still, the knight can kill all the dragons in the limit.

pieces: we consider a computable series $\varepsilon_1, \varepsilon_2, \ldots$ such that $\sum \varepsilon_i < 1/2 - 1/4$; all ε_i are negative powers of 2 (e.g., one may use $1/16, 1/32, 1/64, \ldots$).

To beat the first reduction M_1, Alice uses the economical strategy with parameter ε_1. This means that she analyses the symmetric local game with budget ε_1, finds the point x where the corresponding EXPSPACE-language differs from L and applies the winning strategy in the local game, considering the moves of Bob in the global game as the moves in the local game while it is possible, i.e., while Bob does not exceed the bound ε_1 of the local game. If and when this happens, Alice forgets about this local game, repeats her analysis for the same ε_1 but with current values of k to find new x where the wrong answer can be forced, starts applying the new local strategy until Bob exceeds ε_1-limit, etc.

Alice will do something in parallel against other M_i, but we postpone this discussion. Now we see that the number of restarts is finite, since each restart uses the same ε_1, and Bob cannot spend more than ε_1 infinitely many times. (It does not matter that ε_1 is small as soon as it is not changed during the restart.) And in each game that is abandoned Alice uses less weight than Bob, only in the last game (that is not abandoned; Alice wins in this game) she may use more weight than Bob, and the difference is bounded by ε_1.

How Alice incorporates playing against the next machine M_2 in this scheme? At any moment she may look at the current values of k, perform EXPSPACE-analysis in the ε_2-bounded game against M_2, and start (in parallel) playing this game against M_2-reduction. This game is interrupted if Bob exceeds ε_2 (recall that he does not know anything about ε_i and just plays the global game with budget $1/4$), or if M_1-game changes some of the k-values that are used in both games. In the first case the ε_2-analysis is performed again and the game against M_2 is restarted—maybe, with different x and points where the k-values are decreased, but with the same ε_2. If only interrupts of the first kind happen, then the second game always uses ε_2 and therefore is restarted finitely many times, and at each moment Alice spends (in all the games against M_2) not more than Bob, plus ε_2.

However, if an interrupt of the other type happens (due to the decrease in k caused by the game against M_1), then the second game is also restarted, but with ε_3, not ε_2. (Now it is possible that in the abandoned game Alice used more weight than Bob, but only by ε_2). If again the M_2-game is interrupted due to M_1-game, then the new instance of M_2-game uses ε_3, and so on. The priority argument works: since we do not disturb the games against M_1 by M_2-games, then finally the M_1-game stabilizes. After that only the interrupts of the first type are possible for M_2-games, so they all have the same ε_i, and therefore only finitely many interrupts are possible, and Alice wins the global game against M_2.

Some clarification about shared k-values is needed. When performing M_2-analysis, the value of all $k(x)$ involved in M_1-game are considered as fixed. If Alice or Bob change one of them (in M_1-game both players can do this), then the analysis becomes invalid. In fact, it is easier to agree that *any* move in M_1-game (even in the place that is not used in the M_2-game) causes the interrupt of the second type for M_2-game, so it is restarted (with new limit). Still Bob's moves in places that are not used in the M_1-game do not cause the M_2-game to restart, they are just normal moves of Bob in the M_2-game. The restart of the M_1-game also implies the interrupt of the second type for the M_2-game (it is needed since now M_1-game uses other values of k that should be considered as constants for M_2-game). Note that the reverse direction is safe: in M_2-games the values used in the current M_1-game are considered as constants, so M_1-game cannot be disturbed by their change in M_2-game.

In the same way all the other M_i are added sequentially. When in M_i Bob exceeds his budget (and the game is restarted), or if some move is made in the M_i-game, then all following M_j (with $j > i$) get an interrupt of the second type and should be restarted (sequentially, in the order of increasing j). In the first case the M_i-game is restarted also (before all the M_j), using the same bound. All other games use fresh values in the ε_i-sequence for restart.

In this way the total excess of Alice in the global game will never exceed the sum of ε_i, and the global budget for Bob is $1/4$, so Alice never uses more than $1/2$ and wins against all M_i, as required.

The Generalization for Other Classes. The statement $\mathrm{P}_{tt}^R \subseteq \mathrm{PSPACE}$ has the same proof: one needs to use machines that implement truth-table reduction and the corresponding game belongs to PSPACE. Moreover, we can state the following general statement. Let $\mathcal{M}$ be an enumerable family of Turing machines (for example, polynomial-time Turing machines) with access to some oracle-function. Consider the local game for machines in this family as in Lemma 3. Assume that the language containing all strings x such that there exists a winning strategy to get $M(x) = 1$ belongs to some complexity class $\mathcal{C}$. Then the following theorem holds.

Theorem 10. *Let L be a decidable language. Assume that for every universal U language L is decidable by some machine $M \in \mathcal{M}$ with oracle R_U. Then L belongs to $\mathcal{C}$.*

We affirm that this theorem has the same proof as Theorem 9.

3   Upper Bounds for $\mathbf{P}_{sa}^R$ and $\mathbf{P}_{tt}^R$

Prove that $\mathrm{P}_{sa}^R \subseteq \mathrm{EXP}$ using the technique from the previous section.

Proof. (Proof of Theorem 3). We know that $\mathrm{P}_{sa}^R \subseteq \mathrm{P}^R \subseteq \mathrm{EXPSPACE}$, meaning every language in P_{sa}^R is decidable. Hence, due to Theorem 10 it is enough to prove that the corresponding local game for sub-adaptive reduction belongs to EXP. However, there is a subtle issue in determining if a given machine computes a sub-adaptive reduction, as no algorithm can effectively determine this. But this is not a problem. Instead of enumerating sub-adaptive polynomial-time machines, Alice can enumerate all polynomial-time machines. For every machine

M Alice can either find x $M^R(x) \longleftrightarrow x \notin L$ (for some decidable language $L \notin$ EXP) or conclude that M is not sub-adaptive.

First we explore local game for strong sub-adaptivitely. Note that if a player has a winning position then they can omit their move (it is not worse then making any other move). Thus, we can modify the rules so that players in a winning position are not allowed to make a move. The current position can be described by a path in a reduction tree, see Fig. 3.

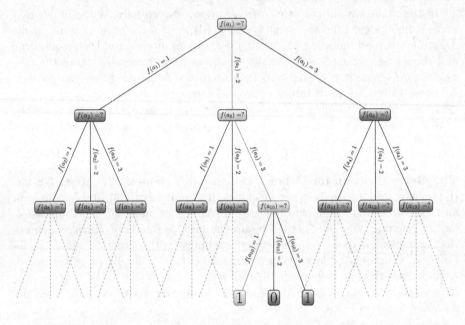

Fig. 3. The current values of oracle f: $(f(a_1) = 2, f(a_3) = 3,$ $f(a_{10}) = 1)$ defines the reduction path. This path defines the output of the machine (here it is 1).

A player (with a losing position) must change the current value of f on the current path of the reduction tree. (In Fig. 3 it is not possible to change $f(a_3)$; the value $f(a_{10})$ is minimal so it is possible to change this value). It is possible that a player may need to make multiple moves to change the value of the output.

Now we will use sub-adaptivity. The key observation is that vertices to the left of the current path will be not change (such moves do not have sense so we can assume that players do not make such moves). Note that sub-adaptivity is crucial here: in general case this is not true (and the corresponding game is EXPSPACE-complete by Theorem 12).

Therefore, the current game position is fully specified by triple consisting of the current path, Alice's current capital, Bob's current capital. We claim that the number of such triples is exponential in the size of the input. Indeed, the tree is exponentially large. The capitals are binary-rational numbers with denominator $2^{\max}$, where max is the maximal number among all numbers $f(y)$ that the machine asks. Since $f(y) \leq 2|y| + c$ and all lengths are bounded by poly(input size) the same is true for max.

Therefore, it is possible to find a winner in exponential time by using dynamic programming.

For general case (for a sub-adaptive reduction, not necessary strictly sub-adaptive) the reasoning is the same: since at the first stage a machine asks polynomially oracle queries non-adaptively the number of possible game-positions is also bounded by an exponent.   □

Now we prove that $\text{BPP}_{tt}^R \subseteq \text{AEXP}^{\text{poly}}$

Proof. (Proof of Theorem 4). Let $L \in \text{BPP}_{tt}^R$. Since $\text{BPP}_{tt}^R \subseteq \text{BPP}^R = \text{P}^R \subseteq$ EXPSPACE the language L is decidable. So, we can use the same technique. As in the previous theorem we can not enumerate all polynomial-time machines that provide a randomized tt-reduction. The problem is that for given random machine M and oracle A the values $\Pr[M^A(x) = 1]$ and $\Pr[M^A(x) = 0]$ depend on A.

But Alice can enumerate all random polynomial-time oracle machines that use this oracle non-adaptively. As in the previous proof for every such machine M she either finds x such that $M^R(x) \longleftrightarrow x \notin L'$ for $L' \notin \text{AEXP}^{\text{poly}}$ or figure that M^R does not provide a randomized tt-reduction.

Note that by an amplification argument if $L \in \text{BPP}_{tt}^R$ then there is a corresponding machine M such that:

- if $x \in L$ then $\Pr[M^R(x) = 1] > 1 - 2^{-|x|}$;
- if $x \notin L$ then $\Pr[M^R(x) = 1] < 2^{-|x|}$.

Therefore, to complete the proof it is enough to show that the following local BPP_{tt}-game belongs to $\text{AEXP}^{\text{poly}}$.

Local Game for BPP_{tt}. There is a polynomial-time random oracle machine M^A that uses oracle A non-adaptively and its input x. Initially the value $\Pr[M^A(x) = 1]$ is greater than $1 - 2^{-|x|}$ or smaller than $2^{-|x|}$. There are two players with some budgets that can change values of A by using their money. Every value can be changed $q(n)$ times only (here n is the length of x and q is some polynomial).

The first player wants $\Pr[M^A(x) = 1] > 1 - 2^{-|x|}$ and second player wants $\Pr[M^A(x) = 1] < 2^{-|x|}$. One (big) move of a player is changing A to make the value $\Pr[M^A(x) = 1]$ "good" for a player.

Prove that BPP_{tt}-game belongs to $\text{AEXP}^{\text{poly}}$. For this it is enough to show the number of (big) moves in this game is bounded by poly(n). Indeed, every big move is described by choosing exponentially many oracle queries.

Choose a polynomial p and show that this game can not continue more than $p(n)$ moves if p is large enough. Consider M as a deterministic machine depending on its input x and random bits r. Note that for every fixing r a machine $M^A(x, r)$ can make at most poly(n) oracle queries; denote this polynomial as $h(n)$.

The game position is depending on a fraction of r such that $M^A(x,r) = 1$. After every big move for at most every r the value $M^A(x,r)$ is changed: after the first big move the fraction of such r is at least $1 - 2^{-|x|+1}$; after $p(n)$ moves the value $M^A(x,r)$ is changed $p(n)$ for $1 - 2^{-|x|+1}p(n)$-fraction of r. However, the value of $M^A(x,r)$ can not be changed more than $h(n)q(n)$ times (recall that $h(n)$ is an upper bound for oracle queries for fixing r and $q(n)$ is an upper bound for possible changing an oracle value by players). So, if $p(n) > h(n)q(n)$ then the number of big moves in this game is bounded by $p(n)$.   □

4   Completeness of Some Games

4.1   Game for tt-Reduction

Here we consider the game like a local game in Lemma 3 but for tt-reduction.

Let M be a polynomial time Turing machine that has access to oracle O. This machine implements tt-reduction, i.e. on inputs of length n the machine M asks poly(n) YES/NO-questions to oracle O. After this machine outputs 1 or 0. Initially O is empty. Let x be some string.

Consider the following game. The goal of Alice is $M^O(x) = 1$, the goal of Bob is $M^O(x) = 0$. Alice and Bob can add strings to O for some cost. Specifically, adding string y costs $v(y)$, where v is some polynomial time computable function $\{0,1\}^* \to \mathbb{N}$. The players take turns, but they can skip their turn if the current value $M^O(x)$ is acceptable for them. Initially Alice has c_A dollars, Bob has c_B dollars.

Theorem 11. *There exists a polynomial-time Turing machine M that implements tt-reduction and a positive polynomial computable function v such that the following is true. The language*

tt-GAME$= \{(x, c_A, c_B)|$ Alice has a winning strategy in the game described above$\}$ is PSPACE-complete.

Note that here we consider an oracle that outputs YES/NO question instead of oracle-function. It is clear that completeness for a binary oracle implies completeness in the more general case.

4.2   Game for Turing Reduction

In this subsection we consider the similar game as in the previous subsection with the following difference: here we consider polynomial time Turing machines realizing Turing reductions instead of tt-reductions.

Theorem 12. *There exists a polynomial-time Turing machine M that realizes Turing reduction and a positive polynomial computable function v such the following is true. The language*

T-GAME$= \{(x, c_A, c_B)|$ Alice has a winning strategy in the game described above$\}$ is EXPSPACE-complete.

Acknowledgements. The authors would like to thank Alexander Shen, Misha Andreev and Dömötör Pálvölgyi [11] for useful discussions, advice and remarks.

References

1. Allender, E., Friedman, L., Gasarch, W.: Limits on the computational power of random strings. Inf. Comput. **222**, 80–92 (2013)
2. Allender, E., Buhrman, H., Koucký, M.: What can be efficiently reduced to the Kolmogorov-random strings? Ann. Pure Appl. Logic **138**, 2–19 (2006)
3. Allender, E., Buhrman, H., Koucký, M., van Melkebeek, D., Ronneburger, D.: Power from random strings. SIAM J. Comput. **35**, 1467–1493 (2006)
4. Babai, L., Fortnow, L., Nisan, N., Wigderson, A.: BPP has subexponential time simulations unless EXPTIME has publishable proofs. Comput. Complex. **3**, 307–318 (1993)
5. Cai, M., Downey, R., Epstein, R., Lempp, S., Miller, J.: Random strings and tt-degrees of Turing complete c.e. sets. Logical Methods Comput. Sci. **10**(3) (2014) lmcs:1126. https://doi.org/10.2168/LMCS-10(3:15)2014
6. Fortnow, L., Santhanam, R., Williams, R.: Fixed-polynomial size circuit bounds. In: Proceedings of the 24th IEEE Conference on Computational Complexity, pp. 19–26
7. Hirahara, S.: Unexpected hardness results for Kolmogorov complexity under uniform reductions. In: Proceedings of the 52nd Annual ACM SIGACT Symposium on Theory of Computing (STOC 2020), pp. 1038–1051 (2020)
8. Impagliazzo, R., Wigderson, A.: P = BPP if E requires exponential circuits: derandomizing the XOR lemma. In: ACM Symposium on Theory of Computing (STOC) '97, pp. 220–229 (1997)
9. Klivans, A., van Melkebeek, D.: Graph nonisomorphism has subexponential size proofs unless the polynomial-time hierarchy collapses. SIAM J. Comput. **31**, 1501–1526 (2002)
10. Li, M., Vitányi, P.: An Introduction to Kolmogorov complexity and its applications, 3rd edn. Springer, Cham (2008). (1st edn, 1993; 2nd edn, 1997), xxiii+790 p. ISBN 978-0-387-49820-1
11. Pálvölgyi, D. https://cstheory.stackexchange.com/questions/41762/what-is-the-complexity-of-ths-game
12. Shen, A., Uspensky V., Vereshchagin, N.: Kolmogorov Complexity and Algorithmic Randomness. ACM (2017)

Inequalities for Entropies and Dimensions

Alexander Shen[(⊠)] [iD]

LIRMM, University of Montpellier, CNRS, Montpellier, France
alexander.shen@lirmm.fr, sasha.shen@gmail.com
https://lirmm.fr/~ashen

Abstract. We show that linear inequalities for entropies have a natural geometric interpretation in terms of Hausdorff and packing dimensions, using the point-to-set principle and known results about inequalities for complexities, entropies and the sizes of subgroups.

Keywords: packing dimension · Hausdorff dimension · Kolmogorov complexity

1 Introduction

Inequalities for Entropies

Let $\xi_1, \ldots, \xi_m$ be jointly distributed random variables with finite ranges. Then, for every nonempty $I \subset \{1, \ldots, m\}$, we may consider the tuple of variables

$$\xi_I = \langle \xi_i \mid i \in I \rangle,$$

and its *Shannon entropy* $H(\xi_I)$. Recall that the Shannon entropy of a random variable ξ that takes s values with probabilities $p_1, \ldots, p_s$ is defined as $H(\xi) = \sum_i p_i \log(1/p_i)$. In this way we get $2^m - 1$ real numbers (for $2^m - 1$ non-empty subsets of $\{1, \ldots, m\}$). Shannon pointed out some inequalities that are always true for those quantities. For example, for every two variables ξ_1, ξ_2 we have

$$H(\xi_1) \leq H(\xi_1, \xi_2) \leq H(\xi_1) + H(\xi_1),$$

and for every triple of variables ξ_1, ξ_2, ξ_3 we have

$$H(\xi_1) + H(\xi_1, \xi_2, \xi_3) \leq H(\xi_1, \xi_2) + H(\xi_1, \xi_3).$$

The latter inequality corresponds to the inequality

$$H(\xi_2, \xi_3 | \xi_1) \leq H(\xi_2 | \xi_1) + H(\xi_3 | \xi_1)$$

for conditional entropies (defined as $H(\xi | \eta) = H(\xi, \eta) - H(\eta)$).

For a long time no other valid inequalities for entropies (except positive linear combinations of Shannon's inequalities) were known. Then Zhang and Yeung [7] found an inequality that is not a positive linear combination of Shannon's inequalities, and since then a lot of other inequalities of this type (*non-Shannon inequalities*) were found. It became clear that the set of all valid linear

G. Della Vedova et al. (Eds.): CiE 2023, LNCS 13967, pp. 120–131, 2023.
https://doi.org/10.1007/978-3-031-36978-0_10

inequalities for entropies has a complex structure (see, e.g., [5]). On the other hand, it became also clear that this set is very fundamental since it can be equivalently defined in combinatorial terms, in terms of subgroups size, and in terms of Kolmogorov complexity (see [6, Chapter 10] for the historical account and references). In this paper we use these characterizations to get one more equivalent characterization of this set, now in terms of Hausdorff and packing dimensions.

Let us recall briefly the characterizations in terms of Kolmogorov complexity and subgroup sizes; more details and proofs can be found in [6, Chapter 10].

Inequalities for Complexities and Subgroup Sizes

For a binary string x, its *Kolmogorov complexity* is defined as the minimal length of a program that produces this string. The definition depends on the choice of programming language, but (as Kolmogorov and Solomonoff noted) there exist *optimal* programming languages that make the complexity function minimal up to an additive constant, and we fix one of them. In this way we define the function $C(x)$ up to a bounded additive term, so to get a meaningful statement we should consider the asymptotic behavior of complexity when the length of the strings goes to infinity. (For more details and proofs about Kolmogorov complexity see, e.g., [6].)

Let $x_1, \ldots, x_m$ be binary strings. A tuple $\langle x_1, \ldots, x_m \rangle$ of strings can be computably encoded as one string whose complexity is (by definition) the complexity of the tuple $\langle x_1, \ldots, x_m \rangle$ and is denoted by $C(x_1, \ldots, x_m)$. The change of the encoding changes the complexity of a tuple at most by $O(1)$, so this notion is well defined. As it was noted by Kolmogorov [3], some inequalities for Shannon entropies have Kolmogorov complexity counterparts. For example,

$$C(x_1) + C(x_1, x_2, x_3) \leq C(x_1, x_2) + C(x_1, x_3) + O(\log n)$$

for all strings x_1, x_2, x_3 of length at most n; this statement corresponds to the inequality for entropies mentioned earlier. Note that this inequality is asymptotic; since $C(x)$ is defined up to $O(1)$ additive terms, some error term is unavoidable. We use $O(\log n)$ term instead of $O(1)$, so the difference between different versions of Kolmogorov complexity (e.g., plain and prefix complexity) does not matter for us.

It is easy to see that every linear inequality for complexities that is true for complexities with logarithmic precision, is also true for Shannon entropies: we replace strings by random variables, Kolmogorov complexity by entropy and omit the error term. It was proven by Romashchenko [2] that the reverse implication is also true and the same linear inequalities are valid for entropies and complexities (the exact statement and the proof can be found in [6, Chapter 10]). This result remains valid if we allow the programs in the definition of complexity access some oracle (set of strings) X (this is called *relativization* in computability theory); in particular, the class of valid linear inequalities for complexities with oracle X does not depend on X (since it coincides with the class of valid inequalities for entropies).

Another characterization of the same class of inequalities (in terms of sizes of subgroups of some group and their intersections) was given by Zhang and Yeung [7]. They have shown that it is enough to consider some special type of random variables that correspond to a group and its subgroups: if a linear inequality is valid for random variables of this type, it is valid for all random variables. (See below Sect. 4 for more details about this class.)

Dimensions and Point-to-Set Principle

The notions of Hausdorff dimension and packing dimension for sets in $\mathbb{R}^m$ are well known in the geometric measure theory, but for our purposes it is convenient to use their equivalent definitions provided by the point-to-set principle formulated by Jack Lutz and Neil Lutz [4]; the references to the classical definitions (and to previous results about effective dimensions) can be found there.

Let $\alpha = 0.a_1a_2a_3\ldots$ be a real number represented as a binary fraction (the integer part does not matter, and we assume that $\alpha \in [0,1]$). Consider the Kolmogorov complexity of the first n bits of α and then consider the limits

$$dim_H(\alpha) = \liminf_{n\to\infty} \frac{C(a_1\ldots a_n)}{n} \quad \text{and} \quad dim_p(\alpha) = \limsup_{n\to\infty} \frac{C(a_1\ldots a_n)}{n}$$

called *effective Hausdorff dimension* and *effective packing dimension* of α. Note that the classical dimension of every point is zero, so these notions do not have classical counterparts. Both dimensions (for every real α) are between 0 and 1.

Now we switch from points to sets and for every set $A \subset [0,1]$ we define the *effective Hausdorff* and *effective packing* dimension of A as the supremum of corresponding dimensions of the points in A:

$$dim_H(A) = \sup_{\alpha\in A} dim_H(\alpha) \quad \text{and} \quad dim_p(A) = \sup_{\alpha\in A} dim_p(\alpha).$$

This definition can be relativized by some oracle X; for that we replace the Kolmogorov complexity C by its relativized version C^X. Adding oracle can make Kolmogorov complexity and effective dimension smaller; we denote the relativized effective dimensions by $dim_H^X(A)$ and $dim_p^X(A)$. The *point-to-set principle* says that for every set A there exists an oracle X that makes the effective dimensions minimal and these minimal dimensions are classical Hausdorff and packing dimensions:

$$\dim_H(A) = \min_X dim_H^X(A) \quad \text{and} \quad \dim_p(A) = \min_X dim_p^X(A)$$

Note that we use "*dim*" (italic) for effective dimensions and "dim" for classical dimensions to distinguish between them (for sets; for individual points only effective dimensions make sense). We take this characterization as (equivalent) definition of Hausdorff and packing dimensions.

Formally speaking, we should first prove that the minimal values are achieved for some oracle X; this is easy to see, because a countable sequence of oracles that give better and better approximations can be combined into one oracle. (Or we could just use "inf" instead of "min" in the definition.)

In the same way the dimensions of a set $A \subset \mathbb{R}^m$ are defined. Now a point $\alpha \in A$ has m coordinates and is represented by a tuple $\langle \alpha_1, \ldots, \alpha_m \rangle$ of binary fractions. To define the effective dimension of α we now consider the Kolmogorov complexity of an m-tuple that consists of n-bit prefixes of $\alpha_1, \ldots, \alpha_m$, and divide this complexity by n. Taking the limits, we get the effective Hausdorff and packing dimension of the point α; they are between 0 and m. Now, taking supremum over all α in A, we define the effective dimensions of $A \subset \mathbb{R}^m$, and their relativized versions $dim_H^X(A)$ and $dim_p^X(A)$ are defined in a similar way. Taking the minimum over X, we get the classical Hausdorff and packing dimensions of the set A.

In the next section we give two examples where the inequalities for Kolmogorov complexities are used to prove some results about (classical) Hausdorff and packing dimensions. Then (Sect. 3) we generalize this approach to arbitrary inequalities for Kolmogorov complexity. Finally (Sect. 4) we prove the reverse statement that shows that this translation can be used to characterize exactly the class of all linear inequalities valid for entropies or complexities.

2   Inequalities for Dimensions: Examples

Example 1. Consider the inequality for Kolmogorov complexities

$$2\,C(x,y,z) \leq C(x,y) + C(x,z) + C(y,z) + O(\log n) \tag{1}$$

that is true for all strings x, y, z of length n (see, e.g., [6, Section 2.3]). We apply it to the first n bits of three real numbers α, β, γ (considered as binary sequences; as we have said, we ignore the integer part and assume that all the real numbers are between 0 and 1).

$$2\,C((\alpha)_n, (\beta)_n, (\gamma)_n) \leq C((\alpha)_n, (\beta)_n) + C((\alpha)_n, (\gamma)_n) + C((\beta)_n, (\gamma)_n) + O(\log n).$$

Here we denote by $(\rho)_n$ the first n bits of a real number ρ considered as a binary sequence. We can divide this inequality by n and take lim sup of both parts: recall that $\limsup(x_n + y_n) \leq \limsup x_n + \limsup y_n$. In this way we get the inequality

$$2\,dim_p(\langle \alpha, \beta, \gamma \rangle) \leq dim_p(\langle \alpha, \beta \rangle) + dim_p(\langle \alpha, \gamma \rangle) + dim_p(\langle \beta, \gamma \rangle). \tag{2}$$

This inequality can be relativized with arbitrary X used as an oracle in the definitions of Kolmogorov complexity and effective packing dimension.

Now instead of one point $\langle \alpha, \beta, \gamma \rangle$ consider a set $S \subset \mathbb{R}^3$. Consider also three its two-dimensional projections onto each of three coordinate planes; we denote them by S_{12}, S_{13} and S_{23}. The point-to-set principle says that the (classical) packing dimension of a set is the minimal (over all oracles) *effective* packing dimension of the set relativized to the oracle, and the latter is the supremum (over all points in the set) of effective packing dimensions of its points. Fix an oracle X that makes the effective packing dimension of all three projections minimal (we may combine the oracles for all three sets) and use it everywhere. Then for every point $s = \langle s_1, s_2, s_3 \rangle$ in S the effective packing dimension of $\langle s_1, s_2 \rangle$ does not exceed the packing dimension of S_{12}, etc. Applying the inequality (2), we conclude that effective packing dimension of every point $\langle s_1, s_2, s_3 \rangle \in S$ satisfies the inequality

$$2\, dim_p^X(\langle s_1, s_2, s_3 \rangle) \le \dim_p S_{12} + \dim_p S_{13} + \dim_p S_{23}.$$

where the effective dimension in the left hand side is taken with the fixed oracle (and classical dimensions in the right hand side do not depend on any oracles). Now we take the maximum of all points $\langle s_1, s_2, s_3 \rangle \in S$ and get the bound for effective packing dimension of S (with oracle X), and, therefore, for the classical packing dimension of S. In this way we get the following result that deals exclusively with classical dimensions:

Proposition 1. *For every set $S \subset \mathbb{R}^3$ and three its two-dimensional projections S_{12}, S_{13} and S_{23} we have*

$$2\dim_p S \le \dim_p S_{12} + \dim_p S_{13} + \dim_p S_{23}.$$

Example 2. Now consider another inequality for Kolmogorov complexities of three strings mentioned earlier:

$$C(x) + C(x, y, z) \le C(x, y) + C(x, z) + O(\log n). \tag{3}$$

We can try the same reasoning, but some changes are necessary. First, we use that

$$\liminf x_n + \liminf y_n \le \liminf(x_n + y_n)$$

(and that $\liminf \le \limsup$) to get an inequality that combines the effective Hausdorff and effective packing dimensions:

$$dim_H^X(s_1) + dim_H^X(\langle s_1, s_2, s_3 \rangle) \le dim_p^X(\langle s_1, s_2 \rangle) + dim_p^X(\langle s_1, s_3 \rangle), \tag{4}$$

for every oracle X. Then, for some strong enough oracle X, we get

$$dim_H^X(s_1) + dim_H^X(\langle s_1, s_2, s_3 \rangle) \le \dim_p S_{12} + \dim_p S_{13}.$$

Still we cannot make any conclusions about the classical dimensions of the projection S_1 and the entire set S, since the point s_1 where the first term is maximal is unrelated to the point $s = \langle s_1, s_2, s_3 \rangle$ when the second term is maximal.

To see what we can do, let us recall that a similar problem appears for the combinatorial interpretation of inequalities for Kolmogorov complexity (see [6,

Chapter 10] for details). The inequality (1) from our previous example has a direct combinatorial translation (a special case of the Loomis–Whitney inequality): if a three-dimensional body has volume[1] V and its three projections have areas V_{12}, V_{13} and V_{23}, then

$$2 \log V \leq \log V_{12} + \log V_{13} + \log V_{23} \qquad (\text{or } V^2 \leq V_{12} V_{13} V_{23}).$$

However, the inequality

$$\log V_1 + \log V \leq \log V_{12} + \log V_{13},$$

written in a similar way for the inequality (3), does not always hold for a three-dimensional body. Consider, for example, the union of a cube $N \times N \times N$ with a parallelepiped $N^{1.5} \times 1 \times 1$: the left hand side is about $1.5 \log N + 3 \log N = 4.5 \log N$, while the right hand side is about $2 \log N + 2 \log N = 4 \log N$ (for large N).

The solution for the combinatorial case is to allow splitting of the set V into two parts: one has (relatively) small projection length, the other has (relatively) small volume. Namely, the following statement is true (see [6, Section 10.7]):

if for some three-dimensional set S the areas V_{12} and V_{13} of its two-dimensional projections onto coordinates $(1,2)$ and $(1,3)$ satisfy the inequality

$$\log V_{12} + \log V_{13} \leq a + b,$$

then the set can be split in two parts

$$S = S' \cup S''$$

in such a way that

$$\log V_1' \leq a \quad \text{and} \quad \log V'' \leq b.$$

Here V_1' is the measure of the (one-dimensional) projection of S' onto the first coordinate, and V'' is the volume of S''.

(Why do we introduce a and b? In a sense, we replace the inequality $u + v \leq w$ by an equivalent statement "for every a, b, if $w \leq a + b$, then either $u \leq a$ or $w \leq b$".)

We use a similar approach for dimensions, and get the following statement.

Proposition 2. *Let $S \subset \mathbb{R}^3$, and let $a, b \geq 0$ be two numbers such that*

$$\dim_p S_{12} + \dim_p S_{13} \leq a + b.$$

Then there exist a splitting $S = S' \cup S''$ such that

$$\dim_H(S_1') \leq a \quad \text{and} \quad \dim_H(S'') \leq b.$$

---

[1] To be more combinatorial, one could consider finite sets and the cardinalities of those sets and their projections.

Here S_1' is the projection of S' onto the first coordinate.

Proof. As before, fix an oracle X that minimizes the effective packing dimensions of S_{12} and S_{13}, and use it everywhere when speaking about complexities and effective dimensions. Then for every point $\langle s_1, s_2, s_3 \rangle \in S$ we have

$$dim_p^X(\langle s_1, s_2 \rangle) + dim_p^X(\langle s_1, s_3 \rangle) \le a + b.$$

The inequality (4) then guarantees that

$$dim_H^X(s_1) + dim_H^X(\langle s_1, s_2, s_3 \rangle) \le a + b$$

for every $\langle s_1, s_2, s_3 \rangle \in S$, and therefore

$$\text{either } dim_H^X(s_1) \le a \text{ or } dim_H^X(\langle s_1, s_2, s_3 \rangle) \le b$$

for every $\langle s_1, s_2, s_3 \rangle \in S$. Therefore we may split S into two sets S' and S'' and guarantee that for all elements $\langle s_1, s_2, s_3 \rangle \in S'$ we have $dim_H^X(s_1) \le a$ and for all elements $\langle s_1, s_2, s_3 \rangle \in S''$ we have $dim_H^X(\langle s_1, s_2, s_3 \rangle) \le b$. This implies that $\dim_H(S_1') \le a$ and $\dim_H(S'') \le b$, as required.

3   Corollaries for Dimensions: General Statement

Proposition 2 can be generalized (with essentially the same proof) to arbitrary linear inequalities for Kolmogorov complexities. Fix some m, and consider an m-tuple of strings $\langle x_1, \ldots, x_m \rangle$. For every non-empty $I \subset \{1, \ldots, m\}$ we consider a sub-tuple x_I that consists of all x_i with $i \in I$. Consider some linear inequality for Kolmogorov complexities $C(x_I)$ for all I; we assume that it is split between two parts to make the coefficients positive:

$$\sum_{I \in \mathcal{I}} \lambda_I \, C(x_I) \le \sum_{J \in \mathcal{J}} \mu_J \, C(x_J) + O(\log n). \tag{5}$$

Here $\mathcal{I}$ and $\mathcal{J}$ are two disjoint families of subsets of $\{1, \ldots, m\}$, and λ_I and μ_J are positive reals defined for $I \in \mathcal{I}$ and $J \in \mathcal{J}$. Assume that this inequality is true for all n and for all tuples $\langle x_1, \ldots, x_m \rangle$ of n-bit strings (with a constant in $O(\log n)$-notation that does not depend on n and $x_1, \ldots, x_m$). As he have mentioned, this assumption can be equivalently reformulated for entropies:

$$\sum_{I \in \mathcal{I}} \lambda_I H(\xi_I) \le \sum_{J \in \mathcal{J}} \mu_J H(\xi_J)$$

for every tuple $\langle \xi_1, \ldots, \xi_m \rangle$ of random variables (Romashchenko's theorem, see [6, Section 10.6, Theorem 211]).

Then we have the corresponding result about dimensions:

Theorem 1. *Under these assumptions, for every set $S \subset \mathbb{R}^m$ and every non-negative reals a_I (defined for all $I \in \mathcal{I}$) such that*

$$\sum_{J \in \mathcal{J}} \mu_J \dim_p S_J \leq \sum_{I \in \mathcal{I}} \lambda_I a_I,$$

where S_J is the projection of S onto J-coordinates, there exist a splitting $S = \bigcup_{I \in \mathcal{I}} S^I$ such that

$$\dim_H(S_I^I) \leq a_I.$$

The number of parts in the splitting is the same as the number of terms in the left-hand side of the inequality; they are indexed by $I \in \mathcal{I}$. By S_I^I we denote the I-projection of the part S^I; it is a set in $\mathbb{R}^k$ for $k = \#I$. The special case considered in Proposition 2 has two terms on both sides of the inequality ($\#\mathcal{I} = \#\mathcal{J} = 2$), and the coefficients λ_I and μ_J are all equal to 1.

Proof. As before, consider some oracle X that makes the effective packing dimensions of all S_J for all $J \in \mathcal{J}$ minimal. Then we have

$$\sum_{J \in \mathcal{J}} \mu_J \, dim_p^X s_J \leq \sum_{I \in \mathcal{I}} \lambda_I a_I,$$

for every point $s = \langle s_1, \ldots, s_m \rangle \in S$; here s_J stands for the projection of s onto J-coordinates. The inequality for Kolmogorov complexities (that we assumed to be true) gives (after dividing by n and taking the limit)

$$\sum_{I \in \mathcal{I}} \lambda_I \, dim_H^X s_I \leq \sum_{J \in \mathcal{J}} \mu_J \, dim_p^X s_J \left[\leq \sum_{I \in \mathcal{I}} \lambda_I a_I \right],$$

as before. (Note that the left hand side uses effective Hausdorff dimensions while the middle part uses effective packing dimensions, because of the limits.) This inequality is true for every point $s \in S$. Therefore, for every point $s \in S$ there exists some coordinate set $I \in \mathcal{I}$ such that

$$dim_H^X s_I \leq a_I,$$

and we can split the set S according to these indices and get sets S^I such that

$$dim_H^X s_I \leq a_I$$

for all points $s \in S^I$, and therefore

$$\dim_H S_I^I \leq a_I,$$

as required.

4   Equivalence

We have shown that every (valid) linear inequality for entropies can be translated to a statement about dimensions. In this section we show that this connection works in both directions:

Theorem 2. *If a linear inequality is not true for entropies, then the corresponding statement about dimensions, constructed as in Theorem 1, is false.*

Proof (sketch). We combine several well-known tools to achieve this result.

1. The first one is the characterization of inequalities in terms of the size of subgroups mentioned above. Let G be some finite group, and let $H_1, \ldots, H_m$ be its subgroups. (We do not require them to be normal.) For every element $g \in G$ consider the cosets $g_1 = gH_1, \ldots, g_m = gH_m$. If $g \in G$ is taken uniformly at random, the cosets $g_1, \ldots, g_m$ become (jointly distributed) random variables with common probability space G. Each ξ_i is uniformly distributed on the family of all cosets gH_i; the size of this family is $\#G/\#H_i$, and the entropy of ξ_i is $\log(\#G/\#H_i)$.

We may consider tuples of them: let g_I be the tuple of all g_i with $i \in I$. It is easy to see that for every I the values of g_I correspond to cosets gH_I for $H_I = \cap_{i \in I} H_i$, and the entropy $H(g_I)$ is $\log(\#G/\#H_I)$.

The result of Chan and Yeung [1] says that the tuples of random variables constructed in this way are enough for testing inequalities: if an inequality

$$\sum_{I \in \mathcal{I}} \lambda_I H(\xi_I) \leq \sum_{J \in \mathcal{J}} \mu_J H(\xi_J).$$

is not universally true (for all tuples of random variables $\langle \xi_1, \ldots, \xi_n \rangle$), then there exists a counterexample with groups, i.e., a finite group G and its subgroups $H_1, \ldots, H_m$ that make the inequality false:

$$\sum_{I \in \mathcal{I}} \lambda_I H(g_I) > \sum_{J \in \mathcal{J}} \mu_J H(g_J).$$

Note that the latter inequality can be reformulated in terms of sizes of a group, its subgroups and their intersections.

So we may assume that the inequality is not true for some group G and its subgroups H_i, and use them to construct a counterexample that shows that the corresponding statement about dimensions is false.

2. For that we use standard results about the dimension of Cantor-type sets. Consider N-ary positional system where every real from $[0, 1]$ is represented by an infinite sequence of digits $0 \ldots N - 1$. (As usual, the double representations for finite N-ary fractions do not matter much, and we ignore this problem.) Let X be a subset of $\{0, \ldots, N - 1\}$. Consider the set C_X of all N-ary fractions with digits only in X (for example, the classical Cantor set is $C_{\{0,2\}}$ for $N = 3$). It is well known that $\dim_H(C_X) = \dim_p(C_X) = \log \#X / \log N$ (and this can be easily derived from the point-to-set principle).

One can consider similarly defined sets in $\mathbb{R}^2, \mathbb{R}^3$ etc. For example, let Y be a subset of $\{0, \ldots, N-1\} \times \{0, \ldots, N-1\}$. Then one can construct a set $C_Y \subset [0,1] \times [0,1]$ that consists of the pairs of N-ary fractions $(u_1 u_2 \ldots, v_1 v_2 \ldots)$ such that $(u_i, v_i) \in Y$ for every Y. The Hausdorff and packing dimensions of the set C_Y are $\log \#Y / \log N$.

For subsets of $[0,1]^m$ the construction goes as follows. Consider some set $A \subset \{0, \ldots, N-1\}^m$. (Later, we let m be the number of variables in the inequality we consider, and construct the set A starting from the group G and its subgroups $H_1, \ldots, H_m$.) Then construct the set $C_A \subset [0,1]^m$ such that $\langle x_1^1 x_2^1 \ldots, x_1^2 x_2^2 \ldots, \ldots, x_1^m x_2^m \ldots \rangle \in C_A$ if and only if $\langle x_i^1, \ldots, x_i^m \rangle \in A$ for all i. The dimension (packing or Hausdorff) of C_A is $\log \#A / \log N$.

The projection of the set C_A on some set $I \subset \{1, \ldots, m\}$ of coordinates is the set C_{A_I} of the same type that is constructed starting from the projection A_I of A onto the same coordinates. Therefore, to find the dimensions of all projections of C_A, we need to know only the size of the projections of A.

3. We can start this construction with a finite set $A \subset U_1 \times \ldots \times U_m$ for arbitrary finite sets $U_1, \ldots, U_m$. Then we identify arbitrarily all U_i with some subsets of $\{1, \ldots, N\}$ for large enough N, and construct the corresponding set $C_A \subset [0,1]^m$. For that we need that $\#U_i \leq N$ for all i; the exact choice of N is not important since the factor $1/\log N$ is the same for all the projections.

Using this remark, we let U_i be the range of g_i, i.e., the family of all cosets with respect to the subgroup H_i, and let

$$A = \{(gH_1, \ldots, gH_m) \colon g \in G\}.$$

Then, as we have seen, the dimension of $(C_A)_I$ is proportional to the logsize of the corresponding projection A_I, which equals the entropy of g_I:

$$\dim(C_A)_I = \frac{H(g_I)}{\log N}.$$

Therefore, we have

$$\sum_{I \in \mathcal{I}} \lambda_I \dim(C_A)_I > \sum_{J \in \mathcal{J}} \mu_J \dim(C_A)_J,$$

assuming that we started with a counterexample to the inequality for entropies that involves group G and subgroups $H_1, \ldots, H_m$. Note that we do not need to specify whether we consider packing or Hausdorff dimensions, since for our sets they are the same.

But this is not what we need: we need to show that a splitting of C_A into sets with bounded dimensions of projections does not exist for some bounds a_I. Let us choose a_I slightly smaller than $\dim(C_A)_I$ so that still

$$\sum_{I \in \mathcal{I}} \lambda_I a_I > \sum_{J \in \mathcal{J}} \mu_J \dim(C_A)_J.$$

We want to show that the assumption about dimensions is false for those a_I, namely, that one cannot split C_A into a family of C^I (for $I \in \mathcal{I}$) in such a way that

$$\dim_H C_I^I \le a_I$$

(here we have to specify the Hausdorff dimension since for the sets C_I^I the Hausdorff and packing dimensions may differ). For that we note that the last inequality implies

$$\dim_H C_I^I < \dim(C_A)_I$$

due to the choice of a_i that are smaller than $\dim(C_A)_I$. It remains to show that the last inequality implies

$$\dim_H C^I < \dim C_A;$$

then we get a contradiction, since the set C_A cannot be represented as a finite union of sets of smaller Hausdorff dimensions.

To get the bound for $\dim_H C^I$ in terms of the dimension of its I-projection we use special properties of the set A that corresponds to the group G and its subgroups $H_1, \ldots, H_m$. Namely, for every set of indices I the projection of A onto A_I is uniform (every element that has preimages has the same number of preimages; we already mentioned a similar property when saying that the variable g_I is uniformly distributed on its image). Indeed, let $H = H_{\{1,\ldots,m\}}$ be the intersection of all subgroups: $H = \bigcap_{i=1,\ldots,m} H_i$, and let H_I be the intersection of some of them: $H_I = \bigcap_{i \in I} H_i$. Then $H \subset H_I$ and we have surjective mappings:

$$G \to G/H \to G/H_I.$$

The projection of A onto A_I is the second mapping; the required property (the same number of preimages) is true since both the mapping $G \to G/H$ and the composition $G \to G/H_I$ have this property. The number of preimages for the projection is $\#H''/\#H' = \#A/\#A_I$.

We use this property and the following lemma.

Lemma 1. *Assume that the projection $\pi_I \colon A \to A_I$ (only I-coordinates remain) is uniform. Consider the set C_A and its projection $(C_A)_I$; let d be the difference in their dimensions: $d = \dim C_A - \dim(C_A)_I$. Then, for every $X \subset C_A$ we have*

$$\dim_H X \le \dim_H X_I + d.$$

Note that this lemma deals with two different projections: mappings $\pi_I \colon A \to A_I$ (finite sets) and $\Pi_I \colon C_A \to (C_A)_I$ (coordinate spaces); the second one applies the first one simultaneously for all positions in N-ary notation.

Proof. The dimension of C_A is equal to $\log \#A / \log N$, and the dimension of $(C_A)_I = \Pi_I(C_A)$ is equal to $\log \#A_I / \log N$, so the difference is equal to

$$\log(\#A/\#A_I)/\log N.$$

The ratio $\#A/\#A_I$ is the size of preimages for the uniform projection $\pi_I \colon A \to A_I$. To specify the first k digits in a point $x \in X$ we have to specify k digits of its projection $x_I \in X_I$, and also for every of k positions choose one of the preimages of some element of A_I. Now we may apply the point-to-set principle to get the desired result.

The application of this lemma, as we have discussed, finishes the proof of Theorem 2.

Discussion. Theorem 1 applies the point-to-set principle to some type of statements in the dimension theory. Why these (rather exotic) statements could be interesting? There are two possible reasons.

First, we get one more reason to consider the class of linear inequalities that are true for entropies of tuples: it can be equivalently characterized in terms of Kolmogorov complexity, in combinatorial terms (size of projections of multidimensional sets), as inequalities for group sizes — and now in terms of dimensions. Second, the point-to-set principle was used to prove results about dimensions using algorithmic information theory. Theorem 2 shows that the reverse direction is also possible, at least in theory (it would be quite surprising to see a proof of some new inequality that goes this way).

Acknowledgments. The author is grateful to all his colleagues, especially to Andrei Romashchenko, the members of the ESCAPE team in LIRMM and the Kolmogorov seminar, and the participants of the meetings organized by the American Institute of Mathematics and Dagstuhl in 2022 where some of the work presented here was discussed. Part of the work was supported by FLITTLA ANR-21-CE48-0023 grant.

References

1. Chan, T.H., Yeung, R.W.: On a relation between information inequalities and group theory. IEEE Trans. Inf. Theory **48**(7), 69–95 (2002)
2. Hammer, D., Romashchenko, A., Shen, A., Vereshchagin, N.: Inequalities for Shannon entropies and Kolmogorov complexities. J. Comput. Syst. Sci. **60**(2), 442–464 (2000)
3. Kolmogorov, A.N.: Logical basis for information theory and probability theory. IEEE Trans. Inf. Theory **14**(5), 662–664 (1968)
4. Lutz, J., Lutz, N.: Algorithmic information, plane Kakeya sets, and conditional dimension. ASM Trans. Comput. Theory **10**(2), 1–22 (2018)
5. Matúš, F., Csirmaz, L.: Entropy region and convolution. IEEE Trans. Inf. Theory **62**(11), 6007–6018 (2016)
6. Shen, A., Uspensky, V.A., Vereshchagin, N.: Kolmogorov complexity and algorithmic randomness, American Mathematical Society, 511 pp. (2017)
7. Zhang, Z., Yeung, R.W.: On characterization of entropy function via informational inequalities. IEEE Trans. Inf. Theory **48**(7), 1440–1452 (1998)

Computational Complexity

Elementarily Traceable Irrational Numbers

Keita Hiroshima$^{(\boxtimes)}$ and Akitoshi Kawamura

Kyoto University, Kyoto, Japan
{keitah,kawamura}@kurims.kyoto-u.ac.jp

Abstract. A function is called *elementary* if it can be computed in time bounded by a tower of powers of constant height. A *trace function* for an irrational number α is a function that maps each rational number r to a rational number that is closer to α than r is. We show, as was conjectured by Kristiansen, that there exists an irrational number that has an elementary trace function but whose continued fraction expansion is not elementary. We also show that there exists an irrational number that has an elementary trace function but whose *sum approximation*, i.e., the function that maps each positive integer n to the index of the nth 1 in the binary expansion of the number, is not elementary.

Keywords: Computable analysis · Elementary functions · Representations for irrational numbers · Trace functions · Continued fractions · Sum approximations

1 Introduction

We write $\mathbb{N}$ for the set of nonnegative integers and $\mathbb{Q}$ for the set of rational numbers. Kristiansen [2] compared several representations of real numbers (or of irrational numbers), including the following, from computational viewpoints.

Definition 1. *1. A* trace function *for a real number α is a function $T \colon \mathbb{Q} \to \mathbb{Q}$ such that $|T(r) - \alpha| < |r - \alpha|$ for each $r \in \mathbb{Q}$.*
2. The sum approximation *of a real number α is the strictly increasing function $S \colon \mathbb{N} \to \mathbb{N}$ such that $\alpha = a + \sum_{i=0}^{\infty} 2^{-(S(i)+1)}$ for some integer a.*
3. The continued fraction *for a real number α is the function $F \colon \mathbb{N} \to \mathbb{N}$ with positive values such that $\alpha = a + \lim_{n \to \infty} f_n$ for some integer a, where*

$$f_n = \cfrac{1}{F(0) + \cfrac{1}{F(1) + \cfrac{1}{\cdots + \cfrac{1}{F(n-1)}}}}. \tag{1}$$

Supported by JSPS KAKENHI Grant Numbers JP18H03203, JP23H03346 and JSPS Bilateral Program Grant Number JPJSBP120204809.

Each irrational number has a trace function, a (unique) sum approximation and a (unique) continued fraction (rational numbers do not have a trace function or a continued fraction).

In terms of computability, these three representations of irrational numbers are equivalent: an irrational number has a computable trace function exactly when it has a computable sum approximation, and also exactly when it has a computable continued fraction. They are also equivalent to representations based on Cauchy sequences, Dedekind cuts [2, Definition 4.1] or binary expansions [3, Definition 5.1]. But they are not equivalent for subrecursive classes, such as that of primitive recursive functions [5, VIII.8].

Kristiansen [2, Theorem 5.4] showed that the sum approximation of a number with a primitive recursive trace function is primitive recursive (and that the converse fails [3, Section 8]). He conjectured that the same implication fails for the subclass of *elementary* (see Sect. 2) functions. We prove this conjecture (in the form relativized by an arbitrary oracle ϕ) in part 1 of the following theorem.

On the other hand, an irrational number has a primitive recursive trace function if and only if it has a primitive recursive continued fraction [2, Corollary 8.5]. Kristiansen [2, Theorem 7.4] showed that an irrational number with an elementary continued fraction has an elementary trace function, and conjectured that the converse fails. We prove this conjecture in part 2 of the following theorem.

Theorem 1. *For each $\phi\colon \mathbb{N} \to \mathbb{N}$,*

1. *there is an irrational number that has a trace function elementary in ϕ but not a sum approximation elementary in ϕ;*
2. *there is an irrational number that has a trace function elementary in ϕ but not a continued fraction elementary in ϕ.*

Part 1 can be generalized easily to *base-b sum approximations from above* and *from below* [3, Definition 7.1] for each integer $b \geq 2$ instead of our notion of sum approximation, which is base-2 sum approximation from below.

Figure 1 summarizes what we know about the six representations mentioned so far. A solid arrow from representation A to representation B means that every irrational number with an elementary A has an elementary B, and a dotted arrow means the analogous relation for primitive recursive functions. Theorem 1 shows that there is no solid arrow from "trace function" to "sum approximation" or to "continued fraction".

2   Elementary Functions

Elementary functions [5, Section VIII.7] are those that can be computed in time bounded by a tower of powers of constant height, such as 2^n, 2^{2^n}, or $2^{2^{2^n}}$, where n is the input size. Here we present a definition relativized with an oracle ϕ:

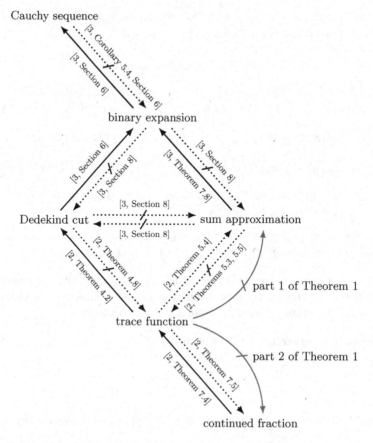

A $\longrightarrow$ B: Every irrational with an elementary A has an elementary B
A $\cdots\blacktriangleright$ B: Every irrational with a primitive recursive A has a primitive recursive B
A $\nrightarrow$ B: There is an irrational with an elementary A but no elementary B
A $\cdots\!/\!\blacktriangleright$ B: There is an irrational with a primitive recursive A but no primitive recursive B

Fig. 1. Some representations of irrational numbers.

Definition 2. *For $\phi\colon \mathbb{N} \to \mathbb{N}$, we define the class of functions* elementary *in ϕ inductively as follows.*

1. *ϕ is elementary in ϕ.*
2. *The functions* zero$\colon \mathbb{N} \to \mathbb{N}$, succ$\colon \mathbb{N} \to \mathbb{N}$, proj$_{i,k}\colon \mathbb{N}^k \to \mathbb{N}$ *(for positive integers k and $i \leq k$),* exp$_2\colon \mathbb{N} \to \mathbb{N}$ *and* max$\colon \mathbb{N}^2 \to \mathbb{N}$, *defined as follows, are elementary in ϕ:*

$$\text{zero}(x) = 0, \qquad \text{succ}(x) = x + 1, \qquad \text{proj}_{i,k}(x_1, \ldots, x_k) = x_i, \qquad (2)$$
$$\text{exp}_2(x) = 2^x, \qquad \text{max}(x, y) = \max\{x, y\}. \qquad (3)$$

3. *If* $h\colon \mathbb{N}^k \to \mathbb{N}$ *and* $g_1, \ldots, g_k\colon \mathbb{N}^l \to \mathbb{N}$ *(for positive integers k and l) are elementary in* ϕ, *so is the function* $f\colon \mathbb{N}^l \to \mathbb{N}$ *defined by*

$$f(\boldsymbol{x}) = h\big(g_1(\boldsymbol{x}), \ldots, g_k(\boldsymbol{x})\big). \tag{4}$$

4. *If* $g\colon \mathbb{N}^k \to \mathbb{N}$, $h\colon \mathbb{N}^{k+2} \to \mathbb{N}$, $j\colon \mathbb{N}^{k+1} \to \mathbb{N}$ *(for a positive integer k) are elementary in* ϕ, *and the function* $f\colon \mathbb{N}^{k+1} \to \mathbb{N}$ *defined by*

$$f(\boldsymbol{x}, 0) = g(\boldsymbol{x}), \qquad f(\boldsymbol{x}, y+1) = h\big(\boldsymbol{x}, y, f(\boldsymbol{x}, y)\big) \tag{5}$$

satisfies $f(\boldsymbol{x}, y) \leq j(\boldsymbol{x}, y)$ *for all* $(\boldsymbol{x}, y) \in \mathbb{N}^{k+1}$, *then* f *is elementary in* ϕ.

Recall that the class of functions primitive recursive in ϕ is obtained by replacing part 4 of this definition by

4' *If* $g\colon \mathbb{N}^k \to \mathbb{N}$ *and* $h\colon \mathbb{N}^{k+2} \to \mathbb{N}$ *(for a positive integer k) are primitive recursive in* ϕ, *so is the function* $f\colon \mathbb{N}^{k+1} \to \mathbb{N}$ *defined by* (5).

Thus, the definition of elementary functions imposes an additional requirement that the function f be bounded by a function j already known to be elementary. As a result, a function growing too fast is not elementary:

Lemma 1. *For a function* $\phi\colon \mathbb{N} \to \mathbb{N}$, *define* $\phi_*\colon \mathbb{N} \to \mathbb{N}$ *by*

$$\phi_*(n) = \sum_{i=0}^{n} \max\big\{\phi(i), 2^i\big\}. \tag{6}$$

Then the function $\Phi\colon \mathbb{N} \to \mathbb{N}$ *given by* $\Phi(n) = \phi_*^n(1)$ *is not elementary in* ϕ.

Proof. We can see by induction that for every $f\colon \mathbb{N}^k \to \mathbb{N}$ elementary in ϕ, there is $l \in \mathbb{N}$ such that $f(n_1, \ldots, n_k) < \phi_*^l(\max\{n_1, \ldots, n_k\})$ for all $n_1, \ldots, n_k \in \mathbb{N}$. Thus, if Φ is elementary in ϕ, there is $l \in \mathbb{N}$ such that $\Phi(n) < \phi_*^l(n)$ for all $n \in \mathbb{N}$, and in particular $\Phi(2l) < \phi_*^l(2l) \leq \phi_*^l(\exp_2^l(1)) \leq \phi_*^l(\phi_*^l(1)) = \Phi(2l)$, a contradiction. $\square$

But the failure of this function to be elementary is, in the following sense, "only" due to its fast growth rate. A function $f\colon \mathbb{N} \to \mathbb{N}$ is said to be (*elementary*) *honest* [4] in ϕ if its graph, i.e., the function $R\colon \mathbb{N} \times \mathbb{N} \to \mathbb{N}$ defined by

$$R(n, m) = \begin{cases} 0 & \text{if } m = f(n), \\ 1 & \text{if } m \neq f(n), \end{cases} \tag{7}$$

is elementary in ϕ. The following is easy to see (analogously to [4, Lemma 5]).

Lemma 2. *The function Φ defined in Lemma 1 is honest in ϕ.*

Lemma 3. *Let $U\colon \mathbb{N} \to \mathbb{N}$ be a function elementary in ϕ, and suppose that $f\colon \mathbb{N} \to \mathbb{N}$ is honest in ϕ and bounded by U, i.e., $f(n) \le U(n)$ for all $n \in \mathbb{N}$. Then f is elementary in ϕ.*

Proof. By the assumption, the graph R of f is elementary in ϕ. So is the function $g\colon \mathbb{N}^2 \to \mathbb{N}$ defined by $g(n,l) = \min(\{\, m \le l : R(n,m) = 0 \,\} \cup \{l\})$, since the class of functions elementary in ϕ is closed under bounded μ-recursion [5, Proposition VIII.7.3]. Thus f is elementary in ϕ because $f(n) = g(n, U(n))$ for all $n \in \mathbb{N}$. $\square$

We extend the notions of elementary and honest functions to functions whose domain and codomain are $\mathbb{Q}$, $\mathbb{Q}^2$, etc., by using a standard encoding of pairs, say $\langle x, y \rangle = (x + y)(x + y + 1)/2 + y$, and a notation $\nu_{\mathbb{Q}}\colon \mathbb{N} \to \mathbb{Q}$ of rational numbers, say $\nu_{\mathbb{Q}}(\langle \langle x, y \rangle, z \rangle) = (x - y)/(z + 1)$.

3   Proofs

We prove the theorem by simply considering the numbers whose sum approximation and continued fraction are the function Φ mentioned in Lemma 1 that grows too fast to be elementary. Interestingly, the fast growth also helps us find a trace function for the number.

Proof (part 1 of Theorem 1). Let $\phi\colon \mathbb{N} \to \mathbb{N}$, and define $S\colon \mathbb{N} \to \mathbb{N}$ to be the function Φ as in Lemma 1 which is not elementary in ϕ. We claim that the real number $\alpha = \sum_{i=0}^{\infty} 2^{-(S(i)+1)}$ with this sum approximation S has a trace function elementary in ϕ. Let $a_n = \sum_{i=0}^{n} 2^{-(S(i)+1)}$ and $b_n = a_n + 2^{-(S(n)+1)}$, so that $[a_0, b_0] \supseteq [a_1, b_1] \supseteq \cdots$ is a sequence of nested intervals containing α.

For every $n \in \mathbb{N}$ and a positive integer $d < S(n)$, we have $2^{S(n)+1}d < 2^{S(n)+1}S(n) \le 2^{2S(n)} \le 2^{\phi_*(S(n))} = 2^{S(n+1)}$; therefore, the closed interval $[a_{n+1}, b_{n+1}] = [a_n + 2^{-S(n+1)-1}, a_n + 2^{-S(n+1)}]$ lies strictly between two consecutive multiples a_n and $a_n + 1/(2^{S(n)+1}d)$ of $1/(2^{S(n)+1}d)$, and thus contains no multiple of $1/d$. This allows us to define a trace function $T\colon \mathbb{Q} \to \mathbb{Q}$ of α by

$$T(r) = \begin{cases} a_{n_0(r)+1} & \text{if } r < a_{n_0(r)+1}, \\ b_{n_0(r)+1} & \text{if } r > b_{n_0(r)+1}, \end{cases} \tag{8}$$

where $n_0(r)$ is the least $n \in \mathbb{N}$ such that the denominator $D(r)$ of the irreducible fraction for r is less than $S(n)$ (and hence the dichotomy on the right-hand side).

To see that T is elementary in ϕ, it suffices to show that the functions mapping each $r \in \mathbb{Q}$ to the numerator and denominator of (the irreducible fractions for) $a_{n_0(r)+1}$ and $b_{n_0(r)+1}$ are elementary in ϕ. It is straightforward to see that they are honest in ϕ, because so is S by Lemma 2. We can thus apply Lemma 3 to see that they are elementary in ϕ, noting that a bound on the denominator $2^{S(n_0(r)+1)+1}$ (and hence on the numerators, which are smaller) can be obtained by $S(n_0(r) + 1) = \phi_*^2(S(n_0(r) - 1)) \le \phi_*^2(D(r))$ by the minimality of $n_0(r)$. $\square$

For the other part of the theorem, we start by observing how the sequence of finite fractions f_n in Definition 1 converges: It can be shown [1, Chapter 1] that

$$f_n = \frac{p_n}{q_n} \quad \text{and} \quad f_{n+1} - f_n = \frac{(-1)^n}{q_n q_{n+1}} \tag{9}$$

for each $n \in \mathbb{N}$, where $p_n, q_n \in \mathbb{N}$ are defined inductively by

$$p_0 = 0, \qquad p_1 = 1, \qquad p_{n+2} = F(n+1)p_{n+1} + p_n, \tag{10}$$
$$q_0 = 1, \qquad q_1 = F(0), \qquad q_{n+2} = F(n+1)q_{n+1} + q_n. \tag{11}$$

Thus $\lim_{n \to \infty} f_n$ converges (for each positive-valued F) to some (irrational) number α because $|f_{n+2} - f_{n+1}|/|f_{n+1} - f_n| = q_n/q_{n+2} \leq q_n/(q_{n+1} + q_n) \leq \frac{1}{2}$, and

$$f_0 < f_2 < \cdots < \alpha < \cdots < f_3 < f_1. \tag{12}$$

Note that the convergence is fast if F is a fast growing function.

Proof (part 2 of Theorem 1). Let $\phi \colon \mathbb{N} \to \mathbb{N}$, and define $F \colon \mathbb{N} \to \mathbb{N}$ to be the function Φ as in Lemma 1 which is not elementary in ϕ. For this F, define f_n, p_n, q_n, for each $n \in \mathbb{N}$, and α, as above, so that F is the continued fraction for α. We claim that α has a trace function elementary in ϕ.

For every nonnegative even number n and a positive integer $d < q_{n+1}$, the closed interval $[f_{n+2}, f_{n+1}]$ lies strictly between two consecutive multiples f_n and $f_n + 1/(q_n d)$ of $1/(q_n d)$ (because of (9)), and thus does not contain any multiple of $1/d$. This allows us to define a trace function $T \colon \mathbb{Q} \to \mathbb{Q}$ of α by

$$T(r) = \begin{cases} f_{n_0(r)+2} & \text{if } r < f_{n_0(r)+2}, \\ f_{n_0(r)+1} & \text{if } r > f_{n_0(r)+1}, \end{cases} \tag{13}$$

where $n_0(r)$ denotes the smallest even number n such that the denominator $D(r)$ of the irreducible fraction for r is less than q_{n+1}.

To see that T is elementary in ϕ, note that since $p_i \leq q_i \leq F(i+1)$ inductively for each $i \in \mathbb{N}$, we have $p_{n_0(r)+2} \leq q_{n_0(r)+2} \leq F(n_0(r)+3) = \phi_*^5(F(n_0(r)-2)) \leq \phi_*^5(q_{n_0(r)-1}) \leq \phi_*^5(D(r))$. Thus, the functions $P, Q \colon \mathbb{Q} \to \mathbb{Q}$ defined by $P(r) = p_{n_0(r)+2}$ and $Q(r) = q_{n_0(r)+2}$ are bounded by $\phi_*^5 \circ D$. Since F and hence P, Q are honest in ϕ by Lemma 2, we can apply Lemma 3 to see that P and Q are elementary in ϕ. Since $f_{n_0(r)+2} = P(r)/Q(r)$, the function that maps each $r \in \mathbb{Q}$ to $f_{n_0(r)+2}$ (or likewise $f_{n_0(r)+1}$) is elementary in ϕ, and thus so is T. □

References

1. Khinchin, A.Y.: Continued Fractions. University of Chicago Press, Chicago (1964)
2. Kristiansen, L.: On Subrecursive Representability of Irrational Numbers. Computability **6**(3), 249–276 (2017)
3. Kristiansen, L.: On subrecursive representability of irrational numbers, part II. Computability **8**(1), 43–65 (2019)
4. Meyer, A.R., Ritchie, D.M.: A Classification of the Recursive Functions. Math. Logic Quarterly **18**(4–6), 71–82 (1972)
5. Odifreddi, P.G.: Classical Recursion Theory, vol. 2. Elsevier, Amsterdam (1999)

Logic vs Topology on Regular ω-languages

Vladislav Orekhovskii[1] and Victor Selivanov[1,2(✉)] [ID]

[1] Department of Mathematics and Computer Science,
St. Petersburg State University, Saint Petersburg, Russia
v.orekhovskii@alumni.nsu.ru
[2] A.P. Ershov Institute of Informatics Systems, Novosibirsk, Russia
vseliv@iis.nsk.su

Abstract. We describe precise relationships between logical and topological classifications of regular ω-languages. In particular, for any level of the Wagner hierarchy we provide a first-order sentence such that the corresponding ω-language is precisely at this level. The structure of the sentence closely mimics a set-theoretic operation describing the level as a Wadge class.

Keywords: Regular ω-language · Boolean operation · Wadge hierarchy · Wagner hierarchy · fine hierarchy

1 Introduction

Automata on infinite words is a well developed part of computer science which is fundamental for the analysis of infinite behaviour of finite-state systems. See e.g. [3,6,15,17,18] for the general theory and applications to verification and synthesis of such systems. In this study people employed different methods, including logical and topological ones.

Logical approach to automata theory was established by Büchi, Elgot and, independently, Trakhtenbrot who have shown that the regular ω-languages coincide with the sets of ω-words satisfying a sentence of monadic second-order logic. There is a similar relation of first order logic to aperiodic regular ω-languages based on the corresponding result of McNaughton and Papert for finite words. This relation leads to interesting logical classifications of aperiodic regular ω-languages similar to the Straubing-Therien and Brzozowski-Cohen hierarchies of languages of finite words. These hierarchies, induced by the quantifier-alternation hierarchies of defining sentences, were thoroughly investigated in the literature. Much of information is also known about difference hierarchies but there are many other interesting hierarchies which were not systematically studied so far. In Sect. 3 we give additional details and new facts about such hierarchies.

Topological approach to automata on infinite words is also well established; it is based on the fact that the set of infinite words carries the natural Cantor

This work was supported by the Russian Science Foundation, project 23-11-00133.

topology. This enables to classify regular ω-languages according to their complexity w.r.t. topological hierarchies known from descriptive set theory [2]. In this context, the Borel hierarchy and Hausdorff-Kuratowski difference hierarchies were thoroughly investigated. All these hierarchies are subsumed by the much finer Wadge hierarchy [19]. In automata theory, some restrictions of these hierarchies to regular ω-languages were considered. A series of papers culminated with introducing the finest possible topological classification of regular ω-languages known as Wagner's hierarchy [20] discovered independently of the Wadge hierarchy. In Sect. 4 we give some additional details about the topological hierarchies.

In this paper we initiate a systematic study of precise relationships between the logical and topological classifications of regular ω-languages. We establish tight syntactic connections between levels of the hierarchies such that each level of a logical hierarchy is contained in the corresponding level of the related topological hierarchy and conversely, for any level of the Wagner hierarchy we provide a first-order sentence such that the corresponding ω-language is precisely at this level. The structure of the sentence closely mimics a set-theoretic operation describing the level as a Wadge class. Informally, the logical hierarchies in a sense "cover" the topological ones. These main results of the paper are presented in Sect. 5.

The close relation between logical and topological hierarchies is heavily based on the so called fine hierarchy (FH) introduced by the second author in computability theory [7] in an attempt to identify "natural m-degrees". In [8] (see also [9,12] better accessible for English-speaking readers) the FH was characterised by set operations which enable to apply it in different contexts, including the logical and topological ones. Since the FH is the main technical tool of this paper, we recall in Sect. 2 its definition and necessary properties, and also establish a new one important for the main results.

After establishing some special properties of the FH in the logical and topological contexts in Sects. 3 and 4, we describe the relationships between them in Sect. 5, with a short discussion of remaining open questions. The established relationships are shown to be useful in proving some properties of logical FHs (notably, the fundamental non-collapse property) which in their statement do not mention topology at all. Some definitions and proofs concerning the logical FHs are rather involved. The main reason are peculiar properties of the corresponding quantifier-alternation hierarchies of sentences, namely the fact that every level of these hierarchies does not have the reduction property [14], in contrast with the finite Borel hierarchy.

2   Fine Hierarchy

Here we recall definition and some basic properties of the general (abstract) FH, and establish a useful new property. This is important for the sequel because all concrete logical and topological hierarchies are instantiations of the abstract FH.

Let $\mathbb{B} = (B, \cup, \cap, ^-, 0, 1)$ be a Boolean algebra. We often use abbreviation $ab = a \cap b$. For any sublattice L of $(B, \cup, \cap, 0, 1)$ and any k, let $L(k)$ be the set of elements of the form $\cup_i(a_{2i} \cap \bar{a}_{2i+1})$, where $a_0 \supseteq a_1 \supseteq \cdots$ and $a_k = 0$. The sequence $\{L(k)\}_{k\in\omega}$ is called the *difference hierarchy over L*.

By a *base in* $\mathbb{B}$ we mean a sequence $L = \{L_n\}_{n<\omega}$ of sublattices of $(B, \cup, \cap, 0, 1)$ such that $L_n \cup \check{L}_n \subseteq L_{n+1}$ for each $n < \omega$, where $\check{L}_n = \{\bar{a} \mid a \in L_n\}$. The base L is *reducible*, if any L_n has the reduction property (i.e., for all $x_0, x_1 \in L_n$ there are disjoint $y_0, y_1 \in L_n$ (*i.e., $y_0y_1 = 0$*) such that $y_i \subseteq x_i$ and $x_0 \cup x_1 = y_0 \cup y_1$.

Typical examples of bases is the finite Borel hierarchy in a topological space (this base is reducible in any second-countable zero-dimensional space [2]) and the quantifier-alternation hierarchies of formulas (these bases are typically non-reducible [14]). The idea of FH is to systematically describe refinements of the base hierarchy L. Well-known refinements are exemplified by the difference hierarchies over any L_n. Along with these, the FH over L subsumes many other refinements (in fact all of them, in some precise sense [9]).

The FH is defined in terms of the (rather exotic) operators $bisep$ and $Bisep$ on subsets of B which are finitary versions of the corresponding infinitary operators popular in the Wadge theory:

$$bisep(X, Y_0, Y_1, Y_2) = \{x_0y_0 \cup x_1y_1 \cup \bar{x}_0\bar{x}_1y_2 \mid x_i \in X, y_j \in Y_j, x_0x_1 = 0\},$$

$$Bisep(X, Y_0, Y_1, Y_2) = \{x_0y_0 \cup x_1y_1 \cup \bar{x}_0\bar{x}_1y_2 \mid x_i \in X, y_j \in Y_j, x_0x_1y_0 = x_0x_1y_1\}.$$

Operation $Bisep$ is more general and applies to FH over arbitrary base, operation $bisep$ leads to an equivalent easier definition of FH over reducible bases (see Lemma 1(6) below).

Definition 1. *The FH over a base L is the sequence $\{S_\alpha\}_{\alpha<\varepsilon_0}$, where $S_\alpha = S_\alpha^0$ and the classes $S_\alpha^n (n < \omega)$ are defined by induction on α:*

$$S_0^n = \{0\}; S_{\omega^\gamma}^n = S_\gamma^{n+1} \text{ for } \gamma > 0;$$
$$S_{\beta+1}^n = Bisep(L_n, S_\beta^n, \check{S}_\beta^n, S_0^n) \text{ for each } \beta < \varepsilon_0;$$
$$S_{\beta+\omega^\gamma}^n = Bisep(L_n, S_\beta^n, \check{S}_\beta^n, S_{\omega^\gamma}^n) \text{ for } \gamma > 0 \text{ and } \beta \text{ of the form } \beta = \omega^\gamma \cdot \beta_1 > 0.$$

In [9,11] one could find many concrete examples of FH which may be considered as the collection of iterated difference hierarchies over the lattices L_n. We recall some known properties of the introduced objects (and formulate one new property).

Lemma 1. *1. If $\alpha < \beta < \varepsilon_0$, then $S_\alpha \cup \check{S}_\alpha \subseteq S_\beta$.*
2. For any $n < \omega$, the sequence $\{S_k^n\}_{k<\omega}$ is the difference hierarchy over L_n.
3. The class $\bigcup_{\alpha<\omega^\omega} S_\alpha$ coincides with the Boolean closure $BC(L_1)$ of L_1.
4. If $\{L_n\}$ and $\{L_n'\}$ are bases in Boolean algebras B and B' respectively and $g : B \to B'$ is a homomorphism satisfying $g(L_n) \subseteq L_n'$ for all $n < \omega$, then $g(S_\alpha) \subseteq S_\alpha'$ for all $\alpha < \varepsilon_0$.
5. Classes of the fine hierarchy over a reducible base L coincide with the corresponding classes obtained by using the operator $bisep$ in place of $Bisep$ in Definition 1.

6. *Let $\alpha < \varepsilon_0$ be a limit ordinal, $a \in S_\alpha^n$ (resp. $a \in \check{S}_\alpha^n$), and $x \in L_{n+1} \cap \check{L}_{n+1}$. Then $ax \in S_\alpha^n$ (resp. $ax \in \check{S}_\alpha^n$).*

7. *Let $\alpha < \varepsilon_0$ be a limit ordinal and $n \in \omega$. Then $S_{\alpha+n} \cdot \check{S}_1 = S_{\alpha+n}$ and $\check{S}_{\alpha+n} \cdot \check{S}_1 = \check{S}_{\alpha+n}$, where $X \cdot Y = \{xy \mid x \in X, y \in Y\}$.*

Proof. Proofs of (1) — (6) may be found in [9,11], so we prove only (7). The proof is by induction on n, for $n = 0$ the statement follows from (6).

Suppose that $S_{\alpha+n} \cdot \check{S}_1 = S_{\alpha+n}$ and $\check{S}_{\alpha+n} \cdot \check{S}_1 = \check{S}_{\alpha+n}$. In the inductive step, we first check that $S_{\alpha+n+1} \cdot \check{S}_1 = S_{\alpha+n+1}$. Let $a \in S_{\alpha+n+1}$, $b \in \check{S}_1$. By Definition 1, $a = x_0 y_0 \cup x_1 y_1$, where $x_0, x_1 \in S_1, y_0 \in S_{\alpha+n}, y_1 \in \check{S}_{\alpha+n}$ and $x_0 x_1 y_0 = x_0 x_1 y_1$. We have $ab = (x_0 y_0 \cup x_1 y_1)b = x_0(y_0 b) \cup x_1(y_1 b)$ and $x_0 x_1(y_0 b) = x_0 x_1(y_1 b)$, $x_0, x_1 \in S_1$. Note that by the induction hypothesis $y_0 b \in S_{\alpha+n}, y_1 b \in \check{S}_{\alpha+n}$. Thus, $ab \in S_{\alpha+n+1}$.

It remains to check that $\check{S}_{\alpha+n+1} \cdot \check{S}_1 = \check{S}_{\alpha+n+1}$. Let $a \in \check{S}_{\alpha+n+1}$, $b \in \check{S}_1$. Notice that $\bar{a} = c \in S_{\alpha+n+1}, \bar{b} = e \in S_1$. We have $ab = \overline{c \cup e}$. It suffices to show that $(c \cup e) \in S_{\alpha+n+1}$. By Definition 1, $c = x_0 y_0 \cup x_1 y_1$, where $x_0, x_1 \in S_1, y_0 \in S_{\alpha+n}, y_1 \in \check{S}_{\alpha+n}$ and $x_0 x_1 y_0 = x_0 x_1 y_1$. We have $c \cup e = (x_0 \cup e)(y_0 \cup e) \cup (x_1 \cup e)(y_1 \cup e)$. Note that:

$(x_0 \cup e), (x_1 \cup e) \in S_1 = L_0$;

$(y_0 \cup e) \in S_{\alpha+n}$ (since $(y_0 \cup e) = \overline{\bar{y_0}\bar{e}}$ and by the induction hypothesis holds $\bar{y_0}\bar{e} \in \check{S}_{\alpha+n}$ (notice that $\bar{y_0} \in \check{S}_{\alpha+n}, \bar{e} \in \check{S}_1$));

$(y_1 \cup e) \in \check{S}_{\alpha+n}$ since $(y_1 \cup e) = \overline{\bar{y_1}\bar{e}}$ and by the induction hypothesis holds $\bar{y_1}\bar{e} \in S_{\alpha+n}$ (notice that $\bar{y_1} \in S_{\alpha+n}, \bar{e} \in \check{S}_1$);

$(x_0 \cup e)(x_1 \cup e)(y_0 \cup e) = x_0 x_1 y_0 \cup e = x_0 x_1 y_1 \cup e = (x_0 \cup e)(x_1 \cup e)(y_0 \cup e)$.

Thus, $c \cup e \in S_{\alpha+n+1}$ and hence $ab = \overline{c \cup e} \in \check{S}_{\alpha+n+1}$. $\square$

Note that by the Stone Representation Theorem, we may (up to isomorphism) think of the L_n's as of lattices of sets (i.e., sublattices of a power-set Boolean algebra $P(X)$) which suffices for the most of concrete examples of FHs. Nevertheless, considering abstract lattices is sometimes useful, e.g. when we deal with hierarchies of formulas, as we do in the next section.

3   Logical Hierarchies

Let A be a finite alphabet containing at least two symbols. We call an infinite sequence of elements of A an ω-*word* over A. A set of ω-words is an ω-*language*. A set of all ω-words over A is denoted by A^ω. Let A^* and A^ω denote respectively the sets of all words and of all ω-words over A respectively. For every $n \in \omega$ denote by A^n the set off all words of length n. Denote by $|v|$ the length of a finite word $v \in A^*$. For every $w \in A^\omega$ and $n > 0$, let $w{\upharpoonright}n \in A^*$ be the initial segment of w of length n. Also we denote by $w(i)$ the i-th letter of the word w. For $w \in A^\omega$ and $a \in A$, let $card(w, a)$ be the cardinality of the set $\{i \in \mathbb{N} \mid w(i) = a\}$.

We associate with $A = \{a, \dots\}$ the signature $\sigma_A = \{\leqslant, Q_a, \dots\}$, where $\leqslant$ is a binary relation symbol and Q_a (for each $a \in A$) is a unary relation symbol. We also consider some expansions of σ_A, namely the signatures $\tau_A = \sigma_A \cup \{p, s\}$

and $\mu_A = \sigma_A \cup \{P_d^r \mid 0 \leq r < d < \omega\}$, where p, s are unary function symbols and every P_d^r is a unary relation symbol.

For any $\rho \in \{\sigma_A, \tau_A, \mu_A\}$, every ω-word $x \in A^\omega$ can be viewed as a ρ-structure $\mathbf{x} = (\mathbb{N}; \leq, Q_a, \ldots)$ where $\leq$ has its usual meaning, for each $a \in A$ $Q_a(i) \leftrightarrow x_i = a$, s is the successor function, p is the predecessor function (with $p(0) = 0$), and P_d^r are true precisely on the positions equivalent to r modulo d. Let Σ_n^ρ be the class of languages $L_\phi = \{x \in A^\omega \mid \mathbf{x} \models \phi\}$ where ϕ ranges over the level Σ_n of quantifier-alternation hierarchy of ρ-sentences. For the sets $FO_\rho = \bigcup_n \Sigma_n^\rho$ we then have the well-known inclusions $FO_{\sigma_A} = FO_{\tau_A} \subset FO_{\mu_A} \subset \mathcal{R}_A$ where $\mathcal{R}_A$ is the class of regular ω-languages over A. By a theorem of McNaughton and Papert (see e.g. [6,15,17]), FO_{σ_A} coincides with the class of aperiodic (star-free) regular ω-languages over A.

Obviously, $\mathcal{L} = \{\Sigma_{1+n}^\rho\}$ is a base in $P(A^\omega)$; let $\{\mathcal{S}_\alpha^\rho\}_{\alpha < \varepsilon_0}$ be the FH over $\mathcal{L}$. As follows from [14], none of the levels $\Sigma_{1+n}^\rho, \Pi_{1+n}^\rho, n \leq \omega$, has the reduction property for $\rho \in \{\sigma_A, \tau_A\}$; we guess that the same applies also to $\rho = \mu_A$. Thus, in the definition of $\mathcal{S}_\alpha^\rho$ we cannot use the operator $bisep$ instead of $Bisep$ (see Definition 1). This is the main reason for some technical difficulties in the proofs of results about the logical FHs $\{\mathcal{S}_\alpha^\rho\}$ below.

We recall clear combinatorial descriptions of Σ_1^ρ (see e.g. p. 348 in [6], for $\rho = \sigma_A$ and p. 6 of [1] for $\rho = \mu_A$) in terms of regular expressions; for higher levels of the quantifier-alternation hierarchies such clear descriptions are not known.

Lemma 2. *1. $L \in \Sigma_1^{\sigma_A}$ iff L is a finite union of language of the form $A^* a_1 A^* \cdots a_k A^\omega$, where $a_i \in A$ for each $1 \leq i \leq k$.*
2. $L \in \Sigma_1^{\tau_A}$ iff L is a finite union of languages of the form $A^* w_1 A^* \cdots w_k A^\omega$, where $w_i \in A^*$ for each $1 \leq i \leq k$.
3. $L \in \Sigma_1^{\mu_A}$ iff L is a finite union of languages of the form $(A^d)^* a_1 (A^d)^* \cdots a_k A^\omega$, where $a_i \in A$ for each $1 \leq i \leq k$.

The sequence $\{\mathcal{S}_\alpha^\rho\}_{\alpha < \varepsilon_0}$ contains many natural logical hierarchies of regular languages as subsequences (e.g., the quantifier-alternation hierarchy $\{\Sigma_{1+n}^\rho\}$ or the difference hierarchy $\{\Sigma_n^\rho(k)\}_{k \in \omega}$ over any fixed level Σ_n^ρ. These hierarchies (and especially their versions for languages of finite words) are rather popular in the literature. Since the logical FHs also subsume many other natural hierarchies, its study seems important, as a natural extension of the well-studied objects. Among the most important questions are the non-collapse problem (the FH $\{\mathcal{S}_\alpha^\rho\}_{\alpha < \varepsilon_0}$ *does not collapse, if* $\mathcal{S}_\alpha^\rho \not\subseteq \check{\mathcal{S}}_\alpha^\rho$ for all $\alpha < \varepsilon_0$) and the decidability problem for any fixed level of the hierarchy (given a deterministic Muller automaton, decide whether the corresponding ω-language is in this level).

Our results below about the logical FHs imply, in particular, their non-collapse for levels $< \omega^\omega$. The main goal of this section is to construct, for each $\alpha < \omega^\omega$, a language N_α that witnesses the non-collapse in level α (more precisely, in this section we only show that N_α is in $\mathcal{S}_\alpha$, and in the subsequent sections, using the relation to topology, that N_α is not in the dual level).

First we specify N_α by a σ_A-sentence for some alphabet A depending on α. We often deal with alphabets $A \subseteq \mathbb{N}$; obviously, sticking to such alphabets do not restrict our considerations. We define some functions used in alphabet encodings below.

Definition 2. *1. For any alphabets $A_1, \ldots, A_n$, define a map $m : A_1^\omega \times \cdots \times A_n^\omega \to (A_1 \cup \cdots \cup A_n)^\omega$ by $m(u_1, \ldots, u_n) = u_1(0) \cdots u_n(0) u_1(1) \cdots u_n(1) \cdots,$ where $u_i \in A_i^\omega$.*

2. For any n and j, define a bijection $\eta : \{0, 1, \ldots, n\} \to \{0, 1 + j, \ldots, n + j\}$ such that $\eta(0) = 0$ and $\eta(x) = x + j$ for $x > 0$. This function induces the function $\eta_j : \{0, 1, \ldots, n\}^\omega \to \{0, 1 + j, \ldots, n + j\}^\omega$ such that $\eta_j(w) = \eta(w(0))\eta(w(1)) \cdots$.

Since the general construction is a bit cumbersome, we start with easy examples of languages in levels $\Sigma_1^\rho, \Sigma_2^\rho$, and in levels of the difference hierarchies over them. We define $\psi_1(x) = \exists y Q_x(y)$ and $\psi_2(x) = \exists y \forall z > y \neg Q_x(z)$. For every $i, n \geqslant 1$ let $L_{1,i}^n$ be the language of all ω-words over the alphabet $\{0, 1, \ldots, n\}$ containing at least i entries of "1". Let also $L_{2,i}^n$ be the language of all ω-words over the alphabet $\{0, 1, \ldots, n\}$ containing only a finite number of entries of "i", where $i \leqslant n$.

Lemma 3. *For every $i, n \geqslant 1$ we have $L_{1,i}^n \in \Sigma_1^\rho$ and $L_{2,i}^n \in \Sigma_2^\rho$ where $\rho = \sigma_{\{0, \ldots, n\}}$.*

Proof. The language $L_{1,i}^n$ is defined by the Σ_1^ρ-formula

$$\phi_i = \exists p_1 \ldots \exists p_i ((p_1 < \ldots < p_i) \wedge (Q_1(p_1) \wedge \ldots \wedge Q_1(p_i)))$$

while the language $L_{2,i}^n$ is defined by the formula $\psi_2(i) \in \Sigma_2^\rho$. $\qquad \square$

Now we define $D_{1,i} = \bigcup_{j \geqslant 1} (D_j \setminus D_{j+1})$, where $D_n = L_{1,n}^1$ if $n \leqslant i$, and $D_n = \varnothing$ otherwise. In other words, if i is even, then $D_{1,i}$ is the union of the languages of all ω-words containing exactly j entries of "1" (where j runs over all odd integers less than i); accordingly, $D_{1,i+1}$ is the union of $D_{1,i}$ and the language of all ω-words containing at least $i + 1$ entries of "1".

Let also $D_{2,i} = \bigcup_{j \geqslant 1} (D_j \setminus D_{j+1})$, where $D_n = L_{2,n}^i$ if $n \leqslant i$ and $D_n = \varnothing$ otherwise. In other words, if i is even, then $D_{2,i}$ is the union of the languages of all ω-words containing an infinite number of entries of "j" and only a finite number of entries of "j-1" (where j runs over all even positive integers less than i).

The next lemma is checked similarly to Lemma 3, using Lemma 1(2) and the following formulas: for any $n \geqslant 1$, let $\psi_{2,n} = (\phi_1 \wedge \neg \phi_2) \vee \cdots \vee (\phi_{2n-1} \wedge \neg \phi_{2n})$, where $\phi_i = \psi_2(i)$, if $1 \leqslant i \leqslant n$ and ϕ_i is the false formula otherwise.

Lemma 4. *For every $i, n \geqslant 1$ we have: $D_{1,i} \in \Sigma_1^\rho(i)$ and $D_{2,i} \in \Sigma_2^\rho(i)$ where $\rho = \sigma_{\{0, \ldots, n\}}$.*

We proceed with the definition of N_α for each $\alpha < \omega^\omega$ (sticking to such ordinals is explained by properties of Wagner hierarchy recalled in the next section). Every such positive ordinal can be uniquely represented in the form $\alpha = \omega^{\alpha_1} + \cdots + \omega^{\alpha_k}$, where $\omega > \alpha_1 \geqslant \cdots \geqslant \alpha_k \geqslant 0$. Denote by $\mathcal{O}$ the class of all limit ordinals less than ω^ω. Let $lh(\alpha) = k$ and let π be the map taking every $\alpha \in \mathcal{O}$ to the corresponding tuple $(\alpha_1, ..., \alpha_k)$, $\alpha_k > 0$. Let l be the function that takes each tuple $(x_1, \ldots, x_n)$ of positive integers to $\sum_{i=1}^{n-1} 2^i + \sum_{i=1}^{n} 2^{n-i} x_i$. For any ρ-sentence ϕ and any $n \geqslant 0$, let $shift_n(\phi)$ be the sentence obtained from ϕ by changing all subformulas of the form $Q_i(x)$ to $Q_{i+n}(x)$. We define the sentence ν_α and the language N_α for every $\alpha \in \mathcal{O}$ by induction on $lh(\alpha)$ as follows.

Definition 3. *1. If $lh(\alpha) = 1$, then $\alpha = \omega^{\alpha_1}$ for some positive integer α_1. We put $\nu_\alpha = \psi_{2,\alpha_1}$.*
If $lh(\alpha) > 1$, then $\alpha = \omega^{\alpha_1} + \cdots + \omega^{\alpha_{n-1}} + \omega^{\alpha_n} = \beta + \omega^{\alpha_n}$, where $n > 1$ and $\beta = \omega^{\alpha_1} + \cdots + \omega^{\alpha_{n-1}}$. We put

$$\nu_\alpha = (\phi_{\alpha,1} \wedge \phi_{\alpha,2}) \vee (\phi_{\alpha,3} \wedge \phi_{\alpha,4}) \vee (\neg \phi_{\alpha,1} \wedge \neg \phi_{\alpha,3} \wedge \phi_{\alpha,5}),$$

where $\phi_{\alpha,1} = \psi_1(1)$, $\phi_{\alpha,2} = \phi_{\alpha,2,1} \wedge \phi_{\alpha,2,2} = shift_1(\nu_\beta) \wedge \neg \psi_1(2 + l(\pi(\beta)))$, $\phi_{\alpha,3} = \psi_1(2 + l(\pi(\beta)))$, $\phi_{\alpha,4} = \phi_{\alpha,4,1} \wedge \phi_{\alpha,4,2} = \neg shift_{2+l(\pi(\beta))}(\nu_\beta) \wedge \neg \psi_1(1)$, $\phi_{\alpha,5} = shift_{2+2l(\pi(\beta))}(\nu_{\omega^{\alpha_n}})$.
2. Let $N_{\alpha,1} = L_{\phi_{\alpha,1}} \cap \{0,1\}^\omega$, $N_{\alpha,2} = L_{\phi_{\alpha,2}} \cap \{0, 2, \ldots, 1 + l(\pi(\beta))\}^\omega$, $N_{\alpha,3} = L_{\phi_{\alpha,3}} \cap \{0, 2 + l(\pi(\beta))\}^\omega$, $N_{\alpha,4} = L_{\phi_{\alpha,4}} \cap \{0, 3 + l(\pi(\beta)), \ldots, 2 + 2l(\pi(\beta))\}^\omega$, $N_{\alpha,5} = L_{\phi_{\alpha,5}} \cap \{0, 3 + 2l(\pi(\beta)), \ldots, l(\pi(\alpha))\}^\omega$ and, finally, let N_α be the language defined by the ρ-sentence ν_α, where $\rho = \sigma_A$ and A is the union of all mentioned alphabets.

Lemma 5. *For every ordinal $\alpha \in \mathcal{O}$ we have $N_\alpha \in \mathcal{S}_\alpha^\rho$.*

Proof. The proof is by induction on $lh(\alpha)$. For $lh(\alpha) = 1$ the assertion holds by Lemmas 4 and 1(2). Let now $lh(\alpha) = n > 1$, then $\alpha = \beta + \omega^{\alpha_n}$, where $lh(\beta) = n - 1$. From Definition 3 it follows that $N_\alpha = (L_{\phi_{\alpha,1}} \cap L_{\phi_{\alpha,2}}) \cup (L_{\phi_{\alpha,3}} \cap L_{\phi_{\alpha,4}}) \cup (\bar{L}_{\phi_{\alpha,1}} \cap \bar{L}_{\phi_{\alpha,3}} \cap L_{\phi_{\alpha,5}})$. Notice that:

1. $L_{\phi_{\alpha,1}}, L_{\phi_{\alpha,3}} \in \Sigma_1^\rho$ (follows from the definitions of $\phi_{\alpha,1}$ and $\phi_{\alpha,3}$);
2. since $L_{\phi_{\alpha,2,1}} \in \mathcal{S}_\beta$ by the induction hypothesis and $L_{\phi_{\alpha,2}} \in \Pi_1^\rho$ by definition, it follows from Lemma 1(7) that $L_{\phi_{\alpha,2}} \in \mathcal{S}_\beta^\rho$;
3. likewise, $L_{\phi_{\alpha,4}} \in \check{\mathcal{S}}_\beta^\rho$;
4. $L_{\phi_{\alpha,5}} \in \mathcal{S}_{\omega^{\alpha_1}}^\rho$ (by the induction hypothesis);
5. $L_{\phi_{\alpha,1}} \cap L_{\phi_{\alpha,2}} \cap L_{\phi_{\alpha,3}} = L_{\phi_{\alpha,1}} \cap L_{\phi_{\alpha,2}} \cap L_{\phi_{\alpha,4}} = \varnothing$.

Thus, $N_\alpha \in \mathcal{S}_\alpha^\rho$ by Definition 1.　　　　　　　　□

Next we define $\nu_{\alpha+n}, N_{\alpha+n}$ for any $\alpha \in \mathcal{O}$ and positive integer n by induction on n. We use the function κ that takes each pair (β, n), where $\beta \in \omega^\omega$, to $2^{n-1}(l(\pi(\beta)) + 2)$. We also use the function

$$\theta(\alpha) = \begin{cases} 1, \alpha < \omega, \\ l(\pi(\alpha)), \alpha \in \mathcal{O}, \\ 2(\kappa(\beta, n)) - 1, \alpha = \beta + n, \text{ where } \beta \in \mathcal{O}, n \geqslant 1. \end{cases}$$

Definition 4. *1. We put* $\nu_{\alpha+n} = (\phi_{\alpha+n,1} \wedge \phi_{\alpha+n,2}) \vee (\phi_{\alpha+n,3} \wedge \phi_{\alpha+n,4})$,
where $\phi_{\alpha+n,1} = \psi_1(1)$, $\phi_{\alpha+n,2} = \phi_{\alpha+n,2,1} \wedge \phi_{\alpha+n,2,2} = shift_1(\nu_{\alpha+n-1}) \wedge$
$\neg\psi_1(\kappa(\alpha, n))$, $\phi_{\alpha+n,3} = \psi_1(\kappa(\alpha, n))$, $\phi_{\alpha+n,4} = \phi_{\alpha+n,4,1} \wedge \phi_{\alpha+n,4,2} =$
$\neg shift_{\kappa(\alpha,n)}(\nu_{\alpha+n-1}) \wedge \neg\psi_1(1)$.
2. Let $N_{\alpha+n}$ *be the language defined by the sentence* $\nu_{\alpha+n}$. *We also define* $N_{\alpha,1} =$
$L_{\phi_{\alpha,1}} \cap \{0,1\}^\omega$, $N_{\alpha,2} = L_{\phi_{\alpha,2,1}} \cap \{0, 2, \dots, \kappa(\alpha, n) - 1\}^\omega$, $N_{\alpha,3} = L_{\phi_{\alpha,3}} \cap$
$\{0, \kappa(\alpha, n)\}^\omega$, $N_{\alpha,4} = L_{\phi_{\alpha,4,1}} \cap \{0, \kappa(\alpha, n) + 1, \dots, 2(\kappa(\alpha, n) - 1)\}^\omega$.

Definitions 3 and 4 provide languages N_α for each infinite $\alpha < \omega^\omega$. For $\alpha < \omega$, let $N_\alpha = D_{1,\alpha}$ be the language from Lemma 4.

Lemma 6. *For every* $\alpha < \omega^\omega$ *we have* $N_\alpha \in \mathcal{S}_\alpha^\rho$.

Proof. For $\alpha < \omega$ the assertion holds by Lemma 4. For a limit ordinal α the assertion holds by Lemma 5. In the case of an ordinal $\alpha + n$ where α is limit and n is a positive integer, we argue by induction on n. From Definition 4 it follows that $N_{\alpha+n} = (L_{\phi_{\alpha+n,1}} \cap L_{\phi_{\alpha+n,2}}) \cup (L_{\phi_{\alpha+n,3}} \cap L_{\phi_{\alpha+n,4}})$. Notice that:

1. $L_{\phi_{\alpha+n,1}}, L_{\phi_{\alpha+n,3}} \in \Sigma_1^\rho$ (follows from the definitions of $\phi_{\alpha+n,1}, \phi_{\alpha+n,3}$);
2. since $L_{\phi_{\alpha+n,2,1}} \in \mathcal{S}_{\alpha+n-1}^\rho$ by the induction hypothesis and $L_{\phi_{\alpha+n,2,2}} \in \Pi_1^\rho$ by the definition, it follows from Lemma 1(7) that $L_{\phi_{\alpha+n,2}} \in \mathcal{S}_{\alpha+n-1}^\rho$;
3. likewise, $L_{\phi_{\alpha+n,4}} \in \check{\mathcal{S}}_{\alpha+n-1}^\rho$;
4. $L_{\phi_{\alpha+n,1}} \cap L_{\phi_{\alpha+n,2}}' \cap L_{\phi_{\alpha+n,4}} = L_{\phi_{\alpha+n,1}} \cap L_{\phi_{\alpha+n,2}} \cap L_{\phi_{\alpha+n,3}} = \varnothing$.

Thus, $N_{\alpha+n} \in \mathcal{S}_{\alpha+n}^\rho$. □

Example: Consider the language $N_{\omega+1}$ over the alphabet $\{0, 1, \dots, 4\}$. From our definition it follows that $N_{\omega+1} = (L_{\phi_1} \cap L_{\phi_2}) \cup (L_{\phi_3} \cap L_{\phi_4})$, where: $\phi_1 = \psi_1(1)$, $\phi_3 = \psi_1(3)$, $\phi_2 = \phi_2(2) \wedge \neg\psi_1(3)$, $\phi_4 = \neg\phi_2(4) \wedge \neg\psi_1(1)$. In other words, it is the language of all ω-words containing at least one entry of "1", zero entries of "3"'s and only a finite number of entries of "2"; or at least one entry of "3", zero entries of "1" and infinitely many of "4".

We constructed languages N_α over alphabets $\{0, 1, \dots, \theta(\alpha)\}$ with properties essential for the sequel. Can we construct similar languages over a fixed alphabet? We currently do not the answer for signature σ_A but we can do that for the signature τ_A, for an arbitrary fixed alphabet, in particular for the binary alphabet $A = \{0, 1\}$. A straightforward coding technique may be used to encode (using also the functions p, s) languages N_α into languages N_α^τ in signature $\tau_{\{0,1\}}$ with the same property.

We do the encoding in three steps. In the first step we encode the language N_α into the language $N_\alpha^{mod} \subseteq \{0,1\}^\omega$, defined by a sentence of the signature $\mu_{\{0,1\}}$. Note that these languages are regular but not aperiodic. In the second step we encode the language N_α^{mod} into the language $N_\alpha^2 \subseteq \{0,1,2\}^\omega$ definable by a sentence of the signature τ. Notice that these languages are aperiodic. This result can be strengthened by further encoding the language $N_\alpha^2 \subseteq \{0,1,2\}^\omega$ into the language $N_\alpha^1 \subseteq \{0,1\}^\omega$ definable by a sentence of the signature $\tau_{\{0,1\}}$.

First step. Let α be an arbitrary ordinal such that $\omega < \alpha < \omega^\omega$. By definition, let ν_α^{mod} be the sentence obtained from ν_α with changing all subformulas $Q_n(i)$ to $Q_1(i) \wedge P_{\theta(\alpha)}^n(i)$.

Example. Consider the languages $N_{\omega+1} \subseteq \{0, 1, ..., 4\}^\omega$ and $N_{\omega+1}^{mod} \subseteq \{0, 1\}^\omega$. An ω-word u over the alphabet $\{0, 1\}$ is in $N_{\omega+1}^{mod}$ if and only if:

1. the set $\{p \in \mathbb{N} \mid p \equiv_4 1 \text{ and } u(p) = 1\}$ is not empty,
2. the set $\{p \in \mathbb{N} \mid p \equiv_4 2 \text{ and } u(p) = 1\}$ is finite,
3. the set $\{p \in \mathbb{N} \mid p \equiv_4 3 \text{ and } u(p) = 1\}$ is empty,

or

1. the set $\{p \in \mathbb{N} \mid p \equiv_4 3 \text{ and } u(p) = 1\}$ is not empty,
2. the set $\{p \in \mathbb{N} \mid p \equiv_4 0 \text{ and } u(p) = 1\}$ is infinite,
3. the set $\{p \in \mathbb{N} \mid p \equiv_4 1 \text{ and } u(p) = 1\}$ is empty.

Thus, every occurrence of the symbol $n > 0$ in a word in the language N_α corresponds to an occurence of a 1 in a position equivalent to n modulo 4.

Denote $s(s^k(x))$ by $s^{k+1}(x)$, where $s^1(x) = s(x)$.

Second step. Let α be an arbitrary ordinal such that $\omega < \alpha < \omega^\omega$. By definition, put ν_α^2 the sentence obtained from ν_α^{mod} with the following rule:

1. if a variable x is bounded by the $\exists$ quantifier, the subformula $Q_n(x)$ is changed to $Q_2(x) \wedge Q_1(s^n(x))$,
2. if a variable x is bounded by the $\forall$ quantifier, the subformula $Q_n(x)$ is changed to $Q_2(x) \to Q_1(s^n(x))$.

Thus, the conditions on entries of "n" correspond to the conditions on entries of "1"'s n positions right of the separator ("2").

Denote

$$\varphi(n, i) = Q_0(i) \wedge Q_1(p(i)) \wedge Q_1(p^2(i)) \wedge ... \wedge Q_1(p^n(i)) \wedge Q_0(p^{n+1}(i)).$$

This formula is true on a position i of a word $x \in A^\omega$ if and only if $x \upharpoonright i = w01^n0$, where $w \in A^*$.

Third step. Let α be an arbitrary ordinal such that $\omega < \alpha < \omega^\omega$.

By definition, put ν_α^1 the sentence obtained from ν_α^2 with changing all subformulas $Q_2(x)$ to $\varphi(\theta(\alpha) + 3, x)$. Summarizing, we obtain the following lemma.

Lemma 7. *For every* $\alpha < \omega^\omega$, *the language* $N_\alpha^\tau = N_\alpha^1$ *is in* $\mathcal{S}_\alpha^\tau$.

4 Topological Hierarchies

Here we discuss some topological FHs related to this paper. Note that for every finite non-unary alphabet A, the set A^ω carries the Cantor topology with the open sets of the form $X \cdot A^\omega$, where $X \subseteq A^*$. This topological space is compact, and for every finite non-unary alphabets A_1, A_2 the spaces A_1^ω, A_2^ω are homeomorphic.

We mostly work with a fixed alphabet A. Let $\mathcal{L} = \{\mathbf{\Sigma}^0_{1+n}\}_{n<\omega}$ be the (finite) Borel hierarchy in A^ω (see e.g. [2] for the definition). As usual, let $\mathbf{\Pi}^0_n = \{\bar{L} \mid L \in \mathbf{\Sigma}^0_n\}$ and let $\{\mathbf{\Sigma}^0_n(k)\}_{k\in\omega}$ be the difference hierarchy over $\mathbf{\Sigma}^0_n$.

The sequence $\mathcal{L}$ is a base (sometimes called the Borel base), hence we can construct the FH $\{\mathbf{S}_\alpha\}_{\alpha<\varepsilon_0}$ over $\mathcal{L}$. As is well known, the base $\mathcal{L}$ is reducible, hence by Lemma 1(5), the FH $\{\mathbf{S}_\alpha\}_{\alpha<\varepsilon_0}$ may be obtained by using in Definition 2 the operation $bisep$ instead of $Bisep$. This is essential for proving an important property of the languages N_α below.

The FH is a very small but important fragment of the Wadge hierarchy in A^ω which is defined in terms of the Wadge reducibility (the many-one reducibility by continuous functions). Let A_1, A_2 be alphabets and $L_1 \subseteq A_1^\omega, L_2 \subseteq A_2^\omega$. We say that the language L_1 is *Wadge-reducible to* L_2 (we use notation $L_1 \leq_W L_2$) if there is a continuous function $f : A_1^\omega \to A_2^\omega$ with $L_1 = f^{-1}(L_2)$. The *Wadge hierarchy* in A^ω is essentially the degree structure of Borel subsets of A^ω under the Wadge reducibility in A^ω (obtained when $A = A_1 = A_2$). The latter structure is semi-well-ordered [19], i.e. well founded and has no antichains of length 3. We the following property of the Wadge hierarchy.

Lemma 8. *Any non-self-dual level $\mathcal{C}$ of the Wadge hierarchy (including the levels $\mathbf{S}_\alpha$ above) have the following property: a language L is in $\mathcal{C} \setminus \check{\mathcal{C}}$ iff L is Wadge complete in $\mathcal{C}$.*

Since we are mostly interested in regular ω-languages, it is natural to restrict the notions and facts recalled above to the class $\mathcal{R} = \mathcal{R}_A$ of such languages over A. In [4] it was shown that $\mathcal{R} \subseteq BC(\mathbf{\Sigma}^0_2)$, i.e. every ω-regular language can be represented as a Boolean combination of $\mathbf{\Sigma}^0_2$-languages. Let $\{\mathcal{R}_\alpha\}_{\alpha<\varepsilon_0}$ be the FH over the base $\{\mathcal{R} \cap \mathbf{\Sigma}_{1+n}\}_{n<\omega}$ (this base is reducible [10]). Then $\mathcal{R}_\alpha = \mathcal{R}$ for all $\alpha \geq \omega^\omega$; this explains why in this paper we mainly deal with levels $< \omega^\omega$ of the FHs. In [10] it was shown that the initial segment $\{\mathcal{R}_\alpha\}_{\alpha<\omega^\omega}$ essentially coincides with the Wagner hierarchy [20] which is the most fundamental topological classification of regular ω-languages. The Wagner hierarchy is essentially the degree structure of regular ω-languages under the Wadge reducibility. We cite some facts from [10].

Lemma 9. *1. The quotient-poset of $(\mathcal{R}; \leq_W)$ has rank ω^ω.*
2. The equivalence classes of $(\mathcal{R}; \equiv_W)$ are precisely $\mathcal{R}_\alpha \setminus \check{\mathcal{R}}_\alpha, \check{\mathcal{R}}_\alpha \setminus \mathcal{R}_\alpha, (\mathcal{R}_{\alpha+1} \cap \check{\mathcal{R}}_{\alpha+1}) \setminus (\mathcal{R}_\alpha \cup \check{\mathcal{R}}_\alpha)$, for all $\alpha < \omega^\omega$.
3. For any $\alpha < \omega^\omega$ we have: $\mathcal{R}_\alpha = \mathcal{R} \cap \mathbf{S}_\alpha$.

We now prove a basic property of the language $N_\alpha \subseteq A$ from Lemma 6.

Lemma 10. *For every $\alpha < \omega^\omega$ the language N_α is $\mathbf{S}_\alpha$-hard, i.e., every $\mathbf{S}_\alpha$-set is Wadge reducible to N_α.*

Proof. For finite α, the assertion is easy and well known. Namely, N_α coincides with the language $D_{1,i}$ from Lemma 4 which is $\mathbf{\Sigma}^0_1(i)$-hard (see e.g. [10,20]). Note that the language $\bar{D}_{1,1}$ is $\mathbf{\Pi}^0_1$-hard. A similar argument applies to language $D_{2,i}$ which is $\mathbf{\Sigma}^0_2(i)$-hard (i.e. $\mathbf{S}_{\omega^i}$-hard). Note that the language $\bar{D}_{2,1}$ is $\mathbf{\Pi}^0_2$-hard.

For infinite α, represented as in Definition 3, the proof is split in two cases. In case $\alpha \in \mathcal{O}$ of a limit ordinal, the proof is by induction on $lh(\alpha)$. When $lh(\alpha) = 1$, there is nothing to prove (the case of $D_{2,i}$ above). Let now $lh(\alpha) = n > 1$ be given. Note that in this case $\alpha = \beta + \omega^{\alpha_n}$, where $lh(\beta) = n - 1$.

Consider an arbitrary $\mathbf{S}_\alpha$-language Q. By Definition 1, $Q = (Q_1 \cap Q_2) \cup (Q_3 \cap Q_4) \cup (\bar{Q}_1 \cap \bar{Q}_3 \cap Q_5)$ for some $Q_1, Q_3 \in \mathbf{\Sigma}_1^0$, $Q_2 \in \mathbf{S}_\beta$, $Q_4 \in \check{\mathbf{S}}_\beta$, $Q_5 \in \mathbf{S}_{\omega^{\alpha_n}}$. Since the Borel base is reducible, we can use the condition $Q_1 \cap Q_3 = \varnothing$.

Note that $Q_1 \leqslant_W N_{\alpha,1}$, $Q_3 \leqslant_W N_{\alpha,3}$ (by Definition 3), and $Q_j \leqslant_W N_{\alpha,j}$ ($j = 2, 4, 5$) (by the induction hypothesis). Let: $f_1 = r_1$, be a continuous function reducing Q_1 to $N_{\alpha,1}$; $f_2 = \eta_1 \circ r_\beta$ where r_β is a continuous function reducing Q_2 to $N_{\alpha,j}$; $f_3 = \eta_{2+l(\pi(\beta))-1} \circ r_1$; $f_4 = \eta_{2+l(\pi(\beta))} \circ r_\beta$; $f_5 = \eta_{2+2l(\pi(\beta))} \circ r_{\omega^{\alpha_n}}$ where $r_{\omega^{\alpha_n}}$ is a continuous function reducing Q_5 to $N_{\alpha,5}$.

The functions $f_1 - f_5$ are continuous, since the functions m and η_j from Lemma 2 are continuous. Notice that $rng(f_i) \cap rng(f_j) = \{0\}$ for all $i \neq j$. It is not hard to check by cases that the continuous function $f(x) = m(f_1(x), f_2(x), f_3(x), f_4(x), f_5(x))$ reduces Q to N_α.

It remains to consider the case of an ordinal $\alpha + n$ where α is limit and n is a positive integer, we argue by induction on n. The proof proceeds in much the same way as above, we omit the details. $\qquad\square$

Using the encodings from the end of Sect. 3 and taking into account that the encoding functions are continuous, we immediately obtain the following.

Corollary 1. *For every $\alpha < \omega^\omega$ the language N_α^τ is $\mathbf{S}_\alpha$-hard.*

5   Relating the Hierarchies

Here we combine the results obtained so far to prove main results of this paper about relationship between logical and topological FHs. Among logical FHs we concentrate on $\{\mathcal{S}_\alpha^\tau\}_{\alpha < \omega^\omega}$, where $\tau = \tau_A$ for any fixed non-unary alphabet A (similar results of course hold for signatures σ_A, μ_A but in the case of σ_A the results are probably alphabet-dependent). By $\{\mathcal{R}_\alpha\}_{\alpha < \omega^\omega}$ we mean the FH of regular ω-languages over A from the previous section.

Theorem 1. *For every $\alpha < \omega^\omega$ we have $\mathcal{S}_\alpha^\tau \subseteq \mathcal{R}_\alpha$ and $\mathcal{S}_\alpha^\tau \not\subseteq \check{\mathcal{R}}_\alpha$.*

Proof. From Lemma 2 it is easy to see that $\Sigma_1^\tau \subseteq \mathbf{\Sigma}_1^0$. By induction on n it is easy to check (using the well-known relation of the existential quantifier to union and of the universal quantifier to intersection) that $\Sigma_{1+n}^\tau \subseteq \mathbf{\Sigma}_{1+n}^0$ for all $n < \omega$. This shows that the identical function g on the power-set $P(A^\omega)$ satisfies the condition of item (4) of Lemma 1 for the bases $\{\Sigma_{1+n}^\tau\}$ and $\{\mathbf{\Sigma}_{1+n}^0\}$. By this item we obtain $\mathcal{S}_\alpha^\tau \subseteq \mathbf{S}_\alpha$ for every $\alpha < \omega^\omega$. We have $\Sigma_{1+n}^\tau \subseteq \mathcal{R}$ for all $n < \omega$ and, by Lemma 9, $\mathcal{R}_\alpha = \mathcal{R} \cap \mathbf{S}_\alpha$ for all $\alpha < \omega^\omega$. Thus, $\mathcal{S}_\alpha^\tau \subseteq \mathcal{R}_\alpha$ for every $\alpha < \omega^\omega$.

The language N_α^τ is in $\mathcal{S}_\alpha^\tau$ by Lemma 7. This language is $\mathbf{S}_\alpha$-hard by Corollary 1, hence it is not in $\check{\mathbf{S}}_\alpha$ by Lemma 8, hence it is not in $\check{\mathcal{R}}_\alpha$ by Lemma 9(3). Therefore, $N_\alpha^\tau \in \mathcal{S}_\alpha^\tau \setminus \check{\mathcal{R}}_\alpha$. $\qquad\square$

Remark 1. The non-inclusion in Theorem 1 does not hold for $\alpha \geq \omega^\omega$ because, as we know from Sect. 4 and Lemma 1(3), $\mathcal{S}_\alpha^\tau \subseteq \mathcal{R} = \mathcal{R}_\alpha$ for every $\alpha \geq \omega^\omega$.

We conclude the paper by some corollaries of Theorem 1 and additional comments.

Corollary 2. *The hierarchy $\{\mathcal{S}_\alpha^\tau\}_{\alpha < \omega^\omega}$ does not collapse.*

Proof. It suffices to check that $N_\alpha^\tau \in \mathcal{S}_\alpha^\tau \setminus \check{\mathcal{S}}_\alpha^\tau$. By Lemma 7 it suffices to check that $N_\alpha^\tau \notin \check{\mathcal{S}}_\alpha^\tau$. Suppose the contrary, then $N_\alpha^\tau \in \check{\mathcal{R}}_\alpha$ by Theorem 1, which is a contradiction. □

Remark 2. The non-collapse results for logical hierarchies are usually proved using specially designed Ehrenfeucht-Fraïssé games (see e.g. [5] where such proofs for some versions of the aforementioned difference hierarchies may be found, or [13,14] where the corresponding questions for languages of finite words are systematically described). But for more complicated levels of the FH the construction of appropriate Ehrenfeucht-Fraïssé games is far from obvious. That is why we used here the Wadge reducibility as a more direct tool. To our knowledge, the idea to use the Wadge reducibility in a similar setting first appeared in Section I.F of [19].

Remark 3. The natural question on the non-collapse of the hierarchy $\{\mathcal{S}_\alpha^\tau\}$ for levels $\alpha \geq \omega^\omega$ (except the difference hierarchies for which the positive answer is known) remains open. It seems quite interesting and technically complex since, by Theorem 1, the method of using the Wadge reducibility does not work for such levels.

Remark 4. Though we established non-trivial relations between logical and topological hierarchies, the latter are of course much courser than the former. E.g., it is not hard to construct open languages in $\Sigma_n^\tau(k) \setminus \Pi_n^\tau(k)$ for all $k, n \geq 1$. We guess that the non-collapse property holds for every level of the FH but showing this is probably hard because the method of using the Wadge reducibility does not apply to levels $\alpha \geq \omega^\omega$.

Corollary 3. *Any regular ω-language is Wadge equivalent to some aperiodic regular ω-language.*

Proof. Let L be a regular ω-language. By Lemma 9(2), L is in precisely one of the classes

$$\mathcal{R}_\alpha \setminus \check{\mathcal{R}}_\alpha, \quad \check{\mathcal{R}}_\alpha \setminus \mathcal{R}_\alpha, \quad (\mathcal{R}_{\alpha+1} \cap \check{\mathcal{R}}_{\alpha+1}) \setminus (\mathcal{R}_\alpha \cup \check{\mathcal{R}}_\alpha),$$

for a unique $\alpha < \omega^\omega$. In the first case we have $L \equiv_W N_\alpha^\tau$, in the second $L \equiv_W \overline{N}_\alpha^\tau$, in the third $L \equiv_W N_\alpha^\tau \oplus \overline{N}_\alpha^\tau$, and the right-hand-side languages are aperiodic. □

Remark 5. The last corollary was established earlier [11] but the syntactic complexity of the corresponding aperiodic witnesses in [11] was not clear because some ad hoc properties of the FH were used to construct them. The witnesses above are more straightforward and defined according to the same Definition 1 as L (but over the logical base instead of the Borel base used in the construction of the topological FH).

Remark 6. In this paper we did not touch the related computability/complexity issues which are of course central in automata theory. They are well understood for the topological hierarchies but most of them are open for the logical hierarchies. E.g., the problem of describing the decidable levels S_α^τ is widely open and seems extremely hard.

References

1. Chaubard L., Pin J.-E., Straubing H.: First order formulas with modular predicates. HAL Id: hal-00112846. https://hal.science/hal-00112846
2. Kechris, A.S.: Classical Descriptive Set Theory. Springer, New York (1994)
3. Khoussainov, B., Nerode, A.: Automata Theory and its Applications. Birkhäuser, Boston (2001)
4. Landweber, L.H.: Decision problems for ω-automata. Math. Syst. Theory **3**, 376–384 (1969)
5. Maklakova, N.A.: Hierarchies of regular quasiaperiodic ω-languages. Bachelor thesis, Novosibirsk State University (2015). (in Russian)
6. Perrin, D., Pin, J.-E.: Infinite Words. v. 141 of Pure and Applied Mathematics series. Elsevier (2004)
7. Selivanov, V.L.: Hierarchies of hyperarithmetical sets and functions. Algebra Logic **22**, 473–491 (1983)
8. Selivanov, V.L.: Fine hierarchies of arithmetical sets and definable index sets. Trudy Mat. Inst. Novosibirsk **12**, 165–185 (1989). (in Russian)
9. Selivanov, V.L.: Fine Hierarchies and Boolean Terms. J. Symb. Log. **60**, 289–317 (1995)
10. Selivanov, V.L.: Fine hierarchy of regular ω-languages. Theoret. Comput. Sci. **191**(1–2), 37–59 (1998)
11. Selivanov, V.L.: Fine hierarchy of regular aperiodic ω-languages. Internat. J. Found. Comput. Sci. **19**(3), 649–675 (2008)
12. Selivanov, V.L.: Fine hierarchies and m-reducibilities in theoretical computer science. Theoret. Comput. Sci. **405**, 116–163 (2008)
13. Selivanov, V.L.: Hierarchies and reducibilities on regular languages related to modulo counting. Theor. Inform. Appl. **43**(1), 95–132 (2009)
14. Selivanov V.L., Shukin A.G.: On hierarchies of regular star-free languages (in Russian). Preprint 69 of A.P. Ershov Institute of Informatics Systems (2000)
15. Straubing, H.: Finite Automata, Formal Logic, and Circuit Complexity. Birkhäuser, Boston (1994)
16. Thomas, W.: Star-free regular sets of ω-sequences. Inf. Control **42**, 148–156 (1979)
17. Thomas, W.: Automata on infinite objects. Handbook of Theor. Computer Science, v. B (1990), 133–191
18. Thomas, W.: Languages, automata and logic. Handbook of Formal Language theory, v. B, 133–191 (1996)
19. Wadge, W.W.: Reducibility and Determinateness on the Baire Space. PhD thesis, University of California, Berkeley (1984)
20. Wagner, K.: On ω-regular sets. Inform. Control **43**(2), 123–177 (1979)

Subrecursive Graphs of Representations of Irrational Numbers

Ivan Georgiev$^{(\boxtimes)}$ iD

Department of Mathematical Logic and Applications, Faculty of Mathematics and Informatics, Sofia University "St. Kliment Ohridski", Sofia, Bulgaria
`ivandg@fmi.uni-sofia.bg`

Abstract. Our goal is to compare the complexity of different representations of irrational numbers. We use the following complexity framework: one representation is subrecursive in another representation if it is possible to convert the latter into the former using an algorithm with no unbounded search. For example, the base-2 expansion is subrecursive in the Dedekind cut, but not conversely. Informally this means that the Dedekind cut provides more information and so it is generally more complex than the base-2 expansion. In the present paper, for any representation of irrational numbers, we consider the characteristic function of its graph as a new representation. The most interesting case is the graph of the continued fraction: we prove that it is strictly subrecursively between the Dedekind cut and the continued fraction itself and also that it is subrecursively incomparable to the left and right best approximations. We also prove that the graphs of the base-b sum approximations from below and from above are subrecursively equivalent to the base-b expansion and that the graphs of the left and right best approximations are subrecursively equivalent to the Dedekind cut.

Keywords: Irrational number representations · Subrecursive classes · Computable analysis

1 Introduction

We are interested in the possibility of efficient conversion between different representations of irrational numbers. In our framework, an algorithm is efficient if it does not use unbounded search. For example, let E_2^α be the enumeration of the base-2 digits of some irrational number $\alpha \in (0, 1)$ and let D^α be the Dedekind cut of α, which decides whether $q < \alpha$ or $q > \alpha$ for any rational number q. The following algorithm converts D^α to E_2^α: assuming we have computed the base-2 digits $D_1, D_2, \ldots, D_n$ of α, we compute the next base-2 digit D_{n+1} by asking the Dedekind cut whether $0.D_1 D_2 \ldots D_n 1$ lies below or above α, so that $D_{n+1} = 1$ or $D_{n+1} = 0$, respectively. The existence of such algorithm which uses no unbounded search shows that E_2^α can be computed efficiently from D^α, or as we shall formally say E_2^α is subrecursive in D^α. Now let us consider the reverse

G. Della Vedova et al. (Eds.): CiE 2023, LNCS 13967, pp. 154–165, 2023.
https://doi.org/10.1007/978-3-031-36978-0_13

conversion from E_2^α to D^α: given a rational number q, we search for the first position p, in which the base-2 expansion of q is different from E_2^α and give answer $q < \alpha$ if $E_2^\alpha(p) = 1$ or $q > \alpha$ otherwise. This is a computable conversion, but it is not efficient since it uses unbounded search. Indeed, it can be shown that any algorithm for converting E_2^α to D^α, which works for all α, necessarily uses unbounded search, so we say that D^α is not subrecursive in E_2^α.

In this paper we consider many different representations, such that any one of them can be computably transformed into any other. But the structure of these representations with respect to subrecursive reducibility is rather interesting and nontrivial. Its general study was initiated in [2,3]. We also refer the reader to the introductory section in [1] for more details on our motivation.

Every representation of an irrational number can be regarded as a function f and we may consider the graph of f (the relation $f(x) = y$) as a $0, 1$-valued function, which uniquely determines f, so it can also be regarded as a representation. For a representation R, let us denote its graph by $\mathcal{G}(R)$. Clearly, $\mathcal{G}(R)$ is always subrecursive in R, but we shall see examples in which R is not subrecursive in $\mathcal{G}(R)$. Moreover, in some cases $\mathcal{G}(R)$ will not be equivalent to any of the representations studied in the literature, so we would like to know how it fits in the already complicated picture of representations.

2 Preliminaries on Subrecursive Classes

Our main objects of study will be total functions of several arguments over the following basic discrete types: the natural numbers $\mathbb{N}$, the rational numbers $\mathbb{Q}$ and the finite strings $\{L, R\}^*$ over the symbols L and R. Of course, in basic computability theory one usually defines codings of all discrete types into the natural numbers. In our framework, we consider these codings to be trivial. In addition, the standard operations with these types, such as the basic arithmetic operations and concatenation, will be allowed in our algorithms. In a similar way, we will freely use finite sequences of elements over the basic types.

As usual, relations will be identified with their characteristic functions. For a function f, we denote by $\mathcal{G}(f)$ the graph of f, considered as a relation, that is $\mathcal{G}(f)$ is the $0, 1$-valued function, given by

$$\mathcal{G}(f)(x, y) = 0 \iff f(x) = y.$$

Given two functions f, g, we denote $f \leq_S g$ and we say that f *is subrecursive in g*, if there exists an algorithm, which given input x computes the value $f(x)$, where the algorithm is allowed to invoke $g(y)$ for any y already computed, but *it is not allowed to use unbounded search*.

Note that we always have $\mathcal{G}(f) \leq_S f$, but we will see that in general $f \not\leq_S \mathcal{G}(f)$.

For a finite set $\mathcal{A}$ of functions, $f \leq_S \mathcal{A}$ if there exists an algorithm as above, but now we can invoke any function from the set $\mathcal{A}$ at any time.

For finite sets $\mathcal{A}$, $\mathcal{B}$ of functions, $\mathcal{A} \leq_S \mathcal{B}$ if $f \leq_S \mathcal{B}$ for all $f \in \mathcal{A}$.

Clearly, if $\mathcal{A} \leq_S \mathcal{B}$ and $\mathcal{B} \leq_S \mathcal{C}$, then $\mathcal{A} \leq_S \mathcal{C}$. Therefore, if we consider $\leq_S$ as a preorder, $\mathcal{A}$ can be regarded as the least upper bound of the set of its elements. We denote:

$$\mathcal{A} \equiv_S \mathcal{B} \text{ if } \mathcal{A} \leq_S \mathcal{B} \text{ and } \mathcal{B} \leq_S \mathcal{A}; \qquad \mathcal{A} <_S \mathcal{B} \text{ if } \mathcal{A} \leq_S \mathcal{B} \text{ and } \mathcal{B} \not\leq_S \mathcal{A}.$$

Definition 1. *A set $S \neq \emptyset$ of functions will be called a subrecursive class if:*

1. *there exists a total computable function U, such that for any $f \in S$ there exists $e \in \mathbb{N}$ with $f(x) = U(e, x)$ for all x;*
2. *if $f \leq_S g$ and $g \in S$, then $f \in S$.*

An important well-known tool when working with subrecursive classes is the following: (for a proof, see the comments below)

Lemma 1. *For any subrecursive class S, there exists a function $f : \mathbb{N} \to \mathbb{N} \backslash \{0\}$, such that $f \notin S$ and $\mathcal{G}(f) \in S$.*

Our main goal here will be to provide a new tool, which will pave the way for the results of Sect. 4.

For a function $f : \mathbb{N} \to \mathbb{N}$, we denote by $f^\Sigma : \mathbb{N} \to \mathbb{N}$ the bounded sum of f, $f^\Sigma(y) = \sum_{x=0}^{y} f(x)$. It is easy to check that $\mathcal{G}(f^\Sigma) \leq_S \mathcal{G}(f)$. Indeed,

$$z = f^\Sigma(y) \iff \exists u \left(\forall x \leq y[(u)_x = f(x)] \ \& \ z = \sum_{x=0}^{y} (u)_x \right)$$

and the code of the sequence u can be bounded by the code of the sequence $z, z, \ldots, z$ of length $y + 1$ (assuming the coding is monotonic).

But the converse is not true:

Theorem 1. *For any subrecursive class S, there exists a function $s : \mathbb{N} \to \mathbb{N}$, such that $\mathcal{G}(s) \notin S$ and $\mathcal{G}(s^\Sigma) \in S$.*

Observe that we have $s \equiv_S s^\Sigma$, but $\mathcal{G}(s) \not\equiv_S \mathcal{G}(s^\Sigma)$. Thus if two functions are subrecursively equivalent, it cannot be inferred in general that their graphs are also subrecursively equivalent.

We will now give the proof of Theorem 1. In order to do that we need a precise notion for an algorithm. The reader may skip the proof and proceed to Sect. 3 if satisfied with the presented level of formality so far.

The formal counterpart of the relation $f \leq_S g$ will be f is primitive recursive in g, that is f can be generated from g and the (initial) primitive recursive functions using the operators composition and primitive recursion.

We will also need the following notions: elementary functions and relations, $f \leq_E g$ (f is elementary in g), honest function, jump of an honest function. The reader is invited to consult Sects. 2, 3 in [1] for their precise definitions and basic properties. The subrecursive classes in the sense of our Definition 1 are precisely the subrecursive classes in the sense of Definition 3.1 in [1], which are closed under primitive recursion. Of course, this holds after coding the basic discrete types into $\mathbb{N}$.

Let S be a subrecursive class. By applying Theorem 3.2 in [1] we obtain an honest function f, such that $g \in S \Rightarrow g \leq_E f$. Therefore, the jump f' of f satisfies $f' \notin S$, since $f' \not\leq_E f$. This proves Lemma 1, because the graph of f' is elementary and therefore $\mathcal{G}(f') \in S$.

Let us also remark that for any honest function f, the ternary relation $y = f^z(x)$ is elementary:

$$y = f^z(x) \iff \exists u \left((u)_0 = x \;\&\; \forall t < z[(u)_{t+1} = f((u)_t)] \;\&\; y = (u)_z \right),$$

where the code of u is bounded by the code of $y, y, \ldots, y$ of length $z + 1$.

We will denote by NF the following ternary elementary function:

$$NF(u, e, x) \;=\; \mathcal{U}\left(\mu t \leq u\, [\mathcal{T}_1(e, x, t)] \right),$$

where $\mathcal{T}_1$ is the elementary Kleene T-predicate and $\mathcal{U}$ is the elementary decoding function from Kleene's Normal Form Theorem. Using Theorem 2.4 in [1] we can employ NF to define a universal function $U_f : \mathbb{N} \times \mathbb{N} \to \mathbb{N}$ for the class of unary functions, which are elementary in f:

$$U_f(a, x) \;=\; NF(f^{(a)_0}(x), (a)_1, x),$$

where a is regarded as the code of the pair $((a)_0, (a)_1)$, $(a)_0 \leq a$, $(a)_1 \leq a$.

Definition 2. *The diagonal function* $d_f : \mathbb{N} \to \{0, 1\}$ *for the honest function* f *is defined by the equalities:*

$$d_f(x) \;=\; \begin{cases} 0, & \text{if } U_f\left(\left\lfloor \frac{x}{2} \right\rfloor, x\right) = 1, \\ 1, & \text{if } U_f\left(\left\lfloor \frac{x}{2} \right\rfloor, x\right) \neq 1. \end{cases}$$

Lemma 2. *For the relation* $R_f \subseteq \mathbb{N}$ *defined by*

$$R_f(x) \iff d_f(x) = 0 \;\&\; Even(x)$$

we have: (i) $R_f \notin S$, (ii) $R_f \leq_E f'$.

Proof. Assume $R_f \in S$. Then $R_f \leq_E f$ and $R_f(x) = U_f(a, x)$ for some a and all x. Consider $x = 2a$. On one hand, $R_f(2a) = U_f(a, 2a)$. On the other hand, the equality $R_f(2a) = 0$ is equivalent to $d_f(2a) = 0$, which by the above definition is equivalent to $U_f(a, 2a) = 1$. So we have a contradiction. As for claim (ii), we can define the auxiliary function $P : \mathbb{N} \times \mathbb{N} \to \mathbb{N}$ by

$$P(x, u) = \mu y \le u \left[\exists z \le x \left(y = f^z(x) \ \& \ z = \left(\left\lfloor \tfrac{x}{2} \right\rfloor \right)_0 \right) \right],$$

which is clearly elementary. Now we have the equality

$$U_f \left(\left\lfloor \tfrac{x}{2} \right\rfloor, x \right) = NF \left(P(x, f'(x)), \left(\left\lfloor \tfrac{x}{2} \right\rfloor \right)_1, x \right), \tag{1}$$

therefore $d_f \le_E f'$ and also $R_f \le_E f'$. □

Remark. We can prove the lemma by using the more natural diagonal function, defined with $U_f(x, x)$ in place of $U_f(\left\lfloor \tfrac{x}{2} \right\rfloor, x)$. But then the proof would depend on the coding, because we must ensure that we can choose a to be even.

Definition 3. *Let us define the unary function s by*

$$s(x) = \begin{cases} f'(x), & \text{if } d_f(x) = 1 \ \vee \ Odd(x), \\ 0, & \text{if } d_f(x) = 0 \ \& \ Even(x) \end{cases}.$$

Proof (of Theorem 1). We will see that the function s we have just defined satisfies the conditions in the theorem. For the first part, assume $\mathcal{G}(s) \in \mathcal{S}$. We have

$$R_f(x) \iff s(x) = 0 \iff \mathcal{G}(s)(x, 0) = 0,$$

which clearly implies $R_f \in \mathcal{S}$, violating (i) in Lemma 2.

For the second part, we give a primitive recursive algorithm for computing $\mathcal{G}(s^\Sigma)(y+1, z)$ using $\mathcal{G}(s^\Sigma)(y, z)$. Of course, we can trivially compute $\mathcal{G}(s^\Sigma)(0, z)$, because $s^\Sigma(0) = s(0)$ is a fixed number.

Given inputs y, z we want to decide if the equality $s^\Sigma(y+1) = z$ holds.

First Case: $f'(y+1) \le z$. Compute $s^\Sigma(y+1)$. If $s^\Sigma(y+1) = z$ return 0, otherwise return 1.

We can check the inequality, because the graph of f' is elementary. For the same reason, we can compute $f'(x)$, $d_f(x)$ for $x \le y+1$ using equality (1) and thus also $s(x)$ for $x \le y+1$. So clearly we can compute $s^\Sigma(y+1)$ and decide the equality $s^\Sigma(y+1) = z$ in this case.

Second Case: $f'(y) \le z < f'(y+1)$. Check the equality $\mathcal{G}(s^\Sigma)(y, z) = 0$. If it does not hold, return 1. If it holds, return 0 if $s(y+1) = 0$ and 1, otherwise.

Assume that $s^\Sigma(y+1) = z$. Then it is not possible that $s(y+1) = f'(y+1)$, therefore $s(y+1) = 0$ and $s^\Sigma(y) = z$. So the first output 1 in this step is correct. Now suppose $\mathcal{G}(s^\Sigma)(y, z) = 0$. Then clearly $\mathcal{G}(s^\Sigma)(y+1, z) = 0$ iff $s(y+1) = 0$, therefore we only need to argue that we can decide $s(y+1) = 0$. To this end, we compute $d_f(y+1)$ using the following equality, similar to (1):

$$U_f \left(\left\lfloor \tfrac{y+1}{2} \right\rfloor, y+1 \right) = NF \left(P(y+1, f'(y)), \left(\left\lfloor \tfrac{y+1}{2} \right\rfloor \right)_1, y+1 \right).$$

Note that we can access $f'(y)$ using the graph of f' and the inequality $f'(y) \leq z$.

Third Case: $z < f'(y)$. Return 1.

Indeed, it is not possible that $s^{\Sigma}(y + 1) = z$, because at least one of the equalities $s(y) = f'(y)$, $s(y + 1) = f'(y + 1)$ is true by the definition of s. □

3   Representations of Irrational Numbers

Let $\alpha \in (0, 1)$ be an irrational number. We follow the denotations from [4].

A fraction $\frac{a}{b}$ in lowest terms is called *a left best approximant of* α if $\frac{a}{b} < \alpha$ and for any other fraction $\frac{x}{y}$, $\frac{a}{b} < \frac{x}{y} < \alpha$ implies $b < y$.

A fraction $\frac{c}{d}$ in lowest terms is called *a right best approximant of* α if $\alpha < \frac{c}{d}$ and for any other fraction $\frac{x}{y}$, $\alpha < \frac{x}{y} < \frac{c}{d}$ implies $d < y$.

Thus in order to provide a better approximation from the left (right) to α than a left (right) best approximant, it is necessary to use a strictly bigger denominator.

Note that $\frac{0}{1}$ is the smallest left best approximant of α and $\frac{1}{1}$ is the largest right best approximant of α.

Definition 4. *The strictly increasing sequence* $L^{\alpha} : \mathbb{N} \to \mathbb{Q}$ *consisting of all left best approximants of* α *will be called* the complete left best approximation *of* α. *The strictly decreasing sequence* $R^{\alpha} : \mathbb{N} \to \mathbb{Q}$ *consisting of all right best approximants of* α *will be called* the complete right best approximation *of* α.

It is easy to see that $\alpha = \lim_{n \to \infty} L^{\alpha}(n) = \lim_{n \to \infty} R^{\alpha}(n)$, so that α is uniquely determined by L^{α} and by R^{α}.

We assume some familiarity with Farey pairs, for reference see Chap. 6 in [7].

For $\tau \in \{L, R\}^{\star}$ we denote $I[\tau] = (\frac{a}{b}, \frac{c}{d})$ the corresponding interval in the Farey pair tree, where $I[\epsilon] = (\frac{0}{1}, \frac{1}{1})$ and $I[\tau L] = (\frac{a}{b}, \frac{a+c}{b+d})$, $I[\tau R] = (\frac{a+c}{b+d}, \frac{c}{d})$.

The fraction $\frac{a+c}{b+d}$ is called *the mediant* of $\frac{a}{b}$ and $\frac{c}{d}$.

For any rational $q \in (0, 1)$ there exists a unique $\tau \in \{L, R\}^{\star}$, such that q is the mediant of the endpoints of $I[\tau]$.

Lemma 3. *The fraction* $\frac{a}{b}$ *is a left best approximant of* α *if and only if there exists* $\tau \in \{L, R\}^{\star}$, *such that* $\alpha \in I[\tau]$ *and* $\frac{a}{b}$ *is the left endpoint of* $I[\tau]$. *The fraction* $\frac{c}{d}$ *is a right best approximant of* α *if and only if there exists* $\tau \in \{L, R\}^{\star}$, *such that* $\alpha \in I[\tau]$ *and* $\frac{c}{d}$ *is the right endpoint of* $I[\tau]$.

Proof. We use the following well-known fact about Farey pairs: if $I[\tau] = (\frac{a}{b}, \frac{c}{d})$, then any rational number q lying in the interval $(\frac{a}{b}, \frac{c}{d})$ has denominator, which is strictly greater than b and d. So if $\alpha \in I[\tau]$ and $\frac{a}{b}$ is the left endpoint of $I[\tau]$, then any fraction $\frac{x}{y}$ with $\frac{a}{b} < \frac{x}{y} < \alpha$ belongs to the interval $I[\tau]$ and thus $y > b$. For the converse, assume that for any $I[\tau]$ with $\alpha \in I[\tau]$, the left endpoint of $I[\tau]$

is different from $\frac{a}{b}$. Since $\frac{a}{b} < \alpha$, there exists τ_0, such that $\frac{a}{b} \in I[\tau_0]$, $\alpha \in I[\tau_0]$, $\alpha \in I[\tau_0 R]$ and $\frac{a}{b} \notin I[\tau_0 R]$. Let $\frac{x}{y}$ be the mediant of $I[\tau_0]$. Observe that our assumption implies that $\frac{a}{b}$ is not equal to $\frac{x}{y}$. But now we have $\frac{a}{b} < \frac{x}{y} < \alpha$ and $b > y$, because $\frac{a}{b} \in I[\tau_0 L]$ (we use again the above fact about Farey pairs). Thus $\frac{a}{b}$ is not a left best approximant.

The proof for right best approximants is symmetric.   □

Definition 5. The Hurwitz characteristic $H^\alpha : \mathbb{N} \to \{L, R\}$ *is the unique infinite string over* $\{L, R\}$, *such that* $\alpha \in I[\tau]$ *for any finite prefix* τ *of* H^α.

Note that the infinite strings H^α, which represent irrational numbers $\alpha \in (0, 1)$ are exactly those, which contain infinitely many occurrences of both L and R.

Lemma 3 implies the following link between the Hurwitz characteristic H^α and the complete best approximations L^α and R^α.

We can write $H^\alpha = L^{A(0)}RL^{A(1)}R\ldots L^{A(n)}R\ldots$ for a unique function $A : \mathbb{N} \to \mathbb{N}$, which is called *the dual Baire sequence* of α.

For any k, let $\tau_k = L^{A(0)}RL^{A(1)}R\ldots L^{A(k-1)}R$, so that τ_k is the shortest prefix of H^α, containing k occurrences of R. Then $L^\alpha(k)$ is the left endpoint of $I[\tau_k]$.

Similarly, $H^\alpha = R^{B(0)}LR^{B(1)}L\ldots R^{B(n)}L\ldots$ for a unique function $B : \mathbb{N} \to \mathbb{N}$, called *the standard Baire sequence* of α.

For any k, let $\tau_k' = R^{B(0)}LR^{B(1)}L\ldots R^{B(k-1)}L$ be the shortest prefix of H^α, containing k occurrences of L. Then $R^\alpha(k)$ is the right endpoint of $I[\tau_k']$.

In fact, as shown in [4] the dual and the standard Baire sequences A and B are subrecursively equivalent to L^α and R^α, respectively.

Let $D^\alpha : \mathbb{Q} \to \{0, 1\}$ be *the Dedekind cut* of α, $D^\alpha(q) = 0 \Leftrightarrow q < \alpha$.

It is not hard to prove that H^α and D^α are subrecursively equivalent, see [5, 6].

Definition 6. *Let* $c : \mathbb{N} \to \mathbb{N} \setminus \{0\}$ *be the unique sequence, such that*

$$\alpha = 0 + \cfrac{1}{c(0) + \cfrac{1}{c(1) + \cfrac{1}{c(2) + \ddots}}}$$

We refer to c *as the continued fraction of* α *and we denote* $c = [\ ]^\alpha$.

We also use the standard notation $\alpha = [0; c(0), c(1), \ldots, c(k), \ldots]$.

It is known that the Hurwitz characteristic of α can be expressed as

$$H^\alpha = L^{c(0)-1}R^{c(1)}L^{c(2)}R^{c(3)} \ldots \tag{2}$$

This is an old result of Hurwitz, cited in [6] in a slightly modified form.

The last three representations concern the expansion of α in a base $b \geq 2$.

The unique function $E_b^\alpha : \mathbb{N} \rightarrow \{0, 1, \ldots, b-1\}$, such that $\alpha = \sum_{n=0}^\infty E_b^\alpha(n)b^{-n}$ will be called *the base-b expansion* of α.

Let us write

$$\alpha = 0 + d_1 b^{-n_1} + d_2 b^{-n_2} + d_3 b^{-n_3} + \ldots,$$

where $d_i \in \{1, \ldots, b-1\}$ and $n_i < n_{i+1}$ for all i. The sequence $\hat{A}_b^\alpha : \mathbb{N} \rightarrow \mathbb{Q}$, which enumerates the terms of this series will be called *the base-b sum approximation from below* of α. *The base-b sum approximation from above* of α is a symmetric sequence $\check{A}_b^\alpha : \mathbb{N} \rightarrow \mathbb{Q}$, which may be defined as $\check{A}_b^\alpha(n) = \hat{A}_b^{1-\alpha}(n)$.

For more on base expansions, sum approximations and their complexity in the subrecursive framework, see [3].

4   Main Results

Let R_1 and R_2 be any two of the above representations.

When we claim below that $R_1 \leq_S R_2$, we always mean that the irrational number α they represent is arbitrary, unless explicitly stated otherwise. In fact, in all proofs in the present paper and in many other cases, $R_1 \leq_S R_2$ is true uniformly in α (satisfying the stated conditions, if present), so that the algorithm does not refer in any way to information, which depends on α.

But when we claim that $R_1 \not\leq_S R_2$, we mean that there exists an irrational number α, for which the claim is true. This distinction is important, because there are irrational numbers (for example, the algebraic irrational numbers), for which all of the above representations have trivial complexity. Therefore, $R_1 \not\leq_S R_2$ can never be true universally in α.

The same comments apply when $\leq_S$ is used with finite sets of representations.

Lemma 4. *Let* $[\ ]^{\alpha,\Sigma}(x) = \sum_{y=0}^x [\ ]^\alpha(y)$ *be the bounded sum of the continued fraction of* α. *Then* $\mathcal{G}([\ ]^{\alpha,\Sigma}) \equiv_S D^\alpha$.

Proof. Since $D^\alpha \equiv_S H^\alpha$, it suffices to prove $\mathcal{G}([\ ]^{\alpha,\Sigma}) \equiv_S H^\alpha$.

First we show $\mathcal{G}([\ ]^{\alpha,\Sigma}) \leq_S H^\alpha$.

Input: natural numbers x, n. *Goal:* check the equality $[\ ]^{\alpha,\Sigma}(x) = n$.

First case: $n = 0$. Return 1.

Second case: $n = 1$. If $x = 0$ & $H^\alpha(0) = \mathtt{R}$ return 0, otherwise return 1.

Third case: $n \geq 2$. Compute $m = n \dot{-} 2$ and $\tau = \mathtt{L}H^\alpha(0)H^\alpha(1)\ldots H^\alpha(m)$. Compute the number x' of all occurrences of substrings $\mathtt{LR}$ and $\mathtt{RL}$ in τ.

If $x = x'$ and $H^\alpha(m+1) \neq H^\alpha(m)$ return 0, otherwise return 1.

End of algorithm.

The correctness of this algorithm is easily seen using equality (2). Note that in the second case, $H^\alpha(0) = $ R iff $[\ ]^\alpha(0) = 1$. In the third case, the inequality $H^\alpha(m+1) \neq H^\alpha(m)$ guarantees that the length n of τ is a value of $[\ ]^{\alpha,\Sigma}$.

Now we show $H^\alpha \leq_S \mathcal{G}([\ ]^{\alpha,\Sigma})$.

Input: natural number n. *Goal:* compute $H^\alpha(n)$.

1. Search for the least $x \leq n+1$, such that $n+2 \leq [\ ]^{\alpha,\Sigma}(x)$.

2. If $Even(x)$, give output L and if $Odd(x)$, give output R.

End of algorithm.

Again equality (2) justifies the correctness. The computed value of x shows whether we find $H^\alpha(n)$ in a sequence of consecutive L-s or in a sequence of consecutive R-s. As for the complexity, the search for x is bounded and we can decide the inequality $n+2 \leq [\ ]^{\alpha,\Sigma}(x)$ using $n+2$ calls to $\mathcal{G}([\ ]^{\alpha,\Sigma})$.   □

Theorem 2.
$$D^\alpha <_S \mathcal{G}([\ ]^\alpha) <_S [\ ]^\alpha.$$

Proof. By Lemma 4 we have $D^\alpha \leq_S \mathcal{G}([\ ]^{\alpha,\Sigma})$ and clearly $\mathcal{G}([\ ]^{\alpha,\Sigma}) \leq_S \mathcal{G}([\ ]^\alpha)$. Now let us take α to be the irrational number, whose continued fraction is the function $c(x) = s(x) + 1$, where s is the function from Theorem 1. It is trivial to see that $\mathcal{G}(c) \equiv_S \mathcal{G}(s)$ and $\mathcal{G}(c^\Sigma) \equiv_S \mathcal{G}(s^\Sigma)$, therefore $\mathcal{G}(c) \notin \mathcal{S}$ and $\mathcal{G}(c^\Sigma) \in \mathcal{S}$. By Lemma 4 we have $D^\alpha \leq_S \mathcal{G}(c^\Sigma)$, therefore $D^\alpha \in \mathcal{S}$. Moreover, $\mathcal{G}(c) \notin \mathcal{S}$, which implies $\mathcal{G}(c) \not\leq_S D^\alpha$. This proves the first part. The second part is easy, because $\mathcal{G}(h) \leq_S h$ for any function h and $[\ ]^\alpha \not\leq_S \mathcal{G}([\ ]^\alpha)$, which can be seen by taking $[\ ]^\alpha = f$, where f is the function from Lemma 1.   □

Lemma 5. *Let A be the dual Baire sequence and B be the standard Baire sequence of α. If $B(x) > 0$ for all x, then we have $L^\alpha \leq_S \mathcal{G}(B^\Sigma)$. If $A(x) > 0$ for all x, then $R^\alpha \leq_S \mathcal{G}(A^\Sigma)$.*

Proof. Let $A(x) > 0$ for all x. We show a reduction $R^\alpha \leq_S \mathcal{G}(A^\Sigma)$.

Input: natural number k. *Goal:* compute $R^\alpha(k)$.

1. Search for the least $y \leq k$, such that $k \leq A^\Sigma(y)$.

First case: $y = 0$. Take $\tau = $ L^k.

Second case: $y > 0$. Compute $A^\Sigma(i)$ for all $i < y$, then $A(i)$ for all $i < y$ and take $\tau = $ L$^{A(0)}$RL$^{A(1)}$R$\ldots$L$^{A(y \dot- 1)}$RL^t, where $t = k \dot- A^\Sigma(y \dot- 1)$.

2. Give output the right endpoint of $I[\tau]$. *End of algorithm.*

The correctness follows from the fact that in both cases τ is the shortest prefix of H^α, which contains exactly k occurrences of L. Note that $A(x) > 0$ is essential in order to have a bound for the search of y. In the case $y > 0$, it is possible to compute $A^\Sigma(i)$ for $i < y$ using the inequality $A^\Sigma(i) < k$ and $\mathcal{G}(A^\Sigma)$. Of course, $A(0) = A^\Sigma(0)$ and $A(i) = A^\Sigma(i) \dot- A^\Sigma(i \dot- 1)$ for non-zero i.

The other part $L^\alpha \leq_S \mathcal{G}(B^\Sigma)$ when $B(x) > 0$ is proven symmetrically.   □

Theorem 3.
$$\mathcal{G}([\,]^\alpha) \not\leq_S L^\alpha, \quad \mathcal{G}([\,]^\alpha) \not\leq_S R^\alpha.$$

Proof. Let us again take the function s from Theorem 1 and let α be the irrational number with dual Baire sequence $a(x) = s(x) + 1$, so that the Hurwitz characteristic of α is $H^\alpha = L^{a(0)}RL^{a(1)}RL^{a(2)}R\ldots$ and by equality (2), the continued fraction of α is $\alpha = [0;\, a(0)+1,\, 1,\, a(1),\, 1,\, a(2),\, 1,\, \ldots]$. Clearly, $\mathcal{G}(a^\Sigma) \in \mathcal{S}$ and by Lemma 5, $R^\alpha \in \mathcal{S}$. We also have

$$y = a(x) \iff (x = 0 \ \& \ y = a(0)) \ \lor \ (x > 0 \ \& \ y = [\,]^\alpha(2x)),$$

which implies $\mathcal{G}([\,]^\alpha) \notin \mathcal{S}$, because $\mathcal{G}(a) \notin \mathcal{S}$. Therefore $\mathcal{G}([\,]^\alpha) \not\leq_S R^\alpha$.

For the first part, take α with standard Baire sequence $b(x) = s(x) + 1$, so that $H^\alpha = R^{b(0)}LR^{b(1)}LR^{b(2)}L\ldots$ and $\alpha = [0;\, 1,\, b(0),\, 1,\, b(1),\, 1,\, b(2),\, 1,\, \ldots]$. $\square$

Theorem 4.

$$L^\alpha \not\leq_S \{R^\alpha, \mathcal{G}([\,]^\alpha)\}, \quad R^\alpha \not\leq_S \{L^\alpha, \mathcal{G}([\,]^\alpha)\}.$$

Proof. Let us take the function f from Lemma 1 and let α be the irrational number with dual Baire sequence f. On one hand, $L^\alpha \notin \mathcal{S}$, since $L^\alpha \equiv_S f$. On the other hand, $\mathcal{G}(f) \in \mathcal{S}$, therefore $\mathcal{G}(f^\Sigma) \in \mathcal{S}$, so Lemma 5 implies $R^\alpha \in \mathcal{S}$. Moreover, we have

$$[\,]^\alpha(x) = y \iff (x = 0 \ \& \ y = f(0) + 1) \ \lor \ (Odd(x) \ \& \ y = 1)$$
$$\lor \ \left(x > 0 \ \& \ Even(x) \ \& \ y = f\left(\left\lfloor \frac{x}{2} \right\rfloor\right)\right),$$

hence $\mathcal{G}([\,]^\alpha) \in \mathcal{S}$. It follows that $L^\alpha \not\leq_S \{R^\alpha, \mathcal{G}([\,]^\alpha)\}$.

The second part is symmetric. $\square$

Results in [1,2] imply that $[\,]^\alpha \equiv_S \{L^\alpha, R^\alpha\}$ and $D^\alpha \leq_S L^\alpha$, $D^\alpha \leq_S R^\alpha$.

According to Theorems 3 and 4, L^α, R^α and $\mathcal{G}([\,]^\alpha)$ are pairwise incomparable with respect to $\leq_S$. It follows that the three representations lie strictly between the Dedekind cut D^α and the continued fraction $[\,]^\alpha$. The following corollary shows that unlike the pair $\{L^\alpha, R^\alpha\}$, the least upper bound of both pairs $\{L^\alpha, \mathcal{G}([\,]^\alpha)\}$ and $\{R^\alpha, \mathcal{G}([\,]^\alpha)\}$ is strictly below the continued fraction $[\,]^\alpha$.

Corollary 1.

$$\{R^\alpha, \mathcal{G}([\,]^\alpha)\} <_S [\,]^\alpha, \quad \{L^\alpha, \mathcal{G}([\,]^\alpha)\} <_S [\,]^\alpha.$$

Proof. We already noted that $L^\alpha \leq_S [\,]^\alpha$, $R^\alpha \leq_S [\,]^\alpha$. It is not possible that $[\,]^\alpha \leq_S \{R^\alpha, \mathcal{G}([\,]^\alpha)\}$, otherwise we would have $L^\alpha \leq_S \{R^\alpha, \mathcal{G}([\,]^\alpha)\}$, which contradicts Theorem 4. The second part is analogous. $\square$

In the last two theorems of this section, we will study the graphs of the other representations, defined in Sect. 3. Of course, $\mathcal{G}(D^\alpha) \equiv_S D^\alpha$, $\mathcal{G}(H^\alpha) \equiv_S H^\alpha$ and $\mathcal{G}(E_b^\alpha) \equiv_S E_b^\alpha$, because $\mathcal{G}(h) \equiv_S h$ for any function h with a finite range.

Theorem 5.
$$\mathcal{G}(\hat{A}_b^\alpha) \equiv_S E_b^\alpha \equiv_S \mathcal{G}(\check{A}_b^\alpha).$$

Proof. First we show that $\mathcal{G}(\hat{A}_b^\alpha) \leq_S E_b^\alpha$.

Input: $n \in \mathbb{N}$ and $q \in \mathbb{Q}$. *Goal:* decide $\hat{A}_b^\alpha(n) = q$.

First case: $n = 0$. If $q = 0$ return 0, otherwise return 1.

Second case: $n > 0$. Search for $m > 0$ and $x \in \{1, \ldots, b-1\}$, such that $q = xb^{-m}$.
    If the search is not successful, return 1. Otherwise, compute the number k of the non-zero digits among $E_b^\alpha(1), E_b^\alpha(2), \ldots, E_b^\alpha(m)$.
    If $n = k$ and $x = E_b^\alpha(m)$ return 0, otherwise return 1.

End of algorithm.
    The correctness is rather easy to see. Note that the search for m can be bounded by $(b-1)d$, where d is the denominator of q.
    Next we show that $E_b^\alpha \leq_S \mathcal{G}(\hat{A}_b^\alpha)$ by a course-of-values recursion.

Input: $n \in \mathbb{N}$. *Goal:* $E_b^\alpha(n)$, assuming we have computed $E_b^\alpha(0), \ldots, E_b^\alpha(n-1)$.
    Let k be the number of non-zero among these computed base-b digits of α.
    Search for $x \in \{1, \ldots, b-1\}$ with $\hat{A}_b^\alpha(k+1) = xb^{-n}$.
    If the search is successful, give output x, otherwise give output 0.

End of algorithm.
    Observe that $E_b^\alpha(n) \neq 0$ iff n is the position of the $(k+1)$-st non-zero base-b digit of α. This justifies that the algorithm correctly computes E_b^α.
    For the second part, $E_b^\alpha \equiv_S E_b^{1-\alpha} \equiv_S \mathcal{G}(\hat{A}_b^{1-\alpha}) = \mathcal{G}(\check{A}_b^\alpha)$. $\qquad\square$

Theorem 6.
$$\mathcal{G}(L^\alpha) \equiv_S D^\alpha \equiv_S \mathcal{G}(R^\alpha).$$

Proof. Here is an algorithm, showing that $\mathcal{G}(L^\alpha) \leq_S H^\alpha$.

Input: $k \in \mathbb{N}$ and $q \in \mathbb{Q}$. *Goal:* Decide $L^\alpha(k) = q$.
    Reduce q to lowest terms. Compute $\tau = H^\alpha(0) \ldots H^\alpha(n-1)$, where n is the denominator of q. Let r be the number of occurrences of R in τ.

First case: $r < k$. Return 1.

Second case: $r \geq k$. Compute $\tau_k = $ the shortest prefix of τ with k occurrences of R. If the left endpoint of $I[\tau_k]$ is equal to q, return 0, otherwise return 1.

End of algorithm.

Only the output in the first case requires explanation. Suppose that the number r of occurrences of R in τ is strictly less than k. Then $L^\alpha(k)$ is the left endpoint of some prefix τ_k of H^α, which ends in R and strictly extends τ. But this clearly implies that the denominator of $L^\alpha(k)$ is strictly greater than the denominators of both endpoints of $I[\tau]$. Moreover, an easy induction on the length n of τ shows that at least one of the endpoints of $I[\tau]$ has denominator $> n$. Therefore, $L^\alpha(k) = q$ is impossible.

And now we give a course-of-values recursion to show $H^\alpha \leq_S \mathcal{G}(L^\alpha)$.

Input: $n \in \mathbb{N}$. *Goal:* $H^\alpha(n)$, assuming we have computed $H^\alpha(0)$, ..., $H^\alpha(n-1)$.

Let $\tau = H^\alpha(0) \dots H^\alpha(n-1)$. Compute the interval $I[\tau]$ and its mediant q, as well as the number r of occurrences of R in τ.

Check: $L^\alpha(r+1) = q$. If true give output R, otherwise give output L.

End of algorithm.

The correctness is easily verified. If $H^\alpha(n) = $ R, then it is clear that $L^\alpha(r+1) = q$. If $H^\alpha(n) = $ L, then $L^\alpha(r+1)$ is the mediant of $I[\tau L^k]$ for some $k \geq 1$. This is possible only if $L^\alpha(r+1) < q$ and thus the output is correct. We succeeded in proving $\mathcal{G}(L^\alpha) \equiv_S H^\alpha$, therefore $\mathcal{G}(L^\alpha) \equiv_S D^\alpha$. The proof of $\mathcal{G}(R^\alpha) \equiv_S D^\alpha$ is completely symmetric. □

Acknowledgements. Thanks to Lars Kristiansen for his useful suggestions on the content of the paper.

This work is supported by the Sofia University Science Fund through continuation of contract 80-10-134/20.05.2022.

References

1. Georgiev, I., Kristiansen, L., Stephan, F.: Computable irrational numbers with representations of surprising complexity. Ann. Pure Appl. Logic **172**(2) (2021). https://doi.org/10.1016/j.apal.2020.102893
2. Kristiansen, L.: On subrecursive representability of irrational numbers. Computability **6**, 249–276 (2017). https://doi.org/10.3233/COM-160063
3. Kristiansen, L.: On subrecursive representability of irrational numbers, part ii. Computability **8**, 43–65 (2019). https://doi.org/10.3233/COM-170081
4. Kristiansen, L.: On subrecursive representation of irrational numbers: contractors and Baire sequences. In: De Mol, L., Weiermann, A., Manea, F., Fernández-Duque, D. (eds.) CiE 2021. LNCS, vol. 12813, pp. 308–317. Springer, Cham (2021). https://doi.org/10.1007/978-3-030-80049-9_28
5. Kristiansen, L., Simonsen, J.G.: On the complexity of conversion between classic real number representations. In: Anselmo, M., Della Vedova, G., Manea, F., Pauly, A. (eds.) CiE 2020. LNCS, vol. 12098, pp. 75–86. Springer, Cham (2020). https://doi.org/10.1007/978-3-030-51466-2_7
6. Lehman, R.: On primitive recursive real numbers. Fundamenta Mathematica **49**(2), 105–118 (1961)
7. Niven, I., Zuckerman, H.S., Montgomery, H.L.: An Introduction to the Theory of Numbers, 5th edn. John Wiley & Sons Inc., New York (1991)

On the Complexity of Learning Programs

Vasco Brattka[1,2]([✉])

[1] Faculty of Computer Science, Universität der Bundeswehr München,
Neubiberg, Germany
`Vasco.Brattka@cca-net.de`
[2] Department of Mathematics and Applied Mathematics, University of Cape Town,
Rondebosch, South Africa

Abstract. Given a computable sequence of natural numbers, it is a natural task to find a Gödel number of a program that generates this sequence. It is easy to see that this problem is neither continuous nor computable. In algorithmic learning theory this problem is well studied from several perspectives and one question studied there is for which sequences this problem is at least learnable in the limit. Here we study the problem on all computable sequences and we classify the Weihrauch complexity of it. For this purpose we can, among other methods, utilize the amalgamation technique known from learning theory. As a benchmark for the classification we use closed and compact choice problems and their jumps on natural numbers, which correspond to induction and boundedness principles, as they are known from the Kirby-Paris hierarchy in reverse mathematics. We provide a topological as well as a computability-theoretic classification, which reveal some significant differences.

1 Introduction

Given a sequence of natural numbers such as $1, 2, 3, \dots$ it is a well-known game to guess how the sequence continues. While the first guess could be that it is the sequence of all positive natural numbers, one has to reconsider this guess when the continuation

$$1, 2, 3, 5, 7, \dots$$

appears. A new guess might be that it is the sequence of all odd numbers together with 2, but when we see

$$1, 2, 3, 5, 7, 11, 13, 17, 19, 23, \dots,$$

then it rather looks like the sequence of prime numbers together with 1. Even if the given sequence is computable, it is easy to see that there is neither a continuous nor a computable way to make the guess converge in general. Questions like this have been extensively studied in algorithmic learning theory [21,27]. More recently, AI approaches to determine programs for given sequences have

---

Vasco Brattka is supported by the National Research Foundation of South Africa.

G. Della Vedova et al. (Eds.): CiE 2023, LNCS 13967, pp. 166–177, 2023.
https://doi.org/10.1007/978-3-031-36978-0_14

been tested [14]. In algorithmic learning theory it is known and easy to see, for instance, that if one restricts oneself to primitive-recursive sequences, then there is an algorithm that makes the guess converge eventually. The crucial problem here is whether it is recognizable that a guess (in form of a Gödel number generating the sequence) represents a total sequence, which is always the case if one restricts everything a priorily to Gödel codes of primitive-recursive sequences. However for general Gödel numbers totality is a Π_2^0-question in the arithmetical hierarchy and hence an oracle such as $\emptyset''$ is required. In fact Gold proved the following result [15].

Theorem 1 (Gold 1967). *The total computable sequences are not learnable in the limit.*

That means that there is no general algorithm that could produce a sequence of Gödel numbers that converges to a correct Gödel number from a total computable sequence that is given as input.

We formalize the underlying problem as follows. The *Gödel (numbering) problem* $\mathsf{G} :\subseteq \mathbb{N}^{\mathbb{N}} \rightrightarrows \mathbb{N}$ can be defined by

$$\mathsf{G} :\subseteq \mathbb{N}^{\mathbb{N}} \rightrightarrows \mathbb{N}, p \mapsto \{i \in \mathbb{N} : \varphi_i = p\},$$

where the domain $\mathrm{dom}(\mathsf{G})$ consists of all computable sequences and $\varphi : \mathbb{N} \to \mathcal{P}$ denotes some standard Gödel numbering of the set of computable sequences $\mathcal{P}$. Briefly we could also define G as φ^{-1} restricted to total computable sequences. If we want to consider G as a theorem whose complexity we aim to classify, then the theorem would be the statement that every total computable function has a Gödel number, i.e.,

$$(\forall \text{ computable } p \in \mathbb{N}^{\mathbb{N}})(\exists i \in \mathbb{N}) \; \varphi_i = p.$$

That is, this theorem states that φ is surjective and hence a numbering of $\mathcal{P}$. This theorem seems to be very simple and does not appear to need particularly powerful resources. However, we will see that it shows some peculiar properties.

Another perspective one could take is to ask what additional useful information is carried by a program i that the sequence p itself does not make accessible? This question has been studied by Hoyrup and Rojas [18] and their answer could be summarized briefly as follows:

Slogan 2 (Hoyrup and Rojas 2017). The only useful additional information carried by a program compared to the natural number sequence it represents, is an upper bound on the Kolmogorov complexity of the sequence.

One of our goals is to study in which sense this slogan can be converted into theorems on the Weihrauch complexity of the Gödel problem. For this purpose we introduce a number of further related problems. For our study the *Kolmogorv complexity* is the function $\mathsf{K} :\subseteq \mathbb{N}^{\mathbb{N}} \rightrightarrows \mathbb{N}$ with $\mathrm{dom}(\mathsf{K}) = \mathrm{dom}(\mathsf{G})$ defined by

$$\mathsf{K} :\subseteq \mathbb{N}^{\mathbb{N}} \to \mathbb{N}, p \mapsto \min \mathsf{G}(p)$$

for all $p \in \mathrm{dom}(\mathsf{K})$. The study by Hoyrup and Rojas also motivates to investigate the following variant of G

$$\mathsf{G}_{\geq} :\subseteq \mathbb{N}^{\mathbb{N}} \times \mathbb{N} \rightrightarrows \mathbb{N}, (p, m) \mapsto \mathsf{G}(p)$$

with $\mathrm{dom}(\mathsf{G}_{\geq}) := \{(p, m) \in \mathbb{N}^{\mathbb{N}} \times \mathbb{N} : m \geq \mathsf{K}(p)\}$. That is $\mathsf{G}_{\geq}$ is the Gödel problem that gets an upper bound on the Kolmogorov complexity as additional input information. We note that the output does not need to satisfy the input bound m according to this definition. Yet another function that one can consider is

$$\mathsf{K}_{\geq} : \mathbb{N}^{\mathbb{N}} \rightrightarrows \mathbb{N}, p \mapsto \{m \in \mathbb{N} : m \geq \mathsf{K}(p)\}$$

that just yields an upper bound on the Kolmogorov complexity of the input sequence, again with $\mathrm{dom}(\mathsf{K}_{\geq}) := \mathrm{dom}(\mathsf{G})$.

In terms of their Weihrauch complexity these problems are in the following obvious relation that is also visualized in the diagram in Fig. 1.

Lemma 3. $\mathsf{G}_{\geq} \sqcup \mathsf{K}_{\geq} \leq_{\mathrm{sW}} \mathsf{G} \leq_{\mathrm{sW}} \mathsf{K}$ *and* $\mathsf{G} = \mathsf{G}_{\geq} \circ (\mathrm{id}, \mathsf{K}_{\geq})$.

Fig. 1. The Gödel problem and its relatives.

Obviously, the Kolmogorov complexity K computes G and G computes $\mathsf{G}_{\geq}$ as well as $\mathsf{K}_{\geq}$. Here $\sqcup$ stands for the supremum with respect to Weihrauch reducibility [8]. A precise definition of Weihrauch reducibility follows in Sect. 2.

Our goal is to classify the Weihrauch complexity and also its topological counterpart of the problems mentioned above. The way we will calibrate this complexity is with the help of the problems

$$\mathsf{K}_{\mathbb{N}} <_{\mathrm{W}} \mathsf{C}_{\mathbb{N}} <_{\mathrm{W}} \mathsf{K}'_{\mathbb{N}} <_{\mathrm{W}} \mathsf{C}'_{\mathbb{N}} <_{\mathrm{W}} \mathsf{K}''_{\mathbb{N}} <_{\mathrm{W}} \mathsf{C}''_{\mathbb{N}} <_{\mathrm{W}} \ldots$$

The so-called *compact choice problem* $\mathsf{K}_{\mathbb{N}}$ and the so-called *closed choice problem* $\mathsf{C}_{\mathbb{N}}$ on the natural numbers play an important role in Weihrauch complexity [8]. As noted by the author and Rakotoniaina [10, §7] they can be seen as Weihrauch complexity analogs of the Kirby-Paris hierarchy

$$\mathrm{B}\Sigma_1^0 \leftarrow \mathrm{I}\Sigma_1^0 \leftarrow \mathrm{B}\Sigma_2^0 \leftarrow \mathrm{I}\Sigma_2^0 \leftarrow \mathrm{B}\Sigma_3^0 \leftarrow \mathrm{I}\Sigma_3^0 \leftarrow \ldots$$

of boundedness and induction principles as it is known from reverse mathematics [11, 16, 17, 22] and we will simply refer to this hierarchy as the (Weihrauch version of the) *Kirby-Paris hierarchy* in the following. They are introduced in Sect. 3.

In Sect. 4 we will classify the topological Weihrauch degree of the Gödel problem and its variants. We will also study the question, which oracle among $\emptyset', \emptyset'', \dots$ is optimal to validate our classification. In Sect. 5 we classify the computability-theoretic Weihrauch degree of these problems, which turns out to be significantly different. In Sect. 6 we discuss closure properties of G that help us to say something on lower bounds on these Weihrauch degrees. This conference version of the material does not contain any proofs. They can be found in the full version of the article [4].

2 Weihrauch Complexity

In this section we introduce some basic definitions of Weihrauch complexity. A more detailed survey can be found in [8]. We recall that a *represented space* (X, δ) is a set X together with a *representation* $\delta :\subseteq \mathbb{N}^{\mathbb{N}} \to X$, i.e., a surjective potentially partial map δ. If $f :\subseteq X \rightrightarrows Y$ is a multivalued partial map on represented spaces (X, δ_X) and (Y, δ_Y), then $F :\subseteq \mathbb{N}^{\mathbb{N}} \to \mathbb{N}$ is called a *realizer* of f, if $\delta_Y F(p) \in f\delta_X(p)$ for all $p \in \mathrm{dom}(f\delta_X)$. We denote the fact that F realizes f by $F \vdash f$. We consider multivalued maps with realizers as problems.

Definition 4 (Problem). *A multivalued map* $f :\subseteq X \rightrightarrows Y$ *on represented spaces with a realizer is called a* problem.

Now we are prepared to define Weihrauch complexity and some variants of it. By $\mathrm{id} : \mathbb{N}^{\mathbb{N}} \to \mathbb{N}^{\mathbb{N}}$ we denote the identity on Baire space $\mathbb{N}^{\mathbb{N}}$, by $\langle . \rangle$ we denote a standard pairing function on $\mathbb{N}^{\mathbb{N}}$. We also use the angle bracket for countable tupling functions, Cantor tupling functions on $\mathbb{N}$ and corresponding pairing functions for $\mathbb{N} \times \mathbb{N}^{\mathbb{N}}$.

Definition 5 (Weihrauch complexity). *Let* $f :\subseteq X \rightrightarrows Y$ *and* $g :\subseteq Z \rightrightarrows W$ *be two multi-valued functions.*

1. f *is* Weihrauch reducible *to* g, *in symbols* $f \leq_{\mathrm{W}} g$, *if there are computable* $H, K :\subseteq \mathbb{N}^{\mathbb{N}} \to \mathbb{N}^{\mathbb{N}}$ *such that* $H\langle \mathrm{id}, GK \rangle \vdash f$ *whenever* $G \vdash g$.
2. f *is* strongly Weihrauch reducible *to* g, *in symbols* $f \leq_{\mathrm{sW}} g$, *if there are computable* $H, K :\subseteq \mathbb{N}^{\mathbb{N}} \to \mathbb{N}^{\mathbb{N}}$ *such that* $HGK \vdash f$ *whenever* $G \vdash g$.

We write $\leq_{\mathrm{W}}^{p}$ *and* $\leq_{\mathrm{sW}}^{p}$ *for the relativized versions of this reducibilities, where* H, K *are only required to be computable relative to* $p \in \mathbb{N}^{\mathbb{N}}$. *Analogously, we write* $\leq_{\mathrm{W}}^{*}$ *and* $\leq_{\mathrm{sW}}^{*}$ *if* H, K *are only required to be continuous.*

We use the usual notations $\equiv_{\mathrm{W}}$ and $\equiv_{\mathrm{sW}}$ for the corresponding equivalences, and similarly also for the relativized versions. The distributive lattice induced by $\leq_{\mathrm{W}}$ is usually referred to as *Weihrauch lattice*.

By $f^*, \widehat{f}$ and $f^\diamond$ we denote the *finite parallelization*, *parallelization*, and *diamond* operations on problems. The definitions can be found in [8], except for the diamond operation that was introduced by Neumann and Pauly [19]. While f^* can be seen as closure under the parallel product $f \times f$, $f^\diamond$ can be seen as closure under the compositional product $f \star f$ by a result of Westrick [25] (see below). Again, the definitions of $\times$ and $\star$ can be found in [8]. For our purposes we just mention the characterization that

$$f \star g \equiv_{\mathrm{W}} \max_{\leq_{\mathrm{W}}} \{f_0 \circ g_0 : f_0 \leq_{\mathrm{W}} f \text{ and } g_0 \leq_{\mathrm{W}} g\},$$

which was proved in [9, Corollary 3.7]. Likewise, we obtain by a theorem of Westrick [25, Theorem 1] that every problem f with $\mathrm{id} \leq_{\mathrm{W}} f$ satisfies

$$f^\circ \equiv_{\mathrm{W}} \min_{\leq_{\mathrm{W}}} \{g : f \leq_{\mathrm{W}} g \star g \leq_{\mathrm{W}} g\},$$

i.e., f° gives us the smallest Weihrauch degree above f that is closed under compositional product. We will also need the *first-order version* of a problem $f :\subseteq X \rightrightarrows Y$ that can be characterized according to [12, Theorem 2.2] by

$$^1f \equiv_{\mathrm{W}} \max_{\leq_{\mathrm{W}}} \{g : g :\subseteq \mathbb{N}^{\mathbb{N}} \rightrightarrows \mathbb{N} \text{ and } g \leq_{\mathrm{W}} f\}.$$

The first-order part ^1f captures the strongest problem with codomain $\mathbb{N}$ that is below f. This concept was recently introduced by Dzhafarov, Solomon, and Yokoyama [12] and has also been studied by Valenti [24] and Valenti and Soldà [23].

Finally, we also need the *jump* f' of a problem that was introduced in [7]. For a problem $f :\subseteq X \rightrightarrows Y$, the *jump* $f' :\subseteq X' \rightrightarrows Y$ is set-theoretically speaking the same problem as f, but the representation of the input set X is changed. If δ is the representation of X, then $\delta' := \delta \circ \lim$ is the representation of X', where $\lim$ denotes the limit map on Baire space. The n–th jump of f is denoted by $f^{(n)}$. More details can be found in [8].

We close this section with the definition of a number of problems that we are going to use in the following. By $\mathrm{Tr} \subseteq \{0,1\}^*$ we denote the set of binary trees and by $[T]$ the set of infinite paths of $T \in \mathrm{Tr}$. By $\widehat{n} = nnn... \in \mathbb{N}^{\mathbb{N}}$ we denote the constant sequence with value $n \in \mathbb{N}$.

The problems LPO and LLPO have been called *limited principle of omniscience* and *lesser limited principle of omniscience*, respectively, by Bishop [1] in the context of constructive mathematics.

Definition 6 (Some problems). *We define the following problems.*

1. $\mathsf{LPO} : \mathbb{N}^{\mathbb{N}} \to \{0,1\}, \mathsf{LPO}(p) = 1 :\Longleftrightarrow p = \widehat{0}$
2. $\mathsf{LLPO} :\subseteq \mathbb{N}^{\mathbb{N}} \rightrightarrows \{0,1\}, i \in \mathsf{LLPO}\langle p_0, p_1 \rangle :\Longleftrightarrow p_i = \widehat{0}$,
   with $\mathrm{dom}(\mathsf{LLPO}) = \{\langle p_0, p_1 \rangle \in \mathbb{N}^{\mathbb{N}} : p_0 = \widehat{0} \vee p_1 = \widehat{0}\}$.
3. $\lim_{\mathbb{N}} : \mathbb{N}^{\mathbb{N}} \to \mathbb{N}, p \mapsto \lim_{n \to \infty} p(n)$ *(limit on natural numbers)*
4. $\mathsf{B} :\subseteq \mathbb{N}^{\mathbb{N}} \rightrightarrows \mathbb{N}, p \mapsto \{m \in \mathbb{N} : (\forall n \in \mathbb{N})\, p(n) \leq m\}$ *(boundedness problem)*
5. $\inf :\subseteq \mathbb{N}^{\mathbb{N}} \to \mathbb{N}, p \mapsto \min \mathsf{C}_{\mathbb{N}}(p)$ *(least number problem)*
6. $\min : \mathbb{N}^{\mathbb{N}} \to \mathbb{N}, p \mapsto \min \mathrm{range}(p)$ *(minimum problem)*
7. $\mathsf{CL}_{\mathbb{N}} :\subseteq \mathbb{N}^{\mathbb{N}} \rightrightarrows \mathbb{N}, p \mapsto \{n \in \mathbb{N} : n \text{ cluster point of } p\}$ *(cluster point problem)*
8. $\mathsf{BWT}_{\mathbb{N}}$ *is the restriction of* $\mathsf{CL}_{\mathbb{N}}$ *to bounded sequences (Bolzano-Weierstraß)*
9. $\liminf_{\mathbb{N}} :\subseteq \mathbb{N}^{\mathbb{N}} \to \mathbb{N}, p \mapsto \min \mathsf{CL}_{\mathbb{N}}(p)$ *(limit inferior problem)*
10. $\mathsf{WKL} :\subseteq \mathrm{Tr} \rightrightarrows 2^{\mathbb{N}}, T \mapsto [T]$ *(Weak Kőnig's lemma)*

All definitions are meant with their natural domains, i.e., $\lim_{\mathbb{N}}$ is defined on converging sequences, B on bounded sequences, $\mathsf{CL}_{\mathbb{N}}$ of sequences with cluster points, etc. The closed choice problem $\mathsf{C}_{\mathbb{N}}$ is defined below.

3   Closed and Compact Choice on the Natural Numbers

Now we want to introduce our benchmark problems, which are *closed choice* on natural numbers and *compact choice* on natural numbers. Choice problems have been studied for a while and they have been uniformly defined for more general spaces than the natural numbers (see [5–8] for more information). For our purposes it is sufficient to define these choice problems on $\mathbb{N}$.

Definition 7 (Closed and compact choice). *We define* closed choice $C_\mathbb{N}$ *and* compact choice $K_\mathbb{N}$ *on natural numbers as follows:*

1. $C_\mathbb{N} :\subseteq \mathbb{N}^\mathbb{N} \rightrightarrows \mathbb{N}, p \mapsto \{n \in \mathbb{N} : (\forall k)\, p(k) \neq n\}$,
   with $\operatorname{dom}(C_\mathbb{N}) = \{p \in \mathbb{N}^\mathbb{N} : \operatorname{range}(p) \subsetneq \mathbb{N}\}$,
2. $K_\mathbb{N} :\subseteq \mathbb{N}^\mathbb{N} \times \mathbb{N} \rightrightarrows \mathbb{N}, (p, m) \mapsto \{n \leq m : (\forall k)\, p(k) \neq n\}$,
   with $\operatorname{dom}(K_\mathbb{N}) = \{(p, m) \in \mathbb{N}^\mathbb{N} \times \mathbb{N} : \operatorname{range}(p) \subsetneq \{0, ..., m\}\}$.

Hence, the task of $C_\mathbb{N}$ is to find a natural number which is not enumerated by the input sequence. Compact choice $K_\mathbb{N}$ has essentially the same task, except that only numbers $n \leq m$ below some additionally given bound m are considered.

The following was proved by Valenti [24, Page 98, Proposition 4.48, Corollary 4.50] and Soldà and Valenti [23, Proposition 7.1, Theorem 7.2, Corollary 7.6]. An independent proof of the first equivalences in each item is due to Dzhafarov, Solomon, and Yokoyama [12, Theorems 4.1 and 4.2]. We did not find an explicit statement of the second equivalence in (2), hence this is probably new. We note that $C_2^* \equiv_{sW} LLPO^* \equiv_{sW} K_\mathbb{N}$ by [7, Proposition 10.9].

Theorem 8 (Closed and compact choice). *For all* $n \in \mathbb{N}$:

1. $^1(\lim^{(n)}) \equiv_{sW} C_\mathbb{N}^{(n)} \equiv_W (LPO^{(n)})^\diamond$,
2. $^1(WKL^{(n)}) \equiv_{sW} K_\mathbb{N}^{(n)} \equiv_W (LLPO^{(n)})^\diamond$.

In [10, Proposition 7.2] it was proved that closed and compact choice and their jumps are linearly ordered in the following way.

Fact 9. $K_\mathbb{N}^{(n)} <_{sW} C_\mathbb{N}^{(n)} <_{sW} K_\mathbb{N}^{(n+1)}$ *for all* $n \in \mathbb{N}$.

Altogether, these properties of closed and compact choice justify to use them and their jumps as benchmark problems for the classification of the complexity of Gödel problem G and its variants, which are all first-order problems.

We close this section with some further characterizations of some of the choice problems. Most of these are well-known, except perhaps the one on the limes inferior.

Proposition 10 (Least number problem, minimum, limes inferior).

1. $K_\mathbb{N} \equiv_{sW} LLPO^* <_{sW} \min \equiv_{sW} LPO^* <_{sW} C_\mathbb{N} \equiv_{sW} \lim_\mathbb{N} \equiv_{sW} \inf \equiv_W B$,
2. $K_\mathbb{N}' \equiv_{sW} BWT_\mathbb{N} <_{sW} \min' <_{sW} C_\mathbb{N}' \equiv_{sW} CL_\mathbb{N} \equiv_{sW} \lim\inf \equiv_{sW} \inf'$.

We emphasize the following fact.

Fact 11. $C_\mathbb{N} \equiv_W B <_{sW} C_\mathbb{N}$.

The separation follows from [8, Proposition 11.6.18].

4   The Topological Classification

The purpose of this section is to classify $G, K, G_\geq$ and $K_\geq$ from a topological perspective. This as such is pretty simple and we obtain the following result.

Theorem 12 (The topological degree). $B \equiv^*_{sW} K_\geq \equiv^*_W G \equiv^*_{sW} K \equiv^*_{sW} C_N$ *and $G_\geq$ is continuous.*

The statement is illustrated in the diagram in Fig. 2 using our benchmark problems K_N and C_N.

The equivalences $K_\geq \equiv^*_W G$ and $G_\geq \equiv^*_W \mathrm{id}$ can be seen as formal versions of the slogan of Hoyrup and Rojas.

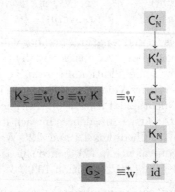

$$
\begin{array}{c}
C'_N \\
\downarrow \\
K'_N \\
\end{array}
$$

$$
\boxed{K_\geq \equiv^*_W G \equiv^*_W K} \quad \equiv^*_W \quad C_N
$$

$$
\begin{array}{c}
\downarrow \\
K_N \\
\downarrow \\
\end{array}
$$

$$
\boxed{G_\geq} \quad \equiv^*_W \quad \mathrm{id}
$$

Fig. 2. The Gödel problem in the topological Weihrauch lattice.

As continuity is computability with respect to some oracle, the question appears whether among the jumps $\emptyset^{(n)}$ there is a simplest one in the place of $*$ that makes the statements of Theorem 12 correct. We recall that the set $\mathsf{TOT} := \{i \in \mathbb{N} : \varphi_i \text{ total}\}$ is a Π^0_2–complete set in the arithmetical hierarchy [20, Proposition X.9.6] and hence $\mathsf{TOT} \leq_T \emptyset''$. Hence it follows easily that $\emptyset''$ is sufficient in place of $*$, as totality of the functions represented by Gödel numbers is a useful property that can be utilized to provide a simple proof of Theorem 12.

Somewhat surprisingly and with a little more effort, we can show that actually the halting problem $\emptyset'$ in the place of $*$ also validates Theorem 12. We start with providing the following equivalences. The upper bound is easy to obtain and for the lower bound the essential idea is to use (a variant) of the set of random natural numbers.

Theorem 13 (With the halting problem as oracle). $B \equiv^{\emptyset'}_{sW} K_\geq \equiv^{\emptyset'}_W$ $G \equiv^{\emptyset'}_{sW} K \equiv^{\emptyset'}_{sW} C_N$.

A close inspection of the proof could reveal that the oracle p has only been used on the input side, i.e., for the computation of the preprocessing operation K in terms of Definition 5. We obtain the following corollary of Theorem 13.

Corollary 14 (Jumps). $\mathsf{B}^{(n)} \equiv_{sW} \mathsf{K}_{\geq}^{(n)}$ and $\mathsf{G}^{(n)} \equiv_{sW} \mathsf{K}^{(n)} \equiv_{sW} \mathsf{C}_{\mathbb{N}}^{(n)}$ for $n \geq 1$.

The next result can be proved using the *amalgamation technique* that is attributed by [27] to Wiehagen [26].

Proposition 15. $\mathsf{G}_{\geq}$ *is computable relative to the halting problem.*

5   The Computability-Theoretic Classification

We now want to explore the unrelativized Weihrauch degree of the Gödel problem and its variants. It turns out that the situation is significantly different in this case and none of G, K and $\mathsf{K}_{\geq}$ is computably Weihrauch equivalent to $\mathsf{C}_{\mathbb{N}}$. Since no other natural candidates of problems are known that are topologically but not computably equivalent to $\mathsf{C}_{\mathbb{N}}$, the best that we can expect for a classification is to obtain optimal upper bounds in terms of the Weihrauch version of the Kirby-Paris hierarchy

$$\mathsf{K}_{\mathbb{N}} <_{\mathrm{W}} \mathsf{C}_{\mathbb{N}} <_{\mathrm{W}} \mathsf{K}_{\mathbb{N}}' <_{\mathrm{W}} \mathsf{C}_{\mathbb{N}}' <_{\mathrm{W}} \mathsf{K}_{\mathbb{N}}'' <_{\mathrm{W}} \mathsf{C}_{\mathbb{N}}'' <_{\mathrm{W}} \dots$$

that are as narrow as possible. We start with some positive results. For the upper bound of $\mathsf{G}_{\geq}$ we use again the amalgamation technique.

Proposition 16 (Upper bounds). *We obtain*

1. $\mathsf{K}_{\geq} \leq_{sW} \mathsf{G} \leq_{sW} \mathsf{K} \leq_{sW} \mathsf{K}' \equiv_{sW} \mathsf{C}_{\mathbb{N}}'$,
2. $\mathsf{G}_{\geq} \leq_{sW} \mathsf{LPO}^* <_{\mathrm{W}} \mathsf{C}_{\mathbb{N}}$.

The result $\mathsf{G}_{\geq} \leq_{\mathrm{W}} \mathsf{C}_{\mathbb{N}}$ is essentially contained in [13] and has also been used in [18]. Our improvement is that we bring the upper bound down to LPO^*. The diagram in Fig. 3 illustrates the situation.

Next we want to show that the upper bounds given in Proposition 16 are minimal, at least with respect to our benchmark problems $\mathsf{K}_{\mathbb{N}} <_{sW} \mathsf{C}_{\mathbb{N}} <_{sW} \mathsf{K}_{\mathbb{N}}' <_{sW} \mathsf{C}_{\mathbb{N}}'$ of the Kirby-Paris hierarchy. We use finite extension constructions for this purpose.

Proposition 17 (Optimality of upper bounds). *We obtain*

1. $\mathsf{K}_{\geq} \not\leq_{\mathrm{W}} \mathsf{K}_{\mathbb{N}}'$,
2. $\mathsf{G}_{\geq} \not\leq_{\mathrm{W}} \mathsf{K}_{\mathbb{N}}$.

As $^1\mathsf{WKL}^{(n)} \equiv_{\mathrm{W}} \mathsf{K}_{\mathbb{N}}^{(n)}$ and $^1\lim^{(n)} \equiv_{\mathrm{W}} \mathsf{C}_{\mathbb{N}}^{(n)}$ by Theorem 8, we obtain the following corollary with respect to WKL and lim.

Corollary 18 (Weak König's lemma and limits). *We obtain*

1. $\mathsf{K}_{\geq} \leq_{sW} \mathsf{G} \leq_{sW} \mathsf{K} \leq_{sW} \lim'$, *but* $\mathsf{K}_{\geq} \not\leq_{\mathrm{W}} \mathsf{WKL}'$,
2. $\mathsf{G}_{\geq} \leq_{sW} \lim$, *but* $\mathsf{G}_{\geq} \not\leq_{\mathrm{W}} \mathsf{WKL}$.

174   V. Brattka

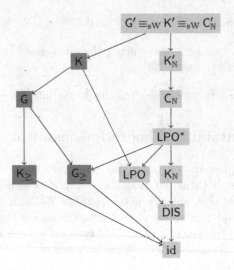

Fig. 3. The Gödel problem in the Weihrauch lattice.

Finally, we still want to separate $K_\geq$ from $G_\geq$ and G. By $|_W$ we denote incomparability with respect to $\leq_W$.

Proposition 19. $G_\geq |_W K_\geq$ *and* $K_\geq <_W G$.

Hence, the diagram in Fig. 3 is complete in the sense that no further Weihrauch reductions to the problems from our Kirby-Paris hierarchy are possible, besides the shown ones (and those that follow by reflexivity and transitivity).

Proposition 19 also shows that the slogan of Hoyrup and Rojas is not true in a computability-theoretic sense. In fact, in this sense Gödel numbers carry strictly more information about the sequences that they represent than just an upper bound of their Kolmogorov complexity.

6   Closure Properties and Lower Bounds

So far we have provided upper bounds to the Gödel problem together with a proof that these upper bounds are optimal with respect to the Weihrauch version of the Kirby-Paris hierarchy. Now we want to provide some closure properties of G, some of which we will utilize to provide optimal lower bounds in a certain sense. By $f|_c$ we denote the restriction of a problem f to all computable instances.

Theorem 20 (Closure properties). *We obtain the following:*

1. $\widehat{G}|_c \equiv_{sW} G <_W^* \widehat{G}$,
2. $(G \star G)|_c \equiv_{sW} G$,
3. $G^* \equiv_{sW} G$.

We note that the above result does not directly show $G \star G \equiv_W G$. This raises the following open problem.

Problem 21. Is $G \star G \equiv_W G$?

Of course, $G \star G \equiv_W^* G$ holds, but the question is whether this is computably true.

A surprising consequence of the parallelization properties of the Gödel problem G is that G is a natural example for a problem that is effectively discontinuous, but not computably so. Such examples where constructed in [3, Proposition 19], but no natural example was known so far. Intuitively, a problem f is *effectively discontinuous*, if given a continuous function $F :\subseteq \mathbb{N}^{\mathbb{N}} \to \mathbb{N}^{\mathbb{N}}$ that is a potential realizer of f, one can continuously determine some input on which F fails to realize f. Analogously, in the case of *computable discontinuity* the input is found in a computable way. See [3] for more precise definition. The *discontinuity problem*

$$\mathsf{DIS} : \mathbb{N}^{\mathbb{N}} \rightrightarrows \mathbb{N}^{\mathbb{N}}, p \mapsto \{q \in \mathbb{N}^{\mathbb{N}} : \mathsf{U}(p) \neq q\}$$

has been defined in [3], where $\mathsf{U} :\subseteq \mathbb{N}^{\mathbb{N}} \to \mathbb{N}^{\mathbb{N}}$ is a standard computable universal function. We are not using the discontinuity problem in any technical way here, hence the definition is not relevant for the following. We have $\mathsf{DIS} <_{sW} \mathsf{LPO} <_{sW} \mathsf{C}_{\mathbb{N}}$ and in [3, Theorem 17] we have proved the following for every problem f.

Fact 22 (Effective discontinuity). *We obtain:*

1. f *is effectively discontinuous* $\Longleftrightarrow$ $\mathsf{DIS} \leq_{sW}^* f$,
2. f *is computably discontinuous* $\Longleftrightarrow$ $\mathsf{DIS} \leq_{sW} f$.

Hence, we obtain the following corollary.

Corollary 23 (Effective discontinuity). $\mathsf{DIS} \leq_{sW}^* \mathsf{K}_{\geq}$, *but* $\mathsf{DIS} \not\leq_W G$. *That is,* G *and* $\mathsf{K}_{\geq}$ *are effectively discontinuous, but not computably so.*

In some well-defined sense DIS is the weakest natural discontinuous problem [2]. That DIS is not computably reducible to G means that the uniform computational power of G is extremely weak. No other standard lower bounds of G (other than related lower bounds such as $\mathsf{K}_{\geq}, G_{\geq}$) are known, besides the trivial lower bound id. The situation is quite different for the Kolmogorov complexity K, where we have the following easy result.

Proposition 24 (Lower bounds for Kolmogorov complexity). $\mathsf{LPO} <_W \mathsf{K}$ *and* $\lim <_W \widehat{\mathsf{K}}$.

As $\mathsf{DIS} \leq_W \mathsf{LPO}$, we have clearly separated the Gödel problem G from the Kolmogorov complexity K. The Gödel problem G is also separated from its bounded counterpart $G_{\geq}$ as the latter is continuous and the former not.

Corollary 25 (Gödel and Kolmogorov). $G_{\geq} <_W G <_W \mathsf{K}$.

7   Conclusions

We have seen that the Gödel problem and its variants have natural classifications in the topological Weihrauch lattice. The halting problem turned out to be the optimal oracle that validates these classifications. With respect to the computability-theoretic version of Weihrauch reducibility the situation was more complex. We established an optimal upper bound with respect to the Weihrauch version of the Kirby-Paris hierarchy that we have used to classify the complexity. We have also discussed closure properties and lower bounds.

References

1. Bishop, E.: Foundations of Constructive Analysis. McGraw-Hill, New York (1967)
2. Brattka, V.: Stashing-parallelization pentagons. Logic. Methods Comput. Sci. **17**(4), 1–29 (2021). https://doi.org/10.46298/lmcs-17(4:20)2021
3. Brattka, V.: The discontinuity problem. J. Symb. Logic (2022). https://doi.org/10.1017/jsl.2021.106
4. Brattka, V.: On the complexity of computing Gödel numbers. arXiv 2302.04213 (2023). https://arxiv.org/abs/2302.04213
5. Brattka, V., de Brecht, M., Pauly, A.: Closed choice and a uniform low basis theorem. Ann. Pure Appl. Logic **163**, 986–1008 (2012). https://doi.org/10.1016/j.apal.2011.12.020
6. Brattka, V., Gherardi, G.: Effective choice and boundedness principles in computable analysis. Bull. Symb. Log. **17**(1), 73–117 (2011). https://doi.org/10.2178/bsl/1294186663
7. Brattka, V., Gherardi, G., Marcone, A.: The Bolzano-Weierstrass theorem is the jump of weak Kőnig's lemma. Ann. Pure Appl. Logic **163**, 623–655 (2012). https://doi.org/10.1016/j.apal.2011.10.006
8. Brattka, V., Gherardi, G., Pauly, A.: Weihrauch complexity in computable analysis. In: Handbook of Computability and Complexity in Analysis. TAC, pp. 367–417. Springer, Cham (2021). https://doi.org/10.1007/978-3-030-59234-9_11
9. Brattka, V., Pauly, A.: On the algebraic structure of Weihrauch degrees. Logic. Methods Comput. Sci. **14**(4:4), 1–36 (2018). https://lmcs.episciences.org/4918
10. Brattka, V., Rakotoniaina, T.: On the uniform computational content of Ramsey's theorem. J. Symb. Log. **82**(4), 1278–1316 (2017). https://doi.org/10.1017/jsl.2017.43
11. Dzhafarov, D.D., Mummert, C.: Reverse Mathematics. Theory and Applications of Computability. Springer, Cham (2022). https://doi.org/10.1007/978-3-031-11367-3
12. Dzhafarov, D.D., Solomon, R., Yokoyama, K.: On the first-order parts of problems in the Weihrauch degrees. arXiv 2301.12733 (2023). https://arxiv.org/abs/2301.12733
13. Freivald, R.V., Wiehagen, R.: Inductive inference with additional information. Elektron. Inform. Kybernetik **15**(4), 179–185 (1979)
14. Gauthier, T., Olšák, M., Urban, J.: Alien coding. arXiv 2301.11479 (2023). https://arxiv.org/abs/2301.11479
15. Gold, E.M.: Language identification in the limit. Inf. Control **10**(5), 447–474 (1967). https://doi.org/10.1016/S0019-9958(67)91165-5

16. Hájek, P., Pudlák, P.: Metamathematics of First-Order Arithmetic. Perspectives in Mathematical Logic. Springer-Verlag, Berlin (1993). https://doi.org/10.1007/978-3-662-22156-3

17. Hirschfeldt, D.R.: Slicing the truth: on the computable and reverse mathematics of combinatorial principles. Lecture Notes Series, Institute for Mathematical Sciences, National University of Singapore, vol. 28. World Scientific, Singapore (2015). http://www.worldscientific.com/worldscibooks/10.1142/9208

18. Hoyrup, M., Rojas, C.: On the information carried by programs about the objects they compute. Theory Comput. Syst. **61**(4), 1214–1236 (2016). https://doi.org/10.1007/s00224-016-9726-9

19. Neumann, E., Pauly, A.: A topological view on algebraic computation models. J. Complexity **44**(Supplement C), 1–22 (2018). http://www.sciencedirect.com/science/article/pii/S0885064X17300766

20. Odifreddi, P.: Classical Recursion Theory - Volume II, Studies in Logic and the Foundations of Mathematics, vol. 143. North-Holland, Amsterdam (1999)

21. Osherson, D.N., Stob, M., Weinstein, S.: Systems That Learn: An Introduction to Learning Theory for Cognitive and Computer Scientists. MIT Press, Cambridge, MA (1990)

22. Simpson, S.G.: Subsystems of Second Order Arithmetic, 2nd edn. Perspectives in Logic, Cambridge University Press (2009)

23. Soldà, G., Valenti, M.: Algebraic properties of the first-order part of a problem. Annal. Pure Appl. Logic **174**, 103270 (2023). https://doi.org/10.1016/j.apal.2023.103270

24. Valenti, M.: A journey through computability, topology and analysis, Ph. D. thesis, Universitá degli Studi di Udine (2021)

25. Westrick, L.: A note on the diamond operator. Computability **10**(2), 107–110 (2021). https://doi.org/10.3233/COM-200295

26. Wiehagen, R.: Zur Theorie der Algorithmischen Erkennung. Dissertation B, Humboldt-Universität zu Berlin (1978)

27. Zeugmann, T., Zilles, S.: Learning recursive functions: a survey. Theoret. Comput. Sci. **397**(1–3), 4–56 (2008). https://doi.org/10.1016/j.tcs.2008.02.021

The Complexity of Finding Supergraphs

Vittorio Cipriani[1]([⊠]) [iD] and Arno Pauly[2] [iD]

[1] Dipartimento di Scienze Matematiche Informatiche e Fisiche, Università degli Studi di Udine, Udine, Italy
vittorio.cipriani17@gmail.com
[2] Department of Computer Science, Swansea University, Wales, Swansea, UK

Abstract. We consider several variations of the following problem: fix a countable graph G. Is an input graph H a(n induced) subgraph of G? If yes, can we find a copy of H in G? The challenge to classify the Weihrauch degrees of such problems was put forth recently by BeMent, Hirst, and Wallace ("Reverse mathematics and Weihrauch analysis motivated by finite complexity theory", Computability, 2021). We report some initial results here, and in particular, solve one of their open questions.

1 Introduction

We explore the complexity of a few problems regarding countable graphs over $\mathbb{N}$. One graph, G, is fixed. The input is another graph H. The decision question is whether G is a supergraph of H. The search problem has a guarantee that the input indeed embeds into G, and the task is to find such an embedding. Both tasks come in a few variations: we can either consider subgraphs or induced subgraphs. The input can be given via its characteristic function or via an enumeration.

The framework for our investigation is Weihrauch reducibility (see [5] for an overview). For the decision problem, this incorporates the effective Wadge degrees of the problem.

This particular line of research was initiated by BeMent, Hirst, and Wallace in [3], where they consider both the present task of asking whether the fixed graph is a supergraph of the input, as well as the dual task of asking whether the fixed graph is a subgraph of the input. It is rather straightforward to verify that if both graphs are given as input, the decision problem is Σ_1^1-complete, and finding the corresponding witness is Weihrauch equivalent to $C_{\mathbb{N}^\mathbb{N}}$. In [3] it is observed that for the totally disconnected infinite graph, the task of deciding whether it is a(n induced) supergraph of a given graph is equivalent to LPO, the simplest discontinuous problem. BeMent, Hirst, and Wallace then raise the question of whether there are graphs for which the corresponding supergraph task is more complicated. We give an affirmative answer here – however, we

---

Cipriani's research was partially supported by the Italian PRIN 2017 Grant "Mathematical Logic: models, sets, computability". He thanks Alberto Marcone and Manlio Valenti for useful discussions about the topics of this paper.

G. Della Vedova et al. (Eds.): CiE 2023, LNCS 13967, pp. 178–189, 2023.
https://doi.org/10.1007/978-3-031-36978-0_15

leave open the companion question of whether there is a graph for which the supergraph task is Σ_1^1-complete open.

At first glance, it may appear as if the second question by BeMent, Hirst and Wallace (and thus the first, too) is already answered in the positive by Hirst and Lempp's [8, Theorem 3.2], which shows that there exists a computable graph H such that the set of indices of computable graphs of which H is a supergraph is Σ_1^1-complete. However, the theorem concerns Σ_1^1-completeness of subsets of $\mathbb{N}$ under many-one reductions, while the question concerns Σ_1^1-completeness of subsets of $2^{\mathbb{N}}$ under effective Wadge reductions. The proof of [8, Theorem 3.2] proceeds by constructing a computable graph, which up to some coding, has exactly those infinite trees as subgraphs that are ill-founded (this can be accomplished by turning failed attempts to build an ill-founded tree into "spurious" cycles). This approach does not relativize in a manner that would be applicable to the open question.

2   The (Induced) Subgraph Problem

The investigation of the dual problem, where the fixed graph is the would-be subgraph, was carried out in a parallel paper by the present authors [7]. For that question, we arrived at a very different picture depending on whether we consider induced subgraphs only, or arbitrary subgraphs. In the former case, we obtained a concise classification: as long as the fixed graph is infinite, the decision problem is Σ_1^1-complete, and the search problem is equivalent to $\mathsf{C}_{\mathbb{N}^{\mathbb{N}}}$ (relative to a suitable oracle at least). The proofs are somewhat non-uniform however, with different constructions being used for different classes of graphs (graphs containing an infinite clique, graphs not containing an infinite ray, and graphs having finitely versus infinitely many vertices of finite degree being the relevant distinctions).

The situation for arbitrary subgraphs is more complicated. If the fixed graph contains an infinite ray, the decision problem is Σ_1^1-complete. On the other hand, by considering trees and forests of finite height, we also give examples of graphs for which the decision problem is complete for levels Σ_{2k+1}^0 and Π_{2k+2}^0. When the task is to actually find the subgraph, having an infinite ray is insufficient to render the problem equivalent to $\mathsf{C}_{\mathbb{N}^{\mathbb{N}}}$. In particular, we show that finding an infinite graph in a given graph is strictly weaker than $\mathsf{C}_{\mathbb{N}^{\mathbb{N}}}$. This may seem surprising, as $\mathsf{C}_{\mathbb{N}^{\mathbb{N}}}$ is the task of finding an infinite path through an ill-founded tree - and thus may look like a special case. However, the difference is that the output of $\mathsf{C}_{\mathbb{N}^{\mathbb{N}}}$ contains the direction of the infinite path (i.e. which way towards infinity), whereas merely knowing which vertices belong to a subgraph that is isomorphic to an infinite ray lacks this extra bit of information. For many other examples (i.e. the bi-infinite line or the full binary tree), finding them as a subgraph is indeed equivalent to $\mathsf{C}_{\mathbb{N}^{\mathbb{N}}}$.

3   Background

3.1   Sequences, Trees, and Graphs

Let $\mathbb{N}^n$ denote the set of finite sequences of natural numbers of length n, where the length is denoted by $|\cdot|$. If $n = 0$, $\mathbb{N}^0 = \{\langle\rangle\}$, where $\langle\rangle$ is the empty sequence. The set of all finite sequences of natural numbers is denoted by $\mathbb{N}^{<\mathbb{N}}$. For $\sigma \in \mathbb{N}^{<\mathbb{N}}$ and $m \leqslant |\sigma|$, let $\sigma[m] := \langle\sigma(0), \ldots, \sigma(m-1)\rangle$. Given $\sigma, \tau \in \mathbb{N}^{<\mathbb{N}}$, we use $\sigma \sqsubseteq \tau$ to say that σ is an *initial segment* of τ, i.e. $\sigma = \tau[m]$ for some $m \leqslant |\tau|$. We use $n^{\mathbb{N}}$ to denote the infinite sequence with constant value n.

We use the symbol $\langle\cdot\rangle$ also to denote a fixed pairing function from $\mathbb{N}^{<\mathbb{N}}$ to $\mathbb{N}$: the context should clarify whether we are referring to a finite sequence or to the number representing it.

A *tree* T is a nonempty subset of $\mathbb{N}^{<\mathbb{N}}$ closed under initial segments. We say that $f \in \mathbb{N}^{\mathbb{N}}$ is a path through T if for all $n \in \mathbb{N}$, $f[n] \in T$ where, as for finite sequences, $f[n] = \langle f(0), \ldots, f(n-1)\rangle$. We say that a tree T is *ill-founded* if $[T] \neq \varnothing$, well-founded otherwise.

A *graph* G is a pair (V, E) where V is the set of *vertices* and E is a binary relation on $V \times V$; a pair $(v, w) \in E$ is called an *edge*. All the graphs we consider in this paper are countable, undirected and without self-loops: that is, $V \subseteq \mathbb{N}$ and E satisfies anti-reflexivity and symmetry.

For a graph G and $n \in \mathbb{N}$, a *line segment of length* n is a sequence of distinct vertices $v_0, \ldots, v_n$ of G such that for every $i < n$, $(v_i, v_{i+1}) \in E(G)$ and we call v_0 and v_n *endpoints*. We say that v *and* u *are connected in* G if there exists a line segment of finite length in G, with endpoints v and u. For a graph G and $v \in V(G)$, we define the *degree* of v in G as $\deg^G(v) := |\{w : (v, w) \in E(G)\}|$.

We now define three particular types of graphs, namely *line segments*, *cycles*, and *complete* graphs. We define L_n, C_n and K_n as graphs having the same vertex set $\{i : i < n\}$, where $n > 0$ in L_n and K_n and $n \geqslant 3$ in C_n. The edge sets are respectively: $E(L_n) = \{(i, i+1) : i < n\}$, $E(K_n) = \{(i, j) : i \neq j \wedge i, j < n\}$ and $E(C_n) = E(L_{n-1}) \cup \{(n-1, 0)\}$. It is immediate that $L_1 = K_1$ and $C_3 = K_3$. Notice that L_n generalizes to the *infinite ray* R, the graph having $\mathbb{N}$ as vertex set and a $\{(i, i+1) : i \in \mathbb{N}\}$ as edge set. Similarly, K_n generalizes to K_ω, the graph having $\mathbb{N}$ as vertex set and $\{(i, j) : i \neq j \wedge i, j \in \mathbb{N}\}$ as edge set.

Given countably many graphs $\{G_i : i \in \mathbb{N}\}$ we define the *disconnected union* $\bigotimes_{i \in \mathbb{N}} G_i$ as the graph having $\bigcup_{i \in \mathbb{N}} \{\langle i, v\rangle : v \in V(G_i)\}$ as vertex set and $\{(\langle i, v\rangle, \langle i, w\rangle) : (v, w) \in E(G_i)\}$ as edge set.

Definition 1. *Given two graphs* $G := (V, E)$ *and* $G' := (V', E')$ *we say that* G *is a supergraph of* G' *if* $V' \subseteq V$ *and* $E' \subseteq E$. *If* G *is a supergraph of* G' *and* $E' = E \cap (V' \times V')$, *then we say that* G *is an induced supergraph of* G'.

We write $G \supseteq_{\mathbf{is}} H$ to denote that $(\exists H' \cong H)(G$ is an induced supergraph of $H')$ (similarly for $G \supseteq_{\mathbf{s}} H$).

3.2   Effective Wadge Reducibility

In this section, we consider the effective counterpart of *Wadge reducibility* and we discuss some well-known results about the level at which some subsets of (products of) the Cantor space are in the lightface hierarchy (the effective counterpart of the boldface hierarchy).

Wadge reducibility introduces a notion of complexity between subsets of topological spaces: in general, its effective counterpart can be defined for effective second-countable spaces, but in this paper we deal only with subsets of $\mathbb{N}^{\mathbb{N}}$ and $2^{\mathbb{N}}$.

Given $A, B \subseteq \mathbb{N}^{\mathbb{N}}$, we say that A is *effectively Wadge reducible* to B (in symbols, $A \leqslant_{\mathsf{EW}} B$) if there is a computable function $f : \mathbb{N}^{\mathbb{N}} \to \mathbb{N}^{\mathbb{N}}$ such that $x \in A \iff f(x) \in B$, where computability is defined in the sense of §3.3. Informally, if $A \leqslant_{\mathsf{EW}} B$ it means that A is "simpler" than B. We refer to the corresponding $\leqslant_{\mathsf{EW}}$-equivalence classes as *effective Wadge degrees*. Given a lightface class Γ, we call B Γ-hard if, for any $A \in \Gamma$, $A \leqslant_{\mathsf{EW}} B$. If in addition $B \in \Gamma$, we say that B is Γ-complete. Notice that if B is Γ-hard (respectively, Γ-complete), then the complement of B is $\check{\Gamma}$-hard ($\check{\Gamma}$-complete), where $\check{\Gamma} := \{\mathbb{N}^{\mathbb{N}} \setminus A : A \in \Gamma\}$. In this paper, we consider both Wadge reducibility and its effective counterpart *effective Wadge reducibility*. of (products of) the Cantor space are in the lightface hierarchy (the effective counterpart of the boldface hierarchy.

In the next proposition (and in the rest of the paper) we use the following abbreviations: $\exists^{\infty} n := (\forall n \in \mathbb{N})(\exists m \geqslant n)$ and $\forall^{\infty} n := (\exists n \in \mathbb{N})(\forall m \geqslant n)$.

Proposition 1. *The following complexity results hold:*

- $\{p : (\forall i)(p(i) = 0)\}$ *is* Π^0_1-*complete;*
- $\{p : (\exists^{\infty} i)(p(i) = 0)\}$ *is* Π^0_2-*complete;*
- $\{p \in 2^{\mathbb{N} \times \mathbb{N}} : (\forall n)(\forall^{\infty} i)(p(n, i) = 1)\}$ *is* Π^0_3-*complete;*
- $\{(p \in 2^{\mathbb{N} \times \mathbb{N} \times \mathbb{N}}) : (\forall i)(\forall^{\infty} j)(\forall^{\infty} n)(p(i, j, n) = 0)\}$ *is* Π^0_5-*complete.*

The proofs for the proposition above can be found in [9, §23.A] (the results are stated for the boldface case, but the same proofs work also in the lightface one).

3.3   Represented Spaces and Weihrauch Reducibility

For more on the topics discussed in this section, we refer the reader to [5,11]. Here computability of functions from $\mathbb{N}^{\mathbb{N}}$ to $\mathbb{N}^{\mathbb{N}}$ is intended as in TTE. A represented space $\mathbf{X}$ is a pair (X, δ_X) where X is a set and $\delta_X :\subseteq \mathbb{N}^{\mathbb{N}} \to X$ is a (possibly partial) surjection. We say that p is a δ_X-name for x if $\delta_X(p) = x$. A computational problem f between represented spaces $\mathbf{X}$ and $\mathbf{Y}$ is formalized as a *partial multi-valued function* $f :\subseteq \mathbf{X} \rightrightarrows \mathbf{Y}$. A *realizer* for $f :\subseteq \mathbf{X} \rightrightarrows \mathbf{Y}$ is a (possibly partial) function $F :\subseteq \mathbb{N}^{\mathbb{N}} \to \mathbb{N}^{\mathbb{N}}$ such that for every $p \in \mathrm{dom}(f \circ \delta_X)$, $\delta_Y(F(p)) \in f(\delta_X(p))$. Realizers allow us to transfer properties of functions on the Baire space (such as computability or continuity) to multi-valued functions on represented spaces in general. Hence, from now on, whenever we say that a multi-valued function between represented spaces is computable we mean that it has a computable realizer.

We now present some of the represented spaces we need thorough the paper. For a represented space $\mathbf{X}$, $\mathcal{A}(\mathbf{X})$ denotes the standard negative representation of closed sets of $\mathbf{X}$. We denote by $\mathbf{Gr}$ and $\mathbf{EGr}$ the represented spaces of graphs represented via characteristic functions and enumerations respectively:

- the representation map δ_{Gr} has domain $\{p \in 2^{\mathbb{N}} : (\forall i, j \in \mathbb{N})(p(\langle i, j \rangle) = 1 \implies p(\langle j, i \rangle) = p(\langle i, i \rangle) = p(\langle j, j \rangle) = 1)\}$. Any graph $G \in \mathbf{Gr}$ has a unique δ_{Gr}-name $p \in 2^{\mathbb{N}}$ such that $i \in V(G) \iff p(\langle i, i \rangle) = 1$ and for $i \neq j$, $(i, j) \in E(G) \iff p(\langle i, j \rangle) = 1$.
- the representation map δ_{EGr} has domain $\{p \in \mathbb{N}^{\mathbb{N}} : (\forall i \neq j \in \mathbb{N})(\exists k \in \mathbb{N})(p(k) = \langle i, j \rangle \implies (\exists \ell_0, \ell_1)(p(\ell_0) = \langle i, i \rangle \wedge p(\ell_1) = \langle j, j \rangle))\}$. A graph $G \in \mathbf{EGr}$ instead has multiple δ_{EGr}-names namely $\{p \in \mathrm{dom}(\delta_{EGr}) : (i \in V(G) \iff (\exists k)(p(k) = i)) \wedge ((i, j) \in E(G) \iff (\exists \ell)(p(\ell) = \langle i, j \rangle))\}$.

To compare the uniform computational content of different problems, we use the framework of *Weihrauch reducibility*. Informally, if f is Weihrauch reducible to g, we claim that there exists a procedure for solving f which is computable modulo a single invocation of g as an oracle. More formally, let $\mathbf{X}, \mathbf{Y}, \mathbf{Z}, \mathbf{W}$ be represented spaces and $f :\subseteq \mathbf{X} \rightrightarrows \mathbf{Y}$, $g :\subseteq \mathbf{Z} \rightrightarrows \mathbf{W}$ be partial multi-valued functions. We say that f is *Weihrauch reducible* (respectively, *strongly Weihrauch reducible*) to g, and we write $f \leqslant_{\mathrm{W}} g$ ($f \leqslant_{\mathrm{sW}} g$) if there are computable maps $\Phi, \Psi :\subseteq \mathbb{N}^{\mathbb{N}} \to \mathbb{N}^{\mathbb{N}}$ such that

- for every name p_x for some $x \in \mathrm{dom}(f)$, $\Phi(p_x) = p_z$, where p_z is a name for some $z \in \mathrm{dom}(g)$ and,
- for every name p_w for some $w \in g(z)$, $\Psi(p_x \oplus p_w) = p_y$ (or just $\Psi(p_w) = p_y$ in case it is a strong Weihrauch reduction) where p_y is a name for $y \in f(x)$.

In other words, a Weihrauch reduction transforms realizers for g into realizers for f. Both Weihrauch reducibility and strong Weihrauch reducibility are reflexive and transitive hence they induce the equivalence relations $\equiv_{\mathrm{W}}$ and $\equiv_{\mathrm{sW}}$: that is $f \equiv_{\mathrm{W}} g$ if and only if $f \leqslant_{\mathrm{W}} g$ and $g \leqslant_{\mathrm{W}} f$ (similarly for $\leqslant_{\mathrm{sW}}$). The $\equiv_{\mathrm{W}}$-equivalence classes are called *Weihrauch degrees* (similarly the $\equiv_{\mathrm{sW}}$-equivalence classes are called *strong Weihrauch degrees*). We can define several natural operations on problems: some of them lift to the $\equiv_{\mathrm{W}}$-degrees and others don't: we only mention the ones that are needed for this paper.

Given a problem f, we define its *infinite parallelization* as $\widehat{f}((x_i)_{i \in \mathbb{N}}) := \{(y_i)_{i \in \mathbb{N}} : (\forall i)(y_i \in f(x_i)\}$.

The *compositional product* $f \star g$ introduced in [4], and proven to be well-defined in [6], captures the informal idea of applying g, possibly doing some computable process, and then applying f. Formally, $f \star g$ is a particular function satisfying $f \star g \equiv_{\mathrm{W}} \max_{\leqslant_{\mathrm{W}}}\{f_1 \circ g_1 : f_1 \leqslant_{\mathrm{W}} f \wedge g_1 \leqslant_{\mathrm{W}} g\}$.

We now define the *jump of a problem*: before doing so, we define the *jump of a represented space*. Given a represented space $\mathbf{X} = (X, \delta_X)$ we define the jump of $\mathbf{X}$ as the represented space $\mathbf{X}' := (X, \delta_X')$ where δ_X' takes in input a sequence of elements of $\mathbb{N}^{\mathbb{N}}$ converging to some $p \in \mathrm{dom}(\delta_X)$ and outputs $\delta_X(p)$. For a problem $f :\subseteq \mathbf{X} \rightrightarrows \mathbf{Y}$ its jump $f' :\subseteq \mathbf{X}' \rightrightarrows \mathbf{Y}$ is defined as $f'(x) := f(x)$.

Informally, f' is the task that, given a sequence converging to a name for an instance of f, produces a solution for that instance. We use $f^{(n)}$ to denote the n-th iterate of the jump applied to f.

We now mention three problems that play a pivotal role in the Weihrauch lattice and that are used extensively during the paper:

- $\mathsf{LPO} : 2^{\mathbb{N}} \to \{0,1\}$ is the function such that $\mathsf{LPO}(p) = 1$ if $(\forall n)(p(n) = 0)$.
- $\mathsf{C_N} :\subseteq \mathcal{A}(\mathbb{N}) \rightrightarrows \mathbb{N}$ is the multivalued function having domain $\{A \in \mathcal{A}(\mathbb{N}) : A \neq \varnothing\}$ and such that $n \in \mathsf{C_N}(A)$ if $n \in A$.
- $\mathsf{lim} :\subseteq (\mathbb{N}^{\mathbb{N}})^{\mathbb{N}} \to \mathbb{N}^{\mathbb{N}}$, $(p_n)_{n \in \mathbb{N}} \mapsto \lim_{n \to \infty} p_n$ is the single-valued function with domain consisting of all converging sequences in $\mathbb{N}^{\mathbb{N}}$.

It is well-known that for every n, $\widehat{\mathsf{LPO}^{(n)}} \equiv_{\mathrm{W}} \mathsf{lim}^{(n)}$.

4 Effective Wadge Complexity of Sets of Graphs

For a fixed graph G, we consider sets of the form

$$\{H \in (\mathbf{E})\mathbf{Gr} : G \supseteq_{(i)s} H\} := \{p \in \mathrm{dom}(\delta_{(E)Gr}) : \delta_{(E)Gr}(p) \supseteq_{(i)s} G\}.$$

Proposition 2. *For any graph G, $\{H \in \mathbf{Gr} : G \supseteq_{(i)s} H\} \leqslant_{\mathsf{EW}} \{H \in \mathbf{EGr} : G \supseteq_{(i)s} H\}$.*

The proof of the above proposition is omitted as it is a direct consequence of $\mathbf{Gr}$ and $\mathbf{EGr}$ definitions. We continue with some results on finite graphs.

Proposition 3. *Let G be a finite graph, and let $\bigotimes^{\infty} G$ the disconnected union of countably many copies of G. The sets $\{H \in (\mathbf{E})\mathbf{Gr} : G \supseteq_{s} H\}$, $\{H \in \mathbf{Gr} : G \supseteq_{is} H\}$, $\{H \in (\mathbf{E})\mathbf{Gr} : \bigotimes^{\infty} G \supseteq_{s} H\}$ and $\{H \in \mathbf{Gr} : \bigotimes^{\infty} G \supseteq_{is} H\}$ are Π_1^0-complete.*

Proof. We prove the claim only for the first three sets, as for the remaining ones the proof is essentially the same.

To show that the first two sets are Π_1^0, we observe that H belongs to them if and only if each of its initial segments describes a finite (induced) subgraph of G. To show that the third set is Π_1^0, the argument applies to the connected components described by the initial segments of H.

We only give the proof that the third set is complete for the class Π_1^0, as the same proof shows also the completeness for the first two sets. By Proposition 1, it suffices to show that $\{p : (\forall i)(p(i) = 0)\} \leqslant_{\mathsf{EW}} \{H \in \mathbf{Gr} : G \supseteq_{is} H\}$. To do so, given $p \in 2^{\mathbb{N}}$, let $G \odot v$ denote the graph consisting of G plus a disconnected vertex. We compute a graph H as follows: as long as p looks like $0^{\mathbb{N}}$, we let H be the empty graph. If at some stage we witness that $p(i) = 1$ for some $i \in \mathbb{N}$, we add to H a copy of $G \odot v$. Since $G \supseteq_{is} \varnothing$ while $G \not\supseteq_{is} G \odot v$, it is clear that $G \supseteq_{is} H \iff (\forall i)(p(i) = 0)$. $\qquad\square$

Proposition 3 does not mention the complexity of the sets $\{H \in \mathbf{EGr} : G \subseteq_{\mathsf{is}} H\}$ and $\{H \in \mathbf{EGr} : \bigotimes^{\infty} G \subseteq_{\mathsf{is}} H\}$ with G being finite: we conjecture that these sets are complete for some class Γ in the *lightface difference hierarchy* (see e.g. [10, §I.2.3] for its definition), and such Γ depends on the particular G.

The following proposition shows a big difference with sets of the form $\{H \in (\mathbf{E})\mathbf{Gr} : G \subseteq_{(\mathrm{i})\mathsf{s}} H\}$. Indeed, in [7] we have shown that for any c.e. graph G such that G contains a copy of R, $\{H \in (\mathbf{E})\mathbf{Gr} : G \subseteq_{(\mathrm{i})\mathsf{s}} H\}$ is Σ_1^1-complete: here we have that $\{H \in (\mathbf{E})\mathbf{Gr} : K_\omega \supseteq_{(\mathrm{i})\mathsf{s}} H\}$ has a significantly lower complexity.

Proposition 4. *The set* $\{H \in (\mathbf{E})\mathbf{Gr} : K_\omega \supseteq_{\mathsf{s}} H\}$ *is computable,* $\{H \in \mathbf{Gr} : K_\omega \supseteq_{\mathsf{is}} H\}$ *is* Π_1^0*-complete and* $\{H \in \mathbf{EGr} : K_\omega \supseteq_{\mathsf{is}} H\}$ *is* Π_2^0*-complete.*

Proof. The fact that $\{H \in (\mathbf{E})\mathbf{Gr} : K_\omega \supseteq_{\mathsf{s}} H\}$ is computable follows from the fact that any graph is a subgraph of K_ω. For the other sets notice that, given a δ_{Gr}-name p for a graph H, $K_\omega \supseteq_{\mathsf{is}} H \iff (\forall v \neq w)(p(\langle v, v \rangle) = p(\langle w, w \rangle) = 1 \implies p(\langle v, w \rangle) = 1)$. To prove completeness, we show $\{p : (\forall i)(p(i) = 0)\} \leqslant_{\mathsf{EW}} \{H \in \mathbf{Gr} : K_\omega \supseteq_{\mathsf{is}} H\}$ (the left-hand-side is Π_1^0-complete by Proposition 1). To do so, given $p \in 2^{\mathbb{N}}$, we compute a graph H as follows: as long as p looks like $0^{\mathbb{N}}$, let H be the empty graph. If at some stage we witness that $p(i) = 1$ for some $i \in \mathbb{N}$ we add to H two disconnected vertices. Clearly, $K_\omega \supseteq_{\mathsf{is}} H \iff (\forall i)(p(i) = 0)$ and this proves the reduction.

To show that $\{H \in \mathbf{EGr} : K_\omega \supseteq_{\mathsf{is}} H\}$ is Π_2^0-complete, first notice that given a δ_{EGr}-name p for a graph H, $K_\omega \supseteq_{\mathsf{is}} H \iff (\forall v \neq w)(\exists k_0, k_1, k_2)(p(k_0) = \langle v, v \rangle \wedge p(k_1) = \langle w, w \rangle \implies p(k_2) = \langle v, w \rangle)$. To prove completeness, we show that $\{p : (\exists^\infty i)(p(i) = 1)\} \leqslant_{\mathsf{EW}} \{H \in \mathbf{EGr} : K_\omega \supseteq_{\mathsf{is}} H\}$ (the left-hand-side is Π_2^0-complete by Proposition 1). To do so, we compute a δ_{EGr}-name q for H as follows. At stage 0 do nothing and at stage $s + 1$:

- if $p(s+1) = 0$, then enumerate in q an isolated vertex to the graph computed up to stage s;
- if $p(s+1) = 1$, then enumerate in q enough edges in the graph computed up to stage s to make it isomorphic to a complete finite graph.

It is clear that if $(\exists^\infty i)(p(i) = 1)$, then $\delta_{EGr}(q) \cong K_\omega$ (and clearly K_ω is an induced supergraph of itself). Otherwise, $\delta_{EGr}(q)$ contains cofinitely many isolated vertices and hence $K_\omega \nsupseteq_{\mathsf{is}} \delta_{EGr}(q)$. $\quad\square$

Proposition 5. *The sets* $\{H \in (\mathbf{E})\mathbf{Gr} : \bigotimes_{i \geqslant 1} L_i \supseteq_{(\mathrm{i})\mathsf{s}} H\}$ *and* $\{H \in (\mathbf{E})\mathbf{Gr} : \bigotimes_{i \geqslant 1} K_i \supseteq_{(\mathrm{i})\mathsf{s}} H\}$ *are* Π_3^0*-complete.*

Proof. We first prove that the sets above are Π_3^0.

For the first set, it is easy to check that $\bigotimes_{i \geqslant 1} L_i \supseteq_{\mathsf{s}} H$ if and only if $\bigotimes_{i \geqslant 1} L_i \supseteq_{\mathsf{is}} H$. Then, notice that $\bigotimes_{i \geqslant 1} L_i \supseteq_{\mathsf{is}} H$ if and only if (1) every vertex in H has degree at most 2 (which is Π_1^0), (2) H contains no cyclic graph (which is Π_1^0) and (3) every connected component of H is finite (which is Π_3^0).

For the second case, we have that $\bigotimes_{i \geqslant 1} K_i \supseteq_{\mathsf{s}} H$ if and only if (3) holds, while $\bigotimes_{i \geqslant 1} K_i \supseteq_{\mathsf{is}} H$ if and only if every connected component is a finite complete graph (which is Π_3^0). It is straightforward to verify that the complexity of all formulas above is the same if $H \in \mathbf{Gr}$ or $H \in \mathbf{EGr}$.

To show that these sets are complete for the class Π_3^0, we show that $\{p \in 2^{\mathbb{N} \times \mathbb{N}} : (\forall n)(\forall^\infty i)(p(n, i) = 1)\} \leqslant_{\mathrm{EW}} \{H \in \mathbf{Gr} : \bigotimes_{i \geqslant 1} L_i \supseteq_{\mathbf{is}} H\}$ (the left-hand-side set is Π_3^0-complete by Proposition 1). For every n, we compute a graph H_n as follows. We start from H_n being a line segment of length 1: then, at stage i, if $p(n, i) = 1$ we increase the length of H_n by 1, otherwise we do nothing. Let $H := \bigotimes_{n \in \mathbb{N}} H_n$ and observe that if $(\exists n)(\exists^\infty i)(p(n, i) = 0)$, then $H_n \cong \mathbb{R}$, and hence $\bigotimes_{i \geqslant 1} L_i \not\supseteq_{\mathbf{is}} H$. Otherwise, if $(\forall n)(\forall^\infty i)(p(n, i) = 1)$, then for every n, $H_n \cong L_m$ for some $m > 0$. This implies that $\bigotimes_{i \geqslant 1} L_i \supseteq_{\mathbf{is}} H$ and so $\{H \in (\mathbf{E})\mathbf{Gr} : \bigotimes_{i \geqslant 1} L_i \supseteq_{(\mathbf{i})\mathbf{s}} H\}$ are Π_3^0-complete.

The same reduction also shows that $\{H \in (\mathbf{E})\mathbf{Gr} : \bigotimes_{i \geqslant 1} K_i \supseteq_{\mathbf{s}} H\}$ is Π_3^0-complete. For $\{H \in (\mathbf{E})\mathbf{Gr} : \bigotimes_{i \geqslant 1} K_i \supseteq_{\mathbf{is}} H\}$, it suffices to modify the construction so that the H_n's are complete graphs instead of line segments.   □

We conclude the results about the effective Wadge complexity discussing $\{H \in \mathbf{Gr} : \mathcal{S} \supseteq_{\mathbf{is}} H\}$, where $\mathcal{S}$ is defined as follows. For any $i \in \mathbb{N}$, S^i is the graph consisting of a special vertex v_i from which is the first vertex of $i + 1$-many copies of $\mathbb{R}$ as well as the first vertex of a copy of L_n for each $n \in \mathbb{N}$: then $\mathcal{S} := \bigotimes_{i \in \mathbb{N}} S^i$. Notice that for every i, $\deg^{\mathcal{S}}(v_i) = \aleph_0$ and, for all $v \neq v_i$, $\deg^{\mathcal{S}}(v) \leqslant 2$

Proposition 6 (^{1}). *Let $\mathcal{S}$ as above: the sets $\{H \in (\mathbf{E})\mathbf{Gr} : \mathcal{S} \supseteq_{(\mathbf{i})\mathbf{s}} H\}$ are Π_5^0-complete.*

Proof. We prove the proposition only for $\{H \in \mathbf{Gr} : \mathcal{S} \supseteq_{\mathbf{is}} H\}$, but the same proof works for the rest of the cases. We first prove that the set is Π_5^0. To do so notice that $\mathcal{S} \supseteq_{\mathbf{s}} H$ if and only if (1) H contains no cyclic graph (which is Π_1^0), (2) there are no distinct connected vertices u, v such that both $\deg^H(v) \geqslant 3$ and $\deg^G(v) \geqslant 3$ (which is Π_1^0) and (3) $(\forall u \in \{k : \deg^G(k) \geqslant 3\})(\forall^\infty v' \in \{k : (u, k) \in E(G)\})(\forall^\infty w)$ every line segment with endpoints v and w passes through u (which is Π_5^0).

Consider the set $\{(p \in 2^{\mathbb{N} \times \mathbb{N} \times \mathbb{N}}) : (\forall i)(\forall^\infty j)(\forall^\infty n)(p(i, j, n) = 0)\}$ and notice that by Proposition 1 such a set is Π_5^0-complete. For any $i \in \mathbb{N}$, we compute a graph T^i as follows. Initially, T^i consists of a special vertex u_i. Then, for every j we add a line segment starting from u_i. If $p(i, j, k) = 1$ we extend the corresponding line segment by 1, otherwise, we do nothing. Let $T := \bigotimes_{i \in \mathbb{N}} T^i$. Notice that for every i, $\deg^{T^i}(u_i) = \aleph_0$ and, for all $u \neq u_i$, $\deg^{T^i}(u) \leqslant 2$ and T^i contains $|\{j : (\exists^\infty n)(p(i, j, n) = 1)\}|$-many copies of $\mathbb{R}$ starting from u_i.

- If $(\exists i)(\exists^\infty j)(\exists^\infty n)(p(i, j, n) = 1)$, notice that T^i has infinitely copies of $\mathbb{R}$ starting from u_i: since no $v^i \in V(\mathcal{S})$ satisfies this property, we immediately obtain that $\mathcal{S} \not\supseteq_{\mathbf{is}} T$.
- Otherwise, if $(\forall i)(\forall^\infty j)(\forall^\infty n)(p(i, j, n) = 0)$, it is immediate that, for every i, T^i has only k-many copies of $\mathbb{R}$ starting from u_i for some $k \in \mathbb{N}$. By definition

---

^{1} The proof that the sets are indeed Π_5^0 was provided to us by a referee.

of S^k, v_k is the unique vertex of infinite degree in S^k and S^k contains k-many copies of R starting from v_i for some $k \in \mathbb{N}$. Furthermore, any path of finite length starting from u_i in T^i can be mapped to some path of finite length in S^i. We now define an increasing function $f : \mathbb{N} \to \mathbb{N}$ such that, for any i, $T^i \subseteq_{\mathsf{is}} S^{f(i)}$: it is clear that if such a function exists, then $S \supseteq_{\mathsf{is}} T$. Let $f(0) = k_0$ where k_0 is the number of copies of R starting from u_0, and at stage $s + 1$ let $f(s + 1) = k_{s+1}$ where k_{s+1} is the minimum $k \geqslant k_s$ such that T^{s+1} has k-many copies of R starting from u_{s+1}. Clearly, for any s, k_s exists as at stage s we have only defined $f(0), \ldots f(s-1)$ and for every k greater than the number of copies of R starting from u_i, $S^k \supseteq_{\mathsf{is}} T^i$.   □

5   The Decision Problems

Now we move to Weihrauch reducibility and the decision problems related to the (induced) supergraph problem.

Definition 2. *For a computable graph G, we define the functions* $\mathsf{IS}^G : \mathbf{Gr} \to 2$ *and* $\mathsf{S}^G : \mathbf{Gr} \to 2$ *by* $\mathsf{IS}^G(H) = 1 \iff G \supseteq_{\mathsf{is}} H$ *and* $\mathsf{S}^G(H) = 1 \iff G \supseteq_{\mathsf{s}} H$. *The same functions having domain* $\mathbf{EGr}$ *are denoted respectively with* $c\mathsf{IS}^G$ *and* $e\mathsf{S}^G$.

Notice that it is well-known that $\mathsf{LPO}^{(n)}$ can be rephrased as the function answering yes or no to questions which are Σ^0_{n+1} or Π^0_{n+1} in the input. The following is a corollary of Proposition 3.

Corollary 1. *Let G be a finite graph. Then,* $(e)\mathsf{S}^G \equiv_{\mathsf{sW}} \mathsf{IS}^G \equiv_{\mathsf{sW}} (e)\mathsf{S}^{\otimes G} \equiv_{\mathsf{sW}} \mathsf{IS}^{\overset{\infty}{\otimes}G} \equiv_{\mathsf{sW}} \mathsf{LPO}$.

The next is a corollary of Proposition 4: the fact that $\mathsf{IS}^{K_\omega} \equiv_{\mathsf{sW}} \mathsf{LPO}$ was already mentioned in [3].

Corollary 2. *The problems $(e)\mathsf{S}^{K_\omega}$ are the constant functions taking value 1 and hence are computable. By contrast,* $\mathsf{IS}^{K_\omega} \equiv_{\mathsf{sW}} \mathsf{LPO}$ *and* $e\mathsf{IS}^{K_\omega} \equiv_{\mathsf{sW}} \mathsf{LPO}'$.

Notice that in [3], the authors left open whether there is a graph G such that $\mathsf{LPO} <_{\mathsf{W}} \mathsf{IS}^G$: the following corollary of Proposition 5 gives a positive answer to this question.

Corollary 3. *The following equivalences hold:*
$$(e)\mathsf{S}^{\otimes_{i\geqslant 1} L_i} \equiv_{\mathsf{sW}} (e)\mathsf{IS}^{\otimes_{i\geqslant 1} L_i} \equiv_{\mathsf{sW}} (e)\mathsf{S}^{\otimes_{i\geqslant 1} K_i} \equiv_{\mathsf{sW}} (e)\mathsf{IS}^{\otimes_{i\geqslant 1} K_i} \equiv_{\mathsf{sW}} \mathsf{LPO}''.$$

It remains open whether there is a graph G such that $\mathsf{IS}^G \equiv_{\mathsf{sW}} \mathsf{LPO}'$. It is also open whether there exists a graph G such that $\mathsf{IS}^G \equiv_{\mathsf{sW}} \mathsf{WF}$, the function that, given in input a tree on $\mathbb{N}$, answers whether T is well-founded or not: indeed, IS^S is the strongest problem of this form we have found. Again, this question is strictly related to the effective Wadge complexity of sets of (names) of graphs considered in this section. The following is a corollary of Proposition 6

Corollary 4. $\mathsf{LPO}^{(4)} \equiv_{\mathsf{sW}} (e)\mathsf{IS}^S \equiv_{\mathsf{sW}} (e)\mathsf{S}^S$.

6   The Search Problem

Before concluding, we offer a brief glimpse at the complexity of the search problem.

Given a fixed graph G (over $\mathbb{N}$), let ISubCopy_G be the problem taking as input a graph H such that G is an induced supergraph of H, and outputs a subset of $\mathbb{N}$ isomorphic to H. The same problem replacing the induced supergraph relation with the supergraph one, is denoted with SubCopy_G. Both H and the output could either be specified via characteristic function or via enumeration, leading to a total of 8 a priori distinct problems per graph G, (4 for ISubCopy_G and 4 for SubCopy_G). It is clear that for the induced supergraph relation (the same holds for the supergraph one), the weakest problem (in terms of Weihrauch reducibility) of the 4 we defined is the one where the input is specified via characteristic function and the output via enumeration, while the strongest is the one in which the input is specified via enumeration and the output via characteristic function. The remaining two problems (the ones in which both the input and the output are specified via characteristic function or enumeration) are clearly above the former and below the latter.

Our first brief observation will be a lower bound of $\text{C}_\mathbb{N}$, using the following graph H_{CN}: the graph H_{CN} has for each $n \in \mathbb{N}$ a dedicated vertex v_n. Moreover, for each $k \neq n$, there is a cycle of length k containing v_n (with all the cycles otherwise disjoint).

Proposition 7. *Let* $(\text{I})\text{SupCopy}_{H_{\text{CN}}}$ *be any of the 8 supergraph problems which are associated to* H_{CN}. *Then* $\text{C}_\mathbb{N} \leqslant_\text{W} (\text{I})\text{SupCopy}_{H_{\text{CN}}}$.

Proof. The input to $\text{C}_\mathbb{N}$ is an enumeration of a set of natural numbers excluding at least one number. The valid outputs are any number absent from the list. From such an enumeration, we built (the characteristic function of) a graph with a central vertex v, and then for any new n appearing in the enumeration, add a fresh cycle of length n around v.

The promise that not all numbers will appear in the enumeration ensures that the resulting graph is indeed isomorphic to an induced subgraph of H_{CN}, and any subgraph it is isomorphic to must contain exactly a special vertex v_n. We can thus observe the enumeration of an answer produced by $(\text{I})\text{SupCopy}_{H_{\text{CN}}}$, wait until we spot a v_n, and then we know that n is a correct answer to the initial $\text{C}_\mathbb{N}$-instance.   □

Our second example takes a somewhat more natural fixed graph as parameter, namely the infinite ray R. A valid input for the problem(s) $(\text{I})\text{SupCopy}_\text{R}$ are graphs consisting either just of finite line segments or of finitely many finite line segments and a copy of the infinite ray. The task is to place those segments into the ray. Whether we consider induced subgraphs or subgraphs has a tangential consequence here, it only impacts slightly when two embedded line segments can be merged and when not. We explore only the version where the output is enumerated, and for our proofs it makes no difference whether the input is given via an enumeration or a characteristic function.

We start by showing that the problem is indeed non-trivial:

Proposition 8. LPO $\leq_W$ (I)SupCopy$_R$.

Proof. As long as the input looks like $0^{\mathbb{N}}$, we build a graph consisting of infinitely many line segments of length 1 and infinitely many line segments of length 2. If we find the first 1 in position k, we keep k line segments of length 1 and merge everything else into an infinite ray.

The output of (I)SupCopy$_R$ on such an input must contain two adjacent vertices, and we can wait until we find such a pair, say $(n, n+1)$. Now there are two options: it could be the case that $(n, n+1)$ is part of a copy of the infinite ray. But then there cannot be more than n isolated vertices (as they have to come before n). Thus, the input to LPO must have a 1 within the first n digits. Alternatively, $(n, n+1)$ forms a line segment of length 2, but then the input to LPO must have been $0^{\mathbb{N}}$. We can distinguish the cases by inspecting the first n digits of the input for LPO, and thereby complete the reduction. $\quad\square$

Proposition 9. (I)SupCopy$_R$ $\leq_W$ $C_{\mathbb{N}} \star \lim \star \lim$.

Proof. Let H be an input for (I)SupCopy$_R$. We can use $\lim \star \lim$ to determine for each $v \in V(H)$ whether its connected component is finite or infinite, and in the former case, how many vertices it is connected to. To do so, notice that $\lim \star \lim \equiv_W \lim' \equiv_W \widehat{\text{LPO}'}$. For any v, we use the $\langle 0, v \rangle$ instance of LPO to ask whether v is connected to infinitely many vertices (a Π_2^0 condition), and for $i > 0$, the $\langle i, v \rangle$ instance of LPO to ask whether v is connected to $i - 1$-many vertices (a Σ_1^0-condition). Hence, $\widehat{\text{LPO}'}$ suffices to answer all of these questions. Then, for any $v \in V(G)$, if the $\langle 0, v \rangle$ instance of LPO answers positively, we know that v belongs to an infinite connected component. Otherwise, the connected component containing the vertex v is finite, and its cardinality, is $\min\{k : \text{the } \langle k + 1, v \rangle \text{ instance of LPO}' \text{ answers negatively}\}$.

With this information available, we can then use $C_{\mathbb{N}}$ to tell us whether there exists a vertex belonging to an infinite component or not, and if so, also tell us the number C of connected components (as the existence of an infinite component necessitates that there be only finitely many components overall).

With all this information available, we can compute a copy of the input graph as an induced subgraph of the infinite ray. For each vertex we encounter belonging to a new finite connected component, we add that entire component to our construction (to the right of where we previously added components). If we do encounter a vertex belonging to an infinite component, then we know that there are exactly C components overall. We wait until we have encountered all of them (and thus have added the $C - 1$ finite components already), and then we add the infinite ray to the right of the previously chosen line segments. $\quad\square$

The style of reasoning employed to specifically attack the complexity of the problem (I)SupCopy$_R$ is reminiscent of the study of the degrees of bi-embeddable categoricity of equivalence relations (as only the number and size of connected components matter), see [1,2].

7 Outlook

We have only scratched the surface of the Weihrauch complexity of the supergraph problem. The central open questions are whether there are graphs for which the supergraph problem is hard (hard meaning, e.g., not on the finite levels of the Borel hierarchy) and whether there are certain classes of graphs for which we can obtain *nice* classifications. In general, supergraph results do not seem to be closely related to analogous subgraph results (cf. [7]).

Additional insight will be required to make further progress. At the present, we do not have conjectures to offer as to what Weihrauch degrees to expect.

References

1. Bazhenov, N., Fokina, E.B., Rossegger, D., San Mauro, L.: Degrees of bi-embeddable categoricity of equivalence structures. Archiv. Math. Logic **58**(5-6), 543–563 (2019). https://doi.org/10.1007/s00153-018-0650-3
2. Bazhenov, N., Fokina, E.B., Rossegger, D., San Mauro, L.: Degrees of bi-embeddable categoricity. Computability **10**(1), 1–16 (2021). https://doi.org/10.3233/COM-190289
3. BeMent, Z., Hirst, J.L., Wallace, A.: Reverse mathematics and Weihrauch analysis motivated by finite complexity theory. Computability **10**(4), 343–354 (2021). https://doi.org/10.3233/COM-210310. arXiv 2105.01719
4. Brattka, V., Gherardi, G., Marcone, A.: The Bolzano-Weierstrass theorem is the jump of Weak Kőnig's Lemma. Ann. Pure Appl. Logic **163**, 623–655 (2012)
5. Brattka, V., Gherardi, G., Pauly, A.: Weihrauch complexity in computable analysis. In: Handbook of Computability and Complexity in Analysis. TAC, pp. 367–417. Springer, Cham (2021). https://doi.org/10.1007/978-3-030-59234-9_11
6. Brattka, V., Pauly, A.: On the algebraic structure of Weihrauch degrees. Logic. Methods Comput. Sci. **14**(4), 2018 (2016). https://doi.org/10.23638/LMCS-14(4:4)2018
7. Cipriani, V., Pauly, A.: Embeddability of graphs and Weihrauch degrees. https://arxiv.org/abs/2305.00935 (2022)
8. Hirst, J.L., Lempp, S.: Infinite versions of some problems from finite complexity theory. Notre Dame J. Formal Logic **37**(4), 545–553 (1996). https://doi.org/10.1305/ndjfl/1040046141
9. Kechris, A.S.: Classical Descriptive Set Theory. Graduate Texts in Mathematics. Springer, NY (2012). https://doi.org/10.1007/978-1-4612-4190-4. https://books.google.co.uk/books?id=WR3SBwAAQBAJ
10. Sacks, G.E.: Higher Recursion Theory. Perspectives in Logic, Cambridge University Press (2017). https://doi.org/10.1017/9781316717301
11. Weihrauch, K.: Computable Analysis: An Introduction, 1st edn. Springer Publishing Company, Incorporated (2013)

Extending Wagner's Hierarchy to Deterministic Visibly Pushdown Automata

Victor Selivanov[1,2]([✉]) [iD]

[1] A.P. Ershov Institute of Informatics Systems, Novosibirsk, Russia
vseliv@iis.nsk.su
[2] Department of Mathematics and Computer Science,
St. Petersburg State University, Saint Petersburg, Russia

Abstract. We extend the Wagner hierarchy of ω-regular k-partitions to visibly pushdown languages on infinite words of bounded stack height. In particular, the structure of Wadge degrees of such k-partitions is shown to be isomorphic to the corresponding structure for the case of finite automata. We show that also computability properties of the Wagner hierarchy survive.

Keywords: Visibly pushdown automaton · Wagner's hierarchy · ω-language · k-partition · stack height · Wadge reducibility

1 Introduction

K. Wagner [16] characterized the structure of regular ω-languages under the continuous reducibility (known also as Wadge reducibility). Later, some results from [16] were extended to languages recognized by more complicated computing devices (see e.g. [4,5,11] and references therein for an extensive study of, in particular, context-free ω-languages). In this wider context, some important properties of the Wagner hierarchy (e.g., the decidability of levels) usually fail.

Motivated by a related study in descriptive set theory, computability and complexity, we extended in [13,15] the Wagner theory from the regular sets to the regular k-partitions $A : \Sigma^\omega \to \{0, \ldots, k-1\} = \bar{k}$ of the set Σ^ω of ω-words over a finite alphabet Σ that essentially coincide with the k-tuples $(A_0, \ldots, A_{k-1})$ of pairwise disjoint regular sets satisfying $A_0 \cup \cdots \cup A_{k-1} = \Sigma^\omega$ (note that the ω-languages are in a bijective correspondence with the 2-partitions of Σ^ω). The extension from sets to k-partitions for $k > 2$ is non-trivial. It required to develop a machinery of iterated labeled trees and of the FH of k-partitions (partially systematized in [15]) which turned out crucial for the subsequent partial extension of the Wadge theory to k-partitions [14] and, as a concluding step, to Q-partitions for arbitrary better quasiorder Q [6].

Among many natural extensions of regular ω-languages, the class of visibly pushdown ω-languages (also known as languages recognized by input-driven

---

V. Selivanov—This work was supported by the Russian Science Foundation, project 23-11-00133.

G. Della Vedova et al. (Eds.): CiE 2023, LNCS 13967, pp. 190–201, 2023.
https://doi.org/10.1007/978-3-031-36978-0_16

automata) [1–3,8] and its subclasses seem especially interesting because they preserve many important properties of regular ω-languages. An investigation of Wagner's hierarchy for this class was initiated in [10] where the hierarchy was successfully extended to the class of languages of well nested words.

In this paper we make the next step by extending the Wagner hierarchy in two directions: from the well nested words to the words of bounded stack height, and from languages to k-partitions. Our main result (Theorem 1 in Sect. 6) gives a complete effective characterization of the corresponding structures. Although DVPA on words of bounded stack height have many common features with DFA, many details are different and require new notions and facts which are interesting on their own. Some of them are formulated in more general form than is needed for this paper in a hope they may be of use for general DVPA (and even for non-deterministic VPA). The proof techniques here are quite different from those in [10] where direct formulations from Wagner's theory apply. As discussed in [15], the effective extensions of Wagner's theory like those in this paper may be of interest not only for automata theory of infinite words but also for the descriptive set theory because they help to identify the constructive part of (in general, very non-constructive) Wadge hierarchy.

The general case of DVPA (of non-deterministic VPA) will probably require new methods and techniques, because the set of Wadge degrees occupied by the corresponding languages and k-partitions is richer than the Wadge degrees of DVP languages of words of bounded stack height, as it follows from the results in [7] and from our paper.

2   Preliminaries

Fix a finite alphabet Σ containing more than one symbol. Let Σ^*, Σ^+, and Σ^ω denote resp. the sets of all words, all nonempty words, and all ω-words over Σ. Let ε be the empty word and $\Sigma^{\leq\omega} = \Sigma^* \cup \Sigma^\omega$. We use standard notation concerning words and ω-words. For $w \in \Sigma^*$ and $\xi \in \Sigma^{\leq\omega}$, $w \sqsubseteq \xi$ means that w is a prefix of ξ, $w \cdot \xi = w\xi$ denote the concatenation, $l = |w|$ is the length of $w = w(0) \cdots w(l-1)$. For $w \in \Sigma^*$, $U, V \subseteq \Sigma^*$, and $A \subseteq \Sigma^{\leq\omega}$, let $w \cdot A = \{w\xi \mid \xi \in A\}$, $U \cdot V = \{uv \mid u \in U, v \in V\}$, and $U \cdot A = \{u\xi \mid u \in U, \xi \in A\}$. For $k, l < \omega$ and $\xi \in \Sigma^{\leq\omega}$, let $\xi[k,l) = \xi(k) \cdots \xi(l-1)$ and $\xi \upharpoonright_k = \xi[0,k)$.

In the context of visibly pushdown automata (i.e., throughout the paper), the alphabet Σ is split into three disjoint sets of *left brackets* Σ_{+1}, *right brackets* Σ_{-1} and *neutral symbols* Σ_0. In this paper, symbols from Σ_{+1} and Σ_{-1} shall be denoted by left and right angled brackets, respectively $(<, >)$, whereas lower-case Latin letters from the beginning of the alphabet $(a, b \ldots)$ shall be used for symbols from Σ_0. Usually we work with a fixed such alphabet which is often omitted from the corresponding notation.

Along with the input alphabet Σ, a visibly pushdown automaton has a non-empty finite *stack alphabet* Γ and a special symbol $\perp \notin \Gamma$ which denotes the bottom of the stack. The variable γ is used below to denote elements of Γ, while variables $x, y, \ldots$ denote finite words over Γ (which are called stack contents).

Following [9], by a *deterministic visibly pushdown automaton (DVPA)* over Σ we mean a tuple $\mathcal{M} = (Q, in, \Gamma, \{\delta^c\}_{c \in \Sigma})$ consisting of a finite non-empty set Q of states, an initial state $in \in Q$, a stack alphabet Γ, and a family $\{\delta^c\}_{c \in \Sigma}$ of transition functions where $\delta^c : Q \to Q$ for $c \in \Sigma_0$, $\delta^c : Q \to Q \times \Gamma$ for $c \in \Sigma_{+1}$, and $\delta^c : Q \times (\Gamma \cup \{\bot\}) \to Q$ for $c \in \Sigma_{-1}$.

We call elements of $Q \times \Gamma^*$ *configurations of* $\mathcal{M}$ and denote them as $(q, x), (r, y), \dots$. Configuration (in, ε) is called the *initial configuration of* $\mathcal{M}$. Any letter $c \in \Sigma$ induces a unary function $(q, x) \mapsto (q, x) \cdot c$ on $Q \times \Gamma^*$ by the following rules: $(q, x) \cdot a = (\delta^a(q), x)$, $(q, x) \cdot <= (r, x \cdot \gamma)$ where $(r, \gamma) = \delta^<(q)$, $(q, \varepsilon) \cdot >= (\delta^>(q, \bot), \varepsilon)$, and $(q, x \cdot \gamma) \cdot >= (\delta^>(q, \gamma), x)$. Note that the top stack symbol in (q, x) is the last symbol of x (or $\bot$, if $x = \varepsilon$), i.e., the push and pop operations are performed on the right end of the stack content x. Subsets of Q (i.e., elements of $P(Q)$) are sometimes called *macrostates of* $\mathcal{M}$.

Any finite word $u \in \Sigma^*$ induces a unary function $(q, x) \mapsto (q, x) \cdot u$ on $Q \times \Gamma^*$ by induction: $(q, x)\varepsilon = (q, x)$ and $(q, x) \cdot (u \cdot c) = ((q, x) \cdot u) \cdot c$. For $\alpha \in \Sigma^\omega$, by $(q, x) \cdot \alpha$ we denote the sequence of configurations $\{(q, x) \cdot \alpha \lceil_i\}_{i < \omega}$ called the α-run of $\mathcal{M}$ starting with (q, x). Abusing the notation $(q, x) \cdot u$ above, we also use it to denote the u-run of $\mathcal{M}$ starting with (q, x), i.e., the sequence $\{(q, x) \cdot u \lceil_i\}_{i < |u|}$. Define also the function $f_{\mathcal{M}} : \Sigma^\omega \to P(Q)$ by setting $f_{\mathcal{M}}(\alpha)$ to be the set of states which occur infinitely often in the α-run $(in, \varepsilon)\alpha$. We say that a configuration (r, y) is *reachable from* (q, x) if $(r, y) = (q, x)u$ for some $u \in \Sigma^*$. The configuration (r, y) is *reachable* if it is reachable from the initial state (in, ε).

Similar to DFA, for DVPA there are natural operations of Cartesian product. We briefly define one of these. Given DVPA $\mathcal{M}_1 = (Q_1, in_1, \Gamma_1, \{\delta^c_1\}_{c \in \Sigma})$ and $\mathcal{M}_2 = (Q_2, in_2, \Gamma_2, \{\delta^c_2\}_{c \in \Sigma})$ with stack bottom letters $\bot_1, \bot_2$, their product $\mathcal{M} = \mathcal{M}_1 \times \mathcal{M}_2 = (Q, in, \Gamma, \{\delta^c\}_{c \in \Sigma})$, with stack bottom letter $\bot = (\bot_1, \bot_2)$, is defined by:

$Q = Q_1 \times Q_2$, $in = (in_1, in_2)$, $\Gamma = \Gamma_1 \times \Gamma_2$,

$\delta^a(q_1, q_2) = (\delta^a_1(q_1), \delta^a_2(q_2))$,

$\delta^<(q_1, q_2) = ((r_1, r_2), (\gamma_1, \gamma_2))$ where $\delta^<_1(q_1) = (r_1, \gamma_1)$ and $\delta^<_2(q_2) = (r_2, \gamma_2)$,

$\delta^>((q_1, q_2), \bot) = (\delta^>_1(q_1, \bot_1), \delta^>_2(q_2, \bot_2))$, and

$\delta^>((q_1, q_2), (\gamma_1, \gamma_2)) = (\delta^a_1(q_1, \gamma_1), \delta^a_2(q_2, \gamma_2))$.

Note that the behaviour of $\mathcal{M}$ "includes" the behaviours of $\mathcal{M}_1$ and $\mathcal{M}_2$, in particular $f_{\mathcal{M}}(\alpha) = f_{\mathcal{M}_1}(\alpha) \times f_{\mathcal{M}_2}(\alpha)$.

A *DVP Muller acceptor* is a pair $(\mathcal{M}, A)$ where $\mathcal{M}$ is a DVPA and $A \subseteq P(Q)$ is a set of macrostates; it recognizes the set $L(\mathcal{M}, A) = f_{\mathcal{M}}^{-1}(A)$. The ω-languages recognized by such acceptors are called *DVP-sets*. The class $\mathcal{D}$ of DVP-sets is closed under the Boolean operations [1] and is contained in the Boolean closure $BC(\Sigma^0_2)$ of the second level Σ^0_2 of Borel hierarchy in Σ^ω.

A *DVP k-partition* is a k-partition $A : \Sigma^\omega \to \bar{k}$ all of whose components are DVP-sets. A DVP k-partition A may be specified by a k-tuple of DVP Muller acceptors which recognize the components $A_0, \dots, A_{k-1}$ but for our purposes we need a slightly different presentation similar to that used in [13,15]. A *DVP Muller k-acceptor* is a pair $(\mathcal{M}, A)$ where $\mathcal{M}$ is a DVPA and $A : P(Q) \to \bar{k}$ is a

k-partition of $P(Q)$. The DVP Muller k-acceptor recognises the DVP k-partition $L(\mathcal{M}, A) = A \circ f_\mathcal{M}$ where $f_\mathcal{M} : \Sigma^\omega \to P(Q)$ is defined above.

Proposition 1. *A k-partition $L : X^\omega \to \bar{k}$ is DVP iff it is recognised by a DVP Muller k-acceptor.*

Proof. We consider only the non-trivial direction. Let L be a DVP k-partition and $k > 2$ (for $k = 2$ the assertion is obvious). Then L_l is DVP for every $l < k$, hence $L_l = L(\mathcal{M}_l, \mathcal{F}_l)$ for some DVP Muller acceptors $(\mathcal{M}_l, \mathcal{F}_l)$. Let $\mathcal{M} = (Q, in, \Gamma, \{\delta^c\}_{c \in \Sigma})$ be the product of $\mathcal{M}_0, \ldots, \mathcal{M}_{k-2}$. We have $pr_l(f_\mathcal{M}(\xi)) = f_{\mathcal{M}_l}(\xi)$ for all $l < k - 1$ and $\xi \in \Sigma^\omega$, where $pr_l : Q \to Q_l$ is the projection to the l-th coordinate. Since L_l are pairwise disjoint, so are also $pr_l^{-1}(\mathcal{F}_l)$. Let $A : P(Q) \to \bar{k}$ be the unique k-partition of $P(Q)$ satisfying $A^{-1}(l) = pr_l^{-1}(\mathcal{F}_l)$ for all $l < k - 1$. Then the DVP Muller k-acceptor $(\mathcal{M}, A)$ recognises L. □

Next we compare the classes $\mathcal{R}_\Sigma$ of regular ω-languages over Σ (the alphabet in this context is considered as a usual non-structured alphabet) and $\mathcal{D}_\Sigma$ of DVP-sets. Following [7], we define the *stack height function* $sh : \Sigma^* \to \omega$ by induction: $sh(\varepsilon) = 0$, $sh(u \cdot a) = sh(u)$, $sh(u \cdot <) = sh(u) + 1$, $sh(u \cdot >) = min\{sh(u) - 1, 0\}$. Let L_{mwm} be the set of *minimally well-matched words*, i.e., words of the form $< w >$ where the last letter $>$ matches the first letter $<$, and $sh(< v)$ is positive for every $v \sqsubseteq w$. Then $W = (\Sigma_0 \cup L_{mwm})^*$ is the set of *well-matched* (also known as *well-nested*) words.

Proposition 2. *For every Σ we have: $\mathcal{R}_\Sigma \subseteq \mathcal{D}_\Sigma$. If at least one of Σ_{+1}, Σ_{-1} is empty then $\mathcal{R}_\Sigma = \mathcal{D}_\Sigma$, otherwise the inclusion $\mathcal{R}_\Sigma \subset \mathcal{D}_\Sigma$ is proper, even for languages of well-nested words. Similarly for the regular and DVP k-partitions.*

Proof. Let $L \in \mathcal{R}_\Sigma$ be recognized by a Muller acceptor $(\mathcal{M}, A)$ where $\mathcal{M} = (Q, in, \{\delta^c\}_{c \in \Sigma})$ and $\delta^c : Q \to Q$ for every $c \in \Sigma$. We can consider $(\mathcal{M}, A)$ as a DVP Muller acceptor $(\mathcal{M}', A')$ (say, with a singleton stack alphabet $\Gamma = \{\gamma\}$) which simulates $(\mathcal{M}, A)$ in the obvious way by extending $\delta^<$ (resp. $\delta^>$) to the function $f : Q \to Q \times \Gamma$ such that $f(q) = \delta^<(q, \gamma)$ (resp. to $g : Q \times (\Gamma \cup \{\bot\}) \to Q$ such that $g(q, \gamma) = g(q, \bot) = \delta^>(q)$). Thus, $\mathcal{R}_\Sigma \subseteq \mathcal{D}_\Sigma$ for every Σ.

If both of Σ_{+1}, Σ_{-1} are empty then any DVPA over Σ (for arbitrary Γ) is in fact a DFA, hence $\mathcal{R}_\Sigma = \mathcal{D}_\Sigma$.

Let now $\Sigma_{+1} = \varnothing \neq \Sigma_{-1}$. Then the stack is never pushed, hence it is always empty and the transitions $\delta^>$ may be considered as functions on Q. Thus, any DVPA over Σ (for arbitrary Γ) is again in fact a DFA, hence $\mathcal{R}_\Sigma = \mathcal{D}_\Sigma$.

Let now $\Sigma_{+1} \neq \varnothing = \Sigma_{-1}$. Then the transitions $\delta^>$ do not exist and the stack is never popped. Replacing any pair $\delta^<(q)$ by its projection to the first coordinate, we see that $\delta^<$ may be considered as functions on Q. Thus, any DVPA over Σ (for arbitrary Γ) is again in fact a DFA, hence $\mathcal{R}_\Sigma = \mathcal{D}_\Sigma$.

Finally, let both of Σ_{+1}, Σ_{-1} are nonempty, hence $< \in \Sigma_{+1}$, $> \in \Sigma_{-1}$ for some $<, >$. Since the language of well-nested ω-words over the alphabet $\{<, >\}$ is in $\mathcal{D}_\Sigma$ but not in $\mathcal{R}_\Sigma$, the inclusion $\mathcal{R}_\Sigma \subset \mathcal{D}_\Sigma$ is proper. □

To avoid trivialities fixed in Proposition 2, below we always assume that both Σ_{+1}, Σ_{-1} are nonempty.

3   Stack Height Factorizations

Since the stack operations of DVPA are completely determined by an input word w, the length of the stack word after reading w will be $sh(w)$ in every DVPA over Σ. Along with set W from the previous section, we also define the sets $W_{-1} = (\Sigma_{-1} \cup \Sigma_0 \cup L_{\mathrm{mwm}})^*$ of words without unmatched left brackets, and $W_{+1} = (\Sigma_{+1} \cup \Sigma_0 \cup L_{\mathrm{mwm}})^*$ of words without unmatched right brackets. Then $W = W_{-1} \cap W_{+1}$ and $W_{-1} = \{u \in \Sigma^* \mid sh(u) = 0\}$. Note that $\Sigma^* = W_{-1} \cdot W_{+1}$, and $(W_{-1}, W_{-1} \cdot (W_{+1} \setminus W))$ is a partition of Σ^*.

The stack height function induces useful partitions of finite and infinite words over Σ which we now carefully describe. For any $n < \omega$, let $H_n = \{w \in \Sigma^+ \mid sh(w) = n\}$ be the set of non-empty words of stack height n. Then $\{H_n\}_n$ is a partition of Σ^+, and H_n coincides with the set of non-empty words which have precisely n unmatched left brackets. The next obvious proposition gives a different description of the sets H_n by induction on n.

Proposition 3. $H_0 = W_{-1} \setminus \{\varepsilon\}$, $H_1 = W_{-1} \cdot {<} \cdot W$, and $H_{n+2} = H_{n+1} \cdot {<} \cdot W$.

For any $n \leq \omega$, let G_n be the set of infinite words which have precisely n unmatched left brackets, then $\{G_n\}_{n \leq \omega}$ is a partition of Σ^ω. Let $\mathrm{wn} = \mathrm{wn}(\Sigma) = (\Sigma_0 \cup L_{\mathrm{mwm}})^\omega$ be the set of well-matched infinite words over Σ. Let also $G_{<\omega} = \bigcup_{n<\omega} G_n$ and $G_{\leq n} = G_0 \cup \cdots \cup G_n$ for $n < \omega$.

The next obvious proposition, which is analogous to the previous one for infinite words, gives a more explicit description of the sets G_n.

Proposition 4. $G_0 = (\Sigma_{-1} \cup \Sigma_0 \cup L_{\mathrm{mwm}})^\omega$, $G_1 = W_{-1} \cdot {<} \cdot \mathrm{wn}$, $G_{n+2} = H_{n+1} \cdot {<} \cdot \mathrm{wn}$ for $n < \omega$, and $G_\omega = W_{-1} \cdot ({<} \cdot W)^\omega$.

For any $w \in \Sigma^+$ (resp. $\alpha \in \Sigma^\omega$), we can group maximal subwords which are in L_{mwm}, and obtain a unique factorization (which we call sh-factorization) $w = w_0 \cdots w_n$ (resp. $\alpha = w_0 w_1 \cdots$) where each factor w_i is in $\Sigma \cup L_{\mathrm{mwm}}$. In the case of an infinite word α, the sh-factorization is also determined by the set $S_\alpha = \{n < \omega \mid \forall m \geq n(sh(\alpha \restriction_m) \geq sh(\alpha \restriction_n))\}$ (see Sect. 3 of [7] where S_α is denoted as $Steps_\alpha$), namely $w_i = \alpha[n_i, n_{i+1})$ for every $i < \omega$ where $S_\alpha = \{0 = n_0 < n_1 < \cdots\}$. A similar description exists to the case of a finite word w, only now the set S_w is finite.

Proposition 5. 1. The sets $L_{\mathrm{mwm}}, W, W_{-1}$ are computable, and H_n is computable uniformly on n.
2. The sh-factorization function on Σ^+ is computable.

Proof. (1) Follows easily from the definitions.

(2) Obviously, the function $sh : \Sigma^* \to \omega$ is computable and $w \in H_{sh(w)}$ for $w \in \Sigma^+$. If $sh(w) = 0$ then, by Proposition 3, we can effectively factorize w to factors from $\Sigma_{-1} \cup \Sigma_0 \cup L_{\mathrm{mwm}}$, and this will be the sh-factorization of w. If $sh(w) = 1$ then we first compute, by Proposition 3, the unique $j < |w|$ such that $w(j)$ is the unmatched left bracket, then factorize $w \restriction_j = u_1 \cdots u_m$ to factors from

$\Sigma_{-1} \cup \Sigma_0 \cup L_{\mathrm{mwm}}$, and $w(j, |w|) = v_1 \cdots v_p$ to factors from $\Sigma_0 \cup L_{\mathrm{mwm}}$ (taking $m = 0$ or $p = 0$ if $w \restriction_j$ or $w(j, |w|)) \in W$ is empty), and obtain the sh-factorization $w = u_1 \cdots u_m w(j) v_1 \cdots v_p$. If $sh(w) > 1$, we proceed in the same way (finding first the rightmost unmatched left bracket $m(j)$), again by Proposition 3. $\quad\square$

4   Cycles of DVPA

A basic notion in the study of Wagner hierarchy is the notion of a cycle of a DFA (see [15,16]). The same applies to DVPA but in this case cycles are a bit more complex.

Definition 1. *A cycle of a DVPA $\mathcal{M}$ is a pair $\mathrm{c} = (u, (q, x))$ where u is a nonempty word from $W_{-1} \cup W_{+1}$, (q, x) is a reachable configuration of $\mathcal{M}$, $x = \varepsilon$ whenever $u \in W_{-1} \setminus W$, and $(q, x)u = (q, y)$ for some $y \in \Gamma^*$. In the case $u \in W_{-1}$, we call $sh(\mathrm{c}) = |x|$ the stack height of c.*

The set of cycles of $\mathcal{M}$ is denoted by $C_{\mathcal{M}}$. The set of states in the run $(q, x)u$ is called the macrostate of c and denoted as $M(\mathrm{c})$, so $M : C_{\mathcal{M}} \to P(Q)$. Let $C_{\mathcal{M}}^{\leq n} = \{\mathrm{c} \in C_{\mathcal{M}} \mid u \in W_{-1} \wedge sh(\mathrm{c}) \leq n\}$ for every $n < \omega$, and $C_{\mathcal{M}}^{<\omega} = \bigcup_{n<\omega} C_{\mathcal{M}}^{\leq n}$. We say that a cycle $\mathrm{d} = (v, (r, y)) \in C_{\mathcal{M}}$ is reachable from c if (r, y) is reachable from (q, x).

Since the reachability relation for DVPA is decidable, we immediately obtain the following.

Lemma 1. *Given $n < \omega$, a DVPA $\mathcal{M}$ and a pair $\mathrm{c} \in \Sigma^+ \times (Q \times \Gamma^*)$, one can effectively test whether $\mathrm{c} \in C_{\mathcal{M}}$, and if yes, compute the macrostate $M(\mathrm{c})$, the stack height $sh(\mathrm{c})$, and test whether $\mathrm{c} \in C_{\mathcal{M}}^{\leq n}$.*

For any $u \in \Sigma^*$ and $q \in Q$, let $\tilde{u}_q$ denote the unique stack content such that $(q, \varepsilon)u = (r, \tilde{u}_q)$ for some $r \in Q$. Note that $\tilde{u}_q = \varepsilon$ whenever $u \in W_{-1}$. For any $\mathrm{c} = (u, (q, x)) \in C_{\mathcal{M}}$ and $n \geq 1$, let $\mathrm{c}^n = (u^n, (q, x))$.

Lemma 2. *Let $\mathrm{c} = (u, (q, x)) \in C_{\mathcal{M}}$ and $n \geq 1$. Then $(q, x)u^n = (u, (q, x \cdot \tilde{u}_q^n))$, the pairs c^n, and $(u, (q, x \cdot \tilde{u}_q^n))$ are cycles of $\mathcal{M}$, and $M(\mathrm{c}^n) = M(\mathrm{c}) = M((u, x \cdot \tilde{u}_q^n))$.*

Proof. Let first $n = 1$, then we have to check that $(q, x)u = (q, x \cdot \tilde{u}_q)$. Indeed, if $u \in W_{-1} \setminus W_{+1}$ then $x = \varepsilon$ and the equality holds by the definition of $\tilde{u}_q$. If $u \in W_{+1}$ then, in any u-run $(r, y)u$, the last (top) letter of y (or $\bot$ if $y = \varepsilon$) is never popped, hence $(r, y)u = (r', y\tilde{u}_q)$ for some $r' \in Q$. In particular, $(q, x)u = (q, x \cdot \tilde{u}_q)$, so this equality holds in any case.

For $n = 2$ we have: $(q, x)u^2 = (q, x \cdot \tilde{u}_q)u$. By the definition of transition functions in a DPDA and by the remark in the previous paragraph, in the runs $(q, x)u$ and $(q, x \cdot \tilde{u}_q)u$ not only the dynamics of stack is the same, but also the sequences of states coincide (moreover, if $u \in W_{-1}$ then the runs coincide; to see this, consider alternatives $u \in W_{-1} \setminus W$ and $u \in W$). Thus, $(q, x \cdot \tilde{u}_q)u = (q, x \cdot \tilde{u}_q^2)$ and therefore $(q, x)u^2 = (q, x \cdot \tilde{u}_q^2)$.

The argument of the previous paragraph enables to use induction on n to show that $(q, x)u^n = (q, x \cdot \tilde{u}_q^n)$, and also implies the remaining assertions. $\quad\square$

We define a function $g_\mathcal{M} : C_\mathcal{M} \to \Sigma^\omega$ by setting $g_\mathcal{M}(c) = u' \cdot u^\omega$ where $c = (u, (q, x))$ and u' is a word with $(in, \varepsilon)u' = (q, x)$. Lemma 2 and its proof immediately imply the following.

Lemma 3. *For any* $c = (u, (q, x)) \in C_\mathcal{M}$ *we have* $f_\mathcal{M}(g_\mathcal{M}(c)) = M(c)$. *Furthermore, if* $u \in W_{-1} \wedge x = \varepsilon$ *(resp.* $u \in W \wedge x \neq \varepsilon$, $u \in W_{+1} \setminus W$) *then* $g_\mathcal{M}(c)$ *is in* G_0 *(resp.* G_{n+1} *for some* $n < \omega$, G_ω).

The importance of cycles is demonstrated by the following lemma which shows that they capture the function $f_\mathcal{M} : \Sigma^\omega \to P(Q)$ by reducing arbitrary ω-words to almost periodic ones.

Lemma 4. *For any* $\alpha \in \Sigma^\omega$ *there is* $c = c_\mathcal{M}(\alpha) \in C_\mathcal{M}$ *such that* $M(c) = f_\mathcal{M}(\alpha)$, *and hence* $\{M(c) \mid c \in C_\mathcal{M}\} = \{f_\mathcal{M}(\alpha) \mid \alpha \in \Sigma^\omega\}$. *Furthermore,* $\alpha \in G_{\leq n}$ *implies* $c_\mathcal{M}(\alpha) \in C_\mathcal{M}^{\leq n}$.

Proof. The second assetion follows from the first one and Lemma 3, so we prove only the first assertion. Let $\alpha \in \Sigma^\omega$ and let $S_\alpha = \{0 = n_0 < n_1 < \cdots\}$ be the set from the end of Sect. 3. Let $(q_i, x_i) = (in, \varepsilon) \cdot \alpha \restriction_i$, then $f_\mathcal{M}(\alpha)$ is the set of states which occur infinitely often in $\{q_i\}$. Let l be the least number such that $\{q_l, q_{l+1}, \ldots\} = f_\mathcal{M}(\alpha)$. We consider cases $\alpha \in G_0$, $\alpha \in G_{k+1}$ for some $k < \omega$, and $\alpha \in G_\omega$.

In the first case, the set $\{i \mid x_i = \varepsilon\}$ is infinite; let $0 = m_0 < m_1 < \cdots$ be the enumeration of this set in increasing order, then $\{m_i\}$ is a subsequence of $\{n_i\}$. Since the set $T = \{(i, j) \mid l < i < j \wedge \{q_{m_i}, \ldots, q_{m_j}\} = f_\mathcal{M}(\alpha)\}$ is infinite and Q is finite, there is $(i, j) \in T$ with $q_{m_i} = q_{m_j}$. Let $v = \alpha \restriction_{m_i}$, $u = \alpha[q_{m_i}, q_{m_j})$, and $q = q_{m_i}$. Then $c = (u, (q, \varepsilon)) \in C_\mathcal{M}$ and $f_\mathcal{M}(\alpha) = f_\mathcal{M}(g_\mathcal{M}(c)) = M(c)$ by Lemma 3. Note that $u \in W_{-1}$.

In the second case, by Proposition 4 there is an infinite subsequence $m_0 < m_1 < \cdots$ of $\{n_i\}$ such that, for every i, x_i is a fixed stack content x of length $k+1$ (hence $\alpha[m_i, m_{i+1}) \in W$). Defining T, v, u, q as in the previous paragraph, we obtain $f_\mathcal{M}(\alpha) = f_\mathcal{M}(g_\mathcal{M}(c)) = M(c)$ where $c = (u, (q, x)) \in C_\mathcal{M}$. Note that $u \in W$.

In the third case we have $n_i < n_{i+1}$ for infinitely many i. By Proposition 4, there is an infinite subsequence $m_0 < m_1 < \cdots$ of $\{n_i\}$ such that $x_{m_0} \sqsubset x_{m_1} \sqsubset \cdots$. Defining T, v, u, q as above, and setting $x = x_{m_i}$, we obtain $f_\mathcal{M}(\alpha) = f_\mathcal{M}(g_\mathcal{M}(c)) = M(c)$ where $c = (u, (q, x)) \in C_\mathcal{M}$. Note that $u \in W_{+1} \setminus W$. $\quad\square$

Remark 1. In the third case above, there might exist c such that $f_\mathcal{M}(\alpha) = f_\mathcal{M}(g_\mathcal{M}(c)) = M(c)$ and $u \in W$.

5 DVP ω-Languages in Borel Hierarchy

In this section we examine the complexity of DVP languages of bounded stack height by means of Borel hierarchy. Similarly to DFA, for this characterization we use preorders $\leq_0$ and $\leq_1$ on $C_\mathcal{M}$ which for DVPA are defined as follows.

Definition 2. *Let* $c = (u, (q, x))$ *and* $d = (v, (r, y))$ *be in* $C_{\mathcal{M}}$. *Then* $c \leq_0 d$, *if for every* $m \geq 1$ *there is* $n \geq 1$ *such that* d^n *is reachable from* c^m *(i.e.,* $(r, y\tilde{v}_r^n)$ *is reachable from* $(q, x\tilde{u}_r^m)$, *see Lemma 2). Let also* $c \leq_1 d$ *mean that* $c \equiv_0 d$ *and* $M(c) \supseteq M(d)$.

A problem with this definition is that the decidability of relations $\leq_0, \leq_1$ is far from obvious. But the relation $c \leq_0 d$ becomes essentially simpler if at least one of u, v is in W_{-1}. Indeed, from Lemma 3 it follows that: if $u, v \in W_{-1}$ then $c \leq_0 d$ iff d is reachable from c; if $u \in W_{-1} \not\ni v$ then $c \leq_0 d$ iff d^n is reachable from c for some $n \geq 1$; if $u \notin W_{-1} \ni v$ then $c \leq_0 d$ iff d is reachable from c^m for every $m \geq 1$.

For any $n < \omega$, the restrictions of $\leq_0, \leq_1$ to $C_{\mathcal{M}}^{\leq n}$ (which we for simplicity denote by the same symbols) are rather simple relations which have important common features with the case of DFA.

Let $\mathcal{C}_i$ be the class of all $\leq_i$-up subsets of $C_{\mathcal{M}}^{\leq n}$ (a set $A \subseteq C_{\mathcal{M}}^{\leq n}$ is $\leq_i$-up if $a \in A$ and $a \leq_i c$ imply $c \in A$; $\leq_i$-down sets are defined similarly). The pair $\mathcal{C} = (\mathcal{C}_0, \mathcal{C}_1)$ is called *the 2-base of up-sets over* $(C_{\mathcal{M}}^{\leq n}; \leq_0, \leq_1)$. According to [15], the 2-base $\mathcal{C}$ is *interpolable* if for every disjoint $\leq_1$-down sets $A, B \subseteq C_{\mathcal{M}}^{\leq n}$ there is a finite Boolean combination C of $\mathcal{C}_0$-sets which separates A from B, i.e., $A \subseteq C$ and $C \cap B = \varnothing$. The structure $(C_{\mathcal{M}}^{\leq n}; \leq_0, \leq_1)$ is a *2-preorder* if both $\leq_0, \leq_1$ are preorders, and $c \leq_1 d$ implies $c \equiv_0 d$; the 2-preorder is *compatible* if $c \equiv_0 d$ implies $\exists e(e \leq_1 c \wedge e \leq_1 d)$.

Lemma 5. *For any DVPA* $\mathcal{M}$ *and any* $n < \omega$, *the structure* $(C_{\mathcal{M}}^{\leq n}; \leq_0, \leq_1)$ *is a compatible 2-preorder. This structure is computably presentable uniformly on* n. *There are only finitely many classes under the equivalence relation* $\equiv_0$ *induced by* $\leq_0$. *The 2-base* $\mathcal{C}$ *is interpolable.*

Proof. The Definition 2 and remarks after it easily imply that $(C_{\mathcal{M}}^{\leq n}; \leq_0, \leq_1)$ is a 2-preorder. For the compatibility, let $c = (u, (q, x))$, $d = (v, (r, y))$, and $c \equiv_0 d$. Since $u, v \in W_{-1}$, there are $u', v' \in \Sigma^*$ such that $(q, x)u' = (r, y)$ and $(r, y)v' = (q, x)$. We define $e = (w, (s, z))$ as follows. Let $w' = u'vv'u$, then $(q, x)w' = (q, x)$. Let (s, z) be a configuration in the run $(q, x)w'$ with the smallest $|z|$ (such a configuration is in general not unique). Let w be the cyclic permutation of w' such that $(s, z)w = (s, z)$. Then $sh(e) \leq sh(c)$, $sh(e) \leq sh(d)$, and e has the desired property. (Notice that the proof of compatibility may be extended to the case when precisely one u, v is in W_{-1}.)

The uniform computable presentability follows from Lemma 1 and the computability of reachability, so it remains to check the interpolability property. Indeed, we can take $C = [A]_0 = \{c \in C_{\mathcal{M}}^{<\omega} \mid \exists a \in A(a \equiv_0 c)\}$. As shown in [15] for a more general case, C is both $\leq_1$-up and $\leq_1$-down, and it separates A from B, hence it remains to check that C is a finite Boolean combination of $\mathcal{C}_0$-sets.

By a property of the difference hierarchy over $\mathcal{C}_0$ (see e.g. Proposition 4.6 in [12]), it suffices to show that there is a finite upper bound on the length m of chains $c_0 \leq_0 \cdots \leq_0 c_m$ of cycles in $C_{\mathcal{M}}^{<\omega}$ such that $c_i \in C$ iff $c_{i+1} \notin C$, $i < m$. We show that $m \leq 2l$ where l is the cardinality of the finite set $Q \times \Gamma^{\leq n}$. Indeed, let

$a_i \in A$ satisfy $a_i \equiv_0 c_i$ for $i \leq m$. Then $a_i \in C$ iff $c_i \in C$. Suppose the contrary: $a_i \in C$ iff $c_i \notin C$. By compatibility, $e \leq_1 c_i \wedge e \leq_1 a_i$ for some cycle e. Since C is $\leq_1$-down, we obtain $e \in C$ and $e \notin C$; contradiction.

Therefore, we have $a_i \in C$ iff $a_{i+1} \notin C$ for $i < m$. Let $a_i = (u_i, (q_i, x_i))$ and suppose, for a contradiction, that $m > 2l$. Then $(q_i, x_i) = (q_j, x_j)$ for some $i < j \leq m$, hence $a_i \equiv_0 a_j$, hence $a_i \equiv_0 a_{i+1}$, hence $a_i \in C$ and $a_i \notin C$; contradiction. This argument also implies the remaining statement that the quotient poset of $C_{\mathcal{M}}^{\leq n}$ under $\equiv_0$ is finite. $\qquad\square$

Remark 2. The structure $(C_{\mathcal{M}}^{\leq \omega}; \leq_0, \leq_1)$ is a computably presentable compatible 2-preorder but the 2-base $\mathcal{C}$ over this 2-preorder is in general not interpolable.

Recall that for subsets $L, M \subseteq X$ of a topological space X, L is *Wadge reducible* to M (denoted by $L \leq_W^X M$) if $L = f^{-1}(M)$ for some continuous function f on X. The sets L, M are *Wadge equivalent* ($L \equiv_W^X M$) if $L \leq_W^X M$ and $M \leq_W^X L$. The equivalence classes under the Wadge equivalence are known as *Wadge degrees* in X. Recall that *Borel sets* in X are generated from the open sets by repeated applications of complement and countable intersection. The Borel sets are organised in the Borel hierarchy; in particular, the $\mathbf{\Sigma}_1$-sets in X are the open sets, $\mathbf{\Pi}_1(X)$ is the class of closed sets, $\mathbf{\Pi}_2(X)$ is the class of countable intersections of open sets, and $\mathbf{\Sigma}_2(X)$ is the class of complements of $\mathbf{\Pi}_2(X)$-sets.

In this paper we mainly use these notions for subspaces $G_{\leq n}$ of the Cantor space Σ^ω. From Propositions 3 and 4 it is easy to see that $G_{\leq n} \in \mathbf{\Pi}_2(\Sigma^\omega)$.

The next lemma is analogous to the corresponding result in [16] (see also Lemma 5 in [15]). Modifications in formulation and proofs are caused by the more complicated definition of cycles in DVPA compared with DFA. Let $(\mathcal{M}, A)$ be a DVP Muller acceptor.

Lemma 6. *1. If the set $\mathcal{A} = \{c \in C_{\mathcal{M}}^{\leq n} \mid M(c) \in A\}$ is $\leq_0$-up then the set $L_A = \{\alpha \in G_{\leq n} \mid f_{\mathcal{M}}(\alpha) \in A\}$ is in $\mathbf{\Sigma}_1(G_{\leq n})$, otherwise L_A is $\mathbf{\Pi}_1(G_{\leq n})$-hard w.r.t. the Wadge reducibility in $G_{\leq n}$.*

2. If $\mathcal{A}$ is $\leq_1$-up then L_A is in $\mathbf{\Sigma}_2(G_{\leq n})$, otherwise L_A is $\mathbf{\Pi}_2(G_{\leq n})$-hard w.r.t. the Wadge reducibility in $G_{\leq n}$.

Proof. (1) Let $\mathcal{A}$ be $\leq_0$-up. For any $\alpha \in \Sigma^\omega$ and any $i < j$, let $c_{i,j} = (\alpha[i, j), (q_i, x_i))$ where $(q_i, x_i) = (in, \varepsilon) \cdot \alpha \restriction_i$. To prove $L_A \in \mathbf{\Sigma}_1^0(G_{\leq n})$ it suffices to show that $L_A = \{\alpha \in G_{\leq n} \mid \exists i < j (c_{i,j} \in \mathcal{A})\}$. Let $\alpha \in L_A$, then for $c = c_{\mathcal{M}}(\alpha)$ we have $c = c_{i,j}$ for some $i < j$. Hence, α is in the right hand set by Lemma 3. Conversely, let α be in the right hand set, $c_{i,j}$ satisfy the corresponding condition, and let $d = c_{\mathcal{M}}(\alpha)$. Then $c_{i,j} \leq_0 d$. Since $\mathcal{A}$ is $\leq_0$-up, $d \in \mathcal{A}$, hence $\alpha \in L_A$ by Lemma 3.

Let now $\mathcal{A}$ be not $\leq_0$-up, i.e. $c \in \mathcal{A} \not\ni d$ for some $c \leq_0 d$; let $c = (u, (q, x))$ and $d = (v, (r, y))$. We construct a Wadge reduction of the $\mathbf{\Pi}_1(G_{\leq n})$-complete language L of words in $G_{\leq n}$ that do not contain factor $<>$, to L_A. By the definition of $\leq_0$, there are $z, w \in \Sigma^*$ such that $(in, \varepsilon) \cdot z = (q, x)$ and $(q, x) \cdot w = (r, y)$. We define a continuous function g on $G_{\leq n}$ as follows. We scan subsequent letters of an input $\alpha \in G_{\leq n}$ waiting for the first occurrence of $<>$; while we do not see it, we construct $g(\alpha)$ as $zuu\ldots$ (thus, if α does not contain factor $<>$ at all then $g(\alpha) = zu^\omega$, hence $f_{\mathcal{M}}(g(\alpha)) = M(c)$); once we see the first entry of $<>$, we further construct $g(\alpha)$ as $zu^{i+1}wv^\omega$, hence $f_{\mathcal{M}}(g(\alpha)) = M(d)$. Then g reduces L to L_A.

(2) Let $\mathcal{A}$ be $\leq_1$-up. To prove $L_A \in \Sigma_2(G_{\leq n})$, it suffices to show that $L_A = \{\alpha \in G_{\leq n} \mid \exists i < j(c_{i,j} \in \mathcal{A} \land \forall l > j(q_l \in \{q_i, \ldots, q_j\}))\}$. Let $\alpha \in L_A$, then for $c = c_{\mathcal{M}}(\alpha)$ we have $c = c_{i,j}$ for some $i < j$. Hence, α is in the right hand set by Lemma 3. Conversely, let α be in the right hand set, $c_{i,j}$ satisfy the corresponding condition, and let $d = c_{\mathcal{M}}(\alpha)$. Then $c_{i,j} \leq_1 d$. Since $\mathcal{A}$ is $\leq_1$-up, $d \in \mathcal{A}$, hence $\alpha \in L_A$ by Lemma 3.

Let now A be not $\leq_1$-up, i.e. $c \in A \not\ni d$ for some $c \leq_1 d$; let $c = (u, (q, x))$ and $d = (v, (r, y))$. We show that the $\mathbf{\Pi}_2(G_{\leq n})$-complete language L of words that contain infinitely many entries of factor $<>$, is Wadge reducible to L_A. By the definition of $\leq_1$, $M(d) \subseteq M(c)$ and there are $z, w, t \in \Sigma^*$ such that $(in, \varepsilon) \cdot z = (r, y)$, $(q, x) \cdot w = (r, y)$, and $(r, y) \cdot t = (q, x)$. We define a continuous function g on $G_{\leq n}$ as follows. We again scan α looking for entries of $<>$; while there are no occurrences, we construct $g(\alpha)$ as $zvv\ldots$ (thus, if α does not contain $<>$ at all, then $g(\alpha) = zv^\omega$, hence $f_{\mathcal{M}}(g(x)) = M(d)$); if we see the first entry of $<>$, we continue to construct $g(\alpha)$ as $zv^{i_0+1}tuwvv\ldots$ (thus, if there is precisely one entry then $g(\alpha) = zv^{i_0+1}tuwv^\omega$, hence $f_{\mathcal{M}}(g(\alpha)) = M(d)$); if we meet the second entry, we continue to construct $g(\alpha)$ as $zv^{i_0+1}tuwv^{i_1+1}tuwvv\ldots$ (thus, if there are precisely 2 entries then $g(\alpha) = zv^{i_0+1}tuwv^{i_1+1}tuwv^\omega$, hence $f_{\mathcal{M}}(g(\alpha)) = M(d)$), and so on (thus, if there are infinitely many entries of $<>$ at positions $i_0 < i_1 < \cdots$ then our construction yields $g(\alpha) = zv^{i_0+1}tuwv^{i_1+1}tuwv^{i_2+1}\ldots$, hence $f_{\mathcal{M}}(g(x)) = M(c)$). Thus, g reduces L to L_A. $\quad\square$

6 Main Result

We formulate the main result of this paper. The formulation and complete proof are rather technical and heavily depend on [15] where a general framework for such kind of results was suggested. For this reason we give only a brief proof sketch with references to the corresponding parts of [15].

The Wadge reducibility for k-partitions $K, L : G_{\leq n} \to \bar{k}$ is defined as follows: $K \leq_W L$, if $K = L \circ g$ for some continuous function g on $G_{\leq n}$. Let $\mathrm{DVP}_{\leq n}$ be the set of such k-partitions recognized by the DVP Muller k-acceptors. Let $\mathcal{T}_k$ be the set of finite $\bar{k}$-labeled trees with the homomorphic preorder (see Sect. 3.2 of [15]). Let $(\mathcal{F}_{\mathcal{T}_k}; \leq_h)$ be the set of finite $\mathcal{T}_k$-labeled forests with the homomorphic preorder.

Theorem 1. *For any $n < \omega$, the quotient posets of $(\mathrm{DVP}_{\leq n}; \leq_W)$ and of $(\mathcal{F}_{\mathcal{T}_k}; \leq_h)$ are computably isomorphic and computably presentable.*

Proof Sketch. We associate with any $L \in \mathrm{DVP}_{\leq n}$ an element of $\mathcal{F}_{\mathcal{T}_k}$ similar to Proposition 8 of [15]. Namely, let F be the forest unfolding of $(C_{\mathcal{M}}^{\leq n}; \leq_0,$

$\leq_1, A)$ where $(\mathcal{M}, A)$ is a DVP Muller k-acceptor which recognizes L. Since every equivalence class in $C_{\mathcal{M}}^{\leq n}/_{\equiv_0}$ has the least element w.r.t. $\leq_1$ and there are only finitely many $\equiv_0$-classes by Lemma 5, we have $F \in \mathcal{F}_{T_k}$. Using Lemma 6 and analogue of Lemma 7 from [15], we obtain that the $G_{\leq n}$-restriction of $A \circ f_{\mathcal{M}}$ is Wadge complete in the level F of the fine hierarchy over the base $(\Sigma_1(G_{\leq n}), \Sigma_2(G_{\leq n})$. The function $(\mathcal{M}, A) \mapsto F$, denoted by g, is computable and induces an isomorphism of the quotient poset of $(\mathrm{DVP}_{\leq n}; \leq_W)$ into that of $(\mathcal{F}_{T_k}; \leq_h)$.

That this isomorphism is surjective follows easily from the results of Sect. 4.1 of [15] where a function $\rho : \mathcal{F}_{T_k} \to \mathcal{R}_k$ was defined where $\mathcal{R}_k$ is the set of ω-regular k-partitions over the binary alphabet. Let this alphabet be $B_2 = \{<>, <<>>\}$, then B_2^{ω} may be considered as a subset of $\mathrm{wn}(\Sigma) \subseteq G_0 \subseteq G_{\leq n}$. This induces an embedding ρ' of the quotient poset of $(\mathcal{F}_{T_k}; \leq_h)$ into that of $(\mathrm{DVP}_{\leq n}; \leq_W)$ such that $g \circ \rho'$ is identical on the quotient poset of $(\mathcal{F}_{T_k}; \leq_h)$. The latter structure is obviously computably presentable. $\square$

Corollary 1. *The quotient posets of* $(\mathrm{DVP}_{\leq n}; \leq_W)$ *and of* $(\mathcal{R}_k; \leq_W)$ *are isomorphic.*

Remark 3. 1. The quotient posets of $(\mathrm{DVP}_{<\omega}; \leq_W)$ and of $(\mathcal{R}_k; \leq_W)$ are not isomorphic. The reason is that, by Remark 2, the 2-preorder $(C_{\mathcal{M}}^{<\omega}; \leq_0, \leq_1)$ may be non-interpolable which yields k-partitions (and even languages) of new Wadge degrees (compared with the degrees of regular ω-languages). Note that these new languages are still finite Boolean combinations of $\Sigma_2(G_{<\omega})$-sets. Also, arbitrary DVP-language is a finite Boolean combination of $\Sigma_2(\Sigma^{\omega})$-sets.

2. From the results in [7] it follows that for the languages recognized by nondeterministic VPA the situation is even more complicated: there are such languages beyond the class $\Sigma_3(\Sigma^{\omega})$, although they are finite Boolean combinations of $\Sigma_3(\Sigma^{\omega})$-sets. The whole picture of the corresponding Wadge degrees, and especially the effectivity and complexity issues, are far from being clear.

Acknowledgement. I am grateful to Alexander Okhotin for many helpful discussions of visibly pushdown automata.

References

1. Alur, R., Madhusudan, P.: Visibly pushdown languages. ACM Symposium on Theory of Computing (STOC 2004, Chicago, USA, 13-16 June 2004), pp. 202-211 (2004). https://doi.org/10.1145/1007352.1007390
2. Alur, R., Madhusudan, P.: Adding nesting structure to words. J. ACM **56**, 3 (2009). https://doi.org/10.1145/1516512.1516518
3. von Braunmühl, B., Verbeek, R.: Input driven languages are recognized in $\log n$ space. Annal. Discr. Math. **24**, 1–20 (1985). https://doi.org/10.1016/S0304-0208(08)73072-X
4. Duparc, J.: A hierarchy of deterministic context-free ω-languages. Theoret. Comput. Sci. **290**(3), 1253–1300 (2003)

5. Finkel, O.: Topological complexity of context-free ω-languages: a survey. In: Dershowitz, N., Nissan, E. (eds.) Language, Culture, Computation. Computing - Theory and Technology. LNCS, vol. 8001, pp. 50–77. Springer, Heidelberg (2014). https://doi.org/10.1007/978-3-642-45321-2_4

6. Kihara, T., Montalbán, A.: On the structure of the Wadge degrees of BQO-valued Borel functions. Trans. Amer. Math. Soc. **371**(11), 7885–7923 (2019)

7. Löding, C., Madhusudan, P., Serre, O.: Visibly pushdown games. In: Lodaya, K., Mahajan, M. (eds.) FSTTCS 2004. LNCS, vol. 3328, pp. 408–420. Springer, Heidelberg (2004). https://doi.org/10.1007/978-3-540-30538-5_34

8. Mehlhorn, K.: Pebbling mountain ranges and its application to DCFL-recognition. In: de Bakker, J., van Leeuwen, J. (eds.) ICALP 1980. LNCS, vol. 85, pp. 422–435. Springer, Heidelberg (1980). https://doi.org/10.1007/3-540-10003-2_89

9. Okhotin, A., Salomaa, K.: Complexity of input-driven pushdown automata. SIGACT News **45**(2), 47–67 (2014). https://doi.org/10.1145/2636805.2636821

10. Okhotin, A., Selivanov, V.L.: Input-driven pushdown automata on well-nested infinite strings. In: Santhanam, R., Musatov, D. (eds.) CSR 2021. LNCS, vol. 12730, pp. 349–360. Springer, Cham (2021). https://doi.org/10.1007/978-3-030-79416-3_21

11. Selivanov, V.L.: Wadge degrees of ω-languages of deterministic Turing machines. Theoret. Inform. Appl. **37**, 67–83 (2003)

12. Selivanov, V.L.: Hierarchies and reducibilities on regular languages related to modulo counting. RAIRO Theoret. Inform. Appl. **41**, 95–132 (2009)

13. Selivanov, V.: A fine hierarchy of ω-regular k-partitions. In: Löwe, B., Normann, D., Soskov, I., Soskova, A. (eds.) CiE 2011. LNCS, vol. 6735, pp. 260–269. Springer, Heidelberg (2011). https://doi.org/10.1007/978-3-642-21875-0_28

14. Selivanov, V.L.: Extending Wadge theory to k-partitions. In: Kari, J., Manea, F., Petre, I. (eds.) CiE 2017. LNCS, vol. 10307, pp. 387–399. Springer, Cham (2017). https://doi.org/10.1007/978-3-319-58741-7_36

15. Selivanov V.: Wadge degrees of classes of ω-regular k-partitions. Journal of Automata, Languages and Combinatorics. Arxiv 2104.10358

16. Wagner, K.: On ω-regular sets. Inf. Control **43**, 123–177 (1979)

On Guarded Extensions of MMSNP

Alexey Barsukov[1,2]($\boxtimes$) [iD] and Florent R. Madelaine[1] [iD]

[1] Univ. Paris Est Creteil, LACL, 94010 Creteil, France
{alexey.barsukov,florent.madelaine}@u-pec.fr
[2] Charles University, Prague, Czech Republic

Abstract. We investigate logics and classes of problems below Fagin's *existential second-order logic* (ESO) and above Feder and Vardi's logic for *constraint satisfaction problems* (CSP), the so called *monotone monadic SNP without inequality* (MMSNP). It is known that MMSNP has a dichotomy between P and NP-complete but that the removal of any of these three restrictions imposed on SNP yields a logic that is Ptime equivalent to ESO: so by Ladner's theorem we have three *stronger sibling logics* that are nondichotomic above MMSNP. In this paper, we explore the area between these four logics, mostly by considering guarded extensions of MMSNP, with the ultimate goal being to obtain logics above MMSNP that exhibit such a dichotomy.

Keywords: descriptive complexity · computational complexity · constraint satisfaction problem · dichotomy · mmsnp

1 Introduction

A consequence of Ladner's theorem [11] is that if P $\neq$ NP, then NP does not have a PvsNP-complete dichotomy. Feder and Vardi proved in [8] that MMSNP captures CSP up to Ptime equivalence and that its three stronger siblings do not have a dichotomy, and conjectured the dichotomy of CSP; a conjecture proved independently by Bulatov and Zhuk in [7,14]. The classes studied in this paper are depicted on Fig. 1, where an arrow from a class $\mathcal{C}_1$ to a class $\mathcal{C}_2$ indicates that any problem from $\mathcal{C}_1$ is Ptime equivalent to a problem from $\mathcal{C}_2$. This means that if $\mathcal{C}_2$ has a dichotomy, then so does $\mathcal{C}_1$. In [4], Bienvenu et al. introduced GMSNP a guarded extension of MMSNP that relaxes the constraint of monadicity, and showed that it is logically equivalent to MMSNP$_2$ [12] an extension of MMSNP which colors edges in the spirit of Courcelle's MSO$_2$. Regarding the constraint of monotonicity, there is no logic in the literature that sits between MMSNP and monadic SNP without $\neq$. There is, however, an extension of CSP on graphs, the so called *Matrix Partition problems* [10], studied on relational structures in [2].

This work was supported by ANR project DIFFERENCE (https://anr.fr/Projet-ANR-20-CE48-0002).

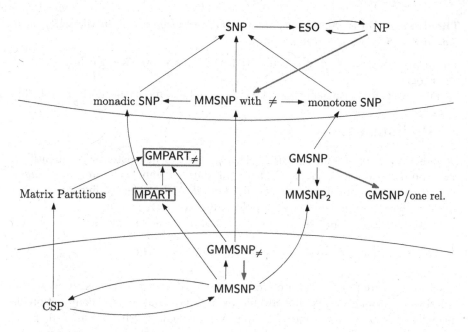

Fig. 1. Classes at the bottom exhibit a PvsNP-complete dichotomy, while those at the top do not, and it remains open for classes in the middle.

Main Contributions. In Sect. 3, we introduce the *guarded extension of* MMSNP *with* $\neq$ (GMMSNP$_{\neq}$) and prove that it exhibits a dichotomy. In this paper, SAT(Φ) denotes the set of finite structures that satisfy a sentence Φ.

Theorem 1. *For any sentence Φ in* GMMSNP$_{\neq}$ *there exists a sentence Φ' in* MMSNP *such that the problems* SAT(Φ) *and* SAT(Φ') *are Ptime equivalent.*

While we are not able to do the same for GMSNP, we establish that it would suffice to prove a dichotomy for a signature with a single input relation in Sect. 4.

Theorem 2. *For any finite relational signature τ there exists a signature τ_1 consisting of a single relational symbol such that, for any* GMSNP τ-sentence Φ *there exists a* GMSNP τ_1-sentence Φ^1 *such that* SAT(Φ) *and* SAT(Φ^1) *are Ptime equivalent.*

We recall Hell's Matrix Partition [10], a graph problem which we recast as a problem on arbitrary relational structure, for which we propose a logic in Sect. 5. Finally, in Sect. 6, we provide a complete proof of one crucial step of Feder and Vardi's argument to establish that the three stronger siblings of MMSNP can not have a dichotomy unless P equals NP. The original argument provides key ideas, in particular using *oblivious Turing machines*, but to the best of our knowledge, nobody in the community has reconstructed a complete proof from their argument, which motivates us to do it here.

Theorem 3. *For each problem Ω in NP there is a sentence Φ in* MMSNP$_{\neq}$ *such that Ω and $SAT(\Phi)$ are Ptime equivalent.*

The interested reader may consult [1] for extensive proofs regarding the two other logics.

Full proofs for statements marked with ⋆ can be found in the arXiv version [3].

2   Preliminaries

Denote by τ a relational signature. Denote the set of existentially quantified second-order variables $\{X_1, \ldots, X_s\}$ by σ. Relation symbols of τ are called *input* and relation symbols of σ are called *existential*. Also, tuples of first-order variables or elements are denoted with bold lower-case letters: $\mathbf{x}, \mathbf{a}, \ldots$

Any τ-sentence Φ in SNP can be rewritten in the following form:

$$\exists X_1, \ldots, X_s \; \forall \mathbf{x} \bigwedge_i \neg(\alpha_i \wedge \beta_i \wedge \epsilon_i), \tag{1}$$

where α_i is a conjunction of atomic or negated atomic τ-formulas, β_i is a conjunction of atomic or negated atomic σ-formulas, and ϵ_i is a conjunction of inequalities $x_i \neq x_j$, for some $x_i, x_j \in \mathbf{x}$. We frequently write "atom" instead of "atomic formula". Every subformula $\neg(\alpha_i \wedge \beta_i \wedge \epsilon_i)$ is called a *negated conjunct*.

An SNP-sentence Φ is called *monadic* if all existential relation symbols have arity 1. It is called *monotone* if every α_i omits negated τ-atoms. Alternatively, one can think of this property as of being closed under inverse homomorphisms, thanks to the following theorem.

Theorem 4 ([9]). *For a sentence Φ in SNP, the class $SAT(\Phi)$ is closed under inverse homomorphisms iff Φ is logically equivalent to a monotone sentence.*

Denote by MMSNP the fragment of SNP consisting of sentences that are monotone, monadic, and *without inequality*, i.e., every ϵ_i is empty.

A sentence Φ is in *guarded monotone strict NP* (GMSNP) if it is written in the form of Eq. (1), where: (a) each α_i is a conjunction of nonnegated τ-atoms, (b) each β_i is a conjunction of σ-atoms or negated σ-atoms, and (c) each ϵ_i is empty.

Also, for every negated σ-atom $\neg X(\mathbf{x}_1)$ from every β_i there exists either (i) a τ-atom $R(\mathbf{x}_2)$ from α_i, or (ii) a nonnegated σ-atom $X'(\mathbf{x}_2)$ from β_i
such that $\mathbf{x}_1 \subseteq \mathbf{x}_2$. In this case, we say that $R(\mathbf{x}_2)$ (or $X'(\mathbf{x}_2)$) *guards* $X(\mathbf{x}_1)$.

Definition 1. *The logic* MMSNP *with guarded $\neq$, denoted by* GMMSNP$_{\neq}$, *is the class of sentences of the form as in Eq. (1), where (a) each α_i is a conjunction of nonnegated τ-atoms, (b) each β_i is a conjunction of unary σ-atoms or negated unary σ-atoms, and (c) for every inequality $x_j \neq x'_j$ of each ϵ_i there exists a τ-atom in α_i that contains both x_j and x'_j.*

Remark 1. For any sentence that we consider, we assume that it is not trivial, i.e., it has some YES and some NO input instances.

For further notions that remain undefined please refer to [5].

3   MMSNP with Guarded Inequality

In this section, we prove Theorem 1, for the sake of simplicity in the case of $\tau = \{R\}$, where R has arity n. In the case of many relations, one should apply the same procedure for each relation independently.

The construction has two main steps. At first, we enrich every negated conjunct of Φ with inequalities and keep the resulting sentence logically equivalent to the initial one. This transformation is the same as the one used in Lemma 4 in [9]. After that, we construct an equivalent MMSNP sentence Φ' by changing the input relational signature. Each new relation symbol is associated with an equivalence relation on an n-element set, where n is the arity of R.

Enriching the Sentence with Inequalities. For every negated conjunct $\neg\phi$ of Φ and for every two variables x, y that appear in the same R-atom of $\neg\phi$, replace this negated conjunct with two negated conjuncts: the first one is obtained from $\neg\phi$ by adding the inequality $x \neq y$ to the conjunction, the second one is obtained from $\neg\phi$ by replacing every occurrence of the variable y with the variable x.

Example 1. If Φ contains a negated conjunct $\neg\big(R(x,y) \wedge X_1(x) \wedge X_2(y)\big)$, then it is replaced by the two following negated conjuncts:

$$\neg\big(R(x,y) \wedge X_1(x) \wedge X_2(y) \wedge x \neq y\big) \wedge \neg\big(R(x,x) \wedge X_1(x) \wedge X_2(x)\big).$$

The following lemma is a direct implication from the construction.

Lemma* 1. *Any* GMMSNP$_{\neq}$ *sentence* Φ *is logically equivalent to a* GMMSNP$_{\neq}$ *sentence* Ψ *such that, for any negated conjunct* $\neg\psi_i$ *of* Ψ *and for any two different variables* x, y *that appear within some* R-atom of ψ_i, *this conjunct contains the inequality* $x \neq y$.

Now, by Lemma* 1, we assume that *w.l.o.g.* for any two variables x, y that appear within the same R-atom in some negated conjunct of Φ, this negated conjunct contains $x \neq y$.

We need to introduce some necessary notations. For n in $\mathbb{N}$, denote by B_n the number of equivalence relations on a set of n elements: $\sim_1, \ldots, \sim_{B_n}$. For each $\sim_k$, denote by $n_k := \big|\{1, \ldots, n\}/ \sim_k\big|$ the number of equivalence classes of this relation. Every n-tuple $(x_1, \ldots, x_n)$ is associated with exactly one $\sim_k$ such that $x_i = x_j$ iff $i \sim_k j$. If $\sim_k$ is associated with $\mathbf{x}$, then we say that $\mathbf{x}$ has *equivalence type* k. For every equivalence class $\{x_{c_1}, \ldots, x_{c_l}\}$ of $\sim_k$, denote it by $[c]_{\sim_k}$, where $c = \min\{c_1, \ldots, c_l\}$ – the smallest number of this set. Then, introduce a linear ordering $\prec_k$ on the set $\{1, \ldots, n\}/ \sim_k$ by setting $[i]_{\sim_k} \prec_k [j]_{\sim_k}$ if $i < j$.

Definition 2. *For a set* X, *define a function* $\mathbf{p} \colon \biguplus_{n=1}^{\infty} X^n \to \biguplus_{n=1}^{\infty} X^n$ *as follows. Let* $\mathbf{x} = (x_1, \ldots, x_n)$ *in* X^n *be an* n-tuple of equivalence type k. *Let* $[s_1]_{\sim_k}, \ldots, [s_{n_k}]_{\sim_k}$ *be the* $\sim_k$-equivalence classes such that $[s_i]_{\sim_k} \prec_k [s_j]_{\sim_k}$ iff $i < j$. *Then, put* $\mathbf{p}(\mathbf{x}) := \big(x_{s_1}, \ldots, x_{s_{n_k}}\big)$.

Example 2. Informally, the function p removes an element from a tuple if it is not its first occurrence. Consider a 3-tuple $\mathbf{t} = (y, x, x)$, it is associated with the equivalence relation $\sim_4$ from Fig. 2, the equivalence classes of $\sim_4$ on the set $\{1, 2, 3\}$ are $[1]_{\sim_4} = \{1\}$ and $[2]_{\sim_4} = \{2, 3\}$. Then, $\mathrm{p}(\mathbf{t}) = (y, x)$ because y is on the first coordinate of $\mathbf{t}$, x is on the second, and $[1]_{\sim_4} \prec_4 [2]_{\sim_4}$.

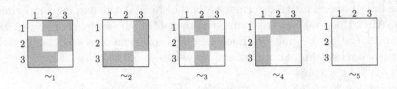

Fig. 2. All the 5 equivalence relations on a 3-element set.

Constructing the MMSNP *Sentence.* The MMSNP sentence Φ' has the same existential signature σ as Φ, however the input signature τ' is not the same. τ' has B_n relation symbols $R_1, \ldots, R_{B_n}$. Each R_i is associated with one of the B_n equivalence relations $\sim_k$ on the set $\{1, \ldots, n\}$, the arity of R_k equals to the number n_k of equivalence classes of $\sim_k$. For example, if $n = 3$, then τ' contains $B_3 = 5$ relation symbols $R_1(\cdot, \cdot, \cdot), R_2(\cdot, \cdot), R_3(\cdot, \cdot), R_4(\cdot, \cdot), R_5(\cdot)$, see Fig. 2. We now describe how to construct the MMSNP sentence Φ' from Φ.

– Firstly, remove all inequalities from Φ.
– Then, replace every τ-atom $R(\mathbf{x})$ with $R_k(\mathrm{p}(\mathbf{x}))$, where k is the equivalence type of $\mathbf{x}$.
– Finally, in order to mimic the inequalities that we have removed, we forbid the same variable to appear within τ'-atoms more than once. For every R_k in τ' and for every $i < j$ in $[n_k]$, add to Φ' the following:

$$\neg R_k(x_1, \ldots, x_{i-1}, x, x_{i+1}, \ldots, x_{j-1}, x, x_{j+1}, \ldots, x_{n_k}). \tag{2}$$

Proof (Theorem 1). Let Φ' be obtained from Φ as above. Let $\mathfrak{A}$ be a τ-structure. The corresponding τ'-structure $\mathfrak{A}'$ has the same domain $A' = A$. And, for every R_k in τ' and for every tuple $\mathbf{a} = (a_1, \ldots, a_n)$ of equivalence type k, we have $\mathrm{p}(\mathbf{a}) \in R_k^{\mathfrak{A}'}$ if and only if $\mathbf{a} \in R^{\mathfrak{A}}$. The remainder of the proof is routine, see [3].
□

4   Guarded Monotone SNP

In this section, we prove Theorem 2 in several stages. In the first one, we check if Φ holds in a structure consisting of a single R-tuple, for R in τ. If not, then we get rid of this relation symbol because we need every relation of an input structure to be allowed to be nonempty. In the second one, we enrich every negated conjunct with τ-atoms so that every relation symbol of τ is present in every conjunct. In the last stage, we construct a suitable sentence over a single relation symbol.

An SNP τ-sentence Φ of the form as in Eq. (1) is called *connected* if no negated conjunct $\neg\phi(\mathbf{x})$ of Φ can be written as $\neg(\psi_1(\mathbf{x}_1) \wedge \psi_2(\mathbf{x}_2))$, where $\mathbf{x}_1$ and $\mathbf{x}_2$ share no variables. By Lemma 2, we can consider only connected τ-sentences Φ in GMSNP and, by Lemma 3, SAT(Φ) is closed under disjoint unions.

Lemma 2 ([6]). *The following statements are equivalent.*

1. *For any τ-sentence Φ in GMSNP, SAT(Φ) is in $P \cup NP$-complete.*
2. *For any connected τ-sentence Φ in GMSNP, SAT(Φ) is in $P \cup NP$-complete.*

Lemma 3 ([5]). *Let Φ be an SNP sentence. Then, SAT(Φ) is closed under disjoint unions iff Φ is logically equivalent to a connected SNP sentence.*

First Stage: Removing Unnecessary Relation Symbols. For a k-ary R in τ, let $\mathfrak{B}_R$ be a τ-structure that consists of one R-tuple $\mathbf{b}_R = (b_{R,1}, \ldots, b_{R,k})$. That is, (a) $\mathfrak{B}_R$ has the domain $B_R = \{b_{R,1}, \ldots, b_{R,k}\}$, (b) $R^{\mathfrak{B}_R} = \{\mathbf{b}_R\}$, and (c) for any other $S \in \tau$, $S^{\mathfrak{B}_R} = \varnothing$.

Lemma* 4. *If, for some R in τ, a connected GMSNP τ-sentence Φ does not satisfy $\mathfrak{B}_R$, then SAT(Φ) is Ptime equivalent to SAT($\Phi^{\mathcal{R}}$), where $\Phi^{\mathcal{R}}$ is a connected $(\tau \smallsetminus \{R\})$-sentence that is obtained from Φ by removing all negated conjuncts that contain an R-atom.*

Second Stage: Enriching Negated Conjuncts With τ-atoms. Call a GMSNP sentence *enriched* if, for any of its negated conjuncts $\neg\phi_i$ and any $R \in \tau$, $\neg\phi_i$ contains at least one R-atom. We now show, for any connected Φ, how to obtain an enriched sentence Φ' such that the corresponding problems are Ptime equivalent. Take any negated conjunct $\neg\phi_i$ of Φ and replace it with $\neg\phi_i' := \neg(\phi_i \wedge \bigwedge_{R \in \tau} R(\mathbf{x}_R))$, where each $\mathbf{x}_R$ is a tuple of new variables. Observe that Φ' is not connected anymore. However, Φ is more restrictive than Φ', as we enrich negated conjuncts of Φ with τ-atoms. That is, for any τ-structure $\mathfrak{A}$, $\mathfrak{A} \models \Phi$ implies $\mathfrak{A} \models \Phi'$. Below, we check the Ptime equivalence of SAT(Φ) and SAT(Φ').

Lemma* 5. *SAT(Φ) is Ptime reducible to SAT(Φ').*

Proof. For a τ-structure $\mathfrak{A}$, put $\mathfrak{A}' := \mathfrak{A} \uplus (\biguplus_{R \in \tau} \mathfrak{B}_R)$. Suppose that $\mathfrak{A} \models \Phi$. By Lemma* 4, we assume that, for R in τ, $\mathfrak{B}_R \models \Phi$. Then, by Lemma* 3, $\mathfrak{A}' \models \Phi$, as $\mathfrak{A}'$ is the disjoint union of structures satisfying Φ. But then, as Φ' is less restrictive than Φ, we have $\mathfrak{A}' \models \Phi'$. For the other direction, see [3]. □

Lemma* 6. *SAT(Φ') is Ptime reducible to SAT(Φ).*

Last Stage: Concatenation. In this part, we construct a τ_1-sentence Φ^1 that is Ptime equivalent to Φ. By Lemmas* 5 and 6, we can assume that Φ is already enriched. Set $\tau_1 := \{P\}$, where $\mathrm{arity}(P) = \sum_{R \in \tau} \mathrm{arity}(R)$. For two tuples $\mathbf{x} = (x_1, \ldots, x_n), \mathbf{y} = (y_1, \ldots, y_m)$, set $(\mathbf{x}, \mathbf{y}) := (x_1, \ldots, x_n, y_1, \ldots, y_m)$. The notation $(\mathbf{x}_1, \ldots, \mathbf{x}_t)$ is defined similarly.

Recall that $\tau = \{R_1, \ldots, R_t\}$. For a negated conjunct $\neg \phi_i$ of Φ, we construct the corresponding negated conjunct $\neg \phi_i^1$ of Φ^1 as follows. The σ-atoms of ϕ_i^1 are the same as in ϕ_i. For every τ-atom $R_j(\mathbf{x})$ of ϕ_i, add to ϕ_i^1 a τ_1-atom $P(\mathbf{y}_1, \ldots, \mathbf{y}_t)$, where $\mathbf{y}_j = \mathbf{x}$ and all other variables of this atomic formula are new and they are used only there. In the rest, we check the equivalence of the corresponding problems. Together, Lemmas* 5 to 8 imply Theorem 2.

Lemma* 7. *SAT(Φ) is Ptime reducible to SAT(Φ^1).*

Proof. For a τ-structure $\mathfrak{A}$, we construct the corresponding τ_1-structure $\mathfrak{A}_1$. The structures have the same domain: $A_1 = A$. The relation $P^{\mathfrak{A}_1}$ is defined by the relations of $\mathfrak{A}$ as follows: $P(\mathbf{x}_1, \ldots, \mathbf{x}_t) \longleftrightarrow R_1(\mathbf{x}_1) \wedge \cdots \wedge R_t(\mathbf{x}_t)$. The remainder of the proof is routine, see [3]. □

Lemma* 8. *SAT(Φ^1) is Ptime reducible to SAT(Φ).*

Proof. For a τ_1-structure $\mathfrak{B}_1$, we construct a τ-structure $\mathfrak{B}$. They have the same domain B, and every τ-relation $R_j^{\mathfrak{B}}$ is defined as follows: $R_j(\mathbf{x}_j) \longleftrightarrow \exists \mathbf{x}_1, \ldots, \mathbf{x}_{j-1}, \mathbf{x}_{j+1}, \ldots, \mathbf{x}_t \ P(\mathbf{x}_1, \ldots, \mathbf{x}_t)$. The remainder of the proof is routine, see [3]. □

5   Matrix Partition

We are not aware of any logic above MMSNP that is still monadic but the "monotone" condition is changed to something less strict. However, there is a well-known class of matrix partition problems [10] that extends graph homomorphisms in this direction. It is not known if this class enjoys a PvsNP-complete dichotomy. In this section, we define corresponding logical classes and discuss what can be an analogue of the "guarded" property for them.

Definition 3 (*[10]*). *Let* M *be an* $(s \times s)$*-matrix with entries from* $\{0, 1, \star\}$. *A loopless graph* $\mathfrak{G}$ *admits* M*-partition if its domain* G *can be split into* s *classes* $X_1, \ldots, X_s$ *such that, for any two distinct* x, y *from any* X_i, X_j, *(a) if* $m_{i,j} = 0$, *then* $(x, y) \notin E^{\mathfrak{G}}$, *(b) if* $m_{i,j} = 1$, *then* $(x, y) \in E^{\mathfrak{G}}$, *(c) if* $m_{i,j} = \star$, *then there is no restriction for* (x, y).

Any matrix partition problem can be expressed in the form of Eq. (1) as follows, this gives rise to a fragment of SNP introduced further in Definition 4.

$$\exists X_1, \ldots, X_s \ \forall x, y \ \neg(\neg X_1(x) \wedge \cdots \wedge \neg X_s(x)) \wedge \bigwedge_{i,j \in [s], i \neq j} (X_i(x) \wedge X_j(x)) \wedge$$

$$\bigwedge_{m_{i,j}=0} \neg(E(x,y) \wedge X_i(x) \wedge X_j(y) \wedge x \neq y) \wedge \bigwedge_{m_{i,j}=1} \neg(\neg E(x,y) \wedge X_i(x) \wedge X_j(y) \wedge x \neq y).$$

Definition 4. *A τ-sentence Φ written in the form of Eq. (1) belongs to the class* GMPART$_{\neq}$ *if: (a) each α_i is either a conjunction only of nonnegated τ-atoms or a conjunction only of negated τ-atoms, (b) each β_i is a conjunction of unary σ-atoms or negated unary σ-atoms, and (c) for every inequality $x_j \neq x'_j$ of each ϵ_i there exists a τ-atom in α_i that contains both x_j and x'_j.*

The class GMPART$_{\neq}$ contains both matrix partition problems and GMMSNP$_{\neq}$ from Sect. 3 but it is not contained in monadic SNP without $\neq$. Denote by MPART the fragment of GMPART$_{\neq}$, where each ϵ_i is empty. This class (strictly) extends MMSNP and belongs to monadic SNP without $\neq$ at the same time.

Proposition 1. *There is a sentence Φ in MPART such that, for any Ψ in MMSNP, Φ is not logically equivalent to Ψ.*

Proof. Let Φ be a sentence that accepts only complete directed graphs with loops: $\forall x, y \; \neg(\neg E(x,y))$. As SAT$(\Phi)$ is not closed under inverse homomorphisms, it can not be expressed by an MMSNP sentence, by Theorem 4. $\square$

Although GMPART$_{\neq}$ is related to MPART in the same way as GMMSNP$_{\neq}$ is related to MMSNP, the methods from the proof of Theorem 1 do not spread to them because now negated conjuncts may contain negated τ-atoms. This means that these two classes might differ *w.r.t.* having a dichotomy.

Question 1. Is it true that for every Φ in GMPART$_{\neq}$ there is Φ' in MPART such that SAT(Φ) is Ptime equivalent to SAT(Φ')?

6   NP Is Ptime Equivalent to MMSNP with Inequality

We prove Theorem 3 and consider a problem Ω in NP: *w.l.o.g.* we may assume that Ω is decided by an *oblivious* Turing Machine M_o, for which the head movement depends only on the size of the input string. We build a sentence Φ in MMSNP$_{\neq}$ that shall operate on an input $\mathfrak{A}$ which ought to describe the space-time diagram of an input string $\mathbf{x}$ of M_o. We use two binary input predicates *succ* and *next* for space and time respectively, together with additional predicates to obtain a grid like structure. Obliviousness allows us to check the computation with monadic predicates only, and it is not hard to prove the following.

Lemma* 9. *There exists a Ptime reduction r_1 from Ω to SAT(Φ).*

The actual subtlety of the proof concerns the converse reduction, and to deal appropriately with structures $\mathfrak{A}$ that are degenerate in the sense that they are not in the image of r_1. It is precisely this part of the proof that is fully absent in [8]. For this part, we need a very uniform oblivious Turing machine for which we can predict the movement of the head. Our construction of Φ ensures that:

- if $\mathfrak{A}$ is over-complete, then $\mathfrak{A} \not\models \Phi$ (checking that the degree of *succ* or *next* is 2 or more is possible in MMSNP$_{\neq}$),

- if $\mathfrak{A}$ is not complete enough either locally – it is like a grid with holes – or globally – too small to simulate a complete run of M_o, then $\mathfrak{A} \models \Phi$ (this is achieved by a monadic marking scheme of $\mathfrak{A}$ by the sentence Φ and a relativization of the verification of M_o's computation to the marked part),
- if $\mathfrak{A}$ is in an appropriate form and can simulate a run of M_o, then $\mathfrak{A} \models \Phi$ iff M_o accepts.

Obliviousness. We use space-time diagrams as input instances of the MMSNP$_{\neq}$ sentence. In order to ensure that an input instance $\mathfrak{A}$ can simulate the whole execution of M_o, we need to know the position of its head at any moment of time and the precise time when the machine will halt. An arbitrary Turing machine can not provide this information, so we need to consider only oblivious ones. Denote by $\mathcal{O}$ a family of Turing machines M_o that satisfy the following.

1. M_o has a one-way infinite tape.
2. The head of M_o is at the first element of the tape at the start.
3. For an input string of length n, the head first moves to the nth cell, then returns to the left end, then moves to the $(n+1)$th cell, then returns to the left end, and so on. At each next round-trip, the tape length increases by one cell. In the end of the run, the head returns to the left end and halts.
4. For some $k \in \mathbb{N}$ there is $f(n) \in O(n^k)$ such that, for any input string of length n, the head makes precisely $f(n)+1$ round-trips as above before it halts. This means that the head makes precisely $g(n) := \frac{1}{2}\big(f(n) + 1\big)\big(2n - 2 + f(n)\big)$ movements during the run.

It is well-known that an oblivious machine can simulate any other one [13]. However, as $\mathcal{O}$ has some additional constraints, we need the following lemma.

Lemma* 10. *For any nondeterministic Turing machine M there is a Ptime equivalent Turing machine M_o in $\mathcal{O}$.*

Construction of the Space-time Diagram. Let M_o have the alphabet Σ_o, and let $\mathbf{x} \in (\Sigma_o \smallsetminus \{\sqcup\})^n$ be an input string. $\mathfrak{A} := r_1(\mathbf{x})$ has a form of a space-time diagram, where the horizontal axis represents "space", and the vertical axis represents "time". It consists of $g(n) + 1$ rows, each row represents the tape at a moment of time from 0 to $g(n)$. The first row has length $n + 1$, and the length increases by 1 each time when the head is at the rightmost element, *e.g.* the nth row has length $n + 1$ but the $(n+1)$th row has length $n + 2$.

$\mathfrak{A}$ has a relational signature:

$$\tau = \big\{s(\cdot) \mid s \in \Sigma \smallsetminus \{\sqcup\}\big\} \uplus \big\{start(\cdot), succ(\cdot,\cdot), next(\cdot,\cdot), row(\cdot,\cdot,\cdot)\big\}, \text{ where}$$

- relations $s(\cdot)$ represent the alphabet Σ_o: the $(i+1)$th element of the first row belongs to $s^{\mathfrak{A}}$ iff the ith cell x_i of the string $\mathbf{x}$ contains $s \in \Sigma_o$;
- $start(\cdot)$ represents the point of reference of the diagram, there is a unique element in $start^{\mathfrak{A}}$ – the first element of the first row;
- $succ(\cdot,\cdot)$ is a horizontal arc: it links two neighbors of the same row and also it connects the last element of a row to the first element of the next row;

- $next(\cdot, \cdot)$ is a vertical arc: for each i, it connects the ith element of a row to the ith element of the next row;
- $row(x, y, z)$ represents the membership of y within the row that starts in x while the next row starts in z.

An example of $\mathfrak{A}$, for the case $n = 3$ and $f(3) = 1$, is displayed on Fig. 3.

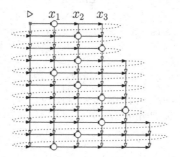

Fig. 3. The structure $\mathfrak{A} = r_1(x_1 x_2 x_3)$, and the positions of the head H.

Construction of Φ. The existential relations of Φ are:

$$\sigma = \big\{ S(\cdot) \mid s \in \Sigma_o \big\} \uplus \big\{ Mark(\cdot), Init(\cdot), H(\cdot) \big\} \uplus \big\{ Q(\cdot) \mid q \in \mathcal{Q} \big\}, \text{ where}$$

- relations S describe the string symbols at any moment of time;
- $Mark$ determines the region, where the head movement is mandatory;
- $Init$ contains the elements of the first row, it is used in order to generate all $Mark$ elements and to assign the initial symbols: $s(x) \to S(x)$;
- H contains all the positions of M_o's head at every moment of time;
- relations Q represent the current state of the machine.

The two most important relations are $Init$ and $Mark$, as other simply imitate the execution of M_o. The relation $Init$ is initiated by the *succ*-neighbor of the *start* and it must spread either until the end of the first row or until an element that is not contained in a relation s, for $s \in \Sigma_o$. The existential relation S is assigned to an $Init$ element x if $s(x)$ holds. The relation $Mark$ is initiated by the $Init$ elements and then it must spread along the vertical *next*-arcs from top to bottom. The *next*-neighbor (red circle) must be in $Mark$ only if its predecessor (black circle) is in $Mark$ and if the neighborhood looks like a two-dimensional grid, see Fig. 4. The head H is forced to move only if it is in $Mark$. If the head is in a rejecting state, then the sentence is false.

The expressiveness of MMSNP$_{\neq}$ permits Φ to have the following *first-order properties*: (a) there is at most one *start* element, (b) the in- and out- degrees of *succ* and *next* are at most 1, (c) an element y can not be in different triples $row(x, y, z)$ and $row(x', y, z')$, (d) loops $succ(x, x), next(x, x)$ are forbidden as well as $row(x, y, x)$, and (e) there can not be 2 symbol relations $s(x), s'(x)$ for the same element.

Lemma* 9 follows from the constructions of Φ and $\mathfrak{A}$.

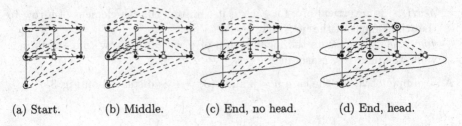

(a) Start.   (b) Middle.   (c) End, no head.   (d) End, head.

Fig. 4. All the four cases when *Mark* is forced to spread to the bottom.

The Difficult Direction. It remains to show the following lemma.

Lemma* 11. *For any τ-structure $\mathfrak{B}$ there exists an input string $\mathbf{x} \in (\Sigma_o \setminus \{\sqcup\})^*$ such that $\mathbf{x}$ is computed in Ptime in $|B|$ and $\mathfrak{B} \models \Phi$ iff M_o accepts $\mathbf{x}$.*

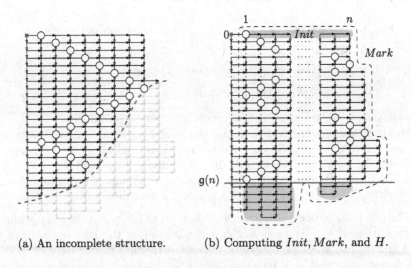

(a) An incomplete structure.   (b) Computing *Init*, *Mark*, and *H*.

Fig. 5. The cases 2 and 3.

As the input structure $\mathfrak{B}$ is arbitrary, there are 3 cases to consider. The first two are easy to deal with.

1. $\mathfrak{B}$ violates one of first-order properties imposed by Φ, *e.g.* the *start* element is not unique, or the degree of *succ* or *next* is 2 or greater, etc. These properties are checked in Ptime, if this is the case, then we reduce $\mathfrak{B}$ to a fixed NO instance of M_o.
2. The set of elements of $\mathfrak{B}$ that are forced to be in *Mark* is not sufficient to simulate the entire run of the machine. For example, if the *start* element does not exist, then no element is forced to be in *Mark*, so the head H will never be in a rejecting state. Or, if the first row contains n elements, and the total

number of rows is lesser than $g(n)$. In any of these situations, $\mathfrak{B} \models \Phi$, so we can reduce it to a fixed YES instance of M_o. See Fig. 5a.

3. $\mathfrak{B}$ allows to simulate M_o's run. In order to check if $\mathfrak{B}$ falls into this case, we find in Ptime all the elements of $\mathfrak{B}$ that are forced to be in $Init$, in $Mark$, and in H. The $Init$ elements are the *succ*-essors of the *start*. Then, we find all the elements that are forced to be in $Mark$, there is the minimal by inclusion set of them. Then, we find all the positions of the head H, it is also done in Ptime because the head movement is deterministic. If, during the first round-trip, the head passes n elements and if the $(g(n) + 1)$th row has an element from H, then, by obliviousness, we are sure that the execution halts there. Otherwise, we are in case 2. In case 3, we reduce $\mathfrak{B}$ to the string consisting of symbols that are present on the first row of $\mathfrak{B}$. See Fig. 5b.

References

1. Barsukov, A.: On dichotomy above Feder and Vardi's logic, Ph. D. thesis, Université Clermont Auvergne (2022)
2. Barsukov, A., Kanté, M.M.: Generalisations of matrix partitions : complexity and obstructions. CoRR (2021). https://arxiv.org/abs/2107.13809
3. Barsukov, A., Madelaine, F.R.: On guarded extensions of MMSNP. CoRR (2023). https://arxiv.org/abs/2305.04234
4. Bienvenu, M., ten Cate, B., Lutz, C., Wolter, F.: Ontology-based data access: a study through disjunctive datalog, CSP, and MMSNP. ACM Trans. Database Syst. **39**(4), 1–44 (2014). https://doi.org/10.1145/2661643
5. Bodirsky, M.: Complexity of Infinite-Domain Constraint Satisfaction. Lecture Notes in Logic, Cambridge University Press (2021)
6. Bodirsky, M., Knäuer, S., Starke, F.: ASNP: a tame fragment of existential second-order logic. In: Anselmo, M., Della Vedova, G., Manea, F., Pauly, A. (eds.) CiE 2020. LNCS, vol. 12098, pp. 149–162. Springer, Cham (2020). https://doi.org/10.1007/978-3-030-51466-2_13
7. Bulatov, A.A.: A dichotomy theorem for nonuniform CSPs. In: 58th IEEE Annual Symposium on Foundations of Computer Science, FOCS, pp. 319–330. IEEE Computer Society (2017). https://doi.org/10.1109/FOCS.2017.37
8. Feder, T., Vardi, M.Y.: The computational structure of monotone monadic SNP and constraint satisfaction: a study through datalog and group theory. SIAM J. Comput. **28**(1), 57–104 (1998). https://doi.org/10.1137/S0097539794266766
9. Feder, T., Vardi, M.Y.: Homomorphism closed vs. existential positive. In: 18th IEEE Symposium on Logic in Computer Science (LICS 2003), pp. 311–320. IEEE Computer Society (2003). https://doi.org/10.1109/LICS.2003.1210071
10. Hell, P.: Graph partitions with prescribed patterns. Eur. J. Comb. **35**, 335–353 (2014). https://doi.org/10.1016/j.ejc.2013.06.043
11. Ladner, R.E.: On the structure of polynomial time reducibility. J. ACM **22**(1), 155–171 (1975). https://doi.org/10.1145/321864.321877
12. Madelaine, F.R.: Universal structures and the logic of forbidden patterns. Log. Methods Comput. Sci. **5**(2) (2009). https://doi.org/10.2168/LMCS-5(2:13)2009
13. Pippenger, N., Fischer, M.J.: Relations among complexity measures. J. ACM **26**(2), 361–381 (1979). https://doi.org/10.1145/322123.322138
14. Zhuk, D.: A proof of the CSP dichotomy conjecture. J. ACM **67**(5), 1–78 (2020). https://doi.org/10.1145/3402029

Turning Block-Sequential Automata Networks into Smaller Parallel Networks with Isomorphic Limit Dynamics

Pacôme Perrotin[1,2(✉)] and Sylvain Sené[1,2]

[1] Université publique, Marseille, France
pacome.perrotin@gmail.com
[2] Aix-Marseille Univ., CNRS, LIS, Marseille, France

Abstract. We state an algorithm that, given an automata network and a block-sequential update schedule, produces an automata network of the same size or smaller with the same limit dynamics under the parallel update schedule. Then, we focus on the family of automata cycles which share a unique path of automata, called tangential cycles, and show that a restriction of our algorithm allows to reduce any instance of these networks under a block-sequential update schedule into a smaller parallel network of the family and to characterize the number of reductions operated while conserving their limit dynamics. We also show that any tangential cycles reduced by our main algorithm are transformed into a network whose size is that of the largest cycle of the initial network. We end by showing that the restricted algorithm allows the direct characterization of block-sequential double cycles as parallel ones.

1 Introduction

Automata networks are classically used to model gene regulatory networks [9,16] [2,4,10]. In these applications the dynamics of automata networks help to understand how the biological systems might evolve. As such, there is motivation in improving our computation and characterization of automata networks dynamics. This problem is a difficult one to approach considering the vast diversity of network structures, local functions and update schedules that are studied. Rather than considering the problem in general, we look for families or properties which allow for simpler dynamics that we might be able to characterize [7,8].

We are interested in studying the limit dynamics of automata networks, that is, the limit cycles and fixed points that they adopt over time, notably since these asymptotic behaviors of the underlying dynamical systems may correspond to real biological phenomenologies such as the genetic expression patterns of cellular types, tissues, or paces. More precisely, we are less interested in the possible configurations themselves than in the information that is being transfered and computed in networks over time. As such, given families of networks, one of our objectives is to count the fixed points and limit cycles they possess.

In this paper, we provide an algorithm that, given an automata network and a block-sequential update schedule, produces an automata network of the

G. Della Vedova et al. (Eds.): CiE 2023, LNCS 13967, pp. 214–228, 2023.
https://doi.org/10.1007/978-3-031-36978-0_18

same size or smaller with isomorphic limit dynamics under the parallel update schedule. After definitions in Sect. 2, this algorithm is detailed in Sect. 3. In Sect. 4, the feasibility of the algorithm on *Tangential Cycles* (TC) is studied, a TC being a set of cycles that intersect on a shared path of automata.

Why Focusing on TCs? Cycles are fundamental retroactive patterns that are necessary to observe complex dynamics [14]. They are present in many biological regulation networks [17] and are perfectly understood in isolation [6,12]. In theory, cycles generate an exponential amount of limit cycles, which is incoherent with the observed behavior of biological systems [9]. The only way to reduce the amount of limit cycles is to constrain the degrees of freedom induced by isolated cycles, which can only be done by intersecting cycles from the purely structural standpoint. This leads us naturally to TCs, as a simple intersection case. Double cycles (intersections of two isolated cycles) in particular are the largest family of intersecting cycles for which a complete characterization exists [5,12]; the present paper generalizes this result to block-sequential update schedules. Moreover, from the biological standpoint, double cycles are also observed in biological regulation networks, in which they seem to serve as inhibitors of their limit behavior [3].

2   Definitions

Let Σ be a finite alphabet. We denote by Σ^n the set of all words of size n over the alphabet Σ, such that for all $1 \leq i \leq n$ and $x \in \Sigma^n$, x_i is the ith letter of that word. An *automata network (AN)* is a function $F : \Sigma^n \to \Sigma^n$, where n is the size of the network. A configuration of F is a word over Σ^n. The global function F can be divided into functions that are local to each automaton: $\forall k, f_k : \Sigma^n \to \Sigma$, and the global function can be redefined as the parallel application of every local function: $\forall 1 \leq i \leq n, F(x)_i = f_i(x)$. For convenience, the set of automata $\{1, \ldots, n\}$ is denoted by S, and will sometimes be considered as a set of letters rather than numbers. For questions of complexity, we consider that *local functions are always encoded as circuits*.

For (i, j) any pair of automata, i is said to *influence* j if and only if there exists a configuration $x \in \Sigma^n$ in which there exists a state change of i that changes the state of $f_j(x)$. More formally, i influences j if and only if there exists $x, x' \in \Sigma^n$ such that $\forall k, x_k = x'_k \Leftrightarrow k \neq i$ and $f_j(x) \neq f_j(x')$.

It is common to represent an automata network F as the digraph with its automata as nodes so that (i, j) is an edge if and only if i influences j. This digraph is called the *interaction digraph* and is denoted by $G_I(F) = (S, E)$, with E the set of edges. The automata network described in Example 1 is illustrated as an interaction digraph in Fig. 1.

Example 1. Let $F : \mathbb{B}^3 \to \mathbb{B}^3$ be an AN with local functions

$$f_a(x) = \neg x_b \vee x_c$$
$$f_b(x) = x_a$$
$$f_c(x) = \neg x_b$$

Fig. 1. Interaction digraph of the AN detailed in Example 1.

An *update schedule* is an infinite sequence of non-empty subsets of S, called blocks. Such a sequence describes in which order the local functions are to be applied to update the network, and there are uncountably infinitely many of them. A *periodic update schedule* is an infinite periodic sequence of non-empty subsets of S, which we directly define by its period. The application of an update schedule on a configuration of a network is the parallel application of the local functions of the subsets in the sequence, each subset being applied one after the other.

For example, the sequence $\pi = (S)$ is the parallel update schedule. It is periodic, and its application on a configuration is undistinguishable from the application of F. The sequence $(\{1\}, \ldots, \{n\})$ is also a periodic update schedule, and implies the application of every local function in order, one at a time.

Formally, the application of a periodic update schedule Δ to a configuration $x \in \Sigma^n$ is denoted by the function F_Δ, and is defined as the composition of the applications of the local functions in the order specified by Δ. For any subset $X \subseteq S$, updating X into x is denoted by $F_X(x)$ and is defined as

$$\forall i \in S, \ F_X(x)_i = \begin{cases} f_i(x) & \text{if } i \in X \\ x_i & \text{otherwise} \end{cases}.$$

Example 2 provides an example of the execution of the network detailed in Example 1 under some non-trivial update schedule.

Example 2. Let $\Delta = (\{b, c\}, \{a\}, \{a, b\})$ be a periodic update schedule, and let $x = 000$ be an initial configuration. For F the AN detailed in Example 1, we have that:

$$F_\Delta(000) = (F_{\{a,b\}} \circ F_{\{a\}} \circ F_{\{b,c\}})(000)$$
$$= (F_{\{a,b\}} \circ F_{\{a\}})(001)$$
$$= F_{\{a,b\}}(101) = 111.$$

A *block-sequential update schedule* is a periodic update schedule where all the subsets in a period form a partition of S; that is, every automaton is updated exactly once in the sequence. If every subset in the sequence is of cardinality 1, the update schedule is said to be sequential. For any AN with automata S, both the parallel update schedule and the $|S|!$ different sequential update schedules are block-sequential. Block-sequential update schedules are *fair* update schedules, in the sense that applying it updates each automaton the same amount of times.

The application of a block-sequential update schedule on an AN can be otherwise represented as an update digraph, introduced in [1,15]. For F an AN

Fig. 2. Update digraph of the AN detailed in Example 1, for $\Delta = (\{a\}, \{b\}, \{c\})$.

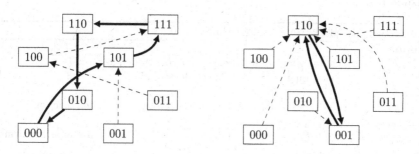

Fig. 3. Two dynamics of the AN F detailed in Example 1. On the left, the dynamics of F under the parallel update schedule. On the right, the dynamics of F under the update schedule $\Delta = (\{a\}, \{b\}, \{c\})$. The limit dynamics are depicted with bold arrows.

and Δ a block-sequential update schedule, the *update digraph* of F_Δ, denoted by $G_U(F_\Delta)$, is an annotation of the network's interaction digraph, where any edge (u, v) is annotated with $<$ if u is updated strictly before v in Δ, and with $\geqslant$ otherwise. An update digraph of the AN detailed in Example 1 is illustrated in Fig. 2.

Given an automata network F and a periodic update schedule Δ, we define the *dynamics* of F_Δ as the digraph with all configurations $x \in \Sigma^n$ as nodes, so that (x, y) is an edge of the dynamics if and only if $F_\Delta(x) = y$. We call *limit cycle of length k* any sequence of unique configurations $(x_1, x_2, \ldots, x_k)$ such that $F_\Delta(x_i) = x_{i+1}$ for all $1 \leq i < k$, and $F_\Delta(x_k) = x_1$. A limit cycle of length one is called a *fixed point*. The *limit dynamics* of F_Δ is the subgraph which contains only the limit cycles and the fixed points of the dynamics. The limit dynamics of the network defined in Example 1 are emphasized in Fig. 3.

Since the dynamics of a network is a graph that is exponential in size relative to the number of its automaton, naively computing the limit dynamics of a family of network is a computationally expensive process.

3 The Algorithm

In this section, we look at an algorithm that can turn any automata network F with a block-sequential update schedule Δ into another automata network F', such that the limit dynamics of F_Δ stays isomorphic to the limit dynamics of F' under the parallel update schedule π. Furthermore, the size of F' will always be the size of F, or *less*.

This algorithm is built from two parts: first, we parallelize the network thanks to a known algorithm in the folklore of automata networks. Second, we remove automata from the networks based on redundancies created in the first step.

First, let us state the usual algorithm that, given an automata network F and a block-sequential update schedule Δ, provides a new automata network F' defined on the same set of automata, such that F_Δ and F'_π have the same exact dynamics.

Algorithm 1. Parallelization algorithm of F_Δ

Input
    F local functions of a network over S, encoded as circuits
    Δ block-sequential update schedule over S
Output
    F local functions of a parallel network over S, encoded as circuits
for (u,v) such that u precedes v in Δ **do**
    apply the substitution $x_u \mapsto \theta_u$ in f_v $\triangleright$ θ is a temporary symbol
let $X \leftarrow S$
while $|X| > 0$ **do**
    let $s \in X$ such that f_s contains no θ symbol
    $X \leftarrow X \setminus \{s\}$
    for $s' \in X$ **do**
        if $f_{s'}$ contains θ_s **then**
            apply the substitution $\theta_s \mapsto f_s$ in $f_{s'}$
    return F

Algorithm 1 proceeds with two waves of subsitutions. First, for every $<$-edge $(u, <, v)$, the influencing automaton u is replaced in the local function of v by a token symbol θ_u. All of these token symbols are then replaced by the corresponding local functions (in this case, f_u) in the correct order: that is, no function is ever used in a substitution if it contains a token character. This way, even if the network contains a complex tree of $<$-edges, the substitutions will be applied in the correct order. It holds that this algorithm always returns, and runs in polynomial time.

Property 1. Algorithm 1 always returns, and does so in polynomial time.

Sketch of Proof. There are no $<$-edge loop in the update digraph by definition, and so the algorithm always ends. Encoding local functions as circuits lets us do all needed substitutions in a straightforward way without increasing the size of the resulting circuits beyond the size of the input.

Proof. Let us denote by $<$-*graph* the subset of the graph $G_U(F_\Delta)$ where only the $<$-edges have been preserved. The $<$-graph of F_Δ is always a tree (or multiple disconnected trees): if this wasn't the case, there would be a cycle of $<$-edges in $G_U(F_\Delta)$, which would mean a cycle of automata that are all updated strictly before their out-neighbor, which is impossible.

Algorithm 1 will place a θ symbol for every edge in the $<$-graph. In the second loop, the selected s is always a leaf of one of the trees contained in the $<$-graph. The applied substitution removes that leaf from the $<$-graph. By the structure of a tree, all the $<$-edges will be removed and the algorithm terminates.

To see that this algorithm can be performed in polynomial time, consider that all of the local functions are encoded as circuits. As such, it is enough to prepare a copy of each local function into one large circuit, on which every substitution will be performed. Any substitution $x_u \mapsto \theta_u$ is performed by renaming the corresponding input gate. Any substitution $\theta_s \mapsto f_s(x)$ is performed by replacing the input gate which corresponds to θ_s by a connection to the output gate of the circuit that computes the local function f_s. These substitutions are performed for every $<$-edge in the update digraph of F_Δ, which can be done by doing one substitution for every pair in the partial order provided by Δ, which is never more than n^2. The resulting circuit is then duplicated for every automaton in the output network, which leads to a total size of no more than k^2, for k the size of the input.   □

Remark 1. This algorithm is not polynomial if the local functions are encoded as formulæ, which is a detail often overlooked in the literature where this parallelization algorithm is always assumed to be polynomial.

Theorem 1. *For any F_Δ Algorithm 1 returns a network F' such that the dynamics of F_Δ is equal to that of F'_π.*

Sketch of Proof. Substitution of the form $x_u \mapsto f_u(x)$ in the local function f_v is equivalent to the presence of a $<$-edge $(u, <, v)$ in the update digraph of the network; in both cases, v is updated using $f_u(x)$ instead of x_u. Altogether this means that both F_Δ and F'_π are the same function.

Proof. Let us consider some configuration $x \in \Sigma^n$, and let us compute its image x' in both systems. Let us consider the initial block X_0 in Δ. For any automaton in X_0, its local function is untouched in F', and thus $F_\Delta(x)|_{X_0} = F'(x)|_{X_0}$. Suppose that $F_\Delta(x)|_{X_0 \cup \ldots \cup X_k} = F'(x)|_{X_0 \cup \ldots \cup X_k}$ for some k, let us prove that is true when including the next block X_{k+1}.

Let $v \in X_{k+1}$. By the nature of updates in Δ, f_v will be updated using the values in $F_\Delta(x)$ for any x_u such that $u \in X_0 \cup \ldots \cup X_k$, and in x otherwise. In F', in the local function f'_v and for any $u \in X_0 \cup \ldots \cup X_k$ that influences v, a substitution has replaced x_u by $f'_u(x)$, which implies that the value of v will be updated using a value of u in $F'(x)$. Pulling this together, we obtain that $f_v(x) = f'_v(x)$ and $F_\Delta(x)|_{X_0 \cup \ldots \cup X_{k+1}} = F'(x)|_{X_0 \cup \ldots \cup X_{k+1}}$, and the recurrence yields $F_\Delta(x) = F'(x)$ for any x.   □

Algorithm 2 is our contribution to this process, and removes automata that are not necessary for the limit dynamics of the network. It proceeds in two steps: first, the algorithm identifies pairs of automata with equivalent local functions, up to some function. In other terms, if one automaton u can be computed as a function g of the local function of another automaton v, then u is not necessary

---

Algorithm 2. Parallelization algorithm of F_Δ, with a possible reduction in size

---

Input
    F local functions of a network over S, encoded as circuits
    Δ update schedule over S

Output
    F local functions of a parallel network over a subset of S,
                   encoded as circuits

let $F' \leftarrow$ apply Algorithm 1 to F_Δ
let $G_I(F') \leftarrow$ the interaction digraph of F'
for $(u, v) \in S^2$ **do**
    if $\forall x \in \Sigma^n, f_u(x) = g(f_v(x))$ **then**   ▷ for some $g : \Sigma \to \Sigma$
        for $(u, w) \in E(G_I(F'))$ **do**
                 apply the substitution $x_u \mapsto g(x_v)$ in f_w
while $\exists u \in S$ such that u has no accessible neighbor in G'_I **do**
    $S \leftarrow S \setminus \{u\}$ ▷ u is removed from the network
  return F'

---

and all references to x_u in the network can be replaced by $g(x_v)$ for an identical result. Of course, this only works under the hypothesis that u and v are updated synchronously, which is the case after the application of Algorithm 1. Second, the algorithm iteratively removes any automaton that has no influence in the network, that is, that has no accessible neighbor in the interaction graph of the network. These automata are not part of cycles and do not lead to cycles, and as such have no impact on the attractors.

Algorithm 2 is non-deterministic, and when the local functions of any pair of automata (u, v) are shown to be equivalent up to some reversible function $g : \Sigma \to \Sigma$, either automata could replace the influence of the other without preference. As such, more than one result network is possible, but all are equivalent in their limit dynamics, as will be shown later.

While it is clear that Algorithm 2 always terminates, its complexity is out of the deterministic polynomial range, as applying it implies solving the coNP-complete decision problem of testing if two Boolean formulæ are equal for all possible pairs of automata and for every possible function $g : \Sigma \to \Sigma$. As such, a polynomial implementation of this algorithm would (at least) imply $P = NP$. This drastic conclusion is softened when looking at restricted classes of networks where redundancies can be easily pointed out, which is the case for the rest of the paper.

Theorem 2. *For any F_Δ, Algorithm 2 returns a network F' such that the limit dynamics of F_Δ and F'_π are isomorphic.*

Sketch of Proof. The local transformations operated by the algorithm preserve the limit dynamics of the network, from which the result naturally follows.

Proof. By Theorem 1, the network F' returned by the application of Algorithm 1 to F_Δ has identical dynamics to F_Δ.

Algorithm 2 operates two kinds of modifications.

The first operation is replacing the influence of any automaton u by another automaton v if they are found to have equivalent local function up to some $g : \Sigma \to \Sigma$, that is, $f_u = g \circ f_v$. For any configuration x, the value of $f_u(x)$ and $g(f_v(x))$ are always equal. Thus, substituting the variable x_u by $g(x_v)$ in the local functions of every out-neighbor of u will lead to an identical limit behavior. After this substitution, the automaton u does not have any influence over the network. Moreover, all its previous out-neighbors in $G_I(F')$ are now the out-neighbors of v.

The second operation is iteratively removing automata that do not influence any automaton. Let u be such an deleted automaton. Consider a limit cycle $(x^1, x^2, \ldots, x^k)$ in G. By definition of a limit cycle, $G(x^i) = x^{i+1}$ for any i, $G(x^k) = x^1$, and $x^i = x^j \implies i = j$. Consider the component x_u^i for some i. Since u does not influence any automaton, x^{i+1} is a function of $x^i|_{S \setminus \{u\}}$. As the entire sequence is aperiodic, the sequence of the subconfigurations $x^i|_{S \setminus \{u\}}$ is also aperiodic, and the attractor is preserved in F'.   □

4   Reductions in Size of Tangential Cycles

In this section, we characterize the reduction in size that our algorithm provides on a specific family of networks. We call *tangential cycles* (TC) any AN composed of any number of cycles $\{C_1, C_2, \ldots, C_k\}$ such that a unique path of automata, called the *tangent*, is shared by all of the cycles. The first automaton of the tangent is the only automaton with more than one in-neighbor, and is called the *central automaton*. A TC is represented as part of Fig. 4, which contains three cycles and a tangent of length 0 (only one node is shared between the cycles).

4.1   Reducing Block-Sequential TCs

The reduction in size provided by Algorithm 2 can be quite large on TCs, as even TCs updated in parallel can be reduced in size by merging the different cycles as much as possible. As such, the reduction power of this algorithm is greater than just removing the redundancies inherent to the block-sequential to parallel update translation. Indeed, Fig. 4 provides an example of a parallel TC, the size of which is greatly reduced by the application of Algorithm 2. But, by this process, the final result of Algorithm 2 is no longer a TC.

As explained above, TCs are studied as the next simplest cases of complex ANs that make biological sense, after automata cycles. Both isolated cycles and double cycles are examples of TCs. To show that the study of TCs under block-sequential update schedules can be directly reduced to the study of TCs under the parallel update schedule, we provide an algorithm that transforms any TC under a block-sequential update schedule into a TC under the parallel update schedule, such that their limit dynamics are isomorphic, and the local functions of their central automaton equivalent. This is done by simply stopping the process of Algorithm 2 earlier to preserve the TC shape of the network.

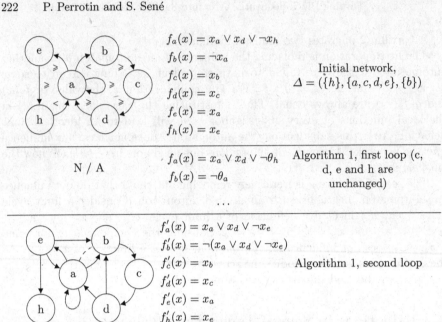

$$f_a(x) = x_a \lor x_d \lor \neg x_h$$
$$f_b(x) = \neg x_a$$
$$f_c(x) = x_b$$
$$f_d(x) = x_c$$
$$f_e(x) = x_a$$
$$f_h(x) = x_e$$

Initial network,
$\Delta = (\{h\}, \{a, c, d, e\}, \{b\})$

N / A

$$f_a(x) = x_a \lor x_d \lor \neg \theta_h$$
$$f_b(x) = \neg \theta_a$$

Algorithm 1, first loop (c, d, e and h are unchanged)

...

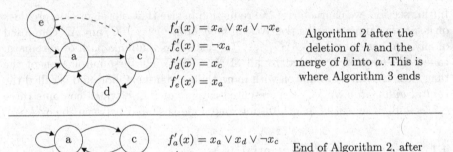

$$f'_a(x) = x_a \lor x_d \lor \neg x_e$$
$$f'_b(x) = \neg(x_a \lor x_d \lor \neg x_e)$$
$$f'_c(x) = x_b$$
$$f'_d(x) = x_c$$
$$f'_e(x) = x_a$$
$$f'_h(x) = x_e$$

Algorithm 1, second loop

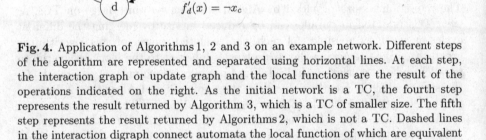

$$f'_a(x) = x_a \lor x_d \lor \neg x_e$$
$$f'_c(x) = \neg x_a$$
$$f'_d(x) = x_c$$
$$f'_e(x) = x_a$$

Algorithm 2 after the deletion of h and the merge of b into a. This is where Algorithm 3 ends

$$f'_a(x) = x_a \lor x_d \lor \neg x_c$$
$$f'_c(x) = x_a$$
$$f'_d(x) = \neg x_c$$

End of Algorithm 2, after the merge of e into c

Fig. 4. Application of Algorithms 1, 2 and 3 on an example network. Different steps of the algorithm are represented and separated using horizontal lines. At each step, the interaction graph or update graph and the local functions are the result of the operations indicated on the right. As the initial network is a TC, the fourth step represents the result returned by Algorithm 3, which is a TC of smaller size. The fifth step represents the result returned by Algorithms 2, which is not a TC. Dashed lines in the interaction digraph connect automata the local function of which are equivalent up to a negation. Only the first graph is represented as an update digraph, as all the other networks are updated in parallel.

Algorithm 3. Parallelization algorithm of a TC F under the block-sequential update schedule Δ, with a possible reduction in size

---

Input
    F local functions of a network over S, encoded as circuits
    Δ update schedule over S
Output
    F' local functions of a parallel network over a subset of S,
            encoded as circuits
let $F' \leftarrow$ apply Algorithm 1 to F_Δ
let $G_I(F') \leftarrow$ the interaction digraph of F'
for $(u,v) \in S^2$, such that either u or v has more than one in-neighbor in $G_I(F')$ **do**
    if $\forall x \in \Sigma^n, f_u(x) = g(f_v(x))$ **then** $\triangleright$ for some $g : \Sigma \to \Sigma$
        for $(u,w) \in E(G_I(F'))$ **do**
            apply the substitution $x_u \mapsto g(x_v)$ in f_w
for $u \in S$ **do**
    if u has no accessible neighbors in $G_I(F')$ **then**
        $S \leftarrow S \setminus \{u\}$ $\triangleright$ u is removed from the network
return F'

The only difference between Algorithms 2 and 3 is that the latter restricts the reductions it operates. If two local functions are found to be equivalent up to some function g, Algorithm 3 removes a node if and only if these local functions are duplicates of the previous local function of the central automaton of the network. Removing duplications of any function that is part of a cycle would merge two cycles and the network would no longer be tangential cycles, in a way that is harder to count the reductions for. Since Algorithm 3 is a variation of Algorithm 2 that only does less reductions, Theorem 2 still applies in its case. An application of Algorithms 2 and 3 is illustrated in Fig. 4 and the difference between the algorithms is highlighted.

Theorem 3. *Let F be a TC and Δ a block-sequential update schedule. The amount of reductions in size that Algorithm 3 operates on F_Δ is the number of $<$-edges in the update digraph of F_Δ, and the result is a TC.*

Sketch of Proof. We show that in a TC, all the local transformations operated by the algorithm result in the removal of exactly one automaton, and that those transformations locally preserve the structure of the TC.

Proof. Algorithm 1 operates a substitution for every $<$-edge in the update digraph of F_Δ. In this proof, we will show that each of the possible transformations implies the removal of exactly one node from the network.

For any such edge $(u, <, v)$, there are two cases. Either u is the central automaton, or not. In any case, $u \neq v$ since the contrary would imply that an automaton is updated strictly before itself.

If we suppose that u is the central automaton, this means that f_v is a local function that only depends on x_u. It can thus be written $f_v(x) = g(x_u)$ for some $g : \Sigma \to \Sigma$. After the application of Algorithm 1, we thus obtain $f_v(x) = g(f_u(x))$, which implies the removal of either u or v (but at this point, not both) by Algorithm 3.

If we suppose that u is not the central automaton, this means that f_v is an arbitrary formula which contains x_u, and f_u is a function of the form $f_u(x) = g(x_w)$ for some g and some $w \in S$. Note that $w \neq u$ by the hypothesis that F is a TC, either w is the previous automaton in the path, or it is the central automaton v. As such, applying Algorithm 1 substitutes any mention of x_u in f_v by $g(x_w)$. Previously, u only had one accessible neighbor, as it was part of a path connecting to the central automaton. This leaves x_u without any accessible neighbors in the interaction digraph of F, which means that it is removed by Algorithm 3. If the removed edge is part of a cycle, this means that this cycle will be reduced in size. If the edge is part of the tangent, this means that the tangent will be reduced in size.

We thus obtain that the number of reductions is at least the number of <-edges in the update digraph of the network. Suppose now that some extra automaton u is removed on top of any <-edge related reduction. First observe that if u has no accessible neighbor, it must have had none from before the application of Algorithm 1, since in none of the two cases are external automaton disconnected from each other. Now suppose that f_u is equivalent to some f_v up to some g. Neither u nor v can be the central automaton, as any duplication of that function is handled in the first case. This proves that the number of reductions is exactly the number of <-edges in the update digraph of (F, Δ).

Let us now show that the result of Algorithm 3 is a TC. If the initial network had a central automata, there still exists a unique central automata at the end of the algorithm, even if the original central automata was removed in a chosen reduction. Paths that exit the central automata in the previous network still exit the central automata in the result, in the same number, and still share some tangent. The paths can be smaller in size, as well as the tangent, but they still end in the central automata.   □

If Algorithm 2 cannot be polynomial in the worst case under the hypothesis that P $\neq$ NP, Algorithm 3 can be simplified to the following rule: taking a TC with a block-sequential update schedule, we obtain the equivalent parallel TC by reducing each cycle by the number of <-edges that its update digraph contains. This process is quadratic, since we only need to check the possible <-edges defined by the partial order defined by Δ, which are no more than n^2.

4.2   Reducing Parallel Boolean TCs Further

Applying Algorithm 2 to its full extent to a Boolean TC (That is, a TC defined over the Boolean alphabet) may result in a larger reduction in size. As any automaton that is not the central one has a unary function as its local function, any pair of non-central local functions is equivalent up to some $g : \Sigma \to \Sigma$ if they are influenced by the same automaton. For example, if the central automaton influences three other automata that represent the start of three chains, these three automata can be merged into one. Continuing this zipping process yields a final network only as large as the longest cycle of the initial TC.

This process is not straightforward for non-Boolean TCs, as the local functions along the chains can be non-reversible using modular arithmetics, for example. Optimizing these networks is still possible, but requires a more complex set of substitutions to do so. It has been proven in general using modules and output functions [13]. The following theorem corresponds to the Boolean case, proven with more classical means. An example of its application is illustrated in the two last steps of Fig. 4.

Theorem 4. *Let F be a Boolean TC. Applying Algorithm 2 to F_π generates a network F' whose size is that of the largest cycle in F.*

Sketch of Proof. All the cycles composing F are merged together in a 'zipping' transformation.

Proof. Starting from the initial TC F, all of the automata directly influenced by the automata at the end of the tangent u (but that are not u) have local functions $f_v(x) = g(x_u), f_w(x) = h(x_u), \ldots$ for $g, h, \ldots : \Sigma = \{0, 1\} \to \Sigma$. All these functions $g, h, \ldots$ are not constant functions, since the automata that they represent are influenced by an automaton by hypothesis. Thus, they can only be defined as the identity or the negation of x_u. As a consequence, all but one of these automata will be removed by the algorithm as they are all equivalent up to some g.

This same argument can be repeated by taking all the automata influenced by the only automaton resulting from the previous iteration, excluding the central automaton. At each step, all of the automata at the same distance from the central automaton are merged. Hence, at the end of this process, whatever the choices made for merging automata along the iterative process, the resulting AN will be composed of k automata, with k the length of the largest cycle of F. □

5 An Application: Disjunctive Double Cycles

As an application of this algorithm and as an example to the algorithm's capacities to reduce the size of the provided network, we turn to the family of disjunctive double cycles. Notice that the result still holds for conjunctive double cycles since conjuctive and disjunctive cycles have isomorphic dynamics [11,12].

In disjunctive automata networks, an edge (u, v) is signed positively if the x_u appears as a positive variable in f_v. An edge (u, v) is signed negatively if x_u appears as a negative variable in f_v. A cycle is said to be positive if it contains an even number of negative edges, and negative otherwise.

A *disjunctive double cycle* is an automata network with an interaction digraph that is composed of two automata cycles that intersect in one automaton. The local function of this central automaton is a disjunctive clause. This family of networks is very simple to define, and is a simple and intuitive next step after the family of Boolean automata cycles, which are composed of a single cycle.

Both families have been characterized under the parallel update schedule [7, 12]; that is to say, given basic parameters concerning the size of the cycles, their sign, and any integer k, an explicit formula (defined as a polynomially computable function) has been given among other to count the number of limit cycles of size k of such networks under the parallel update schedule. In this section, we extend this characterization to the block-sequential equivalents by showing how applying our algorithm reduces the network to a smaller instance of the same family of networks.

Furthermore, as Boolean automata cycles and disjunctive double cycles are TCs, our method can be simplified to the simple following rules: given a TC F, a block-sequential update schedule Δ, count the number of $<$-edges in the update digraph $G_U(F_\Delta)$; for every cycle, substract to its size the number of such edges it contains, while keeping its sign; the final network, under the parallel update schedule, and the initial network under Δ have isomorphic limit dynamics. This is a simple application of Theorem 3, and of the rule of thumb deduced from Algorithm 3.

We denote by $DC(s, s', a, b)$ the disjunctive double cycles with cycle sizes a, b and signs s, s'.

Theorem 5. *Let $D = DC(s, s', a, b)$ be disjunctive double cycles, Δ a block-sequential update schedule. For A (B respectively) the number of $<$-edges on the cycle of size a (b respectively) in $G_U(F_\Delta)$, the limit dynamics of D_Δ is isomorphic to that of D'_π, where $D' = DC(s, s', a - A, b - B)$.*

Proof. This is a straightforward application of Theorem 3.   □

6   Conclusion

In this paper we provide a novel algorithm which allows the reduction in size of automata networks, in particular by passing the network from a block-sequential to a parallel update schedule, while keeping isomorphic limit dynamics. While this algorithm is too computationally expensive for the general case, we study the specific family of intersection of automata cycles, on which this algorithm is easily applied. This study allows the discovery that all block-sequential tangential cycles have isomorphic limit dynamics to parallel tangential cycles. Finally, we apply this fact to Boolean automata double cycles to characterize their behavior under block-sequential update schedules.

It seems now clear to us that the difference between the parallel update schedule and block-sequential update schedules is that the latter changes the timing of the information along sections of the network. In particular, structures such as tangential cycles can be directly translated into an equivalent parallel network with shorter cycles. We are interested in seeing what effects this translation could have in a more general set of families of networks, and if there exists other families in which block-sequential update schedules lead to equivalent parallel networks which are still part of the family.

As a perspective, we would like to characterize more redundancies that can be removed from networks to help with the computation of their dynamics. For example, we are currently interested in more complex compositions of automata cycles, and have already found equivalences that show that many networks are equivalent in their limit dynamics where complex parts of automata networks can be moved alongside cycles without affecting the network's limit dynamics.

Isolated paths are also a strong candidate for size reduction. Isolated paths are paths that lead from cycles to other cycles but can only be crossed once. Our current algorithms conserve such paths, despite it being possible to reduce them completely without changing the limit dynamics of the network in many cases, for example when an isolated path is the only way to go from one part to another. We have to be careful when multiple isolated paths exit from and join onto the same parts, as the synchronicity of the information in the entire network must be preserved.

Acknowledgment. This work has been partially funded by ANR-18-CE40-0002 FANs project (PP & SS), ECOS-Sud CE19E02 SyDySy project (PP & SS), and STIC-AmSud 22-STIC-02 CAMA project (SS).

References

1. Aracena, J., Goles, E., Moreira, A., Salinas, L.: On the robustness of update schedules in Boolean networks. Biosystems **97**, 1–8 (2009)
2. Davidich, M.I., Bornholdt, S.: Boolean network model predicts cell cycle sequence of fission yeast. PLoS ONE **3**, e1672 (2008)
3. Demongeot, J., Elena, A., Noual, M., Sené, S., Thuderoz, F.: "Immunetworks", intersecting circuits and dynamics. J. Theor. Biol. **280**, 18–33 (2011)
4. Demongeot, J., Goles, E., Morvan, M., Noual, M., Sené, S.: Attraction basins as gauges of robustness against boundary conditions in biological complex systems. PLoS ONE **5**, e11793 (2010)
5. Demongeot, J., Melliti, T., Noual, M., Regnault, D., Sené, S.: Boolean automata isolated cycles and tangential double-cycles dynamics. In: Adamatzky, A. (ed.) Automata and complexity: Essays Presented to Eric Goles on the Occasion of His 70th Birthday of Emergence, Complexity, Computation, vol. 42, pp. 145–178. Springer, Cham (2022). https://doi.org/10.1007/978-3-030-92551-2_11
6. Demongeot, J., Noual, M., Sené, S.: On the number of attractors of positive and negative Boolean automata circuits. In: Proceedings of WAINA'10, pp. 782–789. IEEE Press (2010)
7. Demongeot, J., Noual, M., Sené, S.: Combinatorics of Boolean automata circuits dynamics. Discr. Appl. Math. **160**, 398–415 (2012)
8. Gao, Z., Chen, X., Başar, T.: Stability structures of conjunctive Boolean networks. Automatica **89**, 8–20 (2018)
9. Kauffman, S.A.: Metabolic stability and epigenesis in randomly constructed genetic nets. J. Theor. Biol. **22**, 437–467 (1969)
10. Mendoza, L., Alvarez-Buylla, E.R.: Dynamics of the genetic regulatory network for Arabidopsis thaliana flower morphogenesis. J. Theor. Biol. **193**, 307–319 (1998)

11. Noual, M.: Dynamics of circuits and intersecting circuits. In: Dediu, A.-H., Martín-Vide, C. (eds.) LATA 2012. LNCS, vol. 7183, pp. 433–444. Springer, Heidelberg (2012). https://doi.org/10.1007/978-3-642-28332-1_37
12. Noual, M.: Updating automata networks. Ph.D. thesis, École Normale Supérieure de Lyon (2012)
13. Perrotin, P.: Simulation entre modèles de calcul naturel et modularité des réseaux d'automate. Ph.D. thesis, Aix-Marseile Université (2021)
14. Robert, F.: Itérations sur des ensembles Finis et automates cellulaires contractants. Linear Algebra Appl. **29**, 393–412 (1980)
15. Salinas, L.: Estudio de modelos discretos: estructura y dinámica. Ph.D. thesis, Universidad de Chile, Santiago, Chile (2008)
16. Thomas, R.: Boolean formalization of genetic control circuits. J. Theor. Biol. **42**, 563–585 (1973)
17. Thomas, R.: On the relation between the logical structure of systems and their ability to generate multiple steady states or sustained oscillations. In: Della Dora, J., Demongeot, J., Lacolle, B. (eds.) Numerical Methods in the Study of Critical Phenomena. Springer Series in Synergetics, vol. 9, pp. 180–193. Springer, Heidelberg (1981). https://doi.org/10.1007/978-3-642-81703-8_24

Interactive Proofs

Structural Complexity of Rational Interactive Proofs

Daniil Musatov[1,2,3] and Georgii Potapov[1(✉)]

[1] Moscow Institute of Physics and Technology, Dolgoprudny, Russia
`georgy.potapov.0@gmail.com`
[2] Russian Presidential Academy of National Economy and Public Administration,
Moscow, Russia
[3] Caucasus Mathematical Center at Adyghe State University, Maykop, Russia

Abstract. In 2012 P. D. Azar and S. Micali introduced a new model of interactive proofs, called "Rational Interactive Proofs". In this model the prover is neither honest nor malicious, but rational in terms of maximizing his expected reward. In this article we explore the connection of this area with classic complexity results.

In the first part of this article we revise the ties between the counting hierarchy and the hierarchy of constant-round rational proofs. We prove that a polynomial-time machine with oracle access to **DRMA**[k] decides exactly languages in **DRMA**[k], a coincidence unknown for levels of the counting hierarchy.

In the second part we study communication complexity of single-round rational proofs. We show that the class defined by logarithmic-communication single-round rational proofs coincides with **PP**. We also show that single-round rational protocols that treat problems in $\oplus$**P** as black-box samplers of a random variable require at least a linear number of bits of communication.

1 Introduction

Advances in computing technologies not only change our world, but also pave the way to new areas in theoretical computer science. Thus, in 1960s and 1970s emergence of full-scale computers led to evolvement of complexity theory and design of algorithms. Later, in 1980s and 1990s development of computer networks led to invention of interactive proofs and cryptographic protocols. In 2012 a new field that reflects commercial cloud computing was shaped, namely the field of rational interactive proofs.

In cloud computing, a client sends a computational task to a server and receives some response. How can the client be sure that the response is indeed the result of the requested computation? If the task is an **NP** problem, then the server may send a certificate verifiable by the client. But what if the task is harder? The main idea of rational proofs is to create economic incentives for the server to do the computation correctly. To this end, the standard model of interactive proofs is expanded by a polynomially computable probabilistic

G. Della Vedova et al. (Eds.): CiE 2023, LNCS 13967, pp. 231–245, 2023.
https://doi.org/10.1007/978-3-031-36978-0_19

reward paid by the client to the server. In order to maximize the expectation of this reward, the server reveals the correct answer.

Thus, while in standard interactive-proof and cryptographic models the prover may be either honest or malicious, here we consider a single type of the prover, the economically rational one. At the first glance, this does not change much for interactive proofs: the verifier may just pay 1 dollar for an accepted proof and 0 dollars for a rejected one. But things greatly change when we consider round and communication complexity. In our paper, we consider several concrete questions about them.

1.1 History and Related Literature

The area of interactive proofs was introduced in the works of Babai [4] (for public random bits) and Goldwasser, Micali and Rackoff [15] (for private random bits). Then Goldwasser and Sipser showed [16] that a protocol with private bits may be transformed to a 2 rounds longer protocol with public bits. Babai and Moran demonstrated [6] that the number of rounds in a public-bit protocol may be halved. Together these results prove that any language recognizable by a constant-round interactive proof system is in fact recognizable by a two-round public-bit protocol and thus lies in **AM** and hence in the second level of the polynomial hierarchy. The seminal result **IP** = **PSPACE** [19,21,22] showed that a polynomial number of rounds increases the class to **PSPACE**. The case of multiple provers was also analyzed, and it turned out that the respective class **MIP** is equal to **NEXP** [5,7,14].

Meanwhile, Wagner introduced [24] the counting hierarchy, an analog of the polynomial hierarchy, where the existential and universal quantifiers are replaced by majority quantifiers. The famous Toda's theorem [23] implies that the whole polynomial hierarchy lies in the second level of the counting hierarchy.

Interactive proofs and the counting hierarchy meet in the area of rational interactive proofs that was pioneered by Azar and Micali in [2]. They introduced the notion of a rational proof, defined the functional class **FRMA** and the decision class **DRMA** and proved that **DRMA** with constant round complexity equals the counting hierarchy, thus showing the difference from **IP** with constant rounds. On the other hand, if the number of rounds is polynomial, then the respective class, denoted by **RIP**, is still equal to **PSPACE**.

The subsequent analysis went in several directions. Firstly, the concept of rational proofs was also expanded to the case of multiple provers. Since the payoffs of the provers are mutually dependent, the provers play some game with each other and the result depends on the rules of this game. Chen, McCauley and Singh consider both cooperative [10] and non-cooperative [12] approaches and show that the respective classes are not only wider than **RIP** but also wider than **MIP** (the exact characterization depends on fine details of the model). Thus, rationality expands the class of recognizable languages for several provers.

Secondly, various models with computationally limited prover and/or verifier were considered. Azar and Micali introduce [1,3] super-efficient rational proofs, where the verifier is logarithmically time-bounded and the honest prover need not do more computation than to solve the problem. They characterize in these terms classes $\mathbf{TC}^0$, $\mathbf{P}^{\|\mathrm{NP}}$ and $\mathbf{P}^{\|\mathrm{MA}}$. They also show that the verifier needs only a polynomial budget: deviation from the optimal strategy leads to a considerable loss. Guo et al. [17] stepped from $\mathbf{TC}^0$ to $\mathbf{NC}^1$ and Chen, McCauley and Singh [11] improved the bounds for utility gaps. Campanelli and Gennaro constructed a sequentially composable protocol [8] and yet another space-efficient one [9]. Inasawa and Yasunaga explored [18] a variant where both prover and verifier are rational.

1.2   Exposition of the Results

In this paper we return to the original Azar-Micali framework and explore the relations between the counting and the $\mathbf{DRMA}$ hierarchies. In [2] it is shown that a language recognizable by a k-round rational proof lies somewhere between the kth and the $(2k+1)$st levels of the counting hierarchy. We try to shed light on whether these bounds are tight. Is it possible that the two hierarchies coincide?

We answer in the following way: either the hierarchies are different, or their coincidence would lead to resolving a long-time open question.

Result 1 (Corollary 3): $\mathbf{P}^{\mathbf{DRMA}[k]} = \mathbf{DRMA}[k]$.

On the contrary, the equality $\mathbf{P}^{C_k\mathbf{P}} = C_k\mathbf{P}$ is not known: for instance, by Toda's theorem $\mathbf{PH} \subset \mathbf{P}^{\mathbf{PP}}$, but the inclusion $\mathbf{PH} \subset \mathbf{PP}$ is not known.

The next two results show that the levels of the $\mathbf{DRMA}$ hierarchy relate to each other in a way similar, but not equivalent to the counting classes.

Result 2 (Theorem 5): $\mathbf{PP}^{\mathbf{DRMA}[k]} \subset \mathbf{DRMA}[k+1]$.

We do not know whether this inclusion holds as equality. On the contrary, $\mathbf{PP}^{C_k\mathbf{P}} = C_{k+1}\mathbf{P}$ is just the definition of $C_{k+1}\mathbf{P}$ and always holds.

We do not know either whether the equality $\mathbf{DRMA}[k] = \mathbf{DRMA}[k+1]$ implies $\mathbf{DRMA}[k+1] = \mathbf{DRMA}[k+2]$, but we show the following connection between collapses of the two hierarchies.

Result 3 (Corollary 5): If $\mathbf{DRMA}[k] = \mathbf{DRMA}[k+1]$, then the counting hierarchy collapses at most at the $(2k+1)$-st level.

Finally, we estimate the communication complexity of 1-round proofs.

Result 4 (Corollary 6): $\mathbf{PP}$ is equal to $\mathbf{DRMA}[1, O(\log n)]$, i.e., to $\mathbf{DRMA}$ with one round and $O(\log n)$ sent bits.

Thus the question of whether $\mathbf{PP} = \mathbf{DRMA}[1]$ is equivalent to the question whether a polynomial number of communicated bits expands the class compared to a logarithmic number. We also briefly discuss the connection between $\oplus\mathbf{P}$ and $\mathbf{DRMA}[1]$ and limitations of our methods.

1.3   Roadmap

In Sect. 2 we present formal definitions and basic facts about the counting hierarchy and rational proofs. Section 3 and 4 give an exposition of our results about the $\mathbf{DRMA}$ hierarchy and about communication complexity, respectively. In Sect. 5 we provide concluding remarks and pose some questions for further research. Some proofs are omitted and presented in the extended preprint [20].

2 Preliminaries

2.1 Counting Hierarchy

Firstly we remind some basic definitions concerning the counting hierarchy.

Definition 1. *The class* **PP** *is the class of languages A for which there exists a language $B \in \mathbf{P}$ and a polynomial q such that for all x*

$$x \in A \iff \frac{1}{2^{q(|x|)}} \left| \left\{ y \in \{0,1\}^{q(|x|)} : (x,y) \in B \right\} \right| \geq \frac{1}{2}.$$

We will also use an equivalent definition in which the fraction of acceptable certificates y never equals exactly $1/2$. (In order to obtain it, one needs to add 2 new random bits and artificially shift the accepting probability by a tiny amount).

Definition 2. *The relativised class* $\mathbf{PP^C}$ *is defined in the same way but with B being a language in $\mathbf{P}^C$ for some $C \in \mathbf{C}$.*

Definition 3. *The counting hierarchy is defined recursively as follows:*

- $C_0\mathbf{P} = \mathbf{P}$,
- $C_1\mathbf{P} = \mathbf{PP}$,
- $C_{k+1}\mathbf{P} = \mathbf{PP}^{C_k\mathbf{P}}$ *for $k \geq 1$,*
- $\mathbf{CH} = \bigcup_{k \geq 0} C_k\mathbf{P}$.

It is clear that if $C_k\mathbf{P} = C_{k+1}\mathbf{P}$, then $\mathbf{CH} = C_k\mathbf{P}$. Indeed, we have $C_{k+2}\mathbf{P} = \mathbf{PP}^{C_{k+1}\mathbf{P}} = \mathbf{PP}^{C_k\mathbf{P}} = C_{k+1}\mathbf{P}$ and then proceed by induction.

2.2 Rational Interactive Proofs

Rational interactive proofs were introduced by P. Azar and S. Micali in [2]. We will call the prover Merlin and we will call the verifier Arthur. Let us fix a finite alphabet Σ (e.g. $\Sigma = \{0,1\}$) and assume we are working with languages over Σ.

We start from definitions of single-round protocols and the respective classes.

Definition 4. *The class* **FRMA**[1] *(from Functional Rational Merlin-Arthur games with 1 round) is the set of all functions $f : \Sigma^* \to \Sigma^*$, for which there exist polynomial-time computable functions $R : \Sigma^* \to [0,1]$ and $\varphi : \Sigma^* \to \Sigma^*$, such that for all $x \in \Sigma^*$ and for any*

$$m^* \in \mathrm{Argmax}_m \, \mathbb{E}_r R(x; m, r),$$

where r is distributed uniformly on $\{0,1\}^{l(|x|)}$ for some polynomial l, we have

$$f(x) = \varphi(x; m^*).$$

Here m is the Merlin's hint given to Arthur, r is Arthur's randomness, R is the reward paid by Arthur to Merlin given as a finite binary fraction, and φ specifies how to use the hint for computing f. A message m^* maximizing the expected reward must be a hint leading Arthur to the correct value of $f(x)$.

If $f(x)$ has only binary values, it can be treated as a characteristic function of some predicate. It leads to a similar class of languages.

Definition 5. *The class* **DRMA**[1] *(from Decisional RMA) is the set of all languages $S \subset \Sigma^*$ with characteristic functions $\mathbb{I}_S(x) = \mathbb{I}\{x \in S\}$ in* **FRMA**[1].

Azar and Micali show explicitly or implicitly the following results:

Theorem 1 ([2]). $\#\mathbf{P} \subset \mathbf{FRMA}[1]$, $\mathbf{PP} \subset \mathbf{DRMA}[1]$, $\oplus\mathbf{P} \subset \mathbf{DRMA}[1]$.

Now we expand the definitions to multi-round protocols.

Definition 6. *A k-round rational interactive protocol Π consists of polynomial-time computable functions $V : \Sigma^* \to \Sigma^*$, $R : \Sigma^* \to [0,1]$ and $\varphi : \Sigma^* \to \Sigma^*$. For a string $x \in \Sigma^*$ the interaction in protocol Π on input x is defined as follows.*

- *We denote Arthur's messages as $a_1, a_2, \ldots, a_k$ and Merlin's messages as $m_1, m_2, \ldots, m_k$. All messages are required to be of polynomial in $|x|$ length.*
- *Arthur's messages are computed as*

$$a_{i+1} = V(x; m_1, a_1, m_2, \ldots, a_i, m_{i+1}; r_1, \ldots, r_{i+1}),$$

  where $r_1, \ldots, r_k$ are Arthur's private random strings.
- *We call φ the value function and we call the value $\varphi(x; m_1, a_1, \ldots, m_k)$ the value computed in the protocol.*
- *We call R the reward function and we call the value $R(x; m_1, r_1, \ldots, m_k, r_k)$ the reward.*

Remark 1. The value computed in the protocol does not depend on the last message of Arthur, since this dependency can be included in φ. We say that the reward depends only on Merlin's messages and Arthur's randomness, since Arthur's messages can be restored from this information.

Remark 2. In this paper, while describing protocols, we will talk about what messages Merlin sends. This is mostly needed for making a protocol's idea clearer to the reader and should be interpreted as a description of how Arthur processes received strings and what format is expected of Merlin (we assume that messages that deviate from described formats lead to 0 reward).

Definition 7. *In a k-round rational interactive protocol Π with the reward function R, we say that Merlin is rational, if for all $i = 0, 1, \ldots, k-1$ it holds that*

$$m_{i+1} \in \mathrm{Argmax}_m \, \mathbb{E}_{a_{i+1}} \max_{m_{i+2}} \mathbb{E}_{a_{i+2}} \cdots \max_{m_k} \mathbb{E}_{a_k} R(x; m_1, \ldots, a_i, m, a_{i+1}, \ldots, m_k, a_k),$$

i.e. a rational Merlin always chooses a message that maximizes the expected reward, conditional on the currently obtained information.

Definition 8. *We say that a function f is computed in a rational interactive protocol Π, if for all x and for any Merlin's rational behavior it holds that*

$$f(x) = \varphi(x; m_1, a_1, \ldots, m_k).$$

Definition 9. *Class* **FRMA**[k] *is a set of all functions computable in some k-round interactive protocol.*

Definition 10. *Class* **DRMA**$[k]$ *is a class of languages* S *such that their char-acteristic functions* $\mathbb{I}_S(x) = \mathbb{I}\{x \in S\}$ *are in* **FRMA**$[k]$. *When speaking about* **DRMA**$[k]$*-protocols we will often call a corresponding value function a decision function and denote it with* π.

By **DRMA** *we denote the union of all these classes:*

$$\textbf{DRMA} = \bigcup_{k \geq 0} \textbf{DRMA}[k].$$

In the pioneering paper [2], the following connections between the counting hierarchy and the **DRMA** hierarchy were established.

Theorem 2. $C_k \mathbf{P} \subseteq \mathbf{DRMA}[k]$, *for all* $k \geq 0$.

Theorem 3. $\mathbf{DRMA}[k] \subseteq C_{2k+1}\mathbf{P}$, *for all* $k \geq 0$.

Together these two results show that **CH** = **DRMA**.

The following notation simplifies the reasoning about Merlin's rationality.

Definition 11. *Given a rational interactive protocol* Π *and some transcript* $\mathcal{T}_i$, $\mathcal{T}_i = (x; m_1, a_1, \ldots, s), s \in \{m_i, a_{i-1}\}$ *of the first* i *rounds (not necessarily obtained in an interaction with a rational Merlin), denote by* $E_i^{\Pi}(\mathcal{T}_i)$ *the maximal expected reward if Merlin behaves rationally in all future rounds.*

Finally, to construct and analyze protocols, we need the following notion.

Definition 12. *Given a rational interactive protocol* Π *denote by* $\Delta(\Pi)$ *a polynomial-time computable function that gives a positive lower bound for the difference between the expected rewards for an optimal and a second optimal Merlin's messages at the first time he deviates from the rational behavior, i.e. for all* x

$$0 < \Delta(\Pi)(x) \leq \min_{\substack{i, \mathcal{T}_i; \text{ where } \mathcal{T}_i \text{ is obtained in} \\ \text{an interaction with a rational Merlin,} \\ m' \notin \text{Argmax}_m E_{i+1}^{\Pi}(\mathcal{T}_i, m)}} \left(\max_m E_{i+1}^{\Pi}(\mathcal{T}_i, m) - E_{i+1}^{\Pi}(\mathcal{T}_i, m') \right).$$

Remark 3. In the model we are working with, where the reward should be expressed as a finite binary fraction and Arthur's random bits are distributed uniformly and independently, the expected reward can be written as a sum of finite binary fractions (the reward value multiplied by its probability) of length polynomial in input size. This allows us to use $\Delta(\Pi)(x) = 2^{-p(|x|)}$ for some polynomial p dependent on Π. The polynomial $p(n)$ can be taken as $T_R(n) + l_r(n)$, where $T_R(n)$ is the maximal time for the reward to be computed on x with $|x| = n$ (and hence the value of the reward can be expressed as $\frac{k}{2^{T_R(n)}}$ for an integer k), and $l_r(n)$ is the number of random bits Arthur uses on the input of length n. In other models (e.g. the ones where the reward is expressed as a ratio of two integers) the corresponding assumptions about existence of a computable $\Delta(\Pi)$ and adjustments in theorem statements and proofs should be made. It should also be noted that such functions exist for the protocols in [2].

Remark 4. Function $\Delta(\Pi)$ is not the same thing as the reward gap as it used, for example, in [17].

3   Results Concerning DRMA-hierarchy

We start with proving that Arthur can begin an interactive proof with one Merlin and continue it with another one. Moreover, the second Merlin can be asked the expected reward of the first Merlin at the moment of switching.

Lemma 1. *For any integers $i, j \geq 0$, for any* **FRMA**$[i + j]$*-protocol Π for computing function f there exists a function $\widetilde{f}$ that:*

1. *for any x maps any transcript T_i of the first i rounds of interacting with a rational Merlin according to protocol Π on input x to $(E_i^\Pi(T_i), f(x))$,*
2. *maps any transcript T_i of i rounds (i.e. of interaction between Arthur and an arbitrary prover) to $(E_i^\Pi(T_i), v)$ for some v,*
3. *is in* **FRMA**$[j]$.

The idea of the proof is that for a sampleable random variable there is a protocol that determines its expected value, and this protocol can be combined with the original protocol by scaling down the reward in the protocol for expectation.

Proof. Denote by R the reward function in Π and by φ the value function there. The case of $i = 0$ or $j = 0$ is trivial, so we assume $i, j \geq 1$. Consider the following protocol $\widetilde{\Pi}$: in the first round, given the input x and a partial transcript T, Merlin sends $E = E_i^\Pi(T)$ together with $(i + 1)$-st message that Merlin would send in protocol Π, and all other messages are exactly the messages sent by a rational Merlin in Π. In the end Arthur pays Merlin

$$\widetilde{R} = \frac{1}{2}R(T) + \frac{1}{4}\Delta(\Pi)(x)\Big(1 - \big(E - R(T)\big)^2\Big),$$

or he pays 0 if Merlin's message format does not correspond to the format prescribed by the protocol (e.g. if the value E is not in the range $[0, 1]$). Note that $\widetilde{R}$ is polynomial-time computable since R and $\Delta(\Pi)(\cdot)$ are polynomial-time computable by definition (we can use a function of the form $2^{-\,\text{poly}(|x|)}$ for $\Delta(\Pi)$). Since the reward belongs to $[0, 1]$, the value of $(E - R(T))^2$ also lies in $[0, 1]$, which means that, if Merlin ever deviates from the "continuation" of protocol Π at some step, then the expectation of $\frac{1}{2}R(T)$ will decrease at least by $\frac{1}{2}\Delta(\Pi)(x)$, while the expected value of $\frac{1}{4}\Delta(\Pi)(x)\Big(1 - \big(E - R(T)\big)^2\Big)$ will not increase by more than $\frac{1}{4}\Delta(\Pi)(x)$. That means that the rational Merlin may only deviate from the protocol by sending an incorrect E in the first round.

But then he will need to choose E to minimize the functional

$$\mathbb{E}\Big[(E - R(T))^2 \,\big|\, T_i \sqsubseteq T\Big],$$

where $T_i \sqsubseteq T$ means that T is a continuation of T_i. This value is minimized by

$$E = \mathbb{E}\big[R(T) \mid T \sqsubseteq T_i\big] = E_i^\Pi(T_i),$$

where the last equality holds due to the fact that, as we have established, the rational Merlin in protocol $\widetilde{\Pi}$ will behave as the rational Merlin in protocol Π.

Finally, Arthur returns the value $\widetilde{\varphi} = (E, \varphi(T'))$, where T' is just T without the mentioning of E. From the established behavior of a rational Merlin it immediately follows that $E = E_i^{\Pi}(T_i)$ and also, if T_i is produced in the interaction with a rational Merlin, then $\varphi(T') = f(x)$.

Corollary 1. *For all $i, j \geq 0$, the following inclusions hold:*

$$\mathbf{FRMA}[i+j] \subseteq \mathbf{FRMA}[i]^{(\mathrm{FRMA}[j])[1]} \subseteq \mathbf{FRMA}[i]^{\|\mathrm{DRMA}[j]},$$

where "[1]" in the second class means that only one oracle query is allowed.

Proof. The case of $i = 0$ or $j = 0$ is trivial. Let Π be an $\mathbf{FRMA}[i+j]$-protocol for some function $f \in \mathbf{FRMA}[i+j]$. Consider a new protocol Π', which coincides with Π up to Merlin's message in the i-th round. Then Arthur computes his i-th message in protocol Π and sends the current transcript T_i to an $\mathbf{FRMA}[j]$-oracle that corresponds to a function from Lemma 1. The value computed by Arthur and the reward are the ones obtained from the oracle.

The rational Merlin will follow the protocol, because

$$E_{i-1}^{\Pi'}(T_{i-1}) = \max_m \mathbb{E}_r \, R\big((T_{i-1}, m, r)\big) = \max_m \mathbb{E}_r \, E_i^{\Pi}\big((T_{i-1}, m, r)\big) = E_i^{\Pi}(T_i),$$

from which it follows by downward induction that for all $t < i$

$$E_t^{\Pi'}(T_t) = \max_m \mathbb{E}_r \, E_{t+1}^{\Pi'}\big((T_t, m, r)\big) = \max_m \mathbb{E}_r \, E_{t+1}^{\Pi}\big((T_t, m, r)\big) = E_t^{\Pi}(T_t),$$

meaning that the argmaxima, and so the strategies for rational Merlins, coincide for Π and Π'. That means that we can treat the transcript T_i from protocol Π' as the transcript obtained from interaction with a rational Merlin in protocol Π, so by Lemma 1 the oracle will also return the correct value of f.

The second inclusion can be easily obtained by replacing the oracle function $\widetilde{f}$ with the language

$$A_{\widetilde{f}} = \Big\{ (x, i, b) \mid b \text{ is the } i\text{-th bit of } \widetilde{f}(x) \Big\}$$

and calculation of each bit of $\widetilde{f}(x)$ with parallel queries to the $A_{\widetilde{f}}$.

Corollary 2. *For all $i, j \geq 0$, the following inclusions hold:*

$$\mathbf{DRMA}[i+j] \subseteq \mathbf{DRMA}[i]^{(\mathrm{FRMA}[j])[1]} \subseteq \mathbf{DRMA}[i]^{\|\mathrm{DRMA}[j]},$$

where "[1]" in the second class means that only one oracle query is allowed.

Proof. This trivially follows from Corollary 1 because a $\mathbf{DRMA}[k]$ protocol is just a special case of an $\mathbf{FRMA}[k]$ protocol. For the first inclusion, a $\mathbf{DRMA}[i+j]$-protocol is an $\mathbf{FRMA}[i+j]$-protocol for a binary-valued function f, for which, by Corollary 1, there exists a $\mathbf{FRMA}[i]^{(\mathrm{FRMA}[j])[1]}$-protocol that, being a protocol for a binary-valued function, constitutes a $\mathbf{DRMA}[i]^{(\mathrm{FRMA}[j])[1]}$-protocol for the corresponding language. The second inclusion can be proven similarly.

Now we will show that the upper bound of Corollary 2 is tight at least for $i = 0$. In fact, we prove a somewhat stronger result.

Theorem 4. $\mathbf{P}^{\mathbf{FRMA}[k]} = \mathbf{DRMA}[k]$ *for all* $k \geq 0$.

The idea is, again, to scale down the reward for subproblems that depend on the answers to some other subproblems. With carefully performing proof by induction we can see that a fully rational Merlin has no incentive to lie in any of the subproblems.

Proof. The inclusion $\mathbf{DRMA}[k] \subseteq \mathbf{P}^{\mathbf{FRMA}[k]}$ is trivial.

To prove the other inclusion, let A be a language in $\mathbf{P}^f$ for some $f \in \mathbf{FRMA}[k]$, and let Π be a $\mathbf{DRMA}[k]$-protocol for f. Also let M be a polynomial-time Turing machine with access to oracle f that recognizes A. Now consider the following k-round protocol $\widetilde{\Pi}$ for A^f for input string x.

1. In the first round Merlin sends a message m_1, containing a number l, block of l strings $y_1, y_2, \ldots, y_l$ and block of l strings $m_1^{(1)}, m_1^{(2)}, \ldots, m_1^{(l)}$:

$$m_1 = \left(l; y_1, \ldots, y_l; m_1^{(1)}, \ldots, m_1^{(l)} \right).$$

2. Arthur then emulates the machine M on input x, using strings y_i as answers to the oracle queries $x_1, \ldots, x_l$, and interprets strings $m_1^{(j)}$ as first messages of Merlin in the protocol Π for x_i (if emulation of M makes not exactly l queries, the final reward is set to be 0).

3. During all the following rounds, Merlin sends messages of the format $m_i = \left(m_i^{(1)}, \ldots, m_i^{(l)} \right)$, and Arthur sends messages of the format $a_i = \left(a_i^{(1)}, \ldots, a_i^{(l)} \right)$, where Arthur computes each $a_i^{(j)}$ as a response to transcript

$$T_i^{(j)} = \left(x_j; m_1^{(j)}, a_1^{(j)}, \ldots, m_i^{(j)} \right),$$

and Merlin is expected to behave similarly.

4. After all k rounds, Arthur computes $\Delta = \min_j \Delta(\Pi)(x_j)$. and rewards R_j for each "subprotocol", and, if Merlin has not deviated from the protocol in an obvious way, pays him

$$R = \frac{1}{2} R_1 + \frac{\Delta}{4} R_2 + \ldots + \frac{\Delta^{l-1}}{2^l} R_l + \frac{\Delta^l}{2^{l+1}}.$$

Arthur then accepts x if and only if it is accepted by the machine M that gets the strings y_j as answers to queries x_j and in each "subprotocol" Merlin has proven that $f(x_j) = y_j$.

Let us show that a polynomial-time randomized Arthur is capable of following the described protocol. In the protocol, the number of queries and the length of each query x_j are bounded by the time the machine M works on input x, hence for each j we have $|x_j| = \text{poly}(|x|)$ and $l = \text{poly}(|x|)$. That means that each y_j, each message $a_i^{(j)}$, $m_i^{(j)}$ and each composed message a_i, m_i is also of length poly($|x|$). Values $\Delta(\Pi)(x_j)$ are polynomial-time computable values of polynomial length by definition. Computation of R requires a polynomial number of basic arithmetical operations with polynomial length rational numbers, so it can be performed in polynomial time as well.

Now we show that a rational Merlin will not deviate from the protocol. Since R is a strictly positive value, a rational Merlin has no incentive to violate the message format or provide l that does not correspond to the number of queries in simulation of M (which would lead to 0 reward).

By induction on j we will prove that for all j:

(a) the j-th query x_j of the simulation of M is equal to the j-th query of the actual machine M with access to f,

(b) for all $i = 1, 2, \ldots, k$, the string $m_i^{(j)}$ is optimal for a rational Merlin in the corresponding "subprotocol",

(c) $y_j = f(x_j)$.

To prove (a) for j assuming everything is proven for all $j' < j$, notice that (a) and (c) for all $j' < j$ mean that the simulation of M, since it is a deterministic Turing machine, works in the same way as M^f up until the j'-th query to the oracle, including that query.

Now we prove (b) for j assuming it is proven for all $j' < j$. Assume that a rational Merlin did not deviate in the j-th subprotocol until the i-th round. Let $\tilde{m}_i^{(j)}$ be an optimal i-th message in j-th subprotocol, and $\hat{m}_i^{(j)}$ be a message suboptimal for the j-th subprotocol, let $\hat{m}_i$ be the corresponding dishonest message. By the induction hypothesis a rational Merlin would choose optimal messages for all previous subprotocols, so

$$E_{i-1}^{\tilde{\Pi}}(\mathcal{T}_{i-1}) \geq \sum_{j'<j} \frac{\Delta^{j'-1}}{2^{j'}} E_{i-1}^{\Pi}\left(\mathcal{T}_{i-1}^{(j')}\right) + \frac{\Delta^{j-1}}{2^j} E_i^{\Pi}\left(\left(\mathcal{T}_{i-1}^{(j)}, \tilde{m}_i^{(j)}\right)\right)$$

$$\geq \sum_{j'<j} \frac{\Delta^{j'-1}}{2^{j'}} E_{i-1}^{\Pi}\left(\mathcal{T}_{i-1}^{(j')}\right) + \frac{\Delta^{j-1}}{2^j}\left(E_i^{\Pi}\left(\left(\mathcal{T}_{i-1}^{(j)}, \hat{m}_i^{(j)}\right)\right) + \Delta(\Pi)(x_j)\right)$$

$$\geq \sum_{j'<j} \frac{\Delta^{j'-1}}{2^{j'}} E_{i-1}^{\Pi}\left(\mathcal{T}_{i-1}^{(j')}\right) + \frac{\Delta^{j-1}}{2^j} E_i^{\Pi}\left(\left(\mathcal{T}_i^{(j)}, \hat{m}_i^{(j)}\right)\right) + \frac{\Delta^j}{2^j}$$

$$> \sum_{j'<j} \frac{\Delta^{j'-1}}{2^{j'}} E_{i-1}^{\Pi}\left(\mathcal{T}_{i-1}^{(j')}\right) + \frac{\Delta^{j-1}}{2^j} E_i^{\Pi}\left(\left(\mathcal{T}_i^{(j)}, \hat{m}_i^{(j)}\right)\right) + \sum_{j<j'\leq l+1} \frac{\Delta^{j'-1}}{2^{j'}}$$

$$\geq E_i^{\tilde{\Pi}}\left(\mathcal{T}_i, \hat{m}_i\right),$$

here all inequalities are due to the definitions, and the last inequality follows from the induction hypothesis for (b) and an upper bound on geometric series (applying that all the values R'_j do not exceed 1): the expected reward for $(\mathcal{T}, \hat{m}_i)$ is a combination of the expected rewards for partial transcripts $\left(\mathcal{T}_{i-1}^{(j')}\right)$ for $j' < j$ by the induction hypothesis for (b), the expected reward for the partial transcript

$\left(\mathcal{T}_i^{(j)}, \widehat{m}_i^{(j)}\right)$, and the expected rewards for the rest of the subprotocols, which do not exceed 1.

Finally, **(c)** for j follows from **(b)** for j, since a rational Merlin in $\widetilde{\Pi}$ behaves in the j-th subprotocol like a rational Merlin in Π.

Corollary 3. $\mathbf{P^{DRMA}}[k] = \mathbf{DRMA}[k]$, *for all* $k \geq 0$.

Proof. Since a $\mathbf{DRMA}[k]$-protocol is a special case of an $\mathbf{FRMA}[k]$-protocol, the inclusion $\mathbf{P^{DRMA}}[k] \subseteq \mathbf{DRMA}[k]$ follows from Theorem 4. The inclusion in the other direction is trivial.

This corollary shows a plausible difference between the **DRMA** hierarchy and the counting hierarchy. For instance, $\mathbf{P^{PP}}$ is known to contain **PH** due to Toda's theorem, while for **PP** it is unknown, then probably $\mathbf{PP} \neq \mathbf{P^{PP}}$.

Theorem 5. $\mathbf{PP^{FRMA}}[k] \subseteq \mathbf{DRMA}[k+1]$, *for all* $k \geq 0$.

Proof. If A is a language in $\mathbf{PP^{FRMA}}[k]$, then there exists a language $B \in \mathbf{P^{FRMA}}[k]$ and a polynomial q such that for all x:

- $x \in A \Longrightarrow 2^{-q(|x|)} \left| \{y \in \{0,1\}^{q(|x|)} : (x,y) \in B\} \right| > \frac{1}{2}$,
- $x \notin A \Longrightarrow 2^{-q(|x|)} \left| \{y \in \{0,1\}^{q(|x|)} : (x,y) \in B\} \right| < \frac{1}{2}$.

By Theorem 4, there is a $\mathbf{DRMA}[k]$-protocol Π for B with the reward function R and decision function π. We now describe a $\mathbf{DRMA}[k+1]$-protocol Π' for the language A.

1. In the first round Merlin sends one bit b that is supposed to equal $\mathbb{I}\{x \in A\}$.
2. Then Arthur samples a random string $y \sim \mathcal{U}_{q(|x|)}$ and sends it to Merlin.
3. The next k rounds correspond to k rounds of protocol Π for string (x, y).
4. Finally, Arthur computes the value $\Delta = \Delta(\Pi)((x,y))$ as well as the reward R and decision bit π that correspond to the subprotocol for (x, y), pays Merlin the reward $\frac{1}{2}R + \frac{\Delta}{4}\mathbb{I}\{b = \pi\}$ and accepts x if and only if $b = 1$.

The rational Merlin will not deviate from the subprotocol Π, since deviating will decrease $\frac{1}{2}R$ by at least $\frac{1}{2}\Delta$ while increasing $\frac{\Delta}{4}\mathbb{I}\{b = \pi\}$ by at most $\frac{\Delta}{4}$. Hence the rational Merlin in Π' will be replicating the actions of the rational Merlin in the protocol Π, in which case $\pi = \mathbb{I}\{(x,y) \in B\}$. So, to maximize the expected value of $\frac{\Delta}{4}\mathbb{I}\{b = \pi\}$, the rational Merlin will send $\mathbb{I}\{x \in A\}$ in the first round.

Theorem 5 yields an independent proof of Theorem 2 from [2].

Corollary 4. $C_k\mathbf{P} \subseteq \mathbf{DRMA}[k]$ *for all* $k \geq 0$.

Proof. A straightforward induction by k.

The next corollary shows the connection between collapsing of the two hierarchies.

Corollary 5. *If* $\mathbf{DRMA}[k] = \mathbf{DRMA}[k+1]$, *then the counting hierarchy collapses to the* $(2k+1)$-*st level.*

Proof. We will prove by induction on $l \geq 0$ that $C_{k+l}\mathbf{P} \subseteq \mathbf{DRMA}[k]$. The base case is provided by Theorem 2. Induction step is as follows:

$$C_{k+(l+1)}\mathbf{P} = \mathbf{PP}^{C_{k+l}\mathbf{P}} \subseteq \mathbf{PP}^{\mathbf{DRMA}[k]} \subseteq \mathbf{DRMA}[k+1] = \mathbf{DRMA}[k],$$

where the last equality follows from the assumption of the corollary. By Theorem 3 we have $\mathbf{DRMA}[k] \subseteq C_{2k+1}\mathbf{P}$, hence

$$C_{2k+2}\mathbf{P} = C_{k+(k+2)}\mathbf{P} \subseteq \mathbf{DRMA}[k] \subseteq C_{2k+1}\mathbf{P},$$

so $C_{2k+1}\mathbf{P} = C_{2k+2}\mathbf{P}$ and $\mathbf{CH} = C_{2k+1}\mathbf{P}$.

Note that we do not know whether $\mathbf{DRMA}[k] = \mathbf{DRMA}[k+1]$ implies $\mathbf{DRMA}[k+1] = \mathbf{DRMA}[k+2]$, but we still obtain from this corollary that $\mathbf{DRMA}[k] = \mathbf{DRMA}[k+1]$ implies the collapse of the $\mathbf{DRMA}$ hierarchy at some higher level.

4 Communication Complexity of Single-Round Proofs

In this section we study classes of the form $\mathbf{DRMA}[1, c]$, that is, classes of languages that are recognized by $\mathbf{DRMA}[1]$ protocols with at most c bits sent by Merlin. We also assume that Merlin uses the binary alphabet.

Firstly, let us reduce to the case of binary rewards.

Lemma 2. *Every* $\mathbf{DRMA}[1, c]$-*protocol is equivalent to a* $\mathbf{DRMA}[1, c]$-*protocol with the reward function taking values in* $\{0, 1\}$.

Proof. Arthur should, after computing the reward R in the given protocol, send as the reward not the value R, but the i-th bit of R with probability 2^{-i} (which can be done in finite time since for all sufficiently large i the i-th bit of R would be 0), this way Arthur would essentially send 1 with probability R.

Note that this transformation can be applied to any $\mathbf{DRMA}$-protocol without increasing its round or communication complexity.

Lemma 3. *For any two circuits* C_0, C_1 *which compute functions from* $\{0, 1\}^n$ *to* $\{0, 1\}$, *the problem of deciding whether or not* $\mathbb{E}_{x \sim \mathcal{U}_n} C_0(x) \leq \mathbb{E}_{x \sim \mathcal{U}_n} C_1(x)$ *is in* $\mathbf{PP}$. *In other words, the language*

$$\mathsf{Compare - Expectations} = \Big\{ (C_0, C_1) \mid C_i : \{0, 1\}^n \to \{0, 1\},$$

$$\mathbb{E}_{r \sim \mathcal{U}_n} C_0(r) \leq \mathbb{E}_{r \sim \mathcal{U}_n} C_1(r) \Big\}$$

is in $\mathbf{PP}$.

Circuits are used here as a convenient way to describe parameterized functions. in our applications a polynomial-time computable function with a fixed parameter is represented by a polynomial-size circuit. The idea of the proof is to sample both circuits and favor the one with greater value while breaking ties randomly. The proof is presented in the full version of the paper [20].

The following lemma is implicit in [17], but we prove it for completeness.

Lemma 4. PP $\subseteq$ DRMA[1, 1].

Proof. It is well-known that for any language $A \in \mathbf{PP}$ there is a polynomial-time algorithm V such that $\Pr_y[V(x, y) = 1]$ is strictly greater than $\frac{1}{2}$ for $x \in A$ and strictly less than $\frac{1}{2}$ for $x \notin A$.

Consider the following protocol.

1. Merlin sends one bit b that is supposed to be $\mathbb{I}\{x \in A\}$,
2. Arthur runs $V(x, y)$ on random y and pays Merlin $\mathbb{I}\{b = V(x, y)\}$, then accepts x if and only if $b = 1$.

Since there are no ties, a rational Merlin would send the correct bit b.

Finally, to prove the main result of this section, we use the following theorem by Fortnow and Reingold.

Theorem 6 ([13]). *If $A \leq_{tt} B$ and $B \in \mathbf{PP}$, then $A \in \mathbf{PP}$.*

We proceed by the main result of this section.

Theorem 7. DRMA$[1, O(\log n)] \subseteq \mathbf{PP}$.

Proof. Let A be a language in **DRMA**$[1, O(\log n)]$ and Π be the corresponding protocol for A with the reward function R and the decision function π. Since Merlin sends only a message of length $O(\log n)$, there can only be $p(n) = 2^{O(\log n)} = \text{poly}(n)$ possible messages.

Consider an algorithm that, on input x, looks through all possible Merlin's messages and finds the message m^* that maximizes the value $\mathbb{E}_r R(x; m, r)$. This winner can be found in a knockout tournament where messages m_0 and m_1 are compared by feeding the pair $(R(m_0, \cdot), R(m_1, \cdot))$ to the Compare − Expectations oracle. Finally, x is accepted iff $\pi(m^*) = 1$. Clearly, this algorithm provides a polynomial-time truth-table reduction from A to Compare − Expectations $\in \mathbf{PP}$. Hence, by Theorem 6, we have $A \in \mathbf{PP}$.

Corollary 6. PP = DRMA$[1, O(\log n)]$.

Proof. Immediately follows from Lemma 4 and Theorem 7.

Let us now discuss lower bounds on communication complexity of $\oplus \mathbf{P}$ for **DRMA**[1]-protocol. Corollary 6 tells that $\oplus \mathbf{P} \not\subseteq \mathbf{DRMA}[1, O(\log n)]$ would imply $\oplus \mathbf{P} \neq \mathbf{PP}$, while it holds that $\oplus \mathbf{P} \subseteq \mathbf{DRMA}[1, \text{poly}(n)]$ (Theorem 1), so it is interesting to study the communication complexity of **DRMA**[1]-protocols for problems in $\oplus \mathbf{P}$. In all presented proofs so far we have treated certificate verification algorithms that define inclusion in counting classes as samplers from Bernoulli distributions. We now show that this approach cannot yield **DRMA**[1]-protocols with sublinear communication complexity.

Theorem 8. *There is no polynomial-time computable functions $R : \{0,1\}^* \to [0,1]$ and $\varphi : \{0,1\}^* \to \{0,1\}$ such that for any n and $0 \leq k \leq 2^n$ the value of $\varphi(1^n, m^*)$ is equal to the parity of k where $m^* \in \text{Argmax}_m \mathbb{E}_{a,r} R(1^n, m, a, r)$, $|m^*| < \alpha n$ for some constant $\alpha \in (0,1)$, $a \sim \mathcal{U}_s$ with $s = \text{poly}(n)$ and $r \in \{0,1\}^d$ with $d = \text{poly}(n)$ and bits of r being independently sampled from $\text{Bern}\left(\frac{k}{2^n}\right)$.*

The idea is that, for fixed n, m, the reward function is a polynomial in probability of nonuniform bits being equal to 1. If m is short, then some two of these polynomials of polynomial degree have to intersect in exponentially many points. The details are presented in [20].

5   Further Research

In this paper, we show several interesting connections between the counting hierarchy and the **DRMA** hierarchy. But the main question is open: do they coincide or are they different? In case they are different a natural next step would be to construct an example of a language that lies in **DRMA**[k] but seems to not lie in $C_k\mathbf{P}$.

References

1. Azar, P.D.: Super-efficient rational proofs. Ph.D. thesis, Department of Electrical Engineering and Computer Science, Massachusetts Institute of Technology (2014)
2. Azar, P.D., Micali, S.: Rational proofs. In: Proceedings of the Forty-Fourth Annual ACM Symposium on Theory of Computing, pp. 1017–1028. ACM (2012)
3. Azar, P.D., Micali, S.: Super-efficient rational proofs. In: Proceedings of the Fourteenth ACM Conference on Electronic Commerce, pp. 29–30 (2013)
4. Babai, L.: Trading group theory for randomness. In: Proceedings of the 17th Annual ACM Symposium on Theory of Computing, 6–8 May 1985, Providence, Rhode Island, USA, pp. 421–429 (1985)
5. Babai, L., Fortnow, L., Lund, C.: Non-deterministic exponential time has two-prover interactive protocols. Comput. Complex. **1**(1), 3–40 (1991)
6. Babai, L., Moran, S.: Arthur-Merlin games: a randomized proof system, and a hierarchy of complexity classes. J. Comput. Syst. Sci. **36**(2), 254–276 (1988)
7. Ben-Or, M., Goldwasser, S., Kilian, J., Wigderson, A.: Multi-prover interactive proofs: how to remove intractability assumptions. In: Proceedings of the Twentieth Annual ACM Symposium on Theory of Computing, pp. 113–131. ACM (1988)
8. Campanelli, M., Gennaro, R.: Sequentially composable rational proofs. In: Khouzani, M.H.R., Panaousis, E., Theodorakopoulos, G. (eds.) GameSec 2015. LNCS, vol. 9406, pp. 270–288. Springer, Cham (2015). https://doi.org/10.1007/978-3-319-25594-1_15
9. Campanelli, M., Gennaro, R.: Efficient rational proofs for space bounded computations. In: Rass, S., An, B., Kiekintveld, C., Fang, F., Schauer, S. (eds.) GameSec 2017. LNCS, vol. 10575, pp. 53–73. Springer, Cham (2017). https://doi.org/10.1007/978-3-319-68711-7_4
10. Chen, J., McCauley, S., Singh, S.: Rational proofs with multiple provers. In: Proceedings of the 2016 ACM Conference on Innovations in Theoretical Computer Science, pp. 237–248 (2016)

11. Chen, J., McCauley, S., Singh, S.: Efficient rational proofs with strong utility-gap guarantees. In: Deng, X. (ed.) SAGT 2018. LNCS, vol. 11059, pp. 150–162. Springer, Cham (2018). https://doi.org/10.1007/978-3-319-99660-8_14

12. Chen, J., McCauley, S., Singh, S.: Non-cooperative rational interactive proofs. In: 27th Annual European Symposium on Algorithms (ESA 2019). Schloss Dagstuhl-Leibniz-Zentrum fuer Informatik (2019)

13. Fortnow, L., Reingold, N.: PP is closed under truth-table reductions. Inf. Comput. **124**(1), 1–6 (1996)

14. Fortnow, L., Rompel, J., Sipser, M.: On the power of multi-prover interactive protocols. Theoret. Comput. Sci. **134**(2), 545–557 (1994)

15. Goldwasser, S., Micali, S., Rackoff, C.: The knowledge complexity of interactive proof systems. SIAM J. Comput. **18**(1), 186–208 (1989)

16. Goldwasser, S., Sipser, M.: Private coins versus public coins in interactive proof systems. In: Proceedings of the 18th Annual ACM Symposium on Theory of Computing, 28–30 May 1986, Berkeley, California, USA, pp. 59–68 (1986)

17. Guo, S., Hubáček, P., Rosen, A., Vald, M.: Rational arguments: single round delegation with sublinear verification. In: Proceedings of the 5th Conference on Innovations in Theoretical Computer Science. ITCS '14, pp. 523–540. Association for Computing Machinery, New York, NY, USA (2014)

18. Inasawa, K., Yasunaga, K.: Rational proofs against rational verifiers. IEICE Trans. Fundam. Electron. Commun. Comput. Sci. **100**(11), 2392–2397 (2017)

19. Lund, C., Fortnow, L., Karloff, H.J., Nisan, N.: Algebraic methods for interactive proof systems. J. ACM **39**(4), 859–868 (1992)

20. Musatov, D., Potapov, G.: Structural complexity of rational interactive proofs (2023). arxiv.org/abs/2305.04563

21. Shamir, A.: IP=PSPACE. In: 31st Annual Symposium on Foundations of Computer Science, St. Louis, Missouri, USA, 22–24 October 1990, vol. I, pp. 11–15 (1990)

22. Shen, A.: IP=PSPACE: simplified proof. J. ACM **39**(4) (1992)

23. Toda, S.: PP is as hard as the polynomial-time hierarchy. SIAM J. Comput. **20**(5), 865–877 (1991)

24. Wagner, K.W.: The complexity of combinatorial problems with succinct input representation. Acta Inf. **23**(3), 325–356 (1986)

Physical Zero-Knowledge Proof for Ball Sort Puzzle

Suthee Ruangwises[✉] [iD]

Department of Informatics, The University of Electro-Communications,
Tokyo, Japan
ruangwises@gmail.com

Abstract. Ball sort puzzle is a popular logic puzzle consisting of several bins containing balls of multiple colors. Each bin works like a stack; a ball has to follow the last-in first-out order. The player has to sort the balls by color such that each bin contains only balls of a single color. In this paper, we propose a physical zero-knowledge proof protocol for the ball sort puzzle using a deck of playing cards, which enables a prover to physically show that he/she knows a solution with t moves of the ball sort puzzle without revealing it. Our protocol is the first zero-knowledge proof protocol for an interactive puzzle involving moving objects.

Keywords: zero-knowledge proof · card-based cryptography · ball sort puzzle · puzzle

1 Introduction

Ball sort puzzle is a logic puzzle which has recently become popular via smartphone apps [8]. The player is given n bins, each fully filled with h balls. All the hn balls are classified into n colors, each with h balls. The player is also given m additional empty bins, each also with capacity h. The objective of this puzzle is to "sort" the balls by color, i.e. make each bin either empty or full with balls of a single color. Each bin works like a stack; the player can only pick the topmost ball from a bin and place it to the top of another bin that is not full. The additional restriction for each move is that, if the destination bin is not empty, the color of its top ball must be the same as the moved ball. See Fig. 1 for an example.

Very recently, Ito et al. [11] proved that it is NP-complete to determine whether a given instance of the ball sort puzzle has a solution with at most t moves for a given integer t, or even to determine whether it has a solution at all. They also showed that an instance of the ball sort puzzle is solvable if and only if its corresponding instance of a *water sort puzzle* (a similar puzzle with more restrictive rules) is solvable.

Suppose that Philip, a puzzle expert, constructed a difficult ball sort puzzle and challenged his friend Vera to solve it. After trying for a while, Vera could not solve his puzzle and wondered whether it has a solution or not. Philip has to convince her that his puzzle actually has a solution without revealing it (which would render the challenge pointless). In this situation, Philip needs some kind of *zero-knowledge proof (ZKP)*.

G. Della Vedova et al. (Eds.): CiE 2023, LNCS 13967, pp. 246–257, 2023.
https://doi.org/10.1007/978-3-031-36978-0_20

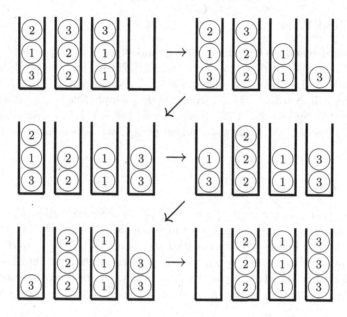

Fig. 1. An example of a ball sort puzzle with $h = 3$, $n = 3$, and $m = 1$ with its solution in five moves

1.1 Zero-Knowledge Proof

Introduced by Goldwasser et al. [7], a ZKP is an interactive protocol between a prover P and a verifier V. Both P and V are given a computational problem x, but its solution w is known only to P. A ZKP enables P to convince V that he/she knows w without leaking any information about w. A ZKP with perfect completeness and perfect soundness must satisfy the following three properties.

1. **Perfect Completeness:** If P knows w, then V always accepts.
2. **Perfect Soundness:** If P does not know w, then V always rejects.
3. **Zero-knowledge:** V gains no information about w, i.e. there is a probabilistic polynomial time algorithm S (called a *simulator*), not knowing w but having access to V, such that the outputs of S follow the same probability distribution as the ones of the actual protocol.

As a ZKP exists for every NP problem [6], one can construct a computational ZKP for the ball sort puzzle. However, such a construction requires cryptographic primitives and thus is not practical or intuitive. Instead, many researchers have developed physical ZKPs for logic puzzles using a deck of playing cards. These card-based protocols have benefits that they require only small, portable objects and do not require computers. They also allow external observers to verify that the prover truthfully executes the protocol (which is a challenging task for digital protocols). Moreover, these protocols are suitable for teaching the concept of a ZKP to non-experts.

1.2 Related Work

Recently, card-based ZKP protocols for several types of logic puzzles have been developed: Akari [1], Bridges [25], Heyawake [17], Hitori [17], Juosan [14], Kakuro [1,15], KenKen [1], Makaro [2,26], Masyu [13], Nonogram [3,20], Norinori [4], Numberlink [23], Nurikabe [17], Nurimisaki [18], Ripple Effect [24], Shikaku [22], Slitherlink [13], Sudoku [9,21,27], Suguru [16], Takuzu [1,14], Usowan [19], and ABC End View [5]. All of them are pencil puzzles where a solution is a written answer.

1.3 Our Contribution

In this paper, we propose a card-based ZKP protocol for the ball sort puzzle with perfect completeness and soundness, which enables the prover P to physically show that he/she knows a solution with t moves of the ball sort puzzle.

By simulating each move by cards, our protocol is the first card-based ZKP protocol for an interactive puzzle (where a solution involves moving objects instead of just a written answer as in pencil puzzles).

2 Preliminaries

We will encode an instance of the ball sort puzzle by cards. Our protocol will enable P to simulate each move of a ball such that V can verify that the move is valid but does not know the color of the moved ball, or which bins the ball is moved to and from. In this section, we will introduce subprotocols that are necessary to hide such information.

2.1 Cards

Each card used in our protocol has a non-negative integer written on the front side. All cards have indistinguishable back sides denoted by $?$.

For $1 \leq x \leq q$, define $E_q(x)$ to be a sequence of consecutive q cards, with all of them being 0s except the x-th card from the left being a 1, e.g. $E_4(3)$ is $0\,0\,1\,0$. This encoding rule was first used by Shinagawa et al. [28] in the context of encoding each integer in $\mathbb{Z}/q\mathbb{Z}$ with a regular q-gon card.

Furthermore, we define $E_q(0)$ to be a sequence of consecutive q cards, all of them being 0s, and $E_q(q+1)$ to be a sequence of consecutive q cards, all of them being 1s, e.g. $E_4(0)$ is $0\,0\,0\,0$ and $E_4(5)$ is $1\,1\,1\,1$.

In some operations, we may stack the cards in $E_q(x)$ into a single stack (with the leftmost card being the topmost card in the stack).

2.2   Pile-Shifting Shuffle

Given a $p \times q$ matrix M of cards, a *pile-shifting shuffle* [28] shifts the columns of M by a uniformly random cyclic shift unknown to all parties (see Fig. 2). It can be implemented by putting all cards in each column into an envelope, and taking turns to apply *Hindu cuts* (taking several envelopes from the bottom of the pile and putting them on the top) to the pile of envelopes [29].

Note that each card in the matrix can be replaced by a stack of cards, and the protocol still works in the same way as long as every stack in the same row consists of the same number of cards.

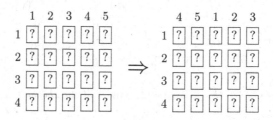

Fig. 2. An example of a pile-shifting shuffle on a 4×5 matrix

2.3   Pile-Scramble Shuffle

Given a $p \times q$ matrix M of cards, a *pile-scramble shuffle* [10] rearranges the columns of M by a uniformly random permutation unknown to all parties (see Fig. 3). It can be implemented by putting all cards in each column into an envelope, and scrambling all envelopes together completely randomly.

Like the pile-shifting shuffle, each card in the matrix can be replaced by a stack of cards, and the protocol still works in the same way as long as every stack in the same row consists of the same number of cards.

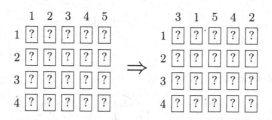

Fig. 3. An example of a pile-scramble shuffle on a 4×5 matrix

2.4   Chosen Pile Cut Protocol

Given a sequence of q face-down stacks $A = (a_1, a_2, ..., a_q)$, with each stack having the same number of cards, a *chosen pile cut protocol* [12] enables P to select a stack a_i he/she wants without revealing i to V. This protocol also reverts the sequence A back to its original state after P finishes using a_i in other protocols.

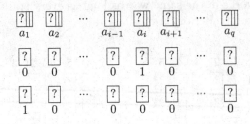

Fig. 4. A $3 \times q$ matrix M constructed in Step 1 of the chosen pile cut protocol

1. Construct the following $3 \times q$ matrix M (see Fig. 4).
   (a) In Row 1, publicly place the sequence A.
   (b) In Row 2, secretly place a face-down sequence $E_q(i)$.
   (c) In Row 3, publicly place a face-down sequence $E_q(1)$.
2. Apply the pile-shifting shuffle to M.
3. Turn over all cards in Row 2. Locate the position of the only $\boxed{1}$. A stack in Row 1 directly above this $\boxed{1}$ will be the stack a_i as desired.
4. After finishing using a_i in other protocols, place a_i back into M at the same position.
5. Turn over all face-up cards. Apply the pile-shifting shuffle to M.
6. Turn over all cards in Row 3. Locate the position of the only $\boxed{1}$. Shift the columns of M cyclically such that this $\boxed{1}$ moves to Column 1. This reverts M back to its original state.

The next two subprotocols are our newly developed subprotocols that will be used in our main protocol.

2.5   Chosen k-Pile Cut Protocol

A *chosen k-pile cut protocol* is a generalization of the chosen pile cut protocol. Instead of selecting one stack, P wants to select $k \leq q$ stacks $a_{\gamma_1}, a_{\gamma_2}, ..., a_{\gamma_k}$ (the order of selection matters). This protocol enables P to do so without revealing $\gamma_1, \gamma_2, ..., \gamma_k$ to V.

1. Construct the following $3 \times q$ matrix M (see Fig. 5).
   (a) In Row 1, publicly place the sequence A.

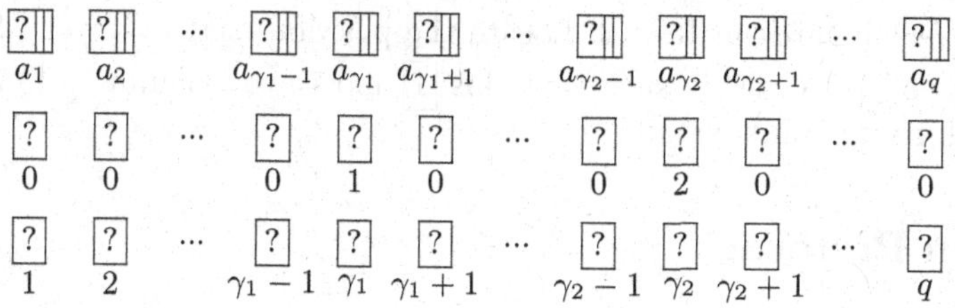

Fig. 5. A $3 \times q$ matrix M constructed in Step 1 of the k-chosen pile cut protocol for the case $k = 2$

(b) In Row 2, secretly place a face-down $\boxed{i}$ at Column γ_i for each $i = 1, 2, ..., k$. Then, secretly place face-down $\boxed{0}$s at the rest of the columns.

(c) In Row 3, publicly place a face-down $\boxed{i}$ at Column i for each $i = 1, 2, ..., q$.

2. Apply the pile-scramble shuffle to M.
3. Turn over all cards in Row 2. Locate the position of an $\boxed{i}$ for each $i = 1, 2, ..., k$. A stack in Row 1 directly above the $\boxed{i}$ will be the stack a_{γ_i} as desired.
4. After finishing using the selected stacks in other operations, place them back into M at the same positions.
5. Turn over all face-up cards. Apply the pile-scramble shuffle to M.
6. Turn over all cards in Row 3. Rearrange the columns of M such that the cards in Row 3 are $\boxed{1}$, $\boxed{2}$, ..., $\boxed{q}$ in this order from left to right. This reverts M back to its original state.

2.6 Color Checking Protocol

Given two sequences $E_q(x_1)$ and $E_q(x_2)$ ($0 \le x_1, x_2 \le q+1$), a *color checking protocol* verifies that

1. $1 \le x_1 \le q$, and
2. either $x_2 = x_1$ or $x_2 = q+1$

without revealing any other information.

1. Construct the following $3 \times q$ matrix M.
   (a) In Row 1, publicly place the sequence $E_q(x_1)$.
   (b) In Row 2, publicly place the sequence $E_q(x_2)$.
   (c) In Row 3, publicly place a face-down sequence $E_q(1)$.
2. Apply the pile-shifting shuffle to M.
3. Turn over all cards in Row 1 to show that there are exactly $q-1$ $\boxed{0}$s and one $\boxed{1}$ (otherwise V rejects). Suppose the only $\boxed{1}$ is located at Column j.
4. Turn over the card at Row 2 Column j to show that it is a $\boxed{1}$ (otherwise V rejects).
5. Turn over all face-up cards. Apply the pile-shifting shuffle to M.

6. Turn over all cards in Row 3. Locate the position of the only $\boxed{1}$. Shift the columns of M cyclically such that this $\boxed{1}$ moves to Column 1. This reverts M back to its original state.

3   Main Protocol

We denote each color of the balls by number $1, 2, ..., n$. For each empty space in a bin, we put a "dummy ball" with number 0 in it, so every bin becomes full. Moreover, we put a dummy ball with number $n+1$ under each bin, and a dummy ball with number 0 right above each bin. Finally, we create an $(h+2) \times (n+m)$ matrix M of stacks of cards, with a stack $E_n(i)$ representing a ball with number i. See Fig. 6 for an example.

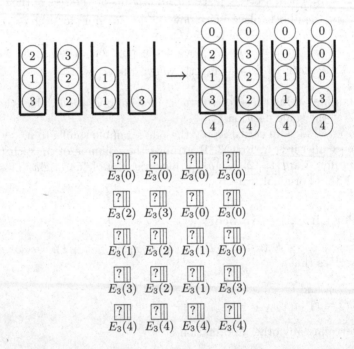

Fig. 6. The way we put dummy balls into an instance of a puzzle, and create a matrix of stacks of cards

The key observation is that, when moving a ball represented by a_x from bin (column) A to bin (column) B, we can view it as swapping a_x with a dummy ball represented by b_y occupying the corresponding empty space in bin B. In each such move, P performs the following steps.

1. Put all stacks in each column of M together into a single big stack. (We now have $n + m$ big stacks of cards.) Apply the k-chosen pile cut protocol with $k = 2$ to select columns A and B from M.
2. Arrange the cards in column A as a sequence of stacks $(a_1, a_2, ..., a_{h+2})$ representing the $h + 2$ balls, where $a_1 = E_n(0)$ is the topmost stack in A and $a_{h+2} = E_n(n + 1)$ is the bottommost stack in A. Analogously, arrange the cards in B as $(b_1, b_2, ..., b_{h+2})$.
3. Apply the chosen pile cut protocol to select a stack a_x from column A and a stack b_y from column B. Note that the chosen pile cut protocol preserves the cyclic order of the sequence, thus we can refer to stacks a_{x-1}, b_{y-1}, and b_{y+1} (where the indices are considered modulo n).
4. Turn over a_{x-1}, b_{y-1}, and b_y to reveal that they are all $E_n(0)$s (otherwise V rejects).
5. Apply the color checking protocol on a_x and b_{y+1}.
6. Swap a_x and b_y.

P performs the above steps for each of the t moves in P's solution. After finishing all moves, P applies the pile-scramble shuffle to the columns of M to shuffle all columns into a random permutation. Finally, P turns over all cards in M. V verifies that there is one column consisting of $(E_n(0), E_n(i), E_n(i), ..., E_n(i), E_n(n + 1))$ for each $i = 1, 2, ..., n$, and there are m columns each consisting of $(E_n(0), E_n(0), ..., E_n(0), E_n(n + 1))$. If the verification passes, V accepts; otherwise, V rejects.

Our protocol uses a total of $\Theta(hn(n + m))$ cards.

4   Proof of Correctness and Security

We will prove the perfect completeness, perfect soundness, and zero-knowledge properties of our protocol.

Lemma 1 (Perfect Completeness). *If P knows a solution with t moves of the ball sort puzzle, then V always accepts.*

Proof. First, we will prove the correctness of our newly developed subprotocols: the chosen k-pile cut protocol in Sect. 2.5 and the color checking protocol in Sect. 2.6.

Consider the chosen k-pile cut protocol. In Step 1(b), for each $i = 1, 2, ..., k$, P places an $\boxed{i}$ in the same column as the stack a_{γ_i}. After applying the pile-scramble shuffle, they will still be in the same column. Therefore, the stacks selected in Step 3 are $a_{\gamma_1}, a_{\gamma_2}, ..., a_{\gamma_k}$ in this order as desired.

Consider the color checking protocol. In Step 3, V verifies that $E(x_1)$ consists of exactly one $\boxed{1}$ and $q - 1$ $\boxed{0}$s, which is an equivalent condition to $1 \leq x_1 \leq q$. In Step 4, V verifies that the x_1-th leftmost card of $E(x_2)$ is a $\boxed{1}$, which is an equivalent condition to $x_2 = x_1$ or $x_2 = q + 1$. Therefore, the protocol is correct.

Now suppose P knows a solution with t moves of the puzzle.

Consider each move of a ball represented by a_x in bin (column) A to an empty position represented by b_y in bin (column) B. Since this is a valid move, the moved ball must be a topmost real ball in bin A, so a_{x-1} must be an $E_n(0)$ (representing either a dummy ball inside the bin or a dummy ball above the bin). As b_y represents a dummy ball inside bin B (not above the bin), b_y and b_{y-1} must also both be $E_n(0)$s. Hence, Step 4 of the main protocol will pass.

Also, since this is a valid move, a_x must represent a real ball, i.e. be an $E_n(\alpha)$ for some $1 \leq \alpha \leq n$, and bin B must either be empty or has the topmost real ball with the same color as the moved ball. In the former case, we have $b_{y+1} = E_n(n+1)$; in the latter case, we have $b_{y+1} = E_n(\alpha)$. Hence, the color checking protocol will pass.

After t moves, the balls are sorted by color such that each bin is either empty or full with balls of a single color. Hence, the final step of the main protocol will pass.

Therefore, V always accepts.   □

Lemma 2 (Perfect Soundness). *If P does not know a solution with t moves of the ball sort puzzle, then V always rejects.*

Proof. We will prove the contrapositive of this statement. Suppose that V accepts, meaning that the verification passes for every move, and the final step of the main protocol also passes.

Consider each move of swapping stacks a_x in column A and b_y in column B. Since the color checking protocol on a_x and b_{y+1} passes, we have that a_x represents a ball with number α for some $1 \leq \alpha \leq n$, i.e. a real ball (not a dummy ball). Since Step 4 of the main protocol passes, we have that a_{x-1} is $E_n(0)$. That means a_x represents a topmost real ball in bin A.

Since Step 4 of the main protocol passes, we also have that b_y and b_{y-1} are both $E_n(0)$s, which means b_y represents a dummy ball inside bin B (not above the bin), so bin B is not full. Since the color checking protocol on a_x and b_{y+1} passes, we have that b_{y+1} represents either a real ball with the same number α or a dummy ball with number $n+1$. In the former case, the topmost real ball in bin B has the same color as the moved ball; in the latter case, bin B is empty. Hence, we can conclude that this move is a valid move in the puzzle.

Since the final step of the main protocol passes, we have that after t valid moves, the balls are sort by color such that each bin is either empty or full with balls of a single color. Therefore, we can conclude that P knows a solution with t moves of the puzzle.   □

Lemma 3 (Zero-Knowledge). *During the verification, V learns nothing about P's solution.*

Proof. It is sufficient to show that all distributions of cards that are turned face-up can be simulated by a simulator S that does not know P's solution.

- In Steps 3 and 6 of the chosen pile cut protocol in Sect. 2.4, due to the pile-shifting shuffle, the $\boxed{1}$ has an equal probability to be at any of the q positions. Hence, these steps can be simulated by S.

- In Steps 3 and 6 of the chosen k-pile cut protocol in Sect. 2.5, due to the pile-scramble shuffle, the order of the q cards are uniformly distributed among all $q!$ permutations of them. Hence, these steps can be simulated by S.
- In Steps 3 and 6 of the color checking protocol in Sect. 2.6, due to the pile-shifting shuffle, the $\boxed{1}$ has an equal probability to be at any of the q positions. Hence, these steps can be simulated by S.
- In the final step of the main protocol, there is one column of M consisting of $(E_n(0), E_n(i), E_n(i), ..., E_n(i), E_n(n+1))$ for each $i = 1, 2, ..., n$, and there are m columns each consisting of $(E_n(0), E_n(0), ..., E_n(0), E_n(n+1))$. Due to the pile-scramble shuffle, the order of the $n + m$ columns are uniformly distributed among all $(n + m)!$ permutations of them. Hence, these steps can be simulated by S.

Therefore, we can conclude that V learns nothing about P's solution.   □

5   Future Work

We developed a card-based ZKP protocol for the ball sort puzzle. A possible future work is to develop such protocol for water sort puzzle, a similar puzzle with more restrictive rules. (In the water sort puzzle, consecutive "balls" with the same color are connected and must be moved together.) We believe it is significantly harder to construct a ZKP for this puzzle as P must also hide the number of moved balls in each move.

Acknowledgement. The author would like to thank Daiki Miyahara for a valuable discussion on this research.

References

1. Bultel, X., Dreier, J., Dumas, J.-G., Lafourcade, P.: Physical zero-knowledge proofs for Akari, Takuzu, Kakuro and KenKen. In: Proceedings of the 8th International Conference on Fun with Algorithms (FUN), pp. 8:1–8:20 (2016)
2. Bultel, X., et al.: Physical zero-knowledge proof for Makaro. In: Izumi, T., Kuznetsov, P. (eds.) SSS 2018. LNCS, vol. 11201, pp. 111–125. Springer, Cham (2018). https://doi.org/10.1007/978-3-030-03232-6_8
3. Chien, Y.-F., Hon, W.-K.: Cryptographic and physical zero-knowledge proof: from sudoku to nonogram. In: Boldi, P., Gargano, L. (eds.) FUN 2010. LNCS, vol. 6099, pp. 102–112. Springer, Heidelberg (2010). https://doi.org/10.1007/978-3-642-13122-6_12
4. Dumas, J.-G., Lafourcade, P., Miyahara, D., Mizuki, T., Sasaki, T., Sone, H.: Interactive physical zero-knowledge proof for Norinori. In: Du, D.-Z., Duan, Z., Tian, C. (eds.) COCOON 2019. LNCS, vol. 11653, pp. 166–177. Springer, Cham (2019). https://doi.org/10.1007/978-3-030-26176-4_14
5. Fukusawa, T., Manabe, Y.: Card-based zero-knowledge proof for the nearest neighbor property: zero-knowledge proof of ABC end view. In: Proceedings of the 12th International Conference on Security, Privacy and Applied Cryptographic Engineering (SPACE), pp. 147–161 (2022)

6. Goldreich, O., Micali, S., Wigderson, A.: Proofs that yield nothing but their validity and a methodology of cryptographic protocol design. J. ACM **38**(3), 691–729 (1991)

7. Goldwasser, S., Micali, S., Rackoff, C.: The knowledge complexity of interactive proof systems. SIAM J. Comput. **18**(1), 186–208 (1989)

8. Google Play: ball sort puzzle. https://play.google.com/store/search?q=ball %20sort%20puzzle

9. Gradwohl, R., Naor, M., Pinkas, B., Rothblum, G.N.: Cryptographic and physical zero-knowledge proof systems for solutions of sudoku puzzles. Theory Comput. Syst. **44**(2), 245–268 (2009)

10. Ishikawa, R., Chida, E., Mizuki, T.: Efficient card-based protocols for generating a hidden random permutation without fixed points. In: Calude, C.S., Dinneen, M.J. (eds.) UCNC 2015. LNCS, vol. 9252, pp. 215–226. Springer, Cham (2015). https://doi.org/10.1007/978-3-319-21819-9_16

11. Ito, T., et al.: Sorting balls and water: equivalence and computational complexity. In: Proceedings of the 11th International Conference on Fun with Algorithms (FUN), pp. 16:1–16:17 (2022)

12. Koch, A., Walzer, S.: Foundations for actively secure card-based cryptography. In: Proceedings of the 10th International Conference on Fun with Algorithms (FUN), pp. 17:1–17:23 (2020)

13. Lafourcade, P., Miyahara, D., Mizuki, T., Robert, L., Sasaki, T., Sone, H.: How to construct physical zero-knowledge proofs for puzzles with a "single loop" condition. Theoret. Comput. Sci. **888**, 41–55 (2021)

14. Miyahara, D., et al.: Card-based ZKP protocols for Takuzu and Juosan. In: Proceedings of the 10th International Conference on Fun with Algorithms (FUN), pp. 20:1–20:21 (2020)

15. Miyahara, D., Sasaki, T., Mizuki, T., Sone, H.: Card-based physical zero-knowledge proof for kakuro. IEICE Trans. Fundam. Electron. Commun. Comput. Sci. **E102.A**(9), 1072–1078 (2019)

16. Robert, L., Miyahara, D., Lafourcade, P., Libralesso, L., Mizuki, T.: Physical zero-knowledge proof and NP-completeness proof of Suguru puzzle. Inf. Comput. **285**(B), 104858 (2022)

17. Robert, L., Miyahara, D., Lafourcade, P., Mizuki, T.: Card-based ZKP for connectivity: applications to Nurikabe, Hitori, and Heyawake. N. Gener. Comput. **40**(1), 149–171 (2022)

18. Robert, L., Miyahara, D., Lafourcade, P., Mizuki, T.: Card-based ZKP protocol for Nurimisaki. In: Proceedings of the 24th International Symposium on Stabilization, Safety, and Security of Distributed Systems (SSS), pp. 285–298 (2022)

19. Robert, L., Miyahara, D., Lafourcade, P., Mizuki, T.: Hide a liar: card-based ZKP protocol for Usowan. In: Proceedings of the 17th Annual Conference on Theory and Applications of Models of Computation (TAMC), pp. 201–217 (2022)

20. Ruangwises, S.: An improved physical ZKP for nonogram. In: Proceedings of the 15th Annual International Conference on Combinatorial Optimization and Applications (COCOA), pp. 262–272 (2021)

21. Ruangwises, S.: Two standard decks of playing cards are sufficient for a ZKP for sudoku. N. Gener. Comput. **40**(1), 49–65 (2022)

22. Ruangwises, S., Itoh, T.: How to physically verify a rectangle in a grid: a physical ZKP for Shikaku. In: Proceedings of the 11th International Conference on Fun with Algorithms (FUN), pp. 24:1–24:12 (2022)

23. Ruangwises, S., Itoh, T.: Physical zero-knowledge proof for numberlink puzzle and k vertex-disjoint paths problem. N. Gener. Comput. **39**(1), 3–17 (2021)

24. Ruangwises, S., Itoh, T.: Physical zero-knowledge proof for ripple effect. Theoret. Comput. Sci. **895**, 115–123 (2021)
25. Ruangwises, S., Itoh, T.: Physical ZKP for connected spanning subgraph: applications to bridges puzzle and other problems. In: Kostitsyna, I., Orponen, P. (eds.) UCNC 2021. LNCS, vol. 12984, pp. 149–163. Springer, Cham (2021). https://doi. org/10.1007/978-3-030-87993-8_10
26. Ruangwises, S., Itoh, T.: Physical ZKP for Makaro using a standard deck of cards. In: Proceedings of the 17th Annual Conference on Theory and Applications of Models of Computation (TAMC), pp. 43–54 (2022)
27. Sasaki, T., Miyahara, D., Mizuki, T., Sone, H.: Efficient card-based zero-knowledge proof for Sudoku. Theoret. Comput. Sci. **839**, 135–142 (2020)
28. Shinagawa, K., et al.: Card-based protocols using regular polygon cards. IEICE Trans. Fundam. Electron. Commun. Comput. Sci. **E100.A**(9), 1900–1909 (2017)
29. Ueda, I., Miyahara, D., Nishimura, A., Hayashi, Y., Mizuki, T., Sone, H.: Secure implementations of a random bisection cut. Int. J. Inf. Secur. **19**(4), 445–452 (2020)

Combinatorial Approaches

Graph Subshifts

Pablo Arrighi[1,2,3]($\boxtimes$), Amélia Durbec[1,2,3], and Pierre Guillon[1,2,3]

[1] Université Paris-Saclay, Inria, CNRS, LMF, 91190 Gif-sur-Yvette,
France and IXXI, Lyon, France
`pablo.arrighi@universite-paris-saclay.fr`
[2] Université Paris-Saclay, CNRS, LISN, 91190 Gif-sur-Yvette, France
[3] Aix-Marseille Université, CNRS, I2M, Marseille, France

Abstract. We propose a definition of graph subshifts of finite type that
can be seen as extending both the notions of subshifts of finite type from
classical symbolic dynamics and finitely presented groups from combinatorial group theory. These are sets of graphs that are defined by forbidding finitely many local patterns. In this paper, we focus on the question
whether such local conditions can enforce a specific support graph, and
thus relate the model to classical symbolic dynamics. We prove that the
subshifts that contain only infinite graphs are either aperiodic, or feature
no residual finiteness of their period group, yielding non-trivial examples
as well as two natural undecidability theorems.

1 Introduction

Subshifts of finite type are well studied objects in symbolic dynamics [17] and
ergodic theory. Given an alphabet Σ, a subshift of finite type (SFT) on $\mathbb{Z}^d$ is a
set of configurations $\mathcal{Y} \subseteq \Sigma^{\mathbb{Z}^d}$ that do not contain a given finite set of forbidden
patterns $\mathcal{F} \subseteq \Sigma^{\{-n,n\}^d}$. In spite of their relatively benign and local definition,
SFT have proven to have complex global behaviours. One example of such results
is the existence of aperiodic SFTs in dimension 2, but not in dimensional 1.
Even some natural problems such as determining whether an SFT contains a
periodic configuration at all, are proven to be undecidable [5]. This local-to-
global complexity is in fact shared by multiple dynamical systems and most
notably with Cellular Automata (CA) [16]. However, the two models are deeply
connected as CA of dimension d can be seen as subshifts of dimension $d+1$. This
connection as been used to prove multiple theorems on different subclasses of
CA [14]. This result is also one of the original motivations of this paper: Graph
subshifts ought to be a means to study a generalization of CA called Causal
Graph Dynamics (CGD) [1]. CGD extend CA in two complementary ways: first
because they are defined on arbitrary graphs of bounded degree m, and second
because they allow for the graph itself to evolve, according to a local, shift-
invariant rule. Graph subshifts aim to encompass CGD spacetime diagrams as
a subclass.

Subshifts have already been generalized to configurations over finitely generated groups. However this is not enough to simulate CGD as all configurations

G. Della Vedova et al. (Eds.): CiE 2023, LNCS 13967, pp. 261–274, 2023.
https://doi.org/10.1007/978-3-031-36978-0_21

share the same support graph. In this paper, we provide a formalism which relaxes this constraint, allowing the support of the graphs itself to also be prescribed by set of forbidden patterns. We introduce and formalize the notion of graph subshifts, i.e. sets of graphs that are defined by forbidding local patterns.

The natural question to ask, then, is whether we may enforce, by means of such local constraints only, that the set of graphs be of a particular shape. In particular, notice that a graph subshift may contain a finite or an infinite number of graphs (up to shift), and that the graphs themselves may be of finite or of infinite size. In this first paper we focus on the question whether there exist subshifts whose graphs are all of infinite size. The question is non-trivial; for instance we prove that the problem whether a given set of forbidden patterns induces a graph subshift without finite configuration is undecidable. The problem whether it uniquely fixes the support graph is also shown undecidable. Still, we prove that the graph subshifts that contain only infinite graphs are either aperiodic, or feature no residual finiteness of their period group, yielding us with non-trivial examples and establishing connections with different areas of mathematics: periodicity from symbolic dynamics; residually finite groups from combinatorial group theory [4,18]; and graph covers as used in graph theory and distributed computing.

All proofs are in the Pre-print version of this paper. A very exploratory version of those results has been presented in the (non-proceedings track of) workshop Automata 2021.

2 Graphs

The notions of graphs and of pointed graphs modulo, together with their operations, are intuitive enough as summarized here, for rigorous definitions see [2]. Let π be the finite set of ports, $\Pi = \pi^2$, and V some universe of names.

Graphs. The graphs denoted by letters $G, H \ldots$ are the usual, connected, undirected, possibly infinite, bounded-degree labelled graphs, but with a few added twists:

- Vertices are connected through their ports. An edge is an unordered pair $\{x : a, y : b\}$ of $V \times \pi$, or a singleton $\{x : a\}$ standing for a self-loop, where x, y are vertices and $a, b \in \pi$ are ports. Each port is used at most once per node: if $e, e' \in E(G)$ intersect, they must be equal. As a consequence the degree of the graph is bounded by $|\pi|$.
- Each vertex x is given a label $\sigma(x)$, taken within a finite set Σ, also referred to as an internal state. Sometimes the function σ is denoted σ_G to emphasize that it belongs to the description of G.

The set of all (finite and infinite) graphs having ports π, vertex labels Σ is denoted $\mathcal{G}_{\Sigma,\pi}$, or simply $\mathcal{G}$. The *support* of graph X is simply the structure of vertices linked by edges with ports, forgetting the labeling σ, or equivalently the graph in which the labeling is changed to the monochromatic one.

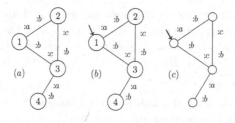

Fig. 1. (a) A graph G. (b) A pointed graph $(G, 1)$. (c) A pointed graph modulo X.

Pointed Graphs Modulo. The goal of this paragraph is to define a set of graphs that is a compact space. Indeed, consider a graph G, a vertex $p \in V(G)$, and $D = G_p^r$ the disk of radius r around p, *i.e.* the subgraph of G induced by the r-neighbors of x in G. Now forgetting about G, this D is one amongst the many possible disks of radius r that can appear in $\mathcal{G}$. In order for the set of graphs to form a compact space, one requirement is that the set of disks of radius r be finite. Morally this is the case, since the degree is bounded by $|\pi|$, but vertex names x, y, z jeopardize this; we must get rid of them. Thus,

- Graphs are endowed with a privileged pointed vertex p playing the role of an origin (in particular, there is no empty graph).
- These pointed graphs (G, p) are then considered modulo isomorphism. Notice that isomorphism rename the pointer in the same way as they rename the vertex upon which it points, i.e. $R : (G, p) \mapsto (RG, R(p))$. Thus the relative position of the other vertices w.r.t to the pointer is unchanged.

Pointed graphs modulo are denoted $X, Y \dots$. The set of all pointed (finite and infinite) graphs modulo is denoted $\mathcal{X}_{\Sigma, \pi}$, or simply $\mathcal{X}$. Given a graph non-modulo G, and a vertex $p \in V(G)$, we write $X((G, p))$ for the corresponding pointed graph modulo. Additionally the set of disks of radius r with states Σ and ports π is written $\mathcal{X}_{\Sigma, \pi}^r$, or simply $\mathcal{X}^r$.

Paths and Vertices. Over graphs modulo isomorphism without pointer, vertices no longer have a unique identifier, which makes designating a vertex a daunting task. Fortunately, our graphs are pointed, so that any vertex $\hat{u}$ can always be designated by some sequence of ports u that leads to it, starting from the origin. Given a pointed graph modulo X, its set of finite paths, starting from the origin, forms a subset $\mathcal{L}(X)$ of Π^* with $\Pi = \pi^2$. Whenever two paths u and v lead to the same vertex, we write $u \equiv_X v$. Thus vertex $\hat{u}$ is really the $\equiv_X$-equivalence class of u, hence the hat notation. The set of these equivalence classes, a.k.a vertices, is denoted $V(X)$. Notice that, starting from origin, following path $v = (ab) \cdots (cd)$ and then path $\overline{v} = (dc) \cdots (ba)$, leads back to the vertex at the origin, namely $\hat{\varepsilon}$, where ε denotes the empty path.

Remark 1. Notice that two paths $u, u' \in \mathcal{L}(X)$ designate the same vertex $\hat{u} = \widehat{u'}$ if and only if for every $v \in \mathcal{L}(X_u)$, $\widehat{uv} = \widehat{u'v}$ (in particular, $v \in \mathcal{L}(X_{u'})$).

Back to Graphs Non-modulo. Sometimes we still need to manipulate usual graphs, where vertices do have names. For this purpose we use a canonical naming function $X \in \mathcal{X} \mapsto G(X) \in \mathcal{G}$, which names each vertex of X by the set of paths that lead to it, starting from ε. This $G(X)$ is referred to as 'the associated graph'. One has $X(G(X), \hat{\varepsilon}) = X$.

Shift. Let $X \in \mathcal{X}$ be a pointed graph modulo. Consider a path $u \in \mathcal{L}(X)$. Then X_u is $X((G(X), \hat{u}))$. The pointed graph modulo X_u is referred to as X *shifted by u.*

From now on we refer to $X \in \mathcal{X}$ as just 'a graph', as it is clear from the notation that it is in fact a pointer graph modulo.

3   Subshifts

Given a pointed graph modulo X, a word in Π^* designates a vertex, and a language $L \subseteq \Pi^*$ designates a set of vertices. If, moreover, L is stable under taking the prefix, then the designated vertices induce a connected pointed subgraph of X which we refer to as 'cut'. Given a set $\mathcal{Z}$ of graphs, one may be interested in selecting those whose cut according to L equals some graph Z, which we refer to as 'cylinder'.

Definition 1 (Cuts and cylinders). *Consider $L \subseteq \Pi^*$ a prefix-stable language, i.e. such that $uv \in L$ implies $u \in L$. The L-cut of a graph $X \in \mathcal{X}$ is the subgraph induced by the vertices $\{\hat{u} \mid u \in L \cap \mathcal{L}(X)\}$. It is denoted $X_{|L}$. Consider $\mathcal{Z} \subseteq \mathcal{X}$, we write $\mathcal{Z}_{|L}$ for $\{X_{|L} \mid X \in \mathcal{Z}\}$. Consider $Z \in \mathcal{Z}_{|L}$, the cylinder of Z within $\mathcal{Z}$ is $\{X \in \mathcal{Z} \mid X_{|L} = Z\}$. It is denoted $[Z]_{\mathcal{Z}}$.*

Definition 2 (Subshift). *Let $\mathcal{F}$ be a set of tuples (F, L), where each F is a finite graph, and each L a finite prefix-stable language. The subshift forbidding $\mathcal{F}$ is*

$$\mathcal{Z} = \left\{ X \in \mathcal{X}_{\Sigma, \pi} \mid \forall v \in \mathcal{L}(X), \forall (F, L) \in \mathcal{F}, (X_v)_{|L} \neq F \right\}.$$

It is of finite type if $\mathcal{F}$ can be chosen finite.

Remark 2. In the pairs (F, L), L cannot always be assumed to be the language labelling the paths of F. For example, requiring every vertex to have an edge with port $a \in \pi$ is a very natural finite-type condition, but this SFT is not of the form $\{ X \in \mathcal{X}_{\Sigma, \pi} \mid \forall v \in \mathcal{L}(X), \forall F \in \mathcal{F}, (X_v)_{|L_F} \neq F \}$ as the L_F do not contain a and hence cannot tell that it is absent.

Yet, this SFT can be defined through our definition by

$$\{ (F, \{\varepsilon, ap\}) \mid p \in \pi, F \text{ 1-node graph} \}.$$

The same remark holds for the dual definitions, *i.e.* through allowed patterns: think of the SFT consisting of those graphs having no port $a \in \pi$.

Lemma 1. *The following are equivalent.*

1. $\mathcal{Z}$ is a subshift of finite type.

2. $\mathcal{Z}$ is the subshift forbidding some $\mathcal{F}' \times \{M\}$ where $\mathcal{F}'$ is a finite set of finite graphs and M a single finite prefix-stable language.
3. $\mathcal{Z}$ is the set of graphs allowing some finite set $\mathcal{A}$ of tuples (A, L), where A is a finite graph and L a finite prefix-stable language—in the sense that:

$$\mathcal{Z} = \left\{ X \in \mathcal{X}_{\Sigma,\pi} \mid \forall v \in \mathcal{L}(X), \exists (A, L) \in \mathcal{A}, (X_v)_{|L} = A \right\}.$$

4. $\mathcal{Z}$ is the set of graphs allowing $\mathcal{A}' \times \{M\}$ where $\mathcal{A}'$ is a finite set of finite graphs and M a single finite prefix-stable language.

Definition 3 (Defining window). *The prefix-stable language M is the same in Conditions 2 and 4 of Lemma 1. It is called a* defining window *for $\mathcal{Z}$.*

Remark 3. The duality between forbidding and allowing no longer holds in general when the subshifts are not of finite type. For example we can think about the set of graphs authorizing exactly those finite graphs which have exactly one red vertex. This set however is not closed topologically (because the red vertex can in some sense vanish to infinity; cf. [2] as summarized by the Appendix) and hence it is not a subshift. Its closure is the so-called *one-dimensional sunny-side-up* subshift, as defined by forbidding those finite graphs having two red vertices.

Remark 4. Given any subshift $\mathcal{Z}$, one can define the subshift of its infinite graphs, by additionally forbidding $(F, L\pi^2)$ for every prefix-stable language $L \in \Pi^*$ and every graph F such that $F_{|L} = F$. Indeed this condition exactly means that L was already describing all possible vertices in F, and longer paths do not add any. Nevertheless, this subshift is very rarely of finite type, as we will see in the following section.

On the contrary, all SFTs presented so far contain finite graphs. It is not obvious a priori whether some SFTs contain only finite graphs, or even whether they are homogeneous, in the sense that all the graphs share a common support. We will discuss these properties in the next sections.

4   Cayley SFTs

The equivalent definitions for SFTs all capture the concept of local constraint, and in the following sections, we often define our SFTs by describing some conditions that graphs must locally satisfy. Among these conditions, *nearest-neighbor constraints* are those defined with a single edge between two vertices, that is $L \subseteq \{\varepsilon\} \sqcup \Pi$.

Example 1. A *directed 2-regular SFT* is an SFT with ports $\pi = \{a, a', b, b'\}$ obtained by imposing nearest-neighbor constraints:

1. enforcing that edges be of the form pp';
2. enforcing that all ports be occupied.

It contains, amongst many others, the Cayley graph of the free group over two generators (a tree), as well as those of all of its quotients.

Example 2 (Locally grid-like SFT). We can define a graph SFT with ports $\pi = \{a, a', b, b'\}$ corresponding to the monochromatic fullshift on $\langle a, b | aba^{-1}b^{-1} = \varepsilon\rangle$, by imposing three families of constraints:

1. enforcing that edges be of the form pp';
2. enforcing that all ports be occupied;
3. enforcing that the subgraph induced by $\{\varepsilon, aa', bb', aa'bb'\}$ obeys the relation *i.e.* form a square as in Fig. 2).

This graph SFT obviously contains the Cayley graph of $\langle a, b | aba^{-1}b^{-1} = \varepsilon\rangle$, but also the Cayley graphs of all quotient groups (excluding really small groups such as the trivial group).

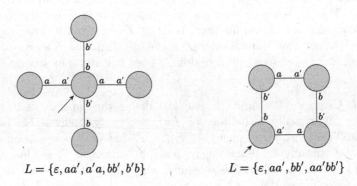

$$L = \{\varepsilon, aa', a'a, bb', b'b\} \qquad L = \{\varepsilon, aa', bb', aa'bb'\}$$

Fig. 2. *Locally grid-like SFT corresponding to the Cayley graph of $\langle a, b | aba^{-1}b^{-1}\rangle$. The SFT is defined by forbidding all but these patterns, on their corresponding languages.*

A similar construction can be performed for any finitely presented group, and via a more precise third constraint, get a cleaner statement (with all possible quotients).

Definition 4 (Cayley SFT). *Consider a finitely presented group $\Gamma = \langle \mathcal{J} | \mathcal{R}\rangle$, that is, a group generated by the abstract finite set $\mathcal{J}$, where $\mathcal{R}$ represents a set of relations, that is words over $\mathcal{J} \sqcup \mathcal{J}^{-1}$ that represent the identity element (and from which all such words can be derived). For example $\mathbb{Z}^2 = \langle a, b | aba^{-1}b^{-1}\rangle$ (it will always be implicitly given by this canonical presentation) and $\mathbb{F}_2 = \langle a, b |\rangle$.*

For every alphabet Σ, there is a canonical way to associate a Cayley SFT $\mathcal{Z}_{\Sigma}^{\Gamma}$ to the group Γ (in fact, to the pair $(\Gamma, \mathcal{J})$, which is a marked group when $\mathcal{J}$ is symmetric and does not contain the identity ε). Define $\pi = \mathcal{J} \sqcup \mathcal{J}^{-1}$ and the following constraints:

1. *each edge involves two inverse ports;*
2. *every vertex must have all possible ports;*

3. *for every word $u \in \mathcal{R}$ and L its language of prefixes, one forbids the pair (Y, L) for every graph Y supported by L in which path u is not a cycle back to the origin.*

Let Γ be a finitely presented group. A SFT over alphabet Σ is defined by Γ-NN constraints *if they include precisely the forbidden patterns defining $\mathcal{Z}_{\Sigma}^{\Gamma}$ and some additional nearest-neighbor constraints. Note that if $\Gamma = \mathbb{F}_k$, then $\mathbb{F}_k$-NN constraints are simply constraints on the edges, provided the correct regularity of the graph.*

Remark 5. The Cayley SFT obviously contains the Cayley graph of Γ, but also all Cayley graphs of its quotient groups, as will be seen in the next section. For example, $\mathcal{Z}_{\Sigma}^{\mathbb{Z}^2}$ contains the infinite grid as well as tori and cylinders, and $\mathcal{Z}_{\Sigma}^{\mathbb{F}_2}$ contains Cayley graphs of all groups with two generators.

Any classical nearest-neighbor SFT defined over some Cayley graph Γ is included in the corresponding graph SFT defined by Γ-NN constraints.

To define a subshift whose unique support is the Cayley graph of Γ, one generally needs to add many constraints imposing that paths that are not labeled by words representing the identity element be not cycles. This usually yields a subshift of infinite type.

Example 3 (Hard-square model). The hard-square model SFT is defined by $\mathbb{Z}^2$-NN constraints: $\mathcal{Z} \subseteq \mathcal{X}_{\{0,1\},\{a,a',b,b'\}}$ such that for every configuration X and edge $\{x : a, y : b\} \in E(X)$, one has that $\sigma_X(x) = 0$ or $\sigma_X(y) = 0$. This can be expressed as an SFT by forbidding the 0/1-coloured versions of Fig. 2 that have two adjacent 1-coloured vertices. This is a direct generalization of a well-known SFT over $\mathbb{Z}^2$. As a graph SFT, it not only contains all the configurations that are already present on $\mathbb{Z}^2$ such as in Fig. 3, but also new infinite configurations such as the cylinder of Fig. 4, and even finite configuration such as tori only containing 0.

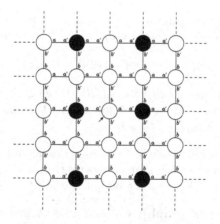

Fig. 3. *Configuration of the hard-square model that is present in $\mathbb{Z}^2$. The colours represent the 0/1 internal states of the vertices.*

Besides finitely presented groups, the notion of quotient of a group can be extended to periodic graphs, which is the subject of the following section.

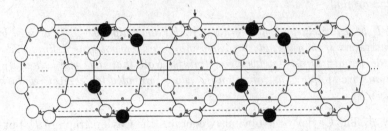

Fig. 4. *Configuration of the hard-square model whose support graph is not* $\mathbb{Z}^2$. *In order to preserve clarity, only half of the ports are written and some edges have been dashed.*

5 Periodicity and Finiteness

5.1 Quotient and Periods

Definition 5 (Period). *Any word* $u \in \mathcal{L}(X)$ *such that* $X = X_u$ *is called a path-period. The corresponding vertex* $\hat{u}$ *is called a* period. *The stabilizer of* X *is its set of periods; it is denoted by* $\mathcal{S}(X)$. X *is called* weakly periodic *if* $\mathcal{S}(X) \supsetneq \{\hat{\varepsilon}\}$, *strongly nonperiodic if* $\mathcal{S}(X) = \{\hat{\varepsilon}\}$.

Notice that if X is weakly periodic, then $\mathcal{S}(X)$ is infinite or every period $\hat{u}$ is *torsion, i.e.* $\widehat{u^n} = \hat{\varepsilon}$ for some $n \geq 2$.

Notice that monochromatic Cayley graphs are exactly the graphs whose all vertices are periods. As we have seen in our Cayley SFT examples, periodic graphs can typically be "folded into smaller graphs" that also belong to the graph SFT. The following formalizes the idea of a graph folding into another one.

Definition 6 (Homomorphism). *A* homomorphism *from graph* $X \in \mathcal{X}$ *to graph* $X' \in \mathcal{X}$ *is a function* φ *from* $V(X)$ *to* $V(X')$ *such that for all* $u \in \mathcal{L}(X)$,

$$\varphi(\hat{u}) = \hat{u} \quad and \quad \sigma_X(\hat{u}) = \sigma_{X'}(\hat{u}).$$

Note the first equality implies $\mathcal{L}(X) \subseteq \mathcal{L}(X')$. *When* $\mathcal{L}(X) = \mathcal{L}(X')$ *(note that this implies that* φ *is surjective and locally injective), we then say that* X covers X' *and that* φ *is a* covering.

Remark 6. A homomorphism sends cycles to cycles and does not change the set of path-periods (i.e. if u' is such that $\hat{u}' = \phi(\hat{u})$, then $X = X_u \iff X' = X'_{u'}$). Hence if $\hat{u}$ is a period of X, $\varphi(\hat{u})$ is a period of $\varphi(X)$.

Definition 7 (Quotient graph). *Consider* $X \in \mathcal{X}$ *and a stabilizer subgroup* H. *We can define a* quotient graph X/H *to be* $X((G, p))$ *where:*

- $V(G) = \{H\hat{u} | \hat{u} \in V(X)\}$, *i.e. each vertex is labelled by a set* $H\hat{u} = \{Hv | v \equiv_X u\}$.
- $p = H$, *i.e. the pointer is the vertex labeled by* H.
- $E(G) = \left\{ (H\hat{u} : a, H\widehat{uab} : b) \middle| uab \in \mathcal{L}(X) \right\}$.
- $\sigma_G(H\hat{u}) = \sigma_X(\hat{u})$.

By stabilizer subgroup, we mean a subgroup of the stabilizer group. As the elements of a stabilizer subgroup cannot be distinguished modulo isomorphism, it follows that a stabilizer subgroup induces a natural covering:

Proposition 1. *For every graph* $X \in \mathcal{X}$ *and every stabilizer subgroup* H *of* X, X/H *is a well-defined graph, and* $\phi : \hat{u} \mapsto H\hat{u}$ *is a covering from* $V(X)$ *to* $V(X/H)$.

On top of being able to"fold" a graph, we can do so while locally preserving it, given that a certain condition on the stabilizer subgroup is met:

Definition 8 (Separated). *If* $U, V \subset \Pi^*$, *then we denote* $UV := \{uv | u \in U, v \in V\}$, *and* $\overline{U} := \{\overline{u} | u \in U\}$. *If* $M \subseteq \Pi^*$ *is a prefix-stable language, we say that a set* H *of vertices is* M-separated *in graph* X *if for every* $\hat{u} \in V(X)$, *there at most one* $\hat{v} \in H$ *such that there exists* $w \in M\overline{M}$ *with* $\widehat{uw} = \hat{v}$.

Proposition 2. *Let* X *be a graph,* $M \subseteq \Pi^*$ *a prefix-stable language, and* $H \le \mathcal{S}(X)$ *a stabilizer subgroup which is* M-separated *in* X. *Then the covering preserves the language of support* M *in the sense that for all* $u \in \mathcal{L}(X)$, $(X_u)_{|M} = (X/H_u)_{|M}$ *(modulo isomorphism).*
In particular, if X *belongs to some SFT* $\mathcal{X}$ *with defining window* M, *then* X/H *also belongs to* $\mathcal{X}$.

5.2   Strong Periodicity

Definition 9 (Density, strong periodicity). *Consider a graph* X *and a finite prefix-stable language* $M \subset \Pi^*$. *We say that a language* $L \in \Pi^*$ *is* M-dense *in* X *if for all* $\hat{u} \in V(X)$, $uM \cap L \ne \emptyset$. L *is said dense in* X *if such a* M *exists. A graph* X *is said to be* strongly periodic *if its stabilizer* $\mathcal{S}(X)$ *is dense in* X. *Equivalently, there are only finitely many distinct (modulo isomorphisms) graphs* X_u, *for* $u \in \mathcal{L}(X)$.

Note that finite graphs are strongly periodic, but may not always be weakly periodic. Apart from this degenerate case, strongly periodic graphs are weakly periodic.

Notice also that strong periodicity is almost equivalent to being a Cayley graph, up to replacement of each vertex by a fixed finite graph (with possible edges between them). This replacement (factor map) corresponds somehow to the application of a causal graph dynamics [2] to the Cayley graph.

Lemma 2. *A graph* X *is strongly periodic if and only if* X/H *is finite for some stabilizer subgroup* H.

The following result establishes a connection between the SFT that admit finite graphs, and the well-established notion (see for instance [7, Chap. 2]) of residual finiteness from group theory:

Definition 10 (Residually finite group). *A group S is residually finite if and only if for any non-identity element $\hat{u} \in S$, there exists a normal subgroup $H \trianglelefteq S$ of finite index such that $\hat{u} \notin H$.*

This notion is very robust. In particular, the property extends to finite sets of non-identity elements I, *i.e.* there exists a normal subgroup $H \trianglelefteq S$ of finite index such that $H \cap I = \emptyset$, simply because any finite intersection of finite-index subgroups is a finite-index subgroup.

Let us relate residual finiteness to quotient graphs, at the intuitive level first. Say X belongs to some SFT $\mathcal{Y}$ and let $\hat{u}_1, \ldots, \hat{u}_n$ be distinct elements of $V(X)$. The above property gives a subgroup H of its stabilizer, and thus X/H is a possible quotient graph; one which maintains that $\hat{u}_1, \ldots \hat{u}_n$ are distinct. The correct choice of $\hat{u}_1, \ldots, \hat{u}_n$ will help us make sure that X/H still belongs to SFT $\mathcal{Y}$.

Theorem 1. *Let $\mathcal{Y}$ be a SFT. $\mathcal{Y}$ contains a finite graph if and only if $\mathcal{Y}$ contains a strongly periodic graph X such that the stabilizer $\mathcal{S}(X)$ is residually finite.*

Thus there are two complementary ways in which a nonempty SFT may have only infinite configurations: either by preventing strongly periodic configurations, or by forcing them to have stabilizers that are not residually finite.

In the latter case (for example when the stabilizer is a Tarski monster group, see for instance [21]), one can build SFTs with strongly periodic configurations that do not fold uniformly onto finite graphs, as shown by the following.

Remark 7. Γ is not residually finite if and only if $\mathcal{Z}^{\Gamma}_{\{0\}}$ includes an SFT containing the Cayley graph of Γ but no finite quotient of it. Indeed, one can consider the SFT $\mathcal{Z}$ included in $\mathcal{Z}^{\Gamma}_{\{0\}}$ defined by the additional constraint that u is never a cycle, where u is a noncyclic path that witnesses that Γ is not residually finite, in the sense that all finite quotients of Γ map u to ε.

5.3 Quotients in Cayley SFTs

We have seen that the notions of quotients and SFTs are linked, because finite-type constraints cannot easily tell a graph from some of its quotients. On the opposite point of view, it is noticeable that some SFTs admit a maximal support with respect to coverings.

Proposition 3. *Let Γ be a finitely presented group, X a graph, and $\mathcal{Z}$ some SFT defined by Γ-NN constraints. The following are equivalent:*

1. *$X \in \mathcal{Z}$.*
2. *X is covered by some colored Cayley graph Y of Γ which is in $\mathcal{Z}$.*

Remark 8. In graphs of $\mathcal{Z}_\Sigma^\Gamma$, all stabilizers are subgroups of Γ (because the concatenation law is coherent with that of the group). One has to be careful though, that quotients of Cayley graphs may not be Cayley graphs, because the stabilizer is not always a normal subgroup. Nevertheless, it is classical that every finite-index subgroup includes a finite-index normal subgroup (see for instance [7, Lemma 2.1.10]), so that a graph of $\mathcal{Z}_\Sigma^\Gamma$ is strongly periodic if and only if some stabilizer subgroup is a finite-index normal subgroup of Γ.

In particular, in graphs of $\mathcal{Z}_\Sigma^{\mathbb{Z}^2}$, all stabilizers are subgroups of $\mathbb{Z}^2$, which makes many properties easier.

Proposition 4. *Let $\mathcal{Z}$ be an SFT defined by $\mathbb{Z}^2$-NN constraints. Then exactly one of the following occurs:*

1. *Every graph in $\mathcal{Z}$ is supported by the infinite grid, and is strongly nonperiodic.*
2. *$\mathcal{Z}$ contains a finite graph and a strongly periodic infinite grid.*

It is already interesting to note that the dichotomy from Proposition 4 is nontrivial, directly from the existence of strongly aperiodic SFTs over the grid (and other ones). But the next subsection will show a stronger result.

5.4 Undecidability

Theorem 2. *The dichotomy from Proposition 4 is undecidable, given a list of $\mathbb{Z}^2$-NN constraints.*

This is a consequence of Theorem 1, allowing us to reduce the previous dichotomy to a classical periodicity problem on $\mathbb{Z}^2$. Consequently, the class of graph SFTs that contains only infinite graphs with the same support is computably unseparable from the class of graph SFTs containing both finite and infinite graphs.

This means the undecidability of any property that is implied by one of the two classes, and which implies the negation of the other one.

Corollary 1. *The problem whether a graph SFT contains only infinite graphs, and the problem whether a graph SFT admits only one support for all its graphs, are both undecidable (even when restricted to graph SFTs with $\mathbb{Z}^2$-NN constraints).*

More precisely, the reduction directly gives that all properties separating the dichotomy are Σ_1^0-hard. The encoding of Cayley graphs into graph SFTs also, more directly, implies the following undecidability result.

Theorem 3. *There exists a finite presentation of a group Γ such that the problem whether a given word $u \in \Pi^*$ represents a cycle from the origin back to itself in every graph of $\mathcal{Z}_{\{0\}}^\Gamma$ is undecidable.*

It is actually Σ_1^0-complete.

6   Conclusion

To sum up, we provided a formalism generalizing SFTs on Cayley graphs by allowing the support graph to be determined by forbidden subgraphs. The generalization also allows the SFT to have finite configurations and we provided examples of such SFT. By defining quotient graphs, we have shown that the only way for an SFT to not have finite configurations is to only have configurations that are either nonperiodic, or with a stabilizer that is not residually finite. Similarly, we have shown that having only one support graph requires configurations to have finite stabilizers. We used both results to prove that the finite configuration problem and the support graph unicity problem are undecidable.

In the future, we wish to study determinism and the relation between causal graph dynamics and graph subshifts, in the perspective of proving structure and complexity results on causal graph dynamics. Moreover, graph subshifts could provide a new point of view for studying group subshifts. On the other hand, many notions and results known over group subshifts such as sofic subshifts, determinism or entropy, would be interesting to lift to graph subshifts.

We have seen that graph subshifts could generalize both classical symbolic dynamics and finite-type group geometry. They could be used to simulate a larger class of objects; let us discuss one example. Let T be a finite set of *tiles*, *i.e.* polygons of the plane $\mathbb{R}^2$. A *tiling* is then a covering of $\mathbb{R}^2$ by translated copies of tiles from T, the intersection of any two of them being either empty, or a vertex, or a whole edge, or the whole tile. Now let us define subshift $\mathcal{Z}_T$ with $\Sigma = T$, π as the set of tile edges up to translation, and the following constraints: each vertex labeled $t \in T$ must have exactly those ports which correspond to the edges of t, and every simple cycle must correspond to a valid vertex in a tiling of the plane by T (*i.e.* it involves tiles that can be put next to each other around this vertex). The fact that the latter condition can be forced by finitely many constraints (so that $\mathcal{Z}_T$ be an SFT) is equivalent to the classical *finite-local-complexity* property of T. With this construction, there is a one-to-one correspondence between tilings by T of the plane and of all surfaces and graphs in $\mathcal{Z}_T$. Now if one is interested in the shift-orbit closure of a single tiling of the plane (*i.e.* the Penrose tiling), it is an interesting question whether this corresponds to an SFT in $\mathcal{Z}_T$. Some work has been devoted to understanding for which tilings one can force locally tilings of the plane to be in the shift-orbit closure [6,9]; one says that the tilings admits *local rules*. Additionnally forbidding (via finite constraints) all possible graphs which represent tilings on surfaces but not on the plane is a new question. Our work shows that if the tiles are rectangles and if we allow some decorations (that could also be encoded locally as small hanging subgraphs), then this is possible. It is tempting to think that this remains possible in the case of general strongly nonperiodic tilings, but the proofs would require a new formalism, because the support is no longer a Cayley graph. The same could be done in the tridimensional space, or in the hyperbolic plane.

Let us make a final remark. Graph theorists are used to considering families of graphs defined by forbidden finite graph minors. Of course, seen as including possibly infinite graphs, these families are subshifts, but they are a priori not SFTs (not even sofic). However, even if the *minor* operation involves vertices at possibly unbounded distance, it is known to have some kind of representation as local constraints [15] (involving a nondeterministic coloring). The relation with our setting could be investigated.

Acknowledgements. We thank the referees for their careful reading of the preliminary version, and helpful remarks. We are indebted to Nicolas Schabanel who encouraged us to study graph subshifts and contributed to the first four definitions. This publication was made possible through the support of the ID# 62312 grant from the John Templeton Foundation, as part of the 'The Quantum Information Structure of Spacetime' Project (QISS). The opinions expressed in this publication are those of the author(s) and do not necessarily reflect the views of the John Templeton Foundation.

References

1. Arrighi, P., Durbec, A., Emmanuel, A.: Reversibility vs local creation/destruction. In: Thomsen, M.K., Soeken, M. (eds.) RC 2019. LNCS, vol. 11497, pp. 51–66. Springer, Cham (2019). https://doi.org/10.1007/978-3-030-21500-24
2. Arrighi, P., Martiel, S., Nesme, V.: Cellular automata over generalized Cayley graphs. Math. Struct. Comput. Sci. **28**(3), 340–383 (2018). https://doi.org/10.1017/S0960129517000044
3. Ballier, A.: Propriétés structurelles, combinatoires et logiques des pavages. Ph.D. thesis, Université de Provence, November 2009
4. Baumslag, G., Solitar, D., Some two-generator one-relator non-Hopfian groups. Bull. Am. Math. Soc. **68**(3), 199–201, 00471 (1962). https://www.ams.org/bull/1962-68-03/S0002-9904-1962-10745-9/, https://doi.org/10.1090/S0002-9904-1962-10745-9
5. Berger, R.: The undecidability of the domino problem. Ph.D. Harvard University (1964)
6. Bédaride, N., Fernique, T.: When periodicities enforce aperiodicity. Commun. Math. Phys. **335**(3), 1099–1120 (2015). https://doi.org/10.1007/s00220-015-2334-8
7. Ceccherini-Silberstein, T., Coornaert, M.: Cellular Automata and Groups. Springer, Heidelberg (2009). https://doi.org/10.1007/978-3-642-14034-1
8. de Menibus, B.H.: Addendum to: tiling an arbitrary amenable group is decidable. draft (2022)
9. Fernique, T., Sablik, M.: Weak colored local rules for planar tilings. arXiv:1603.09485 [cs, math], March 2016. http://arxiv.org/abs/1603.09485
10. Gambaudo, J.-M.: A note on tilings and translation surfaces. Ergodic Theory Dyn. Syst. **26**(1), 179–188 (2006)
11. Gurevich, Y., Koryakov, I.: A remark on Berger's paper on the domino problem. Siberian J. Math. **13**, 459–463 (1972)
12. Hedlund, G.A.: Endomorphisms and automorphisms of the shift dynamical system. Math. Syst. Theory **3**, 320–375 (1969)
13. Jeandel, E., Vanier, P.: The undecidability of the domino problem. In: Akiyama, S., Arnoux, P. (eds.) Substitution and Tiling Dynamics: Introduction to Self-inducing Structures. LNM, vol. 2273, pp. 293–357. Springer, Cham (2020). https://doi.org/10.1007/978-3-030-57666-0_6

14. Kari, J.: The nilpotency problem of one-dimensional cellular automata. SIAM J. Comput. **21**(3), 571–586 (1992)
15. Kuske, D., Lohrey, M.: Logical aspects of Cayley-graphs: the group case. Ann. Pure Applied Logic **131**(1–3), 263–286 (2005). http://linkinghub.elsevier.com/retrieve/pii/S0168007204000831, https://doi.org/10.1016/j.apal.2004.06.002
16. Langton, C.G.: Self-reproduction in cellular automata. Physica D **10**, 135–144 (1984)
17. Lind, D.A., Marcus, B.: An Introduction to Symbolic Dynamics and Coding, p. 03085. Cambridge University Press, Cambridge, New York (1995)
18. Lyndon, R.C., Schupp, P.E.: Combinatorial Group Theory. Classics in Mathematics, p. 04184. Springer, Heidelberg (2001). https://www.springer.com/gp/book/9783540411581
19. Thierry Monteil. Down with hierarchy! (2013). FrAC
20. Novikov, P.S.: On the algorithmic unsolvability of the word problem in group theory. Proc. Steklov Inst. Math. **44**, 1–143 (1955). in Russian
21. Ol'shanskiI, A.Y.: Geometry of Defining Relations in Groups, vol. 70. Springer, Dordrecht (2012). https://doi.org/10.1007/978-94-011-3618-1
22. Piantadosi, S.: Symbolic dynamics on free groups. Discrete Continuous Dyn. Syst. A **20**(3), 725–738 (2008). http://aimsciences.org//article/doi/10.3934/dcds.2008.20.725, https://doi.org/10.3934/dcds.2008.20.725

Improved Complexity Analysis of Quasi-Polynomial Algorithms Solving Parity Games

Paweł Parys[✉][ID] and Aleksander Wiącek

Institute of Informatics, University of Warsaw, Warsaw, Poland
parys@mimuw.edu.pl

Abstract. We improve the complexity of solving parity games (with priorities in vertices) for $d = \omega(\log n)$ by a factor of $\Theta(d^2)$: the best complexity known to date was $\mathcal{O}(mdn^{1.45+\log_2(d/\log_2 n)})$, while we obtain $\mathcal{O}(mn^{1.45+\log_2(d/\log_2 n)}/d)$, where n is the number of vertices, m is the number of edges, and d is the number of priorities.

We base our work on existing algorithms using universal trees, and we improve their complexity. We present two independent improvements. First, an improvement by a factor of $\Theta(d)$ comes from a more careful analysis of the width of universal trees. Second, we perform (or rather recall) a finer analysis of requirements for a universal tree: while for solving games with priorities on edges one needs an n-universal tree, in the case of games with priorities in vertices it is enough to use an $n/2$-universal tree. This way, we allow solving games of size $2n$ in the time needed previously to solve games of size n; such a change divides the quasi-polynomial complexity again by a factor of $\Theta(d)$.

Keywords: Parity games · Universal trees · Quasi-polynomial time

1 Introduction

Parity games have played a fundamental role in automata theory, logic, and their applications to verification and synthesis since early 1990s. The algorithmic problem of finding the winner in parity games can be seen as the algorithmic back end to problems in the automated verification and controller synthesis. It is polynomial-time equivalent to the emptiness problem for nondeterministic automata on infinite trees with parity acceptance conditions, and to the model-checking problem for modal μ-calculus [14]. It lies also at the heart of algorithmic solutions to the Church's synthesis problem [29]. Moreover, decision problems for modal logics like validity or satisfiability of formulae in these logics can be reduced to parity game solving. Some ideas coming originally from parity games allowed obtaining new results concerning translations between automata models for ω-words [5,10], as well as concerning relatively far areas of computer science, like Markov decision processes [15] and linear programming [18,19].

P. Parys—Author supported by the National Science Centre, Poland (grant no. 2021/41/B/ST6/03914).

The complexity of solving parity games, that is, deciding which player has a winning strategy, is a long standing open question. The problem is known to be in UP ∩ coUP [20] (a subclass of NP ∩ coNP) and the search variant (i.e., to find a winning strategy) is in PLS, PPAD, and even in their subclass CLS [9]. The study of algorithms for solving parity games has been dominated for over two decades by algorithms whose run-time was exponential in the number of distinct priorities [2,6,21,30–33], or mildly subexponential for a large number of priorities [4,25]. The breakthrough came in 2017 from Calude, Jain, Khoussainov, Li, and Stephan [7] who gave the first quasi-polynomial-time algorithm using the novel idea of *play summaries*. Several other quasi-polynomial-time algorithms were developed soon after [3,11,16,22,24,26–28].

Fijalkow [17] made explicit the concept of *universal trees* that is implicit in the *succinct tree coding* result of Jurdziński and Lazić [22]. It was then observed that universal trees are not only present, but actually necessary in all existing quasi-polynomial-time approaches for solving parity games [1,8,23]. Namely, it was shown that any algorithm solving a parity game with n vertices, and following existing approaches, needs to operate on an n-universal tree (as defined in the sequel). There is, however, a catch here: this necessity proof is for parity games with priorities on edges, while quite often one considers less succinct games with priorities in vertices. (A general method for switching from priorities on edges to priorities in vertices is to replace each vertex by d vertices, one for each priority, and to redirect every edge to a copy of the target vertex having the appropriate priority; then the number of vertices changes from n to nd.)

The main contribution of this paper lies in a finer analysis of the width of n-universal trees. We improve the upper bound on this width (and thus also the upper bound on the running time of algorithms using such trees) by a factor of $\Theta\left(\frac{d}{\log n}\right)$, where d is the number of priorities.

Then, a second improvement is obtained by recalling from Jurdziński and Lazić [22] that in order to solve parity games with priorities in vertices it is enough to use an $\lfloor n/2 \rfloor$-universal tree instead of an n-universal trees, exploiting the "catch" mentioned above. This allows solving games of size $2n$ in the time needed previously to solve games of size n and, in consequence, improves the complexity of solving parity games (with priorities in vertices) once again by a factor of $\Theta\left(\frac{d}{\log n}\right)$.

Combining the two improvements, we decrease the upper bound on the complexity of solving parity games with $d = \omega(\log n)$ by a factor of $\Theta\left(\frac{d^2}{\log^2 n}\right)$: the best bound known to date [17,22], namely $\mathcal{O}(mdn^{1.45+\log_2(d/\log_2 n)})$, is decreased to the bound $\mathcal{O}(mn^{1.45+\log_2(d/\log_2 n)}/d)$. We remark that both bounds do not display polylogarithmic factors; they are dominated by $n^{\mathcal{O}(1)}$, where the $\mathcal{O}(1)$ comes from the difference between 1.45 and the actual constant $\log_2 e$ which should appear in the exponent (the same style of writing the bound is employed in prior work). Thus, while writing the bounds in such a form, the improvement is by a factor of $\Theta(d^2)$. Simultaneously, the two observations become too weak to improve asymptotics of the complexity in the case of $d = \mathcal{O}(\log n)$.

2   Preliminaries

Parity Games. A *parity game* is a two-player game between players Even and Odd played on a *game graph* defined as a tuple $\mathcal{G} = (V, V_{\mathsf{Even}}, E, d, \pi)$, where (V, E) is a nonempty finite directed graph in which every vertex has at least one successor; its vertices are labelled with positive integer *priorities* by $\pi \colon V \to \{1, 2, \ldots, d\}$ (for some *even* number $d \in \mathbb{N}$), and divided between vertices V_{Even} *belonging to Even* and vertices $V_{\mathsf{Odd}} = V \setminus V_{\mathsf{Even}}$ *belonging to Odd*. We usually denote $|V|$ by n and $|E|$ by m.

Intuitively, the dynamics of the game are defined as follows. The play starts in a designated starting vertex. Then, the player to whom the current vertex belongs selects a successor of this vertex, and the game continues there. After an infinite time, we check for the maximal priority visited infinitely often; its parity says which player wins.

Formally, we define the winner of a game using positional (i.e., memoryless) strategies. An *Even's positional strategy* is a set $\sigma \subseteq E$ of edges such that for every vertex v of Even, in σ there is exactly one edge starting in v, and for every vertex v of Odd, in σ there are all edges starting in v. An *Odd's positional strategy* is defined by swapping the roles of Even and Odd. An Even's (Odd's) positional strategy σ is winning from a vertex v if for every infinite path in the subgraph (V, σ), the maximal priority occurring infinitely often on this path is even (odd, respectively). We say that Even/Odd *wins* from v if Even/Odd has a positional strategy winning from v.

The above definition accurately describes the winning player due to *positional determinacy* of parity games: from every vertex v of a parity game, one of the players, Even or Odd, wins from v [13]. It follows that if a player can win from a vertex by a general strategy (not defined here), then he can win also by a positional strategy.

Trees and Universal Trees. In progress measure algorithms [11,17,22] strategies are described by mappings from game graphs to ordered trees, defined as follows: an *ordered tree* (or simply a *tree*) T of height h is a finite connected acyclic graph, given together with a linear order $\leq_x$ for every node x thereof, such that

- there is exactly one node with in-degree 0, called a *root*; every other node has in-degree 1;
- for every *leaf* (i.e., a node of out-degree 0), the unique path from the root to this leaf consists of h edges;
- $\leq_x$ is a linear order on the *children* of x (i.e., nodes to which there is an edge from x), which describes the left-to-right ordering of these children.

The *width* of a tree T is defined as its number of leaves and denoted $|T|$.

Let T_1 and T_2 be two ordered trees of the same height. We say that T_1 *embeds* into T_2 if there is an injective mapping f preserving the child relation and the $\leq_x$ relations:

- if y is a child of x in T_1, then $f(y)$ is a child of $f(x)$ in T_2, and
- if $y \leq_x z$ in T_1, then $f(y) \leq_{f(x)} f(z)$ in T_2.

A tree $\mathcal{T}$ of height h is *n-universal* if every ordered tree of height h and width at most n embeds into $\mathcal{T}$. Consult Fig. 1 for an example.

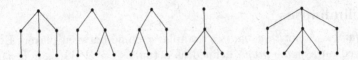

Fig. 1. All four trees of height 2 and width 3 (left); a 3-universal tree of height 2 (right)

3   On the Width of Universal Trees

In this section we prove an improved upper bound on the width of universal trees, as described by the following theorem:

Theorem 3.1. *For all $n, h \in \mathbb{N}$, where $n \geq 1$, there exists an n-universal tree of height h and width at most $f(n, h)$, where*

$$f(n, h) \leq n \cdot \binom{h - 1 + \lfloor \log_2 n \rfloor}{\lfloor \log_2 n \rfloor} \leq n^{2.45 - \varepsilon + \log_2 \left(1 + \frac{h-1}{\log_2 n}\right)}$$

for some $\varepsilon > 0$. Additionally, $f(n, h) = \mathcal{O}(n^{2.45 - \varepsilon + \log_2(h/\log_2 n)})$ if $h = \omega(\log n)$.

We remark that as the height h we usually take (numbers close to) $d/2$, where d is the number of priorities in a parity game. The value $2.45 - \varepsilon$ in the exponent means that the actual constant is slightly smaller than 2.45.

Before giving a proof, let us compare the above bound with bounds known to date: Fijalkow [17, Theorem 4] derives an upper bound of $2^{\lceil \log_2 n \rceil} \binom{h - 1 + \lceil \log_2 n \rceil}{\lceil \log_2 n \rceil}$. The difference is thus in replacing $\lceil \log_2 n \rceil$ by $\lfloor \log_2 n \rfloor$. For "a majority" of n these two values differ by 1, in which case the quotient of the two binomial coefficients is $\frac{h - 1 + \lceil \log_2 n \rceil}{\lceil \log_2 n \rceil}$; this quotient is in $\Theta\left(\frac{h}{\log n}\right)$ if $h = \omega(\log n)$. Coming to the asymptotics, the bound of Fijalkow is in $\mathcal{O}(hn^{2.45 - \varepsilon + \log_2(h/\log_2 n)})$ (see Jurdziński and Lazić [22, Lemma 6] for a proof), which is indeed worse by a factor of $\Theta(h)$ than our bound.

In order to prove Theorem 3.1, we use a construction of Fijalkow [17, Theorem 4] (which is essentially the same construction as in Jurdziński and Lazić [22]). He shows that there exists an n-universal tree of height h and width $f(n, h)$, where the function f (extended to $n = 0$ by setting $f(0, h) = 0$, and to $h = 0$, $n \geq 1$ by setting $f(n, 0) = 1$) is defined by the following recursive formula:

$$f(0, h) = 0 \qquad\qquad\qquad\qquad\qquad\qquad\text{for } h \geq 0,$$
$$f(n, 0) = 1 \qquad\qquad\qquad\qquad\qquad\qquad\text{for } n \geq 1,$$
$$f(n, h) = f(n, h - 1) + f(\lfloor n/2 \rfloor, h) + f(n - 1 - \lfloor n/2 \rfloor, h) \quad \text{for } n, h \geq 1. \quad (1)$$

Compared to Fijalkow [17], we thus perform a more careful analysis of the above recursive formula. First, we provide an explicit formula for $f(n, h)$:

Lemma 3.2. *The function f can be described by the following explicit formula, for all $n, h \geq 1$:*

$$f(n,h) = \sum_{i=0}^{\lfloor \log_2 n \rfloor - 1} 2^i \cdot \binom{h-1+i}{h-1} + (n - 2^{\lfloor \log_2 n \rfloor} + 1) \cdot \binom{h-1+\lfloor \log_2 n \rfloor}{h-1}.$$

While it is possible to confirm the correctness of Lemma 3.2 by an inductive proof, we present here a proof based on generating functions, as it is more instructive.

Proof (Lemma 3.2). Let $F(x,y) = \sum_{n,h \geq 1} f(n,h) x^n y^h$ be a generating function of the two-dimensional sequence $f(n,h)$, excluding the values for $n = 0$ and for $h = 0$. We multiply both sides of Eq. (1) by $x^n y^h$, and then we sum the result over all $n, h \geq 1$; we obtain that

$$F(x,y) = \sum_{\substack{n \geq 1 \\ h \geq 1}} f(n, h-1) x^n y^h + \sum_{\substack{k \geq 1 \\ h \geq 1}} (f(k,h) + f(k-1,h)) x^{2k} y^h$$

$$+ \sum_{\substack{k \geq 0 \\ h \geq 1}} 2f(k,h) x^{2k+1} y^h.$$

Next, in the first sum above we shift h by 1, and we move components with $f(n,0)$ into a separate sum; in the second sum above we split $f(k,h) + f(k-1,h)$ into two separate sums, where in the latter we shift k by 1, and we move components with $f(0,h)$ into a separate sum; in the last sum above, we move components for $k = 0$ into a separate sum. We obtain

$$F(x,y) = \sum_{n \geq 1} f(n,0) x^n y + \sum_{\substack{n \geq 1 \\ h \geq 1}} f(n,h) x^n y^{h+1}$$

$$+ \sum_{\substack{k \geq 1 \\ h \geq 1}} f(k,h)(x^2)^k y^h + \sum_{h \geq 1} f(0,h) x^2 y^h + \sum_{\substack{k \geq 1 \\ h \geq 1}} f(k,h)(x^2)^k y^h x^2$$

$$+ \sum_{h \geq 1} 2f(0,h) xy^h + \sum_{\substack{k \geq 1 \\ h \geq 1}} 2f(k,h)(x^2)^k y^h x$$

$$= \frac{xy}{1-x} + yF(x,y) + F(x^2,y) + 0 + x^2 F(x^2,y) + 0 + 2x F(x^2,y).$$

This gives us the following equation concerning the generating function:

$$F(x,y) = yF(x,y) + F(x^2,y)(1 + 2x + x^2) + \frac{xy}{1-x}. \tag{2}$$

Let $H(x,y) = \frac{1-x}{y} F(x,y)$; then $F(x,y) = \frac{y}{1-x} H(x,y)$. Note that H is the generating function representing the differences between values of f for successive values of n, with h shifted by 1. Substituting this to Eq. (2) we obtain:

$$\frac{y}{1-x}H(x,y) = \frac{y^2}{1-x}H(x,y) + \frac{y}{1-x^2}H(x^2,y)(1+x)^2 + \frac{xy}{1-x},$$

$$\frac{y}{1-x}H(x,y) = \frac{y^2}{1-x}H(x,y) + \frac{y}{1-x}H(x^2,y)(1+x) + \frac{xy}{1-x},$$

$$H(x,y) = yH(x,y) + H(x^2,y)(1+x) + x.$$

Next, let us write $H(x,y) = \sum_{n\geq 1} x^n h_n(y)$. We substitute this to the equation above:

$$\sum_{n\geq 1} x^n h_n(y) = \sum_{n\geq 1} x^n y h_n(y) + \sum_{n\geq 1} (x^{2n} + x^{2n+1}) h_n(y) + x.$$

In order to find h_n, we compare coefficients in front of x^n, on both sides of the equation. For $n = 1$ we have

$$h_1(y) = yh_1(y) + 1, \qquad \text{so} \qquad h_1(y) = \frac{1}{1-y},$$

and for $n \geq 2$ we have

$$h_n(y) = yh_n(y) + h_{\lfloor n/2 \rfloor}(y), \qquad \text{so} \qquad h_n(y) = \frac{h_{\lfloor n/2 \rfloor}(y)}{1-y}.$$

It follows that for all $n \geq 1$ we have a formula

$$h_n(y) = \frac{1}{(1-y)^{\lfloor \log_2 n \rfloor + 1}}.$$

Below, we use the notation $[x^n]A(x)$ for the coefficient in front of x^n in the function $A(x)$. We also use the following formula, where $k \geq 1$:

$$\frac{1}{(1-x)^k} = \sum_{n=0}^{\infty} \binom{n+k-1}{n} x^n. \tag{3}$$

We now conclude the proof (here we assume that $n, h \geq 1$):

$$f(n,h) = [x^n y^h]F(x,y) = [x^n y^h]\frac{y}{1-x}H(x,y)$$

$$= [y^{h-1}]\sum_{j=0}^{n}[x^j]H(x,y) = [y^{h-1}]\sum_{j=1}^{n} h_j(y)$$

$$= [y^{h-1}]\left(\sum_{i=0}^{\lfloor \log_2 n \rfloor - 1} 2^i h_{2^i}(y) + (n - 2^{\lfloor \log_2 n \rfloor} + 1)h_{2^{\lfloor \log_2 n \rfloor}}(y) \right)$$

$$= \sum_{i=0}^{\lfloor \log_2 n \rfloor - 1} 2^i [y^{h-1}]\frac{1}{(1-y)^{i+1}} + (n - 2^{\lfloor \log_2 n \rfloor} + 1)[y^{h-1}]\frac{1}{(1-y)^{\lfloor \log_2 n \rfloor + 1}}$$

$$= \sum_{i=0}^{\lfloor \log_2 n \rfloor - 1} 2^i \cdot \binom{h-1+i}{h-1} + (n - 2^{\lfloor \log_2 n \rfloor} + 1) \cdot \binom{h-1+\lfloor \log_2 n \rfloor}{h-1}.$$

Above, the third line is obtained based on the fact that $h_{2^i} = h_{2^i+1} = \ldots = h_{2^{i+1}-1}$, and the last line is obtained based on Eq. (3). This finishes the proof of Lemma 3.2.

Next, we give two auxiliary lemmata, useful while bounding the asymptotics:

Lemma 3.3. *For all $x \geq 0$ it holds that $\ln(1+x) \cdot (1+x) \geq x$.*

Proof. Denote $h(x) = \ln(1+x) \cdot (1+x) - x$. Because $h(0) = 0$, it is enough to prove that the function h is increasing. To this end, we compute its derivative. We obtain $h'(x) = \ln(1+x)$, so $h'(x) > 0$ for $x > 0$ and indeed the function h is increasing.

Lemma 3.4. *For every $c \geq 0$ the function*

$$\alpha_c(x) = \left(1 + \frac{c}{x}\right)^x$$

is nondecreasing for $x > 0$.

Proof. We compute the derivative of α_c:

$$\alpha_c'(x) = \alpha_c(x) \cdot \left(\ln\left(1 + \frac{c}{x}\right) - \frac{c}{x \cdot \left(1 + \frac{c}{x}\right)}\right).$$

Because $\alpha_c(x) \geq 0$ for $x > 0$, in order to confirm that $\alpha_c'(x) \geq 0$ it is enough to check that

$$\ln\left(1 + \frac{c}{x}\right) \geq \frac{c}{x \cdot \left(1 + \frac{c}{x}\right)}.$$

To show this inequality, we multiply to both its sides $1 + \frac{c}{x}$ and we use Lemma 3.3.

We are now ready to finish the proof of Theorem 3.1:

Proof (Theorem 3.1). In order to obtain $f(n, h) \leq n \cdot \binom{h-1+\lfloor \log_2 n \rfloor}{\lfloor \log_2 n \rfloor}$, we replace all binomial coefficients in the formula of Lemma 3.2 by $\binom{h-1+\lfloor \log_2 n \rfloor}{\lfloor \log_2 n \rfloor}$; obviously $\binom{h-1+i}{h-1} \leq \binom{h-1+\lfloor \log_2 n \rfloor}{h-1} = \binom{h-1+\lfloor \log_2 n \rfloor}{\lfloor \log_2 n \rfloor}$ for $i \leq \lfloor \log_2 n \rfloor$.

Recall that $x^{\log_2 y} = y^{\log_2 x}$ for any $x, y > 0$. The second inequality from the theorem's statement is obtained using, consecutively, the estimation $\binom{n}{k} \leq \left(\frac{en}{k}\right)^k$, the inequality $\log_2 e < 1.45$, and Lemma 3.4:

$$f(n, h) \leq n \cdot \binom{h - 1 + \lfloor \log_2 n \rfloor}{\lfloor \log_2 n \rfloor} \leq n \cdot \left(e\left(1 + \frac{h-1}{\lfloor \log_2 n \rfloor}\right)\right)^{\lfloor \log_2 n \rfloor}$$

$$\leq n \cdot e^{\log_2 n} \cdot \left(1 + \frac{h-1}{\lfloor \log_2 n \rfloor}\right)^{\lfloor \log_2 n \rfloor} = n^{1 + \log_2 e} \cdot \left(1 + \frac{h-1}{\lfloor \log_2 n \rfloor}\right)^{\lfloor \log_2 n \rfloor}$$

$$\leq n^{2.45 - \varepsilon} \cdot \left(1 + \frac{h-1}{\log_2 n}\right)^{\log_2 n} = n^{2.45 - \varepsilon + \log_2\left(1 + \frac{h-1}{\log_2 n}\right)}.$$

Assume now that $h = \omega(\log n)$. Then

$$\log_2\left(1 + \frac{h-1}{\log_2 n}\right) = \log_2\left(\frac{h}{\log_2 n} \cdot (1 + o(1))\right)$$

$$= \log_2\left(\frac{h}{\log_2 n}\right) + \log_2(1 + o(1)).$$

The component $\log_2(1 + o(1)) = o(1)$ can be removed at the cost of decreasing the constant ε, hence we obtain that

$$f(n,h) \leq n^{2.45-\varepsilon+\log_2\left(1+\frac{h-1}{\log_2 n}\right)} = \mathcal{O}\left(n^{2.45-\varepsilon+\log_2\left(\frac{h}{\log_2 n}\right)}\right).$$

$\square$

4   Using Smaller Trees

Papers showing how to solve parity games with use of universal trees [11,17,23, 24] assume that in order to solve games with n vertices one needs n-universal trees. And for games with priorities on edges it can be shown that n-universality is indeed required [1,8]. However most papers (including ours) define parity games with priorities on vertices, in which case the necessity proof does not apply.

Let us come back to the paper of Jurdziński and Lazić [22]. Although it does not mention universal trees explicitly, it uses a very particular universal tree, called succinct tree coding. The important point is that this tree is not n-universal, but rather η-universal, where η can be either the number of vertices of odd priority, or the number of vertices of even priority, whatever is smaller, so clearly $\eta \leq \lfloor n/2 \rfloor$ (formally, throughout their paper η denotes the number of vertices of even priority, but they explain at the beginning of Sect. 4 that priorities can be shifted by 1 ensuring that $\eta \leq \lfloor n/2 \rfloor$). Moreover, by looking into their paper one can see that the only "interface" between Sect. 2, defining the succinct tree coding, and later sections, using the coding, is Lemma 1, where it is shown that the succinct tree coding is an η-universal tree. It is then easy to see that the algorithm of Jurdziński and Lazić works equally well with any other η-universal tree (of appropriate height, namely $d/2$) in place of the succinct tree coding. In particular, we can use the universal trees from our Theorem 3.1, being of smaller width.

Let us now bound the width of a universal tree that is needed for the algorithm, comparing it with previous approaches. In order to avoid the additional parameter η, we replace it in the sequel by $\lfloor n/2 \rfloor$, making use of the inequality $\eta \leq \lfloor n/2 \rfloor$. Substituting $d/2$ for h and $\lfloor n/2 \rfloor$ for n in the formula from Theorem 3.1, we obtain that the width of an $\lfloor n/2 \rfloor$-universal tree $\mathcal{T}$ of height $d/2$ can satisfy

$$|\mathcal{T}| \leq \left\lfloor\frac{n}{2}\right\rfloor \cdot \binom{d/2 - 1 + \lfloor\log_2\lfloor n/2\rfloor\rfloor}{\lfloor\log_2\lfloor n/2\rfloor\rfloor}.$$

To compare, for an n-universal tree T' by Theorem 3.1 we have

$$|T'| \le n \cdot \binom{d/2 - 1 + \lfloor \log_2 n \rfloor}{\lfloor \log_2 n \rfloor}.$$

For natural n we always have $\lfloor \log_2 \lfloor n/2 \rfloor \rfloor = \lfloor \log_2(n/2) \rfloor = \lfloor \log_2 n \rfloor - 1$, so the quotient of the two binomial coefficients is $\frac{d/2 - 1 + \lfloor \log_2 n \rfloor}{\lfloor \log_2 n \rfloor}$, which is in $\Theta\left(\frac{d}{\log n}\right)$ if $d = \omega(\log n)$.

Let us now determine the asymptotics for $d = \omega(\log n)$. First, let us simplify the formula for the n-universal tree T':

$$|T'| = \mathcal{O}(n^{2.45 - \varepsilon + \log_2(d/2/\log_2 n)}) = \mathcal{O}(n^{1.45 - \varepsilon + \log_2(d/\log_2 n)}).$$

For the $\lfloor n/2 \rfloor$-universal tree T we thus have

$$|T| = \mathcal{O}\left(\left\lfloor \frac{n}{2} \right\rfloor^{1.45 - \varepsilon + \log_2(d/\log_2 \lfloor n/2 \rfloor)}\right) = \mathcal{O}\left(\left(\frac{n}{2}\right)^{1.45 - \varepsilon + \log_2(d/\log_2 n)}\right). \quad (4)$$

The second equality above is obtained by replacing $\lfloor \frac{n}{2} \rfloor$ with the slightly greater value of $\frac{n}{2}$, and by observing that

$$\log_2\left(\frac{d}{\log_2 \lfloor n/2 \rfloor}\right) = \log_2\left(\frac{d}{\log_2 n} \cdot (1 + o(1))\right)$$
$$= \log_2\left(\frac{d}{\log_2 n}\right) + \log_2(1 + o(1));$$

the component $\log_2(1 + o(1)) = o(1)$ can be removed at the cost of decreasing the constant ε. We continue by analysing the logarithm of the bound:

$$\log_2\left(\frac{n}{2}\right) \cdot \left(1.45 - \varepsilon + \log_2\frac{d}{\log_2 n}\right) = (\log_2 n - 1) \cdot \left(1.45 - \varepsilon + \log_2\frac{d}{\log_2 n}\right)$$
$$\le \log_2 n \cdot \left(1.45 - \varepsilon + \log_2\frac{d}{\log_2 n}\right) - \log_2\frac{d}{\log_2 n} + \varepsilon$$
$$\le \log_2 n \cdot \left(1.45 - \varepsilon + o(1) + \log_2\frac{d}{\log_2 n}\right) - \log_2 d + \varepsilon; \quad (5)$$

the last equality above was obtained by observing that

$$-\log_2\frac{d}{\log_2 n} = -\log_2 d + \log_2 \log_2 n = -\log_2 d + \log_2 n \cdot o(1).$$

Combining Eq. (4) and (5), we obtain the following bound on $|T|$:

$$|T| = \mathcal{O}\left(n^{1.45 - \varepsilon + o(1) + \log_2(d/\log_2 n)} \cdot \frac{1}{d}\right).$$

The $o(1)$ component can be removed at the cost of decreasing the constant ε again; we can thus write

$$|\mathcal{T}| = \mathcal{O}\left(n^{1.45-\varepsilon+\log_2(d/\log_2 n)} \cdot \frac{1}{d}\right).$$

We now come to the complexity of the algorithm itself. As observed by Jurdziński and Lazić [22, Theorem 7], their algorithm, when using a universal tree $\widehat{\mathcal{T}}$, works in time $\mathcal{O}(m \cdot \log n \cdot \log d \cdot |\widehat{\mathcal{T}}|)$. Using $\mathcal{T}$ as $\widehat{\mathcal{T}}$, and observing that the polylogarithmic function $O(\log n \cdot \log d)$ can be again "eaten" by the $-\varepsilon$ component of the exponent, we obtain the following bound on the complexity, which is our main theorem:

Theorem 4.1. *For $d = \omega(\log n)$ one can find a winner in a parity game with n vertices, m edges, and d priorities in time*

$$\mathcal{O}\left(m \cdot n^{1.45+\log_2(d/\log_2 n)} \cdot \frac{1}{d}\right).$$

Remark 4.2. Compared to the previous bound of $\mathcal{O}\left(m \cdot d \cdot n^{1.45+\log_2(d/\log_2 n)}\right)$ (from Fijalkow [17]), we obtain an improvement by a factor of $\Theta(d^2)$. One $\Theta(d)$ is gained in Theorem 3.1, by improving the bound for the size of a universal tree. A second $\Theta(d)$ is gained by using $\lfloor n/2 \rfloor$-universal trees instead of n-universal trees.

Remark 4.3. The complexity obtained in Fijalkow [17] is the same as in Jurdziński and Lazić [22]: he gains a factor of $\Theta(d)$ by using a better construction of a universal tree instead of the "succinct tree coding", but simultaneously he loses a factor of $\Theta(d)$ due to using n-universal trees in place of $\lfloor n/2 \rfloor$-universal trees.

Let us also use this place to note that there is a small mistake in the paper of Jurdziński and Lazić [22]. Namely, in the proof of Lemma 6 they switch to analysing a simpler expression $\binom{\lceil \log_2 \eta \rceil + d/2}{\lceil \log_2 \eta \rceil}$ in place of $\binom{\lceil \log_2 \eta \rceil + d/2 + 1}{\lceil \log_2 \eta \rceil + 1}$, saying that the simpler expression is within a constant factor of the latter one. This statement is false, though: the quotient of the two expressions is $\frac{\lceil \log_2 \eta \rceil + d/2 + 1}{\lceil \log_2 \eta \rceil + 1}$, which is in $\Theta\left(\frac{d}{\log \eta}\right)$ if $d = \omega(\log \eta)$. Thus, the actual complexity upper bound resulting from their analysis of the algorithm for $d = \omega(\log \eta)$ should not be $\mathcal{O}\left(m \cdot d \cdot \eta^{1.45+\log_2(d/\log_2 \eta)}\right)$ as they claim, but rather $\mathcal{O}\left(m \cdot d^2 \cdot \eta^{1.45+\log_2(d/\log_2 \eta)}\right)$ (and taking $n/2$ for η this gives us the complexity $\mathcal{O}\left(m \cdot d \cdot n^{1.45+\log_2(d/\log_2 n)}\right)$, the same as in Fijalkow [17]).

Remark 4.4. While the current paper was under preparation, Dell'Erba and Schewe [12] published some other improvement of Jurdziński and Lazić's algorithm [22]. A complete discussion is difficult to perform, since the authors have not provided a precise bound.

References

1. Arnold, A., Niwiński, D., Parys, P.: A quasi-polynomial black-box algorithm for fixed point evaluation. In: CSL. LIPIcs, vol. 183, pp. 9:1–9:23. Schloss Dagstuhl - Leibniz-Zentrum für Informatik (2021)
2. Benerecetti, M., Dell'Erba, D., Mogavero, F.: Solving parity games via priority promotion. Formal Meth. Syst. Des. **52**(2), 193–226 (2018)
3. Benerecetti, M., Dell'Erba, D., Mogavero, F., Schewe, S., Wojtczak, D.: Priority promotion with Parysian flair. CoRR abs/2105.01738 (2021)
4. Björklund, H., Vorobyov, S.G.: A combinatorial strongly subexponential strategy improvement algorithm for mean payoff games. Discret. Appl. Math. **155**(2), 210–229 (2007)
5. Boker, U., Lehtinen, K.: On the way to alternating weak automata. In: FSTTCS. LIPIcs, vol. 122, pp. 21:1–21:22. Schloss Dagstuhl - Leibniz-Zentrum für Informatik (2018)
6. Browne, A., Clarke, E.M., Jha, S., Long, D.E., Marrero, W.R.: An improved algorithm for the evaluation of fixpoint expressions. Theor. Comput. Sci. **178**(1–2), 237–255 (1997)
7. Calude, C.S., Jain, S., Khoussainov, B., Li, W., Stephan, F.: Deciding parity games in quasipolynomial time. In: STOC. pp. 252–263. ACM (2017)
8. Czerwiński, W., Daviaud, L., Fijalkow, N., Jurdziński, M., Lazić, R., Parys, P.: Universal trees grow inside separating automata: quasi-polynomial lower bounds for parity games. In: SODA, pp. 2333–2349. SIAM (2019)
9. Daskalakis, C., Papadimitriou, C.H.: Continuous local search. In: SODA, pp. 790–804. SIAM (2011)
10. Daviaud, L., Jurdziński, M., Lehtinen, K.: Alternating weak automata from universal trees. In: CONCUR, LIPIcs, vol. 140, pp. 18:1–18:14. Schloss Dagstuhl - Leibniz-Zentrum für Informatik (2019)
11. Daviaud, L., Jurdziński, M., Thejaswini, K.S.: The Strahler number of a parity game. In: ICALP. LIPIcs, vol. 168, pp. 123:1–123:19. Schloss Dagstuhl - Leibniz-Zentrum für Informatik (2020)
12. Dell'Erba, D., Schewe, S.: Smaller progress measures and separating automata for parity games. CoRR abs/2205.00744 (2022)
13. Emerson, E.A., Jutla, C.S.: Tree automata, mu-calculus and determinacy (extended abstract). In: FOCS, pp. 368–377. IEEE Computer Society (1991)
14. Emerson, E.A., Jutla, C.S., Sistla, A.P.: On model checking for the μ-calculus and its fragments. Theor. Comput. Sci. **258**(1–2), 491–522 (2001)
15. Fearnley, J.: Exponential lower bounds for policy iteration. In: Abramsky, S., Gavoille, C., Kirchner, C., Meyer auf der Heide, F., Spirakis, P.G. (eds.) ICALP 2010. LNCS, vol. 6199, pp. 551–562. Springer, Heidelberg (2010). https://doi.org/10.1007/978-3-642-14162-1_46
16. Fearnley, J., Jain, S., de Keijzer, B., Schewe, S., Stephan, F., Wojtczak, D.: An ordered approach to solving parity games in quasi-polynomial time and quasi-linear space. Int. J. Softw. Tools Technol. Transfer **21**(3), 325–349 (2019)
17. Fijalkow, N.: An optimal value iteration algorithm for parity games. CoRR abs/1801.09618 (2018)
18. Friedmann, O.: A subexponential lower bound for Zadeh's pivoting rule for solving linear programs and games. In: Günlük, O., Woeginger, G.J. (eds.) IPCO 2011. LNCS, vol. 6655, pp. 192–206. Springer, Heidelberg (2011). https://doi.org/10.1007/978-3-642-20807-2_16

19. Friedmann, O., Hansen, T.D., Zwick, U.: Subexponential lower bounds for randomized pivoting rules for the simplex algorithm. In: STOC, pp. 283–292. ACM (2011)

20. Jurdziński, M.: Deciding the winner in parity games is in UP ∩ co-UP. Inf. Process. Lett. **68**(3), 119–124 (1998)

21. Jurdziński, M.: Small progress measures for solving parity games. In: Reichel, H., Tison, S. (eds.) STACS 2000. LNCS, vol. 1770, pp. 290–301. Springer, Heidelberg (2000). https://doi.org/10.1007/3-540-46541-3_24

22. Jurdziński, M., Lazić, R.: Succinct progress measures for solving parity games. In: LICS, pp. 1–9. IEEE Computer Society (2017)

23. Jurdziński, M., Morvan, R.: A universal attractor decomposition algorithm for parity games. CoRR abs/2001.04333 (2020)

24. Jurdziński, M., Morvan, R., Ohlmann, P., Thejaswini, K.S.: A symmetric attractor-decomposition lifting algorithm for parity games. CoRR abs/2010.08288 (2020)

25. Jurdziński, M., Paterson, M., Zwick, U.: A deterministic subexponential algorithm for solving parity games. SIAM J. Comput. **38**(4), 1519–1532 (2008)

26. Lehtinen, K.: A modal μ perspective on solving parity games in quasi-polynomial time. In: LICS, pp. 639–648. ACM (2018)

27. Lehtinen, K., Parys, P., Schewe, S., Wojtczak, D.: A recursive approach to solving parity games in quasipolynomial time. Log. Meth. Comput. Sci. **18**(1), 1–18 (2022)

28. Parys, P.: Parity games: Zielonka's algorithm in quasi-polynomial time. In: MFCS. LIPIcs, vol. 138, pp. 10:1–10:13. Schloss Dagstuhl - Leibniz-Zentrum für Informatik (2019)

29. Rabin, M.O.: Automata on Infinite Objects and Church's Problem. American Mathematical Society, Boston (1972)

30. Schewe, S.: Solving parity games in big steps. J. Comput. Syst. Sci. **84**, 243–262 (2017)

31. Seidl, H.: Fast and simple nested fixpoints. Inf. Process. Lett. **59**(6), 303–308 (1996)

32. Vöge, J., Jurdziński, M.: A discrete strategy improvement algorithm for solving parity games. In: Emerson, E.A., Sistla, A.P. (eds.) CAV 2000. LNCS, vol. 1855, pp. 202–215. Springer, Heidelberg (2000). https://doi.org/10.1007/10722167_18

33. Zielonka, W.: Infinite games on finitely coloured graphs with applications to automata on infinite trees. Theor. Comput. Sci. **200**(1–2), 135–183 (1998)

An $O(\sqrt{k})$-Approximation Algorithm for Minimum Power k Edge Disjoint st-Paths

Zeev Nutov[✉][iD]

The Open University of Israel, Ra'anana, Israel
nutov@openu.ac.il

Abstract. In minimum power network design problems we are given an undirected graph $G = (V, E)$ with edge costs $\{c_e : e \in E\}$. The goal is to find an edge set $F \subseteq E$ that satisfies a prescribed property of minimum power $p_c(F) = \sum_{v \in V} \max\{c_e : e \in F \text{ is incident to } v\}$. In the MIN-POWER kEDGE DISJOINT st-PATHS problem F should contain k edge disjoint st-paths. The problem admits a k-approximation algorithm, and it was an open question whether it admits an approximation ratio sublinear in k even for unit costs. We give a $4\sqrt{2k}$-approximation algorithm for general costs.

Keywords: edge disjoint st-paths · minimum power · wireless networks

1 Introduction

In network design problems one seeks a cheap subgraph that satisfies a prescribed property, often determined by pairwise connectivities or/and degree demands. A traditional setting is when each edge or node has a cost, and we want to minimize the cost of the subgraph. This setting does not capture many wireless networks scenarios, where a communication between two nodes depends on our "investment" in these nodes – like equipment and transmission energy, and the cost incurred is a sum of these "investments". This motivates the type of problems we study here. Specifically, we consider assigning transmission ranges to the nodes of a static ad hoc wireless network so as to minimize the total power consumed, under the constraint that the bidirectional network established by the transmission ranges satisfies prescribed properties.

More formally, in **minimum power network design problems** we are given an undirected (simple) graph $G = (V, E)$ with (non-negative) edge costs $\{c_e \geq 0 : e \in E\}$. The goal is to find an edge subset $F \subseteq E$ that satisfies a prescribed property of minimum total **power** $p_c(F) = \sum_{v \in V} \max\{c_e : e \in \delta_F(v)\}$; here $\delta_F(v)$ denotes the set of edges in F incident to v, and a maximum taken over an empty set is assumed to be zero. Equivalently, we seek an **assignment** $\{a_v \geq 0 : v \in V\}$ to the nodes of minimum total value $\sum_{v \in V} a_v$, such that the **activated edge set** $\{e = uv \in E : c_e \leq \min\{a_u, a_v\}\}$ satisfies the prescribed

G. Della Vedova et al. (Eds.): CiE 2023, LNCS 13967, pp. 287–296, 2023.
https://doi.org/10.1007/978-3-031-36978-0_23

property. These problems were studied already in the late 90's, c.f. [8,16,17,19], followed by many more. Min-power problems were also widely studied in directed graphs, usually under the assumption that to activate an edge one needs to assign power only to its tail, while heads are assigned power zero, c.f. [8,12,14,18]. The undirected case has an additional requirement - we want the network to be bidirected, to allow a bidirectional communication.

In the traditional edge-costs scenario, a fundamental problem in network design is the SHORTEST st-PATH problem. A natural generalization and the simplest high connectivity network design problem is finding a set of k disjoint paths of minimum edge cost. Here the paths may be edge disjoint – the k EDGE DISJOINT st-PATHS problem, or internally (node) disjoint – the k DISJOINT st-PATHS problem. Both problems can be reduced to the MIN-COST k-FLOW problem, which has a polynomial time algorithm.

Similarly, one of the most fundamental problems in the min-power setting is the MIN-POWER st-PATH problem. For this problem, a linear time reduction to the ordinary SHORTEST st-PATH problem is described by Althaus et al. [3]. Lando and Nutov [9] suggested a more general (but less time efficient) "levels reduction" that converts several power problems into problems with node costs. A fundamental generalization is activating a set of k edge disjoint or internally disjoint st-paths. Formally, the edge disjoint st-paths version is as follows.

MIN-POWER k EDGE DISJOINT st-PATHS (MIN-POWER k-EDP)

Input: A graph $G = (V, E)$ with edge costs $\{c_e \geq 0 : e \in E\}$, $s, t \in V$, and an integer k.

Output: An edge set $F \subseteq E$ such that the graph (V, F) contains k edge disjoint st-paths of minimum power $p_c(F) = \sum_{v \in V} \max\{c_e : e \in \delta_F(v)\}$.

A related problem is the NODE WEIGHTED k EDGE DISJOINT st-PATHS problem (a.k.a. NODE-WEIGHTED k-FLOW), where instead of edge costs we have node weights, and seek a min-weight subgraph that contains k edge disjoint st-paths. For unit weights, this problem is equivalent to MIN-POWER k-EDP with unit edge costs - in both problems we seek a subgraph with minimum number of nodes that contains k edge disjoint st-paths. For MIN-POWER k-EDP Lando and Nutov [9] obtained a k-approximation algorithm, improving over the easy ratio $2k$; they gave a polynomial time algorithm for the particular case of MIN-POWER k-EDP when G has a subgraph G_0 of cost 0 that already contains $k - 1$ edge disjoint st-paths, and we seek a min-power augmenting edge set F to increase the number of paths by 1. On the other hand [13] shows that ratio ρ for MIN-POWER k-EDP with unit costs implies ratio $1/2\rho^2$ for the DENSEST ℓ-SUBGRAPH problem, that currently has best known ratio $O(n^{-(1/4+\epsilon)})$ [4] and approximation threshold $\Omega\left(n^{-1/poly(\log\log n)}\right)$ [11]. MIN-POWER k-EDP was also studied earlier on directed graphs in many papers with similar results, c.f. [6,9,10,18]. Specifically, Hajiaghayi et al. [6] showed that directed MIN-POWER k-EDP is LABEL-COVER hard, while Maier, Mecke and Wagner [10] showed that a natural algorithm for unit costs has approximation ratio at least $2\sqrt{k}$.

Summarizing, even for unit costs, the best known approximation ratio for directed/undirected MIN-POWER k-EDP was k, and the problem is unlikely to admit a polylogarithmic ratio. Open questions were to resolve the complexity status for $k = 2$ [1,14], and to obtain a ratio sublinear in k (even just for unit activation costs) [10,13,14].

The MIN-POWER k-EDP problem is closely related to the FIXED COST k-FLOW problem, in which each edge has a fixed capacity and cost, and the goal is to buy the cheapest set of edges to ensure an st-flow of value k. In this context, Hajiaghayi et al. [7] studied the undirected BIPARTITE FIXED COST k-FLOW problem, where the graph $G \setminus \{s,t\}$ is bipartite, and s is connected to one part and t to the other part by edges of infinite capacity and cost 1, and the other edges have cost 0 and capacity 1. They gave for this problem an $O(\sqrt{k \ln k})$-approximation algorithm. One can see that this problem is a very restricted case of MIN-POWER k-EDP with $0,1$ costs. In fact, it was an open question to obtain approximation ratio sublinear in k for MIN-POWER k-EDP even for $0,1$ costs [10,13,14]. Our next result resolves this open question.

Theorem 1. MIN-POWER k-EDP admits a $4\sqrt{2k}$-approximation algorithm.

Theorem 1 is based on the following combinatorial result, that is of independent interest. Given a graph $G = (V, E)$ with edge costs c_e, we denote by $c(G) = c(E) = \sum_{e \in E} c_e$ the ordinary cost of G, and by $p_c(G) = p_c(E) = \sum_{v \in V} \max\{c_e : e \in \delta_E(v)\}$ the power cost of G. It is easy to see that $p_c(G) \leq 2c(G)$. Hajiaghayi et al. [6] proved that $c(G) \leq \sqrt{|E|/2} \cdot p_c(G)$ for any graph G; this bound is tight. We will improve over this bound for inclusion minimal graphs that contain k edge disjoint st-paths as follows.

Theorem 2. Let $G = (V, E)$ be a simple graph with edge costs $\{c_e \geq 0 : e \in E\}$, that contains k edge disjoint st-paths such that no proper subgraph of G contains k edge disjoint st-paths. Then $c(G) \leq 2\sqrt{2k} \cdot p_c(G)$.

The $4\sqrt{2k}$-approximation algorithm will simply compute a minimum cost set of k edge disjoint st-paths, with edge costs c_e; this can be done in polynomial time using a min-cost k-flow algorithm. The approximation ratio $4\sqrt{2k}$ follows from the Theorem 2 bound, and the bound $p_c(G) \leq 2c(G)$; specifically, if F^* is an optimal solution to MIN-POWER k-EDP and F is a min-cost set of k edge disjoint paths, then $p_c(F) \leq 2c(F) \leq 2c(F^*) \leq 4\sqrt{2k} \cdot p_c(F^*)$.

To see that Theorem 2 is indeed of interest, consider the case of unit costs. Then $c(G) = |E|$ and $p_c(G) = V$. Thus already for this simple case we get the following combinatorial result, that to the best of our knowledge was not known before.

Corollary 1. Let $G = (V, E)$ be a (directed or undirected) simple graph that contains k edge disjont st-paths such that no proper subgraph of G contains k edge disjoint st-paths. Then $|E| \leq 2\sqrt{2k} \cdot |V|$.

We now briefly survey some results on related problems. In the MIN-POWER k DISJOINT st-PATHS problem, the k paths should be internally node disjoint. This problem admits an easy 2-approximation algorithm. Based on an idea of Srinivas and Modiano [18], Alqahtani and Erlebach [1] showed that ratio ρ for MIN-POWER 2 DISJOINT PATHS implies ratio ρ for MIN-POWER 2 EDGE DISJOINT PATHS.[1] In another paper, Alqahtani and Erlebach [2] showed that the problem is polynomially solvable on graphs with bounded treewidth. However, it is a long standing open question whether the problem is in P or is NP-hard on general graphs, even for $k = 2$ [1,9,14].

In the more general activation network design problem, we are given a graph $G = (V, E)$ with a pair of activation costs $\{c_e^u, c_e^v\}$ for each uv-edge $e \in E$; the goal is to find an edge subset $F \subseteq E$ of minimum activation cost $\tau(F) = \sum_{v \in V} \max\{c_e^v : e \in \delta_F(v)\}$ that satisfies a prescribed property. This generic problem was introduced by Panigrahi [15], and it includes node costs problems, min-power problems, and several other problems that arise in wireless networks; see a survey in [14] on this type of problems.

2   Proof of Theorem 2

Let $G = (V, E)$ be a simple graph that contains k edge disjoint st-paths such that no proper subgraph of G contains k edge disjoint st-paths. Theorem 2 says that then $c(G) \le 2\sqrt{2k} \cdot p_c(G)$ for any edge costs $\{c_e : e \in E\}$, where $c(G) = \sum_{e \in E} c_e$ and $p_c(G) = \sum_{v \in V} \max\{c_e : e \in \delta(v)\}$ (recall that $\delta(v)$ denotes the set of edges in E incident to v). As was mentioned in Corollary 1, in the case of uniform costs this reduces to $|E| \le 2\sqrt{2k} \cdot |V|$. We will need a slight generalization of this bound to any subset U of V, as follows.

Lemma 1. *Let $G = (V, E)$ be a simple graph that contains k edge disjoint st-paths such that no proper subgraph of G contains k edge disjoint st-paths. Then for any $U \subseteq V$, $|E_U| \le 2\sqrt{2k} \cdot |U|$, where E_U is the set of edges in E with both ends in U.*

The proof of this lemma is long and non-trivial, so it will be proved later. For now, we will use Lemma 1 to prove Theorem 2, namely, that $c(G) \le 2\sqrt{2k} \cdot p_c(G)$. Note that $c(G) \le \sum_{xy \in E} \min\{p_c(x), p_c(y)\}$, where $p_c(v) = \max\{c(e) : e \in \delta(v)\}$. Thus, it is sufficient to prove that for any non-negative weights $\{p(v) : v \in V\}$ on the nodes, the following holds:

$$\sum_{xy \in E} \min\{p(x), p(y)\} \le 2\sqrt{2k} \cdot \sum_{v \in V} p(v) . \tag{1}$$

The proof of (1) is by induction on the number N of distinct $p(v)$ values. In the base case $N = 1$, all weights $p(v)$ are equal, and w.l.o.g. $p(v) = 1$ for all $v \in V$. Then (1) reduces to $|E| \le 2\sqrt{2k} \cdot |V|$, which is the case $U = V$ in Lemma 1.

---

[1] In [1] it is also claimed that MIN-POWER 2 DISJOINT PATHS admits a 1.5-approximation algorithm, but the proof was found to contain an error [5]. Obtaining an approximation ratio better than 2 for MIN-POWER 2 EDGE/NODE DISJOINT PATHS is still a major open problem in the field.

Assume that $N \geq 2$. Let $U = \{u \in V : p(u) = \max_{v \in V} p(v)\}$ and let E_U be the set of edges with both ends in U. Let ϵ be the difference between the maximum weight $\max_{v \in V} p(v)$ and the second maximum weight. Let p' be defined by $p'(v) = p(v) - \epsilon$ if $v \in U$ and $p'(v) = p(v)$ otherwise. Note that $|E_U| \leq 2\sqrt{2k} \cdot |U|$, by Lemma 1, and that p' has exactly $N - 1$ distinct values, so by the induction hypothesis, (1) holds for p'. Thus we have:

$$\sum_{xy \in E} \min\{p(x), p(y)\} = \sum_{xy \in E} \min\{p'(x), p'(y)\} + \epsilon |E_U|$$

$$\leq 2\sqrt{2k} \sum_{v \in V} p'(v) + \epsilon \cdot 2\sqrt{2k}|U|$$

$$= 2\sqrt{2k} \left(\sum_{v \in V} p'(v) + \epsilon |U| \right) = 2\sqrt{2k} \sum_{v \in V} p(v) .$$

The first and last equalities are by the definition of $p'(v)$. The inequality is by the induction hypothesis and Lemma 1. This concludes the proof of Theorem 2, provided that we will prove Lemma 1, which we will do in the rest of this section.

Before proving Lemma 1, let us give an example showing that for $U = V$ the bound in the lemma is tight up to the $2\sqrt{2}$ factor. Consider the (non-simple) graph in Fig. 1 that has q layers of size r each, where any two adjacent layers induce a complete bipartite graph. There are also r edges from s to each node in the first layer and r edges from each node in the last layer to t. Let $k = r^2$. One can easily verify that this graph contains k edge disjoint st-paths. Furthermore, every edge belongs to some minimum st-cut, hence no proper subgraph contains k edge disjoint st-paths. The number of nodes in this graph is $rq + 2$ and the number of edges is $r^2(q + 1)$, but this graph is not simple. To make it a simple graph, for every set of r parallel edges leaving s, subdivide every edge, except of one, by a new node; then apply a similar operation on the edges entering t. The number of nodes increases by $2r(r - 1)$, and so is the number of edges. The obtained graph is simple and every its edge belongs to some minimum st-cut, hence satisfies the conditions of Lemma 1. Furthermore, in this graph:

- The number of nodes is $|V| = rq + 2 + 2r(r - 1) = r[q + 2r + 2/r - 2]$.
- The number of edges is $|E| = r^2(q + 1) + 2r(r - 1) = r(rq + 3r - 2)$.

Consequently, for large enough $q \gg r$ we have

$$\frac{|E|}{|V|} = \frac{rq + 3r - 2}{q + 2r + 2/r - 2} = \frac{r + (3r - 2)/q}{1 + (2r + 2/r - 2)/q} \approx r = \sqrt{k}$$

Now we prove Lemma 1. We need some definitions. For $A \subseteq V$, let $\delta(A)$ denote the set of edges in G that have exactly one end in A, and let $d(A) = |\delta(A)|$. A **nested family** is an ordered (multi-)family of sets $\mathcal{C} = (C_0, C_1, \ldots, C_q)$ such that $C_0 \subseteq C_1 \subseteq \cdots \subseteq C_q$. The general idea of the proof of Lemma 1 is as follows.

(i) We will show that there exists a nested family $\mathcal{C} = (C_1, \ldots, C_q)$ on V such that (see Lemma 3): (a) $d(C_i) \leq k$ for all i and (b) $\bigcup_{C \in \mathcal{C}} \delta(C) = E$.

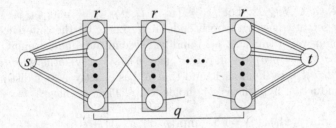

Fig. 1. A tight example for the bound of Lemma 1.

(ii) We will show that any graph that has a family $\dot{\mathcal{C}}$ as in (i) has at most $|E| \leq 2\sqrt{2k} \cdot |V|$ edges. For any $U \subseteq V$, the projection $\mathcal{C}_U = (C_1 \cap U, \dots, C_q \cap U)$ of $\mathcal{C}$ on U is such a family for the subgraph $G[U] = (U, E_U)$ induced by U, implying that $|E_U| \leq 2\sqrt{2k} \cdot |U|$.

(iii) To prove (ii), we partition V into "layers" L_i such that $C_i = L_1 \cup \dots \cup L_i$ for $i = 1, \dots, q$ and $L_{q+1} = V \setminus C_q$. Then every edge goes between two distinct (not necessarily adjacent) layers, see Fig. 2. The length of an edge e from L_i to L_j with $j > i$ is defined by $l(e) = j - i$. We will show that the number of edges of length $< \alpha q/n$ is at most $2\alpha |V|$, while the number of other edges is at most $|V|k/\alpha$. Substituting $\alpha = \sqrt{k/2}$ gives $|E| \leq |V|(2\alpha + k/\alpha) = 2\sqrt{2k} \cdot |V|$; see Lemma 4 and its proof.

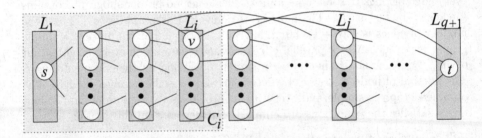

Fig. 2. Illustration to the proof of Lemma 4.

We say that a node subset S of V is a **tight set** if $s \in S$, $t \notin S$, and $d(S) = k$. The next lemma is a folklore, but we will provide a proof for completeness of exposition.

Lemma 2. *Let A, B be two tight sets in a graph $G = (V, E)$ that contains k edge disjoint st-paths. Then $A \cap B, A \cup B$ are both tight and $\delta(A \setminus B) \cap \delta(B \setminus A) = \emptyset$. Consequently, $\delta(A) \cup \delta(B) = \delta(A \cap B) \cup \delta(A \cup B)$.*

Proof. By counting the contribution of various edges to $\delta(A), \delta(B)$ (see Fig. 3(a)) we have

$$
\begin{aligned}
2k &= d(A) + d(B) \\
&= d(A \cap B) + d(A \cup B) + 2|\delta(A \setminus B) \cap \delta(B \setminus A)| \\
&\geq k + k + 0 \ .
\end{aligned}
$$

The first equality is since $d(A) = d(B) = k$, the second is by counting the contribution of various edges to the terms, and the inequality is by Menger's Theorem. Consequently, equality holds everywhere, thus $d(A \cap B) = d(A \cup B) = k$ and $\delta(A \setminus B) \cap \delta(B \setminus A) = \emptyset$. This implies $\delta(A) \cup \delta(B) = \delta(A \cap B) \cup \delta(A \cup B)$, see Fig. 3(b). □

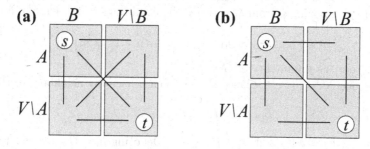

Fig. 3. Illustration to the proof of Lemma 2.

Two sets A, B **cross** if they intersect and none of them contains the other, namely, if each of the sets $A \cap B, A \setminus B, B \setminus A$ is nonempty. We say that a family $\mathcal{C}$ of tight sets is a **witness family** (for the minimality of E) if $\{s\} \in \mathcal{C}, V \setminus \{t\} \in \mathcal{C}$, and $\bigcup_{C \in \mathcal{C}} \delta(C) = E$.

Lemma 3. *Let $G = (V, E)$ be a graph that contains k edge disjoint st-paths such that no proper subgraph of G contains k edge disjoint st-paths. Then there exists a witness family that is nested.*

Proof. By the minimality of G and Menger's Theorem there exists a witness family. Among all witness families of minimum size, let $\mathcal{C}$ be one for which $\sum_{C \in \mathcal{C}} |C|^2$ is maximal. We claim that $\mathcal{C}$ is nested. Suppose to the contrary that there are $A, B \in \mathcal{C}$ that cross. By Lemma 2, $A \cap B, A \cup B$ are both tight and $\delta(A) \cup \delta(B) = \delta(A \cap B) \cup \delta(A \cup B)$. Consequently, $\mathcal{C}' = (\mathcal{C} \setminus \{A, B\}) \cup \{A \cap B, A \cup B\}$ is also a witness family of the same size as $\mathcal{C}$. However, $|A \cap B|^2 + |A \cup B|^2 > |A|^2 + |B|^2$ holds for arbitrary sets A, B that none of them contains the other[2], hence $\sum_{C \in \mathcal{C}'} |C|^2 > \sum_{C \in \mathcal{C}} |C|^2$. This contradicts the choice of $\mathcal{C}$. □

---

[2] To see this, assume w.l.o.g. that $|B| \geq |A|$ and note that $j = |A \setminus B| \geq 1$. Then
$|A \cap B|^2 + |A \cup B|^2 = (|A| - j)^2 + (|B| + j)^2 = |A|^2 + |B|^2 + 2j(|B| - |A| + j) > |A|^2 + |B|^2$.

Now we prove the following lemma, that (as we will show) together with Lemma 3 implies Lemma 1.

Lemma 4. *Let $G = (V, E)$ be a simple graph that has a nested family $\mathcal{C} = (C_1, \ldots, C_q)$ on V such that $\bigcup_{C \in \mathcal{C}} \delta(C) = E$ and such that $d(C) \le k$ for all $C \in \mathcal{C}$. Then $m \le 2\sqrt{2kn}$, where $n = |V|$ and $m = |E|$.*

Proof. Let $L_1 = C_1$, $L_i = C_i \setminus C_{i-1}$ for $i = 2, \ldots, q$, and $L_{q+1} = V \setminus C_q$. The **length of an edge** e that has one end in L_i and the other in L_j where $j > i$ is $l(e) = j - i$. Let ℓ be the maximum length of an edge in E. Let α be a parameter eventually set to $\alpha = \sqrt{k/2}$.

We show that if $\ell < \alpha q/n$ then $m \le 2\alpha n$. Suppose to the contrary that this is not so. Let G be a graph as in the lemma with a minimal number $|V| + |E|$ of edges plus nodes such that $m > 2\alpha n$. We claim that $d(v) \ge 2\alpha$ for all $v \in V$. Otherwise, if G has a node v with $d(v) < 2\alpha$, then the graph $G' = (V', E')$ obtained by removing v from G satisfies the conditions of the lemma, and also satisfies

$$|E'| \ge m - 2\alpha > 2\alpha n - 2\alpha = 2\alpha(n-1) = 2\alpha |V'| \,,$$

contradicting the minimality of G.

Now consider some $v \in L_i$, see Fig. 2. Then v has only neighbors in the sets

$$L_{i-\ell}, \ldots, L_{i-1}, L_{i+1}, \ldots L_{i+\ell} \,,$$

where we let $L_j = \emptyset$ if $j < 1$ or if $j > q + 1$. Denoting $n_i = |L_i|$, we get that

$$d(v) \le n_{i-\ell} + \cdots + n_{i-1} + n_{i+1} + \cdots + n_\ell \,,$$

since G is a simple graph (note that this is the only place where we use the assumption that G is simple). Since $d(v) \ge 2\alpha$ we get

$$n_{i-\ell} + \cdots + n_{i-1} + n_{i+1} + \cdots + n_\ell \ge 2\alpha \quad i = 1, \ldots, q+1 \,.$$

In the sum of these inequalities for $i = 1, \ldots, q+1$, every n_j appears at most 2ℓ times, and since $\sum_{j=1}^{q+1} n_j = n$ we get $2\ell n \ge 2\alpha q$. Consequently, $\ell \ge \alpha q/n$, contradicting the assumption that $\ell < \alpha q/n$.

Now let ℓ be arbitrary. Let $F = \{e \in E : l(e) \ge \alpha q/n\}$. Note that $\sum_{e \in E} l(e) \le kq$, since each edge e appears in exactly $l(e)$ cuts $\delta(C_i)$ and since $|\delta(C_i)| \le k$ for all i. This implies that $kq \ge \sum_{e \in F} l(e) \ge |F| \cdot \alpha q/n$, so $|F| \le nk/\alpha$. The graph $(V, E \setminus F)$ satisfies the conditions of the lemma, and has maximum edge lengths $< \alpha q/n$, hence $|E \setminus F| \le 2\alpha n$. Consequently, for $\alpha = \sqrt{k/2} = \frac{\sqrt{k}}{\sqrt{2}}$ we get

$$|E| = |F| + |E \setminus F| \le nk/\alpha + 2\alpha n = n(k/\alpha + 2\alpha) = 2n\sqrt{2k} \,,$$

concluding the proof. □

Let now $\mathcal{C}$ be a nested family as in Lemma 3. Note that for any $U \subseteq V$, the projection $\mathcal{C}_U = (C_1 \cap U, \ldots, C_q \cap U)$ of $\mathcal{C}$ on U and the subgraph $G[U] = (U, E_U)$ induced by U satisfy the conditions of Lemma 4, implying that $|E_U| \leq 2\sqrt{2k}|U|$.

This concludes the proof of Lemma 1, and thus also the proof of Theorem 2 is complete.

Acknowledgment. I thank anonymous referees for useful comments that helped to improve the presentation of this paper.

References

1. Alqahtani, H.M., Erlebach, T.: Approximation algorithms for disjoint st-paths with minimum activation cost. In: Algorithms and Complexity, 8th International Conference (CIAC), pp. 1–12 (2013)
2. Alqahtani, H.M., Erlebach, T.: Minimum activation cost node-disjoint paths in graphs with bounded treewidth. In: 40th International Conference on Current Trends in Theory and Practice of Computer Science (SOFSEM), pp. 65–76 (2014)
3. Althaus, E., Calinescu, G., Mandoiu, I., Prasad, S., Tchervenski, N., Zelikovsky, A.: Power efficient range assignment for symmetric connectivity in static ad-hoc wireless networks. Wireless Netw. **12**(3), 287–299 (2006)
4. Bhaskara, A., Charikar, M., Chlamtac, E., Feige, U., Vijayaraghavan, A.: Detecting high log-densities: an $O(n^{1/4})$ approximation for densest k-subgraph. In: 42nd ACM Symposium on Theory of Computing (STOC), pp. 201–210 (2010)
5. Erlebach, T.: Personal communication (2022)
6. Hajiaghayi, M., Kortsarz, G., Mirrokni, V., Nutov, Z.: Power optimization for connectivity problems. Math. Program. **110**(1), 195–208 (2007)
7. Hajiaghayi, M.T., Khandekar, R., Kortsarz, G., Nutov, Z.: On fixed cost k-flow problems. Theory Comput. Syst. **58**(1), 4–18 (2016)
8. Kirousis, L.M., Kranakis, E., Krizanc, D., Pelc, A.: Power consumption in packet radio networks. Theoret. Comput. Sci. **243**(1–2), 289–305 (2000)
9. Lando, Y., Nutov, Z.: On minimum power connectivity problems. J. Discrete Algorithms **8**(2), 164–173 (2010)
10. Maier, M., Mecke, S., Wagner, D.: Algorithmic aspects of minimum energy edge-disjoint paths in wireless networks. In: 33rd Conference on Current Trends in Theory and Practice of Computer Science (SOFSEM), pp. 410–421 (2007)
11. Manurangsi, P.: Almost-polynomial ratio ETH-hardness of approximating densest k-subgraph. In: 49th Symposium on Theory of Computing (STOC), pp. 954–961 (2017)
12. Nutov, Z.: Approximating minimum power covers of intersecting families and directed edge-connectivity problems. Theoret. Comput. Sci. **411**(26–28), 2502–2512 (2010)
13. Nutov, Z.: Approximating Steiner networks with node-weights. SIAM J. Comput. **39**(7), 3001–3022 (2010)
14. Nutov, Z.: Activation network design problems. In: Gonzalez, T.F. (ed.) Handbook on Approximation Algorithms and Metaheuristics, vol. 2, 2nd edn., chap. 15. Chapman & Hall/CRC (2018)
15. Panigrahi, D.: Survivable network design problems in wireless networks. In: 22nd Symposium on Discrete Algorithms (SODA), pp. 1014–1027 (2011)

16. Rodoplu, V., Meng, T.H.: Minimum energy mobile wireless networks. In: IEEE International Conference on Communications (ICC), pp. 1633–1639 (1998)
17. Singh, S., Raghavendra, C.S., Stepanek, J.: Power-aware broadcasting in mobile ad hoc networks. In: Proceedings of IEEE PIMRC (1999)
18. Srinivas, A., Modiano, E.H.: Finding minimum energy disjoint paths in wireless ad-hoc networks. Wireless Netw. 11(4), 401–417 (2005)
19. Wieselthier, J.E., Nguyen, G.D., Ephremides, A.: On the construction of energy-efficient broadcast and multicast trees in wireless networks. In: Proceedings of the IEEE INFOCOM, pp. 585–594 (2000)

Author Index

© The Editor(s) (if applicable) and The Author(s), under exclusive license
to Springer Nature Switzerland AG 2023
G. Della Vedova et al. (Eds.): CiE 2023, LNCS 13967, p. 297, 2023.
https://doi.org/10.1007/978-3-031-36978-0

Printed in the United States
by Baker & Taylor Publisher Services